Public Relations

A Values-Driven

Approach

Cases Edition

David W. Guth, APR
University of Kansas

Charles Marsh, Ph.D.
University of Kansas

PEARSON

Boston   New York   San Francisco

Mexico City   Montreal   Toronto   London   Madrid   Munich   Paris

Hong Kong   Singapore   Tokyo   Cape Town   Sydney

Editor-in-Chief: Karon Bowers
Series Editorial Assistant: Suzanne Stradley
Marketing Manager: Suzan Czajkowski
Editorial Production Service: Omegatype Typography, Inc.
Composition Buyer: Linda Cox
Manufacturing Buyer: JoAnne Sweeney
Electronic Composition: Omegatype Typography, Inc.
Cover Administrator: Joel Gendron

For related titles and support materials, visit our online catalog at www.ablongman.com.

Between the time web site information is gathered and then published, it is not unusual for some sites to have closed. Also, the transcription of URLs can result in typographical errors. The publisher would appreciate notification where these errors occur so that they may be corrected in subsequent editions.

ISBN: 0-205-49538-9

Printed in the United States of America

10 9 8 7 6 5 4 3 2 1   10 09 08 07 06

Contents

section one

Foundations of Public Relations

This section of the book lays the foundations for the practice of values-driven public relations. As noted within these pages, public relations is important to the conduct and maintenance of free societies. And it is a discipline that is often misunderstood. These six chapters bring the profession, the issues confronting it, and its values into focus.

section two

The Public Relations Process

Now that the foundations for the practice of public relations have been established, this section of the book focuses on the discipline's four-step process: research, planning, communication, and evaluation. Although this process is both strategic and tactical, an emphasis on values remains at its core. Successful practitioners rely on critical thinking skills introduced in these five chapters.

section three

Public Relations Today and Tomorrow

Public relations practitioners operate in a dynamic and intense environment. We live in a time of great changes that test our values. The final section of this book examines the profession's critical issues. Emerging professionals will confront many, if not most, of these challenges in the coming years. These five chapters bring those challenges into focus.

Case Studies Portfolio

Preface

At the darkest moments of the American Revolution, Thomas Paine wrote, "These are the times that try men's souls." Today, more than four years after the terrorist attacks on the World Trade Center and the Pentagon, we humbly suggest "these are the times that try our values."

Since 9/11, the world we live in has become a much different place. It is not always easy to tell good from evil. Right from wrong. Morality from immorality. People, armed with the same information, can reach conclusions that are polar opposites from one another. That is why, nearly seven years after the publication of the first edition of this book, its authors remain committed to what we call values-driven public relations.

The late and highly respected public relations historian Scott Cutlip wrote about the practitioner's potential for helping what he called "our segmented, scattered society" to replace "misinformation with information, discord with concord." However, he lamented that the profession had fallen short of that goal.

We believe that goal is attainable—even in a world that, at times, has seemingly gone mad. It all comes down to who you are, what you believe, and how you want to be seen by others. It all comes down to whether your actions will match your words.

It all comes down to values.

It has been more than 100 years since the first public relations agency opened in the United States. During the 20th century, the practice of public relations grew from a vague notion to a powerful force in democratic societies. As we begin a new century, the profession has made impressive gains in respect and access to power. Yet, in a very real sense, public relations has a public relations problem. Although its roots date back to the beginning of recorded history, the fact remains that public relations—both as a profession and as a discipline—remains largely misunderstood.

Public relations is an honorable profession with a glorious past and a brilliant future. Like any other human pursuit, it also has its share of flaws. However, at a time when much of the world is embracing democratic institutions for the first time, public relations is an important catalyst for bringing change and promoting consensus. Through the practice of public relations, organizations and individuals communicate their ideas and advance their goals in the marketplace of ideas. This concept is increasingly understood within the nations of Eastern Europe, where, since the fall of communism, the demand for public relations education has skyrocketed.

Public Relations: A Values-Driven Approach introduces this dynamic profession to the practitioners of the 21st century. Through a realistic blend of theory and practical examples, this book seeks to remove the veil of mystery that has shrouded the profession from its very beginnings. Using the conversational style of writing favored by today's college students, this book takes the reader on a journey of discovery, often through the eyes of leading practitioners and scholars.

Values-Driven Public Relations

As the title suggests, however, these pages contain more than just a recitation of facts and concepts. This book champions what we call *values-driven public relations:* an approach that challenges practitioners to align their efforts with the values of their organization, their profession, their targeted publics, and society itself.

Values-driven public relations is a logical response to a dynamic and diverse society in which complex issues and competing values bring different groups of people into conflict. This approach links communication with an organization's values, mission, and goals. Today, public and private organizations are increasingly held accountable for their actions by a variety of stakeholders. No longer is an organization's behavior measured solely by traditional indicators of success, such as profits, stock dividends, and jobs created. Additional measures of social worth now include an organization's relationships with its employees, its communities, its customers, and its physical environment. Stakeholders expect decisions to be made within an ethical framework. *Public Relations: A Values-Driven Approach* prepares future practitioners and the organizations they represent for a world of increased responsibility, scrutiny, and accountability.

Public Relations in the Social Context

Another notable feature of this book is its discussion of relevant issues within a broader social context. Public relations did not develop, nor is it practiced, in a vacuum. Throughout history, the practice of public relations has been shaped by great social forces. Its emergence in the United States was linked to the Industrial Revolution and the related Populist Era reforms. The 20th century's military and social conflicts served as catalysts for the profession's growth. Public relations was also transformed by the economic globalization and technological advances of the 1980s and 1990s. *Public Relations: A Values-Driven Approach* provides this broad social context so that future practitioners can have a clearer understanding of the so-called real world they are about to enter. The book includes full chapters on history, ethics, law, cross-cultural communication, and new technologies. Throughout the book, students are directed to online sources of further information.

Features

A major goal of this book is to strengthen students' problem-solving skills. Every chapter provides two hypothetical but realistic **scenarios:** the opening scenario, at the beginning of the chapter, and It's Your Turn, on the book's web site. Each scenario places students in the shoes of a practitioner and challenges them to create an ethical, values-driven, effective solution. Each chapter also includes relevant case studies that expose students to successful as well as unsuccessful public relations approaches. Following each scenario and case study are questions designed to engage students in a meaningful analysis of the issues raised. The book further promotes problem-solving skills by introducing a variety of processes that guide students through the stages of research, planning, communication, evaluation, and ethical decision making.

Public Relations: A Values-Driven Approach and its web site also contain pedagogical elements that engage students in the subject matter. Each chapter begins with a list of learning **objectives** that set the stage for the topics that lie ahead. **QuickChecks,** a series of questions focusing on the book's content, are interspersed throughout each chapter. **QuickBreaks,** lively and relevant sidebars, bring depth and texture to each chapter. In keeping with the values focus of this text, **Values Statements** from a broad range of organizations are scattered throughout the book. A list of **key terms** appears at the end of each chapter and as web site flash cards. A full **glossary** is provided at the end of the book. Each chapter also includes a **Memo from the Field,** a message to students from one of today's leading public relations professionals. These professionals represent a broad range of public and private interests and reflect the diversity of the society upon which they wield so much influence.

With this special edition, we are pleased to introduce 24 additional case studies at the end of the book as a Case Studies Portfolio. A panel of leading public relations professionals and educators has affirmed that case studies should be an integral part of public relations education. The members of the Commission on Public Relations Education understood the value of learning the real-life lessons of others. Case studies also provide insight into the critical-thinking and problem-solving skills that are essential to successful public relations.

These additional case studies are a mix of the old and the new—updated versions of case studies published in earlier editions of this book and new cases covering recent events still fresh in the reader's mind, such as governmental responses to Hurricane Katrina and the introduction of corporate podcasting. There are stories of good intentions gone wrong. There are also inspirational stories of how the application of sound public relations practices can change the world. All of the case studies provide readers a window to the real world of values-driven public relations.

Acknowledgments

The authors want to thank the dozens of people, many unknown to us before the writing of this book, who contributed greatly to this effort. The authors want to thank former-Dean James Gentry; Dean Ann Brill; and the faculty, staff, students, and alumni of the William Allen White School of Journalism and Mass Communications at the University of Kansas for their advice, support, and patience during this project. A special acknowledgment goes to former student Philippe Stefani, who translated one Memo from the Field from French to English. We want to note the passing of former Memo from the Field contributor Fred Repper—his wit and wisdom are missed. The authors also extend their gratitude to the dozens of companies, agencies, and individuals who gave their permission for the use of photographs, publications, and other artwork used in the text.

Sixteen men and women gave their valuable time to write memos to students who will read this book. The authors gratefully acknowledge the contributions of Judith T. Phair of PhairAdvantage Communications; John Echeveste of Valencia, Pérez & Echeveste Public Relations; Edward M. Block, formerly of AT&T; David A. Narsavage of The Aker Partners, Inc.; René Pelletier of Baromètre, Inc.; Carol Cone of Cone, Inc.; Leslie Gaines-Ross of Burson-Marsteller; Timothy S. Brown of Conectiv; Shirley Barr of Shirleybarr Public Relations; Regina Lynch-Hudson of The Write Publicist; Craig Settles of Successful.com; Wayne Shelor of the Clearwater (Florida) Police Department; Vin Cipolla of HNW, Inc.; Bill Imada of IW Group; James F. Haggerty of The PR Consulting Group, Inc.; and Sarah Yeaney, 2004–2005 national president of PRSSA.

A group of dedicated educators provided many suggestions and, in doing so, helped the authors maintain a focus on the needs of students who read this book: Robert A. Bergman, Lewis University; Jeffrey L. Courtright, Illinois State University; Julie K. Henderson, University of Wisconsin Oshkosh; Jan W. Kelly, University of Scranton; and Jack R. Shock, Harding University.

Once the text was written and the necessary artwork and permissions secured, the burden of this project shifted to the talented editors, designers, and technicians of Allyn and Bacon, including Molly Taylor and Michael Kish, as well as the team at Omegatype Typography, Inc.

Last, and certainly not least, the authors thank their families for their love and unwavering support during this long and challenging process. They are our inspiration and motivation.

With the shadow of terrorism still looming in this uncertain world, this book is dedicated to all those who work to build values-driven relationships.

David W. Guth, APR
Charles Marsh, Ph.D.

About the Authors

The authors of this book come from very different backgrounds but share a passion for public relations education. Both are associate professors at the William Allen White School of Journalism and Mass Communications at the University of Kansas. In addition to this textbook, they have collaborated on two textbooks: *Adventures in Public Relations: Case Studies and Critical Thinking* and, with colleague Bonnie Poovey Short, *Strategic Writing: Multimedia Writing for Public Relations, Advertising, Sales and Marketing, and Business Communication.*

Before becoming an educator, David W. Guth served as a broadcast journalist in six states and won numerous local, state, regional, and national reporting honors, including the prestigious George Foster Peabody Award. He has also served as a public relations practitioner in the public and private sectors, including holding several positions in North Carolina state government. As an educator, Guth coauthored *Media Guide for Attorneys*, a publication that received regional and national awards. In addition to his teaching and research responsibilities, Guth has served as crisis communications consultant to several government agencies and public utilities. Guth is an accredited member of the Public Relations Society of America. His international experience includes public relations work in Japan, Italy, Russia, and Turkmenistan.

Charles Marsh has a Ph.D. in English literature and 20 years of business communications experience. He is the former editor of *American Way*, the in-flight magazine of American Airlines, and the former senior editor of corporate publications for J.C. Penney. He is the author of *A Quick and (Not) Dirty Guide to Business Writing* (Prentice Hall, 1997) and has won national and regional awards for writing and editing. In addition to teaching, Marsh has been a communications consultant to J.C. Penney, Ralston Purina, the USA Film Festival, the United States Information Agency, the American Management Association, and other organizations. His international experience includes public relations work in France, Italy, Spain, Kyrgyzstan, and Costa Rica.

chapter one

What Is Public Relations?

objectives

After studying this chapter, you will be able to

- explain the definition of public relations
- understand the different roles public relations practitioners play
- describe the four-step public relations process
- appreciate the role of personal, organizational, and societal values in the practice of public relations

Bad News on the Doorstep

The first thing you see as you pick up the morning newspaper is a front-page story about your employer. A recent decision to move some of its operations to another location has generated criticism from community leaders, employees, union officials, and area business owners. The article also voices the concerns of several nonprofit organizations that your employer may be backing away from its commitment to local charities.

All of this comes at a time when your employer plans to approach government and business leaders about a new business venture, one that could generate new jobs and help spark the local economy. However, there's a catch: Your employer cannot do it alone. This new venture will require the government's commitment to an expensive upgrade of the city's infrastructure and the chamber of commerce's willingness to assist in the training of new workers.

You also know that your company has no intention of backing away from its support of the local community. The company's values statement says one of its goals is "to bring health and prosperity to the communities where our employees live and work." And until this morning's news story, no one had ever questioned your organization's commitment to its values.

Finishing that first cup of coffee, you know that you have to act. The decisions you make and the advice you give will affect the company's relationships with a wide range of publics. It is a tough job—but you are up to the challenge.

You work in public relations.

Public Relations: Everywhere You Look

Everyone seems to have an opinion about public relations. But a surprising—and alarming—number of these same people have no earthly idea what public relations is.

When you enrolled in class, what did you think public relations was? How do your classmates, friends, and parents define it? There is a good chance that you will get a variety of very different answers—and maybe a few will say, "I don't know."

The purpose of this book is to erase this confusion. By the time you reach the last page of the last chapter, we hope you will understand that a career in public relations can be exciting and rewarding.

The term *public relations* and its abbreviation, *PR*, are often used (and abused) by those who have little or no understanding of its meaning. Some treat *public relations* as a synonym for words such as *publicity, propaganda, spin,* and *hype.* Some use the term as a pejorative, something inherently sinister. Others think of it as fluff, lacking in substance. The news media often contribute to the confusion. According to a study of 100 news stories that used the term *public relations,* fewer than 5 percent of them used it correctly. Researcher Julie K. Henderson wrote that 37 percent of the stories used *public relations* in a negative manner, and only 17 percent contained a positive reference.[1]

There are times when it is easy to see public relations at work. Public relations strategies and tactics helped government agencies and private companies communicate reassuring messages in the frantic hours and days following the September 11, 2001, terror attacks. If you donated blood, gave money to victims' families, or took steps to ensure your own safety, that action may well have been a response to a communication generated by a public relations practitioner. In the months and years following 9/11, public relations has been at the forefront of efforts to restore public confidence and a sense of normalcy.

However, it may be more often that people do not recognize the connection between public relations actions and their outcomes. Concerned that their community lacked a distinctive image to attract tourists and economic development, Richmond,

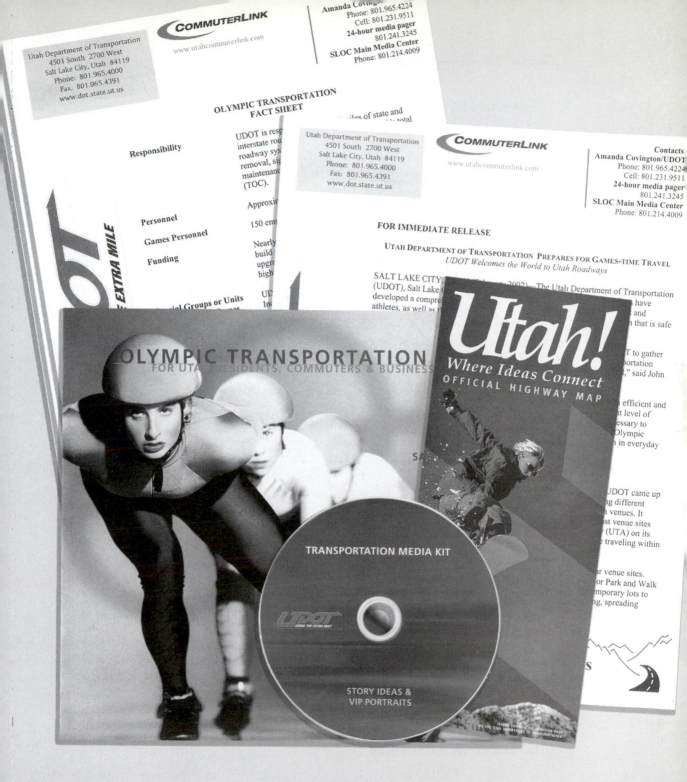

Media Kit Remembering the traffic headaches from previous Olympic games, Utah state officials launched a public awareness campaign to avoid gridlock at the 2002 Winter Olympic Games in Salt Lake City. (Courtesy of the Utah Department of Transportation)

Virginia, officials turned to public relations practitioners, whose solution was a travel and tourism campaign proclaiming that Virginia's capital was "Easy to Love." Requests for information about the Richmond region tripled.[2] Another example of public relations at work involved the 2002 Olympic Winter Games in Salt Lake City. State officials were eager to avoid the traffic headaches that had plagued the 1996 Olympic Games in Atlanta. The Utah Department of Transportation launched the highly successful "Know Before You Go" campaign. Through grassroots communication, media relations, printed materials, and a web site, the traffic volume in Salt Lake City during the games dropped 20–40 percent.[3]

Many try to define public relations strictly in terms of these kinds of high-profile images. However, *publicity* and *public relations* are not synonymous. As you will learn in Chapter 9, publicity is just one of many tactics used by public relations practitioners. Perhaps it is best to think of public relations as a tapestry, with many parts intricately woven into one whole cloth.

Public relations fosters mutually beneficial relationships. During the 1980s, the Adolph Coors Company was under fire from civil rights and feminist groups over its hiring practices. The brewer also was transitioning from a family-owned private company to a stockholder-owned public company. Through a variety of tactics that included the creation of eight employee diversity councils, Coors reached out to publics it once had viewed as its sharpest critics. These initiatives brought both financial and social rewards. Coors is the world's ninth largest brewer, with more than $4 billion in net sales in 2003.[4] *Business Ethics* magazine listed Coors among its 100 Best Corporate Citizens for the fifth straight year in 2004.[5]

Public relations also builds corporate and product identities, a process known as **branding.** In their 2002 book *The Fall of Advertising and the Rise of PR*, authors Al and Laura Ries shook up Madison Avenue with the argument that it was public relations—not advertising—that successfully launched brands such as Starbucks, Palm, The Body Shop, Wal-Mart, and Red Bull. They said the key to this success was the credibility associated with effective public relations.[6]

Some of the best public relations activity occurs when it appears as if nothing at all has happened. Few think to attribute high employee morale, increased productivity, or good corporate citizenship to public relations. But they should. When an orchestra sells out a concert or when a growing number of people decide against drinking and driving, it is easy to forget that these successes may well be benefits of sound public relations strategies. Even knowing where to vote, go to school, and shop is often the result of good public relations.

Public relations casts a broad net.

The Search for a Definition

So what is public relations? To borrow a phrase from a popular 1950s television game show, that is the $64,000 question. Unfortunately, there is no definitive answer. The modern practice of public relations first came under serious study in the early 1900s, and educators and practitioners have struggled ever since with its definition. At the beginning of the 21st century, defining public relations remains an issue.

This confusion was illustrated in a survey of accountants, attorneys, and public relations practitioners. The three groups were selected because they had something in common—a counselor relationship with their clients. Each group was asked about its profession and its place within organizational structures. Although the accountants and attorneys clearly understood their roles, the public relations practitioners did not. This caused the study's authors to raise a pertinent question: If public relations practitioners are unclear about who they are and what they do, why should they expect anyone else to understand?[7]

There isn't even any consensus on what to call the profession. Because of the supposedly negative connotations carried by the term *public relations,* many organizations opt to use euphemisms such as "public affairs," "public information," "corporate communications," or "community outreach" to describe the function. Burson-Marsteller, one of the world's largest public relations agencies, describes itself in its web site as a "global perception management firm."

Other organizations, especially government agencies, try to hide their public relations practitioners from the eyes of jealous rivals and zealous budget-cutters by giving them seemingly innocuous titles, such as "special assistant" or "information manager." One state agency had its listing removed from the North Carolina state government telephone directory in an effort to avoid detection. Instead of answering the telephone by saying "public information office," the staff was instructed to answer by repeating the office's extension number.[8]

Public Relations Defined

In 1976, in an effort to eliminate some of the confusion, public relations pioneer and scholar Rex Harlow compiled 472 different definitions of public relations. From those, Harlow came up with his own 87-word definition, which stressed public relations' role as a management function that "helps establish and maintain mutual lines of communication, understanding, acceptance, and cooperation between an organization and its publics."[9]

Others have sought to define public relations in fewer words. In *Managing Public Relations,* educators Todd Hunt and James E. Grunig opt for a 10-word definition: "the management of communication between an organization and its publics."

One area of agreement among public relations practitioners is the definition of the term **public:** any group of people who share common interests or values in a particular situation—especially interests or values they might be willing to act upon. When a public has a relationship with your organization, the public is called a **stakeholder,** meaning that it has a stake in your organization or in an issue potentially involving your organization.

The fact is that as long as people are people, they will continue to view the world with differing perspectives. That's why it may be best to avoid the debate over the exact wording of a public relations definition and, instead, to concentrate on the

QuickBreak 1.1

THE DEFINITION DEBATE

The struggle to define the profession of public relations continues well into its second century. While many may see this as an intellectual exercise, others say the failure to reach a consensus on what, exactly, public relations is may undermine its future.

The **Public Relations Society of America (PRSA)** has tried to lay the matter to rest on several occasions. The PRSA Assembly adopted an Official Statement on Public Relations in 1982: "Public relations helps our complex, pluralistic society to reach decisions and function more effectively by contributing to mutual understanding among groups and institutions. It serves to bring the public and public policies into harmony."

The statement went on to describe public relations as a management function that encompasses monitoring and interpreting public opinion, counseling management on communication and social responsibility issues, and researching and managing organizational communication.[10]

Recognizing that its own attempt at defining the profession ran more than 400 words, PRSA settled on a more concise and somewhat vague alternative in 1988: "Public relations helps an organization and its publics adapt mutually to each other."[11]

PRSA's efforts to define public relations appear only to have invigorated the debate. The argument over what public relations is and how it should be defined raged throughout the1990s and into the new century. Practitioners, scholars, and textbook writers (including the authors of this book) continue to add fuel to this fire.

The challenge is deceptively simple: Find concise terminology that captures the values, purpose, and spirit of a complex and dynamic profession. The solution, however, remains elusive.

"If the field of public relations wishes to master its own destiny, it must settle on a definition," wrote James G. Hutton of Fairleigh Dickinson University. To that end, he proposed a three-word definition: "managing strategic relationships." While acknowledging his definition's potential drawbacks, Hutton believed that it captured the essential elements of the profession.[12]

Predictably, this attempt to settle the debate was met with skepticism. Writing in *Public Relations Review* in 2001, four European public relations professors found Hutton's approach "commendable, yet a bit flawed." Their major complaint was that Hutton's definition—and most U.S.-based definitions—focus only on U.S. theories and practices. "It is only after we are able to take into consideration the full richness of the present state of thinking and practicing public relations around the globe that we will be able to draw conclusions towards what the public relations profession is in the world at the beginning of the 21st century," the European scholars wrote.[13]

Even with dramatic advances in public relations research and technology during the last century, we are no closer to defining the profession than when Edward L. Bernays first coined the phrase "public relations counsel" in 1923. As one author wrote more than 40 years ago, public relations remains a discipline "of some 100,000 whose common bond is the profession and whose common woe is that no two of them can ever agree on what that profession is."[14]

various elements of the profession itself. Here is where one finds consensus. Common to any comprehensive definition of public relations are the following elements:

■ *Public relations is a management function.* The relationship between an organization and the publics important to its success must be a top concern of the organization's leadership. The public relations practitioner provides counsel on the timing, manner, and form important communications should take. In other words, practitioners aren't just soldiers who follow orders; they're also generals who help shape policy. And like all managers, they must be able to measure the degree of their success in their various projects.

■ *Public relations involves two-way communication.* Communication is not just telling people about an organization's needs. It also involves listening to those same people speak of their concerns. This willingness to listen is an essential part of the relationship-building process.

■ *Public relations is a planned activity.* Actions taken on behalf of an organization must be carefully planned and consistent with the organization's values and goals. And since the relationship between an organization and the publics important to its success is a top concern, these actions must also be consistent with the publics' values and goals.

■ *Public relations is a research-based social science.* Formal and informal research is conducted to allow an organization to communicate effectively, possessing a full understanding of the environment in which it operates and the issues it confronts. Public relations practitioners and educators also share their knowledge with others in the industry through various professional and academic publications.

■ *Public relations is socially responsible.* A practitioner's responsibilities extend beyond organizational goals. Practitioners and the people they represent are expected to play a constructive role in society.

You may have noticed a common theme running throughout this list: the concept of **relationship management.** Farsighted, well-managed organizations know they must have good relationships with publics important to their success. A 1992 study that sought to define excellence in public relations noted that having good relationships with these publics can save an organization money by reducing the likelihood of threats such as litigation, regulation, boycotts, or lost revenue that result from falling out of favor with these groups. At the same time, the study said that an organization makes more money by cultivating good relationships with consumers, donors, shareholders, and legislators.[15] Therefore, nurturing these relationships is one of the most important roles public relations practitioners can play.

However one chooses to frame its definition, there is one other important aspect to public relations: It plays a critical role in the free flow of information in democratic societies. When American colonists declared their independence from Great Britain in 1776, they said, "Governments are instituted among men, deriving their just powers from the consent of the governed."[16] The meaning of this phrase is clear:

For democratic societies to function in a healthy manner, the government and the people must reach a consensus on matters of importance. Consent cannot occur without the exchange of information and ideas. That, in turn, requires communication. Those who cannot communicate effectively in democratic societies are left at a distinct and sometimes dangerous disadvantage.

Public relations plays a critical role in effective communications. Through public relations, individuals and organizations enter the great marketplace of ideas. And, through the proper application of public relations, practitioners participate in the search for consensus.

A Profession Gaining in Respect

It wasn't that long ago that the attitudes of corporate executives toward public relations were ambivalent at best. Former Mobil Corporation executive Herb Schmertz expressed the sentiments of many when he wrote in the mid-1980s that "public affairs is far too important to be left to public affairs professionals."[17] About the same time, survey research identified divergent opinions about the role public relations plays in organizations. While most practitioners surveyed said they saw their jobs as developing "mutual understanding" between management and the public, their bosses said the role of public relations was "persuasion, information dissemination, or propaganda."[18]

But that was then, and this is now. Recent surveys suggest that corporate executives are beginning to see the value of good public relations. A USC Annenberg Strategic Public Relations Center (SPRC) study in 2002 reported that among companies included in *Fortune* magazine's Most Admired list there is greater support for the public relations function than among those of similar size not on the list. The report also said, "There is a demonstrable connection between a company's use of public relations and its own reputation and stature."[19] Another study reported that while many CEOs "still keep their PR executives at arm's length," an increasing number of practitioners are gaining access to upper-level managers.[20] These findings have been confirmed by similar studies in Japan and the United Kingdom.[21]

"There are two very contradictory and simultaneously held views of public relations," said SPRC Director Ian Mitroff. "In short, the profession is doing commendable work but suffers from low-self-esteem. Perception needs to catch up with reality."[22]

Whatever the perception and reality, there is one undeniable fact: Public relations is big business. The Council of Public Relations Firms estimated that the public relations industry had $6.3 billion in revenues during 2001, a 220 percent growth over the previous decade.[23]

The Hunt-Grunig Models of Public Relations

A major reason that recognition of the value of public relations has come so slowly is the many diverse roles practitioners play within different organizational structures. In short, one size does not fit all. Researchers Todd Hunt and James Grunig have identified four models that they say public relations practitioners generally follow:

1. In the **press agentry/publicity model,** the focus of public relations efforts is on getting favorable coverage, or publicity, from the media. In this model accuracy and truth, Hunt and Grunig contend, are not seen as essential.[24] Research showed that this was the most widely practiced model of public relations; however, it ranked third in order of preference among practitioners.[25]

2. In the **public information model,** the focus is on the dissemination of objective and accurate information. Hunt and Grunig say that people following this model serve as "journalists in residence," acting in much the same manner as news reporters.[26] This was the second most practiced model of public relations. It ranked last, however, in order of preference among practitioners.[27]

3. The **two-way asymmetrical model** is a more sophisticated approach in which research is used in an effort to influence important publics toward a particular point of view. Hunt and Grunig describe this as a "selfish" model, one that does not lend itself to conflict resolution.[28] This was the least practiced of the four models. It ranked first, however, in order of preference among practitioners.[29]

4. The **two-way symmetrical model** is the model Hunt and Grunig prefer. It focuses on two-way communication as a means of conflict resolution and for the promotion of mutual understanding between an organization and its important publics.[30] However, this was only the third most practiced model of public relations. It ranked second in order of preference.[31]

Which public relations model an organization chooses to follow depends on several factors. In smaller organizations, which often deal with fewer people and have less-complex issues to address, the practitioner tends to be more a communications technician than a counselor. Organizations that rely on public relations practitioners with relatively little experience usually limit the practitoners' role to technical tasks, such as news release writing and brochure design.

An organization's internal environment also can dictate the degree of influence public relations has. Sometimes corporate culture can inhibit good public relations practices. One study of organizations identified four barriers that practitioners often face in the corporate culture: a lack of access to top management, an unwillingness of management to pay for or grant authority to gather information, a resistance to timely and accurate disclosure, and differences over how managers and practitioners view the role of public relations.[32]

You may be wondering what, if anything, this means to you. If you are planning a career in public relations, it can mean a lot. The Hunt-Grunig models are not abstract concepts. They can help you predict the future. As the previously mentioned research suggests, organizations that embrace public relations tend to be more successful than those that don't. And it doesn't take a rocket scientist to understand that the closer one is to management—the more influence one has—the greater the opportunities for career advancement. Knowing how a potential employer sees the public relations role can make quite a difference in your future.

Public Relations and Marketing

Another definitional issue is whether public relations should be considered a separate discipline at all. Some very learned people argue that public relations is a component of a different field encompassing many persuasive communications: **integrated marketing communications (IMC)**. (This topic is discussed in significant detail in Chapter 13.) However, other, equally learned individuals bristle at the thought of public relations being covered by an all-encompassing IMC umbrella.

The authors of this book support the latter view. We see IMC as a customer-focused marriage of three distinct disciplines: advertising, marketing, and some functions of public relations. As you may have noticed, some people think of public relations as "free advertising" and of advertising as marketing. However, each term represents a distinct discipline:

- **Advertising** is the use of controlled media (media in which one pays for the privilege of dictating message content, placement, and frequency) in an attempt to influence the actions of targeted publics.
- **Marketing** is the process of researching, creating, refining, and promoting a product or service and distributing that product or service to targeted consumers.
- **Public relations** is the management of relationships between an organization and its publics.

Not every marketing situation requires the use of all three disciplines. Marketing, the central concept in IMC, focuses on customers. We respectfully suggest that public relations practitioners engage in relationships that go far beyond customer communications. Although this is a debate that may best be conducted in an atmosphere that includes beverages and peanuts, the debate is indicative of the broader struggle public relations practitioners have faced since the dawn of the 20th century—to have public relations accepted as a separate and significant profession.

The confusion over what public relations is demonstrates why any attempt to define the profession is best done in broad strokes. In truth, public relations is part art and part science. It is a dash of inspiration and a lot of perspiration. It is also very hard work that is often at its best when it goes unnoticed. This, in part, explains why public relations was ranked 12th in a list of the 250 most stressful jobs in the United States—ranked as less stressful than being a police officer or an air traffic controller, but more stressful than being a college basketball coach or a member of Congress.[33]

Quick ✓ Check

1. What are the five essential elements in the definition of public relations?
2. How is public relations related to the concept of relationship management?
3. What are the Hunt-Grunig models of public relations, and why are they significant?
4. How do public relations and marketing differ?

Why a Public Relations Career?

You may already be asking, "Why would anyone want a career in a field as misunderstood and demanding as public relations?" Good question. Now, a better answer: because there is no other job quite like it. Public relations skills are transferable across a broad range of career opportunities. Regardless of a person's career interests—such as health care, sports marketing, environmental management, government and politics, business and finance, or public service—there is no organization that cannot benefit from wise public relations counsel. Every organization has a need to maintain healthy relationships with its important publics. That is where the public relations practitioner exerts influence. Public relations is a profession that demands and rewards creativity and integrity. It's a profession in which you can see the results of a job well done. It is a career in which you can make a difference.

A Profile of Practitioners

Because public relations is not licensed in the United States, no one knows exactly how many people practice it. In its most recent report, the U.S. Bureau of Labor Statistics (BLS) estimated that 158,000 people were employed as "public relations specialists." Some 69,000 were listed as "public relations managers." In comparison, the BLS estimated that there were 85,000 "advertising and promotion managers" and 203,000 "marketing managers" in 1999. According to the BLS publication *Occupational Outlook Handbook, 2004–05 Edition,* "Although employment is projected to increase faster than average, keen competition is expected for entry-level jobs."[34]

In a broad sense, public relations can be practiced within five organizational structures:

- *Public relations agencies:* companies that contract to provide or supplement public relations services for others. These agencies are often affiliated with advertising agencies to provide integrated marketing communications (IMC) services for their clients (see Chapter 13).
- *Corporations:* public relations units within companies. Corporate practitioners are company employees.
- *Government:* public, taxpayer-supported units within government agencies. These units offer counsel on governmental policies and disseminate information vital to the healthy functioning of a democracy. These practitioners are government employees.
- *Nonprofit organizations or trade associations:* public relations units that serve not-for-profit organizations or specific business/interest groups. These practitioners usually are employees of the organizations they serve.
- *Independent public relations consultants:* self-employed public relations practitioners. These practitioners may contract with clients on a per-job basis or may be placed on a retainer, much like a public relations agency.

QuickBreak 1.2

A PROFESSION OR A TRADE?

Adding to the confusion about what public relations is and where it fits into an organization's structure is an ongoing debate: Is public relations a profession or is it a trade? This is a debate over more than mere semantics and prestige. The salaries practitioners earn, their influence on decision making, and the degree to which they are regulated hang in the balance.

Generally recognized qualities that distinguish professions from other career pursuits are

- the need for a certain level of education as a prerequisite to entering the profession;

- support of the profession by ongoing research published in scholarly journals or in professional association publications;

- the establishment of ethical standards, usually in the form of a code of ethics; and

- some form of licensing or government control.

Doctors and lawyers are professionals who clearly meet these criteria. Both have to receive an advanced academic degree and are expected to remain informed on the latest developments in their fields. Both professions are supported by significant bodies of research and have established codes of ethics. And one cannot be a doctor or lawyer until a state licensing board gives its stamp of approval.

When it comes to public relations, the dividing line between profession and trade is not as well defined. In one nationwide survey, there was little consensus on what constitutes a standard of professional performance. Answers varied significantly, depending on the respondent's age, level of education, race, level of experience, and geographic location.[35]

Licensing proponents, including the late Edward L. Bernays, an acknowledged "father" of modern public relations, see licensing as a way of weeding out unqualified practitioners and raising the stature and salaries of those who are licensed. Others see government-sanctioned licensing as burdensome and as an infringement on First Amendment rights to freedom of expression.

Organizations such as PRSA and the **International Association of Business Communicators (IABC)** have sought to promote public relations as a profession through the establishment of voluntary accreditation programs. Practitioners must gain a certain level of experience and demonstrate a certain degree of knowledge before receiving accreditation: **APR,** for **Accredited in Public Relations,** by PRSA and/or **ABC,** for **Accredited Business Communicator,** by IABC. With the creation of the **Universal Accreditation Program** in 1998, PRSA opened its accreditation process to members of eight additional public relations organizations, including the National School Public Relations Association and the Religion Communicators Council.[36] Both IABC and PRSA also promote professionalism with support of scholarly research and through the enforcement of codes of ethics.

With public relations unlicensed, it is nearly impossible to provide an accurate picture of the entire profession. However, available information provides a glimpse of the current state of the industry. In a survey of its membership, IABC reported that 63 percent work in corporate settings, followed by 15 percent in associations/nonprofits, 10 percent in consulting firms, 5 percent self-employed, and 7 percent in some other type of organization.[37] According to a PRSA gender study, women practitioners outnumber men 71 percent to 29 percent. More than 89 percent of those surveyed were white. Six of 10 had bachelor's degrees, and three of 10 had master's degrees. The average salary was $60,935, with male income averaging 31 percent higher than female income.[38] (This raises gender equity issues discussed in Chapter 16.)

Not only is public relations practiced in a wide range of settings, but its practitioners use a broad spectrum of communications skills. Some of the more traditional public relations tasks include news release writing, brochure design, creation of annual reports, and development of marketing materials. In recent years, however, there has been a revolution in communications technologies, and public relations practitioners have been at the cutting edge of change. Practitioners are now engaged in web site development, satellite teleconferencing, and the creation of interactive CDs. Because of the war on terrorism, there is increased emphasis on government information programs, multicultural communications, and crisis communications.

Quick ✔ Check

1. Is public relations a profession? Why or why not?
2. What are the five organizational structures in which public relations is commonly practiced?
3. Is the number of jobs in public relations growing?

Values Statement 1.1

J.C. PENNEY COMPANY

J.C. Penney Company, one of America's largest department store retailers, operates more than 1,230 stores in all 50 states, Puerto Rico, Mexico, and Chile. The company was founded in 1902 in Kemmerer, Wyoming.

The Penney Idea
Adopted in 1913

1. To serve the public, as nearly as we can, to its complete satisfaction.
2. To expect for the service we render a fair remuneration and not all the profit the traffic will bear.
3. To do all in our power to pack the customer's dollar full of value, quality, and satisfaction.

4. To continue to train ourselves and our associates so that the service we give will be more and more intelligently performed.
5. To improve constantly the human factor in our business.
6. To reward men and women in our organization through participation in what the business produces.
7. To test our every policy, method, and act in this wise: "Does it square with what is right and just?"

—From *The Illustrated JCPenney*

The Public Relations Process

Although the technology used in the practice of public relations is constantly changing, the process that guides public relations is one that stands the test of time. Most public relations experts agree that public relations is conducted within the framework of a four-step process. But would this really be public relations if there were agreement on what to label each of the steps? Remember: This is public relations, the profession of a thousand definitions.

The Traditional Four-Step Model of the Public Relations Process

A variety of names have been used to describe the four steps of the public relations process. Some instructors, in an effort to help students memorize the various steps for the inevitable midterm exam, have favored the use of acronyms such as ROPE (research, objective, planning, and evaluation) and RACE (research, action, communication, and evaluation). In adding our two cents' worth to the debate over what to call each of the four steps, we opt for a more straightforward, if less glamorous, approach: research, planning, communication, and evaluation.

- **Research** is the discovery phase of a problem-solving process: practitioners' use of formal and informal methods of information gathering to learn about an organization, the challenges and opportunities it faces, and the publics important to its success.

- **Planning** is the strategy phase of the problem-solving process, in which practitioners use the information gathered during research. From that information, they develop effective and efficient strategies to meet the needs of their clients or organizations.

- **Communication** is the execution phase of the public relations process. This is where practitioners direct messages to specific publics in support of specified goals. But good plans are flexible: Because changes can occur suddenly in the social or business environment, sometimes it's necessary to adjust, overhaul, or abandon the planned strategies. It's worth repeating here that effective communication is two-way, involving listening to publics as well as sending them messages.

- **Evaluation** is the measurement of how efficiently and effectively a public relations effort met the organization's goals.

Although there is a simple elegance in defining the public relations process using this traditional model, it does not reflect the real world. It depicts a linear process: Step two follows step one, step three follows step two, and so forth (see Figure 1.1). How

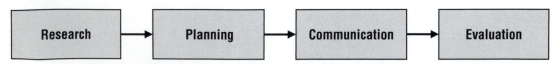

FIGURE 1.1   **The Traditional Four-Step Model of the Public Relations Process**

often does your own life move in such an orderly fashion? If you are like most people, life is constantly changing and full of surprises. Public relations is no different.

The Dynamic Model of the Public Relations Process

In the real world, public relations involves a dynamic process (see Figure 1.2). While practitioners move along a general path of research, planning, communication, and evaluation, it is often necessary to switch directions. They do this because the world is an ever-changing place. To put it another way, what was true yesterday may not be true tomorrow.

For example, the implication of the traditional four-step model is that evaluation is the last thing done. However, in this era of downsizing and increased accountability, evaluation should occur during *every* phase of the public relations process. Research should identify ways to measure the effects of a public relations program. Those measurements should then be built into any plan that is developed. As the plan moves into the communication phase, practitioners should be sensitive to the need to adjust their efforts to any miscalculations or changes in the environment. That, in turn, may require additional research. Finally, the evaluation phase provides critical information on whether the goals of the plan were met. But it also sets the stage for future actions.

The public relations process is not a step-by-step process followed much like a cook follows a recipe. It is a critical-thinking process involving a constant analysis and reevaluation of information.

The Role of Values in Public Relations

Although the dynamic model of public relations more closely resembles the real world, it is still missing a key component: **values.** For the purposes of this discussion,

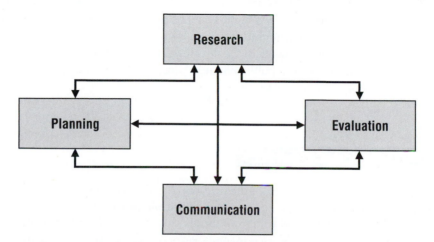

FIGURE 1.2   The Dynamic Model of the Public Relations Process

values are defined as the fundamental beliefs and standards that drive behavior and decision making. To put it another way, values are the filters through which we see the world and the world sees us. Everyone has values. Organizations have values. Actions communicate values. Even thoughtless actions taken without regard to one's beliefs and standards communicate a value.

Think about the process you and your friends follow when planning a spring break trip. As you begin to research where to go, you first identify your values: fun, companionship, safety, price, and so forth. Those core values establish the framework within which you'll gather research, plan your trip, go on your trip, and, finally, evaluate its success.

Let's use a second hypothetical example to illustrate what we mean. If an organization says it values the opinions of its employees, it would not make any sense for that organization to conduct research that doesn't take into account the employees' opinions. And it would make even less sense to launch a plan that, in the pursuit of some other short-term gain, winds up showing that the organization is insensitive to employee concerns. That is why it is necessary to understand an organization's values before engaging in the public relations process. And because good relationships with important publics are critical to any organization's success, it is equally important to understand the values of those publics. Some may argue that this approach limits information gathering and stifles creativity. However, that is exactly what values are supposed to do: establish the boundaries within which we are willing to operate.

This lack of focus on values is perhaps the biggest flaw in the traditional four-step model of public relations. At a time when organizations are being held accountable far beyond the balance sheet, their values-inspired mission and goals must be at the forefront of all their research, planning, communication, and evaluation.

A common complaint against public relations practitioners is that they occasionally act as if the ends justify the means. Some choose to flirt with or even to ignore the boundaries of ethics. Others, failing to pause and consider their organization's core values, sometimes find themselves in the uncomfortable position of trying to place their actions in an ethical framework after the fact. Isn't it much better to snuff out a fire before it causes irreparable damage? Issues of values, ethics, and social responsibility must be addressed throughout the public relations process: The continued growth of public relations as a profession depends on it.

Quick ✔ Check

1. What are the four steps of the traditional public relations process?
2. Why is public relations considered a dynamic process?
3. What are values, and what role should they play in the public relations process?

Actions Speak Louder Than Words—Part I

Too often, unintended actions speak louder than the lofty words found in an organization's mission statement:

■ Following the September 11, 2001, terrorist attacks, American Airlines appeared to be headed toward bankruptcy. Over the next year, the company laid off more than 20,000 employees and successfully lobbied Congress for a $15 billion industrywide bailout. Saying it needed to cut costs to survive, the airline asked for $1.62 billion in labor concessions in April 2003. However, the deal nearly fell through when news leaked that the company had given substantial bonuses to its executives, including a $1.1 million bonus to CEO Donald Carty. American's unions agreed to the new contract—but only after Carty's resignation.[39]

■ Through a life of service as a banker and politician, William Woodard "Hootie" Johnson had developed a reputation as a champion of civil rights. That's why many were surprised when Johnson, chairman of the board of the Augusta National Golf Club, home of the Masters Tournament, became the target of protests in 2002. When he received a four-paragraph letter questioning the club's males-only membership, Johnson responded with a 932-word diatribe that launched a nationwide controversy and placed the club and its policies in the crosshairs of its critics for years to come.[40]

■ Regardless of one's opinion of the recent war in Iraq, few will argue that the U.S.-led coalition's moral authority as liberators was severely undermined by reports of soldiers engaged in a wide range of prisoner abuses at the Abu Ghraib prison outside Baghdad.[41]

Why did these organizations get black eyes? Because their actions—real or perceived—didn't live up to their stated values. Such incidents always leave a stronger impression than the inspirational words of a mission statement.

Values-Driven Public Relations

How can organizations try to ensure that their actions match their words? We advocate an approach we call **values-driven public relations.** Values-driven public relations incorporates a dynamic version of the four-phase process of research, planning, communication, and evaluation into the framework defined by an organization's core values (see Figure 1.3). We offer an alternate definition of public relations: *Public relations is the values-driven management of relationships between an organization and the publics that can affect its success.*

Values-driven public relations is the process of uncovering not just where an organization wishes to go but also the principles the organization will observe in getting there. The process begins with the consideration of values during the research phase—those of the organization and the various publics important to its success. Those values, in turn, are incorporated into planning and communications. Values-driven public relations also means being accountable for adherence to those values when we evaluate our actions.

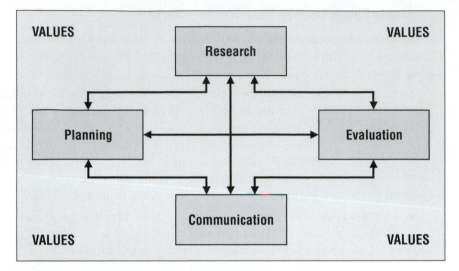

FIGURE 1.3 **Values-Driven Public Relations**

If that sounds easy, it isn't. We live in an increasingly diverse and complex world. New technology and the forces of globalization bring different interests into greater contact—and often into conflict. One need only look at recent history. Violent protests accompany practically every meeting of the World Trade Organization. Much of Seattle's downtown was shut down by pitched battles during WTO meetings in 1999. Four years later, trade talks in Cancun, Mexico, were marred when a South Korean farm leader killed himself to protest the WTO's agricultural trade policies.[42] If anything, these events were the antithesis of values-driven public relations: A lot of heat was generated, but very little light.

Actions Speak Louder Than Words—Part II

At the same time, a variety of publics are holding public and private organizations more socially accountable. No longer is the bottom line seen as the only thing that matters. Although social responsibility may seem idealistic to some, its applications are very real-world:

■ The Church of Jesus Christ of Latter-Day Saints used public relations to improve what had been, at times, a difficult relationship with African Americans. The church teamed with inmates of all races at the Utah State Prison to create the largest collection of slave family records known to exist. A CD containing the records of the Freedman's Bank, an institution created after the Civil War to assist former slaves, provides an estimated 8–10 million slave descendents with clues to their past. For its efforts, the church was awarded the Martin Luther King Jr. Drum Major Award by the Utah Chapter of the NAACP.[43]

■ An outbreak of foot-and-mouth disease in European cattle created a panic among consumers in 2001. During that crisis, poor media relations had made a bad situation worse. Learning from Europe's mistakes, Dairy Management, Inc. (DMI), a marketing coalition created to build demand for U.S. dairy products, launched a proactive campaign of food safety education and training. It involved the creation of a web site, called the Dairy Response Center, designed to go online at a moment's notice.[44] When a single case of mad cow disease was detected in Washington state in 2003, DMI activated its crisis plan. While the cattle industry lost an estimated $1.3 billion because of the outbreak, it could have been much worse.[45] Industry and public relations observers credited DMI's proactive crisis plan with softening the blow.[46]

■ Gap, Inc., set a new standard for corporate candor when it issued its first-ever social responsibility report in May 2004. In it, the retailer acknowledged that many of the clothes it sells are made in overseas sweatshops where workers have been mistreated. The report cited thousands of violations at more than 3,000 factories in 50 countries. It promised to improve conditions at the garment factories that produce merchandise for its Gap, Old Navy, and Banana Republic stores.[47] The Gap told the factories to improve work conditions or risk losing its business. The report said the company cut ties with 136 violators in 2003.[48]

Whose Values Should You Follow?

In the research phase of the public relations process, an organization must, of course, identify and consider its own values—but it must also do more: It must identify the values of involved publics and, perhaps, the values of society itself. Sometimes it can be difficult to decide which values to follow. If there is conflict between organizational and societal values, organizations must make a difficult choice.

This does not imply that one must always adhere to society's values. For example, there was a time in the United States when society condoned slavery, denied women the right to vote, and allowed children to work long hours in unhealthy conditions. An organization may choose to swim against the tide of public opinion. If it chooses to do so, however, it should do so by choice, not chance. Values-driven public relations can be a catalyst for making this crucial decision.

Values-driven public relations is similar to the traditional four-step approach to public relations but it has significant differences. In values-driven public relations the role of organizational, public, and societal values is explicit, rather than implicit. Values-driven public relations also employs a decidedly nonlinear process, in which there are constant checkbacks on values, research, strategies, and execution. Most important, the practice of values-driven public relations answers the most ardent critics of public relations by placing ethical decision making first.

Let's close by returning again to that opening scenario in which your company's actions are under close scrutiny. Faced with several public relations challenges and opportunities, the CEO has just asked, "What do you think we should do?"

QuickBreak 1.3

HOW ORGANIZATIONS ESTABLISH THEIR VALUES

J.C. Penney has *The Penney Idea,* a group of seven governing values written in 1913. One of the values is "To test our every policy, method, and act in this wise: Does it square with what is right and just?"

Hallmark Cards has *This Is Hallmark,* a statement of "Beliefs and Values." One of the statement's five beliefs declares, "We believe that distinguished financial performance is a must, not as an end in itself, but as a means to accomplish our broader mission." One of the statement's four values is "ethical and moral conduct at all times and in all our relationships."

Johnson & Johnson is governed by the one-page *Johnson & Johnson Credo,* which begins, "We believe our first responsibility is to the doctors, nurses, and patients, to the mothers and fathers, and all others who use our products and services."

How did these respected, successful organizations—and others like them—develop their written statements of values? Each organization has its own system, but two ingredients seem common to the values identification process. First, it's a job for a dedicated committee, not an individual. Debating with others helps us clarify what we truly believe. Second, a statement of values must be written, must be well known, and must play an active part in an organization's everyday operations. Only in that way can it be tested and improved.

If an organization lacks a written statement of values, its public relations program is a ship without a rudder. An organization can begin to develop a **values statement** by forming a committee or committees to answer these questions:

1. Why are we in business?
2. What does our organization want to be known for—both today and a generation from now?
3. What should our publics expect from us?
4. What are our highest priorities?
5. Where do we want to go, and whom do we want along for the ride?

Part of your answer should be "research." And to that one word, you'll add a key request: "Let's be sure that our actions reflect our company's values."

Welcome to values-driven public relations.

Quick ✔ Check

1. How do you define *values-driven public relations,* and how does it differ from the traditional definition of public relations?
2. In values-driven public relations, whose values should we follow?
3. What are some examples of public relations decisions in which values played a key role?

6. What should our role be in our community and in our industry?

7. Whose organization is this?

8. To whom do we have obligations?

9. Why should someone want to work for this organization?

The answers to these questions should be used to create a short statement of the organization's core values. Stating each value as a principle can help you move from a values statement to a **mission statement;** in other words, stating each value as a principle can help you move from an idea to a proposed action. For example, J.C. Penney values justice in all its actions. In *The Penney Idea,* that value is stated as a principle: "To test our every policy, method, and act in this wise: Does it square with what is right and just?"

Let's look for a moment at the first question: "Why are we in business?" The obvious answer for many organizations might seem to be "to make money." But it's not money that people crave as much as it is what money can provide:

a nice home, food, education, the ability to help others. Hallmark's statement of beliefs and values notes that money is not an end; rather, it's a means toward accomplishing Hallmark's broader mission.

The *Johnson & Johnson Credo* has served that company particularly well. The company won praise from customers, politicians, journalists, and other key publics for its immediate willingness to put the safety of its customers ahead of company profits during two product-tampering incidents in the 1980s. By adhering to its *Credo,* Johnson & Johnson emerged as one of the most respected companies in the world.

Like many strong, values-driven organizations, Johnson & Johnson periodically evaluates its *Credo* in the context of current business situations. In a values-driven organization, a statement of values or a mission statement should be as much a part of the everyday environment as coffee, meetings, and lunch plans.

Summary

Public relations is a very important but often misunderstood profession. Even those who practice it have difficulty in developing a definition for public relations with which everyone can agree. Despite differences in wording, proper definitions of public relations contain five basic elements: Public relations is a management function, involves two-way communication, is a planned activity, is a social science based on research, and is socially responsible. There is also broad agreement that relationship building is at the heart of good public relations. That requires knowledge of values, the beliefs and standards that govern one's actions. And not just our own values but also those of the various publics important to our success.

The manner in which public relations is practiced depends largely on the structure of the organization it serves. Although public relations should be a major concern of management, some organizations relegate its practitioners to the role of technicians. Some view public relations as an element of integrated marketing communications. However, others—including the authors of this book—view it as a separate and distinct discipline.

The traditional view of public relations is that it is performed through a four-step process: research, planning, communication, and evaluation. The problem with that view is that public relations is a dynamic process in which any of these four phases can occur at any time. When practitioners conduct this process while closely adhering to values—those of the practitioner, the organization, and the society—the process evolves into what is known as values-driven public relations: the values-driven management of relationships between an organization and the publics that can affect its success.

DISCUSSION QUESTIONS

1. Before you read this chapter, how would you have defined *public relations*?
2. Why, in your opinion, is there so much disagreement over a standard definition of public relations?
3. In your opinion, should some form of licensing be mandatory for public relations practitioners?
4. What role does relationship management play in public relations?
5. How would you describe values-driven public relations to a friend who was curious but knew very little about public relations?

Memo *from the* Field

Judith T. Phair, APR, Fellow PRSA, PRSA President 2005, President, PhairAdvantage Communications, Washington, D.C.

Judy Phair, APR, Fellow PRSA, is president of PhairAdvantage Communications, a Washington, D.C.–area public relations and marketing consulting firm, and the 2005 president and chief executive officer of the Public Relations Society of America. Phair is a seasoned public relations executive with extensive experience in marketing, media relations, fund-raising, legislative relations, and communications. Most recently, she was vice president for public affairs at the Council on Competitiveness, a nonpartisan, nonprofit association of corporate chief executives, university presidents, and labor leaders working together to set a national agenda for U.S. leadership in global markets, technological innovation, and education. She has served as an adjunct faculty member at both Goucher College and Towson University and writes and lectures frequently on public relations issues. Phair received her bachelor's degree in communications from Simmons College in Boston and her master's degree in American Studies from the University of Maryland, College Park.

I'll admit to being a bit envious of a new generation of public relations professionals. The reason: This just may be the best time ever to begin a career in our dynamic and demanding business. True, the profession is facing the greatest challenges in its history. But the opportunities are also practically limitless.

The evolution of public relations over just a few short decades is remarkable. We've come a long way from being seen as simply publicity agents whose main job is to get our client's name in the press. Today's public relations professional needs to understand financial spreadsheets and communications theory . . . corporate governance and behavioral science . . . the global marketplace and the 24/7 news cycle.

First, let's take a look at some of the challenges. Americans place a premium on trust and values—in government, in corporations, in nonprofits. Yet trust and confidence in all three of these areas is at its lowest ebb in years. The culprits include corporate and nonprofit scandals, the horrors of 9/11 and the rising tide of terrorism, and a worsening American image abroad. The fact is, all too often as public relations professionals, we have been behind the curve, not ahead of it.

At the same time, we're facing some dramatic changes in our own profession, spurred on by new technology and a shrinking world. In an increasingly specialized society, we are now expected to have highly specialized knowledge in specific market segments, rather than to simply be "generalists." Our clients and employers want us to be accountable and measurable. And the public wants us to be ethical and credible communicators—not "spin doctors" switching our messages every time a new poll shows a shift in opinion.

The stakes are high, but public relations—perhaps more than any other profession—is uniquely poised to make a difference. We can take our profession to a new and higher level—and, in the process, we can play a major role in restoring trust and confidence, at home and abroad.

You can be part of the best generation of public relations professionals ever—ethical, credible, knowledgeable, and ready to show the true power of public relations as an agent of positive change for our nation and our world. Are you ready? Here are a few guidelines, based on observation and hard-won experience, for advancing your career as a professional, as well as our profession.

■ **Think globally.** You are entering a profession that has become global in scope, no matter where you work. Just about every corporation and every organization now has some international connection. Consider the West Virginia utility that was acquired by a Dutch firm—or the tech support for your computer that is based in India. Read international as well as national and local news, travel whenever you can, master another language, or two, or three. Learn—and respect—cultural differences.

■ **Be accountable.** Our profession has become both more specialized and more comprehensive. You will need to know your organization's business from top to bottom if you want to be a truly effective and respected counselor. You'll also be expected to measure and evaluate results—to show how you contribute to the bottom line.

■ **Stay flexible.** Adopt and adapt new technologies, new theories, new approaches to problems and issues. The definition of public relations continues to broaden, and that heightens our value. When I began my career, most of my colleagues shunned marketing tools and techniques. Now we realize that these are important additions to our public relations portfolio. Be willing to take on new assignments that may not "match" your job description or skill set—but can open the door to expanded opportunities.

■ **Listen actively.** Two-way communication is an active process. All too often, we are our own greatest barriers to communication. If we really listened—not just heard—our bosses, our clients, our target audiences, we could engage in real dialogue and set the stage for successful exchange. It's so easy to let our own thoughts and theories crowd out the message we are receiving. The result is that we shortchange ourselves and our clients.

■ **Think strategically.** Ask "why" before "how." Think before doing. When a client presents a problem, it is tempting to focus immediately on specific tasks—or tactics—to turn it around. Without a broader plan—a strategy—individual tactics may end up being temporary patches to make the edifice look good while the foundation is crumbling. Strategic thinking takes care of the long term, so that you can deal with the short term.

■ **Keep on learning.** It's impossible to know "enough." There is always more to learn—both about our profession and about other areas that impact our lives and our careers, our world. Lifelong learning isn't an option; it's a requirement.

■ **Embrace leadership.** In today's world, a solid background in public relations can take you as high as you want to go. Top public relations executives are now becoming presidents and CEOs—an almost unheard-of leap just a few years ago. It makes sense—we possess the skills and sensitivities that can make us great leaders. Take every opportunity—in your community, in your profession, on the job, to learn leadership skills and take on leadership roles. Indeed, PRSSA and PRSA leadership offer excellent opportunities to develop leadership, teamwork, and negotiating skills, along with the chance to get to know other current and potential leaders. Building relationships, after all, is still one of our most important contributions as public relations professionals.

Case Study 1.1

Closing the Gap on Sweatshops

When Paul Pressler became president and CEO of Gap, Inc., in 2002, his teenage daughter confronted him with what could have been an uncomfortable question: "Doesn't Gap use sweatshops?"[49]

However, the question didn't surprise him. The company was just one of many clothing retailers under fire for selling products manufactured in garment factories where workers labor under poor conditions with low wages. Many U.S. corporations have moved their operations overseas to take advantage of lower labor and production costs. This economic globalization has given rise to a growing chorus of labor and human rights advocates voicing concerns about worker safety, child labor, employee harassment and abuse, and less-than-living wages.

So how did Pressler respond to his daughter? He said, "I was able to tell her how the company was working to fight sweatshop practices and improve garment factory conditions around the world."[50]

Gap, Inc., based in San Francisco, owns three of the world's most popular clothing chains: The Gap, Old Navy, and Banana Republic. At the start of 2004, the corporation operated more than 3,000 stores and had more than $15.8 billion in annual net sales.[51] The company's 153,000 full- and part-time employees—as well as its board of directors—are required to follow a corporate code of business conduct. "Gap Inc. was founded in 1969 on the principle of conducting business in a responsible, honest and ethical manner," the code states. "Today, Gap Inc. remains committed to meeting the highest standards of business conduct. Nothing less will do."[52]

The company had set a high standard for itself. The question among many of The Gap's critics was whether the company was willing to keep its word.

An answer came in May 2004, when Gap, Inc., issued its first *Social Responsibility Report*. In it, the clothing retailer acknowledged that workers at many of its overseas suppliers were being mistreated. The company said it uncovered thousands of violations at more than 3,000 factories in 50 countries. "Few factories, if any, are in full compliance all of the time," the report said.[53]

"We believe that garment and other manufacturing workers around the world deserve better than the reality that many unfortunately face," Pressler said. "We recognize and embrace our duty to take a leadership role."[54]

The report detailed the company's ongoing global monitoring program launched in 1996. The 90-person compliance team made 8,500 factory visits in 2003. As a result of these visits, the team cut ties with more than 100 new garment facilities seeking The Gap's business and revoked prior approvals for 136 other factories because of violations of its vendor code of conduct.[55]

Many of The Gap's critics praised the company for its candor. But they also noted that other apparel companies, such as Reebok International, Ltd., had been more forthcoming on the issue. "It's positive that they're coming out with a report that moves this issue of social responsibility forward," said human rights activist Medea Benjamin, who had organized protests and boycotts of Gap products in the 1990s. "But the reality is that the Gap produces in countries where workers don't have basic rights and they leave countries where workers do have basic rights.

"They're coming late to it definitely, and they came kicking and screaming," Benjamin said.[56]

Public relations experts tended to render a kinder judgment. "There was full disclosure with good, key messages embedded, including the news that the company terminated contracts with factories found in violation of its code of vendor conduct," said Katie Delahaye Paine, CEO of KDPaine & Partners. "The resulting PR makes Gap appear ethical, concerned and morally superior to its competitors."[57]

The release of the *Social Responsibility Report* was the latest in a series of moves designed to help Gap, Inc., live up to its code of business conduct. Just a few weeks earlier, company officials and leaders of the nation's largest apparel and textile workers union had announced that they would work together in support of displaced garment workers in El Salvador. Together, they would help open that country's first independent and unionized apparel export factory. Its owners had closed the factory because of labor disputes.

"We've had our differences with Gap in the past, and we may in the future," said union president Bruce Raynor. "But when we started talking with them about this situation and others like it, we realized that we could work together and create positive changes for workers in El Salvador and elsewhere."[58]

However, even this kind of cooperation comes with a price. Raynor said, "My daughter asked me if it was OK to shop at Gap now, and when I said 'yes,' it instantly cost me $80."[59]

DISCUSSION QUESTIONS

1. In your opinion, why did The Gap release its *Social Responsibility Report*?
2. How important are a company's foreign workforce conditions to your personal buying habits?
3. Is social responsibility compatible with making profits?
4. Who do you believe were the most influential stakeholders in The Gap's decision to address working conditions in foreign garment factories?

Case Study 1.2

The Harsh Lessons of History

It is often said that those who fail to learn from history are doomed to repeat it. For evidence to support this statement, look no farther than Bridgestone/Firestone, Inc.

The tire company announced in August 2000 the recall of 14.4 million Firestone-brand ATX, ATXII, and Wilderness tires used on some popular sport utility vehicles (SUVs). This followed widespread reports of tread separation at high temperatures. By March 2004, 271 fatalities had been linked to these tire failures.[60]

In May 2001, the Ford Motor Company, maker of the popular Explorer, announced it would replace all 13 million Firestone tires on its vehicles in what it called a "precautionary" move. Ford President and Chief Executive Officer Jacques Nasser said, "There are early warning signs about these tires, and we will not ignore them."[61]

This move came one day after Bridgestone/Firestone announced it was severing its nearly 100-year business relationship with Ford.

Ford had raised concerns about the safety of the Firestone tires at least two years earlier. The National Highway Traffic Safety Administration (NHTSA) had received its first complaints about the tires as early as 1992. In 1999, Ford began voluntarily replacing Firestone tires on thousands of its SUVs in Saudi Arabia, Venezuela, Thailand, and Malaysia.[62]

From the very beginning of the controversy, Bridgestone/Firestone officials maintained that their tires were safe. They said that no evidence existed to suggest that properly maintained and inflated tires would come apart at high speed in hot weather. The officials blamed consumers, automakers, and even some of their own employees. Not until several national retailers removed the tires from their shelves and Ford had launched its own investigation did Bridgestone/Firestone Executive Vice President Gary Crigger go before reporters to announce the recall and say, "Nothing is more important to us than the safety of our consumers."[63]

Bridgestone/Firestone's public relations agency, Fleishman-Hillard, dropped the $2.5-million-a-month account in September 2000. Critics suggested that this was because of the tire maker's slow response to the crisis and its unwillingness to follow the agency's advice.[64]

Unfortunately, this was not the first time that the Firestone name had been linked to deadly tire-safety issues. In the late 1970s and early 1980s, Firestone endured a similar controversy involving the Firestone 500 tire, which had been one of the most popular brands of its day. But within one year of the start of production, Firestone engineers acknowledged in an internal memorandum that "we are making an inferior quality radial tire, which will be subject to belt-edge separation at high mileage."[65] Instead of dealing with the problem, Firestone engaged in a cover-up by blaming consumers, suing to keep NHTSA from publishing critical research, and even lying to Congress.

Eventually, the company was forced to undertake the largest tire recall in U.S. history, costing $140 million. It also faced more than $2 billion in damage claims from the families of 41 people allegedly killed by the faulty tires. Firestone had to close seven of its North American plants and sell many of its assets to deal with the lawsuits and declining sales. Ironically, Firestone's weakened financial condition helped Bridgestone acquire the company in 1988.

Just as Firestone had a generation earlier, Bridgestone/Firestone eventually had to face the music. On March 15, 2004, a Texas state court judge approved a $149 million settlement of 30 class-action lawsuits against the tire maker. The settlement, involving only plaintiffs who had not suffered any injuries or property damage, could affect up to 15 million people.[66] As of April 2004, other lawsuits remained.[67]

For the first two years following the recall, Bridgestone/Firestone lost $2.2 billion. Firestone-branded tires fell from 10.2 percent of the U.S. consumer replacement tire market in 1999 to 7.2 percent in 2003. However, under new leadership, the company did turn the corner with a modest profit in 2002. Bridgestone-branded tires actually increased their market share. And newspaper reports in April 2004 suggested that the company was trying to repair its relationship with Ford.[68]

DISCUSSION QUESTIONS

1. Is it fair to criticize Bridgestone/Firestone's public relations actions even while the safety of its tires is still under investigation?
2. What might you have done differently in response to the reports of tire failures?
3. What should you do if officials at another company blame your company for product or service failures?
4. Is it fair for the authors to link this problem to one that happened nearly a quarter-century earlier?
5. Bridgestone/Firestone's public relations agency dropped the account at the height of the controversy over the company's tires. Later, the tire maker ended its business relations with Ford. What do you think are appropriate reasons for severing a relationship with a client or customer?

Cyber Coach

Visit www.ablongman.com/guthmarsh3e for these study aids—and more:

- flashcards
- quizzes
- videos
- links to other sites
- real-world scenarios that let you be the public relations professional

KEY TERMS

Accredited Business Communicator (ABC), p. 12

Accredited in Public Relations (APR), p. 12

advertising, p. 10

branding, p. 4

communication, p. 14

evaluation, p. 14

integrated marketing communications (IMC), p. 10

International Association of Business Communicators (IABC), p. 12

marketing, p. 10

mission statement, p. 21

planning, p. 14

press agentry/publicity model, p. 9

public, p. 5

public information model, p. 9

public relations, p. 10

Public Relations Society of America (PRSA), p. 6

relationship management, p. 7

research, p. 14

stakeholder, p. 5

two-way asymmetrical model, p. 9

two-way symmetrical model, p. 9

Universal Accreditation Program, p. 12

values, p. 15

values-driven public relations, p. 17

values statement, p. 20

NOTES

1. Julie K. Henderson, "Negative Connotations in the Use of the Term 'Public Relations' in the Print Media," *Public Relations Review* (spring 1998): 45–54.

2. Jennifer Y. Scott, "Launching A New Brand Identity for Richmond, Va.," *Public Relations Tactics,* April 2003, 18–19.

3. "Know Before You Go," Olympic Transportation Communication Campaign Silver Anvil Awards entry, Utah Department of Transportation with Penna Powers Cutting & Haynes/ProClix, Public Relations Society of America, online, www.prsa.org/_Awards/silver/html/6BW-0315D04.html.

4. Adolph Coors Company, online, www.coors.com.

5. *Business Ethics*, online, www.business-ethics.com/100best.htm.

6. Al Ries and Laura Ries, *The Fall of Advertising and the Rise of PR* (New York: Harper-Collins, 2002).

7. Eric Denig, ed., *A Geography of Public Relations Trends: Selected Proceedings of the 10th Public Relations World Congress* (Dordrecht, the Netherlands: Martinus Nijhoff, 1985), 244–249.

8. David W. Guth, "Crises and the Practitioner: Organizational Crisis Experience As It Relates to the Placement of the Public Relations Function" (master's thesis, University of North Carolina–Chapel Hill, 1990).

9. Rex F. Harlow, "Building a Public Relations Definition," *Public Relations Review* (winter 1976): 36.

10. "Official Statement on Public Relations," *Public Relations Tactics: The Blue Book. The Green Book 2003* (New York: PRSA, 2003), B3.

11. "About Public Relations," Public Relations Society of America, online, www.prsa.org.

12. James G. Hutton, "The Definitions, Dimensions, and Domain of Public Relations," *Public Relations Review* 25, no. 1 (summer 1999): 199–214.

13. Dejan Verçiç, Betteke van Ruler, Gerhard Bütschi, and Bertil Flodin, "On the Definition of Public Relations: A European View," *Public Relations Review* 27, no. 4 (winter 2001): 373–387.

14. John E. Marston, *The Nature of Public Relations* (New York: McGraw-Hill, 1963), 4.

15. James E. Grunig, ed., *Excellence in Public Relations and Communication Management* (Hillsdale, N.J.: Lawrence Erlbaum, 1992), 1–30.

16. *Declaration of Independence* (Washington, D.C.: Commission on the Bicentennial of the United States Constitution).

17. Herb Schmertz with William Novak, *Good-Bye to the Low Profile: The Art of Creative Confrontation* (Boston: Little, Brown, 1986), 5.

18. "Survey Confirms Practitioner/Management Goal Conflicts," *Public Relations Journal*, February 1989, 9.

19. "Public Relations Pays Off for Corporate America, Report Shows," USC Annenberg School for Communication/Council of Public Relations Firms, distributed via Business-Wire, 20 November 2002.

20. "Survey: CEOs Becoming More Confident in their PR Executives," *PR News* 59, no. 16. (April 2003): 21, online, LexisNexis.

21. Yoshikuni Sugiyama, "Top Executive Must Recognize PR role," *Daily Yomiuri* (Tokyo), 20 May 2003, 9, online, LexisNexis; and Graham Sidwell and Michael

Murphy, "Marketing & PR: New Role for Public Relations Industry," *Birmingham Post* (UK), 17 November 2003, online, via LexisNexis.

22. "Public Relations Pays Off for Corporate America, Report Shows."

23. "2001 Public Relations Industry Revenue Documentation and Rankings Fact Sheet," Council of Public Relations Firms, 22 April 2002, online, www.prfirms.org.

24. Todd Hunt and James E. Grunig, *Public Relations Techniques* (Fort Worth, Tex.: Harcourt Brace College, 1994), 8–9.

25. James Grunig and Larissa Grunig, "Models of Public Relations and Communications," in *Excellence in Public Relations and Communication Management,* ed. James F. Grunig (Hillsdale, N.J.: Lawrence Erlbaum, 1992), 304.

26. Hunt and Grunig.

27. Grunig and Grunig.

28. Hunt and Grunig.

29. Grunig and Grunig.

30. Hunt and Grunig.

31. Grunig and Grunig.

32. Michael Ryan, "Organizational Constraints on Corporate Public Relations Practitioners," *Journalism Quarterly* (summer–autumn 1987): 473–482.

33. Les Krantz, *1995 Jobs Rated Almanac,* as cited by *USA Weekend,* 2–4 February 1996, 5.

34. *Occupational Outlook Handbook, 2004–05 Edition,* U.S. Department of Labor Bureau of Labor Statistics, online, http://stats.bls.gov/oco.

35. Glen T. Cameron, Lynne M. Sallot, and Ruth Ann Weaver Lariscy, "Developing Standards of Professional Performance in Public Relations," *Public Relations Review* (spring 1996): 43–61.

36. "Universal Accreditation Board," Public Relations Society of America, online, www.prsa.org.

37. "Executive Summary," *Profile 2002: A Survey of IABC Membership,* IABC Research Foundation.

38. Elizabeth L. Toth and Linda Aldoory, *Year 2000 Gender Study: Report of the Committee on Work, Life and Gender Issues to the Public Relations Society of America National Board,* Public Relations Society of America.

39. "AMR Corporation Form 10-Q for the Quarterly Period Ended March 31, 2003," Securities and Exchange Commission, commission file number 1-8400, online, www.sec.gov.

40. Mark Craig, "2003 Masters Preview: Hootie Johnson," *Star Tribune* (Minneapolis, Min.), 6 April 2003, 6C, online, LexisNexis.

41. "Iraq Prison 'Abuse' Sparks Outrage," CNN, 30 April 2004, online, www.cnn.com.

42. "Suicide Mars WTO talks," CNN, 11 September 2003, online, www.cnn.com.

43. "Bronze Anvil Winners," *Public Relations Tactics* (September 2002): 17.

44. "Maintaining Confidence in Dairy During a Crisis," Dairy Management, Inc., with Weber Shandwick, Silver Anvil Award description, Public Relations Society of America, online, www.prsa.org/_Awards/silver/search2.asp.

45. Alwyn Scott, "Is Beef Industry Reeling? Not Exactly," *Seattle Times,* 29 February 2004, A1.

46. Greg Hazley, "Beef Industry Passes Its First Run-in with Mad Cow," *O'Dwyer's PR Services Report* 18, no. 2 (February 2004): 1.

47. "Gap, Inc. Provides Comprehensive Look at Its Efforts to Improve Garment Factories; First Social Responsibility Report Details Company's Global Monitoring Program and Other Initiatives to Improve Standards in 50 Countries," distributed via PR Newswire, 12 May 2004.

48. "Gap Seeks Better Conditions at Global Garment Factories," *Los Angeles Times,* 13 May 2004, C2.

49. *Gap Inc. 2003 Social Responsibility Report,* online, www.gapinc.com, 2.

50. *Gap Inc. 2003 Social Responsibility Report,* 2.

51. Gap Inc. Securities and Exchange Commission 10-K Report for the Fiscal Year Ending January 31, 2004, Commission File No. 1-7562.

52. *Code of Business Conduct: Doing the Right Thing,* Gap, Inc., 3 (distributed as exhibit 1.4, Gap, Inc. Securities and Exchange Commission 10-K Report).

53. "Gap Seeks Better Conditions at Global Garment Factories."

54. *Gap Inc. 2003 Social Responsibility Report,* 2.

55. "Gap Inc. Provides Comprehensive Look at Its Efforts to Improve Factories."

56. "Gap Seeks Better Conditions at Global Garment Factories."

57. Katie Delahaye Paine, "Gaps PR Fall Into Place While Wal-Mart's Is a Mess," *PR News,* 24 May 2004, online, LexisNexis.

58. "UNITE and Gap Inc. Set Aside Differences to Work Together on Garment Factory Conditions; Unionized Garment Factory Opening in El Salvador, Result of Cooperative Relationship," news release distributed via PR Newswire, 19 April 2004, online, LexisNexis.

59. "UNITE and Gap Inc. Set Aside Differences to Work Together on Garment Factory Conditions."

60. "Bridgestone-Firestone Settlement Approved," CNN, 15 March 2004, online, www.cnn.com.

61. "Ford Motor Company to Replace All 13 Million Firestone Wilderness AT Tires on Its Vehicles," news release issued by Ford Motor Company, 22 May 2001, online, http://media.ford.com/newsroom.

62. Ed Meyer, "Tire Concerns Are Years Old," *Akron Beacon Journal,* 22 August 2000, online, www.ohio.com/bj/news/2000/August/22/doc/024221.htm.

63. "Bridgestone Recalls Tires," CNN, 9 August 2000, online, www.cnn.com.

64. Alison Stateman, Jeff Reese, and John Elsasser, "The Top PR Stories of 2000," *Public Relations Tactics,* January 2000, 16.

65. Dennis L. Wilcox, Phillip H. Ault, and Warren K. Agee, *Public Relations: Strategies and Tactics* (New York: Harper & Row, 1986), 324.

66. "Bridgestone-Firestone settlement approved."

67. Thomas W. Gerdel, "On the Road Again; Tire Company Recovering After Disastrous Recall in 2001," *Cleveland Plain Dealer,* 4 April 2004, G1, online, LexisNexis.

68. Gerdel.

chapter two

Jobs in Public Relations

objectives

After studying this chapter, you will be able to

■ name the basic areas of employment in public relations

■ discuss specific jobs and related duties within public relations

■ explain the differences between public relations managers and public relations technicians

■ describe salaries and levels of job satisfaction within public relations

An Inquisitive Friend

scenario

You've just found a quiet corner in the library, and you feel like putting a sign on the table: "Do not disturb. Serious studying in progress." Just as you open your public relations textbook, a good friend slumps down into the chair across from you.

"Public relations, huh?" he says, tipping back his chair. "Hey, I'm a people person. I love going to lunch. Tell me about public relations."

Stifling the urge to ease a leg forward and push him over, you realize that this could be a good opportunity to review what you know about public relations. You could define the profession for him: Public relations is the values-driven management of relationships between an organization and the publics that can affect its success.

You could tell him that public relations ideally is a function of management and that it's a socially responsible activity based on research, planning, two-way communication, and evaluation.

But what if he looks you in the eye and asks, "So what are the jobs in public relations? What would my duties be? How much money would I make?"

Good questions, you think. And you know that if you could just read Chapter 2, you'd have some answers.

Where the Jobs Are

In the above scenario, as you explained the profession of public relations to your friend, you might also remember to tell him something else you learned in Chapter 1: Broadly speaking, jobs in public relations exist in five different employment settings:

- corporations;
- nonprofit organizations and trade associations;
- governments;
- public relations agencies; and
- independent public relations consulting.

Each of these five areas contains a variety of sometimes startlingly different public relations jobs. Ideally, however, each job helps an organization fulfill its values-driven mission and goals. To help you answer the question about jobs and job duties, let's start by examining the different jobs within these five categories.

Corporations

You could tell your friend that not only do corporations offer most of the jobs in public relations, but they also offer the greatest variety of jobs. Corporations are organizations that produce goods or services for a profit. They include manufacturers such as The North Face, for-profit health-care providers such as Humana, retailers such as The Gap, sports organizations such as NASCAR, and a host of other for-profit organizations.

In most corporations, public relations jobs focus on specific publics. Corporate public relations practitioners often specialize in one of the following: employee relations, media relations, government relations, community relations, business-to-business relations, or consumer relations (or marketing communications). If the corporation is publicly owned—that is, if it sells stock—some practitioners specialize in investor relations. In

Press Box   An important tactic in sports public relations is operating a press box for visiting media, such as those attending this Major League Soccer match. (Courtesy of David Guth)

each of these areas, ideally, practitioners conduct research; advise the organization's top management; and plan, execute, and evaluate relationship-management programs.

Ideally, public relations practitioners should understand and appreciate all sides of a relationship between their organization and a particular public. Practitioners call this function **boundary spanning** because they span the boundaries that separate their organization from important publics. As boundary spanners, practitioners act for the good of relationships, knowing that healthy relationships are vital to their organization's success. And as boundary spanners, practitioners must sometimes ask their own organizations to change to benefit an important relationship.

Although we certainly don't want to downplay the importance of research and counseling, the reality is that most young practitioners begin their careers by creating communications such as newsletter stories and web sites. Therefore, let's look at some of the traditional entry-level tasks.

■ **Employee relations:** Communication tasks in employee relations can include production of newsletters and magazines, video programs, web sites, and special events.

■ **Media relations:** Communication tasks can include production of news releases and media kits (see Chapter 9) and presentation of news conferences. More advanced communication tasks can include speechwriting and preparing scripts for video news releases. Media-related counseling duties can include preparing executives for interviews.

■ **Government relations** (sometimes known as *public affairs*): Communication tasks can include producing brochures, reports, and videos for lobbies and political action committees (see Chapter 9). Advanced duties can include testifying before government fact-finding commissions, monitoring the activities of government units at all levels, and preparing reports.

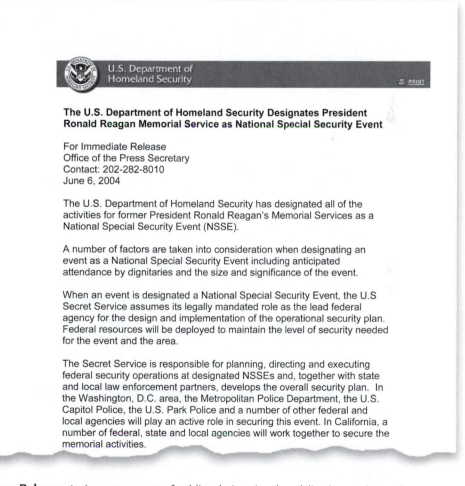

U.S. Department of Homeland Security   PRINT

The U.S. Department of Homeland Security Designates President Ronald Reagan Memorial Service as National Special Security Event

For Immediate Release
Office of the Press Secretary
Contact: 202-282-8010
June 6, 2004

The U.S. Department of Homeland Security has designated all of the activities for former President Ronald Reagan's Memorial Services as a National Special Security Event (NSSE).

A number of factors are taken into consideration when designating an event as a National Special Security Event including anticipated attendance by dignitaries and the size and significance of the event.

When an event is designated a National Special Security Event, the U.S Secret Service assumes its legally mandated role as the lead federal agency for the design and implementation of the operational security plan. Federal resources will be deployed to maintain the level of security needed for the event and the area.

The Secret Service is responsible for planning, directing and executing federal security operations at designated NSSEs and, together with state and local law enforcement partners, develops the overall security plan. In the Washington, D.C. area, the Metropolitan Police Department, the U.S. Capitol Police, the U.S. Park Police and a number of other federal and local agencies will play an active role in securing this event. In California, a number of federal, state and local agencies will work together to secure the memorial activities.

News Release An important part of public relations involves delivering stories to the news media through news releases. Many organizations, including the U.S. Department of Homeland Security, post their news releases on their web sites. (Courtesy of the U.S. Department of Homeland Security)

IN THIS ISSUE ...

Low-cost ideas for adding to your sales team

Is repositioning the right business move for you?

Remaking RFP responses

American Identity uses public relations as a sales tool

Luminary is published by Morningstar Communications Company, providing marketing and brand-building counsel to help leading companies grow. Comments and questions are always welcome at counsel@ morningstarcomm.com. If you would like a digital version, please contact us or sign up on our Web site.

Simply Smart Marketing.

Transcending The Solution Sell

Close your eyes and imagine your best salesperson sitting across the desk from the biggest prospect you've seen since the booming 1990s. Now imagine your salesperson without a single sales "tool." No glossy brochure, no detailed product documentation, no snappy PowerPoint presentation and no business card. Chances are without these, your salesperson doesn't even know how to best position the product or service she represents.

Is this a recurring nightmare or a prophetic dream in your organization? Frequently, sales training consists of equipping the sales team with a briefcase overflowing with printed material and electronic leave-behinds. The theory being, if the salesperson can master the material, a sale will follow. The late '90s brought the "Solution Selling" strategy that tried to meld the prospect's needs with off-the-shelf or customized products.

Now, fast-forward to our post-recession business climate. Prospects no longer want to tell you what "solution" they need to fix their "problem." They need you to figure out the problem. The dilemma of really understanding a prospect's organization takes a new set of skills. Presentation skills, product knowledge and congeniality aren't enough to get you in the front door anymore.

As basic as it sounds, salespeople who put away their laptops and open up their minds will be the "closers" as the economy rebounds. Here are a few strategies to walk away from a sales meeting with more than just a lighter briefcase.

Open your mind. When you are too emotionally involved in the subject, you hear what you want to hear — not what is actually being said. Detach yourself from what you're trying to "sell" and imagine you can use any resources possible to identify and then address the prospect's problems. Remain objective and open-minded.

Focus on content, not delivery. Have you ever noticed the brand of shoes your prospect was wearing or counted the number of times the speaker said "ummm"? If so, you weren't focusing on content. Ask questions and take notes like you are an impartial reporter and need to print a full account of this meeting in tomorrow's paper.

Listen slowly, think quickly and stay quiet. You can think faster than any speaker can talk. Make sure you are listening to exactly what the prospect is saying at that moment. Don't try to anticipate the prospect's next thought or interrupt with a question. When there is a moment of silence, resist the urge to fill it. Wait for the prospect to speak again. Frequently, the next comment will be the most insightful of the entire conversation.

This type of information-rich sales meeting will lead to a deeper understanding of your prospect's long-term needs and open up sales avenues you may never have imagined. Leading organizations will flex beyond product line and service offerings and learn to not only find a solution, but also identify the problem before your prospect asks for help.

You need to figure out the problem.

2004

MORNINGSTAR
COMMUNICATIONS COMPANY

Newsletter Morningstar Communications of Kansas City uses its *Luminary* newsletter to educate current customers and attract new ones. (Courtesy of Morningstar Communications Company)

- **Community relations:** Communication tasks can include maintaining contact with local special-interest groups such as environmental organizations. New practitioners also often help coordinate special events such as tours of their organization's facilities. Upper-level duties can include overseeing a corporation's charitable contributions, organizing employee volunteer efforts, and lending support to special events such as blood drives and United Way fund-raising campaigns.

- **Business-to-business relations,** also known as *B2B:* Communication tasks focus on building strong relationships with related businesses such as suppliers and distributors. Entry-level duties can include writing for newsletters and web sites and helping to plan special events. Management duties can include orientation meetings to discuss shared values and goals.

- **Consumer relations,** also known as *marketing communications:* Communication tasks usually focus on product publicity. Such duties can include preparing news releases and media kits, implementing direct-mail campaigns, organizing special promotional events, enlisting and training celebrity spokespeople, and coordinating communication efforts with advertising campaigns.

- **Investor relations:** Communication activities that target investors and investment analysts can include producing newsletters and other forms of correspondence directed at stockholders, producing an annual financial report to stockholders, planning and conducting an annual meeting for stockholders, maintaining a flow of information to investment analysts, and other activities designed to inform investors about a corporation's financial health and business goals. Investor relations practitioners often oversee the legally required disclosure of financial information to stockholders and to the government.

Nonprofit Organizations and Trade Associations

Let's now tell your friend about public relations jobs in nonprofit organizations and trade associations. And, once again, let's focus primarily on entry-level communication tasks rather than on research and counseling. Nonprofit organizations can include universities, hospitals, churches, foundations, and other groups that provide a service without the expectation of earning a profit. Some nonprofit organizations, of course, are local. Others, such as the United Way, are nationally known. Still others, such as the Red Cross and Amnesty International, have international duties and reputations.

Public relations duties within a nonprofit organization often are similar to public relations duties within a corporation. Well-run nonprofit organizations have practitioners in employee relations, media relations, government relations, community relations, and sometimes marketing communications. However, because nonprofit organizations have no stockholders, they don't engage in investor relations activities. Instead, they have donor relations; fund-raising; and, if appropriate, member relations.

Values Statement 2.1

PUBLIC RELATIONS SOCIETY OF AMERICA

PRSA is the world's largest organization for public relations professionals. Its nearly 20,000 members, organized worldwide in more than 100 chapters, represent business and industry, technology, counseling firms, government, associations, hospitals, schools, professional services firms, and nonprofit organizations.

PRSA Member Statement of Professional Values

This statement presents the core values of PRSA members and, more broadly, of the public relations profession. These values provide the foundation for the Member Code of Ethics and set the industry standard for the professional practice of public relations. These values are the fundamental beliefs that guide our behaviors and decision-making process. We believe our professional values are vital to the integrity of the profession as a whole.

Advocacy

- We serve the public interest by acting as responsible advocates for those we represent.
- We provide a voice in the marketplace of ideas, facts, and viewpoints to aid informed public debate.

Honesty

- We adhere to the highest standards of accuracy and truth in advancing the interests of those we represent and in communicating with the public.

Expertise

- We acquire and responsibly use specialized knowledge and experience.

- We advance the profession through continued professional development, research, and education.
- We build mutual understanding, credibility, and relationships among a wide array of institutions and audiences.

Independence

- We provide objective counsel to those we represent.
- We are accountable for our actions.

Loyalty

- We are faithful to those we represent, while honoring our obligation to serve the public interest.

Fairness

- We deal fairly with clients, employers, competitors, peers, vendors, the media, and the general public.
- We respect all opinions and support the right of free expression.

—From "PRSA Member Code of Ethics 2000," PRSA web site

Communication tasks in donor relations, fund-raising, and member relations can include producing newsletters, videos, and web sites; writing direct-mail solicitations; and organizing special events.

Trade associations are often grouped with nonprofit organizations because, like those organizations, they offer services without the primary motive of earning a profit. Trade associations include such groups as the American Library Association and the

THE VALUES OF SUCCESSFUL EMPLOYERS

What do enduring, successful companies have in common? In the book *Built to Last: Successful Habits of Visionary Companies,* authors James Collins and Jerry Porras examine the workings of companies that have thrived despite occasional adversity and changing environments.[1] One foundation of such companies, the authors say, is a set of clear, strongly held, companywide core values:

Core values [are] the organization's essential and enduring tenets—a small set of general guiding principles; not to be confused with specific cultural or operating practices; not to be compromised for financial gain or short-term expediency. . . .

The crucial variable is not the content of a company's ideology, but how deeply it believes its ideology and how consistently it lives, breathes and expresses it in all that it does. Visionary companies do not ask, "What should we value?" They ask, "What do we actually value deep down to our toes?"

Built to Last examines the long-term success of 20 companies, including IBM, Johnson & Johnson, Motorola, Procter & Gamble, and Walt Disney. "Yes, they seek profits," say the authors, "but they're equally guided by a core ideology—core values and a sense of purpose beyond just making money."

As you consider a career in public relations and as you evaluate the different kinds of employers and job duties, be sure to study the values of those employers. Many organizations now list their values statements on their web sites. What, if anything, do those organizations say they value? Do their actions match their beliefs? Are their values so clear that they can guide public relations policies and actions? In the words of James Collins and Jerry Porras, will you select an employer that's built to last?

International Guild of Professional Butlers. Trade associations offer their members benefits that can include insurance programs, continuing education, networking, and a unified voice in efforts to influence legislative processes. Public relations jobs in trade associations include member relations, media relations, government relations, and marketing communications. Communication tasks in member relations are often designed to educate and update members through newsletters and other publications, web sites, videos, and special events such as annual conventions. The American Medical Association, for example, offers its members the prestigious *Journal of the American Medical Association.* Another task in member relations involves recruiting new members through such actions as direct-mail campaigns.

Governments

Maybe your friend would be more interested in conducting public relations for the government. Tell him not to limit his search to the federal or central government of a nation: Jobs in public relations can also be found within state and local governments. Political parties and independent agencies created by the government, such as the U.S. Postal Service, also employ public relations practitioners.

Public relations jobs within government bodies generally focus on three key publics: voters, the news media, and employees.

Government public relations practitioners operate under a variety of job titles, including **press secretary, public information officer, public affairs officer,** and **communications specialist.** Entry-level communication duties can include writing news releases, responding to constituent concerns, and writing position papers that help politicians articulate their beliefs. Upper-level duties can include speaking with reporters, writing speeches for politicians, and briefing officials on public opinion.

At the federal level in the United States, the term *public relations,* with its connotation of persuasive communication, is rarely used. Public relations practitioners within the federal government prefer euphemisms such as *public information.* One reason for their skittishness is the Gillett amendment, passed by the United States Congress in 1913, which flatly declares, "Appropriated funds may not be used to pay a publicity expert unless specifically appropriated for that purpose." Similar restrictions can exist at state and local levels.

Voters in most countries clearly don't want their tax dollars used for campaigns to persuade them of the wisdom of governmental actions and policies. However, voters also insist that government officials communicate with citizens and respond to their needs and concerns. So public relations *does* exist at all levels of government—but rarely, if ever, is it called by that name.

Public Relations Agencies

Maybe a **public relations agency** is the place for your friend. Public relations agencies assist with the public relations activities of other organizations. Corporations, nonprofit organizations, trade associations, governments, and even individuals hire public relations agencies to help manage and execute various public relations functions. A corporation, for example, may have its own in-house public relations staff—but for its annual report to stockholders or for a complicated overseas venture, it may hire a public relations agency for research, planning, communication, and evaluation. As we'll discuss in Chapter 13, many public relations agencies have merged with advertising agencies to provide a wide range of integrated, consumer-focused communications.

Practitioners in public relations agencies often are assigned to accounts. An account includes all the public relations activities planned and executed for one particular client. Individual accounts are managed by an **account executive** and, often, one or more assistant account executives. Also working on each account are writers, who often are called communications specialists; designers; production supervisors; researchers; and, increasingly, online specialists for web site design and maintenance. Workers within an account sometimes wear more than one hat; for example, a writer may also be a researcher. Additionally, practitioners often are assigned to more than one account.

Public relations agencies can range from small shops with only a handful of employees to divisions within advertising agencies to huge international operations such

When Interstate Brands Corporation—the baker of Hostess Twinkies snack cakes—learned that Lewis Browning had eaten a Twinkie a day since 1941 (20,000-plus Twinkies!), it turned his story into a news release that gained national attention and won a top award in a regional public relations competition. (Courtesy of Interstate Brands Corporation/Hostess Twinkies)

as Hill & Knowlton, Burson-Marsteller, Fleishman-Hillard, and Edelman Public Relations Worldwide.

Independent Public Relations Consultants

Maybe your friend would prefer to work for himself. An **independent public relations consultant** is, essentially, a one-person public relations agency. Organizations or individuals hire the consultant to assist with particular public relations functions. Generally, however, a public relations consultant offers a smaller range of services than an agency. Many consultants, in fact, specialize in a particular area of public relations, such as crisis communications, speechwriting, web site design, or training others in the basics of good public relations.

Some independent consultants, however, thrive as generalists. In the book *Real People Working in Communications,* author Jan Goldberg writes:

> Those who work as generalists in the field must be able to perform a wide array of duties at the same time. On any given week they may write press releases for one client, design a brochure for another, approach an editor for a third, meet with a talk show host for a fourth, implement a promotion for a fifth, set up a press conference for a sixth, put together

a press kit for a seventh, work out the beginnings of a client contract for an eighth, and field media questions for a ninth![2]

Note that eighth duty well. Like public relations agencies, independent consultants often must seek new clients even as they conduct business for current clients. The major appeal of independent consulting is also its biggest burden: The consultant alone bears the responsibility for success or failure.

QuickBreak 2.2

GETTING THAT FIRST JOB OR INTERNSHIP

You may be reading this chapter and thinking, "Great. I'm beginning to understand where and what the jobs are. But how do I get one?" The *Occupational Outlook Handbook* from the U.S. Bureau of Labor Statistics offers some cautious optimism regarding your job search: "Although employment [in public relations] is expected to increase faster than average, keen competition is expected for entry-level jobs."[3]

We'll examine your future in public relations more thoroughly in Chapter 16. But let's preview a few dos and don'ts about communicating with potential employers.

Do This:

- Do thoroughly research a potential employer before applying.

- Do send an error-free application letter and a flawless résumé. Three-quarters of personnel/human resources departments say they disregard job-application letters with grammatical errors or typos.[4] Although organizations say they receive 56 percent of applications via e-mail, an almost equal number—53 percent—say they plan to keep their traditional postal-service methods of acquiring applications.[5] By 2004, however, 28 percent of employers had either eliminated traditional paper applications or were planning to do so.[6]

- Do prepare for a job interview by reviewing your research on the potential employer and developing knowledgeable questions to ask.

- Do create a portfolio of real work done for real clients, including work done as an intern or volunteer.

Don't Do This:

- Don't send a form letter asking for a job. Instead, include specific, organization-related information that shows why you want this particular job.

- Don't ask about salary. Let the potential employer introduce that subject.

- Don't forget to send a brief, typed thank-you letter after each interview.

Comprehensive studies in 1999, 2002, and 2004 confirmed that good writing is the top quality that public relations employers seek in new employees.[7] The 2002 study of almost 1,000 public relations professionals identified the top-three desired qualities for entry-level employees:

1. Strong written/oral communication skills;

2. willingness to learn/enthusiasm; and

3. personality/culture fit.[8]

One more thing, *étudiants.* Experts say "the ability to communicate in a foreign language may open up employment opportunities."[9]
Bonne chance.

1. What are the five broad areas of employment within public relations?
2. Which of those five areas offers the most jobs?
3. What is the Gillett Amendment? How does it affect public relations within the U.S. federal government?

Public Relations Activities and Duties

You've conveyed all this information to your friend, and you've done a great job. But your success generates even more questions: Now he wants to know specifically what kinds of tasks he'll be performing at least five days a week for at least eight hours a day. You *could* excuse yourself for a moment and sneak out of the library—but instead, let's humor him. As a public relations practitioner, how *would* he spend his days?

Since approximately 1970, public relations researchers have devoted a great deal of time to answering that question. Professor David Dozier, who has extensively studied

Time Sheet For billing purposes, public relations practitioners often record how they spend each working day. (Courtesy of Timeslips)

the daily duties and tasks of public relations practitioners, groups public relations practitioners into two broad categories:

1. Public relations managers: They solve problems, advise other managers, make policy decisions, and take responsibility for the success or failure of public relations programs. Public relations managers are most often found in organizations that operate in rapidly changing environments and in organizations that encourage employee input.

2. Public relations technicians: They rarely make key strategic decisions, and they rarely advise others within the organization. Instead, their primary role is to prepare communications that help execute the public relations policies created by others. They are more likely to be found in organizations in which the environment is stable and predictable.[10]

Based on a national survey of PRSA members, Table 2.1 shows that public relations managers and public relations technicians do indeed spend their work-

TABLE 2.1 How Public Relations Practitioners Spend Their Time[11]				
TASK	RANK FOR FEMALE TECHNICIANS	RANK FOR MALE TECHNICIANS	RANK FOR FEMALE MANAGERS	RANK FOR MALE MANAGERS
Disseminating messages	1	1	13	13
Writing, editing, producing messages	2	2	15	15
Implementing decisions made by others	3	6	17	17
Making media contacts	4	3	6	11
Implementing new programs	5	7	3	5
Correspondence/telephone calls	6	4	12	14
Implementing event planning/logistics	7	5	9	7
Managing public relations programs	8	8	2	2
Meeting with peers	9	11	16	16
Planning public relations programs	10	10	1	1
Making communication policy decisions	11	12	4	3
Evaluating program results	12	13	8	8
Conducting or analyzing research	13	15	14	12
Meeting with clients/executives	14	14	7	10
Planning and managing budgets	15	9	5	6
Counseling management	16	17	10	4
Supervising the work of others	17	16	11	9

ing hours in different ways. The most time-consuming task for managers is planning public relations programs, which ranks 10th for public relations technicians. The most time-consuming task for public relations technicians is disseminating (or sending) messages, which ranks 13th for public relations managers. Table 2.1 also suggests that gender may affect how public relations practitioners spend their days.

As you might expect, oftentimes it's not a matter of being always a manager and never a technician, or vice versa. Several studies show that public relations practitioners can have jobs that combine both managerial and technical duties.[12]

Let's mention a final public relations task that's rarely mentioned in surveys of working professionals: recording how you spend your time. Public relations agencies generally bill clients by the hour, and in an agency your supervisors will want to know how you spend each 15-minute block of time. Many corporations, odd as it may seem, also chart time in this manner. For example, a corporation's public relations department may bill the corporation's college recruiting department for the preparation of brochures and videos. An important part of ensuring the financial success of your

QuickBreak 2.3

STUDENT MISPERCEPTIONS OF PUBLIC RELATIONS

As a college student, you probably have realized that professors will study just about anything. Professor Shannon Bowen of the University of Houston studies you: students in introductory courses in public relations.[13] Bowen's research has identified four qualities of the public relations profession that often surprise students in introductory courses.

1. *Diversity of duties.* "You can do more things throughout the field," said one student. "I never realized you can take on so many roles." Bowen's research found that many students had believed that public relations was simply publicity.

2. *Management responsibilities.* "I never realized there was so much management in PR," said another student. Bowen discovered that students in introductory courses had expected simply to learn about news releases and other tactics. The profession's focus on research-based planning surprised many.

3. *Research.* "I didn't know that research and statistics were a part of it or I might not have

taken this course," confessed a candid third student. Despite the occasional difficulty of research, Bowen found that research pleased many students by increasing the legitimacy and credibility of public relations.

4. *Relationship maintenance.* "Now I understand that PR has to manage good relationships by using research, research, research, and getting background knowledge," concluded a fourth student. Bowen found that most new students had viewed public relations simply as a one-way communication process.

Bowen reports that although the unforeseen challenges of public relations discourage some students, they inspire others. "It certainly feels like it is a more difficult and challenging field than I thought," said one student, "but it offers advancement and more responsibility."

organization or your department may well be your scrupulously detailed record of how you've spent your working days.

Quick ✔ Check

1. What specific job duties consume the most time in public relations?
2. How do the job duties of a public relations manager differ from those of a public relations technician?
3. Why do public relations practitioners record how they spend their working hours?

Working Conditions and Salaries

Now that you can exhaustively tell your friend about how public relations professionals get hired and spend their days, you may want to anticipate his next questions: "So what are working conditions like? And how much money will I earn?"

The U.S. Bureau of Labor Statistics reports that public relations technicians work 35 to 40 hours a week—"but unpaid overtime is common." Almost half of public relations managers work more than 40 hours a week, according to the BLS, and "long hours, including evenings and weekends are common." The BLS offers this description of working conditions:

> Occasionally, [public relations practitioners] must be at the job or on call around the clock, especially if there is an emergency or crisis. Public relations offices are busy places; work schedules can be irregular and frequently interrupted. Schedules often have to be rearranged so that workers can meet deadlines, deliver speeches, attend meetings and community activities, or travel.[14]

According to a University of Georgia study, the median starting public relations salary for 2003 graduates of U.S. journalism and mass communication programs was $28,000. Among all graduates of those programs, new employees in the Northeast commanded the highest salaries; new employees in the South commanded the lowest. Slightly under 80 percent of those new hires received medical insurance as part of their salary and benefits package.[15]

In 2000, PRSA and IABC teamed up to administer one of the most extensive surveys of the public relations profession ever conducted. Among the survey's salary findings were:

- The average annual salary for practitioners worldwide is $69,000 in U.S. dollars. In the United States, the average annual salary is $72,000. In Canada, it is $46,000 in U.S. dollars. In other countries, annual salary averages $66,000 in U.S. dollars.

- The median starting salary for entry-level practitioners is $29,000. For low-level managers, it is $43,000; for mid-level managers, $60,000; and for senior managers, $85,000.

- The highest-paid practitioners are consultants, earning an average $160,000 a year. The next highest paid are public relations vice presidents, senior or executive vice presidents, or presidents/executive directors/CEOs, averaging between $130,000 and $160,000 a year.

- Corporations pay the highest annual salaries (median $70,000), followed by public relations agencies (median $52,000), and nonprofit organizations (median $40,000). The study announced no median salary for government practitioners.

- Annual salaries differ by gender, with men earning a median $65,000 and women earning a median $50,000. (Practitioners' length of service may affect this disparity, but gender discrimination remains a reality in many professions.)[16]

Although the PRSA/IABC salary survey provides an extensive review of practitioner salaries, its findings may distort reality a bit. At best, the two organizations represent only a fraction of all public relations practitioners. The people surveyed include many of the profession's best and brightest—meaning that the salary figures could be skewed higher than reality. However, as we'll see in the next section, public relations

QuickBreak 2.4

THE PEOPLE IN PUBLIC RELATIONS

The PRSA/IABC year 2000 worldwide survey of practitioners offers a detailed description of the profession of public relations—including a snapshot of the average practitioner: "The typical respondent to the PRSA/IABC survey is female, 39, responsible for both internal and external communication programs; has been in the profession for 13 years; earns $69,000 annually plus a bonus of $10,000."

Highlights of the survey include the following:[17]

Employment

- On average, public relations practitioners have been with their organization for six years and in their current position for 3.5 years. The average practitioner has worked in public relations for 13.5 years.

On the Job

- Fifty-one percent of respondents have direct access to senior management at least once a day.

- Almost 40 percent of respondents agree that groups or teams make their organization's communications-program decisions.

- The most-reported change in working conditions is the increasing use of computer technology.

Gender

- Forty-eight percent of respondents agreed with the statement "Men still maintain the top job positions over women in the public relations/corporate communications profession."

Accreditation and Education

- Almost 25 percent of respondents are accredited through PRSA or IABC.

- Sixty-six percent of respondents have an undergraduate university degree. Twenty-five percent have a master's degree.

practitioners enjoy their jobs so much that salary is not their top consideration in job satisfaction.

What's Important in a Job?

Finally, you may want to turn the tables and ask your friend a question: What does he want in a job? His answer may surprise you.

According to a survey by PRSA's Counselors Academy, 73 percent of senior public relations executives said that they retain their best employees through "personal satisfaction." Only 12 percent believed that salary was the key to loyalty and motivation.[18]

In the 2000 PRSA/IABC survey, salary was at best seventh on the list of important job-satisfaction attributes.[19] Some 95.5 percent of respondents said that salary was important to job satisfaction—but that high percentage was exceeded by the 99.4 percent who said creative opportunity was important, the 99.2 percent who said access to technology was important, the 97.7 percent who said professional development opportunities were important, and the 96.2 percent who said recognition by colleagues was important.[20]

Public relations practitioners may wish their salaries were higher, but many have discovered something more important than money: A workinpr.com survey found that 73 percent of practitioners are "somewhat satisfied" or "extremely satisfied" with their jobs. Only 16 percent said they were "not satisfied."[21] Even as experienced professionals, they seem to share the enthusiasm of the student in an introductory public relations course who declared, "I feel a lot better about the major now. . . . If you do your job well and do it honestly, you can move up in the PR field. There are a wide variety of employment opportunities . . . and you can move up as far as you will work to go."[22]

That might be a good answer for your friend as you pack up your books and leave the library. Before parting company, you can look your inquisitive friend in the eye and state with confidence that public relations professionals find their careers satisfying and rewarding.

Quick ✔ Check

1. What is the average annual starting salary for entry-level jobs in public relations?
2. Who are the highest-paid public relations practitioners? Do women practitioners earn as much as men practitioners?
3. Is salary the most important aspect of a job in public relations?

Summary

For all their differences, public relations jobs have one thing in common: Ideally, each public relations job has the mission of helping an organization build productive relationships with the publics necessary to its success. Most of the jobs in public relations can be found in five broad settings: corporations, nonprofit organizations and trade associations, government, public relations agencies, and independent public relations consulting.

Within those five broad areas, jobs and job duties vary widely. Public relations practitioners function as managers who counsel other managers and design public relations programs or as technicians who prepare communications. Oftentimes, a practitioner fulfills both roles, depending on the task at hand.

Salaries vary within the profession, with independent consultants earning the highest average salaries. Studies of the U.S. workforce, however, show that salary is not the most important factor in job satisfaction. Such qualities as open communication rank higher than salary in many surveys. Studies of public relations practitioners show that most enjoy their work and believe that they are meeting their personal career goals.

DISCUSSION QUESTIONS

1. Why do corporations have so many different areas of employment for public relations practitioners?
2. Why, in your opinion, have web sites become a standard communication medium in public relations?
3. What are the attractive elements of a public relations manager's job? What are the attractive elements of a public relations technician's job?
4. What do you consider to be the most important element of job satisfaction? How does your answer compare with the findings of national studies?
5. Now that you've read this chapter, what is your opinion of the public relations profession? Does it seem to be an attractive career? Why or why not?

Memo *from the* Field

John Echeveste;
Partner; Valencia,
Pérez & Echeveste
Public Relations;
Pasadena, California

John Echeveste is a partner with Valencia, Pérez & Echeveste Public Relations based in Pasadena, California. Established in 1988, VPE is one of the country's largest Hispanic-owned agencies, handling a diverse roster of consumer, social-marketing, and public affairs accounts. Echeveste has helped develop public relations programs for major national brands such as McDonald's, AT&T, Disneyland, Target Stores, DirecTV, and General Mills. He is a founding member of the Hispanic Public Relations Association and recipient of its Premio Award. He also received the Public Relations Society of America Pioneer Award in 1994. He served as president of the Public Relations Global Network, an association of 30 worldwide PR agencies, in 2003–2004. He is a graduate of California State University Fullerton with a bachelor's degree in communications. He can be reached at john@vpepr.com.

I spent two years in high school and four in college studying for a career in journalism, only to discover after nine months as a reporter that it wasn't the job for me.

What happened? After my short stint as a news and feature reporter at one of the largest dailies in Los Angeles County, I realized that I was too far removed from the center of the action. Nothing wrong at all with being a journalist, but what I discovered all too soon was that reporting was a hands-off job and I was a hands-on person. So I put my journalistic skills to work and bounced around, working for a big corporation (stifling), managing a few political campaigns (exciting, but no future), and writing a documentary film (great fun, little money). In all of these positions, I was developing strategies, testing ideas, making things happen, and seeing results. That, for me, was a lot more satisfying and a lot more challenging than reporting on the things other people were doing. When I combined all these experiences, they pointed in one clear direction: public relations.

I mention this because the road to a PR career isn't always a straight one, and many of us don't end up in the professions we thought we would. But after 30-some years in the profession, the one thing I can tell you is this: Public relations puts you right in the center of the action.

So 16 years after starting an agency, I never regret that early career correction. Every day has brought new challenges, new discoveries, and new opportunities. And what keeps me most energized is working with bright new faces eager to make their own mark in the field.

So what does it take to succeed in this ever-changing profession? Here are the top qualities I look for when interviewing candidates:

- *Learn to write like a reporter.* I can't overemphasize the importance of good writing skills. *I can't overemphasize the importance of good writing skills.* It's essential to everything else in the profession and the foundation of a successful career. The best way to learn good writing is by taking journalism writing classes—learn to write like a reporter and how to write under deadline. Even better, take an internship with a news organization where you can see the inner-workings of a news operation and get some solid writing experience.

- *Be inquisitive.* In public relations, you need to know a little about a lot of things. What I mean by that is that you need to be aware of what's happening in the world and how it impacts your clients or your organization. That means reading a daily newspaper thoroughly, monitoring news and trade magazines, and watching news/public affairs programs. The most effective PR practitioner is the one who arrives in the office every morning knowing what the day's top news stories are. Stay up with trends and with what's happening outside of the office.

- *Show common sense.* This is one they don't teach you in college. I'm convinced that the most effective public relations programs are those that are the most straightforward. Too often, we develop convoluted, confusing initiatives that fall flat on their face. Keep it simple.

- *Be committed.* Anyone expecting PR to be a 9-to-5 job should seek employment elsewhere. Deadlines (and clients) don't wait. You need to be willing to put in the long hours that can make the difference. And on top of that, you need to find the time to be involved in a worthwhile community or charitable cause that exposes you to a whole new universe of contacts and issues.

- *Be an expert.* People who come in with a level of expertise in another field—sports, fashion, health care, a foreign language, music, etc.—are a step ahead of the rest. Your passions and hobbies can be an important personal marketing tool that adds extra value to your credentials.

Public relations is an evolving profession. I've seen it grow to become more inclusive and responsive to our multicultural society; to be used as a powerful marketing tool in launching new products and services and building brand equity; and to become a more valued management function. It is also a profession that thrives on those who are the brightest, most creative, and self-starters. So if you're willing to work long hours, answer to multiple bosses, and make less money than many of your college colleagues in exchange for being where the action is, then welcome to the wild, wonderful, sometimes wacky world of public relations. Enjoy the ride!

Case Study 2.1

Good Guys Finish First: John Graham and the Gold Anvil

Reed Byrum, 2003 president of the Public Relations Society of America, stepped to the lectern. "Our conference theme this year is 'Building Credibility, Confidence, and Respect,'" he told members of the audience at PRSA's annual meeting. "We couldn't have selected better words to describe John Graham, an industry leader whose credibility extends across all audiences."[23]

John Graham is chairman and chief executive officer of St. Louis-based Fleishman-Hillard, one of the world's largest public relations agencies. At PRSA's conference in New Orleans, Graham received the Gold Anvil, the organization's highest individual award, honoring practitioners who have significantly improved the profession of public relations. "Over the past several decades," PRSA declared in its official Gold Anvil statement, "Graham has set a leadership example that has become a benchmark by which other leaders in the industry measure their performance—in ethics, in client satisfaction, in the importance of research, and, above all, in elevating the visibility and perceived value of public relations."[24]

Since 1966, Graham has worked for one employer: Fleishman-Hillard. In 1970, he was promoted to vice president. Four years later, he became president and CEO, and in 1988 he added the title chairman of the board. Under Graham's leadership, Fleishman-Hillard has grown from a one-city agency with a staff of fewer than 50 to a global powerhouse with more than 80 offices in North America, Europe, Asia,

Latin America, Australia, and Africa and more than 2,000 employees. Fleishman-Hillard is now a division of Omnicom, a worldwide marketing and corporate communications company.

"Thirty years ago, I knew Fleishman-Hillard had the potential to do great things on a large scale," Graham says, "but I must say the success we have achieved surpasses anything I anticipated when I took on the responsibilities of chief executive officer."[25]

Fleishman-Hillard's successes include its ranking, for 11 straight years, as the world's top agency in terms of reputation for high-quality work. The Harris/Impulse Research Public Relations Client Survey determines the winner—and since the honor began in 1993, no other agency has won the top award.[26]

Ask John Graham about the future of jobs in public relations, and he'll tell you to expect and work for changes in three areas:

1. *Diversity.* Graham cites daunting statistics: In the United States, African Americans constitute fewer than 5 percent of public relations professionals, Hispanic Americans fewer than 3 percent, and Asian Americans fewer than 2 percent. "Our firm has managed to exceed the industry average," he says, "but we know we have more work to do."[27]

2. *Globalization.* Graham believes that Fleishman-Hillard's dramatic international growth represents the future of public relations. "Our clients . . . expect us to organize and align our global teams to deliver strong and consistent results in any part of the world," he says.[28]

3. *Specialization.* Graham notes that as Fleishman-Hillard has hired individuals with specific areas of expertise, the agency's ability to anticipate client problems and identify client opportunities has increased. "We need to continue to bring more specialized talents and expertise to our clients," he says.[29]

Despite the changes he envisions, Graham adds that public relations must stay rooted in enduring values. "I think the real challenge for PR executives is to continue adapting to these changes without getting distracted from the really critical things our clients need from us that haven't changed," he says. "Things like clear, disciplined writing. Like the obligation to apply our best thinking and analysis to our clients' issues—to offer them strategic insight and honest counsel."[30]

After Graham won the Gold Anvil award, *PR Week* magazine reviewed his career and concluded that his commitment to core values helped explain his success. In an article titled "Graham Embodies the Values That Built Fleishman," the magazine identified three values that Graham has embraced throughout his career: calmness, courtesy, and a respectful, productive corporate culture. "If we don't have the internal focus on culture," he says, "we won't be able to concentrate on work with clients. . . . We can't get off track and forget to emphasize our culture to new hires or when we've made an acquisition."[31]

PR Week could have identified one more value in Graham's life and career: fun. At one point during his interview with the magazine, he burst into laughter and made a brief confession: "There aren't too many things I don't like about this business."[32]

DISCUSSION QUESTIONS

1. What qualities does John Graham have that make him a successful public relations practitioner?
2. What are the advantages of staying with one employer for decades? The disadvantages?
3. Compare Graham's comments on public relations with the PRSA Member Statement of Professional Values (p. 38). On what points do Graham and PRSA agree?
4. Thirty years from now, if *PR Week* were to profile you as a leader in public relations, what specific personal values would you want the magazine to attribute to you?

Case Study 2.2

A List to Avoid

One of the highlights (or lowlights, if it shines on you) of the year for public relations practitioners is the release of an irreverent list of the worst public relations disasters of the past 12 months. Compiled since 1995 by Fineman Public Relations of San Francisco, the list balances an utter lack of mercy with a wicked sense of humor. It offers a wealth of case studies on how *not* to conduct successful public relations.

Among the recent winners of this dubious distinction:[33]

■ *Fox News:* "Television networks are supposed to be pillars of free speech, so no one missed the irony when Fox News sued liberal satirist Al Franken. Fox accused Franken and his publisher of trademark infringement . . . claiming they had violated its 'fair and balanced' trademark. Franken's new book . . . uses 'fair and balanced' in its mocking title. . . . Judge Denny Chin threw the suit out, saying, 'Of course it is ironic that a media company that should be fighting for the First Amendment is trying to undermine it.' "

■ *WPYX-FM, Latham, New York:* "As a promotion, the radio station holds what it calls 'Ugliest Bride' contests. From newspaper wedding announcements, the radio hosts pick the bride they deem the ugliest. Callers win by guessing which photograph was chosen. [Once], in a departure from usual practices, the station aired the bride's full name and place of employment. Hello, $300,000 lawsuit, an AP story, and a mean-spirited image."

■ *Richard Grasso:* "Richard Grasso's $140 million compensation package was a vestige of the bullish 1990s but couldn't stand up to the media scrutiny of the bearish 2000s. Grasso, chairman of the New York Stock Exchange, made several PR blunders after his package was disclosed. . . . *USA Today* opined on Grasso's mistakes of stonewalling the press, while minimizing the payday mess: 'The handling of the scandal may end up in a PR textbook on how not to handle a crisis.' "

■ *Martha Stewart:* "Martha Stewart's 'peaches and cream' reputation seemed to sour in ImClone's insider stock trading scandal because she didn't have a good recipe for responding to the crisis. 'Whether she's guilty or not, she's certainly be-having as if she is,' wrote MSNBC columnist Christopher Byron. Instead of getting out in front of the insider stock trading scandal, Stewart retreated 'into a kind of defensive hunkered down mode that seems to border on paranoia,' Byron wrote of the PR fiasco."

■ *America West Airlines:* "After two America West pilots were fired for allegedly being drunk in the cockpit, the airline was supersensitive about the ensuing barrage of bad publicity. . . . When a woman boarded an America West jet in San Francisco and jokingly asked, 'Have you checked your crew for sobriety?'—the crew overreacted by kicking her off the plane."

■ *Andy Rooney:* "It wasn't just feminists who blitzed Andy Rooney . . . when he said women shouldn't be doing sideline commentary for TV networks at NFL games. . . . Rooney denied he was a sexist in offering what seemed a half-hearted apology, and that led to a second round of negative coverage. 'Well thank goodness he's not a sexist. That leaves being an idiot,' wrote columnist Betty Cuniberti in the *St. Louis Post Dispatch*."

There you have it: how not to conduct successful public relations. If you decide to pursue a career in this wonderful, challenging profession, we hope you'll set many lofty goals for yourself. One of them should be never to appear on the annual Fine-man list.

DISCUSSION QUESTIONS

1. Which of the above public relations blunders is, in your opinion, the worst? Why?
2. Many of the above gaffes were committed by people not in public relations. How could public relations practitioners within the organizations have prevented those errors?
3. Should the organizations cited respond to their presence on the annual Fineman list? Or should they ignore it?
4. Suppose that you're head of public relations for each of the above organizations. The terrible event has just happened. Now the reporters are at your door. What do you tell them?
5. Do you think Fineman Public Relations runs a risk by associating itself with bad public relations?

Cyber Coach

Visit www.ablongman.com/guthmarsh3e for these study aids—and more:

■ flashcards   ■ videos   ■ real-world scenarios that let you be
■ quizzes   ■ links to other sites   the public relations professional

KEY TERMS

NOTES

1. James Collins and Jerry Porras, *Built to Last: Successful Habits of Visionary Companies* (New York: HarperBusiness, 1994), 8, 73, 88.

2. Jan Goldberg, *Real People Working in Public Relations* (Lincolnwood, Ill.: VGM Career Horizons, 1997), 88.

3. *Occupational Outlook Handbook, 2004–2005,* U.S. Bureau of Labor Statistics, online, www.bls.gov.

4. "E-mail Is the Preferred Way to Receive Résumés," *HRFocus,* July 2000, online, Lexis-Nexis.

5. "Help Wanted: Apply Online," news release issued by Accountemps, 9 December 2003, online, LexisNexis; Michael McBride, "Job Hunting in Cyberspace," the (Muncie, Ind.) *Star Press,* 28 March 2004, online, LexisNexis.

6. McBride.

7. Don Stacks, Carl Botan, and Judy Van Slyke Turk, "Perceptions of Public Relations Education," *Public Relations Review* 25 (1999): 9–29; "Workinpr.com State of the Industry Survey 2002," online, www.workinpr.com; "Qualities/Skills Employers Look for in New Hires," National Association of Colleges and Employers, online, www.jobweb.com/joboutlook/2004outlook.

8. "Workinpr.com State of the Industry Survey 2002."

9. *Occupational Outlook Handbook, 2004–2005.*

10. David Dozier, "The Organizational Roles of Communications and Public Relations Practitioners," in *Excellence in Public Relations and Communication Management,* ed. James E. Grunig (Hillsdale, N.J.: Lawrence Erlbaum, 1992), 341–352.

11. Elizabeth Toth, Shirley Serini, Donald Wright, and Arthur Emig, "Trends in Public Relations Roles: 1990–1995," *Public Relations Review* (summer 1998): 145–163.

12. Greg Leichty and Jeff Springston, "Elaborating Public Relations Roles," *Journalism and Mass Communications Quarterly* (summer 1996): 467–468; Toth, Serini, Wright, and Emig; *Occupational Outlook Handbook, 2004–2005.*

13. Shannon A. Bowen, " 'I Thought It Would Be More Glamorous': Preconceptions and Misconceptions among Students in the Public Relations Principles Course," *Public Relations Review* 29 (2003): 199–214.

14. *Occupational Outlook Handbook, 2004–2005.*

15. Lee B. Becker, Tudor Vlad, Amy Jo Coffey, and Heidi Hennink-Kaminski, "2003 Annual Survey of Journalism & Mass Communication Graduates, online, www.uga.edu/centers/frame.AnnualSurveys.asp.

16. "Profile 2000: A Survey of the Profession, Part I," *Communication World,* June/July 2000, A1–A32; "PRSA/IABC Salary Survey 2000," online, www.prsa.org/ppc.

17. "Profile 2000: A Survey of the Profession, Part I"; "PRSA/IABC Salary Survey 2000."

18. "The Satisfaction Factor," *PR News,* 13 January 2003, online, LexisNexis.

19. "PRSA/IABC Salary Survey 2000."

20. "Profile 2000: A Survey of the Profession, Part I."

21. "Workinpr.com State of the Industry Survey 2002."

22. Bowen, 211.

23. "Clarke, Graham Honored During PRSA's Annual Legends Luncheon," Public Relations Society of America, 27 October 2003, online, www.prsa.org/conf2003/102703-5.html.

24. "Clarke, Graham Honored During PRSA's Annual Legends Luncheon."

25. "John D. Graham Honored on 30th Year as CEO of Fleishman-Hillard," news release issued by Fleishman-Hillard, 25 March 2004, online, www.fleishman.com/news.

26. "Fleishman-Hillard Ranked No. 1 in Reputation for Quality Work for 11th Straight Year," a news release issued by Fleishman-Hillard, 13 October 2003, online, Lexis-Nexis.

27. John Graham, "Opportunities for Firms and Clients Abound If We Stick to Our Principles," *PR Week,* 8 December 2003, online, LexisNexis.

28. Graham.

29. Graham.

30. "Q/A: Reflections on Three Decades in Public Relations," *PR News,* 19 April 2004, online, LexisNexis.

31. Julia Hood, "Graham Embodies the Values That Built Fleishman," *PR Week,* 8 March 2004, online, LexisNexis.

32. Hood.

33. Fineman Public Relations' annual list is released through PR Newswire and can be accessed online via LexisNexis.

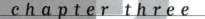

3

A Brief History of Public Relations

objectives

After studying this chapter, you will be able to

■ discuss how public relations evolved before it was formally recognized and given a name

■ identify the forces that have shaped the modern profession's development

■ recognize the major figures and events that influenced the growth of public relations

■ explain the issues and trends that are shaping the future of public relations

Black and White

scenario

In old Western movies, it was always easy to tell who the good guys were—they were always the ones in the white hats. Bad guys wore black hats. When it comes to the practice of public relations, things are not that simple.

Imagine you are at a job fair and have been interviewed by the representative of a multinational corporation. Its operations reach into a wide array of interests, including energy production, health care delivery, food products, and entertainment. The company is well known for its philanthropy and innovative solutions to business problems. However, not all of the news about it has been good. The company is the target of environmental and labor disputes.

The company representative wants you to apply for a job. But you are not sure. On what basis will you make this important decision? Does history provide any examples from which you can learn? Does anyone wear a white hat any more? And is that important?

Why History Is Important to You

At first glance, public relations appears to be a 20th-century invention. It is logical to link the emergence of the profession to the dramatic growth in mass communication technology during the past 100 years.

However, a closer examination reveals a remarkable history—a discipline practiced in many forms long before the nephew of a famous doctor gave it a name. History also tells about a profession that, at its very best, has been a positive force for change and, at its worst, has created challenges we continue to face.

History and the public relations profession are both values-driven. Both are filled with examples of where people acted—or failed to act—on their beliefs and standards. Both are also open to each observer's interpretation—also shaped by values. You faced this challenge in the opening scenario of this chapter: What values will govern your attitudes toward the aforementioned multinational corporation? Do you see it as a good guy or as a bad guy? And does it matter?

The scenario also posed the question "Does history provide any examples from which you can learn?" Here is where the study of our past becomes particularly useful. Not only does it tell us where we have been, but it also provides context for where we are and guidance to where we are going. History is full of examples in which people have learned—or failed to learn—from the actions of others.

William Shakespeare wrote in *The Tempest,* "What is past is prologue." To put it another way: Pay attention to history. You may be watching coming attractions.

Premodern Public Relations

Although the phrase "public relations" did not attain its current meaning until the 20th century, the practice of public relations has been evident since the dawn of recorded history. One example of public relations, in which primitive agricultural extension agents gave advice on how to grow better crops, dates back to 1800 B.C. in what is now Iraq.

Some historians believe that the development of public relations is a direct result of Western civilization's first true democracy: the city-state of Athens led by Pericles from 461 to 429 B.C. The dictatorships of the past had been overthrown, and suddenly the male citizens of Athens were free to debate, create, and implement public policy. In that environment, citizens began to study public opinion and the methods of influencing it. That study, known as **rhetoric,** is often seen as the beginning of public relations as a social science based on research, planning, and two-way communication. The practice of rhetoric fell into disuse with the demise of democratic Athens but flourished again in the freedoms of the final century of the Roman republic (100 B.C.), when a philosophy of *vox populi,* the voice of the people, was embraced.

The spread of Christianity during the Middle Ages could, in a modern context, be linked to the application of public relations techniques. Before the development of mass communication technologies, the faith was passed along by missionaries using word of mouth. Among the most notable of these missionaries was Francis of Assisi, who spread his teachings of self-imposed poverty and service to the poor across Europe and the Middle East. He died in 1226, but his religious order, the Franciscans, survives to this day. Johannes Gutenberg's Bible, printed in 1456 by means of a revolutionary movable type process, heralded the use of mass communication technologies. The Catholic Church's outreach efforts became more formalized in the 1600s when it established the *Congregatio de Propaganda Fide,* or Congregation for the Propagation of the Faith, to spread church doctrine.

Trends Leading to the Development of Modern Public Relations

The growth of modern public relations was not limited to just one nation. Aspects of what we now know as public relations emerged independently in several societies. For example, organized government public relations efforts in the United Kingdom preceded those in the United States by more than a decade. The National Association of Local Government Officers began in 1905, in part to educate the public about the role of local government in British society.[1] However, the earliest development of the profession appears to have emerged in the United States, where privately owned business and industry embraced public relations in the 1880s. In comparison, private sector public relations was not prominent in Britain until after the Second World War.[2]

The march toward modern public relations began in earnest in the United States after the Civil War. To a large degree, this development paralleled the country's transition from an agricultural to an industrial society. The **Industrial Revolution** brought with it growing pains, which, in turn, redefined the relationships among government, business, and the people. Historians often refer to this period of reforms as the **Progressive Era,** which ran from the 1890s to the United States' entrance into World War I in 1917. It was a period in which democracy as well as social and governmental institutions matured. Public opinion grew more important; the nation reexamined and, to a certain extent, redefined itself.

Let's look more closely at how the development of modern public relations is linked to five social trends that had their beginnings in the Progressive Era.

THE GROWTH OF INSTITUTIONS.   The Industrial Revolution spawned the growth of big companies. The resulting concentration of wealth among early 20th-century industrialists such as J. P. Morgan, Andrew Carnegie, and John D. Rockefeller, ran against the traditional American inclination toward decentralized power—as evidenced in the checks and balances established in the Constitution. This, in turn, led to increased regulation of these businesses and consequent growth in the size of government. Led by the University of Michigan in 1897, U.S. colleges and universities began to promote themselves by creating publicity offices.[3] By the 1930s, labor unions began to have clout. As business, government, and labor organizations grew larger, the need for effective communication increased. All three sectors experienced a second growth spurt in the economic boom that followed the end of World War II.

THE EXPANSION OF DEMOCRACY.   Progressive Era reforms such as giving women the right to vote and the direct election of U.S. senators brought more people into the political process and increased the need for public discussion of policy issues. That expansion continued into the mid- to late 20th century. As a result of the civil rights movement, black citizens and other minority groups gained greater access to the political process. During the Vietnam War, 18-year-olds were also given the right to vote. With the fall of communist governments in Europe and Asia near the end of the 20th century came a growing need for effective communication in emerging democratic societies. Because of the increasing importance of persuasion and consensus, public relations has become an integral part of the democratic process.

TECHNOLOGICAL IMPROVEMENTS IN COMMUNICATIONS.   Each new communication medium presents both challenges and opportunities for reaching large audiences. In the early 1900s the growth of national news services such as the Associated Press and the birth of national magazines such as the *Ladies' Home Journal* gave muckraking reporters a wider audience. The introduction of commercial radio in 1920 and commercial television in 1947 launched the era of instantaneous electronic communication. Developments in satellite and computer technology in the second half of the 20th century further revolutionized communications. With the dramatic expansion of the Internet in the 1990s, the power to communicate with mass publics began shifting away from media companies and toward individuals.

THE GROWTH OF ADVOCACY.   In the late 1800s, a wave of immigrants who brought Old World political ideas to the New World—and, to some extent, the reaction of native-born citizens to this human wave from abroad—gave birth to increased political activism. Newspapers evolved from the organs of partisan "yellow journalism" of the 19th century into instruments of social advocacy in the early 20th century. The period after World War II also witnessed the growth of significant social advocacy, including movements for civil rights, women's rights, environmentalism, consumerism, antiwar ideals, children's rights, multinationalism, rights for persons with disabilities,

A great wave of immigrants (shown here receiving health inspections on arrival at Ellis Island) changed U.S. society and helped set the stage for the development of the new profession of public relations. (Courtesy of The Statue of Liberty–Ellis Island Foundation, Inc.)

and gay rights. Both those who advocated change and the institutions forced to deal with it found an increasing need for public relations.

THE SEARCH FOR CONSENSUS.   U.S. society is built upon consensus. The nation at one time believed itself to be a melting pot in which various cultures and philosophies would combine into something distinctly American. In recent decades, however, that concept has been largely discredited. It is now accepted that people can *both* be American and retain other cultural identities. Beyond the United States, the world population is growing at a rapid rate. The emergence of a global economy has highlighted the increasing competition for Earth's dwindling resources. With the threat of thermonuclear war on one hand and global environmental disaster on the other, the need to span cultural and philosophical differences is greater than ever. Organizations and individuals are learning that the positive application of public relations can help bridge those gaps.

As you will read in the coming pages, the development of public relations closely mirrors the growth of the United States. Although the profession evolved in other societies as well, it was in the United States—the great experiment in democracy—that public relations flourished.

BLOWING SMOKE

Public relations has a long—and controversial—association with the tobacco industry. With the help of public relations practitioners, Big Tobacco vigorously protected its multibillion dollar empire in a no-holds-barred defense that often stretched the limits of truth.

One of the most outlandish—and successful—efforts to sell cigarettes to the lucrative and previously untapped female market was on Easter Sunday 1929. Public relations pioneer Edward L. Bernays recruited 10 debutantes to walk down New York's Fifth Avenue carrying lighted cigarettes aloft "to combat the silly prejudice that the cigarette is suitable for the home, the restaurant, the taxicab, the theater lobby, but never the sidewalk."[4] The so-called Torches of Freedom march created a nationwide buzz. Bernays wrote decades later that "a beginning had been made, one I regret today."[5]

A 1952 *Reader's Digest* article, "Cancer by the Carton," dramatically brought home the danger of smoking to Americans. The tobacco industry responded by creating the Tobacco Institute Research Committee (TIRC). In full-page ads in more than 400 newspapers, TIRC announced that it would sponsor research into health issues raised by smoking. Sixty-five percent of the public responded favorably to the advertisements. The TIRC eventually evolved into the Tobacco Institute, which at its height employed more than 120 public relations practitioners and spent more than $20 million annually promoting tobacco.[6]

A major shift in public policy came in the 1990s, fueled by the publication of internal industry documents suggesting that tobacco executives had ignored research showing smoking was harmful. Those documents also raised doubts about industry claims that it doesn't encourage smoking among minors.

Under the threat of a mountain of personal injury lawsuits, the tobacco industry finally admitted in 1997 that cigarettes are addictive and harmful to health. It also agreed to submit to nicotine regulation by the Food and Drug Administration, restrict its marketing tactics, and earmark more than $200 billion for health and antismoking education programs.[7]

It is ironic that public relations practitioners—once scorned for doing Big Tobacco's bidding—are now being praised for their role in reducing the rate of cigarette smoking. A 2003 report in the *Journal of the National Cancer Institute* credited a federal antismoking campaign with a decline in tobacco use. And it said the reason this effort succeeded where others had failed was because of the effective use of public relations.[8]

Pre-20th-Century America

Although it would be more than a century before the discipline had a name, the use of public relations tactics was evident in pre-Revolutionary America. Perhaps the most famous example is the Boston Tea Party, a publicity event designed to focus attention on British taxation without representation. After the Revolution, public relations tactics were used to change the course of history. In what some have described as history's finest public relations effort, the **Federalist Papers** appeared in newspapers between October 1787 and April 1788. Written by Alexander Hamil-

Values Statement 3.1

THE UNITED STATES CONSTITUTION

Delegates from the 13 original states met in Philadelphia from May to September 1787 to draft a constitution for the new nation. Following its ratification by 11 states (North Carolina and Rhode Island ratified it later), the Constitution took effect on March 4, 1789.

We, the people of the United States, in order to form a more perfect union, establish justice, insure domestic tranquillity, provide for the common defence, promote the general welfare, and secure the blessings of liberty to ourselves and our posterity, do ordain and establish this Constitution for the United States of America.

—Preamble, U.S. Constitution

ton, James Madison, and John Jay under the single nom de plume Publius, these essays helped lead the reluctant former colonies to ratify the Constitution of the United States.

The ratification of the Constitution and the Bill of Rights in 1789 remains the most important event in the development of public relations in the United States. The 45 words of the **First Amendment** define the liberties that allow the free practice of this vital profession:

Congress shall make no law respecting an establishment of religion, or prohibiting the free exercise thereof; or abridging the freedom of speech, or of the press; or the right of the people peaceably to assemble, and to petition the Government for a redress of grievances.

This guarantee of free expression, however, is not absolute. It is constantly being interpreted and refined by the U.S. Supreme Court. There have been times, during war or civil unrest for example, when freedom of expression has been severely tested. But more than two centuries after ratification, the First Amendment still stands as the singular liberty that distinguishes U.S. democracy and, as a consequence, the practice of public relations in the United States.

In the 1800s democracy in the United States continued to mature. Public education was introduced, which resulted in a more literate and well-informed society. As the right to vote was extended to men who did not own property, vigorous public debate emerged. The influence of that debate on the government was clear when President Andrew Jackson appointed Amos Kendall to his so-called kitchen cabinet. Kendall was the first presidential press secretary, serving as Jackson's pollster, counselor, speechwriter, and publicist.

Two other figures in the premodern period of public relations are worth noting. During the Civil War, Jay Cooke headed the United States' first fund-raising drive: Through an appeal to patriotism, Cooke sold government bonds to finance the Union's war effort. Better known, but less fondly remembered by practitioners, is Phineas T. Barnum, who created his circus in 1871 and later proclaimed it to be "The Greatest Show on Earth." Barnum was the father of press agentry in this country. A master showman, Barnum generated extensive newspaper coverage of his often bizarre enterprises through exaggeration, distortion, and outright lies. To the shame of the profession, some wanna-be publicists still practice Barnum's "publicity for publicity's sake" approach today.

QuickBreak 3.2

THE AMERICAN REVOLUTION

It is not a stretch to say that the United States owes its existence—at least to some degree—to the successful practice of public relations. The American Revolution was a triumph of ideas and sacrifice, but it could not have happened without public support. While revolutionary leaders may not have called this relationship-building process *public relations,* that is exactly what they were doing.

One example is Thomas Paine, who came to America in 1774 with a passion for liberty and a flair for self-expression. In January 1776, he wrote a 79-page pamphlet, *Common Sense.* In it, Paine laid out the rationale for a permanent separation from the crown.[9] More than 100,000 copies of *Common Sense* were sold within three months of its publication. George Washington credited its "sound doctrine and unanswerable reasoning" with convincing reluctant colonists of the need to break from England.[10]

In its own way, the Declaration of Independence served as a news release, announcing the birth of a new nation and the principles on which it had been founded. When one looks at the drafting of the document and the framing of its messages, it is easy to see its resemblance to modern practice.

Thomas Jefferson was the lead writer, assisted by a committee of editors, fellow delegates to the Continental Congress. As one does when writing a modern news release, Jefferson wrote a lead designed to capture and hold the reader's attention. He wrote, "We hold these Truths to be self-evident, that all Men are created equal, that they are endowed by their Creator with certain unalienable rights, that among these are Life, Liberty, and the Pursuit of Happiness."[11] After the declaration's adoption on July 4, 1776, the Continental Congress ordered copies printed and distributed throughout the new nation. Newspapers reported its contents and, in many cases, published its text in full.[12]

Declaring independence was one thing. Winning it was another. Maintaining popular support was critical. To help in this cause, Paine published a series of 13 pamphlets, *The American Crisis,* in which he urged colonists to continue their struggle for independence. "These are the times that try men's souls," Paine wrote. "The summer soldier and the sunshine patriot will, in this crisis, shrink from the service of their country; but he that stands *now,* deserves the love and thanks of man and woman."[13]

"Methods to move mass audiences that are precious in modern America were vital in early America as well," wrote practitioner and historian Jason Karpf. "The Founding Fathers counted many PR masters among their ranks."

"As a nation, we are most fortunate for their PR triumphs."[14]

Quick ✔ Check

1. What are some of the earliest examples of public relations—even before the profession was known as public relations?
2. What are the major social trends that have influenced the development of public relations?
3. What remains the most important event in the development of public relations in the United States?

The Seedbed Years

The late public relations historian Scott Cutlip called the initial period in the growth of modern public relations, from the dawn of the industrial age to the outbreak of World War I, "the **Seedbed Years.**"[15] It was during this period of growth in U.S. society that organizations first felt the need for formalizing their communications. For example, in 1888 the Mutual Life Insurance Company created a "literary bureau" to publicize its services. One year later George Westinghouse hired a newspaper reporter to help him earn public favor in his battle with Thomas Edison over competing electricity distribution systems. Presidential candidate William Jennings Bryan inaugurated the practice of whistle-stop campaigning during 1896, in large part out of the need for publicity to counter William McKinley's well-financed campaign.

The nation's first public relations agency, the **Publicity Bureau** in Boston, was created in 1900 in recognition of the fact that corporations needed to voice their concerns amid a rising tide of critics. The Publicity Bureau came to epitomize the practice—and the challenges—of modern public relations in its infancy. The Publicity Bureau's clients, which included American Telephone & Telegraph and the nation's railroads, hoped that this new craft known as publicity might stem the increasing demand for government regulation.[16]

Other pioneering practitioners would soon follow. William Wolf Smith opened the national capital's first "publicity business" in 1902. The Parker and Lee agency, the nation's third, opened in New York City in 1904. However, it folded after only four years. That was a common fate of these early agencies.

There were several reasons why early publicity shops met with limited success. First, they were breaking new ground. Although public relations had been practiced in various forms for centuries, the concept of formalized publicity was relatively new. As with advertising on the web today, making public relations profitable in the early days of the 20th century was extremely difficult.

Credibility was also a problem. These early public relations efforts followed a one-way model: Publicity agents were zealous to put forward the view of their clients and often let accuracy fall by the wayside. Sources of information were often hidden, creating a public that was increasingly suspicious of anything carrying a "publicity" label. Real two-way communication did not occur. The ethical divisions between the roles of journalists and practitioners were also not well defined: It was common practice for a journalist to write under his byline (journalists were almost exclusively men in those days) for a newspaper in the mornings and to write anonymous publicity releases in the afternoons.

Early public relations practitioners also faced stiff resistance from newspaper publishers. Some of this hostility stemmed from the tactics of early practitioners, which included bribes, gifts, and outrageous publicity stunts. Journalists also resented the growing number of people at their doorsteps seeking news coverage. Many journalists were contemptuous of former colleagues who switched to public relations careers. This was ironic, because many of the same critics complained bitterly about their own poor wages, negative reputations, and difficult working conditions.[17]

Theodore Roosevelt (1858–1919)

Early publicity efforts—especially those targeted at halting the increasing influence of government regulation—achieved only limited success for yet another reason: Theodore Roosevelt. The youngest person to date to serve as president, Roosevelt dramatically transformed the relationships among the White House, big business, and the electorate. Before Roosevelt's succession to the presidency upon the assassination of William McKinley in 1901, the attitude widely held by Washington officials was, in essence, "What is good for big business is good for America." But Roosevelt saw big business' increasing concentration of power—an estimated 10 percent of the population at that time owned 90 percent of the wealth—as a threat to democracy. Roosevelt's administration proceeded to sue 44 major corporations in an attempt to break up monopolies and increase business competition.

Roosevelt also understood—probably better than any other person of his time—the power of harnessing public opinion. He transformed the presidency into what he called his "bully pulpit." Traditional power brokers were opposed to the reforms of Roosevelt's Square Deal, but the president understood the mood of the people and courted their favor through the muckraking press. As researcher Blaire Atherton French has written,

> Theodore Roosevelt was the first to initiate close and continuous ties with reporters, and may be accurately called the founder of presidential press conferences. He brought the press into the White House literally as well as figuratively. The tale goes that he looked out his window one rainy day and saw a group of reporters manning their usual post by the White House gate. Their purpose was to question those coming and going from the White

Theodore Roosevelt, the nation's youngest president, is best remembered for using the White House as a "bully pulpit," from which he could rally public opinion in favor of his reform policies. (Courtesy of the Library of Congress)

House and in that way to gather news or leads. When T. R. saw them miserable, wet, and cold, he ordered that there be a room in the White House set aside just for them. In doing so, T. R. granted them a status they had never previously enjoyed and would subsequently never lose.[18]

Although many of his proposed reforms were thwarted by a stubborn Congress, much of Theodore Roosevelt's success and widespread popularity was a result of his skillful application of public relations. As another researcher has written, Roosevelt "figured out how a president can use the news media to guide public opinion. He did not just hand out information and leave matters in the hands of reporters. He created news."[19]

Ivy Ledbetter Lee (1877–1934)

A man who deserves more credit for the growth of public relations than he has received is **Ivy Ledbetter Lee.** His was a career that began in triumph and ended in a controversy that outlived him.

The son of a Methodist minister in Georgia, Lee studied at Princeton and worked as a newspaper reporter and stringer. After a brief foray into politics, Lee joined George E. Parker, once President Grover Cleveland's publicity manager, to form a publicity bureau in 1904. The new agency boasted of "Accuracy, Authenticity, and Interest."[20]

This philosophy evolved in 1906 into Lee's "**Declaration of Principles,**" the first articulation of the concept that public relations practitioners (although the term *public relations* had not yet been coined) have a public responsibility that extends beyond obligations to a client. "This is not a secret press bureau," Lee wrote. "All of our work is done in the open."

Lee's "Declaration of Principles" also declared, "In brief, our plan is, frankly and openly, on behalf of business concerns and public institutions, to supply the press and public of the United States prompt and accurate information concerning subjects which it is of value and interest to the public to know about."[21]

Lee's statement, issued at a time when he was representing management's side in a coal strike, changed the direction of the evolving field of public relations. He established ethical standards by which others could judge his work. In doing so, he also brought credibility and professionalism to the field.

Of course, actions speak louder than words, and Lee did not always live up to his own words. Perhaps a kinder interpretation is that he often defined accuracy in very narrow terms. For Lee, accuracy meant correctly reflecting the views of the client—but it did not mean checking to see whether the client's statements were truthful. Because of that questionable logic, during his controversial career Lee often supplied misleading or false information to reporters. The resulting mistrust of Lee and his motives would eventually be his undoing.

Lee had an impressive list of clients. It was Lee who, along with pioneer practitioner Harry Bruno, helped to promote public acceptance of the new field of aviation. Lee was crucial in gaining the needed financial support for a nationwide publicity tour by aviator Charles A. Lindbergh. Lee is also credited for his work with what would

Although his reputation was damaged because of his association with the German Dye Trust, Ivy Lee is more fondly remembered on this historical marker in Rockmart, Georgia, as the "Founder of Modern Public Relations." (Courtesy of Ed Jackson, Carl Vinson Institute of Government, University of Georgia)

eventually become General Mills and the creation of three of its most enduring symbols: Betty Crocker; Gold Medal Flour; and Wheaties, the Breakfast of Champions.[22]

You are judged by the company you keep. The appropriateness of representing controversial clients is an age-old problem for public relations practitioners—for example, would you represent an executive who had stolen from his company? Many of Lee's clients were controversial at the time they retained his services. They included the Anthracite Coal Operators, the Pennsylvania Railroad, and John D. Rockefeller.

However, it would be Lee's worldview and extensive travels that would cause the most damage to his reputation. In many ways Lee was a man ahead of his times. He supported recognition of Soviet Russia at a time when most of his compatriots were fearful of the recent communist revolution in that country. Lee was scorned for his desire for cooperation between the two nations. In less than a decade, however, cooperation between the United States and the Soviet Union would lead to an Allied victory in World War II.

The sharpest criticism was leveled at Lee's work in 1934 on behalf of I.G. Farben, the German Dye Trust. This episode occurred at a time shortly after Adolf Hitler assumed power in Germany. Lee's services were retained by industrialists to help counter a growing anti-German sentiment in the United States. Lee accepted a $25,000 fee with the stipulation that he only provide counsel and not disseminate information for the Germans within the United States. Lee, often referred to by his detractors as "Poison Ivy," was accused of being a Nazi sympathizer. Making matters worse, Lee ignored the advice he had often given others and refused to answer reporters' questions about his German business interests. In what now appears to be a very naive notion, Lee thought he could positively influence the behavior of the government of the Third Reich. In fairness, Lee was not the only person to underestimate the evil embodied in Adolf Hitler. However, this association would stain his name long after his death in 1934.

War and Propaganda

America's entrance into World War I in 1917 had a profound effect on both society and the growth of public relations. The war thrust the United States onto the world stage—a place where many U.S. citizens were reluctant to be. Isolationism grew out of a desire to separate the New World from the problems of Europe. In an earlier time, that had been quite possible. However, with the Industrial Revolution came the growth of U.S. economic power and ties to other nations that were an unavoidable consequence of a growing global economy.

World War I also focused public attention on the use of the mass media as tools of persuasion. People were becoming more familiar with the concept of **propaganda,** which is the attempt to have a viewpoint accepted at the exclusion of all others. The word's etymology stems from the Roman Catholic Church's efforts to propagate the faith during the 17th century. *Propaganda*, as a term, did not carry the negative connotations at the beginning of World War I that it does today. However, its abuse by its most evil practitioner, Nazi Propaganda Minister Joseph Goebbels, discredited propaganda both as a word and as a practice.

To rally the nation behind the war, President Woodrow Wilson established the **Committee for Public Information (CPI).** It became better known as the Creel Committee, after its chairman, former journalist George Creel. Creel was a longtime Wilson friend who had tried to persuade him to run for president as early as 1905, while Wilson was still president of Princeton University. Wilson had been reelected to the White House in 1916 on a promise that he would keep the United States out of the bloody conflict that had been raging across Europe since 1914. With involvement in the war now on the horizon, Wilson leaned toward the advice of his military experts that the press should be strictly censored. Creel, however, as military historian Thomas Flemming has noted, "convinced Wilson that the country needed not suppression but the expression of a coherent pro-war policy."[23]

During the two years that the United States was at war, the CPI churned out more than 75 million pamphlets and books with titles ranging from "Why We Are

Fighting" to "What Our Enemy Really Is." Through what may have been the largest speakers' bureau ever created, the **Four-Minute Men,** 75,000 speakers gave 755,190 talks to drum up home front morale.[24] (The name "Four-Minute Men" came from the length of time volunteers spoke between reel changes at cinemas, which were the most important form of mass entertainment at the time.) CPI filmmakers also produced features such as *Pershing's Crusaders* and *Under Four Flags.* These films not only fanned patriotic fires but also raised $852,744.30—not bad for the days when the price of a movie ticket was only a nickel.[25]

Quick ✔ Check

1. Why did most of the early publicity agencies fail?
2. What contributions did Ivy Ledbetter Lee make to the development of public relations?
3. In what ways did the outbreak of World War I influence the growth of public relations?

Edward L. Bernays (1891–1995)

World War I and the propaganda surrounding it sparked interest in the study and manipulation of public opinion. There was a growing demand for publicity agents to represent the interests of private companies and public agencies. The Creel Committee proved to be a training ground for many of these practitioners. Notable among them was **Edward L. Bernays,** an acknowledged "father" of public relations. Although Bernays had served as a press agent in several capacities before joining the Creel Committee in 1917, it was after the war that he made his indelible mark.

The Austrian-born Bernays was a nephew of Sigmund Freud, and he played a major role in having Freud's theories on psychoanalysis introduced to America. Before joining the CPI, Bernays served as a newspaper reporter and a theatrical press agent. For the most part, Bernays received high marks for his work with the Creel Committee. However, Bernays' lifelong propensity for self-promotion eventually led to the dismantling of the CPI. At the war's end, Bernays traveled with President Wilson to Paris for the Versailles Peace Conference to provide the president with technical assistance in dealing with reporters. Bernays issued a news release upon his departure announcing that he and 15 other employees of CPI were traveling to France as the "United States Official Press Mission to the Peace Conference." In the release Bernays wrote that "the announced object of the expedition is 'to interpret the work of the Peace Conference by keeping up a worldwide propaganda to disseminate American accomplishments and ideals.'"[26] Creel was angry that Bernays had overstated the CPI's role. Wilson's detractors in Congress began to look upon the CPI as the president's personal publicity machine and pulled its plug.

THE SCOPES MONKEY TRIAL

It was one of the great trials of the 20th century. It involved a historic clash between science and religion. The opposing attorneys were giants of their age. Almost 80 years later, it remains a subject of intense debate.

And, oh yes—it was also a publicity stunt.

The State of Tennessee v. John Scopes—better known as the Scopes Monkey Trial—was the flash point of a theological and political struggle over Charles Darwin's theory of evolution. When Darwin published *The Origin of Species* in 1859, he wrote that human beings evolved from apes through a process of natural selection and adaptation. For religious fundamentalists, this theory represented a direct challenge to their belief in divine creation. In a backlash against Darwin, the Tennessee legislature made teaching evolution in public schools a criminal offense in March 1925. The American Civil Liberties Union, eager to test the constitutionality of the law, offered to defend any teacher willing to challenge it.[27]

When Dayton, Tennessee, businessman George Rappleyea read about the ACLU's offer, he immediately recognized an opportunity. Dayton, a small agricultural community located in the southeastern part of the state, had hit hard times.[28] Rappleyea realized that a court battle over evolution would attract national attention that would revive Dayton's economy.[29]

It was in Robinson's Drugstore, a popular gathering spot, that Rappleyea met with local leaders to hatch his plan. But if his scheme to attract publicity was going to work, the conspirators had to identify a defendant—a local teacher willing to be arrested and placed on trial for violating Tennessee's antievolution law. They recruited John Scopes, a popular 24-year-old math

and physics teacher who coached football. After some reluctance, Scopes agreed. Rappleyea—a staunch evolutionist—swore out a warrant for Scopes' arrest and then called the ACLU. When the civil libertarians agreed to defend the coach-turned-defendant, the game was on.[30]

Dayton embraced the controversial trial with a gusto rarely seen before or since. A Scopes Trial Entertainment Committee was established to arrange visitor accommodations. As the trial neared, the town was adorned with pictures of apes and monkeys. Robinson's Drugstore served "simian soda," and the town constable's motorcycle proudly displayed a "Monkeyville Police" sign.[31]

The trial's two lead attorneys dominated the stage, Clarence Darrow for the defense and William Jennings Bryan for the prosecution. Darrow was arguably the most famous trial lawyer in the country and a self-avowed atheist. Bryan was a religious conservative and a three-time Democratic nominee for president. The trial began with jury selection on July 10, 1925.

The nation closely followed proceedings in the Rhea County Courthouse over the next 12 days—it was the first trial ever broadcast over the relatively new medium of radio. Newspaper reporters from around the world descended on Dayton. They included H. L. Mencken of the *Baltimore Sun,* known for his sharp—often cutting—humor.

"Here was an unexampled, almost miraculous chance to get Dayton upon the front pages, to make it talked about, to put it on the map," Mencken wrote. "Two months ago the town was obscure and happy. Today it is a universal joke."[32]

(continued)

QuickBreak 3.3 continued

READ
**"WHY DAYTON
OF ALL PLACES"**

For Sale at
ROBINSON'S DRUG STORE,
On Main Street

Robinson's Drugstore was an important center of action during the Scopes Monkey Trial. At that spot, Dayton, Tennessee, town officials contrived to bring the trial to their community to boost the sagging local economy. (Courtesy of Bryan College)

For the record, Scopes was convicted and fined $100. Five days after the trial, Bryan died and became a martyr for the antievolution cause. Because of technical errors in the proceedings, the case never reached the U.S. Supreme Court. In Dayton, tourists travel to the Rhea County Courthouse every summer to commemorate the trial. Eight decades later, the town remains the focal point of the evolution debate.[33]

Somewhere, George Rappleyea and the folks at Robinson's Drugstore are smiling.

Edward L. Bernays, an acknowledged "father" of public relations, was the nephew of famed psychoanalyst Sigmund Freud and the first person to coin the phrase "public relations counsel." (Courtesy of the Museum of Public Relations, prmuseum.com)

The inevitable finger-pointing ensued. Creel blamed Bernays for undercutting the mission of the CPI in a search for personal glory. For his part, Bernays cast blame on Creel for helping to lose the peace. "Lack of effective public relations between President Wilson and the people of the United States, historians confirm, was one of the reasons for the rejection of the League of Nations by the United States," Bernays wrote. "The final breakdown of the League in the early Thirties was due in large part to the same lack of good public relations."[34]

It was Bernays who, in his 1923 book, *Crystallizing Public Opinion,* popularized the phrase "public relations counsel." He said he used the phrase because of the negative connotations attached to terms such as *propagandist, publicist,* and *press agent:*

> I wanted something broader than publicity or press-agentry. I called what I did "publicity direction," by which I meant directing the actions of a client to result in the desired publicity. A year later Doris [Bernays' wife] and I coined the phrase "counsel on public relations," which we thought described our activity better—giving professional advice to our clients on their public relationships, regardless of whether such an activity resulted in publicity.[35]

Bernays was not the first to use the term *public relations.* President Thomas Jefferson used it in an address to Congress in 1807. Attorney Dorman Eaton also used the term in an 1882 talk before the Yale Law School graduating class.[36] However, Bernays was the first to use it to describe the discipline that bears its name.

In his book, Bernays was also the first to articulate the two-way communication concept of public relations. In the same year that *Crystallizing Public Opinion* was published, Bernays taught the first public relations course, at New York University.

QuickBreak 3.4

THE MOTHER OF PUBLIC RELATIONS

If Edward L. Bernays is most often credited with being the father of public relations, it is both logical and just that his wife, Doris E. Fleischman, be recognized as the profession's mother. Fleischman was more than Bernays' life partner. She was an equal—yet often invisible—business partner in one of history's most important and successful public relations agencies.

The original power couple of public relations met as children at a beach resort on Long Island, where their families had summer cottages.[37] Fleischman, whose father was a prominent attorney, became a women's page writer for the *New York Tribune* in 1914 and a freelance writer in 1916. She went to work for Bernays in the summer of 1919 at $50 a week as a staff writer. (He paid his male staff writers $75 a week.) At that time Bernays was engaged in what he called "publicity direction" for clients such as opera legend Enrico Caruso and the Russian Ballet.[38]

Bernays and Fleischman married on September 16, 1922. In an act that would come to symbolize this partnership, Fleischman—with her new husband's encouragement—registered at the Waldorf-Astoria for their wedding night using her maiden name. "I had an inner fear that marriage (though I wanted it fiercely with Doris) would take away some of my liberties as an individual if there were always a Mrs. added to my name," Bernays wrote in his memoirs. "I wanted both the ties and the freedom."[39] During their 58 years of marriage, Fleischman and Bernays were truly a team. "My relationship

with Doris was at two levels," Bernays wrote. "At the office we were fairly businesslike and professional, but after working hours our relationship became highly personal."[40] Bernays gives credit to his wife for helping him coin the phrase "public relations counsel." Bernays told one interviewer that his wife "played an equally important role with mine, except that her insight and judgment are better than mine."[41]

Although they may have been equal partners, they certainly haven't received equal recognition: Fleischman remains a shadow lingering in the background of Bernays' career. That is largely because of the way this unique partnership operated. Although the couple closely collaborated on all projects, Bernays made all the client contacts and speeches—and not just because of his propensity for self-promotion. It was a time when women were a rarity in the business world. Many companies were uncomfortable and unwilling to embrace women's ideas. Though this reality was a bitter pill to swallow, the couple played the game by the rules of the day and, by all measures, won.

Even though Doris Fleischman has not received the acclaim achieved by her husband, Bernays was his wife's greatest champion. "These are difficult times, being alone after 58 years of happy twenty-four-hour-a-day companionship," Bernays wrote after Fleischman's death in 1980. "She was a rare woman."[42]

Through the years Bernays promoted the interests of a wide variety of clients, including the American Tobacco Company, Lithuanians seeking independence from the Soviet Union, and Procter & Gamble. Bernays took credit for pushing CBS Radio to develop news programming to build up its image. He also acknowledged his role in encouraging women to smoke cigarettes—something he said he regretted much later in life.

Public relations historian Scott Cutlip wrote that Bernays believed in self-promotion to the point that he lost the respect of many of his contemporaries. In one instance, Bernays was fired from an account he had with General Motors because he had gotten more credit for GM's Depression-era relief efforts than had the company.[43] Nevertheless, in recognition of his role in the advancement of public relations, *Life* magazine named Bernays to its list of the 100 most influential Americans of the 20th century.

Bernays remained a leading advocate for professional public relations until his death at the age of 103 in 1995. Late in his life, Bernays favored the licensing of public relations professionals. "Any dumbbell, nitwit or crook can call himself a public relations practitioner," Bernays told an interviewer. "The only way to protect yourself from dumbbells and crooks is to install intellectual and social values that are meaningful and keep out people who only hand out circulars in Harvard Square."[44]

Why Bernays and Not Lee?

Why isn't Ivy Ledbetter Lee, whose "Declaration of Principles" preceded Edward L. Bernays' *Crystallizing Public Opinion* by 17 years, considered the real founder of modern public relations? It appears that timing and circumstances favored Bernays.

That both men deserve recognition is without question. At a time when what was to become known as public relations was in its infancy, Lee gave the profession credibility and ethical standards. Later, Bernays gave the emerging profession a name and direction.

However, it is also true that both men were not saints. Lee proclaimed the value of truth and accuracy, but he didn't always apply those standards to his own work. As for Bernays, his penchant for self-promotion cost him numerous contracts, caused him to be despised by many of his competitors, and may even have helped to dash hopes for a lasting world peace after World War I.

Both men faced a similar fork in the road during their careers. Their choices helped to seal their reputations. With what may have been good intentions, Lee worked for the Nazis. Bernays declined the same opportunity.

Lee's death in 1934 stilled his voice and ended any chance he might have had to salvage his tarnished reputation. Bernays, however, outlived his contemporary critics. In his writings and in his promotional literature, Bernays actively portrayed himself as the "father of public relations," and he was embraced by an industry that had itself sought recognition and acceptance for so long. Now that they are gone, perhaps history will treat both men as the flawed but notable figures they really were.

The Postwar Boom

Government public relations efforts expanded at the start of U.S. involvement in World War II, when a 1942 presidential order created the **Office of War Information**

(OWI). Headed by veteran newspaper and radio commentator Elmer Davis, OWI had a twofold mission: to coordinate and control the flow of information from the battlefield to the home front, and to engage in experiments in psychological warfare against the enemy. The OWI was the forerunner of the United States Information Agency, which had more than 7,300 employees and an annual budget of approximately $1 billion prior to being absorbed by the U.S. State Department in 1999.

Like its predecessor, the Committee for Public Information, OWI became a breeding ground for a new generation of public relations practitioners. During World War II approximately 100,000 people were trained as public information officers.[45] Once the war was over, many of these "battle-hardened" practitioners turned their wartime activities into careers.

The postwar period witnessed a rapid growth in public relations education. It was during this period, in 1948, that the Public Relations Society of America was formed by the merger of the National Association of Public Relations Counsel and the American Council on Public Relations. The International Association of Business Communicators began in 1970 following the merger of the American Association of Industrial Editors and the International Council of Industrial Editors.

Postwar Social Activism

The period following World War II in many ways resembled the period of the Industrial Revolution: It was a time of significant growth in the size of government, businesses, industries, organizations, and population. The United States was the only economic power to emerge from World War II with its industrial base virtually untouched by the destruction of war. A consumer economy that had been slowed by the Great Depression and put on hold by the war was finally unleashed. Great advances were made in telecommunications, including the introduction of the most important mass communication medium of the 20th century, television.

The postwar decades also saw great social reform and upheaval, including the civil rights movement, consumerism, environmentalism, the antiwar movement, women's rights, gay rights, and multinationalism. Looming over all of this was the Cold War and the constant threat of thermonuclear war. Never had there been a time when the need for effective communication among nations, organizations, and individuals was greater.

Consumer advocate Ralph Nader provided one example of how public relations tactics could be used to make big business change the way it operated. Nader burst on the scene in 1965 with his landmark book *Unsafe at Any Speed,* in which he documented safety problems associated with automobiles, especially General Motors' Corvair. Unhappy with the negative publicity, GM sought to discredit Nader, prompting the consumer advocate to sue the company for investigating his private life. General Motors settled out of court and paid Nader $425,000—which he used to create a watchdog group, the Project on Corporate Responsibility. Nader then became a GM shareholder, which gave him access to the company's annual meetings. Although GM management defeated several PCR resolutions placed before shareholders, Nader was successful in coaxing GM to change its operations in several areas, in-

OTHER NOTABLE FIGURES FROM PUBLIC RELATIONS' PAST

Leone Baxter—with her husband and partner, *Clem Whitaker,* formed the first agency specializing in political campaigns in 1933.

Carl Byoir—a Creel Committee veteran; formed one of the earliest public relations firms, Carl Byoir & Associates, which is still prominent today.

Harwood Childs—a Princeton University political scientist who expanded upon Bernays' theories and stressed that practitioners should be students of "social effects and corporate conduct."

Pendleton Dudley—an influential figure in early public relations whose firm evolved through the years to DAY, which was acquired by Ogilvy & Mather.

Rex Harlow—a practitioner and educator; founded the American Council on Public Relations, which evolved into the Public Relations Society of America in 1948.

E. H. Heinrichs—a former Pittsburgh newspaper reporter hired by Westinghouse in 1889 to run the nation's first corporate public relations department.

John W. Hill—with partner *Don Knowlton* created Hill & Knowlton, one of the world's largest public relations firms, in Cleveland in 1927.

George V. S. Michaelis—a leading force behind the creation of the Publicity Bureau, the nation's first public relations agency.

Arthur W. Page—a vice president with American Telephone & Telegraph in 1927 who set the standard for corporate public relations, particularly employee relations.

Theodore Vail—organized the first public relations program for AT&T, based upon the then-revolutionary concept that public utilities had to please their customers through good service and fair rates.

Hamilton Wright—a vigorous promoter of the growing state of Florida and a pioneer in the promotion of land development and in representing foreign nations in the United States.

cluding concessions on minority representation on the board of directors, environmental awareness, and consumer safety.[46]

Ironically, during the Industrial Revolution, many advocates of social change saw public relations as an attempt by big business to maintain the status quo. During the social upheavals of the second half of the 20th century, that view changed. Grassroots organizations adopted public relations tactics to influence the actions of business and government. In many ways, the flow of public relations had reversed.

In the spirit of "if you can't beat 'em, join 'em," well-managed companies came to realize the importance of cultivating important publics through public relations. As Edward Grefe and Martin Linsky note in their book *The New Corporate Activism,*

> A new breed of public affairs professionals began emerging who recognized that to build grassroots constituent support, it was necessary to present potential coalition allies with a positive program they could support. Following the example of grassroots organizers, these professionals fostered strategies that would not be simply against something but equally *for* something.[47]

As has been discussed in earlier chapters of this book, late-20th-century public relations practitioners became increasingly important in a wide variety of areas, including crisis communications, community relations, employee relations, and investor relations. Practitioners also play a part in strategic planning, although the scope of their role varies widely throughout the industry. "Within the public relations profession, the ability to influence strategic planning varies widely," wrote Robert W. Kinkead and Dena Winokur in *Public Relations Journal*. "Some practitioners get involved in developing game plans at the highest corporate level, while others simply implement communications moves once a strategy is set by others."[48]

Quick ✔ Check

1. Why is Edward L. Bernays most often credited as being the "father" of modern public relations?
2. How did the end of World War II influence the growth of public relations?
3. In what ways have social movements such as civil rights, women's rights, and consumerism affected the development of public relations?

The Downsizing of the United States

Changes in the world's economic climate brought dramatic consequences starting in the 1970s. The United States had an aging industrial infrastructure that made it difficult for U.S. businesses to compete with more modern facilities in other nations. Former adversaries Germany and Japan, having risen from the ashes of war, began to compete successfully against U.S. companies both in this country and abroad. Those nations had also adopted many management practices that had been pioneered in the United States but seemingly forgotten here. As a result, business and industry began a sometimes painful process of modernizing and **downsizing.** They trimmed layers of middle management, sold unprofitable divisions, and focused on core enterprises. Jobs that had once seemed certain to last forever suddenly disappeared.

This process was hastened in the 1980s when President Ronald Reagan's New Federalism initiative began the process of downsizing the federal government and shifting many of its responsibilities to the states and to the private sector. In part because of tax cuts, deregulation, and reduced payrolls, the 1980s were a period of sustained economic growth. But they were also a time in which the gap between rich and poor widened in the United States.

The downsizing trend had a major impact on public relations. Many in-house public relations departments were either reduced or eliminated entirely. This, in turn, created opportunities for agencies and private consultants to fill the gaps. The irony, of course, is that this downsizing occurred at a time when organizations needed public relations practitioners more than ever—especially when it came to explaining why people were being laid off while their employers reported record revenues and rising executive salaries. A positive development has been a greater awareness of the need for corporate responsibility and volunteerism—areas in which public relations play a major role.

The Baby Boomers Come of Age

At the same time these economic changes were occurring, a technological revolution was taking place. With the invention of silicon microprocessing chips, computers became more powerful, smaller, and more affordable. Desktop publishing came into existence, along with fax machines, e-mail, and teleconferencing. Information became the nation's top commodity. Workers, especially public relations practitioners, became more productive, and a record number of new jobs were created. Unfortunately, these new information-based jobs often paid lower salaries than the old ones they replaced.

Another important change came in the demographic makeup of the workforce. Women entered the job market in record numbers. Civil rights legislation also created opportunities for African Americans and other minority workers. The face of immigration also changed. A century earlier, the majority of immigrants coming to the United States had been from Europe. The nearly 20 million foreign-born residents counted by the U.S. Census in 1990 presented a different picture. Of that number, 44 percent had been added in the 1980s; and of the new arrivals, almost half came from Latin America and nearly one-third from Asia.

Public relations practitioners began to take on a much higher and sometimes negative profile during the 1970s and 1980s, especially in the area of government and politics. This trend actually had begun in the 1960s, when a large percentage of citizens felt that the Johnson administration was not telling the truth about its conduct of the Vietnam War—creating what commentators often referred to as a "credibility gap." In the 1970s, public relations also was criticized for its role during the Watergate scandal. In reality, many of that scandal's principal figures had advertising, not public relations, backgrounds. Had Richard Nixon followed good public relations principles, he might have been able to avoid the ignominy of becoming the first person to resign the presidency.

Following Bill Clinton's use of rapid-response public relations tactics to defeat incumbent George Bush in the 1992 presidential election, public awareness of political counselors—so-called spin doctors—increased dramatically. Some of these counselors, such as James Carville and George Stephanopoulos, later became network political pundits, a role once exclusively held by reporters. Political public relations took center stage in the presidential election stalemate of 2000. Both George W. Bush and Al Gore, trying to appear presidential and above the fray, relied heavily on surrogate spokespersons during the 36-day deadlock.

The New Millennium

The world is very different from what it was in the days of Teddy Roosevelt, Ivy Lee, and Edward Bernays. And so is the practice of public relations.

The terror attacks of September 11, 2001, have shaped public attitudes toward the profession in many ways. In the days and weeks following 9/11, practitioners won high praise for their efforts to inform a frightened nation, rally public support for victims, and help restore a sense of normalcy. If but for a brief time, the profession appeared to be fulfilling its potential as a catalyst for social consensus.

However, as the months and years passed, there was the inevitable reassessment. The head of the American Red Cross was forced to resign because her agency made misleading statements about how the agency used money raised in the name of the 9/11 victims. The newly created Department of Homeland Security became the object of public ridicule for a color-coded terror alert system that few seemed to understand. The Bush administration's public information campaign prior to the 2003 Iraq war led many to believe that they were misled—especially after the invasion failed to uncover a promised cache of weapons of mass destruction.

If anything, we have become more aware of how much our world is interconnected—and often dysfunctional. For proof, one need look no farther than Iraq's former minister of information, Mohammed Said Sahaf. As the world watched live television images of U.S. forces systematically crushing the forces of Saddam Hussein, Sahaf hurled insults and bragged that Iraq was winning the war. Some American audiences laughed at Sahaf. Some Arab audiences cheered him.[49]

If nothing else, that episode tells us that on the road to global peace and understanding, much work remains to be done. Success in that endeavor may well hinge on a new generation of public relations practitioners. The past is prologue. Will they—will you—have learned from history?

Quick ✔ Check

1. How has corporate downsizing affected public relations practitioners?
2. In addition to downsizing, what other social forces influenced the development of public relations near the end of the 20th century?
3. How can a new generation of public relations practitioners play a role in achieving "global peace and understanding"?

Summary

Although public relations did not acquire its name until the 20th century, it has been practiced in some form since the beginnings of recorded time. At the time the United States was formed, public relations tactics were used to rally colonists to the cause of independence and later to support the adoption of the new nation's Constitution.

Modern public relations was born during the Industrial Revolution and began to take root during the period known as the Progressive Era. Its development throughout the past century has been nurtured by great social trends—the growth of institutions, the expansion of democracy, technological improvements in communications, the growth of advocacy, and the search for consensus. The profession's development has also been advanced by historical figures such as Theodore Roosevelt, Ivy Ledbetter Lee, and Edward L. Bernays.

By the end of the 20th century, public relations had begun to take a more central role in social discourse in the United States. Practitioners began to acquire more public visibility—even on some occasions when they would have preferred otherwise. As organizations downsized in an effort to become more efficient and effective in a global economy, public relations practitioners played a pivotal role. And in a post-9/11 world, the profession is challenged on two fronts: building its own credibility while helping to build global consensus.

DISCUSSION QUESTIONS

1. Whom do you consider the "father of public relations," Ivy Ledbetter Lee or Edward L. Bernays? Why did you choose one man over the other?

2. In addition to Lee and Bernays, who are some of the other major figures who contributed to the development of modern public relations?

3. What major forces have shaped the development of public relations in the 20th century?

4. What is propaganda, and why has its use been largely discredited?

5. What do you consider the most significant lesson to be learned from the history of public relations?

6. Given your knowledge of the history of public relations, on what basis would you decide whether to accept employment at the multinational corporation described in the scenario at the beginning of this chapter?

Memo
from the
Field

Edward M. Block, retired public relations executive

Edward M. Block was senior vice president for public relations, advertising, and employee information at AT&T Corporation for 12 years. He was also assistant to the chairman of the board and a member of the Office of the Chairman. He has received numerous awards for achievements in public relations, including the Public Relations Society of America's Gold Anvil. Most recently, he was cited by *PR Week* magazine as among the 100 most influential public relations people of the 20th century.

On page 77 you will find the names of Theodore N. Vail and Arthur W. Page, two executives whose pioneering ideas remain as enduring principles of corporate relationship building.

Vail is the chief executive whose utterly unique business model built the Bell Telephone System, a quasi-monopoly that created a new industry and dominated telephone service in the U.S. for nearly a century, becoming, at its zenith, the biggest company in the world. He welcomed government regulation, believed that profits need only be sufficient to sustain good service, and established a company-paid pension trust based on identical payout formulas for all employees, management as well as nonmanagement. He invested heavily in research to ensure continuous innovation. He also employed national magazine advertising to explain the policies and plans of the company to the public, no doubt the first demonstration of what would be called "transparency" today. These were remarkable innovations in an era best remembered for its robber barons.

Page elaborated and institutionalized Vail's concepts throughout that giant enterprise. A former magazine editor, he was hired by the parent company, AT&T, in 1926. He thus became the first individual elected to a senior executive position in charge of what we now call public relations. Subsequently, he was elected to the board of directors. He established modern public relations organizations in the Bell companies, delegating to them a cluster of responsibilities still found in most communications departments in U.S. corporations: employee information. Media relations. Community relations. Financial information. Institutional advertising and communications policy. Philanthropy.

Page was above all a counselor, and he made counseling a top priority in the far-flung PR organizations he created. He persistently argued—and demonstrated throughout his career—that when you get your corporate policies and business practices right your public relations programs will succeed. Conversely, he argued, that when your corporate policies are out of sync with the expectations of your publics you cannot sustain effective constituency relationships—so don't bother. Moreover, he warned, communications efforts intended to support wrongheaded policies will only make matters worse.

As an important extension of this focus, Page conceived of public relations as an institutional mind-set, not a functional department, and therefore a priority consideration in every decision, not only by top management, but also by supervisors in the field or on the shop floor. His conception is perhaps best summed up in the modern understanding of the term *corporate culture*. He ardently believed that public relations is everyone's job, a bias, an attitude that strives to fashion policies, actions, and business practices that project integrity and build trust over time.

People employed in the PR departments that Page established were expected to be experts in the communications arts and were hired and incessantly trained in these skills. But more important, they were widely deployed throughout the Bell companies' operating divisions to provide on-the-spot counsel in matters large or small. Their peers in the functional departments routinely took account of their judgments and acted on them.

The Page emphasis on counseling may seem a quaint idea in an era that seems to prize so many of the currently fashionable communications functions such as marketing support and investor relations. But his disciples abound and continue to insist that counseling will sooner or later reassert its importance. Why? Because counseling is by definition a value-added function, providing, as it does, a unique and critical perspective in managing the affairs of businesses whose constituencies are many and varied. Moreover, timely counseling is not overhead. It comes free as part of a total communications package.

Today, a 300-plus member Arthur W. Page Society exists expressly to promote his concepts in a context of contemporary business issues and to serve the needs of senior corporate executives as well as public relations counseling firms.

The Page concepts are captured, albeit cryptically, in the following "principles" espoused by the society's members: Tell the truth. Prove it with action. Listen to the customer. Conduct public relations as if the whole company depends upon it. Remain calm, patient, and good humored, especially in the face of criticism.

When you think about them, these admonitions are nothing more complicated than plain, old-fashioned horse sense. Makes you wonder why so many businesses today seem not to have any.

Case Study 3.1

Remembering the Victims

Reading about history can be educational. Living that history can be hell. And remembering the lives changed and lost on a dark day in history is the job of Kari Watkins.

Watkins is the executive director of the Oklahoma City National Memorial, located on the site of what was at the time the largest mass murder in U.S. history. It was built on the grounds where the Alfred P. Murrah Federal Building once stood. The building was destroyed and 168 innocent people, guilty of no more than being in the wrong place at the wrong time, were killed in an act of terrorism on April 19, 1995.

"There is a reason a lot of memorials have waited 50 years to be built," Watkins said.[50] Different constituencies have different agendas, she noted. And it was the job of those seeking a fitting tribute to the heroes of Oklahoma City to listen to all of them.

In the aftermath of the bombing, Oklahoma City Mayor Ron Norick appointed a 350-member Memorial Task Force. One member of that group was Jeanette Gamba, president and CEO of Jordan Associates, an integrated marketing communications company headquartered in Oklahoma City. But her involvement actually began on the day of the disaster, when she placed telephone calls in a frantic effort to discover whether any of her colleagues or family members were among the dead and injured.[51] Gamba would later head up the memorial's communications subcommittee.

Gamba said that from the very beginning, planning for the memorial was driven by a mission statement developed by people representing a variety of community

The Oklahoma City National Memorial was established to remember the 168 people killed in an act of domestic terrorism on April 19, 1995. (Courtesy of Oklahoma City National Memorial)

interests—especially family members of those killed in the bombing, survivors, and rescue workers so deeply touched by the experience:

> We come here to remember those who were killed, those who survived and those changed forever. May all who leave here know the impact of violence. May this memorial offer comfort, strength, peace, hope and serenity.[52]

"In everything we do and in everything we've done from a public relations standpoint, we try to use the mission statement as our foundation," Gamba said. "Doing the right thing to us means going back and checking to see that it is consistent with the mission statement."

Watkins refers to the mission statement as her "memorial bible" and said it drives all the Oklahoma City Memorial's communications. "We want to communicate that it is a place of remembrance and a place of education," she said. "It is not a place to memorialize the perpetrator of the crime."

That mission statement was put to the test during the weeks and months leading up to the June 11, 2001, execution of Timothy McVeigh, the man convicted of building and exploding the truck bomb that destroyed the Murrah building. It was the first federal execution in nearly four decades. Although McVeigh died by lethal injection at the Federal Penitentiary in Terra Haute, Indiana, much of the world's—and media's—attention focused several hundred miles away in Oklahoma City at the scene of the crime.

"The execution was not our story," Watkins said. "We didn't even want to be a part of it."

However, the reality was that Oklahoma City, once again, could not avoid the limelight. Watkins estimates that she received 2,400 requests for some media presence on the memorial grounds. The best that she could hope for was to manage the onslaught.

To that end, approximately 70 media representatives met with state, local, and memorial officials on April 20, just a few weeks before the execution had originally been scheduled. Its purpose was to discuss common concerns and establish ground rules. Although the media were allowed to use the memorial as a backdrop for their coverage, memorial staff and officials treated June 11 as if it were any other day.

"That was our commitment to the survivors and the families," Watkins said.

More important to the people of Oklahoma City, much of the media's focus shifted from McVeigh to the victims of his terrible deed. At the hour of the execution, several television networks ran moving tributes to those who had died in the blast. "Very little happened by accident," Gamba said. "It was all part of the ongoing relationship we had built with the media."

Successful media relations is just one example of a philosophy that has driven memorial organizers since the days immediately following the bombing. They realized that to honor history, they would have to learn from it.

Members of the Memorial Task Force had extensive conversations with the people who engineered the Vietnam Veterans Memorial in Washington, D.C. Just like the war it commemorates, the Vietnam memorial was a source of intense controversy at the time of its dedication in 1982.

"We met with Jan Skruggs, the head of the Vietnam Memorial Committee early on and asked what mistakes had been made," Watkins said. "One of them was that they didn't involve their constituents as much as they should have."

"We knew we couldn't build this memorial without our neighbors on our side," she added.

In the case of the Oklahoma City memorial, a wide range of constituencies exists. They include family members of the deceased, survivors, rescue workers, government officials, the Oklahoma City community, donors, and the news media. Memorial organizers committed themselves to achieving "buy-in" from each group. "There was never a committee that didn't have one of the co-chairs be either a family member or survivor," Gamba said. "It really gave us a channel of input on everything."

In addition to involving key stakeholders, the Memorial Task Force conducted public and private meetings and gathered thousands of written and Internet survey responses. Once an agreement on the mission statement was reached in March 1996, the focus turned to delivering a message that was both clear and consistent. "Our board has made the commitment that we will say one thing and say it united," Watkins said.

President Bill Clinton helped dedicate the $29.1 million memorial on the fifth anniversary of the bombing. Ten months later, President George W. Bush spoke at the dedication of a museum and interactive media center in what had been the gutted shell of a newspaper office across the street from the Murrah building. "Your loss was great, and your pain was deep," Bush said. "Far greater and deeper was your care for one another."[53]

What was once a scene of unbelievable horror had become a place of "comfort, strength, peace, hope, and serenity."

DISCUSSION QUESTIONS

1. How important was the development of a mission statement in reaching the ultimate goal of building a memorial to the victims of the Oklahoma City bombing?
2. Who were the different constituencies that the Memorial Task Force needed to address and how might each public's point of view differ from the others'?
3. Why did Kari Watkins say that the execution of Timothy McVeigh "was not our (the memorial's) story"? Do you agree or disagree with her statement? Why?
4. What role did research play in this case study, and how was that research conducted?
5. What do you think Kari Watkins meant when she said, "There is a reason a lot of memorials have waited 50 years to be built"?

Case Study 3.2

Too Much Blood and Money

Within minutes of the September 11, 2001, terrorist attacks, the American Red Cross was doing what it had done throughout its 120-year history: helping people in need. Who would have imagined that within a few weeks, the nation's largest charity would be rocked by a scandal—all because it may have been *too* successful?

One problem was that the Red Cross had collected too much blood from tens of thousands of donors eager to help the victims. Blood is perishable and has a shelf life of only six weeks. Within the first 48 hours, the nation's blood supply had tripled.[54] However, it also had become painfully obvious that although approximately 3,000 people had died, very few people were injured and in need of blood.

Jim MacPherson, executive director of America's Blood Center, said, "Even on September 12, the day after the attacks, we called the Red Cross and we said, 'Would you join with us with a message to people that the blood supply is adequate and let's stop the collections right now so we can minimize the wastage.' "[55]

To the dismay of MacPherson and other critics, the Red Cross continued publicizing the need for blood donations. Red Cross official Jerry Squires said the solicitations continued because the future was unpredictable.

"We were hearing that September 11 might not be the end," Squires said. "We really felt that sort of calling a halt to blood donations was probably not the wisest or safest thing to do."[56]

News reports said that directors at several Red Cross blood centers were discarding 20 percent of their donations.[57] Red Cross officials acknowledged that some blood donations could no longer be used for transfusions because the red blood cells had died. But because they were able to use other blood by-products, such as plasma, no donation was wasted.[58]

As difficult as the blood situation was, an even bigger controversy erupted over Red Cross fund-raising. The agency had established a special fund to aid 9/11 victims' families, the Liberty Fund. Within seven weeks of the attacks, it had received an astonishing $547 million in pledges.[59]

By creating the special fund, Red Cross President Bernadine Healy unwittingly sparked a firestorm of criticism. Under normal circumstances, the Red Cross places donations in the National Disaster Fund, a pool of money available to all its chapters. Because the Liberty Fund was separate from the National Disaster Fund, the money was off-limits to local officials.

"My phone has been ringing off the hook with chapters angry about the Liberty Fund," wrote one Red Cross board member. "Creating a separate fund is unacceptable."[60]

Healy also came under fire from victims' families. Less than half of Liberty Fund money collected had gone to the families. Approximately $43.8 million had been dispersed in direct financial aid, with another $66.9 million going to "other immediate disaster relief needs."[61] The families were angered when they learned that the Red Cross planned to set aside more than $300 million for other needs, including a reserve fund for dealing with future terrorist attacks.[62]

"You can't raise the money for purpose A and spend it on purpose B," New York State Attorney General Eliot L. Spitzer told Congress. "My patience has run out."[63]

Healy was forced to resign in late October 2001. Red Cross officials ended active solicitation for the Liberty Fund. From that point on, all contributions were directed into the National Disaster Fund unless specifically earmarked for 9/11 victims.[64]

"We are going to try and be good stewards of the money," said interim Red Cross President Harold Decker. "That is what donors expect."[65]

Red Cross officials took other steps to restore public confidence. By mid-November, the organization reversed course and said that all Liberty Fund money would go to victims' families.[66] A month later, they named former U.S. Senator George Mitchell to oversee the payments.[67] After conducting a series of meetings with family members, Mitchell announced a three-part plan to distribute almost all of the remaining funds before the first anniversary of the attacks.

"The Red Cross deserves credit both for acknowledging its mistakes and changing its policies as necessary," Mitchell said. He also praised the agency "for meeting its historic and traditional role to provide emergency relief to thousands of people at a time of real pain, grief, and need."[68]

The Red Cross changed its advertising and public solicitation policies in June 2002. In doing so, the organization acknowledged that it had not clearly explained to donors that money collected for a local disaster could be used anywhere in the country.[69] The new program was called Donor DIRECT, or Donor Intent REcognition,

Confirmation and Trust. Under it, the Red Cross asks donors to confirm the purpose of their donations.[70]

The Charities Review Council, an industry watchdog, concluded that although the Red Cross was well prepared to address the consequences of the September 11 attack, "by deviating from its traditional policies, it entered uncharted seas." The CRC concluded, "The Red Cross did the right thing by reversing course and openly admitting mistakes."[71]

DISCUSSION QUESTIONS

1. With concerns about the danger of future terrorist attacks, were Red Cross officials wrong to withhold some donations for future use?
2. Were local Red Cross chapter officials justified in their concerns about the creation of the Liberty Fund?
3. What could the Red Cross have done differently to avoid these controversies?
4. What steps did the Red Cross take to restore its credibility? Were they enough to do the job?

Cyber Coach

Visit www.ablongman.com/guthmarsh3e for these study aids—and more:

- flashcards
- quizzes
- videos
- links to other sites
- real-world scenarios that let you be the public relations professional

KEY TERMS

Committee for Public Information (CPI), p. 69
Crystallizing Public Opinion, p. 71
"Declaration of Principles," p. 67
downsizing, p. 78
Edward L. Bernays, p. 70
Federalist Papers, p. 62
First Amendment, p. 63
Four-Minute Men, p. 70

Industrial Revolution, p. 59
Lee, Ivy Ledbetter, p. 67
Office of War Information (OWI), p. 75
Progressive Era, p. 59
propaganda, p. 69
Publicity Bureau, p. 65
rhetoric, p. 59
Seedbed Years, p. 65
vox populi, p. 59

NOTES

1. Jacque L'Etang, "State Propaganda and Bureaucratic Intelligence: The Creation of Public Relations in 20th Century Britain," *Public Relations Review* (winter 1998): 413.
2. L'Etang.

3. Gary A. Warner, "The Development of Public Relations Offices at American Colleges and Universities," *Public Relations Quarterly* (summer 1996): 36.

4. Edward L. Bernays, *Biography of an Idea: Memoirs of Public Relations Counsel Edward L. Bernays* (New York: Simon & Schuster, 1965), 387.

5. Bernays, 387.

6. John Stauber and Sheldon Rampton, "How the American Tobacco Industry Employs PR Scum to Continue Its Murderous Assault on Human Lives," *Tucson Weekly*, 22 November 1995.

7. "States' Attorneys Are Weighing Whether to Sign Deal," Associated Press, as reported in the *Kansas City Star*, 18 November 1998, A4.

8. Frances A. Stillman, et al., "Evaluation of the American Stop Smoking Intervention Study (ASSIST): A Report of Outcomes," *Journal of the National Cancer Institute 95*, no. 22 (19 November 2003): 1681–1691.

9. Norman Foerster, Norman S. Grabo, Russel B. Nye, E. Fred Carlisle, and Robert Falk, eds., *American Poetry and Prose, Fifth Edition/Part One* (New York: Houghton Mifflin, 1970), 139.

10. Foerster, et al., 139.

11. *The Constitution of the United States and the Declaration of Independence* (Washington, D.C.: Commission on the Bicentennial of the United States Constitution, 1992), 35.

12. Jason Karpf, "Adams, Paine and Jefferson: A PR Firm," *Public Relations Tactics*, January 2004, 12–13.

13. Foerster, et al., 146 (emphasis in original).

14. Karpf, 13.

15. Scott M. Cutlip, *The Unseen Power: Public Relations: A History* (Hillsdale, N.J.: Lawrence Erlbaum, 1994), 1.

16. Cutlip, 10–25.

17. Fred Fedler and Denise DeLorme, "Journalists' Hostility Toward Public Relations: A Historical Analysis," paper presented at the Association for Education in Journalism and Mass Communication annual conference, Miami, Fla., August 2002.

18. Blaire Atherton French, *The Presidential Press Conference: Its History and Role in the American Political System* (Lanham, Md.: University Press of America, 1982), 3.

19. Carolyn Smith, *Presidential Press Conferences: A Critical Approach* (New York: Praeger, 1990), 22.

20. Cutlip, 37–45.

21. Cutlip, 45.

22. Cutlip, 139.

23. Thomas Flemming, "When the United States Entered World War I, Propagandist George Creel Set Out to Stifle Anti-War Sentiment," *Military History*, The History Net, online, www.thehistorynet.com.

24. Charles A. Lubbers, "George Creel and the Four-Minute Men: A Milestone in Public Relations History," *Business Research Yearbook: Global Business Perspectives*, vol. III (New York: International Academy of Business Disciplines, 1996), 719.

25. Flemming.

26. Bernays, 161.

27. "The Scopes Monkey Trial," Court TV Online, www.courttv.com/archive/greatesttrials/scopes.

28. "People & Events: The Site of the Trial: Dayton, Tennessee," *American Experience: Monkey Trial,* online, www.pbs.org/wgbh/amex/monkeytrial/index.html.

29. "The Scopes Monkey Trial."

30. Edward Caudill, *The Scopes Trial: A Photographic History* (Knoxville: University of Tennessee Press, 2000), 5–6.

31. Caudill, 6.

32. H. L. Mencken, "The Monkey Trial: A Reporter's Account," *Baltimore Sun,* 9 July 1925, online at "Famous Trials in American History: Tennessee v. John Scopes," University of Missouri–Kansas City Law School, www.law.umkc.edu/faculty/projects/ftrials/scopes/scopes.htm.

33. Caudill, 18–19.

34. Bernays, 177–178.

35. Bernays, 288.

36. Kathleen O'Neill, "U.S. Public Relations Evolves to Meet Society's Needs," *Public Relations Journal,* November 1991, 28.

37. Bernays, 218.

38. Susan Henry, "Anonymous in Her Own Name: Public Relations Pioneer Doris Fleischman," *Journalism History* 23, no. 2 (summer 1997): 52.

39. Bernays, 217.

40. Bernays, 216.

41. Cutlip, 169–170.

42. Cutlip, 170.

43. Cutlip, 159–225.

44. Alvin M. Hattal, "The Father of Public Relations: Edward L. Bernays," *Communication World,* January 1992, 15.

45. Cutlip, 528.

46. Patrick Jackson and Allen H. Center, *Public Relations Practices: Managerial Case Studies and Problems,* 5th ed. (Englewood Cliffs, N.J.: Prentice Hall, 1995), 167–178.

47. Edward A. Grefe and Martin Linsky, *The New Corporate Activism* (New York: McGraw-Hill, 1995), 3 (emphasis in original).

48. Robert W. Kinkead and Dena Winokur, "How Public Relations Professionals Help CEOs Make the Right Moves," *Public Relations Journal,* October 1992, 18–23.

49. David Lamb, "He Wages War—on Reality," *Los Angeles Times,* 8 April 2003, online, www.sunspot.net.

50. Interview, 16 July 2001.

51. Interview, 16 July 2001.

52. Mission Statement, Oklahoma City National Memorial, online, www.oklahomacitynationalmemorial.org.

53. "Bush Praises Oklahoma City as He Dedicates Bombing Museum," CNN Interactive, 19 February 2001, online, www.cnn.com.

54. Transcript, *NewsHour with Jim Lehrer,* 19 December 2001, online, www.pbs.org.newshour.

55. Transcript, *NewsHour with Jim Lehrer.*

56. Transcript, *NewsHour with Jim Lehrer.*

57. Transcript, *NewsHour with Jim Lehrer.*

58. "Red Cross Head Steps Down," CBS News, 26 October 2001, online, www.cbsnews.com.

59. "Liberty Fund Closes Up Shop," CBS News, 30 October 2001, online, www.cbsnews.com.

60. Sharyl Attkisson, "Financial Irregularities at the Red Cross," *CBS Evening News,* 31 July 2002, online, LexisNexis.

61. "Red Cross Closes Liberty Fund, Names Interim Head," CNN, 30 October 2001, online, www.cnn.com.

62. "Defending the Liberty Fund," CBS News, 6 November 2001, online, www.cbsnews.com.

63. Ian Wilhelm, "NY Attorney General Weighs Legal Action Against American Red Cross," *The Chronicle of Philanthropy,* 8 November 2001, online update, http://philanthropy.com.

64. "Liberty Fund Closes Up Shop."

65. "Liberty Fund Closes Up Shop."

66. "Red Cross: Victims Will Get All Liberty Fund Monies," CNN, 14 November 2001, online, www.cnn.com.

67. "Former Senate Leader to Oversee Red Cross Fund," CNN, 27 December 2001, online, www.cnn.com.

68. "Red Cross Unveils Plan for September 11 Funds," CNN, 31 January 2002, online, www.cnn.com.

69. Lena H. Sun, "At 'Turning Point,' Red Cross Picks Chief; New President Says the Organization Needs to Build Trust," *Washington Post,* 28 June 2002, A02, online, LexisNexis.

70. Paul Barbagallo, *Target Marketing* 25, no. 8 (August 2002): 15–16, online, LexisNexis.

71. "September 11: The Philanthropic Response," Charities Review Council, online, http://www.crcmn.org/donorinfo/disaster.htm.

4

The Publics in Public Relations

objectives

After studying this chapter, you will be able to

■ define the term *public* as it is used in public relations

■ name and describe the different kinds of publics

■ list the kinds of information that practitioners should gather about each public

■ identify and describe the traditional publics in public relations

Pop Goes Your Wednesday

scenario

Wednesday starts peacefully at the Kablooie Microwave Popcorn Company, where you are director of public relations. You are planning to spend the morning getting ready for next week's annual meeting of stockholders. Kablooie is a new company, and you are eager to tell stockholders about its recently completed Statement of Values, which begins with these words: "Kablooie Microwave Popcorn Company exists to provide value at a fair price to its customers; to provide a competitive return on investment to its stockholders; and to provide a humane work-place and fair salaries and benefits to its employees."

Then:

- *Your assistant tells you his 13-year-old daughter just telephoned. In instant messaging conversations all over the Internet, she says, kids are suddenly saying that Kablooie Microwave Popcorn is blowing the doors off microwave ovens and injuring teens. One report says that a popular rock star has been hospitalized in critical condition after being injured by a Kablooie explosion. From coast to coast, kids are telling one another to boycott your product.*

- *Your assistant is still talking when a reporter from your local newspaper calls to ask about the rumor that Kablooie Microwave Popcorn is exploding in microwave ovens and injuring people. You emphatically deny the rumor and promise to call back in 15 minutes.*

- *A beep from your computer tells you that a new e-mail message has arrived. It's from a nationally known investment analyst, asking whether there are any new issues you're expecting to deal with at next week's annual meeting for stockholders. Evidently, she hasn't yet heard about the Internet rumors.*

- *Your secretary brings you a letter from a local Boy Scout troop. In two days the troop will begin selling your product door to door as a fund-raising project. The letter is thanking you for the early delivery of 10,000 packages of Kablooie Microwave Popcorn.*

You immediately decide to implement your company's crisis communications plan (see Chapter 12). Like all good public relations plans, it asks you to identify the most important publics with whom you must communicate.

In this scenario, who are your publics? Which are the most important? Can the new Statement of Values help?

What Is a Public?

Public relations. That's what we call this challenging, rewarding business.

Take a good look at that first word: **public.** That's where we start. Publics are literally the first word in our profession.

So what is a public? As you may recall from Chapter 1, a public is any group whose members have a common interest or common values in a particular situation. A political party can be a public. Upper-level managers in a corporation can be a public. Fans of a popular music group can be a public.

The word *stakeholder* often substitutes for the word *public*, but the two words aren't interchangeable. Some publics may have no connection with the organization that a public relations practitioner represents. But as we note in Chapter 1, a **stakeholder,** or stakeholder group, has a stake, or an interest, in an organization or issue that potentially involves the organization. For any given organization, then, all stakeholder groups are publics—but not all publics are stakeholders.

Counting all the publics even in just the United States would be like trying to count the stars—an impossible task. So which publics matter in public relations? With which publics do we build and manage values-driven relationships? Certain publics become important to an organization as its values and values-based goals interact with the environment. Those publics become stakeholders. For example, to fulfill its values-driven goal of healing people, a nonprofit hospital must have a good relationship with the community's physicians. The hospital's values somehow must fit comfortably with the values of the physicians if this vital relationship is to work.

Another example: To fulfill its goal of being a clean, attractive facility, that same hospital must have a good relationship with its custodians. The hospital needs to understand the values of the custodians—such as fair wages—to make that relationship work. As an organization's values interact with the values of different publics, relationships—good or bad—are born. In fact, if we know the specific values-driven goals of an organization and we know the environment in which it operates, we can predict with some accuracy the essential relationships that can help the organization attain its goals.

Sometimes, however, a relationship surprises an organization. A public in the organization's environment can discover a relationship before the organization does. Often, a clash of values triggers that unexpected relationship. For example, a Midwestern county government trying to build a highway around a growing metropolitan area was surprised when Native Americans strongly opposed the proposed route. The highway passed too near, they said, to an area they used for worship. A values-driven goal of the county government—easing traffic congestion within the metropolitan area—had clashed with a religious value of Native Americans in the area. As one values system met another, a relationship was born.

Why Do We Need Relationships with Publics?

Now, what about that second word in public relations: *relations*? Why do organizations build and maintain values-driven relationships with a variety of publics? (We're glad that they do: The relationship-management process provides interesting, rewarding jobs for thousands of public relations practitioners.) But, again, it's worth asking: Why do organizations need relationships with different publics? An excellent answer to this question comes from **resource dependency theory,**[1] which consists of three simple beliefs:

1. To fulfill their values, organizations need resources, such as raw materials and people to work for the organization.
2. Some of those key resources are *not* controlled by the organization.
3. To acquire those key resources, organizations must build productive relationships with the publics that control the resources.

Resource dependency theory tells us that, first and foremost, public relations practitioners must build relationships with publics that possess resources organizations need to fulfill their values-driven goals.

Resource dependency theory can even help us determine which publics will receive most of our relationship-management efforts. Clearly, our most important publics are those that possess the resources our organization needs the most. For example, Pitney Bowes, an international message-management company, focuses on resource dependency theory in the first sentence of its values statement: "Pitney Bowes' relationships with our four constituent groups—customers, employees, stockholders, and the communities—are critical to our success and reputation."[2] In public relations, we build relationships with publics to secure the resources our organizations need to survive and fulfill their values.

Resource dependency theory, therefore, helps explain values-driven public relations. As we describe in Chapter 1, values-driven public relations brings the entire public relations process—research, planning, communication, and evaluation—into a framework defined by an organization's core values. In the planning phase, practitioners establish values-driven public relations goals. To reach those goals, practitioners often must acquire resources held by other publics; this is where resource dependency theory meets values-driven public relations. If our goals are values-driven, the resources we acquire from targeted publics bring our organization closer to fulfilling its values.

Resource dependency theory also helps explain the two-way symmetrical model, the most successful of the four models of public relations (see Chapter 1). Two-way symmetrical public relations works best when there is an exchange of resources. If an organization wants to acquire the resources it needs, it must be willing to give the resource holders something they need. For example, news media have resources most organizations need, including fair and accurate coverage. In return, those organizations have resources news media need, including a willingness to respond to journalists' questions promptly and honestly. In a two-way symmetrical relationship, an organization agrees to exchange resources to fulfill its values-driven goals.

The Publics in Public Relations

Publics may be as impossible to count as the stars, but, like the stars, they can be grouped into categories, including

- traditional and nontraditional publics
- latent, aware, and active publics
- intervening publics
- primary and secondary publics
- internal and external publics
- domestic and international publics

Why bother to group publics into categories? Because knowing which category or categories a public belongs to can provide insight into how to build a productive relationship with it. The thoughtful process of deciding which category or categories a public belongs to can help us learn from our own experiences as well as those of others. So let's examine these categories.

Traditional and Nontraditional Publics

Traditional publics are groups with which organizations have ongoing, long-term relationships. As shown in Figure 4.1, traditional publics include employees, news media, governments, investors, customers, multicultural community groups, and constituents (voters). The fact that these publics are traditional, however, doesn't mean that public relations practitioners can take them for granted. Organizations that

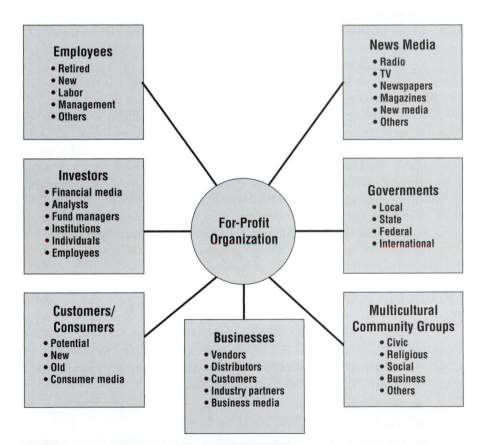

FIGURE 4.1   Traditional Publics in Public Relations A for-profit organization can have dozens of primary publics. Not pictured in this diagram is the most important public for government public relations practitioners: constituents and voters.

ignore the values of employees or of the news media, for example, quickly learn to their sorrow how powerful those publics can be. In Pop Goes Your Wednesday, the scenario that opens this chapter, the investment analyst who e-mails you with a request for information represents a traditional public.

Nontraditional publics are groups that usually are unfamiliar to an organization. For example, in Pop Goes Your Wednesday, the high-tech teenagers with their instant messaging constitute a nontraditional public—a group with which Kablooie hasn't had an ongoing, long-term relationship. Nontraditional publics can be hard to study and may lead you to try some innovative relationship-building strategies. Nontraditional publics are often sparked by changes in a society—such as the growth of instant messaging and related technologies.

Nontraditional publics can be new and challenging, but it's possible that one day they'll become traditional publics. For example, women from an impoverished fishing village in Nigeria shut down a nearby ChevronTexaco oil terminal by entering the facility and refusing to leave. They wanted the corporation to help them improve living conditions in the village. In ensuing negotiations, cultures collided as corporate leaders met with village leaders—but a relationship emerged. "We are friends forever," said a satisfied leader of the protesters.[3]

Closer to home, the ambiguous status of gay and lesbian publics—traditional or nontraditional?—was evident during the 2004 presidential election, with both major political parties divided on the issue of gay marriage. Republican candidate George W. Bush favored a constitutional amendment prohibiting gay marriage while Dick Cheney, his running mate, preferred to leave the matter to state governments. "The Republican Party can't have it both ways," said Patrick Guerriero, executive director of the Log Cabin Republicans, the nation's largest organization of gay and lesbian Republicans.[4] Democratic candidates John Kerry and John Edwards opposed a constitutional amendment—but also opposed gay marriage in favor of civil unions. Meanwhile, Gavin Newsom, the Democratic mayor of San Francisco, directed his city's government to issue marriage licenses to gay and lesbian couples. "It's shameful to play politics with peoples' lives," he said.[5]

In corporate America, United Airlines, Saturn automobiles, and the San Diego Padres baseball teams are among organizations that openly market to gay and lesbian consumers. Other organizations, such as the Walt Disney Company, have extended insurance benefits to the life partners of gay and lesbian employees.[6] But the resultant boycott of Disney products by the Southern Baptist Convention, the largest Protestant denomination in the United States, shows that the terms *traditional* and *nontraditional* are relative. One organization's traditional public can be nontraditional to another.

Latent, Aware, and Active Publics

Public relations scholars often categorize publics as *latent, aware,* or *active*.[7] A **latent public** is a group whose values have come into contact with the values of your organization, but whose members haven't yet realized it; the members of that public are

Congresswoman Kay Granger of Texas addresses the Log Cabin Republicans, the nation's largest organization of gay and lesbian Republicans. In the 2004 presidential election, the Log Cabin Republicans were a traditional public for some, a nontraditional public for others. (Courtesy of Log Cabin Republicans)

not yet aware of the relationship. An **aware public** is a group whose members are aware of the intersection of their values with those of your organization but haven't organized any kind of response to the relationship. An **active public,** however, not only recognizes the relationship between itself and your organization but is also working to manage that relationship on its own terms. In Pop Goes Your Wednesday, the teenagers with their instant messaging are more than just a nontraditional public; they're also an active public.

Intervening Publics

Let's say that in our Kablooie Microwave Popcorn scenario, you wisely keep your promise to the local newspaper reporter who telephoned. You call her back in 15 minutes and report that you've checked with the top five manufacturers of microwave ovens, and none are reporting problems with Kablooie popcorn. In fact, they've said that such a defect in their ovens is impossible. You give the reporter the names

QuickBreak 4.1

YOUR TAX DOLLARS AT WORK

As you're reading this sentence, the federal government of the United States is collecting information about you, your friends, your family—and millions of other Americans.

Sounds scary, right? But that storehouse of information can be incredibly useful to public relations practitioners. Even better, much of the information is online and can be easily accessed at FedStats (www.fedstats.gov).

Need the ethnic makeup of your county? Try the Bureau of the Census. You can reach it through FedStats.

Need employment projections for the coming decades? Try the Bureau of Labor Statistics. You can reach it through FedStats.

Need data on farmers? Try the National Agricultural Statistics Service. On older Americans? Try the Administration on Aging. On prisoners? Try the Federal Bureau of Prisons.

FedStats can connect you to dozens of federal agencies that gather information on the publics that make up public relations. As a taxpayer, you're footing the bill for all those studies, so get your money's worth: Bookmark FedStats for your web browser.

of the public relations officials for those manufacturers, and you fax her a statement from Kablooie's chief executive officer in which he denies the rumors. You even invite her to come tour your factory's quality-control department.

Why spend so much time with one reporter? You know the answer to that: because she has thousands of local readers to whom you want to send the message that Kablooie popcorn is safe. In public relations, any public that helps you send a message to another public is called an **intervening public**. In the Kablooie scenario, one of your most important publics consists of the people of Kablooie Microwave Popcorn's hometown; they're a high-priority public that you're targeting with a specific message to maintain the good relationship between Kablooie and its hometown. If the local newspaper can help you send that message, it is an intervening public.

Primary and Secondary Publics

Publics can also be divided into primary publics and secondary publics. If a public can directly affect your organization's pursuit of its values-driven goals, that public is definitely a **primary public**—a public of great importance. **Secondary publics** are also important. You want to have a good relationship with them—but their ability to affect your organization's pursuit of its goals is minimal. Because resources such as time and money are scarce, public relations practitioners spend most of their time building and managing relationships with primary publics. If resources permit, they also build and manage relationships with secondary publics.

In Pop Goes Your Wednesday, your company's investors are a primary public; your Statement of Values emphasizes that fact. A bad relationship with investors and the people who advise them could immediately and seriously harm the financial security of Kablooie. In this scenario, a secondary public would be local stores that sell microwave ovens. Because they might have to field a few questions, you might telephone them—if time permits. But you wisely decide first to devote your attention to the primary publics that can influence the success of Kablooie Microwave Popcorn.

Internal and External Publics

Publics are either **internal publics** or **external publics;** that is, either they're inside your organization or outside it. Kablooie's employees are an internal public—as well as a primary public. You'd be smart to inform them of the rumors so that they're not surprised by reports in the news media or by inquisitive friends and neighbors. External publics would include investment analysts, news media, the Boy Scouts, and teenagers using instant messaging.

Sometimes, however, the line between internal and external isn't clearly drawn. For example, the alumni of your college or university technically are an external public; they're no longer enrolled, and most have probably moved away. But many of them don't *feel* external—to their dying day, they will be Jayhawks or Tarheels or Longhorns or Horned Toads or whatever mascot brings a tear of pride to their eyes. Smart public relations practitioners identify such feelings and, when appropriate, treat such a public as a member of the organization's family. Although the Kablooie Microwave Popcorn Company is a new organization, imagine it 30 years from now. Will its loyal retired employees feel like an internal or an external public?

Domestic and International Publics

Last but not least, publics are either domestic publics or international publics. **Domestic publics** are those within your own country. But proximity doesn't necessarily mean familiarity. As we saw previously, some domestic publics can be nontraditional publics, requiring effective cross-cultural communication efforts.

International publics are those beyond your country's borders. Increasingly, public relations practitioners are dealing with international publics. For example, suppose that the factory that supplies the packages for Kablooie popcorn is in Mexico. A variety of cross-cultural considerations now confront you. Do you speak Spanish? Does the factory manager there speak English? If your crisis has occurred on May 5 or September 16, will the factory manager answer a telephone call to his or her office? Probably not: Those days are national holidays in Mexico.

What Do We Need to Know about Each Public?

No two publics are the same. And yet the kinds of information we need to gather about each public are remarkably similar. To manage a productive, values-driven relationship with a public, we must be able to answer seven questions about it:

1. *How much can the public influence our organization's ability to achieve our goals?* How dependent is our organization on the resources controlled by this public? In other words, is the public a primary public or a secondary public? As much as public relations practitioners would like to have positive, well-maintained relationships with every public, that ideal is simply too impractical; it would stretch their resources too thin. Public relations practitioners must focus most of their attention and efforts on the relationships that spell the difference between success and failure for their organizations.

2. *What is the public's stake, or value, in its relationship with our organization?* As we noted earlier, a relationship between a public and an organization is born when values intersect. What values does the public hold that have brought it into contact with your organization? For example, investors value steady increases in the price of the stock they own. Customers value getting their money's worth. Employees value, among other things, interesting work and good salaries.

Identifying the value or values a public seeks to realize in its relationship with your organization is one of the most important things you can do in public relations. It allows you to explore the possibility of a relationship in which both sides win: The public's values can be recognized and honored, and your organization can achieve its goal for the relationship. That's the heart of values-driven public relations.

3. *Who are the opinion leaders and decision makers for the public?* Members of a public turn to **opinion leaders** for advice and leadership. Stockholders, for example, often turn to successful investment analysts for advice. Employees may turn to union leaders or trusted supervisors. If we can identify the opinion leaders of a public, perhaps we can build a relationship with them that will strengthen our relationship with the entire public.

Not every public has well-defined, easily identifiable opinion leaders, however. For example, in the scenario that opens this chapter, who are the opinion leaders for the millions of teenagers using instant messaging? That particular public is so large that we might be wise to divide it into smaller publics—based on geography or on the particular chat rooms the teenagers frequent—and look for opinion leaders of those smaller groups.

Decision makers are people who have the authority to dictate actions and establish policies for publics. Some publics have easily identifiable decision makers. For example, decision makers for news media are the editors, publishers, directors, and producers who oversee the content of newspapers, magazines, radio programs, television programs, or web sites. The decision maker of a local environmental group probably would be the group's president or board of directors—though any important decision might involve a vote among members. Decision makers can be determined by the goal your organization is trying to achieve. For example, when a company wants to build a new factory, one set of decision makers from which it needs approval may be a local zoning board.

Some publics, however, don't have easily identifiable decision makers. Latent publics or aware publics (as opposed to active publics) may be only loosely organized at best. For example, suppose your organization wants to improve its relationship with local alternative rock musicians. Who are the decision makers for that diverse group—or for the teenagers in the chat rooms? Perhaps the best we can do is to point to opinion leaders for our targeted public.

Even within a single, well-defined public, opinion leaders and decision makers can vary, depending on the issue. For example, a local taxpayers group may have one opinion leader for issues involving sales taxes but a different opinion leader for property tax issues. And on simple matters such as scheduling meetings, the president of the group may be the decision maker. But on more important decisions, such as organizing a protest at City Hall, the board of directors may have to call for a vote among members.

Despite the difficulties, public relations practitioners seek to identify and to build relationships with decision makers and opinion leaders because they often have influence over publics that may be essential to an organization's success.

4. *What is the demographic profile of the public?* **Demographic information** is data about who a public is. For example, besides telling us how many members a public has, a demographic profile of a public might include information about age, gender, income, education, and number of children per family. For each of these characteristics, we would probably want medians and ranges. For example, we probably would like to know the median age of an important public (the age that represents a halfway point, with half the public younger and half the public older than the median age). The range of ages would specify the age of the youngest member of the public as well as the age of its oldest member. Demographic information can help us understand who a public is, how important that public might be to our organization, and what its values might be.

In our Kablooie Microwave Popcorn scenario, we might consider grocery-store chains that carry our product to be a public. Although demographic characteristics such as age and gender might not influence our communications with that large public, we certainly might rank the members of that public by how much Kablooie Microwave Popcorn each company purchases for resale. That information could help us subdivide our grocery-store chain public into smaller publics and provide direction on which chains we might choose to contact first.

5. *What is the psychographic profile of the public?* **Psychographic information** is data about what members of a public think, believe, and feel. For example, are they politically liberal, moderate, or conservative? Are they religious? Agnostic? Atheistic? Do they like sophisticated technology or fear it—or, perhaps, are they indifferent to it? Psychographic information can be harder to collect and measure than demographic information, but it's no less important. Like demographic information, a psychographic profile can help us understand who a public is and what its values might be.

6. *What is the public's opinion of our organization?* Any television sitcom about high school students eventually has a scene in which one student wants to date another and is desperately trying to find out that person's opinion of him or her. It's the same in public relations, though perhaps a little less stressful. A public's opinion of our organization is one of the foundations of our relationship. That opinion tells us whether we approach the relationship as friends, unknowns, or enemies. It would be an embarrassing waste of resources, for example, to create a communications program for a public that we think is hostile—only to discover that that public has a favorable impression of us and is puzzled by our actions.

7. *What is the public's opinion (if any) of the issue in question?* As we've noted before, sometimes a particular issue creates a relationship between an organization and a public. For example, the false stories about Kablooie Microwave Popcorn have suddenly created a relationship between Kablooie and the teenagers using Internet chat rooms. We need to learn what the public thinks about the issue; in particular, we need to know which of the public's values are supported or threatened by the issue.

Coorientation

Coorientation is a public relations research process that can help us discover where our organization agrees and disagrees with an important public on a particular issue. Coorientation can eliminate damaging misperceptions about what each side believes. (As you'll see, coorientation can get a little like the comedy routine in which one actor says, "I think that you think that I think. . . .") In part, coorientation involves asking these four questions:

1. What is our organization's view of this issue?
2. What is the particular public's view of this issue?
3. What does our organization *think* the public's view is? (Does this agree with reality?)
4. What does the particular public *think* our organization's view is? (Does this agree with reality?)

Let's apply these four basic questions of coorientation to a portion of our Kablooie Popcorn scenario:

1. Our view of the situation is that the rumors are provably false—but we're concerned that the rumors could influence investment analysts.
2. Quick research on our part shows that investment analysts aren't worried at all. They've encountered such rumors before, and they're laughing. They still like our stock.
3. More research shows that our organization's leaders believe investment analysts are troubled by the rumors. Our CEO has asked us to initiate an emergency webcast for the analysts. (Our management team's opinion clashes with reality.)
4. Our research has shown that investment analysts don't think our organization is worried. (That's wrong, but perhaps we can learn from it.)

To honor our CEO's request, we may want to develop a ready-if-needed plan for a webcast—but in the Kablooie case, coorientation can help keep our organization from overreacting to the crisis. Letting the analysts laugh may be our best option. Using coorientation to discover the perceptions and misperceptions of two different publics can help public relations practitioners manage the relationship effectively.

As we said in Chapter 1, the public relations process begins with research. Answering, to the best of our ability, the seven questions listed above is one of the most important parts of public relations research.

Quick ✓ Check

1. In public relations, what is the definition of the word *public*? Of *stakeholder*?
2. What differences separate latent, aware, and active publics?
3. What are the differences between demographic information and psychographic information?
4. What is resource dependency theory?
5. What is coorientation?

The Traditional Publics in Public Relations

Earlier in this chapter we introduced the term *traditional publics*—that is, publics with which organizations have long-term, ongoing relationships. As we noted, *traditional* can be a misleading word. A group that is a traditional public for one organization might be a nontraditional public for another. Many organizations, however, do have long-term relationships with well-established traditional publics, including employees, the news media, governments, investors, consumers, multicultural community groups, constituents (voters), and businesses. In the next several pages, we'll offer brief descriptions of those publics—and, because they change every day, we'll also offer sources you can consult to update your knowledge of these important publics in public relations.

Employees

As the old joke goes, we have good news and bad news. The good news is that two recent surveys show that organization managers consider employee relations and internal communication to be a top priority.[8] So what's the bad news? Almost 50 percent of employees say they first learn about important company news through office gossip—the grapevine.[9] Another survey of the U.S. workforce shows that only slightly more than half of employees believe that their own organizations tell them the truth.[10]

Employees often are the most important publics in public relations. Think about it: If your organization's employees aren't on your side, it doesn't matter how good your relationships with other publics are. So it's good news that organizations are focusing on this key public. But the challenge of building good relationships with employees has never been greater. Employee publics are changing so rapidly that relationship management can seem like building a car while you're driving it. And yet the stakes are huge: Research indicates that companies with good employee relations return three times more value to stockholders than companies with poor employee relations.[11]

What changes are reshaping the employee public? Management consultant Robert Barner identifies five:[12]

- *A distributed workforce:* Employees are scattering. Some work at home and communicate with the office through e-mail, instant messaging, and other electronic

James Cash Penney
His Life and Legacy

Retail genius, philanthropist, "the man with a thousand partners," gentleman farmer, author, lecturer, world traveler, and the founder of the J.C. Penney Company: These are all words and phrases used to describe James Cash Penney.

The man whose name became synonymous with doing business according to the principles of the Golden Rule was born on September 16, 1875, on a small farm outside Hamilton, Mo. Penney's father was a poor farmer and unsalaried Baptist minister. His mother was a devout woman born of a genteel Southern family. Although raised in poverty, he would remain faithful to the rigorous teachings of his parents.

An abiding faith in God, the Christian ethic of the Golden Rule, self-reliance, self-discipline, and honor formed the foundation on which he built his entire life.

Penney showed signs of becoming a merchant as early as age eight,

James Cash Penney, age 59.

Biography A corporate identity booklet, such as this biography of James Cash Penney, founder of the J.C. Penney Company, can help explain organizational culture and values to employees. (Courtesy of J.C. Penney Company)

means. Others work at sites around the world as organizations continue to expand internationally. For generations, studies have shown that employees prefer to get important information about their organizations through face-to-face meetings with their supervisors.[13] Offering that "face time" will become more and more difficult.

Ironically, several important workplace innovations can undermine face-to-face communication. The number of U.S. employers offering flexible work schedules—so-called flex time—to employees soared to 71 percent in 2004, more than double the percentage in 1996.[14] But those nonstandard hours can mean less face time with supervisors. Electronic messages also can reduce the crucial personal element in successful employee communication. "The pervasiveness of e-mail and voice mail makes it more important than ever to make time for face-to-face communication in order to maintain morale," says Donald Ness, of RHI Management Resources in Canada.[15]

■ *The increasing use of temps:* Temporary workers were the fastest-growing part of the U.S. workforce during much of 2003 and 2004, according to the U.S. Bureau of Labor Statistics. By mid-2004, temps represented almost 2.5 million employees in the United States.[16] "Companies increasingly divide their workforces into a core group of permanent, well-paid employees surrounded by less-skilled, lower-wage workers who can be brought in and sent away as demand fluctuates," concluded the *New York Times*.[17] How will organizations build productive relationships with a workforce that increasingly consists of "here today, gone tomorrow" employees?

■ *The growth of information managers:* A generation ago, most workers built products. Today, a rapidly growing percentage of employees manage information—and they need sophisticated technology to do so. As that technology changes literally from day to day, employees will need continuing education throughout their careers. The American Society for Training and Development (ASTD) reports that as overall U.S. employee training increases, traditional classroom training has declined and "e-learning" through web sites and CDs has increased dramatically. Still, in terms of employee training, workers in the United States lag behind Japan, Australia, New Zealand, and other nations.[18] Not surprisingly, ASTD research shows a strong correlation between employee training and financial success.[19] Federal Reserve Chairman Alan Greenspan told U.S. busi-

---

EMPLOYEE PUBLICS: FAQS

1. *What resources do employees have that their organizations need?*
   Primarily commitment. Organizations with committed employees have greater innovation, reduced absenteeism, and significantly greater profits.

2. *What are the greatest challenges to building successful relationships with employees?*
   Poor communications breed distrust and low morale. Employee publics are more diverse than ever. New communications technologies are replacing face-to-face communication.

3. *Where can I find more information on employee publics?*
   - *Communication World* magazine, published by the International Association of Business Communicators
   - U.S. Bureau of Labor Statistics, online at www.bls.gov
   - Society for Human Resource Management, online at www.shrm.org

SABOTAGE IN THE WORKPLACE

Sabotage in the American Workplace: That's the name of a book that caught the public's eye in 1992 with its amazing tales of the destruction committed by bored, unhappy, uninformed employees.[20]

Take Ron, for example, who worked at a well-known chain of toy stores. The job was boring, he said, but he found ways to liven things up for himself and his coworkers:

> One Christmas the store had a Barbie doll house on display. Every night I would create a different scene by dressing the dolls up in strange outfits and setting them in unusual situations. One time I dressed the Ken doll in a clown outfit, tied Barbie against a balcony, and set Ken up so he was whipping her.

And let's not forget Reggie, who worked in the mailroom of a well-known, politically conservative think tank. Reggie was hired without any kind of orientation program, and when he discovered that the think tank's politics were at odds with his own, he—well, let him tell the story:

> People would mail in checks. . . . So I started randomly taking envelopes, opening them, and throwing the checks in the shredder. I started doing it more and more. I could tell if it was a check by holding it up to the light. If it was, I'd toss it or shred it.

Ron and Reggie make a powerful case that values-driven public relations begins with good employee relations. No organization can maintain productive, long-term relationships with important publics if it is crumbling from within. An informed, committed, and respected workforce provides a solid base for all the relationships that an organization must build.

ness leaders in 2004, "We need . . . to discover the means to enhance the skills of our workforce and to further open markets here and abroad to allow our workers to compete effectively in the global marketplace."[21]

■ *The growth of diversity:* The U.S. Bureau of Labor Statistics estimates that by 2012, 65.6 percent of the U.S. workforce will be non-Hispanic white employees, down from 70.5 percent in 2002. Employees from other ethnic groups will increase as a percentage of the workforce: Hispanic employees to 14.7 percent; black employees to 12.2 percent; and Asian American employees to 5.5 percent. By 2012, female employees will constitute 47.5 percent of the workforce, up from 46.5 in 2002.[22] A recent survey of U.S. and Canadian employees concluded that "today's workforce is more diverse than ever. Employees come from different countries and from various ethnic and social backgrounds, each with its own unique mindset and values that impact how they view work."[23]

■ *The aging of the baby boomers:* As baby boomers near retirement, workers 55 and older will jump to 19.1 percent of the workforce by 2012, up from 14.3 percent in 2002.[24] As fewer workers seek early-retirement options, organizations will need new strategies for motivating and training an aging workforce.

We would add one more significant change shaping the new workforce: the impact of employees from Generation X (born 1966 to 1980) and Generation Y (born 1980 to 1994). Employers have gradually learned that different generations have different motivations in the workplace. *Sales & Marketing Management* magazine offers this analysis of generational differences:[25]

- Employees in their 20s want challenging assignments, new responsibilities, and ample continuing education opportunities. They dislike low-tech environments.
- Employees in their 30s want an entrepreneurial and creative environment. They dislike hearing "no" to new ideas.
- Employees in their 40s want time away from work but, still, a chance to shine in the office. They dislike taking orders.
- Employees 50 and older want to mentor younger employees, though they still want learning opportunities. They dislike being considered old.

Age may affect attitude in additional ways. Almost 70 percent of U.S. employees age 35 and younger believe that their companies communicate honestly. However, that statistic plunges to 44 percent for employees 50 and older.[26]

Communication may well be the answer to challenges of trust and motivation. Research shows that more than 80 percent of employees who praise their supervisor's communication skills have high morale; an almost equal number say that morale soars in organizations that request and respond to employee feedback.[27] Unfortunately, research also shows that although 83 percent of managers believe they discuss organizational goals with their staffs, fewer than 50 percent of employees say they know what goal-oriented actions their organizations have undertaken.[28]

Good news and bad news. More than ever before, public relations practitioners recognize the importance of their employee publics. But the challenges of employee relations have never been greater.

The News Media

The numbers are impressive. In the early 21st century, the United States has[29]

- more than 10,739 newspapers
- 407 weekly magazines and other periodicals
- 3,636 monthly magazines and other periodicals
- 3,814 quarterly magazines and other periodicals
- 3,766 AM radio stations
- 5,339 FM radio stations
- 1,332 TV stations
- 1,335 cable TV systems

No reliable figures exist for the number of news-related web sites. However, the Pew Internet & American Life Project reports that news consumers still prefer tradi-

NEWS MEDIA PUBLICS: FAQS

1. *What resources do news media have that organizations need?*

Fair coverage and the willingness to consider news stories offered by public relations practitioners. The relative objectivity and credibility of the news media can provide what is called an **independent endorsement** or **third-party endorsement** of an organization's news.

2. *What is the greatest challenge to building successful relationships with news media?*

A mutual lack of knowledge. A recent study shows that journalists and public relations practitioners alike value accuracy and fairness—but neither party believes the other holds those values.[30]

3. *Where can I find more information on news media publics?*

- American Society of Newspaper Editors, online at www.asne.org
- Poynter Institute for Media Studies, online at www.poynter.org
- *Gale Directory of Publications and Broadcast Media,* published annually by Gale

tional news media to online alternatives: Even among regular Internet users who seek both online and traditional news media, 71 percent prefer traditional media such as television, radio, and newspapers.[31]

Some very important members of those news media are the so-called **gatekeepers:** editors or producers who decide which stories to include and which stories to reject. Without the consent of the gatekeepers, public relations practitioners cannot use the news media as intervening publics. Gatekeepers value news that serves the interests of their audiences. If public relations practitioners can supply that kind of audience-focused news, they should have productive relationships with the gatekeepers of the news media.

Because of the First Amendment and its guarantee of freedom of the press, news media in the United States can, with few limitations, report whatever they perceive to be news. But in emerging democracies around the world, freedom of the press is, so to speak, a hotly contested front-page issue. As new freedoms give rise to modern news media, government officials and journalists around the world are debating the limits of freedom.

In the United States, a continuing problem for the news media is the disproportionately small number of minority journalists. In the wake of violent race riots during the struggle for civil rights, the report of the Kerner Commission in 1968 blasted the U.S. news media for their lack of minority journalists. However, in 1998 the American Society of Newspaper Editors conceded that it would not reach its year-2000 goal of having the minority population of newsrooms reflect the actual minority percentages of the U.S. population.[32] In the first decade of the 21st century, diversity in the U.S. news media looks something like this:

- Almost 13 percent of newspaper journalists are members of minority groups: 5.4 percent are black, 4.2 percent are Hispanic, 2.8 percent are Asian American, and 0.6 percent are Native American.[33]
- Almost 22 percent of television journalists are members of minority groups: 10.3 percent are black, 8.9 percent are Hispanic, 2.2 percent are Asian American, and 0.5 percent are Native American.[34]

When Mount St. Helens in Washington state threatened to erupt in September 2004, volcanologist Cynthia Gardner of the U.S. Geological Survey used the news media as an intervening public to warn a primary public: tourists considering a visit to the active volcano. (Courtesy of David Wieprecht and the U.S. Geological Survey)

■ Almost 12 percent of radio journalists are members of minority groups: 7.3 percent are black, 3.9 percent are Hispanic, 0.4 percent are Native American, and 0.2 percent are Asian American.[35]

Any discussion of 21st-century news media must include the concept of **convergence of media**—that is, a blending of media made possible by digital technology (for more on convergence and digital technology, please see Chapter 11). Simply put, digital technology allows journalists to move words, sounds, and images back and forth among radio, TV, newspapers, magazines, and web sites. As a consequence, members of the news media can offer their news in more than one format. The *Chicago Tribune* newspaper, for example, now works closely with affiliated radio and television stations (broadcast and cable) to offer an online edition of the news gathered by all those media. Radio Margaritaville, a station launched by musician Jimmy Buffett, whose fans are affectionately known as Parrot Heads, exists only online (www.radiomargaritaville.com). The station's digital existence allows it to offer a newsletter, merchandise for sale, play lists, and concert schedules, all of which can be examined online while Parrot Heads listen to their favorite music. Public relations practitioners who can offer journalists stories in digital formats suited to several media will thrive in the new world of convergence.

Values Statement 4.1

PEPSICO

Tracing its origins to a popular soda pop first developed in 1898, PepsiCo emerged in 1965 as a corporation that specializes in soft drinks and snack foods. Its headquarters are in Purchase, New York.

PepsiCo's overall mission is to increase the value of our shareholders' investment. We do this through sales growth, cost controls and wise investment of resources. We believe our commercial success depends upon offering quality and value to our consumers and customers; providing products that are safe, wholesome, economically efficient and environmentally sound; and providing a fair return to our investors while adhering to the highest standards of integrity.

—"Mission Statement,"
PepsiCo web site

No matter what background journalists may have, no matter what news medium they represent, they value one thing that public relations practitioners can supply: information—relevant, accurate, complete, timely information.

Governments

You've probably heard that the nine most feared words in the English language are "I'm from the government, and I'm here to help." Government workers actually *can* help public relations practitioners by providing information and interpreting legislation. But they can also harm a practitioner's organization by adopting unfavorable legislation or regulations. As we note elsewhere in this book, too, a continuing issue in public relations is government licensing of public relations practitioners. That hasn't happened yet, but the debate isn't over.

Who are the members of this influential public? They range from the local chief of police to the president of the United States. Government officials exist at the city/county level, the state level, and the federal level.

THE FEDERAL GOVERNMENT. At the federal level, there were 2.7 million nonmilitary employees in the early years of the 21st century.[36] The U.S. Bureau of Labor Statistics expects that number to increase by 3 percent by 2012, compared with a growth rate of 16 percent for nongovernmental jobs in the United States.[37] Federal employees range from the 535 members of Congress to the 829,587 who work for the postal service and the 4,245 who work in federal libraries.[38]

A survey of federal workers in 2003 revealed that 68 percent were satisfied with their jobs—but one-third said they might leave their federal jobs because of dissatisfaction with the quality of their supervisors, the failure to deal with poor performers, and the lack of incentives for improved performance.[39]

By some measures, the federal workforce is more diverse than the private-sector workforce: 17.6 percent of federal employees are black, compared with 10.4 percent in the private workforce; 7 percent are Hispanic, compared with 13.1 percent in the private workforce; 4.6 percent are of Asian/Pacific Islands origins, compared with 4.5 percent in the private workforce; 2 percent are Native Americans, compared with

GOVERNMENT PUBLICS: FAQS

1. *What resources do governments have that organizations need?*
   Fair, nonrestrictive regulations, protection from unfair competition in the marketplace, and interpretations or explanations of existing laws.

2. *What is the greatest challenge to building successful relationships with government publics?*
   The slow growth of the U.S. federal government is increasing the workload of federal employees and transferring new and sometimes unfamiliar tasks to state and local government employees.

3. *Where can I find more information on government publics?*
   - *The Almanac of American Politics,* published by the U.S. government
   - *Governing: The Magazine of States and Localities,* published by Congressional Quarterly, Inc.; online at www.governing.com
   - FedStats, online at www.fedstats.gov

0.6 percent in the private workforce; and 44 percent are women, compared with 46.5 percent in the private workforce.[40]

Most visible among these employees, of course, are the members of Congress, each of whom has his or her own values and agendas. An excellent source for studying each member of Congress as well as the top issues among each member's constituency is *The Almanac of American Politics,* which offers state-by-state and district-by-district analyses of senators, representatives, voters, and issues.

Lobbyists who work with federal employees, particularly with elected officials, have at least one bit of advice for public relations practitioners: Be well prepared and work fast.[41] Federal employees are busy. In fact, federal employees say that their top job-related need is time away from work to spend with their families.[42]

STATE AND LOCAL GOVERNMENTS. At last measurement, there were 5.1 million state government employees and 11.4 million local government employees in the United States—a total of 16.5 million.[43] The U.S. Bureau of Labor Statistics expects that number to increase to 21.2 million by 2012.[44] In this swirl of numbers, public relations practitioners should appreciate an important trend: State and local governments are growing at a faster rate than the federal government—in many cases taking on functions that formerly existed at the federal level.

Diversity figures for individual state governments generally can be found on state government web sites—often in annual reports to the governor and state citizens. In Wisconsin, for example, 8.6 percent of the state's classified employees (nonelected, nonpolitical, usually long-term) belong to recognized minority groups: 4.4 percent are black; 1.9 percent are Hispanic; 1.6 percent are Asian American; 0.7 percent are Native American; 51.5 percent are women; and 7.2 percent are people with disabilities.[45]

A recent survey of local government employees throughout the nation found that 61 percent are satisfied or very satisfied with their jobs; 17 percent were dissatisfied or very dissatisfied. The strongest factors leading to job satisfaction were departmental pride, good communication with supervisors, and good levels of job-related training. The strongest factors leading to dissatisfaction were low salaries, a lack of opportunities for promotion, and excessive workload. Age had no effect on job sat-

QuickBreak 4.3

JAMES BOND SAVES THE WHALES?

It's a whale of a tale: James Bond (actually Pierce Brosnan, one of the many actors to play Agent 007) and an international group of environmentalists face off against a national president and a powerful multinational corporation. And at the center of it all is resource dependency theory.

The conflict began when Japan's Mitsubishi Corporation and Mexico's national government announced plans to build a salt factory in Mexico's Baja California region. The factory would mean steady jobs for residents of the economically depressed area, but local fisherman opposed it, and the coastline in question was one of the last remaining breeding grounds of the Pacific gray whale, an endangered species. The project involved building a mile-long pier and turning dozens of square miles of the coast into holding ponds and dikes.

Former president of Mexico Ernesto Zedillo held the ultimate resource: the power to grant or withhold permission to build. In nurturing its relationship with Zedillo's government, Mit-subishi pledged an improved economy in return for permission to build the factory. Led by actor Brosnan, the environmentalists urged the Mexican government to honor its earlier commitment to protect the area as a national biosphere reserve. Brosnan also helped organize a boycott against Mitsubishi products—a withholding of resources that Mitsubishi desired.

The first James Bond movie was titled *Dr. No,* which may have been Mitsubishi's nickname for President Zedillo when he declared, "I have taken the decision to instruct the Mexican government . . . to propose the definitive cancellation of the project."

Mitsubishi was gracious in defeat, offering to help find other economic development opportunities for the region. Brosnan was honored by the International Fund for Animal Welfare. And resource dependency remained an important explanation for why groups form relationships with one another.[46]

isfaction for local government employees. However, upper-level employees had higher levels of job satisfaction than did nonsupervisory employees.[47]

Elected officials at all levels of government want to serve their constituents well and be reelected. Public relations practitioners who can help government officials pursue those values will find them to be willing partners in building productive relationships.

Quick ✔ Check

1. Are employees around the world satisfied with their jobs?
2. In media relations, what is an independent endorsement?
3. What does the comparatively rapid growth of state and local government workforces mean for public relations practitioners?
4. For public relations practitioners, what essential resources do employee, media, and government publics possess?

Investors

Companies that sell stock have relationships with investors. The investor public encompasses individual stockholders—and much more:

- Financial analysts study the stock markets to advise investors.
- Financial news media include the *Wall Street Journal, Business Week* magazine, the *Wall Street Week* television show, and web sites such as Value Line, at www.valueline.com.
- **Mutual fund managers** supervise what might be called investment clubs. For a fee, mutual fund managers invest a member's contributions (usually monthly payments) into a diverse collection of stocks and bonds. The popularity of mutual funds has soared in the past 20 years.
- So-called **institutional investors** are large companies or institutions that generally buy huge amounts of stock. The California Public Employees Retirement System, for example, is the largest public pension plan in the United States. It represents almost 1.5 million state and local government employees in California and has assets of approximately $170 billion.
- Employee investors are employees of companies, such as Microsoft, that reward employees with stock in the companies they work for.

If you've studied stock markets at all in recent years, you might guess—correctly—that U.S. investors feel as if they've been riding a roller coaster. But studies show that they're not leaving the amusement park.

"The growth in the investor population has been one of the great demographic stories of the past 15 years," declared *Slate* magazine in 2004. "In 1990, about 23 percent of Americans owned stocks and mutual funds in some form. By last year, a whopping 91 million Americans in 53.3 million households—47.9 percent of the total—owned mutual funds."[48]

Who are these investors? Not, perhaps, who you might think. Table 4.1 lists data on the investing public.[49]

Despite the economic impact of the September 11, 2001, terrorist attacks and the

---

INVESTOR PUBLICS: FAQS

1. *What resources do investor publics have that organizations need?*

Investors purchase stocks. Financial analysts, mutual fund managers, and journalists evaluate stocks and make recommendations to investors.

2. *What are the greatest challenges to building successful relationships with investor publics?*

Investor publics need information and reassurance as stock markets become increasingly volatile. The growing diversity of investors means that old ways of communicating may not be effective.

3. *Where can I find more information on investor publics?*

- Securities and Exchange Commission, online at www.sec.gov
- New York Stock Exchange, online at www.nyse.com
- International Federation of Stock Exchanges, online at www.fibv.com
- The *Wall Street Journal,* published Monday through Friday by Dow Jones and Company, Inc.

TABLE 4.1   U.S. Investors: Who They Are

- Average age is 49.9. Most are ages 40–60.
- 69 percent are college graduates.
- 56 percent are male.
- 83 percent are married.
- 91 percent are white; 2 percent are black; 2 percent are Hispanic; 2 percent are Asian American.
- Median annual household income is $89,000.
- 32 percent live in the South; 28 percent in the Midwest; 21 percent in the West; and 19 percent in the Northeast.

scandals at Enron and other companies, 82 percent of investors still believe that remaining in the stock markets is a good idea.[50] However, 66 percent say that they're more cautious about investment risks than before.[51] In fact, from 2000 to 2004, the Index of Investor Optimism, prepared by the Gallup Organization, declined by 60 percent.[52] One bright spot in the markets is the confidence of investors younger than 40: They remain almost twice as optimistic about the stock markets' future as older investors.[53]

"Weathering the market volatility [2001–2004] was no small feat for the individual investor," says Daniel Leemon, chief strategy officer for Charles Schwab & Company, a financial services firm.[54]

U.S. investors have indeed toughed out some serious storms. Just after the 9/11 terrorist attacks, 75 percent of investors said they would not sell their stocks; 17 percent even said they intended to buy more shares.[55] Slightly more than half of investors now say their investment strategy is to "buy and hold"—to purchase stocks and retain them for years, hoping they'll increase in value.[56]

Almost two-thirds of investors say that they have "high levels of concern" about recent accounting scandals in U.S. corporations.[57] However, almost the same percentage have confidence that new legislation, such as the Sarbanes-Oxley Act, which requires corporate leaders to personally sign financial statements, will reduce the number of such scandals.[58]

Of more concern to U.S. investors than scandals are soaring energy prices. In 2004, investors listed the spike in oil prices and other energy costs as the top threat to the stock markets' stability. In order, investors' next five concerns were

- job losses to overseas employers
- corporate accounting scandals
- instability in Iraq
- the federal budget deficit
- threats of terrorism[59]

Despite their concerns, investors say their top reason for remaining in the stock markets is retirement: 65 percent list retirement plans as their number one reason for investing.[60]

Instability in the markets could be a relationship-building opportunity for investor relations practitioners: More than half of investors can't answer basic questions about their investments—but almost 70 percent say they are trying to learn more.[61] Currently, two-thirds have a broker or financial adviser.[62]

Despite growing popularity, online trading represents only a tiny fraction of market transactions: In 2003, 70 percent of U.S. investors made no online trades; 17 percent made fewer than five.[63] Investors greatly prefer mutual funds. As *Slate* magazine noted, 53.3 million U.S. households own such funds. Most have annual household incomes under $75,000; most mutual fund investors are between the ages of 35 and 54.[64]

Consumers/Customers

The people of the United States are consumers—big-time consumers. Monthly consumer spending in the United States could purchase the entire annual goods-and-services output of Portugal, Finland, Singapore, and Austria—combined.[65]

Consumer spending is the most powerful force in the U.S. economy, accounting for two-thirds of all spending in the United States—twice as much as government and business spending combined.[66] In the words of *American Demographics* magazine, the amount of consumer spending "simply boggles the mind."[67]

Who are these big spenders, and what are they spending all that money on? Some facts:

- The average U.S. household has a before-tax income of $49,430. Its annual expenditures total $40,677. Where does the money go? Table 4.2 gives a partial breakdown.[68]

- The biggest spenders are people aged 45 to 54. Households in which the main earner falls into that age bracket spend $48,748 a year. By way of comparison,

TABLE 4.2	**How U.S Households Spend Their After-Tax Income**
Food	$5,375
Housing	$13,283
Apparel and services	$1,749
Transportation	$7,759
Health care	$2,350
Entertainment	$2,079
Personal care products and services	$526
Alcoholic beverages	$376
Tobacco products and smoking supplies	$320

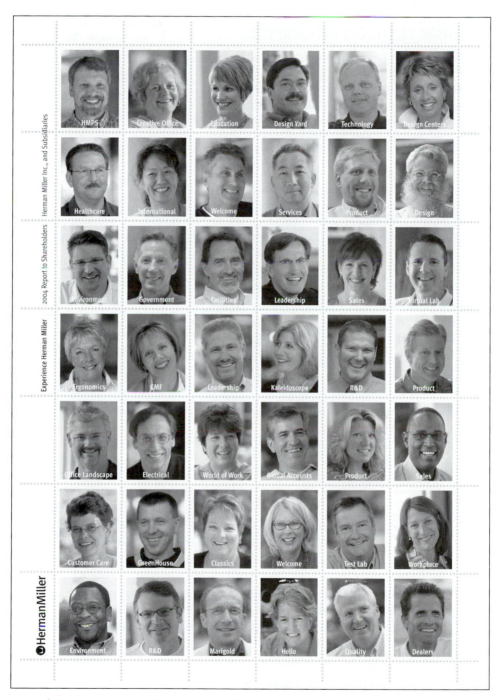

Annual Report Herman Miller, Inc.—an office-furniture design, manufacturing, and maintenance company—has earned praise for targeting investor publics with innovative, visually arresting annual reports. (Courtesy of Herman Miller, Inc.)

CONSUMER/CUSTOMER PUBLICS: FAQS

1. *What resources do consumer/customer publics have that organizations need?*
   Loyalty: a willingness to purchase and repurchase an organization's products. Consumers also possess the resource of publicity: Word-of-mouth cheers or jeers are a powerful force in the marketplace.

2. *What are the greatest challenges to building successful relationships with consumer/customer publics?*
   Forty-seven percent of U.S. consumers say that customer service is fair or poor. Only 8 percent rate it excellent.[69] The diversity of consumers is increasing. Also, public relations must learn to coordinate its tactics with the tactics of marketing, and vice versa (see Chapter 13).

3. *Where can I find more information on consumer/customer publics?*
   - *American Demographics,* published by Crain Communications, Inc., online at www.adage.com
   - U.S. Department of Commerce, online at www.commerce.gov
   - U.S. Bureau of Labor Statistics, online at www.bls.gov

households in which the main earner is under 25 spend only $24,229 a year. For age 65 and older, the total is $28,105.[70]

■ The annual spending power of blacks, Hispanics, and Asian Americans is booming, surging from $600 billion a year in the mid-1990s to more than $1.2 trillion today. In 1990, spending by white U.S. citizens represented 87 percent of annual consumer spending; by 2007, experts estimate that total will dip to 80 percent.[71]

■ Women account for approximately 83 percent of U.S. consumer spending.[72]

■ Generation Y (people born between 1980 and 1994) contributes about 5 percent of annual consumer spending to the U.S. economy.[73] Survey research indicates that Gen Y'ers have less brand loyalty and are more likely to make impulse purchases than any other age group.[74]

Online shopping, also known as **e-commerce** (for electronic commerce), continues to soar in popularity: Since the last quarter of 2001, retail e-commerce has averaged an annual growth rate of more than 20 percent. Midway through 2004, however, e-commerce represented only 1.7 percent of total sales in the United States.[75] The 2004 American Customer Satisfaction Index found that consumers now report higher levels of satisfaction in online shopping than in traditional shopping. Leading the list of companies that satisfy online shoppers was Amazon.com.[76] But the Pew Internet & American Life Project notes that U.S. consumers still vote with their feet: Even regular Internet users do more traditional shopping than online shopping.[77]

Regardless of where and how customers do their shopping, what do they value? Any survey gives you the same answer: quality at a fair price. Customers want to get what they paid for—and more.

Multicultural Communities

Public relations professionals must know the so-called movers and shakers in every community in which their organizations do business. Failing to learn who wields

MULTICULTURAL COMMUNITY PUBLICS: FAQS

1. *What resources do multicultural community publics have that organizations need?*
   The willingness to accept an organization as a community member—to be its employees, supporters, customers, and friends.

2. *What is the greatest challenge to building successful relationships with multicultural community publics?*
   The sheer number of such groups. Organizations' resources are limited, and they usually cannot build relationships with every public within a community. Organizations must determine which relationships in a community are most essential to the fulfillment of their values.

3. *Where can I find more information on multicultural community publics?*
   - U.S. Bureau of the Census, online at www.census.gov
   - U.S. Citizenship and Immigration Services, online at http://uscis.gov
   - *American Demographic,* published by Crain Communications, Inc., online at www.adage.com
   - The *Chronicle of Philanthropy,* published weekly; online at www.philanthropy.com

power in a community can have catastrophic results, as the developer of a proposed landfill site once discovered:

One private developer announced a project that soon drew surprisingly intense environmental opposition from local residents. Only months after announcing the planned facility did the developer learn that the town was home to Ralph Nader.[78]

Besides consumer activist and presidential candidate Ralph Nader, who are the influential publics within our diverse communities? Professor Jerry Hendrix of American University offers a useful breakdown, which appears in Table 4.3.[79] Some of the worst, most expensive public relations fiascoes in recent memory have involved companies perceived as being insensitive to racial or ethnic groups. In the mid-1990s, Denny's, the restaurant chain, faced repeated charges of refusing to seat or serve black customers. In fact, the company paid almost $55 million to settle two class-action lawsuits backed by thousands of reportedly mistreated black customers. Denny's had become "synonymous with discrimination" according to national news media. "It was a hard time for the company," said a Denny's representative. "Morale was so low. Something had to be done."[80]

Something was done. In one of the most dramatic rebounds in the history of values-driven public relations, Denny's changed leadership and committed to diversity in the workforce and in clientele. Today, Denny's restaurant managers earn their salaries in part by showing specifically how they honor the value of diversity in their restaurants. In 2004, *Fortune* magazine ranked Denny's fifth on its list of the nation's top companies for minority employees.

More than ever before, public relations practitioners must foster positive relationships with racial and ethnic publics within their organizations' communities. Otherwise, organizations not only may separate themselves from community goodwill, but they also risk separating themselves from potential employees, customers, investors, donors, and other publics that they depend on to survive. Although the racial/ethnic makeup of every community is different, Table 4.4 shows the U.S. Census Bureau's projections for U.S. population totals and percentages for the year 2008.[81]

QuickBreak 4.4

THE CUSTOMER IS ALWAYS RIGHT?

The reigning master of bizarre customer inquiries is the mysterious Ted L. Nancy (who just might be comedian Jerry Seinfeld).[82] Posing as a clueless customer, Nancy bedevils corporate America with inane letters that usually draw painfully serious responses.[83]

To wit: Nancy wrote to San Francisco's Pan Pacific Hotel, asking if it could accommodate his physical abnormality: "I have three legs. . . . I'll need an ottoman I can place next to the bed when I sleep."

The hotel wrote back, politely noting that "our rooms do have ottoman chairs in them."

Nancy also wrote to the Nordstrom department store chain, asking if he might purchase a store mannequin that resembled his dead neighbor.

"Dear Mr. Nancy," replied a Nordstrom representative.

"Yours is one of the most interesting requests I have ever received. . . ."

Then Nancy wrote to Hanes about its underwear. . . .

Why do companies reply to such off-the-wall requests? Besides good manners, there's good business: A landmark customer-service study shows that most businesses could increase their profits 25–100 percent simply by retaining just 5 percent more of their current customers every year.[84]

Nancy has published three collections of his letters: *Letters from a Nut, More Letters from a Nut,* and *Extra Nutty! Even More Letters from a Nut.*

TABLE 4.3	Influential Community Publics

COMMUNITY MEDIA	COMMUNITY ORGANIZATIONS
Mass media (such as newspapers and television stations)	Civic
	Business
Specialized media (such as entertainment tabloids)	Service
	Social
COMMUNITY LEADERS	Cultural
Public officials	Religious
Educators	Youth
Religious leaders	Political
Professionals (such as doctors and lawyers)	Special-interest groups
Executives	Other groups
Bankers	
Union leaders	
Ethnic leaders	
Neighborhood leaders	

TABLE 4.4	Projected U.S. Population Totals and Percentages for the Year 2008
TOTAL POPULATION	295 million Median age: 37.2 Female: 151 million Male: 144 million
WHITE POPULATION	201 million (68.1 percent) Median age: 40.7 Age 18 & older: 157 million
AFRICAN AMERICAN POPULATION	37 million (12.5 percent) Median age: 32.2 Age 18 & older: 26 million
HISPANIC AMERICAN POPULATION	42 million (14.2 percent) Median age: 27.3 Age 18 & older: 27 million
ASIAN AMERICAN AND PACIFIC ISLANDER POPULATION	14 million (4.7 percent) Median age: 34 Age 18 & older: 10 million
AMERICAN INDIAN, ESKIMO, AND ALEUT AMERICAN POPULATION	2 million (0.7 percent) Median age: 29.5 Age 18 & older: 1.5 million

As noted in Chapter 16, immigration is also changing communities in the United States. The foreign-born percentage of the U.S. population recently reached its highest level since 1930: Of today's residents, 11.7 percent were born citizens of other nations—a total of 33.5 million people. Approximately 37 percent reside in the western United States, followed by 29 percent in the South and 22 percent in the Northeast.[85] But even in small communities in southwestern Kansas, the meatpacking industry attracts immigrants from Vietnam and Somalia.

According to the U.S. Census Bureau, 53 percent of today's immigrants came from Latin America, 25 percent from Asia, and 14 percent from Europe. More than one-third arrived in the United States during the 1990s. Though 67 percent have at least a high school education, immigrants are more likely than nonimmigrants to be unemployed and living in poverty.[86]

In short, communities consist of diverse publics—and diversity within each public is probably increasing.

Constituents (Voters)

Not every organization considers voters to be a traditional public, though many organizations try to influence the legislative process by building relationships with eligible voters. But for public relations practitioners employed by democratically elected governments, voters are the most important public of all.

CONSTITUENT/VOTER PUBLICS: FAQS

1. *What resources do constituent/voter publics have that organizations need?*
   Votes and word-of-mouth endorsements. Constituents who approve of their elected representatives can influence the opinions of other constituents.

2. *What is the greatest challenge to building successful relationships with constituent/voter publics?*
   Voter apathy, which is particularly high among voters aged 18 to 24.

3. *Where can I find more information on constituent/voter publics?*
   - The League of Women Voters, online at www.lwv.org
   - *The Almanac of American Politics,* published by the U.S. government
   - International Institute for Democracy and Electoral Assistance, online at www.idea.int

In a sense, this group includes every citizen of a nation who is of voting age—a huge and diverse public. In countries where voting is compulsory, such as Costa Rica, a description of this public literally would be a description of the country's adult population. In the United States, however, a description of voters is somewhat easier, because not every eligible citizen votes. In the 2004 U.S. presidential election, 60 percent of eligible voters went to the polls—a 36-year high.[87] In voter turnout, the United States ranks 139th among the world's 170-plus democracies.[88]

What do we know about citizens in the United States who *do* vote? According to the U.S. Census Bureau, the most typical voter is a retired, married female homeowner, 65 or older, with a college degree and an above-average household income. Facts from the bureau's analysis of the 2002 elections paint this portrait of American voters:[89]

- *Marriage counts:* 55 percent of married citizens vote compared with 29 percent of single citizens.

- *Education rules:* 61 percent of citizens with a college education vote compared with 28 percent of high school dropouts.

- *Money talks:* 57 percent of citizens with a household income of $50,000 or more vote compared with 25 percent of citizens with a household income of less than $10,000.

The single greatest indicator of regular voting in the United States is age: Voters ages 65–74 are most likely to vote (65 percent). Least likely are voters ages 18–24 (19 percent)—the age group of many readers of this book. In the 2004 presidential election, 52 percent of eligible voters ages 18–29 went to the polls—up from 42 percent in the 2000 election.[90]

Although the civil rights movement in the United States increased opportunities for minority citizens to vote, white voters have the highest turnout at 49 percent. Black voters follow at 42 percent, Asian American voters at 31 percent, and Hispanic voters at 30 percent. Women are more likely to vote than men by the narrow margin of 47 percent to 46 percent.

Eligible voters who *don't* vote offer these Top Eight reasons why they can't make it to the polls (if you're a David Letterman fan, imagine a Top 10 countdown):

8. Transportation problems

7. Confused about registration

6. Forgot

5. Didn't like candidates or key issues

4. Out of town

3. Not interested or believed their vote made no difference

2. Ill, disabled, or had a family emergency

1. Too busy or had conflicting work or school schedules

Businesses

Organizations have relationships with a variety of businesses. Why? Because those businesses have resources that the organizations need if they are to fulfill their values-driven goals. Such relationships involve **business-to-business communication,** often called **B2B** communication. For example, an organization may have relationships with vendor businesses that supply materials to the organization; distributor businesses that help move the organization's products to consumers; customer businesses that purchase the organization's products; and industry partners, which are in the same type of business and work with the organization to help influence legislative and regulation processes at different levels of government. That same organization has sometimes-uneasy relationships with direct competitors. Public relations practitioners communicate with a variety of different businesses to build productive relationships.

B2B communication is big business, and it's growing. Experts estimate that by 2008, B2B spending for traditional media alone—such as magazine advertisements and trade shows—will top $23 billion.[92] According to one estimate, approximately half of all public relations work in England is now B2B communication.[93] In the United States, 100 percent of the Slack Barshinger agency's $10 million in 2003 revenues came from B2B relationship building. "If I were to accept consumer work, it would confuse our staff, our clients, our competitors, and the

---

BUSINESS PUBLICS: FAQS

1. *What resources do business publics have that organizations need?*
Vendor businesses have supplies and loyalty. Customer businesses have the willingness to purchase and repurchase an organization's products. Direct competitors have the resource of competing fairly.

2. *What are the greatest challenges to building successful relationships with business publics?*
One surprising challenge may be the reputation of B2B communications. *Marketing* magazine reports that B2B is thought to be "the least glamorous part" of public relations.[91] Also, the sheer number of business relationships that an organization has poses a challenge to relationship building.

3. *Where can I find more information on business publics?*
- *BtoB* magazine, published monthly by Crain Communications, Inc.; online at www.btobonline.com
- *Sales & Marketing Management* magazine, published monthly by VNU Business Publications; online at www.salesandmarketing.com
- *Business Week* magazine, published weekly by the McGraw-Hill Companies; online at www.businessweek.com

marketplace and blur our image," says Gary Slack, chairman of Slack Barshinger, which won a 2004 *BtoB* magazine award as a top agency. "The first thing people think of when they hear our name is b-to-b."[94]

Quick ✔ Check

1. What is the demographic profile of people in the United States who invest in the stock markets?
2. What age group in the United States spends the most money on consumer goods and services?
3. What does *B2B* mean?
4. For public relations practitioners, what important resources are possessed by investor, consumer, community, constituent, and business publics?

Summary

A public is a group of people who share a common value or values in a particular situation. In other words, publics unite around their values. For employees, the core value may be job security. For an environmental group, maybe it's clean air and water. An organization forms relationships with publics that have the resources it needs to fulfill its values-driven goals. However, when the values of a public intersect with the values of an organization, a relationship—whether the organization wants it or not—is born.

Traditional publics may vary among different organizations. For many organizations, however, long-established traditional publics include employees, the news media, governments, investors, consumers, multicultural community groups, constituents (voters), and businesses.

Publics can and do change constantly, but the questions a practitioner must answer about each public remain the same. Whether a public is latent, aware, or active, if it has the power to influence an organization, a practitioner must answer these questions:

- How much can the public influence our organization's ability to achieve our goals?
- What is the public's stake, or value, in its relationship with our organization?
- Who are the opinion leaders and decision makers for the public?
- What is the demographic profile of the public?
- What is the psychographic profile of the public?
- What is the public's opinion of our organization?
- What is the public's opinion (if any) of the issue in question?

Not until those questions are answered can public relations practitioners strive to build the relationships that will help an organization achieve its values-driven goals.

DISCUSSION QUESTIONS

1. Your authors state that the most important publics in public relations are employee publics. Do you agree? Why or why not?
2. Can you think of examples of nontraditional publics that have become—or are becoming—traditional publics?
3. Why do public relations practitioners try to identify opinion leaders and decision makers for each public?
4. Why is it important to identify a public's stake in an issue of importance to a practitioner's organization?
5. In our opening scenario, how would you classify the local Boy Scout troops? Are they a primary or a secondary public?

Memo
from the
Field

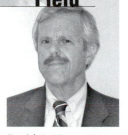

David A. Narsavage;
Senior Partner; The
Aker Partners, Inc.;
Washington, D.C.

A journalism school graduate and former print journalist, Dave Narsavage has been a professional communicator for more than 35 years. Once an Army combat correspondent in Vietnam, he's held communications positions in the U.S. Senate, with a national political party, and as director of employee communications for a 26,000-employee corporation. He now counsels clients of The Aker Partners, a Washington, D.C.–based public affairs firm.

It's all about publics, and messages, and desired effects. And the wheelie video. You've got to figure out who you *want* to see the wheelie video. And who you don't.

My teenaged son was lobbying me for a motorcycle. Not *my* kind of motorcycle: low-slung, no plastic in sight, a throaty "potato potato potato" idle note. Now that's a bike. No, his rocket would be clad in fiberglass, sound like a crazed bee, and hit warp speed in a nanosecond.

"Forget it," I told him. "It's a fatal attraction."

But since we were already *in* a motorcycle showroom during this discussion, I agreed there was no harm in looking. We started chatting with a young salesman, making it clear that my son had a fantasy—and I had a fear of him flying.

The salesman smiled and nodded. Knowingly, I thought. "Dudes!" he blurted suddenly, as if just hit with a truly huge idea. "You've *got* to see this video!" And he took us to a monitor, where we watched young men of little brain race my son's fantasy ride on rear wheel only, front wheel only, and no wheels only. "Isn't that *awesome*!?"

My son, no fool, looked at me and smiled. He knew: *This* was a man who had never read a word from Professors Guth and Marsh.

Know the room. Whether you call them a public or a target audience, know who those people are. Know what will move them: the hot buttons that can either bring them closer to your point of view or push them out of sight.

Remember that they'll have some selfish, self-interest issues, because that's how we humans are. But mostly it will come down to emotions.

One of my relics from a previous life as a U.S. senator's press secretary is a treasured copy of a "Shoe" comic strip, personally signed by the much-missed Jeff Mac-Nelly. It shows the editor bird (just go with me on this if you're not a "Shoe" fan) holding up a sheet of paper and asking the professor bird, "Where should I file this urgent press release from Senator Belfry?" The professor replies, "File it under 'W'— for 'Who cares?'"

Who *cares* about your message? Who *doesn't* care now, and what will it take to rouse them? Because no matter how much your client/employer pays you, no matter how much you buy into his or her fervor and embrace that gospel, if your key audiences don't *care*, you're wasting good professional effort.

Public and *relations*. Of the two, I'd worry about relations. That's where the power is, where the blood, and character, and emotions are. Where the *caring* is. As you'll read in this textbook, the value of our profession comes in the building and nurturing of relationships.

You build those relationships by treating audiences with respect and by communicating with them in the same clear and direct way you would in a letter to a friend. Wait, you don't know what a letter is. In an *e-mail* to a friend, OK? But with capitalization and punctuation.

Do the world a favor. Don't let clients insist on corporate-speak, and puffery, and inflated verbiage whose message seems to be "If you can't understand what I'm saying, then I must be *really* smart."

Have a *conversation* with your audiences. Your authors call it two-way symmetrical public relations. We call that communicating. Anything else is what my father used to call—in mixed company—a bunch of padookey dust.

I love these guys, Guth and Marsh. Not just because they gave me a podium, and as a presentation-trainer friend says, *seize* the podium as your own space, but because they share my concern for employees. Talk about an important audience. These are people who will have a long-term influence on putting meaning behind your message and people who represent a built-in grassroots network for your client.

But more than that, it's simply a basic consideration, a courtesy. People shouldn't have to read the paper or watch the news to know about changes in their work home. Bring them into the communications tent. If that helps you achieve your "values-driven goals," peachy. And even if it doesn't, you'll feel better about looking in the mirror.

I'm getting a "cut" signal from the author guys. Wrap it up.

In time, you *will* need to do some honest work. So before you fold up your "College" sweatshirt, pack your street signs, and leave those hallowed halls—why do we never hear of *un*hallowed halls?—I leave you with this:

- Remember that what seems so vital to your client, and thus to you, probably means jack to most everybody else. So find the people who care. It's better to reach the people who count than count the people you reach.

- Don't use *impact* as a verb. Genuflect before the *AP Stylebook* daily.

- You shouldn't expect any audience to understand and retain any more than about three key messages. If you can't state your position during a routine elevator trip, you need help.

- Laugh in the office every day. Avoid agencies and clients who don't know how.

- If you think you're there to do your client's blind bidding, you're in the wrong gig. If you think you're there to be your client's communications *counsel* and *partner,* welcome to the bond.

- Buy quality hand tools. The cheap stuff won't last. Hey, I'm still seizing the podium here.

What we do serves an honorable purpose: We help people tell their stories. We help them be heard. Then the key audiences have what they need to decide whether to print, buy, vote, move, change, eat, love, hate, or yawn. That's a good thing.

And *your* job is to decide: Should I show the wheelie video?

Case Study 4.1

Criticize Me! Subway and the Crossed-Off Cross-Promotion

The Subway restaurant chain likes to tell its customers to "eat fresh." But in 2004, Subway had to eat something different: a controversial cross-promotional campaign launched by its German franchises.

Cross-promotions occur when two organizations agree to promote each other's products or goals. In the Subway case, the restaurant chain's 100 German franchises contacted the company handling German distribution of *Super Size Me*, a documentary harshly critical of McDonald's, Subway's international rival.[95] To encourage diners to see the film, Subway agreed to use promotional tray liners—ones that featured a chubby Statue of Liberty holding, not a torch and book, but a burger and fries. The liners included the question "Why are Americans so fat?"[96]

"The people in Germany do understand what we want to say and that we do not want to offend anybody," said a representative of the German company that created the liners.[97]

But as Canadian philosopher Marshall McLuhan famously declared, we live in a global village: Unfortunately, a few of Subway's cross-promotional tray liners went cross-country, crossing the Atlantic to the United States, where they made people—well, cross.

"They should feel bad about fanning the flames of anti-Americanism in order to sell more sandwiches," said Jeffrey Mazzella, executive director of the U.S.-based Center for Individual Freedom.[98] The center launched an e-mail campaign, asking supporters to make their feelings known to Subway executives.[99]

"This is every bad stereotype about corporate America come true," railed Tom DeLay, majority leader of the U.S. House of Representatives. "I guess for some companies, corporate patriotism is as flexible as Jared's waistline."[100] (Jared Fogle, well known from Subway television commercials, lost 250 pounds on a diet of Subway sandwiches.)

Not all U.S. observers trashed Subway. "This is a gross example of American overreaction," said Alan Hilburg, president of Porter Novelli Consulting.[101]

But just like an extra-value meal, there's more: The crisis supersized when Subway's cross-promo partner, the German film distributor, sent journalists a media kit that contained a startling image: a giant hamburger crashing into skyscrapers, which spew smoke and topple toward the ground. More than one observer noted a strong resemblance to the September 11 terrorist attacks on the World Trade Center.

"That is not our promotion, and the booklet was never handed out at Subway's German franchises," said a Subway representative in the United States, stressing the fact that the media kit belonged to the film distributor alone.[102]

In fact, officials in Subway's international headquarters in the United States disavowed knowledge of the entire campaign. A Subway representative said the company's leaders were as surprised as others at the cross-promotion. "We try not to put too many restrictions on the franchises to keep up the entrepreneurial spirit of the brand," he explained. But he added that, in the future, Subway's top management would take greater control of the company's many regional marketing campaigns.[103]

Subway's cross-promo partner displayed a disturbing lack of knowledge of modern public relations when a representative expressed surprise that the media kit's controversial images had migrated to web sites.[104]

Others knew better. "Because of the Internet, there's no longer a clear delineation between markets," said Ned Barnett of Barnett Marketing Communications. "Everybody working in PR for a multinational needs to realize that what's said to one person is said to everyone."[105]

The Center for Individual Freedom reported that the media kit even found its way into a Subway restaurant in Munich, where a U.S. citizen saw it and delivered it to the center.[106]

The fast food fiasco had a fast ending when Subway's German restaurants agreed to end the cross-promotion early. A representative from Subway's headquarters apologized for the tray liners, adding that the German restaurants had been in daily contact "because they feel bad."[107]

"We're glad they responded," said a representative from DeLay's office. "But [we're] not exactly sure how you undo the damage."[108]

The Center for Individual Freedom termed the apology "unexpected" and said that Subway's statement "left us very satisfied with their response to this whole thing."[109]

But for some, analysis of Subway's cross-promotion had just begun. "Subway's debacle raises several important questions for PR executives to ponder," declared *PR News*. The magazine graded Subway's response to the crisis and awarded the restaurant chain a D.[110]

"This is a classic case—sure to be chewed on for years by the PR industry and academics alike," wrote Katie Delahaye Paine, CEO of KDPaine & Partners.[111]

Let the chewing begin.

DISCUSSION QUESTIONS

1. What do you know about the values of the Center for Individual Freedom? Should it not have respected Subway's freedom to express itself?
2. How many different publics were involved in this incident? What were the values of each? What resources did each possess?
3. Should international companies such as Subway approve and monitor all of their national or regional marketing campaigns? Why or why not?
4. *PR News* wrote that Subway's cross-promotion generated several questions for public relations practitioners. What are some of those questions? What, in your opinion, are the answers?

Case Study 4.2

Swinging for the Wall: Whirlpool Corporation and Habitat for Humanity

Baseball fans know the story well. In the 1932 World Series, Babe Ruth and the New York Yankees faced the Chicago Cubs. In game three of the fall classic, Ruth homered in an early inning. So when he came to the plate again in the fifth, Chicago fans booed mercilessly and jeered as pitcher Charlie Root zipped two strikes past Ruth.

Then Ruth made the gesture.

He pointed to the centerfield wall. And he hit the next pitch over that wall.

Home run.

In the 21st century, the Whirlpool Corporation just might think it's the Babe Ruth of corporate America. One of the world's best-known makers of home appliances, the company generates annual profits of more than $12 billion. Because Whirlpool is an ambitious company—it sells its products in more than 170 countries—it sought an ambitious new goal.[112]

Then Whirlpool made the gesture.

The company committed, in writing, to this pledge: "Every Home . . . Everywhere. With Pride, Passion, and Performance."[113]

Every home. . . . But what about homeowners who simply couldn't afford Whirlpool appliances—or any appliances for that matter? Figuratively speaking,

Whirlpool had pointed to the centerfield wall. And now it had to deliver or strike out.

Whirlpool delivered. In 1999, the company vowed to donate a refrigerator and a range to every new Habitat for Humanity house in the United States.[114]

Most college students no doubt are familiar with Habitat for Humanity; many have helped build Habitat homes. Habitat for Humanity International is an organization dedicated to ending substandard housing and the lack of homeownership in low-income families. With local branches in more than 3,000 communities in 92 nations, the organization has built more than 150,000 houses for deserving families.[115]

Since 1999, Whirlpool has donated more than 40,000 appliances to Habitat for Humanity.[116]

"Habitat's mission to provide simple, decent, and affordable housing for economically less fortunate families around the world meshes well with Whirlpool's corporate vision of 'Every Home . . . Everywhere,'" says Whirlpool Chairman and CEO David R. Whitwam.[117]

Whirlpool prides itself on being a values-driven company. One of its core values is integrity—matching its words with actions—and the company clearly addresses values in its statements on *Corporate Responsibility* and *Vision & Strategy:*

> At Whirlpool we strongly believe in the principles of Corporate Responsibility—of achieving success in ways that honor ethical values and respect people, communities, and the natural environment. . . . Supporting those in our communities that need support provides our stakeholders with a real sense of Whirlpool's values. . . . Our employees live by the values-based strategy that has made Whirlpool the international leader that we are today. Our values represent who we are to our customers, our investors, and to each other.[118]

To help honor its value of community service, Whirlpool assists Habitat for Humanity with more than donations:

- Whirlpool offers substantial price discounts on additional appliances to Habitat homeowners.[119]

- Whirlpool employees around the world volunteer to help build Habitat homes. In 2003, the company built a Habitat house near the main entrance of its corporate headquarters in Benton Harbor, Michigan, and then transferred the house to a new location.[120]

- In 2004, Whirlpool increased its donations to include new Habitat for Humanity homes in Europe.

In working to fulfill its values, Whirlpool believes that it's being more than a good corporate citizen: The company believes it's strengthening its financial future. Whirlpool's *Corporate Responsibility* statement offers this explanation: "Initiatives such as these help ensure the short-term and long-term viability of our company. . . . We firmly believe the socially responsible actions we take today will produce bottom-line benefits tomorrow."[121]

In pursuing its Every Home pledge, Whirlpool encountered a public it might not have anticipated: deserving individuals who couldn't afford their own homes and appliances. Whirlpool could have changed its goal. Or it could have ignored a public that probably wouldn't have fought back. Instead, like Babe Ruth, Whirlpool stood tall and swung for the wall.

Home run.

Or, maybe, just home.

DISCUSSION QUESTIONS

1. Should an organization establish a goal it can never realistically fulfill?
2. Do you agree with Whirlpool that its commitment to Habitat for Humanity can actually help it financially? If so, how?
3. Do you think "cause marketing" works? How can support for a worthy social cause help a company?
4. Can you name other companies involved in cause marketing?

Cyber Coach

Visit www.ablongman.com/guthmarsh3e for these study aids—and more:

- flashcards
- quizzes
- videos
- links to other sites
- real-world scenarios that let you be the public relations professional

KEY TERMS

active public, p. 98
aware public, p. 98
B2B, p. 123
business-to-business communication, p. 123
convergence of media, p. 110
coorientation, p. 103
decision makers, p. 101
demographic information, p. 102
domestic publics, p. 100
e-commerce, p. 118
external publics, p. 100
gatekeepers, p. 109
independent endorsement, p. 109
institutional investor, p. 114

internal publics, p. 100
international publics, p. 100
intervening public, p. 99
latent public, p. 97
mutual fund managers, p. 114
nontraditional publics, p. 97
opinion leaders, p. 101
primary public, p. 99
psychographic information, p. 102
public, p. 93
resource dependency theory, p. 94
secondary publics, p. 99
stakeholder, p. 93
third-party endorsement, p. 109
traditional publics, p. 96

NOTES

1. Larissa Grunig, James Grunig, and William Ehling, "What Is an Effective Organization?" in *Excellence in Public Relations and Communication Management* (Hillsdale, N.J.: Lawrence Erlbaum, 1992), 77, 80.

2. "Pitney Bowes Statement of Value," online, www.pitneybowes.com.

3. Norimitsu Onishi, "As Oil Riches Flow, Poor Village Cries Out," *New York Times,* 22 December 2002, online, LexisNexis.

4. Carla Marinucci, "Gay Republicans Say They Are Unlikely to Back Bush," *San Francisco Chronicle,* 30 August 2004, online, LexisNexis.

5. Dean E. Murphy, "California Attorney General Is Pressed on Gay Marriage," *New York Times,* 25 February 2004, online, LexisNexis.

6. Cherie Jacobs, "More Companies Extend Benefits to Same-Sex Partners," *Tampa Tribune,* 12 August 2001, online, LexisNexis.

7. James E. Grunig and Fred C. Repper, "Strategic Management, Publics, and Issues," in *Excellence in Public Relations and Communication Management,* ed. James E. Grunig (Hillsdale, N.J.: Lawrence Erlbaum, 1992), 125.

8. "CEOs Have New Appreciation for Internal Communications," *Public Relations Strategist* (winter 2003): 26; "Annual Defined-Contribution Survey," *Pension Benefits,* May 2001, online, Expanded Academic Index.

9. "Workplace Grapevine Is Like Kudzu," news release issued by Randstad North American, 17 June 2003, online, www.randstad.com.

10. "Towers Perrin Survey Finds Almost Half of American Workers Doubt the Credibility of Employer Communications," news release issued by Towers Perrin, 7 January 2004, online, www.towersperrin.com.

11. "Effective Employee Communication Linked to Greater Shareholder Returns," news release issued by Watson Wyatt Worldwide, 3 November 2003, online, www.watsonwyatt.com.

12. Robert Barner, "The New Millennium Workplace: Seven Changes That Will Challenge Managers—and Workers," *The Futurist,* March–April 1996, 14–19.

13. "You Can't E-mail Face Time," news release issued by Randstad North America, 24 June 2003, online, www.us.randstad.com.

14. "Employers Increase Work/Life Programs, According to Results of Mellon Survey," news release issued by Mellon Financial Corporation, 15 January 2004, online, www.mellon.com.

15. John Milne, "We Need to Talk," *Canadian Manager* (spring 2000): online, LexisNexis.

16. Louis Uchitelle, "Companies Hold off on Hiring Until Demand Rises," *New York Times,* 6 March 2004, online, LexisNexis.

17. Uchitelle.

18. "ASTD 2003 State of the Industry Report," American Society for Training and Development, February 2004, online, www.astd.org.

19. "Federal Reserve Chairman Calls for Enhancing Worker Skills," news release issued by the American Society for Training & Development, 25 February 2004, online, www.astd.org.

20. Martin Sprouse, ed., *Sabotage in the American Workplace* (San Francisco: Pressure Drop Press, 1992).

21. "Federal Reserve Chairman Calls for Enhancing Worker Skills."

22. "Civilian Labor Force by Sex, Age, Race, and Hispanic Origin," U.S. Bureau of Labor Statistics, 11 February 2004, online, www.bls.gov/emp.

23. "Effective Managers Must Evolve Their Generational Stereotypes: Findings from the 2001 Randstad North American Employee Review," online, www.us.randstad.com.

24. "Civilian Labor Force by Sex, Age, Race, and Hispanic Origin."

25. Jennifer Gilbert, "Motivating Through the Ages," *Sales & Marketing Management,* November 2003, 34–40.

26. "Towers Perrin Survey Finds Almost Half American Workers Doubt the Credibility of Employer Communications," news release issued by Towers Perrin, 7 January 2004, online, www.towersperrin.com.

27. "New Year's Resolution for the Boss," news release issued by Randstad, 20 December 2003, online, www.randstad.com.

28. "Growing Confusion about Corporate Goals Complicates Recovery," news release issued by Watson Wyatt Worldwide, 9 September 2002, online, www.watsonwyatt.com.

29. *Gale Directory of Publications and Broadcast Media, vol. 3,* 136th ed. (Farmington Hills, Mich.: Gale, 2002), xxvii.

30. Lynne Sallot, Thomas Steinfatt, and Michael Salwen, "Journalists' and Public Relations Practitioners' News Values: Perceptions and Cross-Perceptions," *Journalism and Mass Communication Quarterly* (summer 1998): 369–370.

31. Deborah Fallows, "The Internet and Daily Life," Pew Internet & American Life Project, 11 August 2004, online, www.pewinternet.org.

32. Felicity Barringer, "Editors Debate Realism vs. Retreat in Newsroom Diversity," *New York Times,* 6 April 1998, online, LexisNexis.

33. "Newsroom Employment Drops Again; Diversity Gains," news release issued by the American Society of Newspaper Editors, 20 April 2004, online, www.asne.org.

34. Bob Papper, "Recovering Lost Ground," *Communicator,* online, www.rtnda.org.

35. Papper.

36. "Federal Government Civilian Employment by Function," U.S. Census Bureau, March 2002, online, www.census.gov.

37. *The 2004–2005 Career Guide to Industries,* U.S. Bureau of Labor, 27 February 2004, online, www.bls.gov.

38. "Federal Government Civilian Employment by Function."

39. Tim Kauffman, "What Feds Like and Don't Like," *Federal Times,* 31 March 2003, online, www.federaltimes.com.

40. "Working for America: Annual Report to Congress," Federal Equal Opportunity Recruitment Program, March 2004, online, www.opm.gov/feorp.

41. James D. McKevitt, "Making Friends on the Hill," *Association Management,* October 1996, online, LexisNexis.

42. Marcella Kogan, "All Worked Up: The Demand for Family-Friendly Workplaces Is Growing," *Government Executive,* November 1996, online, LexisNexis.

43. "2002 Public Employment Data: State Governments," U.S. Bureau of Labor Statistics, online, www.bls.gov; "2002 Public Employment Data: Local Governments," U.S. Bureau of Labor Statistics, online, www.bls.gov.

44. "Employment by Major Industry Division," U.S. Bureau of Labor Statistics, 11 February 2004, online, www.bls.gov.

45. "Affirmative Action Annual Report for Wisconsin State Government, 25th Edition," State of Wisconsin Office of State Employee Relations, April 2004, online, http://oser.state.wi.us.

46. Diana Marcum, "The Footprint of a Whale," *Los Angeles Times Magazine,* 29 April 2001, online, LexisNexis; "IFAW Honors Pierce Brosnan for Efforts to Protect Wildlife," PR Newswire, 15 November 2000, online, LexisNexis; "After Five-Year Battle, Mitsubishi Ends Baja Mexico Salt Plant Project," PR Newswire, 2 March 2000, online, LexisNexis.

47. Mark Ellickson and Kay Logsdon, "Determinants of Job Satisfaction of Municipal Government Employees," *State and Local Government Review* (fall 2001): 173–184.

48. Daniel Gross, "Buy Stock, Vote Bush," *Slate,* 27 August 2004, online, LexisNexis.

49. "Annual SIA Investors Survey: Investors' Attitudes Toward the Securities Industry, 2003," Harris Interactive and the Securities Institute Association, online, www.harris interactive.com; "Equity Ownership in America," Investment Company Institute and the Securities Industry Association, 2002, online, www.ici.org.

50. "Today's Investor Expresses New Attitudes, New Experiences," news release issued by Charles Schwab & Company, 21 January 2004, online, LexisNexis.

51. "Today's Investor Expresses New Attitudes, New Experiences."

52. "Will 'Stealth' Issues Determine the U.S. Investment Climate, Election," news release issued by the Gallup Organization, 23 August 2004, online, www.gallup.com.

53. Mary Jo Feldstein, "Bull or Bear," *St. Louis Post-Dispatch,* 4 April 2004, online, LexisNexis.

54. "Today's Investor Expresses New Attitudes, New Experiences."

55. "Equity Ownership in America."

56. "Annual SIA Investors Survey: Investors' Attitudes Toward the Securities Industry, 2003."

57. "Annual SIA Investors Survey: Investors' Attitudes Toward the Securities Industry, 2003."

58. "Movaris Sponsored Poll Shows That 59% of Individual Investors Believe That the Sarbanes-Oxley Law Will Protect Their Investments," news release issued by Movaris, 27 January 2004, online, LexisNexis.

59. "Will 'Stealth' Issues Determine the U.S. Investment Climate, Election."

60. "Equity Ownership in America."

61. "7th Annual Ariel Mutual Funds/Charles Schwab & Co. Black Investor Survey Results Are In," news release issued by Charles Schwab & Company, 23 June 2004, online, LexisNexis; "Today's Investor Expresses New Attitudes, New Expectations."

62. "Annual SIA Investors Survey: Investors' Attitudes Toward the Securities Industry, 2003."

63. "Annual SIA Investors Survey: Investors' Attitudes Toward the Securities Industry, 2003."

64. "Investment Company Institute Research in Brief," *Fundamentals,* October 2003, online, www.ici.org.

65. "The World Economic Outlook Database," International Monetary Fund, online, www.imf.org.

66. Louis Uchitelle, "Why Americans Must Keep Spending," *New York Times,* 1 December 2003, online, LexisNexis.

67. Christopher Reynolds, "Spending Trending," *American Demographics,* 1 April 2004, online, LexisNexis.

68. "Consumer Expenditures in 2002," U.S. Bureau of Labor Statistics, February 2004, online, www.bls.gov.

69. "What Consumers Want from Businesses," *Sales & Marketing Management,* August 2000, 78.

70. "Consumer Expenditures in 2002."

71. Rebecca Gardyn and John Fetto, "Race, Ethnicity, and the Way We Shop," *American Demographics,* 1 February 2003, online, LexisNexis.

72. Kristi Turnquist, "Memo to Marketers: Wise Up about Women," (Portland) *Oregonian,* 26 May 2004, online, LexisNexis.

73. James Morrow, "X-It Plan," *American Demographics,* 1 May 2004, online, LexisNexis.

74. Michael J. Weiss, "To Be about to Be," *American Demographics,* 1 September 2003, online, LexisNexis.

75. "Retail E-Commerce Sales in Second Quarter 2004 Were $15.7 Billion," news release issued by the U.S. Department of Commerce, online, www.commerce.gov.

76. Susan Posnock, "Customer Satisfaction Up Online," *American Demographics,* 1 April 2004, online, LexisNexis.

77. Fallows.

78. David McDermitt and Tony Shelton, "The 10 Commandments of Community Relations," *World Wastes,* September 1993, online, LexisNexis.

79. Jerry A. Hendrix, *Public Relations Cases,* 4th ed. (Belmont, Calif.: Wadsworth, 1998), 18–19.

80. Tannette Johnson-Elie, "Denny's Turnabout Means Fair Play for Minority Employees," *Milwaukee Journal Sentinel,* 31 October 2000, online, LexisNexis.

81. "Resident Population of the United States," U.S. Bureau of the Census, online, www.census.gov.

82. Oliver Burkeman, "Is Jerry the Joker?" (London) *Guardian,* 3 July 2002, online, www.guardian.co.uk.

83. All examples are from Ted L. Nancy, *Letters from a Nut* (New York: Scholastic, 1997).

84. Frederick F. Reichheld, *The Loyalty Effect* (Boston: Harvard Business School Press, 1996), 33.

85. Luke J. Larsen, "The Foreign-Born Population in the United States: 2003," U.S. Census Bureau, August 2004, online, www.census.gov.

86. Larsen.

87. "Voter Turnout Highest Since 1968," Associated Press, 3 November 2004, online, LexisNexis.

88. "Voter Turnout from 1945 to Date," International Institute for Democracy and Electoral Assistance, 2004, online, www.idea.int.

89. Jennifer Day and Kelly Holder, "Voting and Registration in the Election of November 2002," U.S. Census Bureau, July 2004, online, www.census.gov. Unless otherwise noted, voting data are from Day and Holder.

90. Jose Antonio Vargas, "Vote or Die?" *Washington Post,* 9 November 2004, online, LexisNexis.

91. "PR League Tables: Why Trade PRs Are Hooked on the Net," *Marketing,* 25 May 2000, online, LexisNexis.

92. "VSS Forecasts Solid Growth Across All Communications Sectors—First Time in Four Years," Veronis Suhler Stevenson Media Merchant Bank, 2004, online, www.vss.com.

93. "PR League Tables: Top 50 Business-to-Business," *Marketing,* 21 May 1998, online, LexisNexis.

94. Kate Maddox, "2004 Top Agencies," *BtoB,* 8 March 2004, 29, 34.

95. Nathan Burchfiel, "German Film Defends Subway Restaurant Press Kit," Cybercast News Service, online, www.cnsnews.com.

96. Eric Pfanner, "Subway Stirs the Ire of Patriots," *International Herald Tribune,* 9 August 2004, online, LexisNexis.

97. Burchfiel.

98. "Subway Ends Anti-American Promotion," news release issued by the Center for Individual Freedom, 3 August 2004, online, LexisNexis.

99. John N. Frank, "Subway Under Pressure to Apologize for Insulting U.S.," *PR Week,* 9 August 2004, online, LexisNexis.

100. Pfanner, "Subway Pulls German Promo Featuring Large Lady Liberty," *Los Angeles Times,* 3 August 2004, online, LexisNexis.

101. "Subway's 'Humorous' Promotion Is No Laughing Matter for PR Execs," *PR News,* 23 August 2004, online, LexisNexis.

102. Pam Dawkins, "Subway Disavows 'Fat' Promo," (Bridgeport) *Connecticut Post*, 5 August 2004, online, LexisNexis.

103. "Subway's 'Humorous' Promotion Is No Laughing Matter for PR Execs."

104. Burchfiel.

105. "Subway's 'Humorous' Promotion Is No Laughing Matter for PR Execs."

106. Dawkins.

107. "Subway Pulls German Promo Featuring Large Lady Liberty."

108. Frank.

109. Dawkins.

110. "Subway's 'Humorous' Promotion Is No Laughing Matter for PR Execs."

111. Katie Delahaye Paine, "Image Patrol—Subway/McDonald's," *PR News*, 16 August 2004, online, LexisNexis.

112. "Whirlpool Brand Announces 2004 Reba McEntire Tour Dates," news release issued by Whirlpool Corporation, 10 May 2004, online, LexisNexis.

113. "Vision & Strategy," Whirlpool Corporation, online, www.whirlpoolcorp.com.

114. "Whirlpool and Habitat for Humanity," Whirlpool Corporation, online, www.whirlpoolcorp.com.

115. "Whirlpool Brand to Sponsor Reba McEntire Concert Tour That Will Benefit Habitat for Humanity," news release issued by Whirlpool Corporation, 22 March 2004, online, www.whirlpoolcorp.com.

116. "Whirlpool Brand to Sponsor Reba McEntire Concert Tour That Will Benefit Habitat for Humanity."

117. "Whirlpool Corporation Sponsors Habitat for Humanity Blitz Build on Headquarters' Campus," news release issued by Whirlpool Corporation, online, www.whirlpoolcorp.com.

118. "Our Commitment to Corporate Responsibility," Whirlpool Corporation, online, www.whirlpoolcorp.com; "Vision & Strategy."

119. "Whirlpool and Habitat for Humanity."

120. "Whirlpool and Habitat for Humanity"; "Whirlpool Corporation Sponsors Habitat for Humanity Blitz Build on Headquarters' Campus."

121. "Our Commitment to Corporate Responsibility."

chapter five

Communication Theory and Public Opinion

After studying this chapter, you will be able to

- understand the process of communication and some of the theories of how people react to what they encounter in the mass media

- identify the forces that motivate people

- describe the power of public opinion and the process under which it develops

- recognize the differences between the use of persuasion and manipulation in public relations

Growing Pains

scenario

The local state university was founded as an agricultural college in the late 19th century. At that time, it was located on farmland several miles from a small town. However, times have changed, and both the school and the community are experiencing growing pains—apparently at each other's expense.

The latest controversy involves the university's purchase of three dilapidated houses on the edge of one of the town's oldest neighborhoods. School administrators want to tear down the houses and build a much-needed residence hall. The neighbors object, saying the structure will increase noise and traffic. Also opposed are members of the local historical society, who believe the dormitory would have a negative impact on a nearby historic site. It seems as if everyone has a dog in this fight, including the university, its students, the neighborhood, the historical society, the local zoning board, and even the governor, who also chairs the state historical commission.

If you were a public relations counselor to one of the many sides in this dispute, how would you proceed?

The Power of Public Opinion

Anyone with even a passing knowledge of history knows of the Holocaust and the unspeakable horror that confronted Jews living in Europe. German Führer Adolf Hitler and his Nazi henchmen committed history's worst crimes against humanity in a twisted effort to purge the world of Jews.

Lesser known, however, is the role that *German* public opinion had in sparing the lives of 2,000 Jewish prisoners in March 1943. These prisoners, mostly men, had non-Jewish German spouses. The prisoners had been scheduled for transport to Auschwitz, the most notorious of the Nazis' death camps. However, the power of public opinion—something you might not expect to be a concern of a totalitarian regime—forced the Nazis to halt the shipment and release the prisoners, most of whom survived the war.

Hundreds of women staged protest rallies outside the Berlin jail in which the prisoners were held—right in the very heart of the capital of the Third Reich. The women gathered every night for a week shouting, "Give us our husbands back!" Guards fired gunshots on several occasions in an attempt to disperse the crowd. However, the protests continued until the authorities gave in and released the prisoners. With the tide of the war turning against the Nazis, Gestapo Chief Heinrich Himmler did not want to risk German public support for the nation's war effort.[1]

If public opinion could force the Nazis to change their policies, think of its power in a peaceful democracy. The very essence of a democratic society is that public policies are created as a result of words, not weapons. Effective communication is a key to success. So is the ability to persuade others to accept or at least respect your point of view. Both are at the heart of the practice of public relations.

As we've said before and will say again, good public relations involves two-way communication between an organization and the publics important to its success. Responding to the concerns and needs of others is a big part of public relations. Ultimately, you want to create a mutually beneficial environment in which both an organization and its publics can flourish. That environment is achieved through the give-and-take that characterizes two-way communication. It is not enough for an organization to be a good listener. It also must be a good communicator. Successful companies and individuals excel in letting others know their values and preferences. And in today's results-oriented environment, success is often measured by one's ability to persuade others to come around to a certain way of thinking.

In this chapter's opening scenario, local residents and university officials are at loggerheads over plans to build a dormitory. School officials see the construction as a good deal for the community. More students on campus means more money for local merchants. Construction would also remove some community eyesores. However, the residents have a different perspective. They fear a dormitory would change the nature of their neighborhood and lower their property values. As a result, each side has certain values it does not want to compromise.

Because public relations focuses on building and maintaining relationships, it is important for practitioners to understand how the processes of communication and persuasion work—and how to use that knowledge to achieve values-driven and mutually beneficial solutions.

A Communication Model

Before we discuss how public opinion is formed, let's look at the process that makes it happen, communication. It is a process familiar to all and completely understood by none. Since Aristotle's day, scholars have tried figure out how it works. They have developed what are called "communication models," graphic representations helpful in understanding the dynamics of the communication process. Some of these models are simplistic. Others look like the schematic drawing of an MP3 player. For our purposes, we have chosen a model based on the writings of David Berlo.[2] The elegance of this model is its simplicity. It breaks down the communication process into six basic ingredients: noise, source, message, channel, receiver, and feedback (Figure 5.1).

NOISE.   Sometimes referred to as static, **noise** envelops communication and often inhibits it. Noise can take both physical and intangible forms. It can have a physical quality, such as that experienced when a person is trying to talk with someone in a large crowd. The crowd noise can make it difficult to understand everything being said. However, noise does not have to be audible to inhibit communication. A person's state of mind can also block effective communication. An example is the mental "static" experienced by a person who is reeling from an emotional event and is not really listening to what is said. There are also times when for a variety of reasons—cultural, religious, and generational among them—we erect barriers to

FIGURE 5.1
A Communication Model

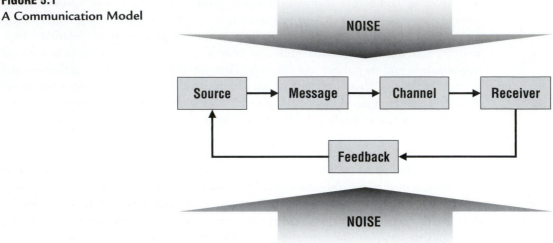

communication. In these instances, we often generate "noise" because we don't like either the message or the messenger.

SOURCE.   The **source** is where a communication originates. The source is also the first part of the coorientation model mentioned in Chapter 4. How a source views its audience—and is viewed by an audience—can help or hinder communication. Source credibility can be influenced by a variety of factors, including reputation, context, and communication ability. For example, a particular elected official was once seen as a leading advocate for strong family values. His subsequent arrest on a morals charge, however, undermined his credibility and ultimately ended his political career.

MESSAGE.   The **message** is the content of the communication. To a large degree, successful formation of the message relies on knowledge of both the purpose of the message and its intended receiver. If the message is not relevant or is not in language understood by that receiver, it will probably be misunderstood or ignored. It wouldn't make sense for your professor to speak to the class in French—unless, of course, it was a French class.

CHANNEL.   The **channel** is the medium used to transmit the message to the intended receiver. The selection of the most appropriate channel or channels is a key strategic decision. Like the source, the channel must be relevant and credible to the intended receiver. And much like a broadcast channel on an old-time radio, the channel can be susceptible to static. In this case, static is defined as physical and psychological forces that can make it difficult for the receiver to acquire the message. For example, many public relations practitioners have had their well-planned efforts at obtaining

Even Ronald Reagan, considered one of the best communicators to live in the White House, faced the challenge of overcoming noise in the environment when promoting his administration's policies. (Photo by David Guth)

publicity foiled by breaking news stories that have caused reporters to focus their attentions elsewhere. One of your authors had three painstakingly planned news conferences derailed by attempted political assassinations in the same year.

RECEIVER.   The **receiver** is the person or persons for whom the message is intended. The receiver is also the second part of the coorientation model mentioned in Chapter 4. How the receiver views the source—and is viewed by the source—can help or hinder communication. The most effective communications are those that specifically target the intended receiver. For reasons already stated, the communicator must select the source, message, and channel with the needs of the receiver in mind. That, in turn, requires a thorough knowledge of the receiver, including its needs, values, predispositions, and communication ability. After all, what good does it do to communicate if the intended audience is not listening?

FEEDBACK.   Feedback is the receiver's reaction—as interpreted by the source—to the message. Without this final step, true communication does not occur. Feedback lets you know whether the message got through and how it was interpreted. Think of a stand-up comedian: If the audience laughs, the joke was funny. If there is silence, the joke failed. Good communicators, especially public relations practitioners, actively seek feedback. Feedback, often in the form of telephone calls and letters, can be spontaneous. However, that isn't always the case. Sometimes special mechanisms are established to generate feedback, such as toll-free telephone numbers and public opinion polls.

As stated before, social scientists have developed a variety of communication models. However, the models all have something in common: Communication is a lot like an electrical circuit—if a short or break occurs anywhere along the wire, nothing happens. No communication takes place if the source is not seen as credible, the message is not relevant, the channel is filled with static, the receiver is not listening, or feedback is lacking.

A breakdown in the communication process was evident in May 1970, when President Richard Nixon attempted to reach out to anti–Vietnam War protesters. The president made a predawn visit to the Lincoln Memorial, where antiwar ac-

QuickBreak 5.1

MOKUSATSU

Communication fails when a source sends a message that cannot be understood or is misinterpreted by the receiver. Never has that fact had more tragic consequences than at the end of World War II, when the decision to use atomic bombs may have hinged on a misunderstanding over the meaning of a single Japanese word.

The decision to use the recently developed bomb against Japanese targets was not an easy one for President Harry Truman. On the one hand, the bomb might shock the Japanese military into surrendering, thus avoiding the bloody consequences of a full-scale military invasion of the island nation. On the other hand, Truman also knew that many civilians would be killed in an atomic attack. However, the signs coming out of Tokyo were not good. Although the Japanese military had been crushed as a result of three years of terrifying and unrelenting warfare, its leaders said Japan would never surrender.

Truman decided to give the Japanese one last chance before unleashing the bomb. In what has become known as the Potsdam Declaration, Truman told the Japanese that they had to surrender unconditionally or face unspecified consequences. Japanese Prime Minister Kantaro Suzuki, an aging civilian aristocrat, wanted to

negotiate peace quickly with the Americans. But Suzuki also knew that the military, which dominated the government, would not let him.

When asked by the military press for his response to the Potsdam Declaration, the prime minister said, "We *mokusatsu* it." Suzuki thought he had been clever. *Mokusatsu* is a Japanese word that has a variety of interpretations, largely dependent on who is perceived as its source. In saying "We *mokusatsu* it," Suzuki was speaking for himself and asking the Americans to keep negotiations open and make another peace offer. However, Truman believed the prime minister was speaking on behalf of the military. In that context, *mokusatsu* was interpreted as meaning "hold in silent contempt."

Believing that the Japanese had rejected the United States' last olive branch, Truman authorized the use of atomic bombs. Hiroshima was attacked on August 6, 1945. An estimated 92,000 people were killed and an unknown number suffered long-term effects from radiation. Another 40,000 people died three days later in the atomic bombing of Nagasaki. One week later, the Japanese surrendered.

tivists, mostly college students, were camped out awaiting the start of a major protest rally. The meeting didn't go well. Nixon said he spoke to the students about his and their mutual desire to end the war—but he said they didn't really listen. The students told reporters that the president talked about sports and surfing and "wasn't really concerned about why we were here." Whichever version of the event you accept, the outcome was undeniable: a communication breakdown that reinforced the mistrust that Nixon and the students had of one another.[3] For true communication to take place, it must be a two-way process.

Quick ✔ Check

1. What are the six elements of the communication model used in this text?
2. What are some of the things that can block communication?
3. Why is listening essential to good communication and effective public relations?

Mass Communication Theories

Public relations practitioners are, in some respects, the race car drivers of mass communication. Aside from the obvious comparisons—that speed, accuracy, and winning are desired—there's also a critical need to know what makes things work. Drivers know what makes their machines tick. That knowledge gives them the edge they need to gain maximum performance from their cars. For the same reason, practitioners need to understand the processes of mass communication—what makes it tick. Over the past century, a variety of mass communication theories have evolved for just that reason.

The Magic Bullet Theory

World events had a great influence on early theories of mass communications. As you may remember from the history chapter of this book, research interest in persuasion and public opinion heated up in the wake of the use of propaganda techniques during World War I. The growth of fascism in Europe and Asia during the 1930s largely paralleled the growth of the first electronic mass medium, radio. Out of these developments came the first mass communications theory, the **magic bullet theory** of mass communications. This theory, illustrated in Figure 5.2, is grounded in a belief that the mass media wield great power over their audiences. It was thought that if a sender developed just the right message, the so-called magic bullet, people could be influenced

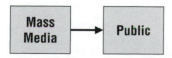

FIGURE 5.2   The Magic Bullet Theory of Mass Communications

to do almost anything. The problem with this approach to mass communications is that it supposes that people are weak-willed robots unable to resist finely sculptured appeals.

The Two-Step Theory

By the end of World War II, the magic bullet theory had been largely discredited. Social scientists began to understand better the role of intervening publics in influencing public opinion. From this realization evolved the **two-step theory** of mass communications, the foundation of which is the belief that the mass media influence society's key opinion leaders, who in turn influence the opinions and actions of society itself (Figure 5.3). These key opinion leaders were said to include elected public officials, powerful business executives, and religious figures. Although the opinion leaders were seen as powerful, this theory remained based on the belief that the mass media were powerful forces in molding public opinion.

FIGURE 5.3   Two-Step Flow of Mass Communications

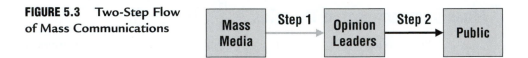

The N-Step Theory

Recognizing that different people may be credible in different contexts, communication researcher Wilbur Schramm developed the **n-step theory** of mass communications (Figure 5.4). It was similar to the two-step theory in that it stressed the role of opinion lead-

FIGURE 5.4   N-Step Flow of Mass Communications

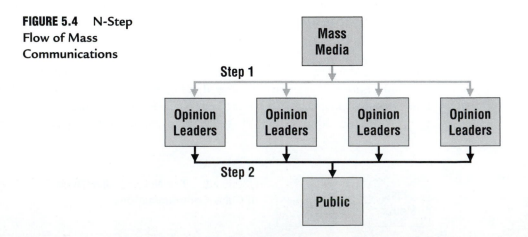

ers. However, under the n-step theory, key opinion leaders may vary from issue to issue. For example, you may turn to slugger Barry Bonds if you want to learn how to hit a baseball. However, it is more likely that you would seek insight from a finance expert if you actually wanted to buy some bonds.

Diffusion Theory

Unlike its predecessors, the **diffusion theory** of mass communications was based on a belief that the power of the mass media is not as much to motivate people as it is to inform them (Figure 5.5). Under this theoretical view of mass communications, people have the power to influence members of their own peer groups. Agricultural extension agents have followed this approach for decades. The agents provide farmers with information on how they can improve their crop yields. If a farmer adopts an approach that works, he or she spreads the word of this success to other farmers. In other words, the idea is passed along through a diffusion process. In a sense, everyone can become an opinion leader.

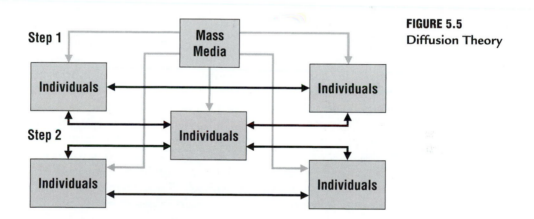

FIGURE 5.5
Diffusion Theory

The Agenda-Setting Hypothesis

The most significant and widely accepted view of how the mass media interact with society is currently the **agenda-setting hypothesis.** It is based on the simple principle that the mass media tell people not what to think, but what to think about. In other words, the media set the public agenda (Figure 5.6).

FIGURE 5.6   **The Agenda-Setting Hypothesis**

QuickBreak 5.2

WHY PUBLIC RELATIONS IS NOT PROPAGANDA

Few words in the English language are as emotionally and ethically charged as *propaganda*.[4] That's why public relations practitioners bristle when people—especially journalists—suggest that public relations and propaganda are one and the same.

The problem is that propaganda—just like public relations—is hard to define. Historian Brett Gray wrote, "Propaganda as a label suffered (and suffers) from a certain imprecision; it is not unlike Justice Potter Stewart's fabled definition of pornography: 'I don't know how to define it, but I know it when I see it.'"[5]

Many see propaganda as an umbrella covering all forms of persuasive communication, including advertising and public relations. Even the man considered the father of modern public relations, Edward L. Bernays, gave credence to this interpretation when he defined *public relations*—the term he coined in *Crystallizing Public Opinion*—as "the new propaganda."[6]

Some researchers lump all persuasive communication into two broad categories. One is *revealed propaganda,* messages that are overt in their effort to persuade, such as those in conventional advertising. The other is *concealed propaganda,* such as publicity generated from the distribution of news releases. However, if this approach is followed to a logical conclusion, it could be argued that *all* communication is propaganda.[7] One wonders how journalists would feel about that.

Since its earliest days, practitioners have tried to differentiate public relations from propaganda by placing it within an ethical framework. That was certainly the intent of Ivy Lee, whose "Declaration of Principles" in 1906 spoke of providing "prompt and accurate information."[8] But public relations historian Scott M. Cutlip wrote that Bernays' efforts to further define public relations in his 1928 book *Propaganda* served only to muddy the waters and "handed the infant field's critics a club with which to bludgeon it."[9]

Gray argued that propaganda should not be confused with advertising and public relations. "For my part, I try to maintain that distinction by defining propaganda as the organized manipulations of key cultural symbols and images (and biases) for the purposes of persuading a mass audience to take a position, or move to action, or remain inactive on a controversial matter," he wrote.[10]

Propaganda researchers Garth S. Jowett and Victoria O'Donnell prefer an even narrower definition. "Propaganda is the deliberate, systematic attempt to shape perceptions, manipulate cognitions, and direct behavior to achieve a response that furthers the desired intent of the propagandist."[11] In contrast, they argue that persuasion "is interactive and attempts to satisfy the needs of both the persuader and persuadee."[12] These interpretations are in line with more widely accepted definitions of public relations that stress two-way communication, as well as the building and maintaining of mutually beneficial relationships.

As is discussed at the end of this chapter, there's a big difference between persuasion and manipulation. Public relations practitioners know this.

We see examples of the agenda-setting hypothesis at work in every morning's newspaper. Have you ever noticed how one issue can dominate the newspapers—and public debate—for several weeks, only to be replaced by another? For example, look at media coverage of missing or abducted children. The problem has been around for many years. However, only when a dramatic incident occurs does the issue move to the top of the public agenda. That was the case in 2002, when a 14-year-old girl was kidnapped from her Salt Lake City home. With the help of a local public relations firm, the family kept the issue in the media spotlight for nearly a year until she returned safely home.[13] However, it didn't take long for the issue of missing children, once again, to slip into the shadows of public consciousness.

If you take the agenda-setting hypothesis to its next logical step, it raises an important question: If the media tell us not what to think but what to think about, who tells the media what to think about? Media in democratic societies have the independence to report on any topic they choose, so who sets the media's agenda?

The answer is equally important: Organizations and individuals are free to use public relations techniques to influence the media and thereby to put their imprint on the public agenda. And many organizations and individuals do just that. Historically, presidents of the United States have been particularly good at setting the media's agenda. Because of the power and prestige of the White House, almost anything a president does or says is news. Every president from Washington on has tried to influence news coverage in an attempt to control the public agenda. However, because presidents are not alone in understanding these dynamics, each has enjoyed only mixed success.

The experiences of recent presidents has been typical. Bill Clinton succeeded in convincing the majority of the public that the Republican-controlled Congress was responsible for a January 1996 shutdown of the federal government, even though his veto of the budget precipitated it. On the other hand, Clinton was unsuccessful in his effort to win public support for a comprehensive health-care package, largely because his opponents successfully framed the issue as government intrusion on personal liberties. This pattern of mixed results in controlling the agenda continued with Clinton's successor. A Gallup poll reported that President George W. Bush's job approval rating hit 90 percent in September 2001, largely in response to his actions following the 9/11 terrorist attacks. However, his popularity ratings dropped to the lowest levels of his first term in 2004 amid charges that he was losing the War on Terrorism.[14]

Uses and Gratifications Theory

This brings us to yet another evolution in communications theory. In recent years, theorists have noted that the agenda-setting hypothesis is based on a model in which the receiver is seen as a passive participant in the communication process. If this model is correct, theorists point out, then the source has the ultimate power of persuasion over the receiver. However, this concept of a passive receiver is being challenged by what is known as the **uses and gratifications theory.** The technological advances of recent years have resulted in an explosion of available mass communications channels. Researchers say that the real power now rests in the ability of receivers to pick and choose their channels of information. Although many communicators may seek to persuade the audience to take a particular course of action, the

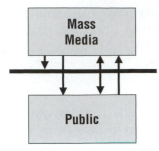

FIGURE 5.7   Uses and Gratifications Theory

audience serves as a gatekeeper—in effect, deciding to whom it will grant influence (Figure 5.7).[15]

A Two-Way Process

Mass communications theory appears to have undergone a complete reversal. It has evolved from a belief that people are powerless to resist the mass media to an acknowledgment of the public's supremacy over media. This new view suggests that persuasion, like communication, is a two-way street. According to *Excellence in Public Relations and Communication Management,* a publication of the IABC Research Foundation, "The concept of negotiation, rather than domination or persuasion, is the key to understanding the effects of communication and public relations programs."[16]

Let's go back to the opening scenario of this chapter. Each side of the dormitory debate has its merits. The university says construction will bring important economic benefits to the community as well as remove unwanted dilapidated housing. Opponents of the plan fear it will disrupt the peace and quiet of their neighborhood and possibly harm a historically significant site. If each side enters the debate unwilling to listen to the other, sparks will, no doubt, fly. Eventually, one side will win and the other side will lose. But the controversy will not end there. The lingering effects of

QuickBreak 5.3

SPINNING AND FRAMING

As already noted several times in this book, many find public relations a difficult concept to define. That's why one often hears practitioners referred to by a variety—and sometime unflattering array—of nicknames. They have been called press agents, flacks, mouthpieces, fronts, shills—and a few names of which your mother would not approve.

However, public relations practitioners were given a new handle in an October 21, 1984, *New York Times* editorial: **spin doctors.** Editorial writer Jack Rosenthal coined the phrase on the eve of that year's second presidential campaign debate:

Tonight at about 9:30, seconds after the Reagan–Mondale debate ends, a bazaar will suddenly materialize in the press room of the Kansas City Municipal Auditorium. A

dozen men in good suits and women in silk dresses will circulate smoothly among reporters, spouting confident opinions. They won't be just press agents trying to impart a favorable spin to a routine release. They'll be the Spin Doctors, senior advisers to the candidates, and they'll be playing for very high stakes. How well they do their work could be as important as how well their candidates do theirs.[17]

In his book *New Political Dictionary,* political columnist William Safire defined **spin** as "deliberate shading of news perception; attempted control of political reaction."[18] In essence, spin doctors try to influence perceptions by emphasizing certain aspects of events that reinforce their point of view. An example of spin would

the ill will created by such a controversy could have political, social, and economic ramifications for years. However, if the two sides enter the discussion willing to listen to each other's concerns, a compromise is possible. Neighborhood preservation and campus growth are not necessarily mutually exclusive concepts. However, the key to keeping the peace is two-way communication.

Motivation

Having discussed the communication process and the various theories on how mass communications influence people, we now focus on the individual. What motivates a given individual to do something? What forces are in play when we try to influence someone's behavior? What kind of appeals can spark action? These are questions psychologists and sociologists have pondered for centuries.

Although many theories explain why people do the things they do, one simple explanation is best: People usually act in their own self-interests. This may not seem, on the surface, to be an earth-shattering revelation. However, this simple truth is at the heart of molding public opinion. But how do people determine their self-interests? You can look to your own parents for the answer.

As strange as it may seem, your parents were once teenagers. If they grew up in the late 1960s and early 1970s, it is very possible that they owned bell-bottom jeans, wore long hair, and spoke of a desire for a peaceful world governed by a loose-knit

be the classic difference between a pessimist and an optimist: The pessimist sees the glass half-empty while the optimist sees the glass half-full.

While *spin* is the popular term-of-art, a more appropriate word to describe this kind of activity is **framing.** It is a concept first articulated by Canadian sociologist Erving Goffman in 1974. In his book *Frame Analysis: Essays on the Organization of Experience,* Goffman wrote that all of us "actively classify and organize our life experiences to make sense of them."[19] Researcher Robert Entman has defined framing as communicating an idea in such a way that an audience is influenced, either intentionally or unintentionally, by the way it is expressed.[20]

Regardless of whether we call it spinning or framing, is it ethical and something public relations practitioners should do? If done in an ethical manner—using accurate information within an appropriate context—there is no problem. Spinning or framing an issue is no different from articulating mutual interests and values. It is only when one attempts to distort, hide, or mislead that ethical concerns arise.

Of course, everyone operates within his or her own frame of reference. For that reason, one person's "facts" may be another's "spin." So next time talk show host Bill O'Reilly says guests on his cable television program are in a "no spin zone," he's probably right. However, it is also likely that they are doing a lot of framing.

philosophy known as "flower power." At the center of this popular culture was the most successful rock band the world had ever known, the Beatles. John, Paul, George, and Ringo had a generation believing that if you sought peace and tranquillity, "all you need is love."

If only it were that simple. Unfortunately, the Beatles were wrong.

Maslow's Hierarchy of Needs

Long before the Fab Four sang that love is the central force behind everything, psychologist Abraham Maslow developed a theory to explain how people determine their self-interests: **Maslow's Hierarchy of Needs** (Figure 5.8). The basis of the theory is that some needs are more basic than others and, therefore, must be fulfilled first.[21] On Maslow's list, love comes in only third.

According to Maslow, the lowest (most basic) order of needs is our *physiological* needs. These are the biological demands our bodies make for food, water, rest, and exercise. He included sex among our most basic needs, but only as it related to the continuation of our species. Love and romance had nothing to do with it. By Maslow's way of thinking, if humans do not fulfill their physiological needs, little else matters.

According to Maslow, *safety* is the next order of need. By "safety needs" he means things such as personal security, comfort, and orderly surroundings. To understand Maslow's ranking, assume for a minute that you are in a shelter in the middle of a war zone. Bombs and bullets are flying all around you. The shooting is expected to last for weeks. As long as you stay in that shelter, you are safe. However, suppose that shelter has no food or water. Maslow believed that, eventually, you will

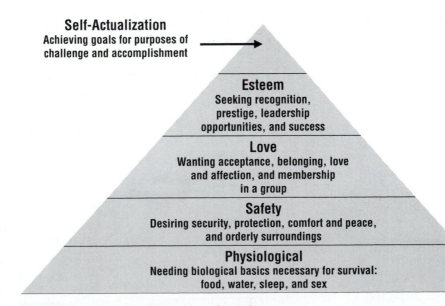

FIGURE 5.8   Maslow's Hierarchy of Needs

leave that shelter and forgo personal safety to fulfill your physiological needs. Otherwise, you will die anyway.

The third order of need is *acceptance,* or what Maslow referred to as love and belongingness. This is where the Beatles come in. At this level, we seek out love, a sense of belonging, an affiliation with others through group memberships. Still, this is only third on the list. Pretend that you have entered our imaginary bomb shelter only to find that it is filled with people you do not like and vice versa. Under Maslow's hierarchy, you are willing to endure any annoyance and indignity that may occur from these uncomfortable arrangements because of the safety the shelter provides.

Next on Maslow's hierarchy is *self-esteem* needs, for which we strive to earn recognition and view ourselves as being successful. Everyone wants to be seen as a winner. However, people are often willing to let their self-esteem suffer if doing so provides some measure of acceptance. That is why some people choose to remain in abusive, unhealthy relationships. It isn't until the victim understands that this isn't true acceptance or that physiological or safety needs are threatened that the abusive relationship ends.

The highest order is *self-actualization* needs. We reach self-actualization when we achieve a goal just for the sake of achieving that goal. Climbing a mountain "because it is there" is an expression of self-actualization. Some people never achieve self-actualization because they haven't fulfilled the requirements imposed by lower-order needs. In some ways, self-actualization is like the Great American Novel that many people say they will write but never do—because their attention is constantly focused on more pressing needs.

Examples of Maslow's Theory at Work

Just a guess: You are not reading about Maslow's Hierarchy of Needs as an expression of self-actualization. Your motivation is probably a result of a need to fulfill your safety needs: Failure to read the material assigned by your professor could well put your grade at risk! However, there is more to this stuff than just passing your next test. Maslow's theory figures prominently in the practice of public relations.

We can see Maslow's theories at work by looking at recent U.S. presidential elections. National security issues were always prominent on the campaign trail during the Cold War years. That's because the electorate felt it had reason to fear for its survival. But with the fall of the Berlin Wall and the dissolution of the Soviet Union, the threat of thermonuclear war evaporated. By the early 1990s, voters defined survival in terms of rising interest rates, high unemployment, and low wages. Bill Clinton's campaign advisers recognized that in 1992. A major Clinton campaign theme—taken from a poster on his campaign headquarters wall—was "It's the economy, stupid," and it was a key to his victory over the first President Bush. With the Cold War over, national security did not play significant roles in either the 1996 or 2000 elections.

September 11, 2001, changed everything. American voters suddenly felt vulnerable. The danger of terrorist attacks on U.S. soil seemed very real. As a result, public

MONROE'S MOTIVATED SEQUENCE

In an era in which change is the only constant, it is refreshing to see an idea that has stood the test of time. In the mid-1920s, Purdue University Professor Alan H. Monroe developed an organizational pattern for persuasive messages that has come to be known as **Monroe's Motivated Sequence.**[22] Nearly 80 years later, it remains a standard for persuasive communication.

Building persuasive messages using Monroe's Motivated Sequence involves a five-step process. Let's look at that process using a real-world example: a company executive trying to motivate employees to improve quality by reducing workplace errors:

1. *Attention.* Get the attention of the audience through a dramatic story, quote, or statistic. Tell the audience why the topic is important to it.

> "One of our competitors has been forced to cut back production and lay off some of its employees. Its sales have dropped because of consumer complaints of shoddy products. We can't afford to have that happen here."

2. *Need.* Show that a significant problem exists and that it won't go away by itself. Document the need with relevant examples.

> "There is a great deal of competition in today's global economy. Consumers are demanding quality. If they don't get it from us, they have plenty of other options."

3. *Satisfaction.* Now that a need has been shown, offer solutions. They should be reasonable solutions that adequately address the need.

> "By working together, the management and employees of this company can de-velop reasonable training programs to improve the quality of our products and reduce production-line errors."

4. *Visualization.* Tell what will happen if nothing is done to solve the problem. Explicitly tell the audience the consequences of its choices.

> "In recent weeks, our research department has noticed an increasing number of consumer complaints. We are headed down the same road as our competition. If we don't make changes, it is likely that some of us will lose our jobs."

5. *Action.* Tell the audience members what they, personally, can do to solve the problem. It is important that the actions requested are explicitly stated.

> "I am asking you to make a personal commitment to quality. Don't be afraid to share your ideas for improving our products. Volunteer to serve on the various committees we are establishing to examine this issue. Help make this company's mission statement—'providing quality products and services'—a reality."

It is not a coincidence that the example cited here is closely linked to the company's mission statement. Values should serve as the foundation of all persuasive communication.

In today's world of the six-second soundbite, the art of persuasive speaking may seem irrelevant. But it is just as important today as it was in Monroe's time. Monroe's Motivated Sequence is a tried-and-true method of making one's points in a logical and persuasive manner.

opinion polls showed national security at the top of the list of voter concerns during both the 2002 midterm and 2004 presidential elections.

We can see the practical use of Maslow's theory in other ways. When environmental groups such as Greenpeace seek public support, their messages focus on physiological needs—specifically, the survival of the planet. When social service organizations seek additional funding, they realize that an appeal to the public's unfulfilled safety needs will be more effective than one based in either acceptance or self-actualization. By the same token, an appeal to personal self-esteem will have a greater chance of success among affluent audiences, whose physiological and safety requirements have been met, than among lower-income audiences struggling to fulfill basic needs.

Do people stop and think, "What would Maslow have me do under these circumstances?" Of course not. However, we instinctively follow Maslow's model. Self-interest is at the heart of motivation. Understanding the needs of the public being targeted is the key to successful communication and persuasion.

Persuasion and Public Opinion

Since the beginning of recorded history, people have pondered the question of how to persuade others to take a desired course of action. And it is a very important question. The persuasion of others and the molding of public opinion are central to our concept of a society, the manner in which people choose to organize themselves.

In democratic societies, we organize ourselves around a core belief in fulfilling the will of the people. However, history has shown us that democratic societies operate best when there is a willingness to seek consensus on matters of importance to all. That, in turn, requires a willingness among the members of these societies to engage in public debate. It is during this debate that we either persuade others to come over to our point of view or are persuaded to accept the opinion of someone else. A measure of these ongoing discussions is what we commonly refer to as public opinion.

Persuasion and public opinion are vital elements in the practice of public relations. As has been stressed in many places throughout this textbook, public relations is a two-way process of both communicating and listening. Sometimes the need to convince others about the advisability of a certain course of action arises. In that situation, we try to persuade others to adopt our point of view. However, we must also be sensitive to public opinion and the concerns of others. At its best, public relations is not about winning or losing. Instead, it is about building and maintaining mutually beneficial relationships. That is why understanding the dynamics of persuasion and public opinion is so critical to successful public relations.

Aristotle, Persuasion, and Public Relations

Aristotle said that **persuasion** takes three forms: **logos,** or an appeal to reason; **pathos,** or an appeal to emotions; and **ethos,** or an appeal based on personality or character.

He said that a persuasive argument may use one of these forms exclusively or in any combination with the others.

Aristotle believed the decision to choose one form of persuasion over another depended on several factors: the circumstances in which the appeal is made, the specific nature of what is being argued, and the makeup of the audience being addressed.[23] To state this concept in simpler terms: The selection of an appropriate persuasive appeal depends on determining what you are saying, where and when you are saying it, and to whom you are saying it. This concept should sound familiar to you. It is pivotal to the practice of public relations.

Aristotle did believe that ethos, the persuasive value of a communicator's character, is often the most powerful of the three modes of persuasion. In his classic book *Rhetoric,* he says that a communicator's character "may almost be called the most effective means of persuasion he possesses."[24] That's one reason why practitioners should strive to practice ethical, values-driven public relations: Their well-earned good name can help build the relationships that are essential to their organization's success.

Aristotle's analysis of persuasion raises an important question that is currently being debated within professional and academic circles: Is persuasion an appropriate activity for public relations practitioners? Some people believe that the goal of persuasion is inconsistent with the two-way communication requirement for effective public relations. Two-way communication, by definition, implies a willingness to listen to the needs and concerns of the targeted public and act accordingly. Persuasion linked to one-way communication tends to ignore a central tenet of motivation, that people act in their own self-interests. Any effort at persuasion that does not first take into account the public's point of view is poor public relations—and probably won't work. However, when practiced at its highest levels, public relations identifies common interests and promotes actions that are mutually beneficial. Therefore, in that context, persuasion is a **compliance-gaining tactic** appropriate for public relations practitioners.[25]

Public Opinion Defined

In much the same way that an atom is the basic building block of matter, **belief** is the basic building block of public opinion. A belief is one's commitment to a particular idea or concept based on either personal experience or some credible external authority. For example, many people who have traveled to and experienced Paris believe that it is the most beautiful city in the world. However, others who have never been to France may feel the same way because they have heard it from sources they consider credible, such as friends, travel guides, and popular culture.

When a belief starts affecting the way we behave, it creates an **attitude.** To put it another way, an attitude is a behavioral inclination. For example, if a belief that Paris is a beautiful city causes you to start reading about Paris, encourages you to enjoy French cuisine, or just encourages you to look positively upon all things Parisian, you have developed an attitude.

If that attitude is strong and inspires you to share it with others, you have developed an **opinion.** By definition, an opinion is an expressed behavioral inclination. That opinion can be expressed verbally, by telling others how much you admire Paris, or nonverbally, by adopting French fashion as your own preferred style.

That takes us to **public opinion,** the average expressed behavioral inclination. Public opinion takes into account a wide range of positions that people may have on the same issue. For example, a majority of people may feel that Paris is a beautiful city. A small minority may disagree. Yet another group may have no opinion at all. Together, those three groups constitute public opinion on the issue of the beauty of Paris.

As noted in Chapter 4, the publics of public relations can be divided into what are known as latent, aware, and active publics. Which one of these defines a particular public depends on the degree to which the public realizes and cares about the intersection of its values with an issue. The same can be said for public opinion. **Latent public opinion** is the result of people having varying degrees of interest in a topic or issue but being unaware of the interests of others. **Aware public opinion** occurs when people grow aware of an emerging interest. **Active public opinion** occurs when people act—formally or informally, and often not in unison—to influence the opinions and actions of others.

The Evolution of Public Opinion

Although persuading one person to adopt a particular point of view can be difficult, the true challenge is to persuade large numbers of people. That is the essence of decision making in a democratic society—a public debate that leads to a public consensus and, eventually, to public policy. The evolution of public opinion can be outlined as follows:[26]

1. Public opinion starts with an *already present mass sentiment,* a consensus that developed as a result of earlier public debates.
2. Public opinion begins to evolve when an *issue* is interjected into that consensus. For something to be considered an issue, it has to affect a variety of groups and be seen as evolving.
3. Like-minded individuals coalesce into a *public.* Often these publics can be characterized as being either pro or con. However, many issues are complex and have more than two sides.
4. The various publics engage in *public and private debate* over the issue. This debate can take many forms. It is at this stage that the practice of public relations has its greatest influence among publics that have not yet formed a strong opinion.
5. There is an unspecified period of *time* during which the debate occurs and people make up their minds. The amount of time needed for this to happen varies from issue to issue. With some issues, such as gun control and abortion, the debate seems never to end.
6. Eventually the debate leads to a consensus, which is known as *public opinion.*

7. In turn, that public opinion precipitates some form of *social action,* such as a policy change, an election, or the passing of a new law.

8. At this point the issue evolves into a *social value;* this, in turn, becomes a part of the already present mass sentiment, and the public opinion process begins anew.

You can see the public opinion process at work in the events that followed the death of racing legend Dale Earnhardt at the 2001 Daytona 500. The tragedy reopened

---

QuickBreak 5.5

A PUBLIC OPINION CHECKLIST

Volumes have been written about how to influence public opinion, but here are 10 key guidelines you should remember:

1. *You may not be the best judge of public opinion.* Don't trust hunches or gut reactions. They could be wrong. Base your decisions on solid research and analysis.

2. *People resist change.* Change is often viewed as a threat. For that reason, do not assume that a targeted public understands the benefits of a proposal. Spell them out.

3. *WIIFM (What's In It For Me?).* Social psychologist Hadley Cantril wrote, "Once self-interest is involved, opinions are not easily changed."[27] Don't tell targeted publics why something is good for you. Instead, describe how the desired action benefits them.

4. *People believe what they want to believe.* When people have their minds made up on an issue, they tend to seek out information that reinforces their position. They also tend to avoid or block out what social scientists call **cognitive dissonance**—the mental disturbance resulting from encountering information that runs contrary to their beliefs.

5. *Plant seeds in fertile ground.* It is easier to provide information than it is to shape an opinion. It is also easier to shape an opinion than it is to change an opinion. You can't afford to waste limited time and resources on those who have already decided against you. You can achieve greater suc-

cess by directing public relations efforts to those who are already on your side and those still willing to listen.

6. *KISS (Keep It Simple and Straight).* In the clutter that makes up mass communications, it is the simplest of messages that are most likely to get through and register with a public. Symbolism is often more effective than a complex explanation of concepts.

7. *Demonstrate knowledge of the issue.* When public opinion is undecided or running against you, presenting all sides of the issue tends to be the most effective approach. It also provides an opportunity to demonstrate the comparative strength of your position.

8. *When among friends, preach to the choir.* When public opinion is on your side, stick to your message. In this case usually no need arises to discuss the other side of the issue. Your job isn't so much to change public opinion as to solidify it into action.

9. *Actions speak louder than words.* People are impressed when you actually do what you say you are going to do. Empty promises breed mistrust; keeping your word builds credibility.

10. *Get in the last word.* When there is little to choose from between opposing views, a determining factor tends to be the argument heard last.

Values Statement 5.1

a long-simmering conflict between personal privacy rights and the public's right to know (*an already-present mass sentiment*). An Orlando newspaper investigating the accident filed a public records request to view Earnhardt's autopsy photos. The driver's family objected and went to court to have them sealed (*an issue*). This created a legal, political, and ethical debate, with news organizations on one side and victims' rights groups on the other (*like-minded individuals coalesce into a public*).

The two sides sparred in Florida's courts, in the state legislature, and in the court of public opinion (*public and private debate*).[28] Public reaction was swift and decidedly one-sided (*time passes*). There was an outpouring of support for the Earnhardt family—due, in part, to a well-orchestrated campaign created by the Burson-Marsteller public relations agency (*public opinion*). Just 39 days after the Earnhardt crash, the state legislature passed and the governor signed the Florida Family Protection Act, a law restricting access to autopsy photos (*social action*).[29] The U.S. Supreme Court rejected a challenge to the law in December 2003, bringing an end to the debate (*social value*).[30] However, it is a virtual certainty that media groups will continue to pursue public records containing sensitive personal information (*the public opinion process begins anew*).

The dynamics of the public opinion process point out the need for companies and organizations to conduct ongoing programs of public relations. Because public opinion is always evolving, one-shot efforts at influencing it are rarely effective. Sometimes public opinion crystallizes very quickly, as it did in the Earnhardt autopsy photos controversy. Public opinion is also very fluid and can evolve over time, as with the dramatic change in public attitudes toward civil rights since the early 1960s. Public relations practitioners need to keep their fingers constantly on the pulse of public opinion. Only then are they properly prepared to guide their organizations through potentially stormy seas.

Persuasion versus Manipulation

Understanding the dynamics of public opinion is essential to the practice of public relations. However, as is true with most things in life, it is possible to get too much of a good thing. Although it is often desirable to win people over to a particular point of view, there is a great temptation to try to manipulate public opinion to achieve one's goals. The 1997 movie *Wag the Dog* gave us a glimpse of that behavior. In the film presidential spin doctors, eager to avoid political fallout from an embarrassing scandal, manufactured a fake war to divert public opinion. The ruse worked—but only for a brief period of time. By the end of the movie, the moviegoer was left with the impression that the web of lies was beginning to unravel.

Of course, that was just a movie—for which we should be grateful. But *Wag the Dog* does, nevertheless, illustrate two valuable lessons for public relations practitioners. First, it suggests the need to draw the line between influencing and manipulating public opinion. **Manipulation,** by its very nature, suggests something underhanded. It is true that one may reap short-term gains by telling half-truths or by putting narrow interests ahead of broader ones, but it is also true that those gains are short-lived. Manipulation, whether real or perceived, comes with a cost: credibility. No one likes to feel as if he or she has been used. Manipulation also runs contrary to the ideal of public relations as a problem-solving discipline whose practitioners seek alternatives that are mutually beneficial to all parties concerned.

A second valuable lesson is that those who seek to master public opinion often become a slave to it. This results in a lack of leadership. A common complaint we hear these days about politicians and corporate executives is that they are too often driven by public opinion polls. Instead of acting on what they believe, they seek to do what is popular. Although public opinion is important in democratic societies, so are values. It is often necessary to forgo what is popular for what is right. Think how different human history would be if certain special individuals had not, at critical moments, put their values ahead of public sentiment. Public relations is a values-driven discipline. Those values are determined by what we believe, not necessarily by what is popular.

Quick ✔ Check

1. What are the three kinds of persuasive appeals identified by Aristotle?
2. How does public opinion develop?
3. What is the difference between manipulation and persuasion?

Summary

History has shown us that communication is a fragile process. It can fail in a variety of ways, including a lack of source credibility, an irrelevant message, an inappropriate channel, an inattentive receiver, the absence of feedback, or the presence of physical or psychological noise.

With the growth of communications technology in the 20th century, people initially feared that mass media could dominate public opinion. This fear led to the development of what came to be known as the magic bullet theory. However, as the technology of mass communications evolved, so did our understanding of mass media. Now we realize that mass media do not tell us what to think, but rather influence what we think about. That concept is known as the agenda-setting hypothesis. However, even that theory is evolving. According to uses and gratifications theory, the *real* power to persuade resides with individuals, who can pick and choose from thousands of information sources and are driven by their own self-interests—especially their need to survive.

The evolution of public opinion is a dynamic process that never ceases; for this reason, organizations need to stay attuned to changes in public attitudes and conduct ongoing programs of public relations.

Although efforts to win people over to a point of view are legitimate, manipulation of public opinion by underhanded means is counterproductive. Those who engage in manipulation lose credibility and may become slaves to the public mood.

DISCUSSION QUESTIONS

1. Can and should public relations practitioners try to influence public opinion? Does our ability to persuade have any limits?
2. Describe the process of communication. What are some factors that can cause communication to break down?
3. Does an explanation exist for why some things serve as stronger motivations to action than others?
4. To what degree do you think mass media influence you? How does your personal experience relate to the various theories of mass communications?
5. What would be a good example of an issue that has undergone a rigorous public debate and emerged as a social value? Describe the process by which this happened.

Memo *from the* Field

René Pelletier;
President; Baromètre,
Inc.; Montreal,
Canada

René Pelletier has worked in the research field for nearly 30 years. He has held senior executive positions with firms such as CROP, Inc., Sorécom (of which he was president for 15 years), and Gallup before founding his own company, René Pelletier Groupe-Conseil, Inc., in 1990, and assuming the leadership of Baromètre, Inc., in 1996. He has conducted more than 700 research studies on behalf of different levels of government, as well as for a wide variety of clients in fields such as public services, private service industries, consumer goods, food products, communications, and public affairs.

Pelletier has a master's degree in sociology, with a specialization in applied communications research. A former president of the Professional Association of Marketing Researchers, he is also a founding vice president of CAMRO (Canadian Association of Marketing Research Organizations), a group that establishes strict standards for the industry.

For public relations practitioners, the main role of surveys is to enable them to make decisions based upon facts—as accurately as possible. Those facts concern their publics' beliefs and behaviors about the situation they are dealing with or the company for which they manage public relations.

When should we conduct a survey? Unless an unexpected crisis happens, most successful practitioners conduct public opinion surveys before, during, and after their communication work. I intentionally exclude crisis management surveys in order to concentrate on the most productive and intelligent use of surveys in normal situations.

Before Communicating

Most observers, including public relations practitioners, usually have an inaccurate picture of public opinion. In more than 30 years of professional experience, I have witnessed most of my clients either underestimating or overestimating public support for their projects; I have seen them emphasizing wrong arguments, thinking they would have an immediate and important influence upon public opinion. I have also seen clients neglecting the most powerful lever because they underestimated its influence upon public opinion. Every public relations practitioner concerned about managing a client's image or a project, and who hopes for success, should work with an exhaustive and accurate picture of public opinion before taking any action. This picture will ideally include such information as

1. Who knows or doesn't know your client or product?
2. What are the perceived strengths or weaknesses of the client or product?
3. How credible is your spokesperson (or spokespeople)?
4. Among the arguments you intend to use to influence public opinion, which is or which are the most powerful arguments, the most powerful levers able to influence opinion?
5. What is the profile (both demographic and psychographic) of your primary intervening public—that is the public most likely to have an influence on your targeted public?
6. How big is the gap between reality and your goal? For instance, if only 3 percent of your client's targeted public knows about your client, you won't use the same strategy you would use if your client is known by 60 percent or 70 percent. In the same way, if 70 percent of your client's targeted public has a negative opinion, your challenge will be very different than if that opinion were favorable.
7. What are the losses and damages your client's targeted publics fear most? Why? Can your client counterbalance those possible losses? Are those feared losses real? Are they accurately assessed or overvalued by the public?*

The more accurate and exhaustive the portrait, the better the choice of messages, targeted publics, and communication channels; the final results, too, will be

*It is probably the most important information to survey when organizing a lobby about a specific project (mall in a residential area, possible closing of a factory, building of a possible pollutant factory in a region, use of green areas for industrial means, etc.).

better. Planning a campaign without such a picture of public opinion is like hunting blindfolded and without any knowledge of what prey to search for!

During Communication

Most professional communicators don't measure public opinion during the communication process. Why should we do so? To check the basics: Is the public reached the same one we targeted? Is our message understood and interpreted as planned? Do the people exposed to our message have a more favorable perception of our client or product? Overall, are we on the way to reaching our objectives, or do we have to make some adjustments?

After Communication

Unless you work with a client or brand image on a long-term basis, you will have to conduct your actions within a timeframe, with goals that have to be attained by precise deadlines.

Having a precise deadline will enable you to understand better than anyone else the dynamic of public opinion, how much it changed (or didn't change) since the beginning of the communication process, and how you could most efficiently communicate with your publics during the next months or years.

Clients too often consider a final measurement as being of little use, whereas public relations practitioners often dread it, as it will be seen, in part, as an evaluation of their work. However, I know that the best communication agencies propose that final measurement. It becomes an important tool in understanding the way public opinion changes.

In Finishing . . .

—Never believe that you know what people think before asking them.

—Never believe that public opinion is logical. It often contains paradoxes, and that's normal.

—If people don't understand your message, it is easier to change the message than to change people!

—Simplicity and conciseness of the message are the hardest elements to create, but they are the most effective in the end. The most common mistake among communicators without experience is failing to speak in the language of the public. Successful politicians know the power of short, image-laden sentences or one liners.

—Today's crisis is often the result of yesterday's negligence.

The three elements a public relations practitioner should take into account before making decisions concerning a client are public opinion, public opinion, and public opinion.

Case Study 5.1

I Decide

The Centers for Disease Control and Prevention estimates that on any given day, 4,400 youths age 12–17 will try their first cigarette. That's one every 20 seconds. Of those, one in three will eventually die from a smoking-related disease. That's one every minute.[31]

The problem of teenage smoking is a major concern of the Illinois Department of Public Health (IDPH). According to one study, nearly 36 percent of Illinois high school students (grades 9–12) smoke cigarettes. That is almost eight percentage points above the national average.[32] State health officials have said teenage smoking is part of a much bigger problem. They estimate that tobacco-related illnesses take the lives of more than 16,500 Illinois residents each year and cost the state $6.7 billion annually in medical care and lost productivity.[33]

"Most of these people began using tobacco in early adolescence, typically by age 16," said Dr. John R. Lumpkin, state public health director. "To prevent another generation from being plagued by tobacco addiction, we must try innovative ways to encourage young people not to take up smoking or to quit if they have already started.

"Studies have demonstrated that if young people don't smoke as teenagers, it is unlikely they will ever do so."[34]

Using money obtained as the state's share of a settlement agreement between tobacco companies and 46 state attorneys general, IDPH launched "I Decide," a youth-focused antitobacco organization, in 2000. The effort had two major goals: to reduce smoking rates among teens in a one-county pilot program and "to demonstrate that a comprehensive social marketing campaign aimed at lowering teen tobacco use can be successful."[35] In terms of a long-term strategy, IDPH officials hoped that success of the pilot project would translate into a permanent, statewide effort.

Winnebago County, which includes Rockford and is approximately 80 miles northwest of Chicago, was selected for the program. Focus group and survey research yielded alarming results. Only one-third to one-half of middle and high school students said that they had been taught about the dangers of tobacco in school. An even lower number reported talking about the subject with their parents. An estimated 35 percent of Winnebago County high school students and 15 percent of middle school students smoked.[36]

With the assistance of Golin/Harris International, IDPH launched a $15.5 million peer-to-peer campaign to mobilize teens in their communities. A variety of media and disciplines, including advertising and promotions, were used to achieve campaign objectives.[37]

Inspired by the popular MTV program *TRL: Total Request Live*, campaign officials introduced their own TRL, as in Tobacco Reality Live. It was a traveling event designed to encourage awareness and increase participation in antismoking activities. These daylong summits featured trained teenagers conducting peer-to-peer presentations on tobacco's manipulative effects. Other peer-to-peer efforts included teen-written articles for the I Decide bimonthly newsletter. Campaign organizers also developed educator kits containing membership cards, teaching materials, brochures, temporary tattoos, book covers, and posters. I Decide organizational information was also available through a campaign web site.

To broaden the reach of the campaign, officials targeted the high-profile state boys and girls basketball tournaments. I Decide rally towels and headbands branded with the names of the qualifying teams were distributed at the arena. Other promotional activities included an overnight lock-in at an athletic center, ice skating events, and movie nights.[38]

Supplementing these public relations efforts was a satirical advertising campaign created by Hadrian's Wall, a Chicago-based advertising agency. A fictitious "All Smoke High"—or A.S.H.—where students were *required* to smoke. Those who rebelled and chose not to smoke were the hip ones. Television ads were broadcast in the Rockford market within programs such as *Friends* and *The Gilmore Girls*.[39] A series of outdoor and local transit bus ads also complemented the campaign.[40]

"We know that teenagers do not react well when told what to do and that, typically, they end up making better decisions than adults give them credit for," said ad writer Kevin Lynch. "So we used a little reverse psychology."[41]

By June 2002, more than 6,000 teens were members of I Decide. The program had expanded to another six Illinois counties. Follow-up studies showed that 78 percent of targeted teens knew about the movement. Among those, 86 percent rated I Decide as "excellent" or "good." More significantly, teenage smoking rates in Winnebago County schools dropped from 35 to 28.5 percent.[42]

However, not everything went as organizers had hoped. Faced with an economic recession, the Illinois legislature voted to cut the program from the 2003 state budget. This action evoked an outpouring of public support for the program. That, in turn, prompted IDPH to look for alternative funding sources and to launch a new, smaller scale teen antitobacco program.

DISCUSSION QUESTIONS

1. Using the theories and issues discussed in the chapter that precedes this case study, why do you think it is difficult to deliver antismoking messages to teenagers?
2. What research was conducted in support of the I Decide campaign?
3. What role did peer-to-peer communication play in this campaign? Why do you think this strategy was used?
4. How was the success of this campaign evaluated? Was it, in your opinion, successful?
5. What would you do differently if the target audience for this campaign were a slightly older group: your college classmates?

Case Study 5.2

Color-Coded Confusion

If Homeland Security Secretary Tom Ridge happened to be watching David Letterman's "Top Ten List" on February 20, 2003, it is easy to imagine that he winced when Dave reached item number two.

That evening's category was "Top Ten Ways Dumb Guys Are Preparing for a Terrorist Attack." Number two on that list was "creating elaborate color-code systems to alert citizens to threat levels."[43]

Letterman's jab was aimed at the Homeland Security Advisory System (HSAS), a five-level, color-coded system designed by Ridge's agency to prepare public officials and private citizens for possible terrorist attacks. The comedian's joke came at a time when the nation was under "orange alert," a period in which the nation's security and intelligence agencies rated the threat of a terrorist incident as "high." Many people felt that the terror alert system was a wise precaution. Others ridiculed it as being a counterproductive and costly effort that unnecessarily alarmed the population.

This very easily could have been a "Thumbs Up" case study. The ideas and values behind Homeland Security's efforts were based on sound theory and presented with the best intentions. "The Homeland Security Advisory System is designed to measure and evaluate terrorist threats and communicate them to the public in a timely manner," Ridge said when he introduced the terror threat system on March 12, 2002. "It provides clear, easy to understand factors which help measure threat."[44]

However, it was the last point—that it was "easy to understand"—that drew the most criticism. The HSAS established five terrorist threat conditions: green (low condition), blue (guarded condition), yellow (elevated condition), orange (high condition), and red (severe condition). Each of these levels was accompanied by a list of protective measures that the government and private sectors were advised to take. For example, during an orange alert, public and private agencies were advised to take "additional precautions at public events" and to prepare "to work at an alternative site or with a dispersed workforce."[45]

In announcing the system, Ridge said, "It provides a common vocabulary, so officials from all levels of government can communicate easily with one another and to the public."[46] As noted in Chapter 12, the idea of using a "common vocabulary" is sound crisis management practice. However, the HSAS left unanswered a question on the minds of people outside of the national security and defense establishment: "What is it, *specifically,* that I am supposed to do?"

Government officials tried to answer that question during a February 7, 2003, orange alert announcement. U.S. Attorney General John Ashcroft said that the U.S. intelligence community had concluded that there was an increased likelihood of a terrorist attack coinciding with the end of the Hajj, the annual period of Muslim pilgrimages to Mecca. At the same news conference, Ridge said, "For individual Americans, we ask that you remain aware and remain alert."[47]

With the nation's nerves on edge, officials decided to reassure the American people a couple of days later. They outlined precautionary steps individuals could take to protect themselves. These included storing a three-day supply of food and water, and creating emergency supply kits for both homes and automobiles. The list of materials for the kit included plastic sheeting and duct tape for sealing windows and doors against a terrorist gas attack.[48]

If anything, the attempt to reassure the country appeared to have had the opposite effect. Within hours of the announcement, stores nationwide reported a run on duct tape. A hardware store in Alexandria, Virginia, sold every roll it had in stock. Another Alexandria store announced that its sales of duct tape had tripled. "Everything that was on that newscast, we are selling a lot of it," said one Washington area store employee.[49]

Officials who had sought to prepare the public for possible dangers found themselves trying to avert a public panic and keep people from sealing themselves in their homes with duct tape and plastic. "God forbid, there may come a time when the local authorities or national authorities will tell you that you've got to use them," Ridge said. "But for the time being, we just don't want folks sealing up their doors or sealing up their windows."[50]

Just two days before the February 2003 orange alert, Congress had chided Homeland Security for its flawed warning system. Representative Chris Cox of California, Republican chairman of the House Homeland Security Committee, called it a "senseless, unfocused, nationwide response" too often created by "unspecified threat alerts." Representative Jim Turner, a Texas Democrat, complained "state and local governments spend hundreds of thousands of dollars—perhaps millions—to defend against an amorphous threat." Committee members also scolded the agency for not giving the public information on what it should do when the threat level is raised.[51] Of course, that is exactly what Homeland Security did a few days later—and it prompted a nationwide run on duct tape.

And just in case you are wondering about David Letterman's number one way a dumb guy prepares for a terrorist attack, it was "Taping a duck."[52]

DISCUSSION QUESTIONS

1. Do you agree with the authors that this a difficult case to designate as a definitive "Thumbs Up" or Thumbs Down"? Why or why not?
2. What do you consider to be the Department of Homeland Security's key failure in explaining the color-coded terror alert system to the public?
3. What communication and persuasion theories discussed in this chapter can explain how this case evolved in the manner it did?
4. What values should government officials consider when weighing a decision to inform the public about potential dangers?
5. What, if anything, would *you* have done differently in this case?

Cyber Coach

Visit www.ablongman.com/guthmarsh3e for these study aids—and more:

- flashcards
- quizzes
- videos
- links to other sites
- real-world scenarios that let you be the public relations professional

KEY TERMS

active public opinion, p. 155

agenda-setting hypothesis, p. 145

attitude, p. 154

aware public opinion, p. 155

belief, p. 154

channel, p. 141

cognitive dissonance, p. 156

compliance-gaining tactic, p. 154

diffusion theory, p. 145

ethos, p. 153

feedback, p. 141

framing, p. 149

latent public opinion, p. 155

logos, p. 153

magic bullet theory, p. 143

manipulation, p. 158

Maslow's Hierarchy of Needs, p. 150

message, p. 141

Monroe's Motivated Sequence, p. 152

noise, p. 139

n-step theory, p. 144

opinion, p. 155

pathos, p. 153

persuasion, p. 153

public opinion, p. 155

receiver, p. 141

source, p. 141

spin, p. 148

spin doctor, p. 148

two-step theory, p. 144

uses and gratifications theory,
    p. 147

NOTES

1. Nathan Stoltzfus, "Dissent in Nazi Germany," *The Atlantic Monthly*, September 1992, 87–94.
2. David Berlo, *The Process of Communication: An Introduction to Theory and Practice* (New York: Holt, Rinehart and Winston, 1960).
3. Richard M. Nixon, *RN: The Memoirs of Richard Nixon* (New York: Grosset & Dunlap, 1978), 460–466.
4. This Quickbreak is based on the academic paper "Propaganda v. Public Diplomacy: How 9/11 Gave New Life to a Cold War Debate," by David W. Guth, presented at the annual conference of the Association of Educators in Journalism and Mass Communications, August 2003, Kansas City, Mo.
5. Brett Gray, *The Nervous Liberals: Propaganda Anxieties from World War I to the Cold War* (New York: Columbia University Press, 1999), p. 8.
6. Scott M. Cutlip, *The Unseen Power: Public Relations, A History* (Hillsdale, N.J.: Lawrence Erlbaum, 1994), 82–183.

7. Gayle Mertz and Carol Miller Lieber, *Conflict in Context: Understanding Local to Global Security,* Educators for Social Responsibility, 1991, online, www.esrnational.org/whatispropaganda.htm.

8. Cutlip, 45.

9. Cutlip, 182.

10. Gray, 8.

11. Garth S. Jowett and Victoria O'Donnell, *Propaganda and Persuasion,* 3rd. ed. (Thousand Oaks, Calif.: Sage Publications, 1999), p. 6.

12. Jowett and O'Donnell, 1.

13. Carol-Lyn Jardine, "PR's Role in Bringing Elizabeth Home," *Public Relations Tactics,* May 2003, 1.

14. Presidential Job Approval Ratings, Gallup Organization, online, www.gallup.com.

15. James E. Grunig et al., eds., *Excellence in Public Relations and Communication Management* (Hillsdale, N.J.: Lawrence Erlbaum, 1992), 165.

16. Grunig.

17. Jack Rosenthal, "Spin Doctors," *New York Times,* 21 October 1984, as quoted by "Present at the Creation: Spin," National Public Radio, 4 November 2002, online, www.npr.org/programs/morning/features/patc/spin/index.html.

18. "Present at the Creation: Spin."

19. Erving Goffman, *Frame Analysis: Essays on the Organization of Experience* (New York: Harper & Row, 1974), 21.

20. Robert Entman, "Framing: Toward Clarification of a Fractured Paradigm," *Journal of Communication* 43, no. 3, 51–58.

21. Abraham Maslow, *Motivation and Personality* (New York: Harper & Row, 1954), 9.

22. Raymie E. McKerron, Bruce E. Gronbeck, Douglas Ehninger, and Alan H. Monroe, *Principles and Types of Speech Communication,* 14th ed. (Boston: Allyn & Bacon, 2000), 153–164.

23. Edward P. J. Corbett, *Classical Rhetoric for the Modern Student* (New York: Oxford University Press, 1971), 50.

24. Aristotle, *Rhetoric,* trans. W. Rhys Roberts (New York: Modern Library, 1954), 25.

25. Grunig, 331.

26. Based on Lang and Lang's *Collective Dynamics,* cited in *PRSA Accreditation Study Guide* (New York: Public Relations Society of America, 1993), 38.

27. Hadley Cantril, *Gauging Public Opinion* (Princeton, N.J.: Princeton University Press, 1972), 226–230.

28. "Earnhardt Autopsy Review—A Collision with the Truth," *Salisbury Post,* 13 April 2001, online, www.salisburypost.com/2001april/041301ed.htm.

29. HB 1083, Florida General Assembly, online, www.leg.state.fl.is.

30. Gina Holland, "Florida Newspaper Loses Appeal over Earnhardt Autopsy Photos," *USA Today,* 1 December 2003, online, www.usatoday.com.

31. Centers for Disease Control and Prevention, "Tobacco Use Among Middle and High School Students—United States, 2002," *Morbidity and Mortality Weekly Report,* 14 Nov 2003, 1096.

32. Centers for Disease Control and Prevention, "Illinois Highlights," online, www.cdc.gov/tobacco/statehi.

33. "Tobacco Kills 16,500 in State; Economic Damage in Billions," Illinois Department of Public Health, news release, 27 May 2004, online www.idph.state.il.us.

34. "Ryan Proposal Doubles Tobacco Prevention Funding," Illinois Department of Public Health news release, 21 February 2001, online, www.idph.state.il.us.

35. *I Decide, The First Year 2000–2001,* Illinois Department of Public Health, online, www.idph.state.il.us.

36. *I Decide, The First Year 2000–2001,* 3.

37. "I Decide: Illinois Teens Talk Back to Big Tobacco," Silver Anvil award summary 6BW-0301C06, Public Relations Society of America, online, www.prsa.org.

38. "I Decide: Illinois Teens Talk Back to Big Tobacco."

39. Megan Larson, "Hadrian's Wall," *Adweek,* 23 Jun 2003, 18–20.

40. "Anti-Tobacco Bus Ads Unveiled," Illinois Department of Public Health, news release, 17 February 2001, online, www.idph.state.il.us.

41. Megan Larson.

42. "I Decide: Illinois Teens Talk Back to Big Tobacco."

43. "Top Ten Ways Dumb Guys Are Preparing for a Terrorist Attack," *The Late Show with David Letterman,* 20 February 2003, online, www.cbs.com/latenight/lateshow/top_ten/archive.

44. "Remarks by Governor Ridge Announcing Homeland Security Advisory System," White House transcript, 12 March 2002, online, www.whitehouse.gov.

45. "Gov. Ridge Announces Homeland Security Advisory System," White House news release, 12 March 2002, online, www.whitehouse.gov.

46. "Remarks by Governor Ridge Announcing Homeland Security Advisory System."

47. "Homeland Security Threat Level Raised to Orange," White House transcript, 7 February 2003, online, www.whitehouse.gov.

48. "Administration: Prepare, Don't Panic," CNN, 11 February 2003, online, www.cnn.com.

49. Jeanne Meserve, "Duct Tape Sales Rise Amid Terror Fears," CNN, 11 February 2003, online, www.cnn.com.

50. "Ridge Tries to Calm America's Nerves," CNN, 14 February 2003, online, www.cnn.com.

51. Shaun Waterman, "Lawmakers Lambaste Color-Coded Alert System," United Press International, 5 February 2003, online, LexisNexis.

52. "Top Ten Ways Dumb Guys Are Preparing for a Terrorist Attack."

chapter six

Ethics and Social Responsibility in Public Relations

After studying this chapter, you will be able to

- define what is meant by the word *ethics*

- specify categories of ethics codes

- understand the most common ethical challenges

- describe the ethics codes of important philosophers from Aristotle to John Rawls

- use the Potter Box to analyze ethical dilemmas

Choose and Lose

scenario *You are an upper-level public relations practitioner for an international manu-facturing company. Your primary duty is internal (employee) public relations. Three days ago, the CEO of your company told the news media that a much-publicized though minor environmental hazard in your company's production process had been eliminated. The person responsible for eliminating the hazard is one of your best friends. And right now, she really needs your friendship: Because of a death in her family, she's going through a rough time.*

As your concern for her grows, you learn, by accident, that she hasn't eliminated the environmental hazard; it still exists. In her distraught condition, she doesn't even realize that she hasn't corrected it. You're afraid that telling her will damage your friendship, one of the few positive things in her life right now. But if the CEO discovers the oversight, he may fire her—which, you fear, would deepen her depression. And, of course, you're concerned that the news media will find out that they were given, albeit unintentionally, false information.

What do you do?

What Are Ethics?

In the 1990s comedy *Bill and Ted's Excellent Adventure*, two young slackers travel through time to learn about history. If you could do the same (not that you're a slacker), you could round up some of the great minds of philosophy to help you learn about ethics. Imagine bringing Aristotle, Immanuel Kant, and John Stuart Mill to your local pizza joint.

"We don't seem to agree on much about ethics," Kant says.

"I disagree," says Mill as Aristotle rolls his eyes. "We agree on a lot."

"The truth is somewhere in the middle," says Aristotle. "We *do* agree that more than anything else, human beings want happiness. Pass the pizza."

"Right," says Kant. "And we agree that unless we're ethical, we can never be truly happy."

"And we agree that being ethical means acting on our values," Aristotle says. "Ethics are values in action."

"Perfect," says Mill. "But we disagree on how to find those values."

"But we agree that Aristotle eats too much pizza," Kant shouts, banging his fist on the table.

And the debate would go on. But you've probably read enough philosophy in your other classes to know that this fantasy is fairly accurate: **Ethics** are values in action. And without ethics, philosophers say, we cannot achieve our goal of happiness. Consider the ethics scandals of the early 21st century: Enron, Martha Stewart, Halliburton, and so many more. None seemed to lead to happiness for those involved.

Being ethical means identifying our values and acting on them. The late John Ginn, a journalism professor at the University of Kansas, often told his students, "Ethics are not something that we *have*. They're something that we *do*." Ideally, once we decide what our values are, we embrace guidelines for behavior that will help us reach those values. Those guidelines become our ethics code. Our ethics code governs what we're willing to do—and what we're unwilling to do. Ethics aren't something we occasionally think about and then toss into a dark closet. Instead, we use

QuickBreak 6.1

THE ETHICS CODES OF PRSA AND IABC

Members of the Public Relations Society of America pledge to abide by the *Member Code of Ethics 2000*. Based on the values of advocacy, honesty, expertise, independence, loyalty, and fairness (see p. 38), the PRSA ethics code specifies six "Core Principles," including the following two:

- "Free flow of information: Protecting and advancing the free flow of accurate and truthful information is essential to serving the public interest and contributing to informed decision making in a democratic society."
- "Safeguarding confidences: Client trust requires appropriate protection of confidential and private information."

Each core principle includes guidelines that define in greater detail the principle's intent. For example, the following list reproduces the guidelines for the "free flow of information" principle.

A member shall:

- Preserve the integrity of the process of communication.
- Be honest and accurate in all communications.
- Act promptly to correct erroneous communications for which the practitioner is responsible.

- Preserve the free flow of unprejudiced information when giving or receiving gifts by ensuring that gifts are nominal, legal, and infrequent.

Members of the International Association of Business Communicators are governed by the *Code of Ethics for Professional Communicators*. Like PRSA's code, the IABC code specifies guidelines for ethical conduct. Its values echo those of PRSA in many areas, especially in the realms of truth and accuracy. According to the IABC code, "Professional communicators uphold the credibility and dignity of their profession by practicing honest, candid, and timely communication and by fostering the free flow of essential information in accord with the public interest." IABC also maintains an Ethics Committee to "offer advice and assistance to individual communicators regarding specific ethical situations." Both organizations can enforce sanctions against members who do not adhere to their ethical standards.

The complete text of the PRSA ethics code can be found in the appendix of this book.

them every day to help us honor and attain our values. In other words, ethical behavior isn't a distant goal. Rather, it's a part of daily life.

Ethics Codes for Values-Driven Public Relations

Ethics codes identify core values. They also specify ways of acting that honor those values. Therefore, ethics codes offer guidelines for values-driven actions. Public relations professionals live their lives under the guidance of several ethics codes: international codes, societal codes, professional codes, organizational codes, and personal codes. Let's look at examples of each.

INTERNATIONAL CODES.   As more organizations build relationships with publics in other nations, international codes of business ethics are emerging. For example, the Global Alliance for Public Relations and Communication Management drafted an outline for an international public relations code in 2003. Members of this consortium of 150,000-plus public relations professionals pledge to act on five key values: advocacy, honesty, integrity, expertise, and loyalty. The Global Alliance's code is online at www.globalpr.org.

SOCIETAL CODES.   The Ten Commandments, a foundation of Judeo-Christian culture, are an example of a societal ethics code that influences the lives of millions of people throughout the world. Other religions, of course, have codes to help their believers achieve obedience to divine will. Eighteenth-century historian Edward Gibbon said of the Koran, the holy book of Islam, "From the Atlantic to the Ganges, the Koran is acknowledged as the fundamental code, not only of theology, but of civil and criminal jurisprudence; the laws which regulate the actions and property of mankind are guarded by the infallible and immutable sanction of the will of God."[1]

PROFESSIONAL CODES.   Unlike members of some professions, public relations practitioners have no central, binding code of ethics. We're not licensed by a central organization, as are doctors and lawyers. Many public relations practitioners, however, voluntarily join organizations that do have binding ethics codes. The two largest such organizations in the world are the Public Relations Society of America (PRSA) and the International Association of Business Communicators (IABC). Unfortunately, not everyone is familiar with public relations ethics codes. "Recently," say public relations scholars Hugh Culbertson and Ni Chen, "we commented to a journalist friend that we'd been asked to write a paper on public relations ethics. 'There aren't many,' he joked. 'Your paper ought to be quite brief.'"[2] Ouch.

ORGANIZATIONAL CODES.   Many organizations have written ethics codes that employees are asked to read, sign, and follow. Often, members of an organization's public relations staff are asked to help draft, evaluate, and revise these codes. Facing criticisms of biased coverage of the war in Iraq, the Al-Jazeera news channel—a major news network in the Arab world—announced in 2004 that it would write and follow an ethics code "to uphold journalistic values."[3]

PERSONAL CODES.   Truett Cathy, founder of the Chick-fil-A restaurant chain, closes his 1,500-plus restaurants on Sundays. The company's web site makes it clear that the policy stems from Cathy's personal values:

> Admittedly, closing all of our restaurants every Sunday makes us a rarity in this day and age. But it's a little habit that has always served us well, so we're planning to stick with it.
>   Our founder, Truett Cathy, wanted to ensure that every Chick-fil-A employee and restaurant operator had an opportunity to worship, spend time with family and friends, or just plain rest from the work week. Made sense then, still makes sense now.[4]

Truett Cathy, founder of the Chick-fil-A restaurant chain, follows his personal ethics code by sponsoring more than 100 foster children. They call him Grandpa. (Courtesy of Chick-fil-A, Inc.)

Cathy's son Dan, president of the company, said that his father "didn't want to have to wash dishes on Sunday afternoon like he had to when he was a kid in a boardinghouse, and he didn't want to ask others to do what he didn't want to do himself."[5]

Objectivity versus Advocacy: A Misleading Ethics Debate

In addition to identifying the values specified in ethics codes, we can learn more about ethics in public relations by studying the values of related professions. An enduring debate in public relations comes from comparing the roles of public relations practitioners with those of lawyers and journalists. At the heart of this debate lies this question: Are public relations practitioners ethically obligated to communicate the *full* truth of a matter? In all our different relationship-building activities, do we strive to present an unbiased view of the complete truth as we know it? Or do we strive to present only the information that benefits our organization—in other words, do we deliver only selective truth? To oversimplify, are public relations practitioners objective communicators, like journalists, or are we advocates, like lawyers?

Some practitioners charge that total objectivity would lead us to tell the truth but ignore the consequences of what we say. Imagine, for a moment, the consequences of telling every public everything you know about the organization you represent. Surely, not every public has a right to know everything. Legally, some information, such as employee health records, must be confidential. And surely you wouldn't betray strategic secrets that help your organization stay competitive. Advocacy, with its focus on the consequences of communicating, can seem more suitable than objectivity for public relations.

If, however, we choose to operate solely as advocates, we soon encounter the sticky issue of selective truth. In attempting to build relationships with publics, are we allowed to withhold damaging information that certain publics have a right to know? Sometimes we can withhold such information legally—but can we do so ethically? Some practitioners say yes. They maintain that our society has become adversarial, like a courtroom. Public relations practitioners engaged in a debate, they say, need present only the facts that help them, trusting that opponents will present other facts and that a judge—the public—will decide the truth of the matter.[6]

Objectivity versus Advocacy: A Solution

In recent years, public relations practitioners have worked hard to develop an ethical solution to the objectivity–advocacy debate. That solution, as we discussed in Chapter 1, is the growing role of public relations as a management function.

How does being a manager—instead of being someone who simply carries out orders—help solve the ethical nightmare of 100 percent truth versus selective truth? Increasingly, public relations practitioners are helping to create their organizations' policies before those policies are implemented. Studies show that more than 80 percent of practitioners in the United States and Canada meet with their organization's top management at least once a week.[7] Public relations professionals can advise other leaders within their organization about the impact policies may have on various publics. They can vigorously discourage unethical proposals by noting the impact such proposals could have on key publics—such as news media.

The entire objectivity-versus-advocacy debate seems to be based on a misleading question: Are public relations practitioners objective communicators or are they advocates? What if the answer is "neither"? Many practitioners respond to the debate by saying that public relations practitioners are, first and foremost, relationship managers. Their priority is building honorable, ethical relationships between an organization and the publics that are essential to its success. Sometimes relationship management calls for delivering unpopular truths, either to a public or to the organization itself. And sometimes relationship management involves being an advocate—even if that means advocating the viewpoint of an important public within your own organization. In all their actions, however, public relations practitioners are acting for the good of the relationships that sustain an organization.

Quick ✔ Check

1. What does the word *ethics* mean?
2. In our society, who establishes ethics standards?
3. What problems are associated with an advocacy–selective truth philosophy of public relations?

ARISTOTLE, CONFUCIUS, AND THE GOLDEN MEAN

Is it all right to tell a lie? If we answer quickly, most of us will probably answer no. Telling a lie, we will say, is wrong. It's unethical.

Let's complicate the situation. Is it unethical to tell a lie to save someone's life? Here's a classic ethical question: If you were hiding an innocent victim of political persecution in your attic and representatives of the corrupt regime asked whether you were hiding that individual, would you lie? Or would you tell the truth and betray an innocent person?

Moral absolutes can be troublesome. We can almost always think of exceptions to the moral guidelines we generally follow. Those exceptions can help us understand the concept of the **golden mean,** developed by the Greek philosopher Aristotle (384–322 B.C.).

Aristotle believed that ethical conduct existed at a point of balance and harmony between the two extremes of excess and deficiency. That point

of balance is the golden mean. For example, Aristotle would contend that it's unethical *never* to lie (one extreme), just as it's unethical *always* to lie (the opposite extreme). The challenge of the golden mean lies in answering the crucial question *when:* When is it all right to lie? In what specific circumstances could lying be considered an ethical course of action?

A century before the birth of Aristotle, the Chinese philosopher Confucius (551–479 B.C.) established much the same principle with his *Doctrine of the Mean:* "The superior man . . . stands erect in the middle, without inclining to either side."[8]

Finding the golden mean isn't easy. But as we seek to discover the ethical course between absolutist extremes, we learn more about the values that govern and will govern our lives.

Challenges to Ethical Behavior

Identifying our values is one thing; acting on them is another. Many kinds of challenges stand in the way of ethical behavior. For one thing, some ethical questions aren't easy. They can keep you lying awake at night, staring at the ceiling and trying to select the right course of action amid four or five unappealing options. Also, overwork sometimes conceals ethical obligations while the damage has already begun. Still another challenge is being aware of the mistaken assumption that something legal is always ethical. Or perhaps the business practices of an international client lead you into unfamiliar cross-cultural ethical territory. Or perhaps the challenge lies in the dangers of short-term thinking, or of working in a so-called virtual organization in which values clash. Let's discuss each of these challenges.

Dilemmas

Some ethical challenges are called *dilemmas*—meaning difficult quandaries in which important values clash and every potential solution will cause pain. A dilemma isn't simply a problem; it's a problem that lacks a good, painless solution. The Choose and Lose scenario that opens this chapter is an example of a dilemma. No matter which course of action you select, you seem to hurt or betray someone who trusts you: your CEO, your friend, the news media, or the publics that might suffer from the environmental hazard.

In real life, PepsiCo, Northwest Airlines, and other large international companies encountered clashing values when the government of Burma, a country (also know as Myanmar) in which the companies operated, began a series of increasingly brutal crackdowns on opposition political parties. Should the companies honor the value of justice and leave the country, refusing to help the government through taxes? Or should they honor the value of supporting their local employees, who desperately need their jobs, and stay? By 2004, PepsiCo, Northwest Airlines, and nearly 100 other international companies had made the difficult decision to leave Burma.[9]

Overwork

Is it possible to work too hard? Yes, if doing so clouds your judgment. You, and your organization, have an ethical obligation regarding workload: You should shoulder only the work that you can efficiently handle in a typical 40- to 50-hour workweek. Hard work is probably a value within your organization—but so are quality and accuracy. You have an ethical obligation to control the quality of your work. Overwork can also rob you of time you ideally would devote to self-analysis—that is, to thinking about your organization's values and your own values and checking to see whether all your actions are working toward those values.

Legal/Ethical Confusion

What is legal isn't always ethical—and, to a lesser degree, what is ethical may not always be legal. For example, does any law prevent you from remaining silent when you're mistakenly praised for someone else's work? Your silence wouldn't be illegal—but, by most standards, it would be unethical. Or perhaps your supervisor asks you whether a particular project is done. You're a little behind, but you're certain you can finish it this afternoon; because you know she won't ask for it until tomorrow, you say it's done. The small lie isn't illegal, but is it a breach of your personal ethics code? Probably. Simply following the law isn't enough to guarantee ethical behavior.

When Tylenol capsules laced with cyanide killed seven people in the Chicago area in 1982, executives at Johnson & Johnson had no legal obligation to launch a nationwide recall of the product. Company lawyers may even have feared that such an action would be an admission of liability. However, Johnson & Johnson recalled the product out of what company officials felt was a moral obligation to their customers. Despite substantial short-term financial damage, the economic impact of the recall was temporary. In the long run, Johnson & Johnson was praised for its business ethics and was able to save its position as the maker of this country's premier over-the-counter pain reliever.

Can something illegal be ethical? Can doing the right thing involve breaking the law? In a recent protest march in Washington, D.C., anti-AIDS activists deliberately broke the law and demanded to be arrested for illegal assembly. They justified their actions by claiming that the benefits of media attention for AIDS victims and AIDS policies outweighed the value of honoring the law.[10] The concept of **civil disobedience** involves peaceful, unlawful actions designed to help change government policies.

Cross-Cultural Ethics

Let's say you're doing business overseas and you're given an expensive vase by one of the many companies seeking to establish a partnership with your organization. Giving gifts to new acquaintances is standard in the culture you're visiting. Can you ethically accept the gift? Or do you reject it as a bribe?

Professor Thomas Donaldson of the Wharton School of Business notes two extremes in the range of your possible responses to the gift: **cultural relativism** and **ethical imperialism.** Both, he says, are wrong. Cultural relativism involves the belief that no set of ethics is superior to any other set. With cultural relativism, you could accept the gift, saying, "It may violate my sense of ethics, but I'm just honoring the ethics of my host nation." Ethical imperialism is the belief that your system of ethics has no flexibility and no room for improvement; your system overrules every other system. With ethical imperialism, you would quickly reject the gift, saying, "Sorry, but this looks like a bribe to me."

Donaldson suggests a middle ground:

When it comes to shaping ethical behavior, companies should be guided by three principles:
- Respect for core human values, which determine the absolute moral threshold for all business activities.
- Respect for local traditions.
- The belief that context matters when deciding what is right and what is wrong.[11]

In other words, be clear on your own beliefs but willing to explore the beliefs of others. Is that lavish gift a bribe—or is it a genuine gift of friendship, an important part of the culture you're visiting? If it's clearly a bribe, you politely but firmly explain that you can't accept it. If it's a genuine gift, perhaps your organization's policy allows you to accept it on behalf of the company. Maybe you can donate it to charity when you return home.

Short-Term Thinking

The classic example of someone engaged in short-term thinking is the person who plugs a leaking dam with a lit stick of dynamite. The short-term problem is solved, but at too high a cost. A public relations practitioner who deceives members of any public, from reporters to employees, is guilty of short-term thinking. Eventually, the deception may be revealed, damaging the long-term relationship between the practitioner and the public.

Virtual Organizations

An emerging threat to ethical behavior comes from **virtual organizations,** which are temporary organizations formed by smaller units to complete a specific job. For example, an independent public relations consultant might team up with an architectural agency and a developer to try to persuade a community that it needs a new shopping center. These different units would consider themselves part of one organization for the duration of the project; when the project ends, so does the organization.

Dramatic improvements in communications technology have spurred the growth of virtual organizations, allowing them to include partners from different locations throughout the world. But unfamiliar partners or a lack of internal communication can lead to clashing values and ethics. In *Marketing Ethics: An International Perspective,* Professor Bodo Schlegelmilch writes, "How such organizations can create a sense of shared values and ethics, and how such organizations can be controlled by any external bodies, will constitute one of the key challenges in business ethics in the future."[12]

The Rewards of Ethical Behavior

Let's ask a blunt question: What's the payoff for ethical behavior? What's in it for you?

Payoffs for ethical behavior, of course, are many, but among the most important is simply the deep satisfaction of doing the right thing. This chapter is based on the assumption that you want to be an ethical person who works for an ethical organization. Virtue, you've heard, is its own reward.

However, ethical behavior has other bonuses—compensation, perhaps, for the sheer difficulty of behaving ethically. There's growing evidence that ethical behavior can lead to promotion within your organization. A Harvard University study of successful leaders concluded that a powerful correlation exists between leadership and "strong personal ethics."[13] Many public relations practitioners believe that good ethics positively affect an organization's financial success. In recent years, in fact, more than 30 studies have shown a direct link between good ethics and good profits. And ethical companies may have superior employees: One recent survey showed that 65 percent of U.S. employees felt truly loyal to employers who "subscribed to ethical practices."[14] However, the 2000 National Business Ethics Survey of U.S. companies concluded that a code of ethics alone has no effect on profits. Instead, values-based ethics must truly be a part of an organization's culture.[15] "If you are going to have a values statement and not follow it," says Shane McLaughlin of the Best Practices in Corporate Communications organization, "it does much more damage to a company than not having a values statement at all."[16]

Not everyone is persuaded by the many studies that tie an organization's profits to its good ethics. "There is not one scintilla of evidence to demonstrate that having a good ethics policy increases profits," a professional ethics consultant recently told the *Wall Street Journal.* But, he added, "there are some modicums of evidence to show that a lack of one is extraordinarily costly."[17]

QuickBreak 6.3

IMMANUEL KANT AND THE CATEGORICAL IMPERATIVE

The German philosopher Immanuel Kant (1724–1804) contributed the concept of the "categorical imperative" to the study of ethics. Despite the fancy name, the concept is fairly simple. Let's say that you're experiencing an ethical crisis that has several different possible solutions. Kant would tell you to imagine that a universal maxim—a clear principle designed to apply to everyone in the world—will be the outcome of whichever course of action you choose. For example, one course of action might be for you to make a promise that you know you can't keep. Kant would ask you to imagine such an action becoming standard behavior for everyone. Clearly, the consequences would be disastrous.

In *Fundamental Principles of the Metaphysic of Morals*, Kant writes, "Act only on that maxim whereby thou canst at the same time will that it should become a universal law."[18] When you discover a course of action that could and probably should be a universal law, that is a **categorical imperative.** And a categorical imperative, says Kant, is a course of action that you must follow.

How would you apply Kant's theory of categorical imperatives to the scenario that opens this chapter? You would imagine that each possible course of action created a maxim that everyone in the world would follow. You would then reject any course of action that created a maxim that could lead to undesirable behavior if it were truly adopted by everyone. For example, one such maxim might be "It's all right to deceive the news media to protect our employees." Would that be a categorical imperative you'd want the world to follow every day?

At the very least, we can say that good ethics are probably good for business—and that bad ethics are probably bad for business. The odds favor doing the right thing.

Quick ✔ Check

1. What is a golden mean? How does that concept apply to ethics?
2. How is a dilemma different from a problem?
3. Is legal behavior always ethical? Is illegal behavior always unethical?
4. In the business world, is ethical behavior financially profitable?
5. What is a categorical imperative?

Trust and Corporate Social Responsibility

The business scandals of the early 21st century damaged an essential ingredient for ethical relationships: trust. Professors Gene Laczniak and Patrick Murphy say trust is the logical outcome of ethical behavior.[19] In a landmark report titled *Restoring Trust in Business: Models for Action*, the PR Coalition—a consortium of more than 20 leading public relations organizations—concluded: "Trust has become an overriding concern for business leadership around the globe. It has been identified as a key factor in successful leadership and management. By contrast, lack of trust in a business is seen as crucially debilitating."[20]

Unfortunately, 74 percent of those polled in a 2004 Reputation Institute survey rate the reputation of U.S. businesses as "not good" or "terrible."[21] Almost half the respondents in a recent survey of public relations managers maintain that "the biggest issue facing PR today is credibility/trust."[22]

In its report, the PR Coalition recommended that public relations practitioners help their organizations establish trust with key publics through three values-driven actions:

1. Articulate a set of ethical principles that are closely connected to their core values and business processes and are supported with deep management commitment and enterprise-wide discipline.
2. Create a process for transparency and disclosure that is appropriate for their company and industry in both current and future operations. (**Transparency** involves doing business openly and honestly without hidden agendas.)
3. Make trust and ethics a board-level corporate governance issue and establish a formal system of measuring trust that touches all parts of the organization.[23]

"Trust is built over time, based on what companies do, not say," says Chris Atkins, founder of the Reputation Laboratory, part of the Ketchum public relations agency.[24]

Corporate Social Responsibility

One way to build trust over time involves a philosophy known as **corporate social responsibility,** or CSR. Organizations that embrace CSR are "a positive force for change to help improve the quality of people's lives" in the words of the International Business Leaders Forum (IBLF). In other words, such organizations are good corporate citizens. According to the IBLF, corporate social responsibility strives for high standards in seven areas:

1. human rights, labor, and security;
2. enterprise and economic development;
3. business standards and corporate governance;
4. health promotion;
5. education and leadership development;
6. human disaster relief; and
7. environment.[25]

"Eighty-nine percent of Americans say that in light of the Enron collapse and WorldCom financial situation, it is more important than ever for companies to be socially responsible," reports public relations agency Cone, Inc.[26]

Cone's research shows that CSR is more than an ethical imperative; it is a social expectation. Around the world, publics increasingly expect organizations to be good citizens, contributing to the social well-being of their communities. As Cone, Inc.,

President Carol Cone notes in this chapter's "Memo from the Field," companies that embrace CSR fare better in the marketplace.

As a values-driven, relationship-oriented philosophy, CSR fits perfectly into the broad profession of public relations. A generation ago, Harold Burson, founder of the Burson-Marsteller public relations agency, offered these thoughts on CSR and public relations in a speech at Columbia University: "My subject pertains to the relationship between public relations and corporate social responsibility. I do not believe there is a relationship between the two. They are not cousins or even siblings. They are even closer than identical twins. They are one and the same."[27]

Beyond CSR: Strengthening Ethical Behavior

Ethical behavior and CSR in an organization must start with top management. Public relations practitioners can monitor and counsel on ethical matters, but ultimately an organization's top managers must lead by example. Leadership carries with it a special ethical burden. Today's business climate doesn't tolerate executives who have a "do as I say, not as I do" attitude. When it comes to accountability, executives do well to remember the sign on President Harry Truman's White House desk: The Buck Stops Here.

Executives, with the assistance of public relations counsel, should create an environment that helps the organization to focus constantly on the importance of ethical behavior in its relationships with others. Creating this environment involves CSR and more:

- periodic ethics audits to help you assess the current state of affairs in your organization;
- integration of values into the four-step public relations process (described in Chapter 1); and
- a system such as the Potter Box (see p. 183) for analyzing ethical challenges when they do occur.

Ethics Audits

An audit is a process of examination, evaluation, and recommendations. Most of us, probably, have heard of financial audits, in which a professional auditor examines an organization's income and expenditures and makes recommendations for improvement. In an **ethics audit,** we should ask and answer six basic questions:

1. What is our organization's ethics code?
2. How do we communicate that code to ourselves and others?
3. What do key publics—including employees—know about our ethics code?
4. What successes in ethics have we recently had, and why?
5. What setbacks in ethics have we recently had, and why?
6. What can we do to bolster strengths and reduce weaknesses in our ethics?

FEEDING CHILDREN BETTER

National Evaluation of ConAgra Foods Kids Cafes

Center on Hunger and Poverty
Heller School for Social Policy and Management
Brandeis University

November 2003

An analysis prepared for the
ConAgra Foods Feeding Children Better Foundation
Sponsor of Kids Cafes in communities across the nation

Evaluation Report To verify compliance with the social responsibility goals of its Kids Café program, ConAgra Foods Feeding Children Better Foundation asked the Center on Hunger and Poverty at Brandeis University to conduct an independent investigation of the Foundation's free meal program for needy children. (Courtesy of ConAgra Foods Feeding Children Better Foundation)

Periodically answering these questions and correcting any seeming deficiencies can help your organization build the necessary foundation for ethical behavior.

Integrating Ethics into the Public Relations Process

As we'll discuss in Chapter 12, the best time to solve a problem is before it starts. That's certainly true of challenges to ethical relationships: The best time to solve them is before they become problems. How can you attempt to do that? By ensuring that a focus on values is at the heart of your four-step public relations process.

In the *research* phase, as you scan the horizon searching for issues that may affect your organization, you should be well aware of your organization's written values. When you begin to research a particular issue, you should both remind yourself of those values and gather information on the values of the involved publics. Any clashes among those sets of values should alert you to a potential ethics problem.

In the *planning* phase, you should test every proposed action against your organization's values and against the values of important publics.

In the *communication* phase, you should implement every action with a clear understanding of how it reflects the values of your organization and the involved publics.

In the *evaluation* phase, you should study whether your completed actions were indeed in accordance with your organization's values. You should also consider the impact of the actions on the values of the involved publics. Any lapses or clashes should initiate a study to see whether problems stemmed from the actions or from your organization's values.[28]

Table 6.1 (p. 184) summarizes the key questions at each stage of the process.

The Potter Box

With CSR, periodic ethics audits, and your values-driven public relations process, you've established a foundation. But let's be realistic: Some challenges, like the hypothetical case study that begins this chapter, appear out of the blue. We can't prevent them. All we can do is try to react effectively and ethically. A helpful tool in such situations is the **Potter Box.** Designed by Ralph Potter, a former professor of divinity at Harvard University, the Potter Box helps people analyze individual ethical crises.[29] It derives its name from its boxlike format (see Figure 6.1).

To analyze an ethical problem with the aid of the Potter Box, you follow a six-step process:

1. Define the situation as objectively as possible. What *don't* you know? Would anyone define the situation differently? Who and why? (Definition box).
2. State the different values that you see involved in the situation and compare the merits of the differing values (Values box).

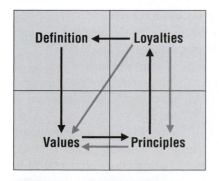

FIGURE 6.1   **The Potter Box**

TABLE 6.1	**Incorporating Values into the Public Relations Process**
	Incorporating values into each step of the public relations process can help an organization achieve ethical behavior.

I. RESEARCH

- In this problem or opportunity, which of our organization's values are affirmed or challenged?

- In this problem or opportunity, what are the relevant values of the key publics involved?

II. PLANNING

- Are the goals, objectives, and tactics under consideration consistent with our organization's values?

- Are the goals, objectives, and tactics under consideration consistent with the values of our targeted publics? If not, could effective alternative courses of action honor our targeted publics' values?

III. COMMUNICATION

- As we enact our plan, are our actions consistent with our organization's values?

- As we enact our plan, are our actions consistent with the values of our targeted publics? If not, could effective alternative courses of action honor our targeted publics' values?

IV. EVALUATION

- Are the methods of evaluation we propose consistent with our organization's values?

- Are the methods of evaluation we propose consistent with the values of our targeted publics? If not, could other effective methods of evaluation honor our targeted publics' values?

- Were all our actions in addressing this problem or opportunity consistent with our organization's values? If not, why not? Were inconsistencies avoidable?

- Did any of our actions in addressing this problem or opportunity violate the values of our targeted publics? If so, why? Was the violation avoidable?

3. Consider traditional ethics principles and approaches from relevant ethics codes and from this chapter's QuickBreak philosophers: Aristotle, Kant, Mill, and Rawls (Principles box). Do these principles suggest any new values?

4. Identify all the stakeholders. What obligations do you have to each? Who most deserves your loyalty? (Loyalties box). Do these loyalties suggest new principles and values that you haven't considered? Are there individuals or groups noted in the definition toward which you feel no loyalty? If so, why?

5. Select a course of action that embraces the most compelling values, principles, and loyalties. Examine it in the light of your definition. If it still seems to be the best choice, implement it. Again, this is not easy. But in each possible course of action, you can now see which values, principles, and loyalties you're honoring.

6. Evaluate the impact of your decision.

Values Statement 6.1

GOODWILL INDUSTRIES OF ORANGE COUNTY

Goodwill Industries of Orange County, California, helps people with disabilities find rewarding employment that benefits employers and employees alike. Founded in 1924, Goodwill Industries of Orange County is accredited by Goodwill Industries of America, Inc.

Mission

The mission of Goodwill Industries of Orange County is to provide people with disabilities the opportunity to achieve their highest levels of personal and economic independence.

Vision

We envision a world where all individuals with disabilities and other barriers to employment will have opportunities to enjoy the full benefits of competitive employment. Goodwill will focus on being the leader in providing quality education, training, and employment services. The core of Goodwill programs will empower individuals to be productive and independent, based on their abilities and interests.

Values

We believe in the inherent value of work; work has a greater value than charity.

We trust and respect the dignity and creative potential of every person.

We strive for superior quality in our programs and services.

—Goodwill Industries of Orange County web site

This six-step process won't automatically tell you what the most ethical course of action is. But it can help you dissect the situation so that you can examine the relevant values, principles, and loyalties to justify your decision to yourself and to others. The Potter Box can help you practice values-driven public relations.

The Potter Box at Work

Let's apply the Potter Box to Choose and Lose, the scenario that opens this chapter:

1. *Definition box:* Three days ago, the CEO of my company told the news media that a much-publicized environmental hazard in our company's production process had been eliminated. The person responsible for eliminating the hazard is one of my best friends. Right now, she really needs me because she's going through a rough time dealing with the death of her oldest child. Yesterday I learned that she hadn't eliminated the environmental hazard; it still exists. In her condition, she doesn't even realize that she hasn't corrected it. I'm afraid that telling her will damage our friendship, which is one of the few positive things in her life right now. But if our CEO discovers the oversight, he may fire her—which, I'm afraid, could deepen her depression to a dangerous level.

2. *Values box:*

A. Friendship

B. Duty to CEO and company

C. Duty to environment

D. Honesty with news media

3. *Principles box:* Using the philosophy of Immanuel Kant, you could turn each value into a possible categorical imperative (see QuickBreak 6.3):

A. Honor friendships. Never damage a friendship.

Ethics Helpline Poster   Mired in an ethics dilemma? If you're an employee of Sprint Corporation, help—or at least understanding—may be just a phone call away. (Courtesy of Sprint Corporation)

B. Support the integrity of the CEO and the company in all your actions. Do nothing to undermine the integrity of the CEO and the company.

C. Take every possible action to protect the environment. Do nothing that hurts the environment.

D. Be absolutely truthful with the news media. Never lie to them. Correct every factual error.

Now you ask whether other, standard ethical principles apply. Aristotle's golden mean (QuickBreak 6.2)? Mill's principle of the greatest good for the greatest number (QuickBreak 6.4)? John Rawls' demand for unbiased social justice for all, with special consideration for society's least powerful (QuickBreak 6.5)?

Mill and Rawls help you to realize that you've left out a key value: the health and welfare of people who may be affected by the uncorrected environmental hazard. You now add this as value E, and you add a corresponding principle to the Principles box.

Now you examine the ethics codes of public relations and your organization. Those codes, you decide, strongly emphasize honesty and CSR.

At this point, you may decide that the strongest principles are A, B, D, and E: support of your friend, your CEO/company, the news media, and people at risk from the environmental hazard, respectively. You can think of minor exceptions to C—such as damaging the environment slightly by building a new home. As you think more, you begin to wonder about A: Never damage a friendship. Don't you sometimes have to tell a true friend something she doesn't want to hear? Are some values more important than the very important value of friendship? You reluctantly begin to think yes, some are.

JEREMY BENTHAM, JOHN STUART MILL, AND UTILITARIANISM

The English philosophers Jeremy Bentham (1748–1832) and John Stuart Mill (1806–1873) helped develop the philosophy of utilitarianism. **Utilitarianism** holds that all our actions should be directed at producing the greatest good for the greatest number of people.

The obvious question here is What is the greatest good? According to utilitarianism, the greatest good is the action that produces the greatest happiness. "Actions are right in proportion as they tend to promote happiness, wrong as they tend to produce the reverse of happiness," writes Mill in *Utilitarianism*.[30] Bentham and Mill don't mean cheap, momentary, sensual happiness. They mean profound, lasting happiness, the kind produced by justice and love.

Utilitarianism asks us to consider courses of action that may not benefit us. "As between [a person's] own happiness and that of others," writes Mill, "utilitarianism requires him to be as strictly impartial as a disinterested and benevolent spectator."[31]

You might consider utilitarianism when you face a dilemma—that is, when you face an ethical problem in which every option has a downside. Utilitarianism would suggest that you select the solution that creates the greatest happiness—or perhaps the least unhappiness—for the greatest number of people.

How might you apply utilitarianism to the Choose and Lose scenario that opens this chapter? Simply put (though hard to do), you would examine which course of action creates the greatest good for the greatest number of people.

Regarding value E, you can think of companies whose processes create environmental hazards, but this doesn't excuse your company's processes because you've pledged to eliminate the hazard in question. You believe you must honor principle E, which might be phrased as *Do not initiate or continue manufacturing processes that injure the health and welfare of others.*

4. *Loyalties box:* Reviewing the situation, you determine that there are six primary stakeholders:

A. your friend;

B. the CEO and the company;

C. the environment;

D. the news media and their audiences;

E. people affected by the environmental hazard; and

F. yourself.

As you seek to determine the most ethical action in this situation, you begin to see that if you remain loyal only to your friend and say nothing, you're damaging the environment, hurting your company's important relationship with the news media, hurting those affected by the hazard, and perhaps hurting your future with the company. You realize that such damage will affect your organization's ability to reach its goals. Failure to reach those goals will affect your coworkers' ability to send children to college, to plan for retirement, to assist elderly parents, and other important concerns.

Utilitarianism's philosophy of the greatest good for the greatest number of people urges you to act out of loyalty to the environment and three large groups: your company, the news media, and people affected by the hazard. But you still wonder: Now that the choices and consequences are clearer, must you be disloyal to your friend?

5. *Decision and action:* You decide that the highest of the clashing values is honesty and that the most important stakeholders are the environment and the people affected by the hazard. Aristotle helps you realize that you can't always be loyal to friends, and Rawls influences you to consider who has the most to lose. You decide to tell the CEO, help correct the problem, and inform the news media. You approach an official in the company's human resources department with the following plan:

A. You will gently inform your friend of the problem and help her correct it.

B. The human resources official will inform the CEO of the death in your friend's family and the consequent depression your friend is experiencing. The official will inform the CEO that your friend needs to meet with him on an important matter—but the official will not reveal the failure to correct the environmental hazard. Your friend will do that.

QuickBreak 6.5

JOHN RAWLS AND SOCIAL JUSTICE

What do we owe to those less fortunate than we are? In decision-making processes, who speaks for the powerless who may be affected by the decisions? These questions concern advocates of social justice such as John Rawls.

In his book *A Theory of Justice*, Rawls urges decision makers to recognize and consider the values of all affected publics, not just those who have the power to influence decisions. Rawls recommends two particular techniques for an ethical decision-making process:[32]

1. Rawls suggests that before a decision is made, decision makers figuratively don a **veil of ignorance** that strips away their rank, power, and status. The veil of ignorance strategy asks decision makers to examine the situation objectively from all points of view. In particular, it asks them to imagine lifting the veil of ignorance only to discover that they are now a member of one of the affected publics instead of the decision maker.

2. Rawls suggests that to redress social injustice, the most disadvantaged publics in a situation should receive the most advantages—with the exception of freedom. Freedom, he says, is an advantage that must be shared equally. All other resources, however, should flow to those who have the least. Power should flow to the powerless, and wealth should flow to the poor.

Rawls' theory of social justice may sound extreme, but it shares some similarities with values-driven public relations. It asks us to identify, respect, and build relationships with the publics whose values come into contact with the values of our organizations.

C. Along with the official from the human resources department, you will accompany your friend to the CEO's office, and she will tell him of the omission and of her corrective actions.

D. You will help prepare a news release to be sent to all appropriate news media. In that release, the company will announce the error and state what it is doing to ensure that such temporary inaccuracies never happen again. Your strategy is to explain that the uncorrected problem was the result of an inadvertent human error and that steps are being taken to correct the possibility of a recurrence.

E. You will increase your efforts to support your friend and, with the official from human resources, will explore what company policies and programs are available to help her.

6. *Evaluation:* Most publics—including the news media—are impressed by honesty and will forgive unintended errors. But you'll still evaluate the reaction of important publics such as employees and journalists. You'll also evaluate your friend's progress in dealing with her grief. Your evaluation of this episode will also, no doubt, lead you to establish procedures to verify information before it is distributed throughout your company and to the news media.

Quick ✔ Check

1. What is CSR?
2. In the four stages of the public relations process, where should we consider values?
3. What is an ethics audit? What questions should we ask in the course of an ethics audit?
4. What ethical principle is the foundation of utilitarianism?
5. In order, what are the four quadrants of the Potter Box?
6. What is meant by the veil of ignorance? How can it assist ethical decision making?

Summary

No thinking person will ever say that living an ethical life is easy. But the rewards of ethical behavior are substantial. We can attain those rewards by constantly examining our ethics codes and how well our actions live up to our high standards. Sometimes our only reward is the satisfaction of knowing that we analyzed a tough situation and followed the most ethical course of action. Hardly a day goes by, on the other hand, that we read our morning paper without finding evidence of unethical behavior in the business world. The penalties for unethical behavior can be substantial, leading to lost profits and, often, lost jobs. And for public relations practitioners, unethical behavior can mean the loss of credibility, which is one of our most valuable possessions.

The ethics that affect public relations come from five general sources: international codes, societal codes, professional codes, organizational codes, and personal codes.

Practitioners must know these codes and should be familiar with ethical decision-making processes such as the Potter Box if they hope to tackle successfully traditional ethical challenges that arise from dilemmas, overwork, legal/ethical confusion, values of other cultures, short-term thinking, and virtual organizations. Practicing CSR and examining your organization's values, as well as those of important publics, at every stage of the public relations process can help you achieve ethical, values-driven behavior.

It's hard to write about ethics and not sound preachy. That's not our purpose in this chapter. But ethical behavior is indispensable in values-driven public relations. For our society, for our organizations, for our important publics, and for ourselves, we should strive for nothing less.

DISCUSSION QUESTIONS

1. Where do you stand in public relations' objectivity–advocacy ethics debate? Should practitioners always tell 100 percent of what they know? Or is selective truth telling acceptable? If so, when?
2. What organizations have news media recently featured for ethical behavior? For unethical behavior?
3. From what you know of Johnson & Johnson's Tylenol crisis, how might that company have applied the utilitarian philosophy? How might it have applied categorical imperatives? How might it have applied the Potter Box?
4. Are John Rawls' theories of social justice unrealistic for profit-making businesses? Why should for-profit businesses care about powerless, disadvantaged publics?
5. What companies are well known for CSR? Do their reputations affect your purchasing decisions?

Memo
from the
Field

Carol Cone; CEO; Cone, Inc.; Boston, Massachusetts

Carol Cone is nationally recognized for her work in the Cause Branding and strategic philanthropy arenas. As the CEO of Cone, Inc., she has embraced a steadfast commitment to building substantive and sustainable partnerships between companies and social issues for more than 20 years. Cone has pioneered new alliances for private/public partnerships to create signature programs for a host of *Fortune* 500 companies, including the Avon Breast Cancer Crusade, ConAgra Foods' Feeding Children Better Program, PNC Grow Up Great Program, the American Heart Association's Go Red for Women Program, Reebok's Human Rights Awards, Rockport's Fitness Walking Program, Gillette Women's Cancer Connection, and Polaroid's Project KidCare, among others. Overall, Cone's signature cause programs have raised

more than $500 million for various social causes. Today, Cone, Inc. is acknowl-
edged as the nation's leading Cause Branding consultancy. A magna cum laude
graduate of Brandeis University, Cone has been named one of the "50 Most Powerful Women in Public Relations" by *PR Week* magazine.

"What do you stand for?"

For over a decade, our Cone research has confirmed the powerful influence
of corporate social actions on American attitudes and behavior. "What do you
stand for?" is a resounding question asked of corporations by key stakeholders—
employees, consumers, communities, governmental officials, and shareholders. The
pressure on companies to answer this question has become more intense through a
confluence of business challenges. These include ongoing corporate scandals following Enron's demise; a hypersensitive post–September 11 climate in which employees and consumers constantly reevaluate their relationship with the companies
they work for and do business with; the need for true organizational and brand dif-
ferentiation that is long-lasting; and the power of the Internet to unveil corporate
operations. In this new reality of conducting business, companies must bring their
humanity, indeed their values, to life.

No matter what you call it—strategic philanthropy, corporate citizenship, community relations, corporate social responsibility, cause branding—companies today
are strategically approaching their relationship to society in a whole new way. This
is an extremely exciting time for public relations practitioners, as the elevation of this
practice to strategy brings the function directly into the center of the corporation and
into the "C" suite—the office of the chairman and chief executive officer.

Key findings from our ongoing research (the Cone Corporate Citizenship Study)
include:

- 78 percent of Americans say that companies have a responsibility to support social issues;

- 89 percent of Americans say that in light of the Enron collapse, it is more important than ever for companies to be socially responsible;

- 85 percent of Americans say that even during an economic downturn, it is important for companies to continue to support causes;

- 77 percent of Americans say a company's commitment to social issues is important when they decide where to work;

- 75 percent of Americans say a company's commitment to social issues is important when they decide which products and services to recommend to other
  people;

- 84 percent of Americans say a company's commitment to social issues is important when they decide which companies they want to see doing business in
  their community; and

- 66 percent of Americans say a company's commitment to social issues is important when they decide which stocks/mutual funds to invest in.

How a company brings its values to life depends on how it views its responsibility to society and how it sees this function as a means to deepen its relationships with stakeholders. Early adopters, McDonald's and The Home Depot, had CEOs who keenly understood the social contract—to take from a community, employee, or consumer meant that you also had to give back. From their mission statements, both companies developed operating policies to improve their communities in ways strategically aligned with their businesses: McDonald's provides a myriad of children's programs, from its Ronald McDonald houses to high school scholarships, while The Home Depot rebuilds local neighborhoods hit by disasters or communities in extreme need of physical rehabilitation. Both organizations' CEOs know these efforts tie them to their employees, communities, and customers in highly unique and powerful ways—ways that pay off in hiring and retaining the best employees, customer loyalty, community support, and increased sales.

While McDonald's and The Home Depot were early practitioners of corporate citizenship, today's companies practice a range of actions that fall along the spectrum of corporate social responsibility. These include a variety of strategic internal and external functions, from corporate governance to environmental responsibility, employee and community relations, cause branding, philanthropy, responsible product development, and sourcing.

While select leadership companies have established powerful brands rooted in their values, and many more have implemented corporate citizenship initiatives in the past few years, most are playing catch-up to keep pace with rapidly shifting business and stakeholder pressures. As a public relations practitioner, you can play a leadership role in guiding corporate management toward an understanding of the power of putting values in action, through words, but even more importantly, through credible and lasting deeds.

To do this, you will need a wide range of skills. First, gain a solid knowledge of the public relations profession through school, extensive reading, and internships. Next, gain on-the-job training in a variety of areas from communications (all communications, not just media relations) to community, from employee and investor relations to philanthropy—even spend some time in various business units learning about product development, distribution, marketing, and sales. Then broaden your capabilities beyond work by volunteering for nonprofits.

Concurrently, read, read, read, books and trade publications on business, corporate citizenship, and various social issues of interest to you. A few of my favorites include *Built to Last* by Jim Collins and Jerry Porras, *A New Brand World* by Scott Bedbury and Stephen Fenichel, and *Pour Your Heart into It: How Starbucks Built a Company One Cup at a Time* by Howard Schultz.

Next, get involved in an ongoing corporate citizenship initiative. To eventually earn the mantle of leading a corporate program, you will need to be part of a team executing one or many program elements.

What an exciting journey! Any practitioner who has led this charge has emerged a much more satisfied individual, having brought this critical new business practice into the center of the organization. Recognizing the power of values in action brings a new purpose to the corporation and to each individual the program touches, either internal or external.

Corporate citizenship could indeed become the new golden era for PR professionals, if it is embraced strategically and with deep commitment and honesty to help the CEO and the organization fulfill their mission to their stakeholders.

Case Study 6.1

Cappuccino with Values, Please: Starbucks Coffee Company

Every now and then, Starbucks Coffee Company probably makes a bad cup of coffee. And every now and then, like every organization, it makes a bad decision. What separates Starbucks from many other organizations, however, is its values-driven willingness to publicly evaluate its actions.

In the frenzied first hours after the September 11, 2001, terrorist attack on the World Trade Center, a Starbucks employee in New York City sold bottled water to a paramedic. Starbucks had meant to donate the water, but, in the chaos, a company employee made a mistake.

When Starbucks President Orin Smith learned of the error, he phoned the ambulance company to apologize and to reimburse the paramedic. He instructed his public relations team to issue a news release apologizing for the action. He then did his best to ensure that Starbucks employees were donating water, coffee, and other products to rescue workers and to the injured.[33]

Ironically, he was communicating with employees who could have chosen to stay home: After the terrorist attacks in New York and Washington, D.C., Starbucks temporarily closed its North American stores to allow employees to be with their families. But Starbucks stores in New York City chose to remain open, honoring one of the company's six "guiding principles": "Contribute positively to our communities and our environment."[34]

Starbucks' commitment to its values has helped place it on *Business Ethics* magazine's annual list of the "100 Best Corporate Citizens" every year since the list began in 2000—one of only 29 companies to claim that honor.[35] In 2003, *Fortune* magazine ranked Starbucks eighth in its list of "America's Most Admired Companies" and 34th in its list of the "100 Best Companies to Work for."[36] Since 1996, the company has won more than a dozen national and regional awards for ethical behavior.

"How does [Starbucks] inspire ethics in its employees?" asked one journalist? "By promoting its values. The company starts with a mission statement, which includes six guiding principles."[37] Starbucks mission statement reads as follows.

Starbucks Mission Statement and Guiding Principles: Establish Starbucks as the premier purveyor of the finest coffee in the world while maintaining our uncompromising principles as we grow.

The following six Guiding Principles will help us measure the appropriateness of our decisions:

- Provide a great work environment and treat each other with respect and dignity.
- Embrace diversity as an essential component in the way we do business.
- Apply the highest standards of excellence to the purchasing, roasting, and fresh delivery of our coffee.
- Develop enthusiastically satisfied customers all of the time.
- Contribute positively to our communities and our environment.
- Recognize that profitability is essential to our future success.

Starbucks' mission statement and principles almost guarantee conflict. Striving for profits, quality, and good citizenship can pull a company in at least three different directions. Such was the case in 2000 when protestors began demanding that Starbucks supply Fair Trade coffee. Fair Trade means that individual farmers in developing nations grow the beans and receive a fair price for them—a price higher than traditional market value.

In response, Starbucks began to seek Fair Trade beans that met its quality standards. Within four years, Starbucks was annually purchasing almost 7 million pounds of Fair Trade, organic, and shade-grown beans—the latter two categories being environmentally friendly procedures.[38] In 2004, Starbucks launched CAFÉ Practices—Coffee and Farmer Equity Practices—to support Fair Trade and environmentally conscious coffee bean farmers.[39] The corporation even has begun to feature Fair Trade coffee as its Coffee of the Week.

"Maintaining the trust of our stakeholders will never be taken for granted," wrote Starbucks Chairman Howard Schultz and President Orin Smith in the company's 2003 *Corporate Social Responsibility Annual Report.* "We know it's something to be earned every day and happens only if we uphold our core values."[40]

Starbucks' willingness to act its stated values earns admiration even from potential detractors. "Starbucks Fair Trade Coffee of the Week is a wonderful step towards strengthening the relationships among students, producers, and business," said Isaac Grody-Patinkin, a national organizer for United Students for Fair Trade.[41]

Not all Starbucks evaluators are as complimentary, however. When Starbucks increased its presence in Portland, Oregon, it drew a stinging rebuke from Portland's Independent Media Center web site: "The first day of this parasitic corporate invasion is also the first day of Starbucks Resistance," declared a message on the site. "We will stop at nothing but the complete withdrawal of this unjust corporation from our community." Vandals broke windows in Portland Starbucks stores and threw a firebomb at one.[42]

Aristotle wrote that true virtue lies in finding the point of ethical balance and harmony among extremes. Starbucks' values-driven willingness to seek a golden mean among its obligations to many publics—including employees, stockholders, customers, surrounding communities, and coffee bean farmers—provides an example of ethical public relations in a world that lacks easy answers.

DISCUSSION QUESTIONS

1. What is your opinion of Starbucks' mission statement and guiding principles?
2. After the terrorist bombing of the World Trade Center, the news media reported that Starbucks sold, instead of donated, water to a paramedic. How might Starbucks have responded? What is your opinion of Starbucks' actual response?
3. Starbucks presumably could have purchased Fair Trade beans earlier than it did. Does its failure to do so make it an unethical company?
4. What advice do you think John Rawls would have offered Starbucks as it considered its decision whether to buy Fair Trade beans?
5. What advice do you think Immanuel Kant would have offered Starbucks as it considered its decision whether to buy Fair Trade beans?

Case Study 6.2

Appearance of Obfuscation? Digene Corporation and European Women for HPV Testing

Cervical cancer kills. In Europe, it annually takes more than 12,000 lives.[43]

In recent years, Europeans have rallied to conquer the cancer second only to breast cancer in terms of occurrence.[44] They have demanded services for early identification of the disease. In 2001, the European Society for Infectious Diseases in Obstetrics and Gynecology called for improved testing.[45] Nine months later, the European Parliament announced that its insurance program would support screening tests for female members and employees.[46]

Instrumental in both victories was a Brussels-based organization called European Women for HPV Testing. HPV stands for human papilloma virus, which can be an early indicator of potential cervical cancer. Digene Corporation, the U.S.-based manufacturer of a leading test for HPV, acknowledged the support of European Women for HPV Testing in at least two news releases.[47] In one of those releases, Digene reported,

> Women's health advocates throughout Europe today launched European Women for HPV Testing, a campaign that seeks to ensure that all European women have access to HPV testing. The campaign is composed of over 100 high-profile women from the fields of politics, education, media, sports, the arts and entertainment from 11 countries across Europe.

Digene Chairman and CEO Evan Jones added, "The launch of European Women for HPV Testing reinforces the belief that women are interested in knowing if they harbor a cancer-causing virus."[48]

Only one thing prevents this story from being a solid example of a successful third-party endorsement: Digene and public relations agency Burson-Marsteller launched and paid for European Women for HPV Testing. The corporation failed to mention that fact in its early news releases, and critics charge that Digene and Burson-Marsteller disguised their connection to the grassroots lobbying group.

Claims of a "clandestine lobbying campaign" first surfaced in the *Observer,* a British newspaper. In 2004, the *Observer* fired off this headline: "Revealed: How Stars Were Hijacked to Boost Health Company's Profits; Famous Women Have Backed Up [a National Health Service] Screening Test Unaware They Were Being Set Up by a Biotech Corporation and Its PR Agency." In an article even longer than the headline, the *Observer* charged that "celebrities have been duped into supporting a sophisticated lobbying campaign secretly orchestrated from Brussels by one of the world's largest public relations firms."

The *Observer* further reported that an early letter from European Women for HPV Testing was signed by a woman who, the newspaper learned, was an employee in Burson-Marsteller's Brussels office.

In the article, representatives from Burson-Marsteller acknowledged their connection to European Women for HPV Testing. "This is not a cloak-and-dagger operation," said one. "We make sure everything is very transparent, and we clearly state that Digene funds the campaign." But the *Observer* noted a lack of such transparency in documents from Digene and European Women for HPV Testing. The newspaper also reported that celebrities it contacted, women who allegedly endorsed European Women for HPV Testing, "had never heard of the group—let alone . . . being members, as its Web site claims."[49]

In its "Member Code of Ethics 2000," the Public Relations Society of America directs members to "Reveal the sponsors for causes and interests represented." And under "examples of improper conduct," the PRSA Code includes this entry: "Front groups: A member implements a 'grass-roots' campaign or letter-writing campaigns to legislators on behalf of undisclosed interest groups."[50]

Digene Corporation's Mission Statement includes this sentence: "All of our actions are guided by our responsibility to act as good citizens in the global community."[51] Perhaps that declaration led to Digene's eventual decision to post this announcement on all news releases from European Women for HPV Testing as well as on the organization's web site: "European Women for HPV Testing is made possible by an unrestricted grant from Digene Corporation."[52]

As the dust of the controversy settled and Digene publicized its connection to European Women for HPV Testing, *PR Week* magazine wondered why the "duplicitous appearance" occurred in the first place: Why would Digene act as if it had "something to hide" when, it reality, it had developed a popular, life-saving medical procedure? "That's cause for celebration," wrote Paul Holmes, president of Holmes Group public relations agency, "so why even risk the appearance of obfuscation?"[53]

DISCUSSION QUESTIONS

1. If Digene was effectively promoting a test that can save lives, did it really do anything wrong by sponsoring European Women for HPV Testing?

2. Imagine that Digene had asked for your ideas on what advice the great philosophers—Aristotle, Kant, Mill, and Rawls—might have had regarding quiet sponsorship of European Women for HPV Testing. What do you think each would have advised?

3. Were Digene's actions in supporting European Women for HPV Testing consistent with its Mission Statement?

4. What is your personal reaction to the full story of European Women for HPV Testing? Do you agree with Paul Holmes?

5. Can you think of any instances in which a so-called front organization is ethically defensible?

Cyber Coach

Visit www.ablongman.com/guthmarsh3e for these study aids—and more:

- flashcards
- quizzes
- videos
- links to other sites
- real-world scenarios that let you be the public relations professional

KEY TERMS

categorical imperative, p. 179

civil disobedience, p. 177

corporate social responsibility (CSR), p. 180

cultural relativism, p. 177

ethical imperialism, p. 177

ethics, p. 170

ethics audit, p. 181

golden mean, p. 175

Potter Box, p. 183

utilitarianism, p. 187

transparency, p. 180

veil of ignorance, p. 188

virtual organizations, p. 178

NOTES

1. *New Standard Encyclopedia*, vol. 5 (Chicago: Standard Education Society, 1947).

2. Hugh N. Culbertson, Ni Chen, and Linzhi Shi, "Public Relations Ethics: Some Foundations," *Ohio Journalism Monographs*, no. 7 (January 2003): 2.

3. "Al-Jazeera Pledges 'Truth' in War Coverage" (Kitchener-Waterloo, Ontario), *Record*, 15 July 2004, online, LexisNexis.

4. Chick-fil-A, online, www.chick-fil-a.com.

5. L. M. Sixel, "Five Questions with Dan Cathy," *Houston Chronicle*, 25 June 2004, online, LexisNexis.

6. Ralph D. Barney and Jay Black, "Ethics and Professional Persuasive Communication," *Public Relations Review* 20, no. 3 (fall 1994): 189.

7. "Profile 2000: A Survey of the Profession," *Communication World*, June/July 2000, A10.

8. Confucius, *The Doctrine of the Mean,* online, http://classics.mit.edu/Confucius/doctmean.html.

9. Free Burma Coalition, online, www.freeburmacoalition.org.

10. Karlyn Barker, "98 Arrested in Capitol Hill AIDS Protest," *Washington Post,* 21 May 2004, online, LexisNexis.

11. Thomas Donaldson, "Values in Tension: Ethics Away from Home," *Harvard Business Review,* September–October 1996, online, LexisNexis.

12. Bodo Schlegelmilch, *Marketing Ethics: An International Perspective* (London: International Thomson Business Press, 1998), 11.

13. Shlegelmilch, 145.

14. "National Workplace Study Shows Employees Take Dim View of Current Leadership Ethics," news release issued by Walker Information, 1 September 2003, online, www.walkerinfo.com.

15. Shane McLaughlin, "A New Era for Communicating Values," *The Public Relations Strategist* (winter 2003): 10.

16. Thomas Donaldson, "Adding Corporate Ethics to the Bottom Line," *Financial Times,* 13 November 2000, online, LexisNexis.

17. Clay Chandler, "Ambivalent about Business," *Wall Street Journal,* 12 May 1996, B1.

18. Immanuel Kant, *Fundamental Principles of the Metaphysic of Morals,* in *Harvard Classics,* vol. 32 (New York: P. F. Collier and Son, 1910), 352.

19. Gene Laczniak and Patrick Murphy, *Marketing Ethics: Guidelines for Managers* (Lexington, Mass: Lexington Books, 1985).

20. PR Coalition, "Restoring Trust in Business: Models for Action," Arthur W. Page Society, 2003, online, www.awpagesociety.com.

21. "Johnson & Johnson Tops Reputation Rankings," *PR Week,* 8 March 2004, 8.

22. Mark Weiner, "Proving Your Worth," *Communication World,* April–May 2003, 26.

23. "Restoring Trust in Business: Models for Action."

24. Chris Atkins, "Restoring Trust in Business," *The Public Relations Strategist* (winter 2003): 11.

25. International Business Leaders Forum, online, www.csrforum.com.

26. "2002 Cone Corporate Citizenship Study," Cone, Inc., online, www.coneinc.com.

27. Harold Burson, "Social Responsibility or 'Telescopic Philanthropy': The Choice Is Ours," speech to the Columbia University Graduate School of Business, 20 March 1973.

28. For more information on integrating ethics into the public relations process, see Thomas Bivins, "A Systems Model for Ethical Decision Making in Public Relations," *Public Relations Review* (winter 1992): 365–384.

29. See Clifford Christians, Mark Fackler, Kim Rotzoll, and Kathy Brittain McKee, *Media Ethics: Cases and Moral Reasoning,* 5th ed. (New York: Longman, 1998).

30. John Stuart Mill, *Utilitarianism,* searchable text online, www.library.adelaide.edu/etext/m/m645u.

31. Mill, online.

32. John Rawls, *A Theory of Justice* (Cambridge, Mass.: Harvard University Press, 1971).

33. "Starbucks President and CEO Orin Smith Addresses Starbucks Customers," news release issued by Starbucks Coffee Company, 27 September 2001, online, www.starbucks.com.

34. Starbucks Coffee Company, online, www.starbucks.com.
35. "29 Firms Make 100 Best Corporate Citizens List Five Years in a Row," news release issued by *Business Ethics* magazine, 3 May 2004, online, LexisNexis.
36. "Starbucks Recognized as One of the Most Valued Global Brands," news release issued by Starbucks, 30 March 2004, online, LexisNexis.
37. Meredith Alexander, "Do You Need an Ethics Officer?" *The Industry Standard,* 10 July 2000, online, LexisNexis.
38. "Starbucks Validates Commitment to Transparency in New Corporate Social Responsibility Annual Report," news release issued by Starbucks, 7 April 2004, online, LexisNexis.
39. "Starbucks Recognized as One of the Most Valued Global Brands."
40. *Living Our Values: Corporate Social Responsibility Fiscal 2003 Annual Report,* Starbucks Coffee Company, online, www.starbucks.com.
41. "Fair Trade Certified Coffee Takes Center Stage as Starbucks' 'Coffee of the Week' May 3–9," news release issued by Starbucks Coffee Company, 29 April 2004, online, LexisNexis.
42. Joseph Rose and Stephen Beaven, "Firebomb Hits New Starbucks," *The Oregonian,* 6 May 2004, online, LexisNexis.
43. "Major European Medical Society Includes Broad Use of HPV Testing in Cervical Cancer Screening Guidelines," news release issued by Digene Corporation, 20 September 2001, online, www.digene.com.
44. Digene Corporation, online, www.digene.com.
45. "Major European Medical Society Includes Broad Use of HPV Testing in Cervical Cancer Screening Guidelines."
46. "European Parliament to Include HPV Testing in Its Cervical Cancer Screening Program," news release issued by Digene Corporation, 17 June 2002, online, www.digene.com.
47. "Major European Medical Society Includes Broad Use of HPV Testing in Cervical Cancer Screening Guidelines"; "European Parliament to Include HPV Testing in Its Cervical Cancer Screening Program."
48. "Major European Medical Society Includes Broad Use of HPV Testing in Cervical Cancer Screening Guidelines."
49. Antony Barnett, "Revealed: How Stars Were Hijacked to Boost Health Company's Profits; Famous Women Have Backed Up an NHS Screening Test Unaware They Were Being Set Up by a Biotech Corporation and Its PR Agency," *Observer,* 25 January 2004, online, LexisNexis.
50. Public Relations Society of America, online, www.prsa.org.
51. Digene, online, www.digene.com.
52. European Women for HPV Testing, online, www.womenforhpvtesting.org.
53. Paul Holmes, "Digene's Duplicitous Appearance Counteracts the Accolades Its Cervical Cancer Test Merits," *PR Week,* 2 February 2004, online, LexisNexis.

chapter seven

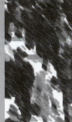

Research and Evaluation

objectives

After studying this chapter, you will be able to

■ describe the value of research and evaluation in the public relations process

■ recognize the differences between formal and informal research

■ develop a strategy for conducting research

■ explain the basics of conducting the five most common forms of public relations research

■ glean valuable information through effective analysis of survey results

City Hospital Faces Competition

scenario   *City Hospital has served the people of your community for more than 100 years. It is a public institution run by a board of directors appointed by the city council. The people have come to depend on its inpatient, outpatient, and emergency care facilities. For most of its existence, the hospital has had no direct competition.*

However, things have changed. Two years ago a nationwide health-care corporation opened a same-day surgical clinic in your community. City Hospital officials decided that the best strategy was to ignore the newcomer. "The people in our community know us," said the hospital administrator. "They don't want their health in the hands of strangers." Although City Hospital has remained the community's predominant health-care provider, the number of same-day surgical procedures performed has steadily declined. Some of City Hospital's best doctors, nurses, and medical technicians have been hired away by the competition.

The nationwide health-care corporation has now announced it will seek government permission to build a modern full-service hospital in the community. "Competition is a good thing," says the mayor. City Hospital's management doesn't see it that way. It fears a substantial loss of income that could force City Hospital either to close its doors or to merge with some other hospital—possibly even with the competition. That is why the board of directors has hired you as a public relations consultant.

What is the first thing you are going to do?

Did the Needle Move?

Public relations practitioners finally get it.

There once was a time when practitioners were comfortable in saying, "You can't really measure the good things we do." The rationale was that public relations contributes to an organization in ways that cannot be measured on an accountant's balance sheet. After all, how much are good relationships with key publics worth to a company? That argument often succeeded—at least until economic conditions soured. And then guess who were the first employees laid off? You've got it: the "you can't really measure the good things we do" practitioners.

However, as documented in Chapter 1, the profession's star is on the rise. There is newfound respect for the role public relations plays in marketing products and in managing reputations. But if you think that means the need to measure the effectiveness of public relations activities has waned, think again.

"Research continues to demonstrate that public relations is either not validated or the methodologies used are considered suspect," writes Michael Fairchild, a leading British practitioner. "Convergence with service industries, notably management consultancy, accountancy and law, means public relations will face growing competition from others who can stake a claim to advisory areas like communication and reputation."[1]

Just as it is with most things in life, the bigger public relations gets and greater its reputation grows, the more it has to prove itself.

Measuring Intangibles

Spurred by organizations such as the Institute for Public Relations (IPR), practitioners have increasingly focused on putting hard numbers into public relations evaluation.

QuickBreak 7.1

ROI AND AVE

What is the value of publicity, and how do you know that the public relations budget yielded a favorable financial **return on investment (ROI)**?

Organizations have struggled to demonstrate that their public relations efforts add to their bottom line. Some practitioner associations, such as the Institute for Public Relations, believe that ROI is not the best measure. A 2004 IPR survey showed that a majority of communications directors believe it is possible to show that public relations efforts can make more money for an organization than they cost. However, only one-third of those surveyed said they actually consider public relations budgets in ROI terms.[2]

Facing pressures to demonstrate public relations ROI, many practitioners have turned to **advertising value equivalency (AVE),** a calculation based on advertising rates and the amount of media coverage. For example, suppose a public relations agency distributed a news release that generated a story that took up 10 column-inches of space in the local newspaper. If the newspaper charges $100 per column inch, the math would be simple: 10 inches times $100 equals an AVE of $1,000.

Because of third-party endorsement, some note that publicity is more credible—and therefore more valuable—than advertising. They argue that there should be a multiplier in the AVE formula to account for publicity's added value. For example, the Texas Commission on the Arts advises its stakeholders that "a good rule of thumb is to mark up the advertising value by a factor of three for a general story."[3] Using this formula, the AVE of our news story would balloon to $3,000.

You may be asking yourself how this credibility multiplier was determined. That's the heart of the controversy. "The weightings for 'third-party' endorsement are totally made up," wrote Professor James Grunig.[4] The Institute for Public Relations Research has gone so far as to suggest that these "arbitrary weighting schemes" are "unethical, dishonest, and not supported by the research literature."[5]

The use of AVE raises other issues. Is a story in a local medium as important as one in a national medium? How do you quantify the value of a story that depicts your organization in a positive, negative, or neutral light? Did the readers, viewers, or listeners take a desired action as a result of the story? As a practitioner, can you ethically tell a journalist that your news release contains news—but then evaluate it using advertising rates?

Gary Getto, vice president of Surveillance Data, embraces AVE. He told one publication that the public relations industry runs the risk of throwing "the baby out with the bath water" by rejecting AVE. Citing research conducted by his and two other firms, Getto said, "We think this study helps to put to rest the claim that AVE is not as valid a tool as audience impressions and article counts."[6]

IPR cosponsored the Public Relations Evaluation Summit in New York in October 1996. Out of that meeting of leading professionals and academics came a series of guiding principles for public relations measurement and evaluation.[7]

In the past decade, interest in public relations research and evaluation has intensified. You need only look at IPR's web site, www.instituteforpr.com, to see the wealth of public relations research and evaluation literature generated since that summit. Among the most notable papers published on the subject was 1999's *Guidelines for Measuring Relationships in Public Relations* by Linda Childers Hon and James Grunig (see QuickBreak 7.3). It marked the first serious attempt to quantify the strength of the relationships an organization has with its key stakeholders.[8] Recently, much of this academic theory has been put to practical use. Edelman, the world's largest independent public relations agency, announced the development of what it calls the Relationship Index, based on the Hon-Grunig research, in April 2003. Edleman's Bob Kornecki said the new measurement tool will help clients "benchmark, monitor and manage stakeholder relations."[9]

As IPR's Commission on PR Measurement and Evaluation noted in a 2003 report, every practitioner must be prepared to answer this question: "Will those public relations and/or advertising efforts that we initiate actually have an effect—that is, 'move the needle' in the right direction—and, if so, how can we support and document that from a research perspective?"[10]

The Value of Research and Evaluation

The first step in the public relations process is research. The fourth, or last, step is evaluation. Nothing in public relations research could be more important than those two assumptions. Or more wrong.

Some are tempted to view these two steps as necessary "evils" that allow practitioners to get to the "really important" parts of the public relations process—planning (where strategy and tactics are developed) and communication (where plans are executed). Sometimes, we bypass research and evaluation out of a sense of presumed knowledge: We think we already know everything we need to know to act and that we will know whether we have been successful. Other popular excuses for bypassing the research and evaluation steps are lack of time, lack of personnel, lack of money, and lack of how-to knowledge. At face value, these may seem like logical excuses. But that's all they are: excuses. "Clients have difficulty swallowing $20,000–$50,000 on research when most PR budgets are around $100,000 a year," said Paul Owen, president of Seattle's Owen Media. "But $20,000–$50,000 is a drop in the bucket for a $10 million ad campaign."[11]

Research and evaluation are cornerstones of good public relations practice. They lead us to explore two areas essential to success in any public relations effort:

1. *What we think we know:* Do our assumptions hold up under closer examination? If nothing else, research and evaluation can remove lingering doubts by validating the accuracy of information.
2. *What we don't know:* Are pieces missing from the puzzle? By exploring terra incognita—unknown territory—we can open doors of opportunity that may otherwise remain closed.

Why not have separate chapters on research and evaluation? We link those parts of the public relations process in this chapter for two reasons. First, as we noted in

QuickBreak 7.2

ISSUES MANAGEMENT AND THE AIDS EPIDEMIC

An increasingly significant form of problem–opportunity research (see pp. 206, 208) is known as **issues management.** Instead of trying to determine the nature of the *present* environment, practitioners engage in issues management as a means of predicting and managing *future* issues and concerns. Issues management often begins with **scanning,** which is short for "scanning the horizon." In the days before satellites and radar, scanning the horizon was the only way to determine whether any potential threats were approaching. This is the concept behind issues management: Through a process of analyzing emerging trends and issues, practitioners can prepare their organizations to respond in a timely and appropriate manner.

For example, many organizations failed to take note of news reports in the late 1970s about a mysterious and fatal disease that claimed its victims by destroying their ability to ward off infections. Even when the disease, AIDS (Acquired Immune Deficiency Syndrome), was finally identified, many felt that its impact was limited to those persons identified as being most at risk. By the mid-1980s, the AIDS epidemic was at the center of a public policy debate in the United States. It had—and continues to have—a dramatic impact on a wide variety of social issues, ranging from health care to public education. Inevitably, the organizations quickest to identify AIDS as an emerging issue were the best prepared to address it.

The Florida Dental Association was one such organization. When it was reported that a Stuart, Florida, woman had died from an HIV infection passed to her during a routine procedure by her dentist, both patients and doctors reacted with alarm. Some state legislators proposed sweeping changes in the law, including mandatory AIDS testing of all health-care providers. Although the Florida Dental Association favored some changes in regulations, it was also concerned that a shadow had been cast upon the entire profession by one isolated incident.

To its credit, the association had already researched the AIDS epidemic. It knew that procedures were already in place to halt the spread of HIV. In news releases and letters to Florida public officials, the association reminded a nervous public that Florida's dentists were responsible professionals who always put the health and safety of their patients first. Through effective issues management, the association was able to defuse volatile public opinion and allow public policy to be made in a calm and reasoned environment.

Issues management involves both scanning and **monitoring.** Scanning, as we said before, means actively looking for issues that could eventually affect your organization. This requires a keen eye and an open mind. Scanning can involve everything from reading local and national newspapers to holding periodic meetings with traditional stakeholder groups. The goal is to scan for all issues and trends with potential for having an impact—whether positive or negative—on your organization. Once an issue is identified, active monitoring should begin. Keep track of the latest developments. When you have gathered sufficient information, your organization can develop a response that is consistent with its values. And this is where the *real* value of issues management is demonstrated: Issues management gives an organization time to act in a manner that allows it to dictate its own course rather than having its course dictated by events.

Chapter 1, public relations is a dynamic, nonlinear process. The traditional four-step process implies a straight-line approach: research, followed by planning, followed by communication, followed by evaluation. However, public relations does not work that way. The four steps are intertwined. Research and evaluation occur at every phase of the public relations process. It's not unusual for practitioners, in the midst of planning, to decide they need more information. Nor is it unusual for public relations professionals to adjust strategy in the midst of its execution based on either feedback or new information.

The second reason we combine the two steps here is that the processes of research and evaluation are closely related. Both involve using similar methods to gather information. It could be said that research is gathering information before the fact and evaluation is gathering information after the fact. That notion has an element of truth, but it's an oversimplification. Instead, we constantly gather information, evaluate it, and seek new information to test a developing hypothesis. Remember your first school dance? You probably picked a dance partner based on an ongoing process of research and evaluation. At first glance across a dimly lit gymnasium, you may have been interested in dancing with a particular person. However, on closer inspection, appearance and behavior may have changed your mind. You may then have sought new information on someone else. Several cycles of research and evaluation may have occurred before you took that big step and ventured onto the dance floor. Public relations is no different—although it is often less traumatic.

No one, certainly not the authors of this book, expects you to become an expert researcher based on the information you find in this chapter. Later in your career, it may be that you rarely do in-depth research—it may be someone else's job to do it for you. Nevertheless, it is important that you know enough to be a good consumer of research.

"As communicators, we need to learn how to measure," said Julie B. Chughtai, director, executive communication, DePaul University. "Unfortunately, I had to learn on the job. We should be teaching the next generation of communicators both the art and the science of what we do."[12]

And that's *exactly* what we are going to do.

Quick ✔ Check

1. Why has there been an increased emphasis on public relations research and evaluation during the past decade?
2. What are ROI and AVE?
3. What is issues management?

Developing a Research Strategy: What Do I Want to Know?

Getting started in almost any endeavor can be difficult. Research is no different. Before setting out on any journey, it is important to know the destination. A journey into research is no different. That is why the first step when you embark on a research project is to develop a **research strategy.** That involves asking yourself two important questions:

1. What do I want to know?
2. How will I gather that information?

By answering these questions, you develop a research strategy. Your research strategy, in turn, begins to lay the foundation for a successful public relations program. Let's take a closer look at how we might answer the first question.

What we need to know in public relations research falls into one of four categories: client research, stakeholder research, problem–opportunity research, and evaluation research. Quite often research findings can fit into more than one category. However, the information itself is far more important than how it is categorized.

Client Research

Client research focuses on the individual client, company, or other organization on whose behalf the practitioner is working. Efforts are geared toward discovering an organization's size; the nature of the products or services it offers; and its history, staffing requirements, markets and customers, budget, legal environment, reputation, and beliefs about the issue in question. It is also essential to understand a client organization's mission and consequent goals. As noted in Chapter 1, an organization's mission statement is based on the organization's core values. Goals are general statements indicating the direction the organization wants to take and are consistent with an organization's values and mission statement.

Stakeholder Research

Stakeholder research focuses on identifying the specific publics important to the success of the client. These various constituencies are known as stakeholders, for each has a different stake in how the organization responds to various issues. The people important to your organization are not a homogeneous mass. They are a wide range of constituencies, each having its own values, attitudes, concerns, needs, and predispositions. How these stakeholders relate to an organization can change from issue to issue. For example, a teachers' union may oppose proposed tax increases for new roads but favor higher taxes for educational programs. Also, people are often members of more than one stakeholder group. Building on the prior example, a member of the teachers' union may favor new road taxes if the funds are earmarked for the area in which that member lives. Stakeholder research helps you better target the message and the media for that message to the needs of each constituency.

Problem–Opportunity Research

Put in the simplest terms, **problem–opportunity research** is research designed to answer two critical questions: What is at issue, and what stake, if any, does our organization

MEASURING RELATIONSHIPS

We bet that you have heard at least one of your professors say something like this: "Your grade is not based on the amount of work you do. It is based on the quality of the work you submit." That's another way of saying that you will be judged by results.

Judging results is a very real-world approach to evaluating success. And it focuses on the most important—and difficult—aspect of evaluation: deciding what constitutes an appropriate measure of success.

For example, how does one measure the success of a news release? Sometimes we measure **outputs,** such as the number of news releases we send to the media. Other times, we measure **outcomes.** Although this could mean the amount of media coverage our news release generates, it is important to remember that we are using the news media as an intervening public. For that reason, a more meaningful measure would be the response of the primary public, the people we are trying to reach through the media. In this case, we may want to measure the number of people who called a toll-free number mentioned in the news release.

Both approaches have their limitations. At best, they measure our public relations activities and the consequent short-term changes in the public relations environment. They also tend to focus only on the target audience's response to a specific program or event. Missing is an understanding of the long-term effects a public relations program has on relationships with key publics.

To address this broader issue, the Institute for Public Relations, based at the University of Florida, established a panel of educators and professionals to search for more meaningful ways to measure the effectiveness of public relations. One of its reports, released in 1999, recommends a process through which practitioners measure the quality of important relationships.

Linda Childers Hon of the University of Florida and James E. Grunig of the University of Maryland wrote that the evaluation of long-term relationships rests on examining six key **components of relationships:**[13]

1. Control mutuality: the degree to which parties agree on who has the power to influence the actions of the other. In an ideal relationship, the parties share a degree of control.

2. Trust: the willingness of one party to open itself to the other. This depends on perceptions of each party's integrity, dependability, and competence.

3. Satisfaction: the degree to which the benefits of the relationship outweigh its costs.

4. Commitment: the extent to which each party feels the relationship is worth the time, cost, and effort.

5. Exchange relationship: the giving of benefits to one party in return for past benefits received or for the expectation of future benefits.

6. Communal relationship: the provision of benefits to each other out of concern and without expectation of anything in return.

Hon and Grunig believe that by administering a questionnaire that includes agree/disagree statements focusing on these six aspects of a relationship, practitioners will have a more meaningful measure of the effectiveness of public relations programs. Grunig has published a follow-up paper in which he said qualitative methods, such as in-depth interviews or focus groups, can sometimes provide more insight into the dynamics of a relationship.[14] In short, it is the difference between generating numbers or intimate detail.

Values Statement 7.1

INSTITUTE FOR PUBLIC RELATIONS

The Institute for Public Relations (IPR) was founded in 1956 as the Foundation for Public Relations Research and Education. Located at the University of Florida, IPR is dedicated to improving the professional practice of public relations around the world and encouraging academic and professional excellence in the field of public relations.

The Institute for Public Relations: Our Purpose

No real profession attains that status without a substantial body of codified professional knowledge, as well as educational systems to help create and disseminate that knowledge. This is as true of public relations as it is of medicine, law, accounting or teaching. There is science underlying the art, and it is the working knowledge of that science combined with creativity that marks the best professionals.

The Institute for Public Relations is focused on the science beneath the art of public relations. We exist to expand and document the intellectual foundations of public relations, and to make this knowledge available and useful to all practitioners, educators, researchers and client organizations.

—IPR web site

have in this issue? Problem–opportunity research develops background information on a particular topic or issue. It also identifies related trends that may have developed. Ultimately, problem–opportunity research answers a key question: Why is it necessary—or unnecessary—for our organization to act? Sometimes organizations are reactive, responding to events that could shape their destiny. Other times they are proactive, launching those destiny-shaping events. There are even times when doing nothing is the best course of action. Problem–opportunity research helps the organization decide whether and how to act.

Evaluation Research

Although evaluation is listed last among the four steps in the traditional public relations process, today's climate demands attention to **evaluation research**—procedures for determining the success of a public relations plan—from the very beginning. With practitioners facing greater demands for accountability, every public relations plan must achieve an impact that is measurable.

Research shows that evaluation is closely tied to public relations planning. More than half of practitioners questioned in a joint PRSA-IABC survey said they measure program performance against specified objectives. Nearly 9 out of 10 also said that their public relations objectives are tied to overall business objectives. The survey also showed that organizational executives understand that the value of public relations cannot be measured by merely looking at a profit–loss statement. Only 1 percent of those surveyed said the effectiveness of their communications program was measured by sales results.[15]

Evaluation research cannot be an afterthought; practitioners are expected to articulate at the outset of any campaign how success is defined. A clear understanding of the environment before and after the campaign must be achieved. It is not always possible to recreate the original conditions once a campaign has begun. For that reason, determining ways to evaluate success must always be among the first things good public relations research addresses.

Institute for Public Relations

Institute for Public Relations Through its web site (www.instituteforpr.com), the Institute for Public Relations provides both scholars and practitioners with the latest research on a wide range of topics important to the profession. (Courtesy of the Institute for Public Relations)

Quick ✔ Check

1. What are the six key components of relationships?
2. When developing a research strategy, what two questions should you ask yourself?
3. What are the four major categories of public relations research?

Developing a Research Strategy: How Will I Gather Information?

First we asked the initial question, "What do I want to know?" Having done that, our next major strategy decision has to do with the methods we will use to gather information. To a large degree, the answer to the question "How will I gather that information?" depends on the time and resources at our disposal. Those factors, in turn, determine whether the research we are planning to conduct will present a reasonably accurate picture of reality or just a snapshot of some smaller aspect of it.

Using the vocabulary of researchers, this is the essential difference between **formal research** and **informal research.** Formal (also known as quantitative or scientific) research presents an accurate picture. That is because it uses scientific methods designed to create a representative picture of reality. In public relations, formal research generally is used to create an accurate portrayal of a stakeholder group. On the other hand, informal (also known as nonquantitative or nonscientific) research describes some aspect of reality but doesn't necessarily develop an accurate picture of the larger reality as a whole. In public relations, informal research is very useful—but it should not lead us to conclusions about an entire stakeholder group.

Now, back to the question at hand: How will I gather the information I need? Public relations practitioners commonly employ five research methods, some of which are already familiar to you: secondary (library) research, feedback research, communication audits, focus groups, and survey research.

Secondary (Library) Research

Secondary research is probably a research method you know well. It utilizes materials generated by others—sometimes for purposes entirely different from your own. The alternative to secondary research is **primary research,** which is new research you generate from scratch. Sources used in secondary research include

■ *Published materials,* such as newspaper and magazine articles, library references, various directories, and trade association data. This also includes information available through online databases and services such as LexisNexis, Dow Jones News Service, and various sites on the web.

■ *Organizational records,* such as annual reports, statistics, financial reports, and other disclosures that organizations with publicly held stock are required by law to release. For example, check out the disclosure documents that have been filed with the Securities and Exchange Commission and are available online through the EDGAR search engine, at www.sec.gov.

■ *Public records generated by governments:* With few exceptions, government agencies in the United States are required to operate in the open. These agencies often generate a wealth of useful information, such as the U.S. Census and monthly reports on the nation's economy. Much of this information is available through federal and state depository libraries located in communities and on college campuses around the country. Now that the Internet has gone from being a private tool of researchers to an everyday information source for all, an increasing amount of this information is also available online. For example, check out the FedStats database, at www.fedstats.gov.

Secondary research is especially valuable in providing information you might never have the means to gather on your own.

Feedback Research

Feedback research enables an organization to receive tangible evidence—often unsolicited—of stakeholder groups' responses to its actions. This evidence can mani-

Bacon's Clipping Bureau Brochure Clipping services, such as Bacon's Clipping Bureau, can help organizations keep track of what is being said about them in the news media. (Courtesy of Bacon's Information, Inc., Chicago, Illinois)

fest itself in many forms, most commonly through letters and telephone calls to the organization. For example, every time the president of the United States speaks on television, White House operators keep a running tally of the number of calls expressing support for or disapproval of what was said. Proactive organizations monitor all media, including the Internet, to track what others say about them. Web monitoring products include eWatch, NetCurrents, CyberAlert, and CyberScan. Organizations also encourage feedback through a variety of tactics, including point-of-sale surveys and e-mail links on their web sites. Although feedback research is not a formal research method, it can give very strong indications of the public relations environment.

The Communication Audit

Communication audits are research procedures used to determine whether an organization's communications are consistent with its values-driven mission and goals. In completing a communication audit, we review an organization's communications and records, and we conduct interviews with key officials.

A communication audit could have saved Wal-Mart executives from having to explain to the Federal Election Commission why it distributed a company publication to 200,000 North Carolina residents featuring U.S. Senate candidate Elizabeth Dole on the cover just two weeks before that state's 2002 Republican primary. In an article titled "Elizabeth Dole would like you to read this article," the former American Red Cross president was promoting literacy. Dole wasn't even Wal-Mart's first choice for its annual literacy issue: Oprah Winfrey had declined.[16]

A communication audit should answer five questions:

1. What are the organization's stated goals in relation to its stakeholder groups?
2. What communication activities has the organization used to fulfill those goals?
3. Which communication activities are working well and are consistent with those goals?
4. Which communication activities are not working well toward the achievement of those goals?
5. Given the findings of this audit, what revisions in goals or communication activities are recommended?

THE COMMUNICATIONS GRID.   One illustrative method of conducting a communication audit is a **communications grid.** The various media used by an organization are listed on one axis. Stakeholders important to the organization are listed on the other. An X is placed everywhere a particular stakeholder is reached by a particular medium. This exercise graphically illustrates where efforts have been directed and which stakeholders may have been overlooked.

Figure 7.1 shows a simplified version of a communications grid using the City Hospital scenario that opened this chapter. Each mark on the grid represents communication between the hospital and a key stakeholding public. We know from the scenario that City Hospital officials are concerned about the threat of increased competition. Six of the hospital's many stakeholder publics are its employees, the city officials who appoint the hospital board, the news media, the patients, the doctors who practice at the hospital, and a local health advocacy group. For the purposes of this example, let's assume that the only channels the hospital uses for communication are a weekly newsletter, an annual report, advertising, media kits, e-mail, and the hospital's web site.

The grid illustrates that all publics represented here have access to the hospital's web site. But this is a passive form of communication—the only people who see the web site are those who seek it out. All these publics are exposed to the hospital's advertising. However, the advertising messages may not be well targeted to each of these audiences. Advertising also lacks the credibility that comes with independent third-party endorsement.

The grid also shows us that most of the hospital's communication channels are very selective and may be underutilized. For example, perhaps the hospital should use e-mail in communicating with the news media—reporters often prefer it. The hospi-

MEDIA USED BY CITY HOSPITAL

CITY HOSPITAL'S STAKEHOLDERS	weekly newsletter	annual report	broadcast and print ads	media kits	e-mail	Internet web site
employees	X		X		X	X
city officials		X	X			X
news media			X	X		X
patients			X			X
doctors		X	X			X
health advocates			X			X

FIGURE 7.1   City Hospital's Communication Channels

tal also may want to consider placing its media kits on its web site, making the kits available to reporters whenever they may be needed. If the hospital values keeping its workers informed about current issues affecting their jobs, it may want to share the annual report with employees.

The grid also shows a serious communication gap with two of the hospital's stakeholder publics. First, if one goal is to encourage doctors to refer their patients to City Hospital, sending them just an annual report is probably not enough. And second, the local health advocacy group—which may be very influential with some of the hospital's other stakeholders—is receiving no direct communication. Do you see other similar communication gaps in the grid?

In short, a communications grid is a good way to audit visually whether an organization is reaching all the publics important to its success. However, there is one significant drawback: A grid does not address the messages contained in the various media. Those can be determined only through an analysis of their content.

Focus Groups

Focus groups are an informal research method in which interviewers meet with groups of selected individuals to ascertain their opinions. Although focus group results should not be seen as representative of any particular public, they can indicate a public's knowledge, opinions, predispositions, and behavior.

Focus groups are a popular research method because, compared with survey research (that is, formal questionnaires), they are relatively inexpensive. They also have the advantage of giving the researcher immediate feedback. Focus groups are often

Focus groups are small, informal gatherings where the participants are encouraged to discuss their concerns, attitudes, and predispositions about the subject at hand. (Courtesy of Consumer Research Associates/Dallas, San Francisco)

used in advance of survey research. The interaction among focus group participants often raises issues that merit further study. Focus groups can even test the clarity and fairness of survey questions.

Focus group research was a key element in an award-winning public relations campaign developed by Hill & Knowlton for the Florida Hospital Association during 2004. The hospitals wanted state lawmakers to limit the amount of money awards in medical liability lawsuits. Insurance premiums for hospitals had doubled—and for doctors had quadrupled—in just two years. Researchers conducted focus groups among registered voters—people who could influence legislators. They found voters confused by the complexities of tort reform but willing to listen to targeted messages that explained the issue in meaningful terms. By the end of the campaign, newspaper polls showed that 74 percent of Floridians supported some limits. Over well-funded opposition from trial lawyers, the legislature voted to cap noneconomic damages for physicians and hospitals.[17]

HOW TO CONDUCT A FOCUS GROUP.   When preparing to conduct focus group research, we suggest you follow this 10-step process:

1. *Develop a list of general questions based on information needs.* The questions usually should be open ended, avoiding simple yes/no answers.

2. *Select as a moderator someone skilled in interviewing techniques.* The moderator must be strong enough to keep the discussion on track.

3. *Recruit 8 to 12 participants.* Because of the problem of no-shows (people who promise to participate in the focus group but fail to show up), it is necessary to invite a larger number than you need. You can dismiss any extras with a small reward. As to who should be invited to attend, decide on a selection strategy. From what kind of people do you want to hear opinions? Sometimes a screening questionnaire will narrow the field. Participants are often compensated (with money, a free meal, etc.) for their time. An important rule: Avoid inviting people who have sharply divergent points of view. You are interested in gathering information; you are not interested in conducting a debate. Too much clash can stifle participants who may speak up in a friendlier environment. Even if it means conducting additional focus groups, it is best to keep people with sharply different opinions separated.

4. *Record the session on audiotape or videotape (or both).* Make certain participants know that the session is being recorded. It may be necessary to reassure them that the tape provides a record of what was said and will not be used for any other purposes.

5. *Observe the session.* In addition to the moderator, others should watch the focus group. They should record their impressions in notes. They do not participate in the session. Some facilities allow these observers to watch the proceedings from behind two-way mirrors. In many cases, however, observers sit quietly along the wall of the room in which the session is being held.

6. *Limit the discussion to 60–90 minutes.* When the conversation starts repeating itself, that is a sign to wrap it up.

7. *Discuss opinions, problems, and needs—not solutions.* It is very likely that participants are not qualified to discuss solutions.

8. *Transcribe the tape of the session.* This makes it much easier to analyze participants' comments.

9. *Prepare a written report on the session.* Identify participants by name, age, occupation, hometown, and any other pertinent information. Where possible, use direct quotations.

10. *Remember that focus groups are informal research.* Opinions stated in a focus group do not necessarily represent everyone else's view. At best, they serve as indicators of public opinion. However, they can be considered even stronger indicators if multiple focus groups yield the same comments.

Although these are the recommended steps for conducting focus group research, we also realize that sometimes it is necessary to bend the rules. For example, time and distance may make it difficult to get everyone together in the same room at the same time. Under those circumstances, the use of teleconferencing technology may provide a viable alternative. How one gathers information isn't really the issue. What matters is whether the information gathered is useful and reliable.

Quick ✔ Check

1. What is secondary research?
2. What is the purpose of a communication audit?
3. What are some of the reasons a researcher may choose to conduct a focus group rather than a survey?

Survey Research

When you are unable to gather the information you need through secondary research or informal research methods, conducting a formal survey may be your best choice. Although **survey research** can be both expensive and time consuming, it can also be a highly accurate way to gauge public opinion. Through the use of specifically worded questionnaires and a carefully selected list of people, researchers are able to make judgments about a much larger population. In essence, surveys provide a snapshot of what people are thinking on a particular subject at a moment in time.

With the practice of public relations becoming more results driven and cost conscious than ever before, surveys are a very useful tool in targeting communications and measuring results. Through computer analysis, survey research makes it easier to select the right target, use the appropriate message, communicate through the most effective channels, and measure the results.

Of course, some surveys are better than others. When the local newspaper asks its readers to vote on a "question of the day," is that a valid survey? When the local television station conducts "person-on-the-street" interviews, do those interviews necessarily reflect the opinions of the larger community? The answer to both questions is no. But if you change the question and ask whether any useful information can be gleaned from those two approaches, the answer is yes.

The degree to which survey results can be seen as an accurate reflection of a larger population depends on two key factors: the composition of the people we are surveying and the structure of the survey instrument.

The Survey Sample

A sample is a portion of a public that we select for the purpose of making observations and drawing conclusions about the public as a whole. In other words, when

QuickBreak 7.4

THE FLORIDA FOLLIES

Although U.S. citizens will remember Election Night 2000 for a long time, many in the television industry would just as soon forget it.

All the major broadcast and cable networks initially projected at 7:50 P.M. (Eastern Time) that Vice President Al Gore had won the pivotal state of Florida. They recanted around 10 P.M., saying the race was too close to call. By midnight, it became apparent that whoever won Florida would become the next president of the United States. Armed with new numbers, the networks declared shortly after 2 A.M. that Texas Governor George W. Bush had won. However, a little more than one hour later, the networks pulled Florida back into the undecided column for a second time. There it would stay until the U.S. Supreme Court settled the dispute five weeks later.

NBC News anchor Tom Brokaw said, "Not only do we have egg on our face, we have the whole omelet." At CBS, Dan Rather was telling his viewers, "To err is human, but to really foul up requires a computer." CNN anchor Bernard Shaw looked around the studio in amazement and asked his colleagues, "Do you like your crow well done?"[18]

In hindsight, it is easy to see where the seeds of the debacle were planted. The five networks and the Associated Press had all relied on the same data. In a cost-cutting move, they created the Voter News Service (VNS) in 1990. The idea was simple: VNS would collect the raw data samples and project election winners. The system had worked well over the years, although it had resulted in at least two incorrect projections in races for the U.S. Senate.[19]

Unfortunately, an internal audit conducted after the election showed that VNS operated with bad data. The number of absentee ballots was twice as high as had been anticipated. Sampling errors in 45 precincts inflated Gore's numbers. VNS also used a flawed model, basing its projections on Florida's 1998 gubernatorial election instead of the 1996 presidential election. By basing its projections on flawed exit poll data rather than on real numbers, VNS inflated Gore's lead by 16 percentage points.[20]

The journalists who lived through the embarrassment of the Florida Follies can take comfort in the fact that they were not the first to blow the big story based on faulty survey data. A *Literary Digest* survey predicted in 1936 that Kansas Governor Alf Landon would beat incumbent President Franklin D. Roosevelt by a margin of 57 to 43 percent. Roosevelt won reelection in a landslide. Twelve years later, an even more memorable blunder occurred. Most of the nation's pollsters boldly predicted that New York Governor Thomas E. Dewey would easily defeat President Harry Truman in the 1948 election. However, Truman won by more than 2 million votes. Out-of-date samples were to blame in both survey disasters. The pollsters failed to take into account major shifts in the makeup of the population.

The lesson of these and other Novembers is that a survey is only as good as the sample on which it is based. Just ask the networks.

we question members of a large stakeholder group, we generally don't question every member. Instead, we question a portion, or sample, of that public. A sample is said to be a **representative sample** of a targeted population when it is of sufficient size and when every member of the targeted population has an equal chance of being selected for the sample. Although surveying a representative sample provides a more accurate picture, it is not always practical because of time, cost, and personnel considerations.

For example, which would give you a better picture of U.S. public opinion regarding gun control: an informal poll of your classmates or a formal nationwide survey? Clearly, the latter would provide the more accurate picture. However, the informal poll would at least have its advantages in terms of time, money, and effort. And informal results aren't necessarily worthless. To the contrary, they provide an indication of what public attitudes may be—within the limitations of the sample. In this case, those limitations are the size of your sample and the fact that not everyone in the nation has an equal opportunity of being chosen for questioning. You would not be able to say that your classroom poll was an accurate reflection of national opinion. However, if everyone in your class had the same opportunity to express his or her opinion, those results would be representative of the class' views on gun control.

How big should the sample be? No one answer is correct. Nor does a simple explanation exist. At issue here are what statisticians call **confidence levels,** the statistical degree to which we can reasonably assume the outcome is an accurate reflection of the entire population. As a general rule, the larger the sample, the more accurate the outcome is. However, we do come to a point where additional numbers do not significantly improve accuracy. Statistical accuracy within two or three percentage points is usually the best one can hope for.

DEVELOPING A SAMPLING STRATEGY.   Developing a sampling strategy is a step critical to the administration of an accurate survey. Sampling can be as much an act of creativity as writing the survey instrument itself. However, as mentioned earlier, it is not always possible or practical to administer a formal survey. Issues such as cost, time, and staffing often come into play. Before we discuss some of the more common sampling strategies, a few definitions are in order:

- **Sample:** the segment of a population or public a researcher studies to draw conclusions about the public as a whole.
- **Sampling frame:** the actual list from which the sample, or some stage of the sample, is drawn. The sampling frame is important because the accuracy of your list will affect the accuracy of the survey. For example, using the local telephone book as a sampling frame may underrepresent the attitudes of either the very rich or the very poor. Survey results should always be reported in the context of the limitations of their sampling frame.
- **Units of analysis:** what or whom you are studying to create a summary description of all such units. It is important to be clear about units of analysis because you don't want to make a common error in analyzing results—comparing apples to oranges. The results of a survey of attitudes of students in your classroom should not be used to describe the attitudes of all students because the units of analysis in your sample were students in your classroom, not all students. The views of students in your classroom may not be representative of those of all students.

- **Probability sampling:** the process of selecting a sample that is representative of the population or public being studied. The sample is considered to be representative when it is large enough and when all members of that population or public have an equal chance of being selected for the sample. Usually within a few percentage points, known as the sampling error, the results of a survey of a representative sample are considered an accurate reflection of the sampling frame.

- **Nonprobability sampling:** the process of selecting a sizable sample without regard to whether everyone in the public has an equal chance of being selected. This sampling technique is often chosen because of time, cost, or personnel considerations. This does not mean that the results are without value. To the contrary, nonprobability sampling results can give researchers an indication of public opinion. However, those results cannot be said to be an accurate reflection of the attitudes of any particular public.

It is important for you to understand these concepts because they are central to your selection of a sampling strategy. The challenge of survey research is to use a sampling technique that serves two masters: a desire for accuracy and a need to achieve it in a logistically realistic and cost-effective manner. Using some techniques, it is possible to be both accurate *and* cost effective.

NONPROBABILITY SAMPLING.   In the real world of public relations, practitioners are often challenged to conduct survey research with little time, money, or staffing at their disposal. This often leads to using a form of nonprobability sampling known as **convenience sampling**—the administration of an informal survey based on the availability of subjects. As the name suggests, this approach has the advantage of being easy to do. However, it also sacrifices accuracy.

The so-called person-on-the-street interviews seen in newspapers and on television are examples of convenience sampling. Reporters often ask a "question of the day" to passersby in an attempt to gauge the mood of their community on a particular topic. But instead of getting an accurate picture of community attitudes, these reporters are only measuring the opinions of the people who happen to be walking by that spot at that time. A reporter standing on an inner-city sidewalk may get answers to questions about the state of the economy that differ greatly from answers obtained in a suburban shopping mall. Even the time of day can make a difference.

Does this mean that data obtained from an informal survey are useless? No, it doesn't. Data obtained from such a survey can provide an *indication* of public opinion. The more indicators you have pointing in the same direction, the greater the chance that your data are accurate.

In the same breath, however, we'd like to repeat that all informal surveys should be taken with a grain of salt. In and of itself, an informal survey should not be considered an accurate picture of reality. At best, it is just one interpretation of the world, an interpretation that may or may not be correct.

PROBABILITY SAMPLING. When planning to conduct formal probability sampling, you have a choice of several techniques. All of them have one important element in common: *Every person within the sampling frame has an equal chance of being selected for the sample.* In other words, surveys based on these sampling techniques have a high probability of being an accurate reflection of public opinion. These are some of the most common probability sampling strategies used by public relations practitioners:

■ **Simple random sampling** (Figure 7.2) is the most basic form of probability sampling. But often it is not practical. Simple random sampling involves assigning a number to every person within the sampling frame. By making a random selection of numbers, as in drawing numbers out of a hat, you develop a representative sample. However, think how tedious it would be to assign a number to every name in the local telephone book. Because simple random sampling can be a cumbersome process, especially with large sampling frames, this technique is seldom used in practice.

■ **Systematic sampling** (Figure 7.3) is a more practical approach to probability sampling. Through a standardized selection process, it is possible to create a sample that is both representative and easy to develop. At its most basic level, systematic sampling involves the selection of every Kth member of a sampling frame. For example, let us assume that your college or university has 25,000 students. The sampling frame for your survey is a computer printout of enrolled students. If you are seeking a sample of 250 names from a sampling frame of 25,000, then K = 25,000/250, or 100. In this scenario, you would select every 100th name from the enrollment printout for the

FIGURE 7.2   Simple Random Sampling
In this example, every individual is assigned a number—in this case, a number from 1 to 100. To achieve a sample of 20 individuals, 20 numbers are selected at random.

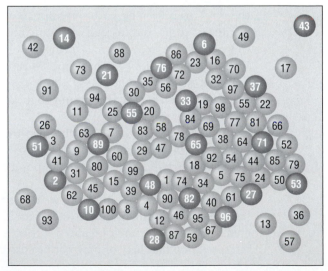

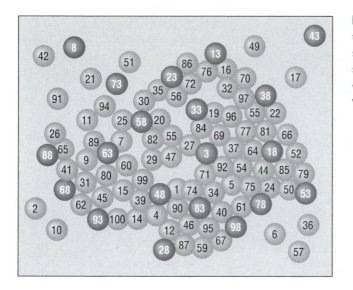

FIGURE 7.3   Systematic Sampling In this example, we want to achieve a sample size of 20. There are 100 individuals in the sampling frame. The value of K is 100/20, or 5. Therefore, we pick every fifth individual for our sample.

sample. Compare this with the work involved in simple random sampling, and it is easy to see why many researchers choose to go this route.

■ It is often hard to identify a perfect sampling frame. Although a city telephone directory gives you the names of most city residents, it excludes those who do not have a telephone, who tend to be poor, and those with unlisted numbers, who tend to have higher incomes. In this case, the extremely rich and extremely poor may be underrepresented. One way to overcome a flaw in a sampling frame is by using what is known as **cluster sampling** (Figure 7.4). This technique involves breaking the population into homogeneous clusters and then selecting the sample from individual clusters. For example, pretend that your sampling frame is students enrolled in public relations courses. If your school is typical of the national trend, there is a strong probability that women will easily outnumber men. To achieve a sample that is half men and half women, you group the students' names into different gender pools and select an equal number of names from each pool. Cluster sampling is generally not as accurate as simple random sampling or systematic sampling. Under certain conditions, however, it can be the most practical.

■ One way to ensure that a sample is an accurate reflection of a specific population is to survey *everyone*. That is what is known as taking a **census** (Figure 7.5)—that is, surveying every member of the sampling frame. A well-known census is the decennial U.S. Census, in which an attempt is made to count and analyze every person living in the United States. Although a properly done census has the advantage of accuracy, this technique comes up short when it comes to practicality. It may be easy to administer a questionnaire to everyone in your class, but how easy would it be for you to survey everyone in your college or university?

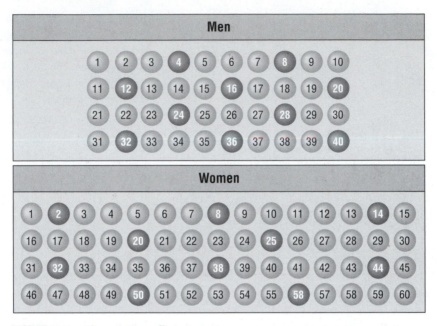

FIGURE 7.4   Cluster Sampling In an attempt to correct an imbalance in the sampling frame, individuals with similar characteristics are clustered. In this example, systematic sampling is used within each cluster to develop a sample containing 10 from each group.

FIGURE 7.5   Census In a census, everyone in the sampling frame is selected.

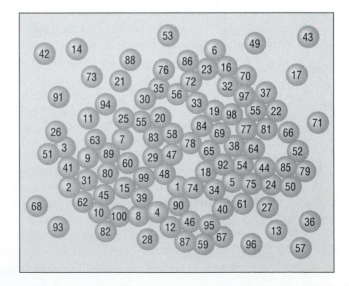

Quick ✓ Check

1. What two elements are critical to the administration of an accurate survey?
2. How does a sample differ from a sampling frame?
3. What is the major difference between probability and nonprobability sampling?

The Survey Instrument

Creating a good survey instrument is just as important as having a good survey sample. Even if you identify a sample that is representative of the population you want to study, a faulty questionnaire can render your results meaningless. It is not just *whom* you ask the questions, but also *how* you ask them that matters.

There are many considerations you need to keep in mind when developing survey questions. The questionnaire should use language that is appropriate for and readily understood by the public for whom the survey is intended. Researchers wouldn't ask elementary school students, homeowners, and nuclear scientists the same questions about nuclear power. Each group has a different level of understanding of the issue; therefore, the questions need to be tailored to the knowledge level of each group. In certain situations it may be necessary to provide background information before asking a question.

Questions asked on surveys cannot be vague if they are to have any real meaning. Questions have to be explicit, not indirect. Ask exactly what you want to know. If respondents are guessing at what a question means, their answers cannot serve as an accurate measure of anything (except, of course, of someone's inability to write clear questions).

Use words that have clear and specific meanings. For example, let's consider a question about presidential job performance. Suppose respondents are given the choice of answering the question using these options: gnarly, groovy, super, cool, and awesome. Can these survey results have any real meaning? The problem is that what may be gnarly to one person could be groovy to another. For the survey results to have real meaning, the words used in the survey must have precise definitions. A good survey instrument also keeps the questionnaire reasonably short. The longer the survey, the more likely that people will decline to participate because they "don't have the time."

Avoid bias in the wording or ordering of questions. The manner in which a question is worded can influence the response. Even the placement of the question can influence responses to questions that follow. For example, suppose you are answering a survey that poses a series of questions about high taxes, then asks, "What is the most important issue facing government today?" Because of the earlier questions, you may be primed to answer, "High taxes, of course!"

Don't ask objectionable questions. Even the most sensitive information can be obtained if questions are worded tactfully. Also, save the toughest questions for last.

QuickBreak 7.5

FIVE WAYS TO ASK QUESTIONS

1. **Contingency questions:** Whether a respondent is expected to answer a specific question is often contingent upon the answer to an earlier question. For example, if a respondent indicates that he or she doesn't like ice cream, it would make no sense to ask that person in the next question to identify his or her favorite flavor of ice cream. Therefore, the second question is a contingency question. Respondents who answer yes about liking ice cream will answer the next question. Those who answer no will be instructed to skip it.

2. **Dichotomous questions:** These are either/or questions such as true/false, yes/no, and positive/negative. They are sometimes used to set up contingency questions. In the previously cited example, a no answer would make it unnecessary for the respondent to answer the next question about favorite flavor. The respondent would be instructed to skip that question.

3. **Rating scale questions:** These questions measure the range, degree, or intensity of attitudes, something a dichotomous question cannot do. An example of a rating scale question is one that news and polling organizations often ask about the president's job performance. Respondents are asked to respond to the statement "I think the presi-

dent is doing a good job." Their options are to strongly agree with the statement, agree, disagree, strongly disagree, or express no opinion. These kinds of questions can give researchers a more detailed read on public opinion than dichotomous questions can provide.

4. **Open-ended questions:** These questions don't define a range of possible answers (called a response set). In other words, the respondent is left to fill in the blank. Answers to these questions can provide detailed information. However, they are the most difficult to analyze because they can't be tabulated as quickly as answers to questions in which the response set is specifically defined.

5. **Closed-ended questions:** These are questions in which the response set is specifically defined. To put it another way, respondents are required to select their answer from a predetermined menu of options. The risk with these questions is that researchers may leave out certain options or may overemphasize other options. Another problem to watch for is answers that overlap slightly. However, these questions are significantly easier to analyze than open-ended questions.

Asking the toughest questions first could abruptly end the process or bias subsequent responses. Demographic questions regarding matters such as age, income, and political affiliation can also be sensitive. Often, researchers place demographic questions at the end of the questionnaire in the belief that members of the sample won't skip them because they've already invested time in filling out the rest of the survey.

A way to avoid problems is to pretest the questionnaire. If the survey instrument has any bugs, it is best to find them before distributing surveys on a large scale. Run a small test first to make sure that the questions are understandable, all biases corrected, and objectionable questions removed.

When it comes time to administer the survey, logistics must be considered as well. Can the personnel requirements be met? Can the survey be administered within the desired time frame? Does the survey plan fit into the budget? The people who administer the survey, the data collectors, must be trained. Will they use the telephone, or meet with members of the sample face to face? Or, as is common, will you simply mail out the survey and dispense with data collectors?

Analyzing Survey Results

Once all the data are collected, the time has come to analyze and report the results. This is a public relations text, not a statistics text, so any attempt at this point to offer a detailed explanation of statistical analysis would not do the subject justice. However, we do not want to ignore the subject entirely. Raw data without structure or purpose are meaningless. Analysis gives data context so that their meaning can be understood.

The truth is that the overwhelming majority of public relations practitioners never conduct survey research. Instead, they pay someone else to do it for them. That's OK. But how do you know whether the research you are buying is good? That's why this discussion of sampling and questionnaire development is important. If you plan to make a career in public relations, you need to be a good consumer of this and all kinds of research.

For the purposes of this discussion, let's start with two basic definitions:

1. **Attributes:** characteristics or qualities that describe an object. In the case of an individual, attributes can be gender, age, weight, height, political affiliation, church affiliation, and so on.
2. **Variables:** a logical grouping of qualities that describe a particular attribute. Variables must be exhaustive (incorporating all possible qualities) and mutually exclusive. For example, the variables associated with the attribute of gender are female and male.

The purpose of analysis is to get a clearer picture from the data. The deeper the analysis, the clearer the picture. The most basic form of analysis is **univariate analysis.** As the name suggests, it is the examination of only one variable. An example of a univariate analysis would be the examination of responses to the question Do you like ice cream? By counting the responses to that question, we would know the total number of people who said yes and the total number who said no. But that is all that we would know.

If we were to examine the same question using two variables, however, the results would become more meaningful. This is what is known as **bivariate analysis.** A bivariate analysis of the question Do you like ice cream? could look at two variables: whether respondents like ice cream and the respondents' gender. We might find that men answer the question differently from women. That, in turn, could affect a variety of marketing decisions.

If we turn to **multivariate analysis,** the examination of three or more variables, our survey results would have even greater depth. Carrying our example to its logical conclusion, let's add the variable of age to our analysis of the ice cream question. Such an analysis could find that younger men and older women like ice cream more than their counterparts in other age groups. If our goal is to promote the sale of ice cream, these results suggest that we need to work harder to attract younger women and older men to the frozen delight. That information is far more valuable to us than only knowing the raw numbers.

Again, we acknowledge that this is an elementary approach to a very complex subject. If you are interested in numbers-crunching, more power to you. Take some research and statistics courses. However, if you don't see yourself in that role, please remember that this information is offered as a reminder that survey analysis is conducted on many levels and can yield a lot of valuable information.

Back to City Hospital

Let's close by returning to the City Hospital scenario that opened this chapter. What would be your first steps in addressing the public relations problems and opportunities before you? We hope you'd begin determining your research strategy by asking those two all-important questions:

1. What do I want to know?
2. How will I gather that information?

You'd soon decide, perhaps, that you want to know what the values of the hospital are as articulated in its mission statement. You'd want to know who the key stakeholder groups are and what they think of both City Hospital and its new competition. You'd also want to learn as much as you could about City Hospital. And you'd want to learn as much as possible about the hospital's new competition. Finally, you'd want to learn what the desired outcome of this situation is—so you can measure your ultimate success.

Where will you find the answers to those questions? Both primary and secondary research would be useful in this scenario. You'd start with secondary research—but, if resources allow, you'd certainly do primary research as well. An initial survey of the opinions of important stakeholder groups seems appropriate. And how might you use focus groups?

After your public relations plan has been executed, you may want to survey the important stakeholder groups again to see whether you have changed any opinions or strengthened any relationships. And that suggestion brings us full circle in this chapter. With that second survey, you'd be using research to conduct evaluation—and that evaluation may well prompt new research that launches a new public relations campaign on a newly discovered issue. As we noted earlier, research and evaluation are intertwined in values-driven public relations.

Quick ✔ Check

1. When writing a survey questionnaire, what should you consider in wording questions?
2. What are some of the logistical considerations you should take into account before administering a survey?
3. What are the differences among a univariate analysis, a bivariate analysis, and a multivariate analysis? Why would you want to do any of them?

Summary

As organizations become more results-oriented, public relations practitioners are increasingly expected to defend their decisions and measure the effectiveness of the actions they propose. That is why research is critical to the practice of public relations. Research enables a practitioner to understand a client, the problems/opportunities facing the client, and the stakeholders important to the client's success. Evaluation research enables a practitioner to determine the success of communication strategies and the strength of relationships.

Not all research is created equal. Formal research has the advantage of providing a more accurate picture of reality. However, conducting informal research may be necessary because of time, cost, or staffing considerations. Although not as accurate a reflection of reality, informal research results still can help you piece together a picture of the world. Before embarking on research, it is important to have a clear understanding of what kinds of information you are seeking and what is the best way for you to gather it. That is known as developing your research strategy.

The five most common forms of public relations research are secondary (library) research, feedback research, communication audits, focus groups, and surveys. Secondary research is making use of material generated by someone else, sometimes for a purpose other than that for which it was originally intended. Feedback research involves analyzing both solicited and unsolicited communications an organization receives from its stakeholders. Communication audits indicate whether an organization's communications are consistent with its values-driven mission and goals. Focus groups are an informal research method in which a small group of people are brought together to discuss their values, concerns, needs, attitudes, and predispositions. The successful use of survey research depends on both a good sample and a good survey instrument or questionnaire. The value of survey research is that, when properly conducted and analyzed, it provides a reasonably accurate snapshot of reality. That, in turn, provides a solid foundation for a public relations plan.

DISCUSSION QUESTIONS

1. How might evaluation research be used to launch a new public relations campaign?
2. Which research should you ordinarily conduct first: primary research or secondary research? Why?

3. How is issues management a part of problem–opportunity research?

4. Why aren't focus groups necessarily representative of a larger public?

5. What is the difference between probability sampling and nonprobability sampling? What is the advantage of probability sampling? Is nonprobability sampling without value?

6. Using the City Hospital scenario at the beginning of this chapter, what research technique(s) would you use to discover the attitudes and opinions of one of the key stakeholders? Which stakeholder would you select and why? What kinds of information would you seek?

Memo *from the* Field

Dr. Leslie Gaines-Ross, Chief Knowledge and Research Officer (U.S.), Burson-Marsteller, New York, New York

In her role as chief knowledge and research officer, Dr. Leslie Gaines-Ross leads Burson-Marsteller's thought leadership and research capability. Gaines-Ross is one of the world's most widely recognized experts on how CEO reputations are built, maintained, enhanced, and defended. Gaines-Ross is the architect of CEOgo.com, a web site devoted exclusively to CEO news and information. Her book, *CEO Capital: A Guide to Building CEO Reputation and Success,* was published in January 2003 by John Wiley & Sons.

Few public relations firms have as sterling a reputation for research as Burson-Marsteller. Established in 1952 by Harold Burson, a legend in his own time and a recognized "founding father" of modern public relations, the firm is one of the world's leading public relations and public affairs firms.

I had often noticed Burson-Marsteller's research while heading *Fortune*'s Marketing, Communications, and Research Department. Burson-Marsteller distinguished itself from other public relations firms by acknowledging the central role research and informed opinion play in successful client solutions. Ironically, Burson-Marsteller contacted me in 1996 to expand its research department. The firm's commitment to continuing research excellence could not have been more timely. Looking back over the past eight years of creating research for Burson-Marsteller and its clients, I would have to say that two areas that deserve special distinction are CEO/corporate reputation management and online influence.

CEO/Corporate Reputation Management

The demands on public relations firms were beginning to change when I joined Burson-Marsteller as chief knowledge and research officer. With the approaching millennium came a new need to reassess the corporate environment. Companies were clearly recognizing that their stakeholders were becoming more numerous and diverse. With the rise of the Internet came a deeper interest in corporate affairs. A company's constituencies were expanding beyond traditional groups such as Wall Street, the media, and government regulators to encompass organizations such as Greenpeace and the Sierra Club. Technology empowered newly powerful stakeholders to voice their opinions and demand access to top management. News was instantaneously communicated around the world through the proliferation of cable stations and new media. Every nook and cranny of a company's affairs were now wide open to critique and scrutiny.

As the business world changed, so did research. While mass audiences remained a survey's target audience, many smaller and previously neglected audiences suddenly rose to new levels of importance. Companies wanted to understand not only the perceptions of Wall Street and the media but also those of employees, company alumni, customers, regulators, web activists, management gurus, and individual investors. As an investor class quickly grew (nearly six out of 10 households own stock), the public became more interested in corporate performance and strong leadership. Within no time, business became everyone's business.

In response to the fragmentation of the audiences just noted, Burson-Marsteller's 1997 reputation research survey was the first to include a wide range of influential business audiences—CEOs, top executives, financial analysts, the media, and government officials. We mailed surveys to these hard-to-reach business influentials—who are rarely reachable by telephone—to ensure that our findings were valid and could withstand media scrutiny. Over the years we added nongovernmental organizations (NGOs), consumers, and executive recruiters to our stakeholder groups.

In Burson-Marsteller's first survey, we found that CEO reputation was inextricably linked to company reputation. The average estimated contribution of the CEO to a company's reputation stood at 40 percent in 1997. In 2003, this figure jumped to 50 percent. The tremendous importance attached to CEO reputation reaches far and wide, and its value has been proven in countries and across continents. Even among consumers, a segment often considered less informed about business matters, the CEO effect was strong. In both the United States and United Kingdom, Burson-Marsteller's research of the general public found that a CEO's reputation accounted for 48 percent of a company's reputation. CEO reputation continues to matter the world over.

As a result of this pioneering research, Burson-Marsteller now advises companies on how to best manage company and CEO reputation. Our recommendations are valued because they are based on reliable stakeholder research. In addition to establishing a link between CEO and corporate reputation, we identified the top three drivers of a favorable CEO reputation—credibility, ethical behavior, and the ability to communicate internally. These factors serve as the foundation of Burson-Marsteller's client work. They have also opened up new offerings in internal leadership communications and social responsibility. Without a doubt, Burson-Marsteller professionals and clients have learned how to navigate in this evolving new world of communications because of the agency's unwavering commitment to research.

Online Influentials

Reputation management is not the only type of research in which Burson-Marsteller is invested. Another new avenue of investigation involves the Internet and its role in modern communications. In 1998, as the Internet was just taking hold in business circles, we began surveying the general public to determine how word-of-mouth was affected by this new medium. As a public relations firm, we understood off-line influence, but we knew that we needed to learn more about the evolution of online influence.

Through a series of telephone interviews and online research with a panel of consumers, we soon discovered that a small segment of Internet users—perhaps no more than 10 percent—were disproportionately more influential than others. We dubbed these online influentials "*e*-fluentials"™ and now know how they influence friends, family, and colleagues.

E-fluentials were among the first to explore the Internet frontier, and they remain today's most prominent online trailblazers. While they are extremely influential online, *e*-fluentials also spread their opinions in the off-line world as well. Civic-minded *e*-fluentials are more likely to vote, attend public meetings, serve on local committees, and make speeches. Their families and peers regularly approach them for information, opinions, and advice on a wide range of subjects—from business and politics to entertainment and health/lifestyle issues. *E*-fluentials' influence has been proven to run far and wide.

The expansive effect of this powerful group of men and women can make or break a brand, marshal or dissolve support for business and consumer issues, and provide insight into events as they unfold. For companies and marketers, there is an urgent need to earn *e*-fluentials' trust, approval, and support. *E*-fluentials are today's information brokers. Not surprisingly, many companies and other organizations now ask us to help them identify their *e*-fluentials and learn how to harness *e*-fluentials' power to shape perceptions about products and services.

Conclusion

These examples demonstrate the far-reaching results that can be achieved when a firm such as Burson-Marsteller commits time, personnel, and resources to research. In addition to informing clients, attracting new business, and building employee pride, our research supports the firm's thought leadership and differentiates us in the industry. Burson-Marsteller's reputation as a trail blazer in public relations research builds on Harold Burson's legacy of listening carefully and solving problems with facts, not fancy.

Case Study 7.1

Betting on Terror

"You know, I've been around this building 12 years," the reporter told Defense Department spokesman Lawrence Di Rita. "It seems so absurd that anything like this could ever see the light of day."

"But I just—there's really—I don't think I have much more to say on that," Di Rita responded.[21]

Based on that unusual exchange at a July 29, 2003, Pentagon briefing, you must be wondering what it was that had the reporter so befuddled and the spokesman so rattled? The subject of such confusion and amazement was a tactic in the War on Terrorism that, even today, sounds so outlandish that you may believe it was a hoax. But it wasn't. And some still believe it was a good idea.

What they were talking about was the Policy Analysis Market (PAM), an online trading market designed to help predict terrorist attacks. Speculators could go on the Internet and place wagers on a probability of a wide range of terrorist activities. These included an attack on western tourists at the pyramids in Egypt, the assassination of Middle East political figures, or even a North Korean missile attack.

PAM was the brainchild of the Defense Advanced Research Projects Agency (DARPA), the Defense Department's Research Arm. According to one of its creators, Robin Hanson of George Mason University, it was based on the same market forces that drive agricultural and financial futures markets.

"Prediction markets are speculative markets created for the purpose of aggregating information on topics of interest," Hanson said on a statement on his web site. "Previous field studies had found that such markets out-predict co-existing institutions regarding the weather, printer sales, movie sales, elections and much more."[22]

Stanford University economics professors Justin Wolfers and Eric Zitzewitz wrote in the *Washington Post* that the concept of a "terrorist futures market" merited public support. "The reason markets work so well is that they reflect our collective wisdom. And your opinion will be reflected only to the extent that you are willing to put your money where your mouth is."[23]

"There is good reason to believe that a market set up to forecast the sort of political instability that leads to terrorism might well work," wrote Information and Management Systems Professor Hal R. Varian of the University of California–Berkley. "At least, there is enough reason to warrant an experiment, given the high payoff to having better forecasts of these events."[24]

That experiment did not come. It was short-circuited when two U.S. senators highlighted the plan in a congressional budget debate over defense intelligence spending. Senator Ron Wyden, an Oregon Democrat, said, "spending taxpayer dollars to create terrorism betting parlors is as wasteful as it is repugnant. Clearly, this is morally wrong." Senator Byron Dorgan, North Dakota Democrat, called the scheme "incredibly stupid."[25]

Even members of the Bush administration appeared surprised by the plan. "I share your shock at this kind of program," said Deputy Defense Secretary Paul Wolfowitz. He told the Senate Foreign Relations Committee that he first learned of PAM by reading his morning newspaper.

"The agency is brilliantly imaginative in places where we want them to be imaginative," Wolfowitz said. "It sounds like maybe they got too imaginative."[26]

In the face of a flood of public criticism, the Pentagon moved quickly to kill the program. "No one from Congress asked us if the accusations were correct, or if the more offending aspects could be cut from the program," Hanson said. "The next morning the secretary of defense announced that [PAM] was cancelled."[27]

Retired Rear Admiral John M. Poindexter, who as head of DARPA's Terrorism Awareness Office had conceived the program, resigned under pressure. Many Washington observers had a sense of déjà vu: Poindexter had been forced to resign as President Reagan's national security adviser over his role in the Iran-Contra "weapons for hostages" scandal nearly two decades earlier.

"The war against terrorism is not likely to be won by hiring more economists," wrote *Washington Post* columnist Steven Pearlstein. "It is going to have to be won the old-fashioned way, improving the government's intelligence network one spy at a time."[28]

DISCUSSION QUESTIONS

1. What does this story have to do with public relations research and evaluation?
2. What values were in conflict in this controversy?
3. What could the Pentagon have done to make this program more publicly acceptable?
4. What do you feel about a terrorist futures market as a means of predicting future terrorist activities?

Case Study 7.2

Fighting Back with Facts

Do you know anybody who drinks to get drunk? If you don't, your experience may soon change. Recent research suggests that your chances of knowing a binge drinker are improving.

Research at more than 100 U.S. colleges helped define the problem. For the purposes of a Harvard School of Public Health study, *binge drinking* was defined as five drinks in a row for males and four drinks in a row for females. A *drink* was defined as 12 ounces of beer or wine cooler, 4 ounces of wine, or a 1.25-ounce shot of liquor. During that same 2002 study, 29.4 percent said they went on a binge at least *three* times in the two weeks prior to the survey.[29]

The problem of binge drinking on college campuses is not about a traditional rite of passage. It is about young people dying. According to the *Journal of Studies on Alcohol,* 1,400 college students between 18 and 24 die each year from alcohol-related unintentional injuries, including motor vehicle crashes. Another 500,000 are injured. More than 600,000 students are assaulted by another student who had been drinking. Another 70,000 students are victims of alcohol-related sexual assault or date rape. And the list goes on and on.[30]

The Higher Education Center for Alcohol and Other Drug Prevention reports that drinking behavior became increasingly polarized during the past decade. More students are abstaining from drinking, up from 16 percent in 1993 to 19 percent in 2001. However, the percentage of students who say they drink to get drunk rose from 39.9 percent in 1993 to 48.2 percent in 2001.[31]

The good news is that the truth can save lives. At Hobart and William Smith Colleges in Geneva, New York, researchers have discovered that college students drink less when they learn their classmates drink less. That message is the basis of a model program that resulted in a 21 percent reduction in drinking on the Hobart and William Smith campus over a two-year period.

"No matter how much alcohol is being consumed, students almost uniformly across campuses exaggerate what they think is typical of their peers," said Professor Wesley Perkins of Hobart and William Smith.[32]

To change this misconception, Hobart and William Smith officials incorporate alcohol research findings into "campus factoids" displayed on campus computer screen savers. They use an electronic media campaign and incorporate alcohol-abuse awareness issues into the classroom. They have also received federal funds to expand the program to other schools.

Professor Terry L. Rentner, head of the public relations sequence at Bowling Green State University (Ohio), decided to use Perkins' research to tackle the problem of binge drinking on her campus. But she chose to go about it in a nontraditional manner.

"Most universities have developed educational programs which address alcohol related issues," Rentner said. "Those programs convey information about the physical and psychological effects of alcohol, and they are designed for a mass audience."

"They usually are not effective."[33]

The Bowling Green approach, which has been judged by the U.S. Department of Education as one of the top six in the country, attacks the problem on a smaller, more targeted scale. The program focuses on small groups of students considered at high risk for binge drinking. Those groups have included freshmen, athletes, and members of fraternities and sororities. In small groups, students are asked to complete a survey on how much alcohol they consume and how much they think their peers consume. After the surveys are tabulated, a second meeting is held to discuss the results.

"Without fail, students think their peers are drinking more than they actually are," Rentner said. She said that once the truth is exposed, students feel less pressure to drink to "fit in."[34]

The program appears to be working. During a two-year period in which binge drinking rose by 4 percent nationwide, the rate dropped by 2.5 percent on the BGSU campus. Rentner does not take full credit for the improvement, noting that the program is part of a comprehensive community–campus effort to curb binge drinking.

The battle is also being waged on other fronts. At Dartmouth College, students returned to campus to find advertisements describing a campus survey conclusion: 58 percent of students don't think alcohol is important to have at a party. The University of Arizona has been spreading the word that most students don't drink heavily. Approximately 1,600 resident assistants at the 15 state universities in Michigan have been trained in alcohol intervention. The University of Delaware, as well as other schools, contacts parents when students violate alcohol policies.[35]

To their credit, many student organizations have chosen to tackle the problem, as well. One example can be found at Michigan State, which has established a vigorous antialcohol campaign. Following a binge-drinking death and an alcohol-fueled riot, many in MSU's Greek community sobered up. The taps have been turned off.

"Our overall living conditions improved," said Lambda Chi fraternity member Ben Glime. "Our overall academic [grade point average] went up."[36]

DISCUSSION QUESTIONS

1. Why do you think the authors of this book placed this case study at the end of the chapter on research and evaluation?
2. What makes the alcohol-abuse program at Bowling Green State University different from traditional programs? What prevents more colleges and universities from taking this approach?
3. What are some of the research methods cited in this case?
4. Is binge drinking a problem on your campus? How do you know? How can you find out? Are any programs addressing the issue; if so, how effective are they?

Cyber Coach

Visit www.ablongman.com/guthmarsh3e for these study aids—and more:

- flashcards
- quizzes
- videos
- links to other sites
- real-world scenarios that let you be the public relations professional

KEY TERMS

advertising value equivalency (AVE), p. 202
attributes, p. 225
bivariate analysis, p. 225
census, p. 221
client research, p. 206

closed-ended questions, p. 224
cluster sampling, p. 221
commitment, p. 207
communal relationship, p. 207
communication audits, p. 211

NOTES

1. Michael Fairchild, "An Opportunity to Raise the Standing of PR," *Journal of Communication Management* 6, no. 4 (June 2002): 305–307.
2. "Return on Investment Is an Inadequate Expression of PR Value," news release issued by the Institute of Public Relations, 19 May 2004, online, www.ipr.org.uk/Nedws/stories/197.htm.
3. "The Power of Public Relations: A Basic Guide to Getting Noticed—Measurement/Evaluation/Wrap-up," Texas Commission on the Arts, 1999, online, www.arts.state.tx.us/news/prpower/measure.htm.
4. James Grunig, "Evaluation," International Public Relations Association e-group, 4 August 2000.
5. *Guidelines and Standards for Measuring and Evaluating PR Effectiveness,* Institute for Public Relations, University of Florida, 2000, online, www.instituteforpr.com.
6. "Ad Value Equivalency Comes Out of the Shadows, but Is It Still Considered 'PR Witchcraft'?" *Ragan Media Relations Report,* 1 October 2001.
7. *Guidelines for Measuring the Effectiveness of PR Programs and Activities,* Institute for Public Relations Commission on PR Measurement and Evaluation, 2002, 1.
8. Linda Childers Hon and James E. Grunig, *Guidelines for Measuring Relationships in Public Relations,* Institute for Public Relations Commission on PR Measurement and Evaluation, 1999.
9. "Edelman Offers New Relationship Index," news release issued by Edelman, 29 April 2003, online, www.edleman.com.
10. *Guidelines for Measuring the Effectiveness of PR Programs and Activities,* 2.

11. Sherri Deatherage Green, "Up-Front Research Doesn't Yet Have a Permanent Place in PR," *PR Week* U.S. edition, 4 August 2003, 15.

12. John Finney, "Assessing the Value of Communication," *Communication World,* January/ February 2004, 36–40.

13. Hon and Grunig.

14. James E. Grunig, *Qualitative Methods for Assessing Relationships between Organizations and Publics,* Commission on PR Evaluation and Measurement, online, www. institutefor.pr.com.

15. "Profile 2000—A Survey of the Profession," *Communication World,* June–July 2000, A15–A17.

16. "Wal-Mart: Timing of Cover Was Mistake," Associated Press, 31 August 2002, online, LexisNexis.

17. "Help Heal Florida's Healthcare," 2004 Silver Anvil Award summary no. 6BW-0406B11, Public Relations Society of America, online, www.prsa.org.

18. Rich Noyes, "How Election Night Became a Sit-Com," Human Events Online, 17 November 2000, www.humaneventsonline.com/articles/11-17-00/noyes.html.

19. Noyes.

20. "Polling Service Errors Distorted Florida Election Night Projections, VNS Report Says," CNN Interactive, 22 December 2000, online, www.cnn.com.

21. Department of Defense briefing transcript, 29 July 2003, online, www. defenselink.mil.

22. Robin Hanson, "The Policy Analysis Market Archive," 9 January 2004, online, http:// hanson.gmu.edu/policyanalysismarket.html.

23. Justin Wolfers and Eric Zitzewitz, "The Furor Over Terrorism Futures," *Washington Post,* 31 July 2003, A19.

24. Hal R. Varian, "A Good Idea with Bad Press," *New York Times,* 31 July 2003, online, www.nytimes.com.

25. Richard Sisk, "Gambling on Terror," *New York Daily News,* 29 July 2003, online, www.nydailynews.com.

26. "Pentagon Axes Online Terror Bets," BBC News, 29 July 2003, online, http://news.bbc. co.uk.

27. Hanson.

28. Steven Pearlstein, "Misplacing Trust in the Markets," *Washington Post,* 30 July 2003, E01.

29. R. W. Hingson, T. Heeren, R. C. Zakocs, A. Kopstein, and H. Wechsler, "Magnitude of Alcohol-Related Mortality and Morbidity among U.S. College Students Ages 18–24," *Journal of Studies on Alcohol* 63, no. 2, 2002, 136–144.

30. Hingson, et al.

31. Daniel Ari Kapner, "Alcohol and Other Drugs on Campus: The Scope of the Problem," *Infofacts Resources,* Higher Education Center for Alcohol and Other Drug Prevention, June 2003.

32. "Frequent Binge Drinking Rises among U.S. College Students, but Abstaining Also Increases," CNN Interactive, 14 March 2000, online, www.cnn.com.

33. "BGSU Program to Curb Binge Drinking to Serve as National Model," Bowling Green State University News Service, 2 November 1999, online, www.bgsu.edu/offices/pr/news/1999/binge.html.
34. "BGSU Program to Curb Binge Drinking to Serve as National Model."
35. "College Binge Drinking Kills," About: The Human Internet, 22 September 1999, http://alcoholism.about.com.library/weekly/aa990922.htm.
36. "College Town Takes Sober Look at Drinking Problem," CNN Interactive, 8 March 1999, online, www.cnn.com.

8

Planning:
The Strategies of
Public Relations

objectives

After studying this chapter, you will be able to

■ describe the different kinds of public relations plans

■ discuss why public relations practitioners create plans

■ explain the process of creating a public relations plan

■ summarize the qualities of a good plan

■ explain where and how values enter into the planning process

The Art of Planning

You're the director of public relations for an art museum in a city in the southwestern United States. Your museum is renowned for its collection of contemporary Native American art, but the museum also has other, diverse artwork and a growing national reputation.

Like many successful public relations operations, your three-person staff has a well-organized issues-management process. You're constantly scanning the environment for potential problems and opportunities. When you spot a potential issue, you monitor it to see whether action is desirable. Last week, you discovered a possible issue: One of your assistants attended a luncheon sponsored by the Hispanic American Leadership Conference. During dessert, a participant asked her why the museum didn't promote Hispanic artists. Another participant overheard the question and agreed that the museum tended to overlook Hispanic artists.

At your weekly issues-management meeting, you and your team discuss that possible perception within your city's Hispanic community. You agree to monitor the situation. Two days later, another staff member shows you an advertisement that a local corporation placed in Hispanic Plus, *a national magazine that targets graduating seniors. The ad boasts of the exciting Hispanic influence on your city's cultural attractions. Your museum is not mentioned in the ad's list of cultural highlights.*

You're puzzled, because the museum recently hosted a very successful exhibition on mid-20th-century Mexican artists, Frida Kahlo and her husband, Diego Rivera. But you're also concerned: Almost one-third of your city's residents are of Hispanic origin. If influential members of that broad public believe that your museum is not serving their interests, consequences for future attendance as well as future budgets could be disastrous. Almost 40 percent of your museum's budget comes from city tax revenues.

You assemble a focus group, and a clearer picture of the potential problem emerges. Members of the focus group loved the Kahlo-Rivera exhibition, but they were unanimous in believing that your museum does nothing to promote Hispanic artists now living and working in your city. Additional in-depth interviews with opinion leaders in the Hispanic public echo that belief. One of the opinion leaders says, "Please don't limit yourself to modern Hispanic art—but don't ignore it, either."

More research turns up some startling misperceptions. You learn that almost 65 percent of your museum's small cash grants to up-and-coming artists went to city residents of Hispanic origin—but that you haven't publicized that fact. And you discover another misperception: The head curator of the museum—herself of Hispanic origin—says to you, "No one can say there's a problem here. We're doing more than enough to support Hispanic-influenced art."

On the wall in your office is a poster that contains the museum's statement of values and its mission statement. One of the values is "Diversity." Below that, part of the mission statement says, "This museum will diligently nurture the artistic interests of the residents of our city."

Given your values-based mission and the damaging misperceptions that your research has revealed, you decide that you must address this emerging problem.

What do you do?

The Basics of Values-Driven Planning

The appearance of certain phrases in the news media can make public relations practitioners want to dig a deep hole and pull the dirt in after them. Those devastating phrases include "public relations disaster," "public relations gaffe," "public relations fiasco" and, last but certainly not least, "bad planning."[1] In the first weeks of the new millennium, the British news media launched those criticisms and more at the public relations plans of the United Kingdom's Millennium Dome.

Built to host year 2000 celebrations, the enormous domed stadium near London began as an enormous public relations opportunity. As a government project, the Millennium Dome could not justify a hefty advertising budget. Instead, officials chose to promote the Dome primarily through public relations, particularly media relations. Thus, on opening night—the magical last night of the old millennium—Dome officials invited the United Kingdom's best-known journalists to the festivities. At least, that was the plan. However, Dome officials chose to route the journalists through the crowded London subway system, where, with their families, they were stranded for three hours. They missed most of the Dome celebration and spent much of that memorable night in an underground station.

In retrospect, journalists reported, they should have anticipated the most frustrating evening of their lives. Said one reporter, "[The Dome's] public relations team habitually treated the most innocent inquiry with a combination of paranoia and defensiveness that caused relations with the press to sour long before virtually every national newspaper editor and TV chief was trapped in Stratford station on New Year's Eve."[2]

With that kind of a relationship, media reaction to the Dome's opening-night transportation travesty was predictable:

- "One also marvels at the Dome's public relations, which must have broken the first lesson on day one at PR school: make sure the opinion formers get their tickets on time and get good seats."[3]

- "The organizers could not have planned a worse public relations disaster if they had tried."[4]

Because the Dome consumed substantially more government funding than anticipated, the United Kingdom's National Audit Office investigated Dome finances.

The auditors' report took an unusual detour into public relations practices, gently but clearly blaming poor media relations planning for a portion of the Dome's failure. In a section titled "Contingency Planning," the National Audit Office concluded:

- "On any major project managers need as much flexibility as possible to respond if things do not go to plan."
- "Managers may find it difficult to respond to major unforeseen events unless they have already developed crisis plans. This is not planning for failure. It is planning to make the best of a bad situation."

Near the end of its report, the National Audit Office analyzed the impact of the poor media relations planning:

> The [Dome] Company considered that negative media coverage of the Dome . . . had a significant depressing effect on visitor numbers. . . . The Company estimates that each time the Dome received "bad press," sales inquiries dropped by 30 percent to 50 percent in the following week.[5]

The saddest conclusion of all, however, may have come from a Dome media relations official as he led a group of politicians and journalists through the exhibits. "There hasn't been a dull moment at the Dome," he said, "but I think I'll be getting out of public relations after this."[6]

Lessons Learned

Now *there's* an optimistic start to a chapter on planning: international failure and personal career crisis. But as you've no doubt already realized, the Dome's doom was avoidable. Perhaps you've already considered some key questions: Did the Dome's media relations plan have a goal? Did that goal reflect the government's values? Did anyone measure progress toward the goal? Did the public relations team do *any* research on the values of journalists? As you know from the basic public relations process, a good plan begins with good research.

Let's look at a public relations challenge that we can still salvage: the Art of Planning, the scenario that opens this chapter. Scanning and monitoring, which are *problem–opportunity research* techniques, have revealed the Hispanic community's belief that the museum isn't supporting local Hispanic artists. *Client research* has shown that the museum is doing a good job of supporting local Hispanic artists—but that the museum isn't publicizing that success. Last but certainly not least, *stakeholder research*—particularly coorientation (p. 103)—has identified disturbing differences in what key publics think of the situation: Leaders of the Hispanic community think there's a problem; the curator of the museum doesn't.

By this point, you (the public relations director) have studied the issue. You know what the important publics think about it. So you're ready to begin planning, right? Wrong. You still need to answer one more question before you begin planning: *What values-based outcome do you seek?* You're about to take action, so what results do you seek? And will those results be consistent with your organization's values, mission, and goals? In the scenario, the outcome you seek is an improved relationship between your museum and the Hispanic residents of your city. Is that outcome consistent with the museum's values? Indeed it is. One of your organization's stated values is "Diversity." Furthermore, the values-based mission statement poster in your office includes these words: "This museum will diligently nurture the artistic interests of the residents of our community." The improved relationship you seek definitely would help your organization fulfill its mission.

Now you're finally ready for some values-driven planning.

Different Kinds of Public Relations Plans

To attain their organizations' public relations goals, public relations practitioners devise different types of plans. These fall into three basic categories: ad hoc plans, standing plans, and contingency plans.

Ad Hoc Plans

The plan you will create to end the misperceptions surrounding your museum will target a temporary (we hope) situation; therefore it's called an **ad hoc plan.** *Ad hoc* is a Latin phrase that means "for this purpose only." When you and your friends make plans for a party, for example, that's an ad hoc plan. Your plan is important, but it's temporary. It's not something you're going to live with for years (unless your party is truly legendary).

Standing Plans

Because many important relationships are ongoing and long-term, wise organizations have ongoing and long-term plans to nurture those relationships. A plan of this type is often called a **standing plan.** Your museum, for example, probably would devise a standing plan to maintain a positive relationship with Hispanic residents once your ad hoc plan had succeeded.

A weekly newsletter that a multinational corporation publishes for its upper-level managers is part of a standing plan. The newsletter helps the organization fulfill its values-based goal of maintaining a good relationship with some very important employees. Ideally, another part of that standing plan would be frequent opportunities for those upper-level managers to express their concerns to the corporation's top leadership. Remember: Successful public relations is built on two-way communication and on an organization's willingness to change when necessary.

One danger of standing plans is that they sometimes stand too long. The plan becomes tradition, and we continue carrying out its directives because, we are told, "That's what we've always done." A plan that stands too long can become divorced from its original values-based goal. For example, we may be publishing a great weekly newsletter for those upper-level managers, but perhaps it's no longer effective because they now need daily, not weekly, updates.

Conducting evaluation research can reduce the danger of obsolete standing plans. As we noted in Chapter 7, evaluation research can help us see whether our plan is meeting its goals. A communication audit, for example, is a form of evaluation research that would examine our organization's communications goals and then check to see how well our communications actions are reaching those goals. An effective communication audit would be the death of an obsolete standing plan.

Contingency Plans

A third kind of public relations plan is called a **contingency plan.** Such plans are used for "what if" scenarios. Through good scanning and monitoring, organizations often spot issues that may require action if they suddenly gather strength. If any such

QuickBreak 8.1

PLANNING FOR THE ENTIRE ORGANIZATION

Besides creating ad hoc, standing, and contingency plans, public relations practitioners ideally help create plans at an even higher level: They help determine their organization's values, mission, and specific business goals. A 2004 survey of Chicago-area public relations practitioners found that 71 percent provided significant counsel in organizational policy meetings. Some 54 percent agreed that "companies are giving more thought to PR when they make business decisions."[7] In its 2004–2005 analysis of the public relations profession, the U.S. Bureau of Labor Statistics reported, "As managers recognize the growing importance of good public relations to the success of their organizations, they increasingly rely on public relations specialists for advice on the strategy and policy of such programs."[8]

Public relations practitioners should contribute to organizational planning for two important reasons:

1. Realistic values, missions, and business goals depend on a clear understanding of relationships with employees, partners, competitors, and other powerful groups. No organization can achieve its goals without cooperation from its publics. And no one has a better understanding of those essential groups than public relations practitioners.

2. A good public relations plan contributes to the fulfillment of an organization's highest aspirations: its values, mission, and business goals. An organization's public relations team, therefore, must thoroughly understand and eagerly accept those aspirations. The best way for public relations practitioners to achieve understanding and acceptance is to help the organization establish those same values, mission, and business goals. Put this in terms of your own life: You're a lot more likely to support a spring break trip if you get to help plan it.

In a well-run organization, public relations practitioners have frequent and easy access to the organization's top management. That access is particularly important when an organization is creating its values, mission, and business goals. "It's not just about creating press releases," says Herbert Heitmann, chief of global communications for SAP, a software maker. "It's about being thought leaders."[9]

The well-informed voice of the public relations team must be heard when an organization is planning its future.

issue has the potential to become powerful, a smart organization prepares a contingency plan. One of the best-known examples of a contingency plan is a crisis communications plan, which is discussed in Chapter 12. Many (though not enough) organizations have a basic crisis communications plan that they practice and can quickly adapt to meet the needs of an emerging crisis.

For example, an animal-feeds manufacturer in Canada recently faced an impending strike by its factory workers. Had the workers walked out, the company's public relations team was prepared to present the company's position immediately to a variety of publics: to the news media (and, through the media, to customers); to non-striking employees; to veterinarians, who often recommend the manufacturer's products; to suppliers; to retailers; to large agricultural customers; and to other key publics. News releases and personal letters were ready to be delivered, a news conference was ready to go, and many other tactics simply awaited the announcement of a strike. The company had taken its standard crisis communications contingency plan and adapted it to the specific circumstance of a factory-worker strike. Fortunately, a last-minute settlement averted the strike. So were all the preparations wasted? No: Planning for possibilities that don't materialize sharpens an organization's readiness for the possibilities that *do* happen.

Despite the different natures of these three kinds of plans—ad hoc, standing, and contingency—they share many characteristics, which we'll discuss next. But one shared characteristic is so important that we'll emphasize it now as well as later: *All public relations plans should be values-driven.* Any public relations plan that you propose should strive to fulfill some area of your organization's values-based mission statement. A good way to win the enthusiastic support of your organization's top managers is to show them exactly how your plan helps to achieve an important business goal. It's not enough to say, "This plan is great! It's going to help us build better relationships with important publics." Instead, show the top managers how those improved relationships help fulfill the organization's values-based mission.

Quick ✔ Check

1. How do an organization's values relate to the public relations planning process?
2. What kinds of research should precede the creation of a public relations plan?
3. What are the three kinds of public relations plans? How do they differ?
4. Why should public relations practitioners help an organization establish its values, mission, and related business goals?

Why Do We Plan?

Effective public relations practitioners spend a great deal of their time making ad hoc, standing, and contingency plans. So it's logical to ask *why?* Why is planning so indispensable to successful public relations? We can think of five good reasons, which we'll detail below.

To Keep Our Actions in Line with Our Organization's Values-Based Mission

As we'll discuss shortly, a good plan is a series of proposed actions designed to produce a specific result. That specific result should advance our organization toward the fulfillment of its values-based mission. Planning prevents random, pointless actions that don't promote our values or our mission. Planning helps us ensure that all our actions are ethical and productive.

Let's put this same philosophy in terms of your own life. Why are you attending college? Chances are, your presence on campus isn't a random action. Instead, your collegiate studies are part of a plan that's consistent with several values in your life: a good education, a good career, and so on. You wouldn't dream of investing so much time and money in something that took you nowhere. It's the same in public relations. We plan in order to avoid waste as we energetically pursue our broader mission.

To Help Us Control Our Destiny

You have surely heard the sports cliché "We control our own destiny." Athletes say it when their team can make it to the playoffs simply by winning—that is, when they don't need the assistance of losses by other teams in other games. Planning helps an organization control its destiny by proactively managing issues rather than just reacting to them. Planning can help an organization ensure that its relationships with key publics are a source of strength, not of weakness.

To appreciate the link between planning and positive relationships, simply apply the link once again to your own life. Imagine that you'd like to spend more time with a particular someone. Are you going to call that person and, with no warning, ask him or her to go out immediately to who knows where because you haven't yet decided? Or are you going to ask a few days in advance with a specific social agenda? Spontaneity can be fun, but a little planning is indispensable in most good relationships.

Public relations departments that create and implement ad hoc, standing, and contingency plans increase their organization's options in a constantly changing environment. In doing so, they increase their value to the organization.

To Help Us Better Understand and Focus Our Research

Planning puts our research to the test. A detailed plan quickly shows us what we know—and what we don't know. For example, before we plan a specific relationship-building action with an important public, we must know several things:

- Does the relationship really require an adjustment?
- Does our organization want to make the adjustment?

- How will the public probably react to our proposed action?
- Do we have adequate resources to implement the action successfully?

You can probably think of other questions, but note what these have in common: They force us to look closely at our research. Planning helps us ascertain what we truly know, and it identifies areas that require more research.

To Help Us Achieve Consensus

As public relations practitioners transform research into a plan, they seek feedback. Many people, especially an organization's managers, provide input as the plan takes shape. When the planners are satisfied, the plan often goes to the client or top management for formal approval. Thus, when the final plan is drafted, there's a sense of joint ownership and consensus. The organization's decision makers and its public relations team also share a commitment to the success of the plan. Consensus and commitment help an organization avoid misunderstandings regarding relationship-building activities.

To Allow Effective Management of Resources

Resources are finite. (Think of your own entertainment budget, for example.) Public relations managers rarely have enough time, money, equipment, and staff to pursue every public relations issue affecting their organizations. Therefore, any waste of resources is painful. Public relations practitioners create plans because they want every fraction of every resource to move the organization toward its values-driven goals.

It may seem odd to you that the five reasons for planning we've just outlined don't include the notion that we plan in order to change other people's behavior. In reality, much of public relations planning *does* seek to change the behavior of particular publics. A plan designed to motivate a public to do something that it's predisposed to do may well be successful—but recent research suggests that plans that seek dramatic or rapid behavioral changes rarely succeed. In the mid-1990s, the Research Foundation of the International Association

---

Values Statement 8.1

BOEING COMPANY

Boeing, based in Chicago, develops and produces aircraft, space systems, and missile systems for commercial and national defense purposes.

In all our relationships we will demonstrate our steadfast commitment to:

- Leadership
- Integrity
- Quality
- Customer Satisfaction
- People Working Together
- A Diverse and Involved Team
- Good Corporate Citizenship
- Enhancing Shareholder Value

—Excerpt from "Vision,"
Boeing web site

of Business Communicators completed a comprehensive study of effective public relations and came to what may be a disappointing conclusion: "[C]ommunication programs seldom change behavior in the short term, although they may do so over a longer period."[10]

Behavior or even opinions *may* change, then, but it's a long process. So what do public relations practitioners do? Through research and planning, we build relationships to gain resources (resource dependency theory). After all, this profession is called public *relations*. Good relationships, built on trust, cooperation, and two-way communication, can gradually produce the kinds of behavior that an organization desires from its important publics. Those good relationships can even cause our organization to change its own behavior. The IABC study confirmed that when we seek partnerships with particular publics—partnerships in which both sides win—we stand the best chance of gaining those publics' cooperation as we pursue our business goals. As noted in Chapter 1, this win-win philosophy is called two-way symmetrical public relations.

Public relations practitioners may understand the wisdom of this "partnership" approach to planning, but there's no guarantee that the top leaders of an organization will share that understanding. They may still expect practitioners to design and implement plans aimed at producing immediate behavioral changes. When such changes are possible and ethical, we should try to bring them about. But we also need to educate—diplomatically—our organizations' top leaders. We should seek opportunities to inform them about the wisdom and legitimacy of two-way symmetrical public relations.

How Do We Plan?

Public relations planning usually begins after an organization establishes its mission-related business goals. In an ideal setting, public relations managers help establish those business goals. Once those goals are clear, however, the focus of the public relations team shifts to the development of relationship-management plans that help the organization reach its business goals.

A public relations goal is a general statement of the outcome we want a public relations plan to achieve. The goal of our museum scenario, for example, might be *To improve our museum's relationship with Hispanic residents of this city.*

The sections below describe the phases of the planning process, from consensus building to brainstorming to the creation of a written plan.

Consensus Building

Agreement on the need for action must be reached before planning can proceed. In the museum scenario, do museum managers agree with the above goal? Your research has revealed that the head curator doesn't think there's a problem in the museum's relationship with Hispanic residents. Thus, before you can plan for an improved relationship, you need to persuade her, and perhaps other museum officials, that the museum indeed has a problem. Otherwise, you lack agreement on your goal.

Fortunately, you have solid research you can use to show the curator that a growing problem does exist. Is that enough to win agreement on the goal? Perhaps not. You also need to show her that fulfilling this public relations goal will help the museum fulfill its broader goal. When the curator understands that vital connection, you will probably win her enthusiastic endorsement of your goal. Again, public relations practitioners must clearly link their public relations plans to the broader goals of their organizations.

Brainstorming

Once we've achieved consensus on a goal, we move to a speculative phase in which we explore our options for action: **brainstorming.** We ask tough questions about the quality of our research. We ponder what conclusions we can draw. We discuss what specific actions would be the best relationship builders. A good brainstorming session might even prompt us to revise our goal. In short, we have a wide-ranging, no-holds-barred session in which we frequently ask, "Do we know that for sure?" and "What if we tried this?" One Dallas-based agency tries to ensure creative brainstorming sessions by holding them on a basketball court, mixing planning and playing as practitioners work for some slam-dunk ideas.

To guide a brainstorming session, we recommend—in addition to a basketball court—a system based on a planning grid (see QuickBreak 8.2). A planning grid is a tool that public relations practitioners use to develop communication strategies. It's a systematic approach to the planning process. As a prelude to a formal, written plan, a brainstorming grid highlights four areas for discussion:

■ *Publics:* Which publics are or must be involved in the issue? For each public, who are the opinion leaders and decision makers?

■ *Values:* What are each public's interests, stakes, or involved values? In other words, why does each public care about this situation?

■ *Message:* What message should we send to each public? A successful message addresses a public's values and attempts to get a specified response that would help your organization achieve a particular public relations goal.

■ *Media:* Note that the word *media* is plural. You're not limited to just one channel of communication when you send a message to a targeted public.

As a brainstorming session starts to generate ideas, you can write them in a grid. The beginning of a brainstorming grid (p. 249) for our museum scenario would articulate a clear goal:

GOAL: *To improve our museum's relationship with Hispanic residents of this city.*

In our museum scenario, one *public* we could identify would be opinion leaders within the Hispanic community. We might decide that from the museum's standpoint, the key *value* held by that group is a strong interest in seeing more support for

GOAL: To improve our museum's relationship with Hispanic residents of this city.			
PUBLIC	**VALUE(S)**	**MESSAGE**	**MEDIA**
Opinion leaders in the Hispanic community.	They want more support for local Hispanic artists.	The museum *is* actively supporting those artists—and it's willing to do more.	Address Hispanic Chamber of Commerce.

local Hispanic artists. Our *message* could focus on the little-publicized fact that the museum actively supports local Hispanic artists. Finally, we might discuss using face-to-face meetings and a special event as *media* to send that message.

As you brainstorm and begin to formulate a specific plan, be sure to test all the options against your organization's values-based mission statement and goals. As we've noted before, actions that become divorced from values are counterproductive and a waste of resources.

The wonderful thing about brainstorming is that you're not yet making firm commitments. Instead, you're just thinking on paper, or on a chalkboard or a flip chart. However, the brainstorming grid does provide the basic information we need for the next step: the written plan, consisting of goal(s), objectives, and tactics.

Quick ✔ Check

1. Should public relations plans focus on quickly changing the behavior of a public or publics? Why or why not?
2. What strategies should public relations practitioners use to win top management's support for a public relations plan?
3. What is brainstorming? Why is it useful in planning?
4. How does understanding a particular public's values help public relations practitioners create a message for that public?

Goals, Objectives, and Tactics: The Written Plan

A written public relations plan consists of three main elements, as shown in Figure 8.1. However, practitioners often disagree on what to call those elements and

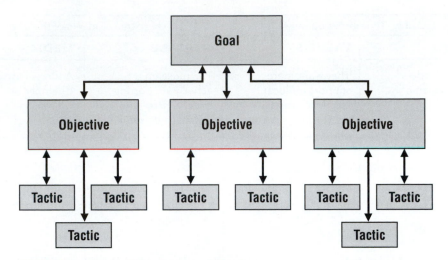

FIGURE 8.1   Goal, Objectives, and Tactics
In a public relations plan, a goal determines the necessary objectives, which, in
turn, determine the necessary tactics. In executing the plan, a public relations
practitioner first executes the tactics; this leads to the fulfillment of the objectives,
which, in turn, leads to the fulfillment of the goal.

how to define them. "Practitioners have almost as many different definitions of
goals, objectives, strategies, and activities as we have for defining the profession itself," says Tom Hagley, a practitioner with 30-plus years of experience.[11] This book
will use three commonly accepted terms:

1. a *goal* or goals,
2. *objectives,* and
3. *tactics,* or recommended actions.

The order of the three is important. Not until you've clearly established the goal and
shown that it's consistent with your organization's values can you move to objectives.
And not until you've specified the objectives and shown that they, too, are consistent
with organizational values can you move to tactics, or recommended actions—which,
again, must be consistent with organizational values. The Public Relations Society of
America notes that some plans include **strategies,** which are general descriptions of
how we propose to achieve the objectives. In those plans, practitioners specify strategies after objectives but before the more specific tactics.

Let's look at goals, objectives, and tactics in more detail.

GOALS.   Your starting point, the **goal,** is a generalized statement of the outcome you
hope your plan achieves. For example, in our museum scenario, you've diplomatically persuaded the management team that the goal is

To improve our museum's relationship with Hispanic residents of this city.

Goals often begin with infinitives, such as *to improve* or *to increase*. By beginning your plan with a verb, you place an immediate focus on action.

OBJECTIVES.   Once you have agreement on a well-written goal, you move to the next part of a written plan: the **objectives**. Whereas goals are general statements, objectives define particular ambitions. Objectives, in the words of the PRSA Accreditation Board, are "specific milestones that measure progress toward achievement of a goal."[12] For example, we earlier mentioned an ad hoc plan for a party that you and your friends might throw. Your goal, of course, would be to throw a great party. Your objectives would include activities such as identifying and inviting guests; creating a fun, social atmosphere; and so on. You'd have to meet each of these objectives in order to meet your goal.

According to the Institute for Public Relations, good objectives have five qualities. They must

1. specify a desired outcome (increase awareness, improve relationships, build preference, adopt an attitude, generate sales leads, etc.)
2. directly specify one or several target audiences
3. be measurable, both conceptually and practically
4. refer to "ends," not "means"
5. include a time frame in which the objective is to be achieved, for example, by July 1[13]

In the book *Using Research in Public Relations*, Professors Glen Broom and David Dozier write, "The most frequently asked question in our classes and workshops is 'How much change do you know how to call for in an objective?' The simple response is 'By researching the situation to learn what is possible.'"[14] To that solid beginning, we offer these additional pointers:

- Remember that changing a public's behavior, if it can be done at all, is a long-term process.[15] Measuring resource acquisition or the quality of relationships may be easier (see QuickBreak 7.3, p. 207).

- When appropriate, consider targeting opinion leaders and decision makers with your objectives. It may be easier to create and measure results with a smaller group.

- As you enact your plan, conduct ongoing evaluation to see if your objectives were realistic. You may have time to change course.

In a public relations plan, objectives often focus on the targeted publics. If your plan involves six publics, the plan may well have at least six objectives—because you're seeking to build six different relationships to achieve your goal. However, it is also true that some objectives can serve more than one public. Unfortunately, no magic formula exists that can help you determine the right number of objectives for a goal. The only true test of whether your objectives are sufficient is this question: If I fulfill each objective and manage my resources wisely, will I reach the goal? If the answer is yes, you have the right number of objectives.

QuickBreak 8.2

THE PRSA PLANNING GRID

Ready for a healthy dose of alphabet soup? The Accreditation Board of the Public Relations Society of America recommends that you use PIPP, POST, and TASC grids as part of a three-step planning process.[16]

PIPP, POST, and TASC are memory aids to help you complete three fill-in-the-blank planning grids. The PIPP acronym stands for a process that helps you identify and define the publics your plan may target. It stands for **P**ublic, **I**mportant Segments, **P**rofile, and **P**riority. A PIPP grid looks like this:

Public	Important Segments	Profile	Priority

For each public that you identify, you note the important segments of that public, such as influential members and decision makers, that may require special attention. You then profile each public: You describe its "unique issues, needs, concerns, special demographics, . . . etc."[17] Profile information helps you determine what communication tactics you'll recommend for that specific group. Finally, you assign each public a priority: Which of the identified publics is the most important to your organization? Which is least?

After PIPP comes POST, which helps you develop specific communication actions. The acronym stands for **P**ublic/Segment, **O**bjectives, **S**trategies, and **T**actics. A POST grid looks like this:

Public/ Segment	Objectives	Strategies	Tactics

In our museum scenario, your objectives might look something like this:

Objective 1: To improve the museum's outreach program to Hispanic artists by November 1.

Objective 2: To increase the Hispanic community's knowledge of the museum's programs by December 1.

Objective 3: To establish a continuing program, by January 1, that informs museum personnel of the museum-related values of this city's Hispanic residents.

If you can fulfill these objectives, you'll surely meet your goal. One of your challenges, however, may be measurability. In particular, you have to decide exactly what you mean by "To improve" and "To increase the Hispanic community's knowledge. . . ." As we stated in Chapter 7, evaluation must be considered and conducted at every step of the public relations process.

The specificity of your objectives will, in all likelihood, be familiar to top managers within your organization. Many organizations practice a philosophy called

You begin by naming the identified publics and their important segments. For each public, you then specify objectives, strategies, and tactics. Objectives, which we describe in detail in the text under the heading Goals, Objectives, and Tactics, are measurable results that you hope to achieve with each public. Strategies are general descriptions of the actions you'll take to reach each objective. For example, a strategy in our museum scenario might be "Seek face-to-face opportunities to demonstrate to local Hispanic opinion leaders how our museum is supporting local Hispanic artists." Finally, tactics are specific actions that help you fulfill your strategies.

Having worked through PIPP and POST, you're ready to move to the final step of the three-phase process: outlining the logistics of each tactic. The third acronym, TASC, stands for **T**actic, **A**mount, **S**chedule, and **C**oordinator. A TASC grid looks like this:

Tactic	Amount	Schedule	Coordinator

For each tactic, you list the amount it will cost, when it is scheduled to occur, and who will coordinate its implementation.

From the identification of key publics to the naming of a coordinator for a specific action, the three-part PRSA planning grid can help you assemble the information you need for an effective public relations plan.

management by objectives, or MBO for short. MBO involves having managers commit to specific performance objectives for their particular departments. MBO is also used in performance evaluations for employees. Working with their managers, employees agree to specific objectives for the quality and quantity of their work in the coming year. The employees are then judged by how close they came to meeting those objectives. Public relations plans that focus on goals, objectives, and specific tactics are clearly part of the MBO philosophy favored by many of today's organizations.

TACTICS.   When you're satisfied with your goal(s) and objectives, it's time to suggest specific tactics. **Tactics,** or recommended actions, make up the third and final part of a written plan. To fulfill each objective, you need to take specific actions. Thus, you can list recommended actions under each objective. That placement is important. You don't gather your tactics and place them at the end of the plan. Instead, you put one or more recommended actions under each objective to show how you plan to achieve that specific ambition.

Unlike goals and objectives, tactics don't begin with infinitives. They begin with active verbs; they're commands. Thus, in the museum scenario, your first tactic under your second objective might be something like this:

Objective 2: To increase the Hispanic community's knowledge of the museum's programs by December 1.

Tactic 1: Address the November meeting of the city's Hispanic Chamber of Commerce.

That tactic is a good command, but it's not very complete. Who should address the Hispanic Chamber of Commerce? When is the meeting? How can you get on the meeting's agenda? What presentation materials will the speaker use? Besides being expressed as a brief command, each tactic should provide enough specific details to enable someone to implement it. It's common under each tactic to give the following information:

- *Brief description* (specifying only what is essential for the action to be executed)
- *Deadline*
- *Budget*
- *Special requirements* (specifying anything out of the ordinary, such as a need for unusual technology)
- *Supervisor* (name of the person in charge of seeing that the action is executed)

Our tactic might now look something like this:

Tactic 1: Address the November meeting of the city's Hispanic Chamber of Commerce.

- *Brief description:* Request permission for curator to give a 10-minute presentation on the museum's support for local Hispanic artists. Permission is generally granted if we provide two-weeks' advance notice. Use handouts and computer-generated slides to show the scope of the museum's support for local Hispanic artists. To demonstrate our willingness to change and to be accommodating, the curator should begin her presentation in Spanish (which she does speak) before switching to English. Handouts and slides should be in Spanish and English.
- *Deadline:* Contact Hispanic Chamber of Commerce by November 1. November meeting date is November 21.
- *Budget:* $300 for preparation of handouts and computer graphics.
- *Special requirements:* Take grant-application forms to meeting so that Hispanic Chamber of Commerce members can help distribute them to local Hispanic artists. Ensure that forms are written in Spanish and English.
- *Supervisor:* Public relations director.

Having supplied this much detail, you're ready to move on to your next tactic under Objective 2.

SHEDD SHARKS GO WILD

With a limited budget and high expectations for opening its largest, most expensive exhibit ever, the Shedd Aquarium knew that its success would rely on effective public relations to build anticipation and excitement for the opening of *Wild Reef* in April 2003. The $48 million underground exhibit not only featured an eye-to-eye look at reef aquatic life, but it brought to Chicago two dozen sharks.

Research

Communications planning began in early 2002 for Wild Reef and started with market research that identified five key audiences and the messages to which they would be likely to respond. For example, Young Urban Explorers would respond to messages that the exhibit was "the newest thing" and wasn't just for families or kids, while Fun-Loving Suburbanites want to get up close to the animals and need activities with kid-friendly features.

In addition, the Aquarium identified a sixth audience. Chicago has a vital Filipino community, which would take a keen interest in this exhibit, since it re-creates a Philippine island and the surrounding coral reefs. Through interviews and secondary research, team members learned about this community, especially its opinion leaders and media outlets, to build awareness about the opening of *Wild Reef*.

Planning

Using the marketing research, the communication team prepared a 12-month media plan starting in April 2002, culminating with the exhibit's opening on April 15, 2003 and continuing into the summ...
Throughout the campaign, the communication team worked closely with the aquarium's ani...
facilities staffs to identify several key story opportunities in the year leading up to the exhi...

The key objectives established for the campaign were to 1) increase the awareness amon...
and tourists by 20 percent that *Wild Reef* was opening in April, 2) to raise annual attend...
and 3) to expand annual membership revenue for 2003 by 8 percent and to garner a 1 ...
direct mail. Because of limited advertising dollars, the public relations team was char...
"buzz" about the exhibit to carrying the public awareness.

Although the exhibit featured a life around a coral reef, the communications strate...
the sharks. Although nearly 1 million animals are in the exhibit (if you count the ...
what captured people's imaginations and interested. Media materials and story p...
the sharks. To ensure as much favorable exposure as possible, the outreach sta...
opening date with a tour of the empty shark tank that is three stories tall. Start...
helped position *Wild Reef* as the major "must-see" in Chicago.

Throughout the construction of the exhibit, Shedd and PCI worked with the animal care and fac...
at the aquarium and pitched an average of one story every month during the last six months before the
exhibit opened. The resulting news stories served as periodic media previews to build excitement in
prospective visitors for the opening.

In addition, to gauge the effect that the impending war in Iraq was having on national television news,
Shedd and PCI made some initial "soft soundings" to producers with the national television networks to
evaluate the chances of landing a feature story on *Wild Reef*. As a result of these calls, it was determined
that the best strategy to deal with the impending war in Iraq was to minimize national TV public relations
efforts early on, but to start targeting the national TV network morning shows after the war had been fought
and the initial aftermath had subdued.

Public Relations Plan The John G. Shedd Aquarium and Public Communications, Inc., won a 2004 Silver Anvil Award from the Public Relations Society of America for their "Shedd Sharks Go Wild" campaign to promote a new exhibit at the aquarium in Chicago. (Courtesy of the John G. Shedd Aquarium and Public Communications, Inc.)

QuickBreak 8.3

THE SWOT ANALYSIS

Imagine the success you would enjoy as a public relations professional if you could create relationship-building plans that helped your organization or clients

- improve strengths;
- diminish weaknesses;
- seize opportunities; and
- avoid threats.

SWOT analysis can help you achieve that ambition.

SWOT is an acronym for strengths, weaknesses, opportunities, and threats. For an organization, those qualities can be internal or external.

- *Strengths* are an organization's current assets, including issues and social conditions, that can help the organization achieve its goals. Strengths can include employee expertise, public opinion, and new legislation.
- *Weaknesses* are an organization's current disadvantages, including issues and social conditions, that can prevent the organization from achieving its goals. Weaknesses can include a lack of internal resources and a public scandal.
- *Opportunities* are emerging assets, issues, and social conditions that, in the future, could help the organization achieve its goals. Op-

portunities can include new products and services the organization is developing, pending legislation, and new international markets.

- *Threats* are emerging disadvantages, issues, and social conditions that could prevent the organization from achieving its goals. Threats can include the upcoming retirement of key employees, growing competition in the marketplace, and pending legislation.

A SWOT analysis is a bridge between research and planning. It helps sort out your data about an organization and the social environment in which it operates. Using specific information from a SWOT analysis, public relations practitioners can create plans to boost positives and reduce negatives. A highly focused SWOT analysis that identifies the strengths, weaknesses, opportunities, and threats in a particular situation can serve as a situation analysis for a proposal (page 257).

Whether broad or narrow in scope, a SWOT analysis must be factual. Avoid opinions and the temptation to overstate positives and understate negatives. Be realistic. Be objective.

And be ready to bring SWOT analysis into the planning process.

Fleshing out each tactic helps give us the road map we need to reach our goal. When we're finished, we have a highly detailed, realistic, workable plan—in writing.

Expanding a Plan into a Proposal

Even with your written plan completed, your writing may be unfinished. Some plans exist alone as plans. Sometimes, however, you need to "sell" your plan to a client or a supervisor who may want a greater amount of background information. Often, therefore, a plan is inserted into a larger document called a **proposal.** Agencies often prepare proposals for their clients, and even within corporations public relations practitioners often prepare proposals for top management. A public relations proposal generally contains, in order, these sections:

1. A title page
2. An **executive summary** that briefly, in one page, describes the problem or opportunity, identifies the targeted publics, lists the specific tactics for addressing the situation, and includes a budget summary
3. A **situation analysis** that accurately and fairly describes the current situation in such a way that action seems advisable
4. A **statement of purpose** announcing that the proposal presents a plan to address the described situation
5. A list and description of publics that the plan targets
6. A plan that specifies your goal(s), objectives, and tactics
7. Other sections as appropriate, such as
   - campaign theme and key messages
   - line-item budget
   - timetable
   - evaluative measures
   - supporting documents (usually in the appendices)

A proposal, as you can see, can be an extensive document. But at its heart is a clear plan consisting of a goal or goals, objectives, and tactics.

Quick ✔ Check

1. How is a goal different from an objective?
2. What are the qualities of a well-written objective?
3. What are tactics? What is their relationship to objectives?
4. How is a plan different from a proposal?

Qualities of a Good Plan

We've covered why we plan and how we plan, and we've seen how a plan can be incorporated in a proposal. Let's turn now to the qualities of a good plan. We've already mentioned some: A good plan seeks measurable results, and it has specific deadlines. What other qualities should a good plan have?

■ *A good plan supports a specific goal of your organization.* As we've said before, don't take for granted that your organization's leaders automatically recognize the value of good public relations. Show them how your plan can help the organization reach a specific business goal.

■ *A good plan stays goal-oriented.* Remember the problem with some standing plans? They stand for so long that we forget why we're following them; instead, we just execute the actions, such as an employee newsletter, because we've always done them. That won't happen if we stay goal-oriented, finding ways to remind ourselves of why we're executing these particular actions.

■ *A good plan is realistic.* Don't promise more than you can achieve. It's OK to dream an impossible dream, but you should plan for an achievable reality. Unrealistic goals and objectives often involve quickly changing a public's behavior. That's not necessarily always impossible, but public relations is much better at building the open and honest relationships that foster gradual changes. Unrealistic tactics include those that require more resources or expertise than your organization can supply.

■ *A good plan is flexible.* Things change. Sometimes important elements of a situation change just as you're launching a plan. If you constantly evaluate the situation, as you should do, you may need to adjust your plan to fit the new circumstances.

■ *A good plan is a win-win proposition.* Whenever possible, the success of your plan should benefit the target publics just as much as it benefits your organization. Forcing a public to change against its will is rarely possible and is almost always bad public relations. A good plan tries to honor each important public's values. When that's not possible, a good plan seeks to minimize damage to important relationships.

■ *Finally, and most importantly, a good plan is values-driven.* As we've noted more than once, if your plan isn't helping your organization achieve its values, it's pointless. It's wasting resources. A good plan resonates with the well-known values of your organization.

Summary

Plans usually fit into one of three categories: ad hoc, standing, or contingency. Successful public relations plans have many qualities, but they share one in particular: They must be clearly tied to an organization's goals. In other words, public relations practitioners must show an organization's top managers how a proposed relationship-building plan aligns with the organization's values and mission. If that connection is not established, the plan will probably die for lack of consensus and approval.

Good public relations plans consist of a general goal or goals; measurable objectives; and specific tactics, or recommended actions. Often, a written plan becomes part of a larger document called a proposal, which practitioners use to present a plan to a client or to their organization's top management.

Good, creative planning is an art—but it's an art based on science. A good plan is goal-directed and research-based. It is realistic and flexible, and it aims for a win-win outcome. Above all, a good public relations plan helps an organization fulfill its values.

DISCUSSION QUESTIONS

1. At what specific points do values enter the public relations planning process?
2. What unique characteristics differentiate ad hoc plans, standing plans, and contingency plans from one another?

3. Can you think of examples—in public relations or otherwise—of standing plans that have stood too long?

4. Why should you go to the effort of producing a written plan if you've already completed a planning grid? If you have a written plan, when should you consider expanding it into a proposal?

5. Why are measurable objectives important to the evaluation phase of the public relations process? What are the advantages of measurable objectives? What are the disadvantages?

Memo
from the
Field

Timothy S. Brown, APR, Ph.D., Director, Corporate Communications, Conectiv, Carneys Point, New Jersey

Timothy S. Brown is an accredited public relations professional with more than 20 years of communications experience in public relations, public affairs, and marketing communications. Brown currently serves as director, corporate communications, for the mid-Atlantic energy company Conectiv, a subsidiary of Pepco Holdings, Inc. In this capacity, he is responsible for directing all public relations activities of the organization, including strategic communications planning, media relations, crisis communications, and employee communications. Brown also teaches a business writing course at Wesley College in New Castle, Delaware. He holds a Ph.D. in English and rhetoric from the University of Maryland at College Park, a master's degree in English from George Mason University, and a bachelor's degree in journalism from Pennsylvania State University. Brown lives in Newark, Delaware— a great college town, he says—with his wife and two children.

When I was in college, sitting where you are, one of my favorite professors began one of my favorite classes by writing a time line on the board. The time line charted the length of time between major technological advances in the history of man—from the invention of simple tools, to the domestication of fire, to the use of the wheel, and so on up to modern times. My favorite professor's point was that the pace of change had accelerated dramatically over time. While it had been thousands of years between the domestication of fire and the invention of the wheel, these days major technological changes are measured in years, if not months or weeks. Such well-known history is behind the well-known maxim that life is change.

This chapter offers a wealth of valuable advice on public relations planning. It explains why planning is important, lays out a sensible approach to planning, offers useful examples of effective plans, and defines the qualities of a good plan. One particular point the authors made in the last section struck a chord with me. They note that "a good plan is flexible" because "things change," making it important for you to "constantly evaluate the situation . . . [so you can] adjust your plan to fit the new circumstances."

If I were you, I'd underline, highlight, and asterisk that passage. My 20 years of experience as a communications professional has underscored the power behind the simple truth that "things change." I've seen the electric industry where I now work change dramatically with the onset of "deregulation." I've seen dozens of executive leaders come and go. I've seen my latest organization significantly change its business strategy three times in six years. Such experiences have left me convinced that the best public relations plans must both anticipate and accommodate change.

Let me give you an example that illustrates the importance of adapting your public relations plans to accommodate change. It is my good fortune to be able to coordinate the strategic communications planning process for my company, Pepco Holdings, Inc. My colleagues and I ground that planning process in the needs of the business units that we support. We also factor in what is happening in our industry and the broader environment in which we do business. All of these elements are combined in a matrix that identifies the goals, objectives, strategies, messages, and tactics that we will use to execute our plan over the next several years.

I'm sure you can guess the flaw in that process. You got it: Things change. Most recently, for example, our company was hit by a major hurricane that disrupted service to nearly one million of our 1.8 million customers. Those customers had questions and issues that weren't anticipated in our plan. To address those new public relations challenges, we had to adapt our well-established plans.

We followed the basic process that we used in developing the initial plan. We conducted research, including surveys and focus groups with customers that had been hardest hit by the hurricane. Based on that research, we reformulated our strategies and objectives for our matrix communications plan. Those new strategies, in turn, translated into adaptations of previously planned communications tactics. For example, we modified a long-running advertising campaign to reflect the lessons of the hurricanes, including, especially, the desire for more information about when power would be restored, which customers expressed via our research. This process resulted in a "new and improved" version of our matrix communications plan that we are currently implementing.

You will likely find in your career that you will have to accommodate similar new developments. If anything, change will be even more of a constant for you. You will be judged in large part by how well you adapt to such a climate in which change is the norm. It will of course be important for you to follow the sound advice that you have received about planning in this chapter and this course. But it will be equally important for you to be adaptable enough to adjust those plans to the ever-changing conditions that will be a constant reality in your public relations career.

Unfortunately, I can't tell you exactly how to do that. You will need to develop the experience, expertise, and judgment to know when and how to adapt your plans based on changing conditions. Doing so will be one of the most challenging and yet satisfying aspects of your career.

There is, however, one piece advice with which I would leave you. No matter how much you have to change your *plans* to adapt to new challenges, you should not feel that it is necessary to change your *values*. As the title of this textbook suggests, your public relations practices must ultimately be grounded in the values that define you and your organization. In fact, it is only by identifying the values that most matter to you and your organization that you can decide how to most appropriately adapt existing public relations plans in the face of inevitable changes.

Hopefully, as you look back on your own college experience in the future, you'll consider this class to be part of the formative process of the way you approach public relations. If so, I'll hope you'll agree with the importance of always being ready to change your plans but never being too quick to change your values.

Case Study 8.1

Boeing, Boeing, Gone

Good public relations planning usually is invisible: The plan unfolds, relationships begin or improve, and organizations move closer to reaching their goals. Only rarely does the world stand back and say, "Wow, what a great public relations plan." But that's what happened in 2001 when Boeing Company's public relations team helped plan the company's move from Seattle to . . . well, to *where?* The *where* is half the story.

"Boeing approached the process with engineers' precision, considering a range of options and eliminating the weaker choices. [It] brought a flair for public-relations drama . . . which has received global news coverage," reported the *Dallas Morning News*.[18] That assessment joined a chorus of praise from journalists, public relations practitioners, business leaders, and politicians.

The decision to leave Seattle became the first remarkable event in Boeing's relocation. In the corporate world, Boeing and Seattle were almost synonymous. William Boeing, a lumber millionaire, founded the company in 1916 in Seattle as the Pacific Aero Company. Within a year, he had changed the name to Boeing Airplane Company. By the end of the 20th century, Boeing's Seattle-based commercial airplane manufacturing unit employed almost 80,000 workers. In 2000, its annual revenues topped $50 billion for the third consecutive year. In 2001, Boeing had customers in 145 countries and employees in more than 60 countries.

Because of the local, national, and international implications of Boeing's impending move, its public relations officials were among the first to learn of the closely guarded secret. To support the move, the public relations team created a plan to secure resources held by four key publics:

1. Employees, who held the resources of continued commitment to the company and a willingness to move to a new city, if asked. Some employees would be moving, some would be staying, and some might even lose their jobs. In all, however, only about 500 top-level jobs would move with the headquarters. Virtually all the manufacturing jobs would remain in Seattle.

Employee relations tactics included asking employees to refer all media questions to Boeing's public relations team; scheduling the move for late summer so that employees' children would be able to begin the school year in the new city; ensuring that employees would be the first to learn of the new location; and offering severance pay to employees who would lose their jobs.[19]

2. Nonprofit groups in Seattle, which had benefited from Boeing's philanthropy. Boeing donated almost $70 million to charitable causes in 2000, most of it in the Seattle area.[20] The recipients of that generosity would soon be in the national media spotlight; thus, they held the resource of helping to preserve Boeing's good name.

Local community relations tactics included a prominent assurance that Boeing's Seattle philanthropy would continue. "The impact [of the move] will be zero," said Boeing's senior executive in charge of corporate philanthropy. "We have a values statement that says we support communities where our people live and work."[21]

3. Publics in the cities Boeing was considering for a new home. These stakeholders included community groups, local governments, businesses, and the news media. These groups held the resource of accepting Boeing as a community member.

Tactics for these publics included news conferences and ensuring that members of Boeing's public relations team were accessible. Boeing appointed top managers to visit each city to meet with community groups and to negotiate for tax breaks and office space.

4. The national and international news media, which, like local media, held the resource of fair, balanced coverage of the move.

Tactics for the news media included news conferences, news releases, the accessibility of the public relations team, and, most important of all, an attention-grabbing way of announcing Boeing's final decision.

When Boeing officials narrowed their clandestine search to three cities—Chicago, Dallas, and Denver—the public relations plan called for removing the veil of secrecy. As the media clamored to learn the winner of the three-way race, Boeing public relations practitioners made it clear that they were following a well-ordered plan. "We have a plan and a process in place, and we're going to stick to that," Boeing spokesman Ken Mercer told reporters.[22]

Public relations practitioners quickly recognized the depth and quality of Boeing's plan. "I'm sure they played out all the scenarios like a war game and were able to guess what people would start checking on next," said a Dallas-based practitioner. "It's a good model."[23]

PRNews magazine noted that the entire relocation plan proceeded smoothly because Boeing's top public relations officials had joined the planning process from the beginning: "The company's three highest communications executives . . . all had seats at the executive table from the beginning planning stages, and it shows."[24]

The most attention-grabbing aspect of Boeing's plan was the tactic for announcing the winning city. Boeing's CEO at the time, Philip Condit, would board a private jet in Seattle after filing flight plans to all three cities. Once in the air, he would announce his destination city, which would become Boeing's new home.

"You talk about an old-fashioned stunt," said one admiring public relations professional. "You send your chairman up in a plane with three different flight plans and announce that you'll call the governor [of the winning state] from the air. That's straight out of P. T. Barnum. It's like the corporate version of the 'Survivor' finale. . . ."[25]

Even politicians and business leaders in the contending cities praised the plan. "What Boeing has done is nothing short of brilliant," said a spokesman for Denver's mayor. A representative of Dallas' Chamber of Commerce added, "The Boeing Company is keeping the suspense up."[26]

When CEO Condit finally picked up that phone in his jet, whom did he call? Governor George Ryan of Illinois. Boeing would move to Chicago.

Boeing's search had ended, but praise for its public relations expertise continued. "Boeing's relocation strategy elevates PR to new heights," proclaimed a headline in *PRNews*. A headline in the *San Diego Union-Tribune* stated, "Boeing's way of moving earns high PR marks."[27]

But the most accurate praise came from Dallas-based public relations professional Teresa Henderson. "I think you will find the Boeing case will go into . . . public relations textbooks," she said.[28]

She was right.

DISCUSSION QUESTIONS

1. Boeing officials tried to ensure that company employees were the first public to learn about new developments related to the move. Why?
2. In this case study, where do you find evidence of Boeing employees following the company's clearly defined values?
3. Public relations practitioners and journalists praised Boeing's public relations planners for anticipating problems. What negative issues might have arisen during Boeing's relocation process?
4. Of the three kinds of planning—ad hoc, standing, and contingency—which do you find in this case study?
5. How does Boeing's relocation planning illustrate resource dependency theory, discussed in Chapter 4?

Case Study 8.2

Mess at Maryville: A Private Plan Goes Public

Maryville Academy was earning headlines for all the wrong reasons. The Catholic-run institution for troubled youth, the largest such program in Illinois, faced allegations of beatings, sexual misconduct, and suicide among its residents. Investigators cited a lack of cooperation from academy officials and even claimed that Maryville employees had tried to smear their reputations.[29] Unfortunately, an 11-page public relations plan to rebuild key relationships became part of the problem rather than the beginning of a solution.[30]

"Maryville Academy officials have publicly rejected a proposed public relations plan to conduct a smear campaign against critics of the Roman Catholic child-care institution," the *Chicago Sun-Times* reported.[31] Two days earlier, the *Sun-Times* had trumpeted this headline: "Cardinal [Francis George] Rips Maryville P.R. Plan as 'Fiasco.'"[32]

Two passages in the public relations plan, prepared by Serafin & Associates of Chicago, drew fire from client and critics alike: "Conduct opposition research" and "Utilize a third-party organization to question unnamed insiders and sources and their motives in questioning Maryville's leadership."[33]

Reaction to those passages was immediate. "After I read it, I felt like taking a bath . . . ," said Patrick Murphy, a Cook County (Chicago) public official. "It's clear what they're saying. They don't come right out and say 'smear,' but that's what they mean. . . . I don't think that's what the Catholic Church should be all about."[34]

Reaction from within Maryville was equally harsh. "I refused it, and I don't want to discuss it," said the Reverend John Smyth, Maryville's founder.[35]

James Guidi, Maryville's head of operations, added, "I read it and came back the next day, sat with Father Smyth and said, . . . 'Father, as a practicing Catholic, I don't want to be involved in anything like that, and as a Catholic organization, we should not be involved in anything like that.'"[36]

How could a public relations plan designed to improve relationships worsen them? The answers may lie in a lack of research, a lack of clarity, and a lack of confidentiality.

Serafin & Associates had been working with Maryville for less than a year, and a lack of client knowledge may have affected the plan. Regarding planning sessions with top Maryville officials, Thom Serafin, president of Serafin & Associates, said, "I never had any discussions—no discussions—with anyone."[37] The *Sun-Times* reported that some critics believed that Serafin was trying to protect his client by taking sole responsibility for the plan.[38]

But Guidi also cited a lack of research as a cause for rejecting the plan: "It's unfortunate that the public relations firm has not done their research well enough to realize that as a Catholic institution it would be immoral to do this kind of research."[39]

Lack of clarity may also have hampered parts of the report. Serafin told *PR Week* magazine that, to him, "conduct opposition research" meant that Maryville should study similar institutions to better understand the statewide conditions of child care.[40] But Herbert Simons, a Temple University professor of speech communication, disagreed with that definition: "You find out all kinds of nasty things about your opponents," he said, describing opposition research. "You spread it around."[41]

"The language is wrong, but the intent is good," Serafin said. "One of the problems and the principle issues with Maryville is, organizationally, they need to communicate better. This was an effort to communicate internally so you can communicate better externally."[42]

In addition, Serafin had submitted a confidential draft to Maryville, not a finished product—and the draft had leaked to the media. "I rejected it outright," Smyth reasserted to the *Chicago Daily Herald,* adding that someone must have taken the plan from his desk.[43]

Serafin reacted quickly to the public disclosure of the work in progress. "This draft has been misinterpreted," he said. "[Critics] decided to focus on three words in the report. Full disclosure is always best."[44] To ensure full disclosure and to allow the controversial passages to be seen in context, Serafin posted the entire plan on his agency's web site.

"If you read the entire plan," he said, "it's a great plan to put more scrutiny on Maryville."[45]

One tactic in the plan did call for weekly meetings with area news media to inform them of progress at Maryville.

In the swirl of charges and countercharges regarding the public relations plan, the Maryville–Serafin partnership received a bleak appraisal from Cardinal Francis George of the archdiocese of Chicago. "The very fact that you're hiring people who would think about this is not encouraging," he said. "I think we have to reconsider the whole relationship."[46]

Maryville Academy did reconsider—and chose to retain Serafin & Associates as its public relations agency.[47]

DISCUSSION QUESTIONS

1. How might better knowledge of stakeholder values have prevented this problem?
2. In public relations, is it unethical to conduct research on hostile publics? Why or why not?
3. In your opinion, should Serafin & Associates have shown a draft version—rather than the final version—of its plan to the client?
4. In your opinion, did Serafin & Associates do a good job of responding to the crisis? Why or why not?

Cyber Coach

Visit www.ablongman.com/guthmarsh3e for these study aids—and more:

- flashcards
- quizzes
- videos
- links to other sites
- real-world scenarios that let you be the public relations professional

KEY TERMS

ad hoc plan, p. 242
brainstorming, p. 248

contingency plan, p. 243
executive summary, p. 257

goal, p. 250

objectives, p. 251

proposal, p. 256

situation analysis, p. 257

standing plan, p. 242

statement of purpose, p. 257

strategies, p. 250

SWOT analysis, p. 256

tactics, p. 253

NOTES

1. Patrick Wintour and Anthony Browne, "The Dome: Triumph or Disaster?" *Observer,* 9 January 2000, online, LexisNexis; Mark Fox, "We Need a Moan-Free Zone for the Dome," *Sunday Express,* 9 January 2000, online, LexisNexis; Dominic Kennedy, "Now for a Few Dome Truths," *Times,* 7 January 2000, online, LexisNexis.

2. John Rees, "Doomed Saucer Crashes to Earth," *Sunday Business,* 10 September 2000, online, LexisNexis.

3. David Lister, "Media: The Editors and the Queuing Zone," *Independent,* 11 January 2000, online, LexisNexis.

4. Wintour and Browne.

5. "National Audit Office: The Millennium Dome," 9 November 2000, online, www.nao. gov.uk.

6. John Chapman, "Tory Julie Roams the Dome," *Express,* 25 May 2000, online, Lexis-Nexis.

7. Jonathan Lehrer, "Survey Says PR People Gain Influence in the Boardroom," 3 March 2004, online, www.publicity.org.

8. *Occupational Outlook Handbook 2004–2005,* U.S. Bureau of Labor Statistics, online, www.bls.gov.

9. Andrew Gordon, "SAP Retools Global Comms," *PR Week,* 9 August 2004, 1.

10. James E. Grunig, "Communication, Public Relations, and Effective Organizations: An Overview of This Book," in *Excellence in Public Relations and Communication Management,* ed. James E. Grunig (Hillsdale, N.J.: Lawrence Erlbaum, 1992), 14.

11. Tom Hagley, "Lead with Integrity," *Public Relations Strategist,* winter 2003, 40.

12. *Accreditation Study Guide, 1993* (New York: Public Relations Society of America, 1993), 81.

13. "Guidelines for Setting Measurable Public Relations Objectives," Institute for Public Relations Commission on PR Measurement and Evaluation, 1999, online, www. instituteforpr.com/printables/objectives.htm.

14. Glen M. Broom and David M. Dozier, *Using Research in Public Relations: Applications to Program Management* (Englewood Cliffs, N.J.: Prentice Hall, 1990), 40.

15. Grunig, 14.

16. *Accreditation Study Guide, 1993,* 89.

17. *Accreditation Study Guide, 1993,* 90.

18. Alan Goldstein, "Boeing Move to Chicago Began with CEO's Chat with His Wife," *Dallas Morning News,* 11 May 2001, online, LexisNexis.

19. Michael Mecham, "A New Headquarters: Boeing Says, 'Chicago's It,'" *Aviation Week & Space Technology,* 14 May 2001, online, LexisNexis; Kyung Song, "Boeing Deftly Builds Suspense over Move," *Seattle Times,* 10 May 2001, online, LexisNexis.

20. Marsha King and Sheila Farr, "Generous Giant Vows It Will Keep on Giving," *Seattle Times,* 22 March 2001, online, LexisNexis.

21. King and Farr.
22. Angela Shah and Alan Goldstein, "Rumors Put Boeing's New Headquarters in Chicago," *Dallas Morning News,* 10 May 2001, online, LexisNexis.
23. Crayton Harrison, "Dallas–Fort Worth Still Buzzing about Boeing's Decision," *Dallas Morning News,* 11 May 2001, online, LexisNexis.
24. "Boeing's Relocation Strategy Elevates PR to New Heights," *PRNews,* 21 May 2001, online, LexisNexis.
25. "Boeing's Relocation Strategy Elevates PR to New Heights."
26. Shah and Goldstein; Song.
27. "Boeing's Relocation Strategy Elevates PR to New Heights"; Victor Godinez, "Boeing's Way of Moving Earns High PR Marks," *San Diego Union-Tribune,* 25 June 2001, online, LexisNexis.
28. Godinez.
29. Cathleen Falsani, "Maryville Critics Say They Are Targets of Smear," *Chicago Sun-Times,* 19 August 2003, online, LexisNexis.
30. John N. Frank, "Criticism Forces Firm to Make PR Plan Public," *PR Week,* 25 August 2003, online, LexisNexis.
31. Falsani, "Maryville Critics Say They Are Targets of Smear."
32. Cathleen Falsani, "Cardinal Rips Maryville P.R. Plan as 'Fiasco,'" *Chicago Sun-Times,* 17 August 2003, online, LexisNexis.
33. Falsani, "Cardinal Rips Maryville P.R. Plan as 'Fiasco.'"
34. Amy McLaughlin, "Maryville, Public Guardian Square off Over Report, Fight," *Chicago Daily Herald,* 16 August 2003, online, LexisNexis; Cathleen Falsani, "DCFS Probes Charges of Cover-Up at Maryville," *Chicago Sun-Times,* 16 August 2003, online, LexisNexis.
35. Ofelia Casillas, "Proposed Tactics Deemed Immoral," *Chicago Tribune,* 17 August 2003, online, www.prwatch.org.
36. Falsani, "DCFS Probes Charges of Cover-Up at Maryville."
37. Falsani, "Maryville Critics Say They Are Targets of Smear."
38. Falsani, "Maryville Critics Say They Are Targets of Smear."
39. Casillas.
40. Frank.
41. Casillas.
42. "Critics Say Draft Plan Shows Shelter's Intent to Hide Trouble," *Northwest Indiana News,* 17 August 2003, online, www.thetimesonline.com/articles/2003/08/17/news.
43. McLaughlin.
44. Frank.
45. McLaughlin.
46. Falsani, "Cardinal Rips Maryville P.R. Plan as 'Fiasco.'"
47. "Maryville Officials Stick with PR Firm for Now," *Chicago Tribune,* 19 August 2003, online, www.poynter.org/dg.lts/id.46/aid.44966/column.htm.

9

Communication: The Tactics of Public Relations

objectives

After studying this chapter, you will be able to

- understand what makes a tactic effective

- discuss the traditional tactics in public relations

- select tactics that seem particularly appropriate for specific publics

- describe how to carry out tactics efficiently and effectively

scenario

You are assistant director of public relations for a small but profitable international manufacturing firm based in California. Your company is publicly held; that is, it sells shares of ownership to stockholders throughout the world. Today you helped other members of the management team make a decision that's good news for some of your publics and bad news for others: To save money, your company is going to move a factory from Toronto, Canada, to San José, Costa Rica.

During the decision-making process, you advised the company's leaders about the move's impact on different publics. You suggested specific public relations tactics to be deployed if the company did vote to move the factory to Costa Rica. You even pointed out that some publics would be bitterly disappointed no matter what kinds of relationship-building tactics your company undertook. The best your company could do in those situations, you said, would be to minimize the unavoidable damage to these relationships.

After voting to move the factory, the leaders praised your assistance in helping them understand the wide-ranging impacts of such a decision. Now they've asked you to draw up a plan that recommends specific relationship-building tactics for each affected public. And they've asked you to hurry. The move will be announced next week.

Time to get started. Who are the relevant publics, and what relationship-building tactics do you suggest for each one?

Communicating with Specific Publics

A public relations plan is launched for one of two reasons: either to maintain or to change a relationship with an important public or publics. In Chapter 4 we examined the traditional publics in public relations, such as employees and the news media. In this chapter we examine specific **tactics** you can undertake to influence relationships with those publics. Accomplishing the tactics—often called communication—is the third phase of the public relations process, coming after research and planning. A tactic, once again, is a public relations action designed to have a particular effect on an organization's relationship with a particular public. In this chapter we also examine *how* you can accomplish tactics in a way that helps ensure their efficiency and effectiveness. This chapter also has a crucial link to the previous chapter, on planning: It describes specific tactics you could include as part of your plan. As you'll recall, a plan consists of

- a goal or goals;
- objectives that focus on particular publics; and
- recommended tactics.

This chapter examines traditional (and sometimes not-so-traditional) public relations tactics and offers a strategy for executing them.

Tactics as Messages and Channels

In Chapter 5, as you'll recall, we presented a basic communication model, which looks like this:

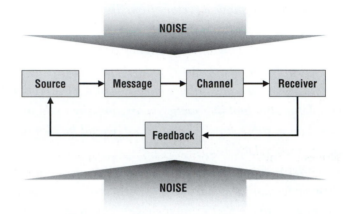

Public relations tactics enter this model as messages and channels. Messages have tactical value because they can influence a relationship. In our Canada to Costa Rica scenario, for example, management (source) could refuse to help (message) the unhappy workers in Toronto (receivers). That message certainly would influence the relationship. On the other hand, management could send a message that it will help the workers find new jobs. That message probably would have a different, more beneficial impact on the relationship. Because public relations tactics are designed to influence relationships, messages definitely are tactics.

More commonly, however, tactics are thought of as channels. A presentation from your company's top official in Toronto to the unhappy workers would be a channel—a tactic—designed to deliver a message and influence the relationship. A brochure that specifies exactly what the company will do for the Toronto workers could be another channel. Sometimes channels and messages are so intertwined that the channel becomes the message. For example, let's say your message to the unhappy workers in Toronto is *We'll help you find new jobs.* One channel for that message could be the creation of a training and placement center to help the employees polish their résumés and brush up on new job skills. In this case, the channel (the training and placement center) is so intertwined with the message *(We'll help you find new jobs)* that the two are indistinguishable.

If this seems overly complicated, let's remember our definition of a tactic: a public relations action designed to have a particular effect on an organization's relationship with a particular public. The messages we create can affect relationships; so can the channels that we use to send messages. Thus, both messages and channels can be tactics. Generally, a tactic is a channel with a message.

Successful messages and channels must respect the receiver's needs and preferences. An effective message, as we noted in Chapter 8, clearly addresses the receiver's values and interests. Likewise, an effective channel is one that appeals to the receiver. We can't rely exclusively on the channels that are cheapest or easiest, though that may be very tempting. Instead, our messages must flow through channels that our targeted receivers prefer.

So what are the available channels for our messages? A message can be sent through a special event, such as an open house or sponsorship of a particular charity's festival, or it can be sent through controlled or uncontrolled media. Let's take a closer look at these channels.

Special Events

You've certainly heard the cliché that actions speak louder than words. That cliché describes the message-sending power of a **special event.** For example, in our opening scenario, you could simply *tell* the upset employees in Toronto that your company cares

Special events, such as an appearance by the RayWatch "safe-sun" models (see Case Study 9.1, p. 302), can appeal to a variety of publics, including news media. (Courtesy of Canadian Dermatology Association and GCI Group)

about them and that the company will help them. But actions speak louder than words—so what "wordless" actions could *prove* that you'll help? You could offer a generous pay package that includes an extra three months of salary after the employees have been let go. And you could establish that training and placement center to help the workers prepare for new jobs with other employers. Those special events would clearly demonstrate that you're not abandoning your former employees. Instead, your special events would send the message that you value those individuals and that you'll help them through this difficult transition. Special events often weave together the message and the channel.

Special events are designed for the participants, of course, but in many cases they're also designed for observers. Your training and placement center in Toronto, for example, is clearly meant for the workers there—but it also sends a powerful message to workers in your other factories throughout the world: Your company takes care of its employees. That reassuring message should help strengthen relationships with the people who are best able to increase your company's productivity.

Another example of a special event that could target both participants and observers would be a student group's sponsorship of a Halloween party for underprivileged children. The party may send a message to the children, though that seems doubtful; they probably will be enjoying themselves too much to find any kind of message in their fun. But with a little help from the news media, the Halloween party definitely can send a message to important observers: potential members of the student group; university officials; and, perhaps most important, community members who may not have realized the contributions that college students can make to the community. One special event can help build relationships with many different important publics.

When public relations practitioners create a special event designed only to attract the attention of the news media, some practitioners call it a **pseudoevent.** However, as we discuss in QuickBreak 9.1, that term may be misleading. Public relations practitioners do not have the final say in what is news. Journalists who cover special events determine what is pseudo and what is not—and what is news and what is not.

Controlled Media

Media channels send words and images to the receiver. Some of those channels, such as newspapers and television news programs, are beyond the direct control of public relations practitioners; we can only give their editors information and hope that they use it. But with other media channels, such as various forms of advertising, employee newsletters, speeches, brochures, and web sites, we control the message. Such media are called **controlled media.** In controlled media, not only do we control the words and images; we also control when the message is sent and how often it's repeated.

Special events often use controlled media to emphasize their main point. For example, you might inaugurate your Toronto training and placement center with a speech from your company's district manager. In that speech, he or she would directly deliver the message to the factory employees: *We appreciate all you've done for us, and we'll help you find new jobs.* You might also produce and distribute a brochure

KISSES, TEA PARTIES, AND PSEUDOEVENTS

You may have seen it live: Madonna, Britney Spears, and Christina Aguilera heating up the MTV Video Music Awards when—cover your eyes, grandparents—Madonna kissed Britney on the lips. Uproar ensued, and Fox News quickly labeled the kiss a "pseudoevent."[1]

In recent decades, *pseudoevent* has become a term meaning an activity created solely to generate publicity. Historians have suggested that the Boston Tea Party was an early example of a U.S. pseudoevent. Critics have applied the same term to such activities as marches for and against abortion legislation.

So-called pseudoevents raise at least two interesting questions: What is the dividing line between a "real" event and a publicity stunt? And does it matter?

Regarding the first question, an activity's purpose may help separate the real from the fake. The Miss America pageant began as a publicity ploy to extend the tourist season of Atlantic City. Should that event, swimsuits and all, be compared to the Boston Tea Party?

Surely the goal of the desired publicity can separate one event from another.

But a more important factor may be the news coverage itself: If journalists report an event, they have deemed it newsworthy, nothing pseudo (from the Greek word *pseudes,* or "fake") about it. And this leads to the second question: Does it really matter if we call a public relations tactic a pseudoevent?

It does matter. Credibility is essential to effective public relations. The label *pseudoevent* suggests fakery on the part of public relations practitioners and gullibility on the part of journalists who report such an activity. Those qualities are not the hallmarks of a healthy relationship or a healthy democratic society that relies on the integrity of the two professions.

As more than one scholar has written, news is what journalists say it is. Madonna's kiss made worldwide headlines—nothing *pseudo* about that.

that describes the extended-salary policy as well as the features of the new training and placement center.

You could also use controlled media to manage your relationships with several other affected publics. You could send letters from the chief executive officer to all your stockholders, explaining how they'll benefit from the move. You could place articles in employee newsletters in your other factories around the world, telling employees there that their jobs are not in danger. You could place advertisements in the news media in San José, Costa Rica, notifying residents of the move and seeking employment applications. Such nonproduct advertising is often considered to be part of public relations. You could even include a message from the CEO on your web site. That message could help you manage relationships with publics that initiate contact with you, rather than vice versa.

Uncontrolled Media

Not all media, of course, are controlled. We can't tell television and radio stations which news stories to broadcast. We can't tell web sites such as Yahoo! which news headlines to feature on their homepages. Yet those media can be valuable channels in our quest to send messages to our targeted publics. By **uncontrolled media,** we often mean the news media: newspapers, radio and television stations, magazines, and on-line news providers. Each of those news providers employs individuals who act as gatekeepers—that is, editors who decide which stories to include and which stories to reject. Even if the gatekeepers decide to publish or broadcast our story, we can't control exactly what information they'll use or what other sources of information they'll seek out. Nor can we control when or how often they will publish or broad-cast our story.

Furthermore, uncontrolled media can initiate a story against your wishes. For ex-ample, perhaps a television station in Toronto has learned about your factory's planned move to Costa Rica before you're ready to announce it. The station sends a camera crew to your California headquarters with a request to interview the CEO. Should the CEO tell the reporters about the move? Ideally, you've planned for this possibility, and you have a tactic ready. For example, the CEO might simply say, "We'll be making an announcement about that in a few days." That won't satisfy re-porters, but at least you haven't allowed a definite message to reach your publics ahead of schedule; just as important, you haven't violated your values by lying. Be-cause the reporters will keep digging, you'd be wise to speed up your timetable to make the announcements as soon as possible.

Not every form of media is easily classified as controlled or uncontrolled. Some-times a channel can be both. For example, suppose that your organization's director of investor relations initiates a telephone conference call to several investment ana-lysts at the same time. She could begin with a prepared statement about the move to Costa Rica, using the conference call as a controlled medium. But after the statement she might invite the analysts to ask questions. Although she can control the wording of her answers, she can't control the questions. The conference call now becomes, at least partially, an uncontrolled medium.

Controlled versus Uncontrolled Media

So which are better: controlled or uncontrolled media? Neither. Each has its own ad-vantages and disadvantages. The advantages of controlled media include your abil-ity to select the exact words and images that get sent. A possible disadvantage is a lack of credibility. Receivers know that you're controlling the message, and they may wonder whether you're telling the whole truth. Another disadvantage of con-trolled media is cost: Generally, you pay for control, especially when using adver-tising to send a message. Unlike public relations, advertising purchases space or time in the news media; and, within legal limits, advertising controls the content of what it purchases.

Credibility and costs are lesser problems with *un*controlled media. Receivers know that you're not controlling the message; that key fact tends to give the message more credibility. As we've noted before, one reason media relations is such an important part of public relations is that the news media can provide a **third-party endorsement** or **in-dependent endorsement** of a news story. That is, in public relations, news media are

JOHNSON & JOHNSON

Johnson & Johnson is a manufacturer and provider of health-care products and services. The company was founded in 1886 and is headquartered in New Brunswick, New Jersey.

Our Credo:

We believe our first responsibility is to the doctors, nurses and patients, to the mothers and fathers and all others who use our products and services. In meeting their needs everything we do must be of high quality. We must constantly strive to reduce our costs in order to maintain reasonable prices. Customers' orders must be serviced promptly and accurately. Our suppliers and distributors must have an opportunity to make a fair profit.

We are responsible to our employees, the men and women who work with us throughout the world. Everyone must be considered as an individual. We must respect their dignity and recognize their merit. They must have a sense of security in their jobs. Compensation must be fair and adequate, and working conditions clean, orderly and safe.

We must be mindful of ways to help our employees fulfill their family responsibilities.

We are responsible to the communities in which we live and work and to the world community as well. We must be good citizens—support good works and charities and bear our fair share of taxes. We must encourage civic improvements and better health and education. We must maintain in good order the property we are privileged to use, protecting the environment and natural resources.

Our final responsibility is to our stockholders. Business must make a sound profit. We must experiment with new ideas. Research must be carried on, innovative programs developed and mistakes paid for. New equipment must be purchased, new facilities provided and new products launched. Reserves must be created to provide for adverse times. When we operate according to these principles, the stockholders should realize a fair return.

—"Our Credo,"
Johnson & Johnson web site

third parties—neither the sender nor the receiver—that can implicitly offer independent verification of a story's newsworthiness.

Sending messages through uncontrolled media usually costs less than doing so through controlled media. Using uncontrolled media may call for a written news release or a time-consuming meeting with a reporter, so it's not fair to say that uncontrolled media are free—but they generally are significantly less expensive than controlled media.

The disadvantage of uncontrolled media is clearly stated in their name: *uncontrolled*. Public relations practitioners can do their best to ethically influence the messages sent through uncontrolled media, but ultimate control of the message rests with others.

Public relations campaigns generally use both controlled and uncontrolled media. The trade-off is that controlled media ensure precise messages, whereas uncontrolled media are less expensive and offer stronger credibility.

Tactics and Traditional Publics

Public relations tactics range from low-tech, such as face-to-face meetings, to high-tech, such as online interactive videos. However, successful public relations tactics have several qualities in common:

- Successful tactics are part of a written, approved public relations plan that is tied to an organization's values-based mission.

- Successful tactics target publics one at a time. What works for one public may be completely inappropriate for another. However, if a tactic would be effective with more than one primary public, using it for all the appropriate publics could save time and money. A newsworthy special event, for example, could target event participants while also targeting other publics through the intervening public of the news media.

- Successful tactics are based on research about the targeted public's values, interests, and preferred channels of communication.

- Successful tactics send a clear message that targets a public's values and interests even as it strives to achieve an organization's objective. In other words, successful tactics try to create win-win situations in which both the sender and the receiver benefit.

- Successful tactics are evaluated as they're performed and after they're executed.

It would be impossible—and unwise—to create a list of standard public relations tactics to fit every situation. Every public relations challenge is different and requires special, even sometimes unique, tactics. But there are traditional tactics that every practitioner should know. Because successful tactics are directed toward specific publics, let's organize a discussion of traditional tactics around the publics that they might target. Table 9.1 presents a capsule summary of the discussion that follows.

Employees

We'll start with employees, who usually constitute one of every organization's most important publics. If employees aren't well informed and motivated, the quality of an organization's relationships with other publics may not matter; the organization is in danger of collapse.

FACE-TO-FACE MEETINGS.   Virtually every study of internal communications shows that employees' favorite channel for receiving information about their organizations is face-to-face meetings with their immediate supervisors. To use this channel, you may need to work with your organization's human resources or personnel department to create communication training programs for supervisors. Perhaps your organization could use the approach known as MBWA—management by walking around. Managers who aren't "chained" to their desks can initiate spontaneous face-to-face meetings with employees. However, as more organizations allow employees to work

TABLE 9.1	**Traditional Tactics for Traditional Publics**

Employees	*Investors*	*Customers*
face-to-face meetings	newsletters	product-oriented news releases
newsletters	magazines	product-oriented media kits
magazines	letters	special events
videos	annual meetings	open houses and tours
bulletin boards	annual reports	responses to customer contacts
speeches	web sites	bill inserts
intranets	facility tours	cell-phone text messaging
e-mail	conference calls	
instant messaging	news releases to financial news	*Constituents (Voters)*
special events	media	letters
	media advisories to financial	newsletters
News Media	news media	news releases
news releases	webcasts	media advisories
media kits		news conferences
fact sheets	*Community Groups*	speeches
backgrounders	volunteering	face-to-face meetings
photo opportunity sheets	donations	web sites
media advisories	sponsorships	responses to constituent
pitch letters	cause marketing	contacts
video news releases	speeches	
actualities	open houses and tours	*Businesses*
news conferences	face-to-face meetings	stories in trade magazines
public service announcements		extranets
guest editorials and	*Governments*	
commentaries	lobbies	
letters to the editor	grassroots lobbying	
interviews	political action committees	
satellite media tours	soft money	
stories for trade or association	disclosure documents	
magazines		

at home and "telecommute" by computer, organizing face-to-face meetings with immediate supervisors is becoming more difficult.

NEWSLETTERS.   Newsletters are generally inexpensive, and they have the virtue of putting a message in writing so that employees can review it. Newsletters should be frequent; if they appear infrequently, they run the risk of delivering old news—which means, of course, that they won't be read. Newsletters needn't be limited to paper. If everyone in your organization has easy access to a computer, a newsletter can be on-line and can include videos, sound clips, links to other sites, and an archive of former issues.

MAGAZINES.   Because they're more difficult than newsletters to produce, magazines usually aren't used to communicate breaking news stories to employees. Instead, magazines contain less time-sensitive stories, such as broad overviews of the organization's values and goals, stories about key employees, and updates on continuing issues. Some organizations mail their magazines to employees' homes, often in hopes that other family members will read them and feel goodwill toward the organization. Like newsletters, magazines can also exist online.

VIDEOS.   A message-bearing video can be used in several ways. Special videos or video newsletters might be shown on monitors in employee cafeterias and break rooms. Or, though this is more expensive, a video containing a particularly important message might be mailed to employees' homes or individually distributed at work. New video production technology makes downloading videos onto web sites fairly easy.

BULLETIN BOARDS.   Low-tech doesn't mean ineffective. Some organizations use controlled-access bulletin boards—often with the messages under a locked glass cover—to deliver daily news to employees. Some large organizations place the cafeteria's daily lunch menu on the bulletin board. Employees checking out the daily desserts just may stop and read other important announcements. Bulletin boards can help organizations meet legal requirements to post information regarding new labor laws or changes in employee benefits.

SPEECHES.   Employees generally like to see and be seen by the big boss. If an organization's leader is a good speaker, a face-to-face speech containing an important message can be highly effective as well as complimentary to an organization's employees. Such a speech means that the leader cares enough to look employees in the eye and tell them about the future of their organization. Copies of speeches can be distributed to specific employees; short speeches and excerpts of longer speeches can also be reprinted in employee newsletters.

INTRANETS.   We all know about the Internet, but what's an **intranet**? It's an organization's controlled-access internal computer network. A well-designed intranet not only provides e-mail processing; it includes an internal web site with department descriptions, links to other web sites, and an area for the latest news. As noted above, it also can contain newsletters, magazines, and videos.

E-MAIL.   According to recent studies, **e-mail** usage has soared to become organizations' most-used employee communications tactic. However, employees still consider face-to-face meetings more effective.[2] Employees report feeling overwhelmed by the volume of e-mail—and they know that it allows supervisors to relay bad news without the awkwardness of a face-to-face meeting. E-mail's convenience can also be its danger: Misunderstandings—or worse—can arise if one doesn't think before posting a message.

INSTANT MESSAGING.   As most teenagers and young adults know, **instant messaging** is a network-based computer system that allows several individuals to instantly exchange typed messages with one another. For example, five employees in different locations could conduct an instant messaging meeting on an important project. All five employees could see and respond to messages from one another. In the United States, more than 24 million employees who began using instant messaging in their personal lives now use IM for workplace communication (though two-thirds say they also use it to chat with family and friends during the workday).[3] As with e-mail, users of instant messaging should not sacrifice clarity and diplomacy for speed and convenience.

SPECIAL EVENTS.   Special events for employees can range from company picnics to special nights at sporting events to more complex tactics, such as the hypothetical training and placement center for your former employees in Toronto. Remember: controlled media such as brochures can often emphasize the message sent by a special event. For example, a groundbreaking ceremony for your new factory in Costa Rica would be a special event for government officials and the news media. A short speech—ideally in Spanish—by your CEO could be a controlled medium within that special event to help ensure that participants and observers receive the message that your company pledges to be a good corporate citizen.

Quick ✔ Check

1. What is a public relations tactic? In what stage of the public relations process do tactics play a role?
2. What's the difference between a message and a channel? When are they the same? When are they different?
3. What are the differences between controlled media and uncontrolled media?
4. What is an intranet?

News Media

Public relations practitioners generally target the news media as an intervening public—that is, as a go-between public that helps carry a message to a primary public. To place a message in the news media, practitioners use a variety of tactics to appeal to the media's so-called gatekeepers: the editors and producers who decide which stories to report and which to reject.

NEWS RELEASES.   The **news release** is one of the most important yet misused documents in all of public relations. A news release, ideally, is an objective, straightforward, unbiased news story that a public relations practitioner writes and distributes to appropriate news media. For example, in our Canada to Costa Rica scenario, you would issue news releases to news media in Costa Rica, in Toronto, in your hometown in California, and in any other cities where your organization has operations. In addition, because you have stockholders, you would issue news releases to the major financial news media around the world. News-release distribution services such as PR Newswire and BusinessWire could help circulate the news releases, and you could post the stories on your organization's web site as well.

Why do we say that news releases are among the most misused documents in public relations? Studies show that gatekeepers throw away more than 90 percent of the news releases they receive. Why? Many news releases commit one or both of two deadly sins: They have no local interest—that is, no appeal to a particular gatekeeper's audience—and/or they're too promotional; they lack the strict objectivity that characterizes good news reporting. An effective news release uses its headline and first paragraph to show a gatekeeper that it contains local interest. For example, your news release to the Toronto news media would be slightly different from your California news release. And far from being promotional, an effective news release sounds as if it were written by an objective reporter, not a public relations practitioner.

Though news releases go to print, broadcast, and online news media, most are written in newspaper style. Nonprint news media take such news releases and, if they use them, rewrite them in their own formats (see Chapter 10). The news media rarely publish or broadcast news releases word for word. If they use a news release, they generally rewrite it, often shortening it or including additional sources.

News releases reach the news media in a variety of ways. They can be mailed, faxed, e-mailed, or distributed through services such as PR Newswire. Occasionally, an organization's news releases are in such demand that it need only post them on its web site. That's the approach used by the Kansas City Chiefs of the National Football League.

MEDIA KITS.   Public relations practitioners use media kits to publicize complex stories that have many newsworthy elements. For example, television networks use media kits to publicize their upcoming programming seasons. A **media kit** packages at least one news release with other supporting documents. Two of the most common types of supporting documents are called *fact sheets* and *backgrounders*. A **fact sheet** is usually a what-who-when-where-why-how breakdown of the news release. Unlike the news release, however, the fact sheet is not written as a story; instead, it's just a well-organized list of the facts. Why include a fact sheet when the media kit already has a news release? Some journalists don't want to see your version of the story; they think you're biased. They want just the facts, and the fact sheet delivers those.

A **backgrounder** is a supplement to the news release. It contains useful background information on, for example, a person or organization mentioned in the news release. Like news releases, backgrounders usually are written as stories. Unlike news releases, however, backgrounders aren't news stories. Some feature testimonials from satisfied customers. Many others read like biographies. For example, you might choose to send media kits to Costa Rican news media so that they can learn more about your company. Your backgrounders might include a short history of the company that

Media Kit Morningstar Communications created this innovative media kit for CommunityAmerica Credit Union's "Stuff the Bus" campaign, which donates school supplies to needy children. (Courtesy of Morningstar Communications Company and CommunityAmerica Credit Union)

expands the brief description contained in your news release. Another backgrounder might be a biography of the CEO that, again, expands the briefer biography contained in your news release.

Media kits can have other documents. If the media kit is publicizing a visually attractive event, such as a groundbreaking ceremony for your new factory in Costa Rica, you might include a **photo opportunity sheet.** Photo opportunity sheets aren't meant for publication, so they can include a little bit of fact-based promotional writing designed to spark a gatekeeper's interest. Photo opportunity sheets tell what, who, when, and where. They can include special instructions for photographers as well as maps showing the location of the event.

Media kits can also include brochures, product samples, and any other document or item that can help gatekeepers make well-informed decisions about the newsworthiness of the story.

Media kits ordinarily are mailed to the news media. Increasingly, entire media kits—including news releases, backgrounders, fact sheets, videos, and photographs—are placed on **CD-ROMs** or **DVDs** and distributed to the news media (see Chapter 11).

MEDIA ADVISORIES.   Some newsworthy stories take shape so quickly that there's not time to write and distribute a news release. In such situations, public relations practitioners often issue a **media advisory.** Media advisories are also issued to remind the news media about events they may want to cover. Like a fact sheet, a media advisory isn't written as a story; instead, it simply lists the necessary information about what, who, when, where, why, and how. Media advisories are generally faxed or e-mailed to the news media.

PITCH LETTERS.   A **pitch letter** is, in certain circumstances, a replacement for a news release. A pitch letter is a letter to a journalist, a gatekeeper, that "pitches" a story that may not be important but still is interesting. Pitch letters often are used for softer human-interest stories that don't merit the "hard news" approach of a news release yet are newsworthy and would generate favorable publicity for an organization. Unlike news releases, which are sent to several news media at the same time, pitch letters usually are sent to only one news medium at a time. In other words, they offer an exclusive to the news medium.

VIDEO NEWS RELEASES.   **Video news releases,** commonly called **VNRs,** are distributed to television stations. As online news media become more sophisticated, however, we may see public relations practitioners arranging the online transfer of videos to news media. Video news releases are designed to look like television news stories. Like news releases, VNRs ideally are finished products; they're ready to broadcast. However, most VNRs include a section called **b-roll,** which contains unedited video footage of the news story. Many television stations prefer to create their own version of the story, using b-roll instead of the finished VNR. B-roll, they believe, gives them more control over the presentation of the story.

VNRs are distributed on videocassette, on floppy disk, on CD, and via satellite. A VNR can be beamed to a satellite at a particular time and downloaded by interested television stations, which have been notified, often by media advisories, about the timing and the correct satellite coordinates. Unlike print news releases, VNRs are expensive to produce and distribute. They should be used only for highly visual, highly newsworthy stories.

ACTUALITIES.   **Actualities** are sound bites for radio stations. They're catchy quotes and sometimes accompany written news releases. Actualities usually are placed on cassette tapes and mailed to radio stations, but they also can be distributed through telephone menu systems and through an organization's web site.

NEWS CONFERENCES.   News conferences are like dynamite. They should be used only when necessary—and even then with caution. A **news conference** is a scheduled meeting between an organization's representative(s) and the news media. Your organization should consider scheduling a news conference when—and *only* when—three conditions exist:

1. You have a highly newsworthy breaking story. A breaking story is extremely timely; it can't wait on a news release, media kit, or VNR.
2. It is advantageous to meet with reporters as a group, instead of individually.
3. You know that journalists will be glad they came; the story is that good.

If your story meets the above three criteria, no problem; your news conference is a productive media relations tactic. But if your story *doesn't* meet those criteria, get ready for trouble: Either journalists will be angry that you didn't use a different communication tactic that shows more respect for their time—or they simply won't come, damaging your reputation as a public relations practitioner. If journalists can get the same information in another form—such as a VNR or a media kit—without being disappointed, use that other form instead of a news conference.

News conferences should be used with caution because they are the ultimate experience in uncontrolled media. You can try to set the agenda with an opening statement, but following that, reporters generally get to ask questions—and there is no guarantee that they'll ask questions that you want to answer or are prepared to answer.

President George W. Bush uses news conferences as a communications tactic to build relationships with voters, political leaders, and other important publics. (Courtesy of the White House)

When a news conference definitely is the media relations tactic to use, however, consider these guidelines:

- Invite news media to the news conference with media advisories and follow-up telephone calls.

- Schedule the news conference strategically. By this we mean that you should balance your organization's interests against those of the news media. The news media generally prefer a mid-morning schedule. That's the best time for TV journalists who want to broadcast the story on the evening news, and it also benefits newspaper journalists with late-afternoon deadlines for the next morning's paper. A mid-*afternoon* news conference, on the other hand, limits immediate media coverage of the story to your organization's message; it reduces journalists' time for investigation. In scheduling a news conference, you must balance the needs of your organization against the value of a good relationship with the news media.

- Rehearse your presenters. Ask them the toughest questions that reporters may pose, and help them develop honest, credible answers.

- Have very few presenters—ideally, just one. Don't muddle the news conference with several speakers.

- Hold the news conference in a location that's easily accessible and has plenty of parking spaces.

- Hold the news conference in a room that has plenty of electrical outlets for television crews and photographers.

- Begin with a prepared statement. After that, accept questions from journalists. Avoid answering, "No comment." If you can't or won't answer a question, explain why.

- Don't let the news conference run more than one hour.

- Distribute media kits that reinforce and supplement the news story.

- Film and record the conference to provide video- and audiotapes to TV and radio stations that couldn't attend. These recordings also allow you to keep a record of exactly what was said.

PUBLIC SERVICE ANNOUNCEMENTS. Public service announcements, often called **PSAs,** are advertisements created by nonprofit organizations to publicize their services. The news media do not charge for PSAs as they do for commercial announcements. PSAs for the broadcast news media exist in a variety of formats. A broadcast PSA might be simply a short script for a radio announcer to read, or it might be produced like a commercial and distributed on audio- or videocassettes or compact discs. Radio and television stations broadcast PSAs to meet legal public service requirements. Just as with news releases, however, there's no guarantee that the media will use your PSA.

PSAs also target the print media, where they're sometimes called *public service advertisements* or *public service messages*. In newspapers and magazines, PSAs are similar to print advertisements. Organizations provide them in standard advertising sizes and "camera ready," which means ready to be photographed with the rest of the magazine page to make a plate for a printing press. Or, for pages designed on computer screens, print PSAs are distributed on disk and online for easy transfer to a computer file.

PSAs also exist for web sites. In the United States, the Ad Council, a group of corporations and other organizations that creates and distributes PSAs, offers thin horizontal online advertisements called "banners" that promote Smokey Bear, seat-belt safety, education, and other social needs. Organizations wanting to support those causes can, with permission, download a banner from the Ad Council's web site and place it on their own web site.

GUEST EDITORIALS/COMMENTARIES.   Most news media, especially newspapers, are willing to consider guest editorials or commentaries on issues important to the medium's audience. In our Canada to Costa Rica scenario, for example, you might want to consider having your chief executive officer prepare an editorial for a Toronto newspaper. The editorial could defend the move, describing the actions your company took to try to stay in Toronto and explaining why those efforts failed. In reality, the CEO might ask you to write the editorial. He or she might then make a few changes, and the editorial would be sent to the newspaper under the CEO's name.

Unlike news releases, guest editorials or commentaries aren't sent to several different news media at once. Instead, news media are approached one at a time and asked whether they would be interested in such an editorial. Editorials are offered as exclusives. Editors and producers can be contacted by a business letter that's quickly followed up with a phone call.

A related tactic involves meeting with a news medium's editorial board. That board doesn't exist to do favors for your organization, but it should be interested in fairness and fact-based opinions. Some news media have community editorial boards in which selected nonjournalists help a news medium formulate the editorials it publishes or broadcasts. Members of such boards occasionally write the editorials themselves.

LETTERS TO THE EDITOR.   Like a guest editorial or commentary, a letter to the editor allows a member of your organization to express an opinion on an important issue. Unlike an editorial, however, a letter to the editor doesn't require you to contact the news medium first. You simply mail a well-written letter and hope for the best. Though most of us think of sending letters to print media such as newspapers and magazines, radio stations and television stations also sometimes read, on air, letters from members of their audiences. For example, the show *All Things Considered*, on National Public Radio, reads letters from its listeners every Thursday afternoon.

INTERVIEWS.   Yet another way for your organization to publicize its point of view is to offer a high-ranking official to different news media for interviews. Occasionally, interviews for television stations can involve a tactic called a **satellite media tour (SMT)**. During a satellite media "tour," your organization's official actually never leaves a local television studio. Instead, he or she links one at a time, via satellite, with television stations around the world for live or recorded interviews. In the Canada to Costa Rica scenario, for example, your organization's CEO could offer individual interviews to the major television stations in Costa Rica without ever leaving California. Satellite media tours often are publicized by means of media advisories or phone calls to specific television stations.

STORIES FOR TRADE OR ASSOCIATION MAGAZINES.   If your organization is known for its expertise in a particular area, trade or association magazines may well be interested in publishing a story written by one of your experts. **Trade magazines** target members of particular trades and professions: construction companies, farmers, veterinarians, and so on. **Association magazines** are similar, being a benefit of belonging to an organization such as the American Library Association. If your organization offers a product or service that might benefit members of a trade, profession, or association, you can contact these magazines' editors with story ideas. You can also offer your experts should the magazine editors have story ideas for which they're seeking writers. Unlike news releases, such stories are not distributed to several magazines at once. Instead, the story is an arrangement between your organization and one particular magazine.

Investors

Investors are an important traditional public in public relations. By purchasing stock, they represent a source of capitalization for an organization—and because they own stock, they technically are the organization's owners. As we note in Chapter 4, investors include individual stockholders; institutional investors, such as the huge California Public Employees Retirement System; investment analysts; mutual fund managers; and the financial news media. We now know the traditional ways to communicate with the news media, but what are the standard tactics for other members of the investment community? A warning before we proceed: As we discuss in Chapter 15, communications with the investment community are closely regulated by such organizations as the Securities and Exchange Commission and the major stock exchanges.

NEWSLETTERS AND MAGAZINES.   Some companies have periodic publications that they distribute to investors. Such publications can discuss company goals, changes in leadership, new product lines, or anything else that might affect the performance of the company's stock. The publications also can steer investors to the company's web site or its investor relations office for more current information.

LETTERS.   Databases allow companies to send personal letters to stockholders, addressing them by name and noting the number of shares they have as well as how much they're earning in dividends. These letters can be more intimate than comparatively impersonal newsletters and magazines. A company might use personal letters for sensitive situations, as in an effort to get minor shareholders either to buy more of the company's stock or to sell their few shares back to the company.

BEATING THE ODDS: SUCCESSFUL NEWS RELEASES

Studies show that journalists have a favorite place for 92 to 98 percent of the news releases they receive: their wastebaskets, online or otherwise.

That's the bad news. The good news is that a tiny minority of well-written news releases do succeed. But what makes a good news release?

Journalism professor Linda Morton has conducted several national studies of what journalists seek in news releases, and she offers this advice:[4]

- Write in a simple style. Use short sentences and paragraphs and common words.

- Focus your news release on one of the four topics that succeed best with editors: consumer information, a coming event, interesting research, or a timely issue.

- Localize the news release. Practitioners often call such news releases "hometowners,"

because they clearly target an editor's specific audience.

- Above all else, serve the editor's audience. Research the information needs of each editor's audience, find a way in which your organization can address those needs, and then write an objective news story on that crucial link.

Morton's research shows that public relations practitioners who follow these basic guidelines place almost one-third of their news releases. That's about 700 percent better than the success rate of practitioners who ignore the needs of journalists and their audiences.

Page 1—or the wastebasket? You can make the difference.

ANNUAL MEETINGS.   The Securities and Exchange Commission requires every U.S.-based company that sells stock to hold an annual meeting for its stockholders. Most stock exchanges also require annual meetings as a prerequisite for membership. Not only stockholders but investment analysts and members of the financial news media attend annual meetings. The **annual meeting** can be an excellent channel to investors; it allows a company to use controlled media tactics such as speeches, videos, and brochures.

Not every element of an annual meeting is controlled, however. Question-and-answer periods with investors can rattle even the toughest executives. Some investors, known as gadflies, buy a few shares of a company's stock just to earn the right to attend the annual meeting, where they ask confrontational questions. In the Canada to Costa Rica scenario, for example, you should prepare for the possibility that former employees or other residents of Toronto who own shares in your company may attend your next annual meeting and launch emotional attacks on your rationale for the move.

ANNUAL REPORTS.   Like annual meetings, annual reports are required by the Securities and Exchange Commission and by most stock exchanges. Anyone who owns even a single share of stock in a company receives its annual report, which often looks like a glossy magazine but can also exist in a second, complementary form

QuickBreak 9.3

THE VNR THAT WENT TOO FAR?

The television news report showed President George W. Bush earning a standing ovation as he signed the new Medicare law of 2004. The story included footage of a pharmacist telling an elderly customer that the new law "helps you better afford your medications." At the end of the news spot, the reporter signed off with "In Washington, I'm Karen Ryan reporting."[5]

But Karen Ryan wasn't a reporter. She was a public relations practitioner, and the news story was a video news release (VNR) produced by the federal Department of Health and Human Services—and that's where the trouble began.

Video news releases can be as controversial as they are popular. As television news staffs decrease in size, TV journalists increasingly rely on video supplied by public relations practitioners.[6] However, in its position paper on video news releases, the Radio-Television News Directors Association states:

> RTNDA does not endorse the use of so-called video news releases, but neither do we reject their use, as long as that use conforms to the association's Code of Ethics. . . . RTNDA believes that sound journalistic practice calls for clear identification of all material received from outside sources."[7]

As critics denounced the Medicare VNR, an angry Ryan responded, "Shame on me for practicing my profession and engaging in a standard, acceptable practice, namely narrating a VNR."[8] Other public relations practitioners agreed that Ryan had followed standard procedures for video news releases.[9]

But this VNR was for the federal government—and under the Gillett amendment (p. 40) and Congress' annual "Consolidated Appropriations Resolution," which helps establish the federal budget, "no part of any appropriation contained in this or any other Act shall be used

for publicity or propaganda purposes within the United States not heretofore authorized by Congress."[10]

After studying three versions of the VNR, the federal Government Accountability Office, which reviews federal programs and expenditures, concluded that the Medicare VNR "violated the publicity or propaganda prohibition" because the ready-to-play news story and script did not identify the federal government as the story's creator.[11] The GAO did note that Health and Human Services had correctly labeled every other aspect of the VNRs, including b-roll—but had neglected to identify itself as the source of the Karen Ryan story.[12]

As the controversy spread to CNN, MSNBC, *USA Today,* and the *New York Times,* the Public Relations Society of America responded. In a written statement, PRSA issued these guidelines for VNRs:

- Organizations that produce VNRs should clearly identify the VNR as such and fully disclose who produced and paid for it at the time the VNR is provided to TV stations.

- PRSA recommends that organizations that prepare VNRs should not use the word "reporting" if the narrator is not a reporter.

- Use of VNRs or footage provided by sources other than the station or network should be identified as to source by the media outlet when it is aired.[13]

In recommending both that public relations practitioners identify themselves as such and that TV journalists take more responsibility for the quality of their newscasts, *American Journalism Review* magazine concluded, "The truth is, there's plenty of blame to go around in the aftermath of the Medicare video news release flap."[14]

such as a video, CD, or web site. By law, an **annual report** features recent financial information, a year-to-year comparison of financial figures, a description of the organization's upper-level management, and a letter from the company's leader that discusses the organization's health and direction.

Annual reports are also sent to investment analysts, mutual fund managers, the major financial news media, and any potential investor who requests a copy. Many organizations post their annual reports on their web sites.

WEB SITES.   Web sites are an excellent way for companies to communicate with their investors. Live **webcasts** regarding important announcements can be broadcast. Stock prices can be updated continuously; e-mail links can be provided; special statements and news releases can be indexed; video tours can be offered; the text of recent speeches can be featured; and the annual report can be included, as can the quarterly updates filed with the SEC. A good, interactive web site can function as a daily newsletter for investors, investment analysts, and the financial news media.

OTHER TACTICS FOR INVESTMENT ANALYSTS, MUTUAL FUND MANAGERS, AND THE FINANCIAL NEWS MEDIA.   Investment analysts, mutual fund managers, and financial journalists don't like to be surprised. They require current information on a company and immediate updates about any events that might affect the company's financial performance. Investor relations practitioners can ensure rapid, frequent communication through such tactics as live webcasts, factory or other facility tours, telephone conference calls, and letters. News releases and media advisories can be distributed to the financial news media, often through services such as PR Newswire and Business-Wire, which can electronically transfer these documents to news media throughout the world. Often, timely news releases are required by the SEC and the major stock markets (see Chapter 15).

Quick ✔ Check

1. How is a news release different from a media advisory? From a backgrounder? From a fact sheet? From a VNR?
2. What advice would you have for a friend who wants to hold a news conference?
3. What is an annual report? What publics does it target?

Community Groups

Community groups include churches, schools, professional organizations, clubs, chambers of commerce, and other local groups whose values somehow intersect with those of an organization. Relationship-building tactics for such groups can be high-tech; more often, however, community relations tactics fall into the roll-up-your-sleeves-and-get-involved category.

VOLUNTEERING.   Many organizations encourage employees to volunteer at schools, churches, hospitals, senior centers, libraries, and other important local institutions. Some organizations allow time off for volunteer activities, and others make cash donations to community groups based on how many volunteer hours their employees donate. Volunteerism is a powerful, rewarding way to build positive relationships with community groups.

DONATIONS AND SPONSORSHIPS.   After organizations have rolled up their sleeves and volunteered, they sometimes open their wallets and donate. Sometimes those donations take the form of sponsorships—for example, paying the bills for a local literacy program's fund-raising carnival. Such generosity can create goodwill for an organization, but letting someone else spend your money sometimes leads to unpleasant surprises. Be sure to specify in writing exactly what the donated money is for, and then monitor the situation to ensure that your donation was spent correctly.

Instead of money, some organizations donate goods or services or even the expertise of their employees. For example, a community bank might lend a tax expert to a local nonprofit organization to help it prepare its tax returns. Or a local manufacturing company might allow an executive to work half-time temporarily as the coordinator of the community's United Way campaign.

CAUSE MARKETING.   Organizations sometimes devote money, goods, services, and volunteerism to particular social needs, such as literacy or cancer research. In a sense, the organizations adopt a particular social need as their primary philanthropy. Such a community relations tactic is called **cause marketing.** Like special events, cause marketing often addresses more than one public. It certainly addresses people affected by the social need; most organizations that adopt a cause genuinely want to help. But the tactic also is designed to create goodwill among government officials, consumers, current and potential employees, and other important publics that can help the organization achieve its goals.

SPEECHES.   Professional and civic groups such as the Kiwanis Club, the Rotary Club, and the League of Women Voters often seek community leaders to speak on current issues at weekly or monthly meetings. If an organization has a stake in a local issue, a speech followed by a question-and-answer session can promote the organization's point of view and collect information about how other people feel.

OPEN HOUSES/TOURS.   Organizations that produce interesting goods or services can build goodwill in the community by sponsoring open houses and offering tours of company facilities. Open houses and tours often provide opportunities to use controlled media such as speeches, brochures, and videos. They also provide opportunities to distribute so-called specialty advertising products such as coffee mugs, Frisbees, ball caps, and other items that feature an organization's name and logo.

FACE-TO-FACE MEETINGS.   Community groups sometimes are activist groups. For example, an environmental group in Costa Rica may wonder how your company's new factory will dispose of toxic waste. At the first sign that such a group is studying your organization, it's vital that you open lines of communication with its members—ideally through face-to-face meetings. Many activist groups gather their research before they assume a firm public stance. If you can demonstrate your organization's good intentions before the activist group solidifies its position, you may defuse a crisis before it begins.

In community relations, face-to-face meetings need not be limited to activist groups. An organization can conduct such meetings with a variety of neutral or friendly community groups in hopes of paving the way for alliances or partnerships on future problems or opportunities. Such a process is called **coalition building.**

Governments

Governmental action at any level—federal, state, county, or city—can profoundly affect an organization. Public relations practitioners thus use a portfolio of tactics to make their organizations' voices heard in the halls of government.

LOBBIES AND LOBBYISTS.   A **lobby** is a special-interest group that openly attempts to influence government actions, especially federal and state legislative processes. One of the most effective lobbies at the turn of this century, for example, has been AARP, formerly the American Association of Retired Persons, which advances the interests of people age 50 and older. A *lobbyist* is someone who, acting on behalf of a special-interest group, tries to influence various forms of government regulation. Lobbies and lobbyists generally pass persuasive information along to government officials. They host special events for officials and their staffs, and they often respond to government officials' requests for information on particular issues.

At the federal level in the United States, lobbies and lobbyists are regulated by the Lobbying Disclosure Act, which mandates that people who are paid to lobby Congress or the executive branch of the federal government must register with the government. Paid lobbyists must specify whom they represent and how much they are being paid.

GRASSROOTS LOBBYING.   Not all lobbyists must register with the federal government. If you write a letter to your congressional representatives asking them to increase funding for student loans, you're acting as a lobbyist for a special interest, but you need not register. Such informal, infrequent, "unprofessional" lobbying is often called **grassroots lobbying,** especially if you're acting with others to show legislators broad support for your opinion. Because grassroots lobbying is the "voice of the people," it can be highly influential with elected government officials.

POLITICAL ACTION COMMITTEES.   **Political action committees,** often called **PACs,** have one purpose: to donate money to candidates and political parties. Political action committees are sponsored by corporations, labor unions, special-interest groups, and other organizations. In 2003, more than 4,000 PACs were registered with the federal government; such registration is required for PACs that donate money to presidential or congressional candidates.[15] State governments also have laws that govern PAC donations.

Corporations and labor unions aren't allowed to donate money directly to candidates for federal offices. But they can form PACs, which can accept voluntary—not mandatory—donations from employees, members, and others and route the money to candidates who support their views.

SOFT MONEY.   So-called **soft money** was money donated to political parties to be spent not on individual candidates but on noncandidate projects such as get-out-the-vote drives, voter education, and issues-oriented advertising. Critics of soft money contended that political parties often illegally used it to support candidates. In 2002, Congress passed legislation that stopped the flow of soft money to political parties. Proponents and opponents of soft money alike attacked the legislation. Proponents claimed it violated First Amendment guarantees of freedom of speech. Opponents of soft money claimed the legislation left open many loopholes, including hefty donations to national political conventions and to local branches of political parties. Proponents and opponents of soft money also agree that the legislation will change in the future. Public relations practitioners who specialize in government relations are well advised to monitor the legality of soft money.

DISCLOSURE DOCUMENTS.   In the United States, companies that sell stock must, by law, communicate with the government. Often, investor relations practitioners help write and file a comprehensive annual report—called a 10-K—with the federal Securities and Exchange Commission. Other SEC forms that practitioners often help prepare or review are the 10-Q (quarterly financial report) and the 8-K (used to announce an event that might affect the price of the company's stock). Disclosure law is covered more fully in Chapter 15.

Customers

Customer relations is where public relations overlaps with marketing (see Chapter 13). Marketing, simply put, is the process of getting a customer to buy your product or service. Most marketing tactics lie outside the boundaries of traditional public relations; marketing tactics include advertising, direct-mail letters, coupons and other sales promotions, and face-to-face sales encounters. But public relations can add several tactics to what is called the *marketing mix*.

PRODUCT-ORIENTED NEWS RELEASES AND MEDIA KITS.   We discussed news releases and media kits earlier in this chapter. When news releases or media kits focus on a newsworthy aspect of a product or service, they target customers and are part of the so-called marketing mix. The news media become an intervening public between an organization and the customers it's hoping to reach.

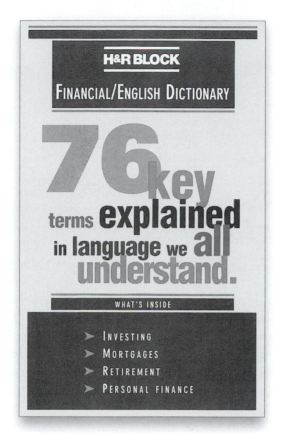

Brochure A popular brochure by H&R Block, a financial services company, builds relationships by addressing customers' often-insufficient knowledge of financial and tax terms. (Courtesy of H&R Block)

SPECIAL EVENTS.   There's no telling who the next fictional hero for young children will be. We've already seen an aardvark named Arthur and a school principal who can become Captain Underpants. One thing is certain: Whoever or whatever the next heroes are, costumed actors who portray them will visit our bookstores. Such a visit is a special event, which is any out-of-the-ordinary occurrence designed to attract customers.

OPEN HOUSES AND TOURS.   An organization with interesting products or services or unusual production technology can attract customers by inviting them to tour its facilities. During open houses and tours, customers often get to sample or test products or services. Wineries, for example, often offer tours and free samples to visitors of legal drinking age.

RESPONSES TO CUSTOMER CONTACTS.   Smart organizations respond quickly to phone calls, letters, and e-mail messages from customers and potential customers. Such two-way communication not only builds customer loyalty; it also helps an organization know what its customers are thinking.

FOR IMMEDIATE RELEASE

FOR MORE INFORMATION:
Mirna Aceituno, McDonald's
(630) 623-6432

Michael Delgado, VPE Public Relations
(626) 403-3200, Ext. 217

McDONALD'S® NEW *SIZZLING* McGRIDDLES® BREAKFAST SANDWICHES ARE TRULY INNOVATIVE

Customers Now Have A New Convenient Way To Eat Their Favorite Breakfast Tastes

OAK BROOK, Ill. (June 9, 2003) – Question: What's ingenious, innovative and yummy all over? **Answer:** McDonald's new McGriddles breakfast sandwiches! A new, permanent menu item, McGriddles breakfast sandwiches provide an innovative way for customers to eat warm golden griddle cakes (with the sweet taste of maple syrup baked right in), and different combinations of savory sausage, crispy bacon, fluffy eggs and melted cheese in a convenient sandwich. Beginning June 10, 2003, McDonald's customers nationwide can enjoy these one-of-a-kind creations at participating McDonald's restaurants.

The three varieties of these new, hot breakfast sandwiches consist of two soft and warm golden griddle cakes -- with the yummy taste of maple syrup baked right in -- and a choice of sausage, sausage, egg & cheese, or bacon, egg & cheese. The sausage McGriddles breakfast sandwiches are available at a suggested retail price of $1.59 and the other two tasty varieties are available for a suggested price of $2.19 (prices and participation may vary).

"These new breakfast sandwiches are truly unique to the breakfast category," said Max Gallegos, director of marketing, McDonald's USA. "No other restaurant has them and in test restaurants across the nation, McGriddles have wowed our customers with their one-of-a-kind combination of sweet and savory tastes. It's another way McDonald's is responsive to evolving consumer tastes and providing a novel breakfast option."

News Release McDonald's Corporation used news releases to help explain the ingredients of McGriddles breakfast sandwiches. For a Spanish-language version of this news release, see page 474.
(Courtesy of Valencia, Pérez & Echeveste Public Relations)

NET GAINS

As the Internet grows in influence and popularity, it can seem like the magic tactic, the high-tech solution to all public relations needs. Data from the Pew Internet & American Life Project, however, indicate that cyber magic has its limits:

- The Internet plays a daily role in the lives of 88 percent of U.S Internet users; one-third of users report that it plays "a major role" every day. But a clear majority of daily users prefer off-line alternatives for almost any service the Internet can provide. The only clear advantage for the Net? Supplying maps.[16]

- Slightly more than three-fourths of Internet users go online to communicate with government officials. Internet users are three times more likely to contact government agencies than nonusers, and half of Internet users say their online access has improved their relationship with governments. But, for the majority of Americans, personal visits and telephone calls to government officials outrank online access.[17]

- Internet users are increasingly becoming on-line content suppliers—but these creators remain a small minority. In the United States, 13 percent of Internet users have their own web sites, and 7 percent have web cameras attached to their computers. Approximately 7 percent of U.S. users have their own blogs, and 11 percent read blogs.[18]

The Internet can be a stunningly effective tactic for relationship building—and it can be utterly inappropriate for some publics. A former print ad for a telecommunications company said it best: "The Internet is your friend—but not your only friend."

BILL INSERTS.   Organizations that regularly mail bills or other financial statements to customers often include **bill inserts:** brochures or newsletters that focus on customer interests. Occasionally, short messages, such as *For more information, visit our web site at www.whatever,* are printed directly on a bill.

CELL-PHONE TEXT MESSAGING.   Organizations can use **text messaging** to notify customers of special offers—even using global positioning devices and satellites to contact customers as they near favorite stores.

Constituents (Voters)

As we noted in Chapter 4, many organizations try to influence the legislative process by building relationships with eligible voters. But for public relations practitioners employed by democratically elected governments, voters are the most important public of all. We're already familiar with many of the tactics that government practitioners use to build productive relationships between elected or appointed officials and their constituents: letters and newsletters; news releases, media advisories, and news conferences; speeches; face-to-face meetings; and interactive web sites.

Although every organization should respond quickly to letters, phone calls, and e-mail messages from members of important publics, such responses are particularly significant in the relationship between elected or appointed government officials and voters. A quick, personalized reply, even if a more detailed follow-up response is necessary, is one of the most important tactics in constituent relations. These responses encourage constituents to feel connected to and valued by their representatives. Members of Congress, for example, have staff members who spend the majority of their working hours addressing constituent concerns. Contacts from constituents can also be an excellent source of research data regarding issues that concern potential voters.

Businesses

Business-to-business communication is big business in the 21st century. If organizations are to reach their goals, they must use a variety of tactics to build relationships with other businesses such as suppliers and business customers. Just like tactics for individual customers, business-to-business tactics sometimes more closely resemble marketing than public relations. Such tactics include personal selling, price discounts, trade shows, and direct-mail advertising. But some business-to-business tactics are pure public relations.

MAGAZINES.   Businesses that offer products to other businesses sometimes publish glossy magazines with articles that feature product applications. Targeted customers receive the magazines at no charge.

STORIES IN TRADE MAGAZINES.   Businesses can attract new customers as well as new suppliers by writing and submitting stories to trade, or professional, magazines. Often, such stories present a company official as an expert on a particular topic. Many magazines focus on trades or professions such as law, carpentry, and farming. Those magazines accept and publish well-written stories of interest to their readers. Such magazines also publish news releases, which generally are shorter than featured stories and do not include a byline.

EXTRANETS.   Extranets are controlled-access computer networks, similar to intranets. At a minimum, they usually include web sites and e-mail capabilities. Unlike intranets, extranets are for businesses outside the host business. For example, winemaker Robert Mondavi purchases NASA satellite photos of vineyards and posts them on its extranet so that its independent grape suppliers can spot problems before they become serious.[19]

Accomplishing the Tactics

Most of the research has been done. The plan has been written and approved. Now it's time to carry out the tactics. Though this section appears near the end of the chapter, it is, in reality, the center of gravity, the focus of this chapter. Simply selecting a tactic does not create communication. Rather, communication begins

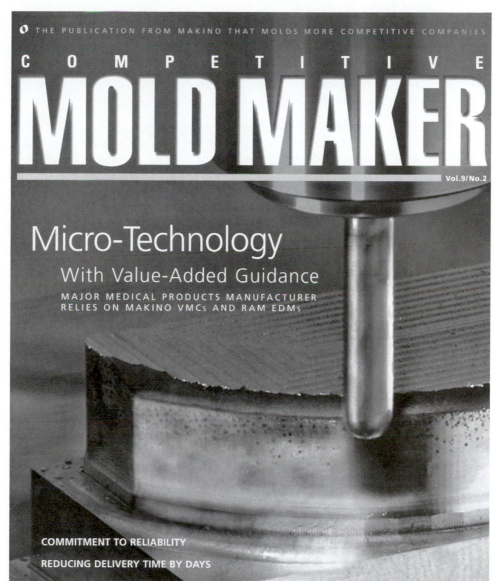

◊ THE PUBLICATION FROM MAKINO THAT MOLDS MORE COMPETITIVE COMPANIES

COMPETITIVE
MOLD MAKER

Vol. 9/No. 2

Micro-Technology
With Value-Added Guidance
MAJOR MEDICAL PRODUCTS MANUFACTURER
RELIES ON MAKINO VMCs AND RAM EDMs

COMMITMENT TO RELIABILITY

REDUCING DELIVERY TIME BY DAYS

DEVELOPING A PARTNERSHIP

**SPECIALIZATION SETS THE PATH
FOR SUCCESS**

Business-to-Business Magazine Makino publishes *Competitive Mold Maker,* and its accompanying web site, to promote its technological abilities to the die- and mold-making industry. (Courtesy of Makino and HSR Business to Business, Inc.)

when the tactic is executed. High standards are essential at this point of the public relations process. No amount of research or planning can overcome sloppy communication efforts. Public relations practitioners, therefore, tend to stress six key factors as they execute a plan's tactics: delegation, deadlines, quality control, communication within the team, communication with clients or supervisors, and constant evaluation.

1. *Delegation.*   Delegate the responsibility for a tactic's execution to a particular individual. With every tactic in a written plan, include the responsible individual's name. For example, in the Canada to Costa Rica scenario, your plan would charge one individual with the responsibility of creating a job-training and placement center. That individual wouldn't have to act alone—but he or she, ultimately, would bear the responsibility of creating the center. Naming names in this manner helps ensure successful results: No one wants to be the highly visible manager of a failed tactic.

2. *Deadlines.*   In the written plan, establish a deadline for the completion of each tactic. For example, each local-interest news release necessary in the Canada to Costa Rica scenario would have a mailing or transmission deadline. The named manager of each tactic would be responsible for meeting that deadline.

3. *Quality control.*   Conduct quality control. Have more than one editor and proofreader examine every document. Attend photo shoots to ensure that photographers are getting the picture you planned. Visit printing companies to ensure that the colors of your brochures and magazines are correct. (You may even get to shout, "Stop the press!") Look over a lot of shoulders as the tactics progress. In public relations for the move to Costa Rica, part of quality control would include double-checking the quality of Spanish-language news releases. And because the Spanish of Costa Rica is different from the Spanish of Spain, you would be wise to seek the assistance of native Costa Rican public relations professionals.

4. *Communication within the team.*   Encourage communication among the practitioners who are executing the tactics. Frequent short meetings in which teammates update one another can be a good idea. For example, the manager of one of the news releases on the Costa Rica move may need to know that the job-training and placement center will indeed open on a particular date; it may be an important point in her news release. Good communication within your team can ensure that the tactics of your plan complement one another as they are accomplished.

5. *Communication with clients or supervisors.*   Communicate frequently with the clients and/or supervisors as the execution of the tactics progresses. Be sure to inform them of any problems, and try to present realistic solutions. In our scenario, perhaps a company executive phones you at the last moment, wanting to change some of the job-training and placement brochures from two colors to full color. You will need to communicate as quickly as possible with your supervisor, detailing the impact of the proposed change on budget and scheduling.

6. *Constant evaluation.* Evaluate the process as it progresses. Are news releases, videos, and web sites professional in every respect? Are deadlines being met? Do any sudden changes within your targeted publics or within the social or political environment require a change of tactics? Perhaps a video news release prepared for San José television stations, for example, doesn't run because, as you later discover, the stations wanted a longer Spanish-language question-and-answer session on the VNR's b-roll. If your plan calls for a second VNR, you can remedy that situation in hopes of improved media coverage.

Carrying out the tactics of a public relations plan is exciting. You've worked hard to create a realistic, effective plan, and now you're giving it your best shot. But even after the tactics are completed and you heave a heartfelt sigh of relief, the public relations process isn't over. Now it's time to evaluate the impact of the tactics. It's time to see whether your plan met its objectives and goals.

Quick ✔ Check

1. What is cause marketing?
2. What are the differences between a lobby and a political action committee?
3. What can you include in a written plan to help ensure that tactics are completed on schedule?

Summary

Accomplishing the tactics—often called communication—is the third phase of the public relations process, coming after research and planning. During this phase, practitioners complete well-defined actions to achieve a written plan's objectives. Each tactic targets a particular public and sends a message that does two things: appeals to the receiver's values and promotes the sender's objective. An effective tactic helps build a relationship that benefits a message's receiver as well as its sender.

A wide range of effective tactics can help organizations communicate with their traditional publics, including employees, the news media, investors, community groups, governments, customers, and constituents (voters). Ranging from low-tech face-to-face meetings to high-tech satellite media tours, such tactics strive to create win-win situations that benefit both an organization and the targeted public.

As public relations professionals execute the tactics of a plan, they are guided by the principles of delegation, deadlines, quality control, communication within the team, communication with clients or supervisors, and constant evaluation.

Public relations tactics, after all, are values in action. An organization's values lead to a mission statement. That mission statement leads to goals. Those goals lead to objectives. And those objectives lead to tactics. Tactics are actions that allow an organization to strive toward its highest values.

DISCUSSION QUESTIONS

1. In the Canada to Costa Rica scenario, what publics besides employees, stockholders, investment analysts, and the news media would you target with a public relations plan?
2. What message would you send to each public you identify in your answer to question 1? Can you create win-win messages?
3. What tactics could you use to send the messages that you described in your answer to question 2?
4. Why should tactics be evaluated as they're being implemented?

Memo
from the
Field

Shirley Barr, APR,
President, Shirleybarr
Public Relations,
Houston, Texas

Shirley Barr, APR, president of Shirleybarr Public Relations in Houston, is a consumer marketing specialist. She has won PRSA Excalibur Awards for services as diverse as the Women at Risk: Breast Implants program (an educational, informational, and practice-development campaign) and product introductions for Ben & Jerry's Ice Cream and Wolfgang Puck Frozen Pizzas. Other clients include American Express and the Smithsonian Institute.

Her clients have appeared on *Larry King Live,* the *Today Show,* and other national television programs, as well as in *Newsweek, USA Today,* the *New York Times,* and the *Wall Street Journal.*

Rather than looking beyond news releases, media kits, special events, media tours, and other tactics for "creative ideas," my technique for the past 30 years (time flies when you're having fun) has been to stay within those frameworks, making the very tactics fresh and inventive.

Not all of them have been as much fun as using a pizza box as our media kit for Wolfgang Puck Frozen Pizza with the accompanying Interview Opportunity sheet: "Here's an interview you can sink your teeth into." But a colorful chef like Puck deserved a flamboyant Texas launch for his new frozen pizza.

Not all of them have been as difficult to arrange (or as successful!) as bringing the Martini & Rossi 100 Years of the Martini exhibition of vintage posters and celebrity photos into Morton's of Chicago restaurants when it had previously been displayed only in galleries and museums. (Note to students: read/clip/save. I read about the Martini & Rossi exhibit when it was at the Art Institute of Houston two years before I presented the idea to Morton's for its two Dallas steakhouses.)

Not all of them have been a natural: Who wouldn't think of inviting journalists to test drive Chrysler-Plymouth's "America" car with a Drive Safe America rally? But fleshing out the idea took a team. My team worked with the Houston Police Department to design a route through the city and convert that into a map our media drivers would use. We worked with Rice University to secure the parking lot of the football field as the rally point for the new vehicles and expanded our Houston media list to include auto and lifestyle writers from as far away as Beaumont. We brought in car mechanics and AAA safety experts, which led to a cover story in the *Houston Chronicle* and five smaller Texas papers.

Essay contests have worked for selling American Express services and even diamonds! "What the Statue of Liberty Means to Me" essays by immigrants and third graders helped Amex showcase its support for the restoration of the venerable sculpture and of Ellis Island. They made for some nice coverage, but nothing spectacular. But one year the Houston winner of the annual Why My Mom Deserves a Diamond contest, sponsored by the Diamond Information Center, turned out to be a Chinese child prodigy pianist who had been taught by his concert violinist mother. The contest winner copped a front-page color photo with the headline "Jewel of an Essay Wins Mom a Diamond of a Deal" in many Texas daily newspapers plus TV news coverage on Mother's Day and the week after.

The venue and timing for announcing contest winners is also a critical element in media success. The Adam's Mark Hotel agreed to host the young essay finalists and their parents at its Mother's Day Buffet, where media were invited to photograph the winners and hear them read the essays.

Piggybacking a crowd also worked for the Baileys Dessert Heaven contest. Finalists (local chefs) were invited to bring dessert samples for media judges to taste at the opening party for the Nutcracker Market (a huge event at the convention center each December that benefits the Houston Ballet). All the media judges arrived with cameras to document the gorgeous desserts in the glitzy setting teeming with people. Baileys Original Irish Cream and its distributors drank a toast to the success of their contest and subsequent rise in sales.

Alliteration, gerundial leads, double entendres (e.g., "Jamba Juice Lemonade Stands for Charity"), and freshening old sayings with new twists all work well. Staying close to universal values is the key. Sometimes, writing simply and tightly is the most creative aspect of all.

California Pizza Kitchen had been providing pizzas on Christmas Eve to Salvation Army Centers in its key markets for several years. When I was given the project in Florida, Georgia, and Texas, we added a few "creative toppings" that turned out the media: We bought Santa hats for the line cooks to wear while they prepared those hundreds of pizzas; we quoted Salvation Army majors saying, "Other people send turkey and dressing on Christmas Day, but CPK is the first company to remember the shelter on Christmas Eve." And we created the headline "Pizza on Earth, Good Will toward Men."

Case Study 9.1

The Great Canadian Cover-Up

Few organizations try to discourage business, especially among the highly desirable age 15–35 consumer group. But that's exactly what the Canadian Dermatology Association (CDA) is doing. Its doctors would like to see fewer young Canadians with skin cancer.

The CDA's goal of reducing cancer and reducing business is values-driven. Among the core values that unite the more than 500 dermatologists of the CDA is "a lifetime of healthier skin" for Canadians.[20]

The CDA reports that cases of a skin cancer called melanoma, one of the most common forms of cancer for Canadians 15 to 35 years old, have almost doubled since 1989. Excessive, unprotected exposure to sunlight, the association adds, is a leading cause of skin cancer.[21] Floppy hats and sunblock would do much to combat the problem—but try telling that to millions of teenagers seeking the perfect tan.

In describing the challenges that confronted the CDA's campaign to protect teens, the newsletter *PRNews* reported, "Teens are notorious for two things: their sun-worshipping ways and their deep-seated belief that they are Teflon-coated with respect to anything health threatening. Unfortunately, traditional PR tactics (i.e., news releases and primetime PSAs) have little impact on their behavior."[22]

GCI Group, the public relations agency hired by the CDA, also realized that standard public relations tactics wouldn't impress or even reach a teen audience. "Getting a bunch of articles in the paper is nice," said Nancy Croitoru, president of GCI Group's Canadian operations, "but teenagers don't read the papers; their parents do. And it's not like teens to listen to their parents."[23]

The CDA's budget presented another challenge. The association could provide $80,000 (in U.S. dollars) for the campaign: a sizable amount of money, but not enough for an expensive advertising campaign or enough to cover the expenses of a celebrity spokesperson.

When traditional public relations tactics seem inadequate, one alternative is the untraditional. That's the route GCI Group chose for an award-winning campaign it called "It's Cool to Cover Up." Tactics for the campaign included

- The "RayWatch" team, a group of well-toned, untanned teens who hit beaches, music festivals, sporting events, and other locations where young Canadians gathered in the sun. Attired in beachwear, the RayWatch teens clearly spoofed the popular *BayWatch* television show. Team members distributed containers of sunblock as well as fact sheets on skin protection. A professional dermatologist discreetly trailed the team to answer any technical questions. Before each RayWatch appearance, GCI Group notified local news media through media advisories that stressed photo opportunities.

  RayWatch gained additional publicity when two members of the team appeared in the *Toronto Sun* as "Sunshine Girl" and "Sunshine Boy." These two aspects of the newspaper generally feature nearly nude models who often praise a fun-in-the-sun way of life. The RayWatch teens put a safe-sun spin on that message.

- GCI Group also persuaded the MuchMusic channel, a Canadian version of MTV, to air a safe-sun commercial at reduced rates. The ad depicted a 16-year-old girl's smooth hand withering into a wrinkled, sun-scorched claw. MuchMusic's French-speaking sister station, Musique Plus in Quebec, also ran the ad. The ad's production and airing costs consumed nearly half the campaign's budget. Suzie McMeans, a GCI executive, said that MuchMusic was "the fastest way to reach the youth in Canada."[24]

- GCI Group sent "It's Cool to Cover Up" media kits to Canada's top youth-oriented radio stations. In addition to safe-sun facts, the kits included safe-sun packages containing RayWatch clothing, sunblock, and coupons for indoor activities such as movies. The radio stations used the kits to create their own "It's Cool to Cover Up" promotional giveaways.

By the end of the summer of 2000, GCI Group believed that the tactics were succeeding. "Young adults are traditionally the most difficult demographic to reach," Croitoru said. "This is especially true for a message about sun safety, which asks youth to give up their summer tans for their future health. Our team rose to the challenge by using humor and sex appeal to position sun safety as 'cool,' a life choice you can make without compromising your looks."[25]

GCI Group and the Canadian Dermatology Association are realistic about the likelihood of immediately changing teen behavior. "We don't expect teenagers to change their minds overnight," said CDA dermatologist Lynn From. "But we've reached an awful lot of people."[26]

PR practitioners noted the big impact of the moderately priced campaign. "Witty Campaign Puts PR Where the Sun Don't Shine" declared a headline in *PRNews*.[27]

Dermatologists also applauded the innovative campaign. In 2001, "It's Cool to Cover Up" won the Gold Triangle Award from the American Academy of Dermatology—the first time a Canadian campaign had won that award.[28]

The next step in evaluative research is to see whether teen behavior changes and cancer rates decline—but that's a long-term process. For now, GCI does know that its safe-sun message reached millions of teens. "We were extremely effective as a team," said GCI Group's McMeans. "And we had a lot of fun doing something fulfilling and for the greater good."[29]

DISCUSSION QUESTIONS

1. Imagine that GCI Group conducted an "It's Cool to Cover Up" campaign in the United States. What other tactics would you suggest to reach U.S. teens?
2. Although GCI Group emphasized public relations tactics, it also used advertising. What does GCI's choice of tactics say about the relative merits of public relations and advertising?

3. GCI's commercial on MuchMusic used an emotional appeal (*pathos*) to teens. In your opinion, was that an effective choice? How might *logos* and *ethos* have been used in a commercial?

4. To attract news media to RayWatch events, GCI used media advisories that emphasized excellent photo opportunities. If you were writing a photo opportunity sheet for the RayWatch events, what information would you include to attract photographers?

Case Study 9.2

"Emily, Get Out of the Way."

The TV screen showed serene palm trees and gentle waves on Jordan's Dead Sea. Unfortunately, the camera was supposed to be focused on U.S. Secretary of State Colin Powell—and the conversation offscreen was anything but serene.

In Jordan for talks with Middle Eastern leaders, Powell was taping an interview with journalist Tim Russert for later broadcast on NBC's influential Sunday-morning news program *Meet the Press.*

As Russert neared the end of his allotted time without showing signs of stopping, Powell's staff phoned the NBC control room: Powell's schedule was tight, and other journalists awaited their turn on the satellite link.[30] As Russert went into overtime, by the calculations of Powell's staff, he began a final, hard-hitting question about the justification for the war in Iraq:

"Finally, Mr. Secretary, in February of 2003, you placed your enormous credibility before the United Nations and laid out a case against Saddam Hussein citing. . . ."[31]

And then the camera, controlled by a Jordanian crew hired by Powell's staff, swerved from Powell's face to the palms trees and waves. Microphones captured this conversation:

> Emily Miller, a Powell media relations aide: "You're off."
> Powell: "I am not off."
> Miller: "No, they can't use it; they're editing it."
> Powell: "Emily, get out of the way. Bring back the camera, please."[32]

Journalists offered an array of tough verbs to characterize Powell's tone: He *snapped, snarled, dressed down, chastised,* and *ordered.*[33]

When the camera swung back to him, Powell candidly answered Russert's question about Iraq: "It turned out that the sourcing was inaccurate and wrong and in some cases, deliberately misleading. And for that, I am disappointed and I regret it."[34]

When his other interviews had ended, Powell telephoned Russert to apologize.[35]

"Secretary Powell was really stand-up," said Russert, praising Powell's actions. "He was a general and took charge."[36]

However, Russert had different feelings about Miller. He aired the unedited tape on *Meet the Press,* and the recriminations began—beginning with Russert. "This is attempted news management gone berserk," he declared in a *Washington Post* article.[37] Meanwhile, officials in the administration of President George W. Bush told journalists that a White House aide may have authorized an extra five minutes for Russert, a message not relayed to Powell and his staff.[38] Russert's staff maintains that Powell was 45 minutes late for the interview, and that journalists already had had to reschedule satellite links.[39]

"So what's a press secretary to do?" asked Jim Kennedy, communications director for former President Bill Clinton. "First, remember that agreements [about time] are about as solid as Hollywood wedding vows or a deficit projection by the Office of Management and Budget." Kennedy called the episode "a now-infamous debacle."[40]

In a highly partisan exchange on CNN's *Crossfire,* Bush administration critic Paul Begala and supporter Robert Novak each bashed Miller:

> Begala (to the audience): A Bush administration [aide] turned NBC's camera off of Secretary of State Colin Powell to try to stop him from answering a question from Mr. Russert about how the Bush administration misled you and your fellow Americans before taking us to war in Iraq. . . .
>
> Novak: A woman named Emily, a third-ranking hack at the State Department, not a Bush administration official, did it."[41]

Headlines also focused on Miller: "Press Aide Tries to Halt Powell Interview," wrote the *Frontrunner,* a daily political newsletter.[42] "Aide Charges in, Cuts Camera to Colin's Chagrin," declared the alliterative *Boston Herald.*[43]

State Department officials were more forgiving. "I think she's great, and she's doing a good job for us," said the leader of the department's media relations team. "Russert went on and on and on. We asked the cameraman to help us cut it off."[44]

But *PR Week* magazine labeled Miller "DC's Scandal Queen of the Week,"[45] and *Cablefax* magazine accused her of a "toxic mixture of bad timing and horrible judgment."[46]

Journalists have long memories. *Roll Call,* a Capitol Hill newspaper, recalled an earlier episode in which a *Washington Post* writer reported that Miller, angry about one of his stories, telephoned him and said, "You are dead to us."[47]

Miller seemingly accepted her notoriety with good humor—and got in one last dig at Russert. "My 15 minutes of fame are over now," she said. "And unlike NBC, I don't want any more time."[48]

DISCUSSION QUESTIONS

1. What alternatives to Miller's action of redirecting the camera can you think of?
2. In your opinion, did this episode help or hurt the reputation of Colin Powell?
3. In your opinion, should Russert have shown the unedited video? Was it newsworthy?
4. As a general rule, when journalists irritate public relations practitioners, how should the practitioners respond?

Cyber Coach

Visit www.ablongman.com/guthmarsh3e for these study aids—and more:

- flashcards
- quizzes
- videos
- links to other sites
- real-world scenarios that let you be the public relations professional

KEY TERMS

actualities, p. 282
annual meeting, p. 287
annual report, p. 289
association magazines, p. 286
backgrounder, p. 280
bill inserts, p. 295
b-roll, p. 282
cause marketing, p. 290
CD-ROMs, p. 281
coalition building, p. 291
controlled media, p. 272
DVDs, p. 281
e-mail, p. 278
extranets, p. 296
fact sheet, p. 280
grassroots lobbying, p. 291
independent endorsement, p. 274
instant messaging, p. 279
intranet, p. 278
lobby, p. 291

media advisory, p. 282
media kit, p. 280
news conference, p. 282
news release, p. 279
photo opportunity sheet, p. 281
pitch letter, p. 282
political action committees (PACs), p. 291
pseudoevent, p. 272
public service announcements (PSAs), p. 284
satellite media tour (SMT), p. 285
soft money, p. 292
special event, p. 271
tactics, p. 269
text messaging, p. 295
third-party endorsement, p. 274
trade magazines, p. 286
uncontrolled media, p. 274
video news releases (VNRs), p. 282
webcasts, p. 289

NOTES

1. *Fox News Watch,* 6 September 2003, online, LexisNexis.
2. "New Survey Shows High Trust Levels among New Jersey Employees," news release issued by the New Jersey Chapter of the International Association of Business Communicators and Berry Associates Public Relations, 4 December 2003, online, LexisNexis.
3. "America Online Inc.'s Second Annual Instant Messaging Trends Survey Shows Instant Messaging Has Gone Mainstream," news release issued by America Online, 24 August 2004, online, LexisNexis.
4. Linda Morton, "Producing Publishable News Releases: A Research Perspective," *Public Relations Quarterly* 37, no. 4 (22 December 1992), online, LexisNexis.

5. Robert Pear, "U.S. Videos, for TV News, Come Under Scrutiny," *New York Times,* 15 March 2004, online, LexisNexis.

6. Anthony H. Gamboa, "Decision: Matter of Department of Health and Human Services, Centers for Medicare & Medicaid Services—Video News Releases," U.S. General Accounting Office, 19 May 2004, online, www.gao.gov.

7. "RTNDA Urges Caution and Disclosure When Using Video News Releases," news release issued by the Radio-Television News Directors Association, 18 March 2004, online, www.rtnda.org.

8. Jay Rosen, "Flacks Cannot Say They're 'Reporting' Anymore," Pressthink, 20 April 2004, online, www.journalism.nyu.edu/pubzone/weblogs/pressthink.

9. Pear; Gamboa.

10. Gamboa.

11. Gamboa.

12. Gamboa.

13. "Statement of the Public Relations Society of America (PRSA) on Video News Releases (VNRs)," Public Relations Society of America, 20 April 2004, online, www.prsa.org.

14. Deborah Potter, "Virtual News Reports," *American Journalism Review,* June/July 2004, online, LexisNexis.

15. "PACs Maintain Growth Trend in 2003," news release issued by the U.S. Federal Election Commission, 23 March 2004, online, www.fec.gov.

16. "The Internet Has an Impact on Americans' Everyday Lives," news release issued by the Pew Internet & American Life Project, 11 August 2004, online, www.pewinternet.org.

17. "Use of E-Government Increases 50%," news release issued by the Pew Internet & American Life Project, 24 May 2004, online, www.pewinternet.org.

18. "44% of American Internet Users Have Contributed Their Thoughts and Digital Content to the Online World," news release issued by the Pew Internet & American Life Project, 29 February 2004, online, www.pewinternet.org.

19. Andy Reinhart, "Extranets: Log On, Link Up, Save Big," *Business Week,* 22 June 1998, online, LexisNexis.

20. "RayWatch Team Spreads Sunscreen and Safe Sun Messages at Halifax Buskers' Festival," news release issued via Canada NewsWire, 4 August 2000, online, LexisNexis.

21. "Witty Campaign Puts PR Where the Sun Don't Shine," *PRNews,* 9 April 2001, online, LexisNexis.

22. "Witty Campaign Puts PR Where the Sun Don't Shine."

23. "Witty Campaign Puts PR Where the Sun Don't Shine."

24. "Witty Campaign Puts PR Where the Sun Don't Shine."

25. "GCI Group Receives Prestigious Gold Triangle Award," news release issued via PR Newswire, 29 March 2001, online, LexisNexis.

26. "Witty Campaign Puts PR Where the Sun Don't Shine."

27. "Witty Campaign Puts PR Where the Sun Don't Shine."

28. "GCI Group Receives Prestigious Gold Triangle Award."

29. "Witty Campaign Puts PR Where the Sun Don't Shine."

30. Douglas Quenqua, "Powell Press Aide Meets the Press' Wrath," *PR Week,* 24 May 2004, online, LexisNexis; John Bresnahan, "Heard on the Hill," *Roll Call,* 18 May 2004, online, LexisNexis.

31. *Deborah Norville Tonight,* MSNBC, 17 May 2004, online, LexisNexis.

32. Andrew Miga, "War on Terror; Aide Charges in, Cuts Camera to Colin's Chagrin," *Boston Herald,* 17 May 2004, online, LexisNexis.

33. "Press Aide Tries to Halt Powell Interview," *The Frontrunner,* 17 May 2004, online, LexisNexis; James Gordon Meek, "Colin Airs Rage at Aide in Live Dispute," (New York) *Daily News,* 17 May 2004, online, LexisNexis; Howard Kurtz, "Colin Powell Interview with Russert Is Cut Off," *Washington Post,* 17 May 2004, online, LexisNexis.

34. "Effort to Muzzle Powell Fresh Attack on the Truth," *Traverse City* (Mich.) *Record-Eagle,* 20 May 2004, online, www.record-eagle.com.

35. Meek.

36. "Press Aide Tries to Halt Powell Interview."

37. Quenqua.

38. "Powell Aide Laughs Off Meet the Press Controversy," *The White House Bulletin,* 18 May 2004, online, LexisNexis.

39. "Press Aide Tries to Halt Powell Interview."

40. Jim Kennedy, "Meeting the Press and Surviving It," *New York Times,* 23 May 2004, online, LexisNexis.

41. *Crossfire,* CNN, 17 May 2004, online, LexisNexis.

42. "Press Aide Tries to Halt Powell Interview."

43. Miga.

44. Richard Leiby, "Ever Consider a Career in Diplomacy?" *Washington Post,* 17 May 2004, online, www.washingtonpost.com.

45. Quenqua.

46. M. C. Antil, "M. C. Antil's Cablefolks," Cablefax, 18 May 2004, online, LexisNexis.

47. Bresnahan.

48. "Powell Aide Laughs Off Meet the Press Controversy."

chapter ten

Writing and Presentation Skills

objectives

After studying this chapter, you will be able to

- describe and follow the different stages of the writing process

- identify and use techniques that increase the effectiveness of spoken language

- describe and follow the process of making a successful presentation

Publicizing Volunteer Clearinghouse

scenario — *A college internship has led to your first job: You're now an assistant account executive with a public relations agency. As an intern, you impressed the agency's partners with your character, work ethic, team spirit, and writing abilities. At the end of your internship, the partners asked you to stay in touch, which you did, occasionally sending them class projects and successful assignments from other internships. One week before you graduated, the partners rewarded your talent and persistence with a job offer, which you accepted.*

Your first task at the agency involves writing a news release for Volunteer Clearinghouse, which coordinates volunteer recruitment for nonprofit social-service agencies in your county. Volunteer Clearinghouse is one of your agency's pro bono clients, meaning the agency doesn't charge for its services. Offering unpaid services to Volunteer Clearinghouse helps your agency honor one of its founding values: a commitment to building a better community through social responsibility.

The board of directors of Volunteer Clearinghouse has just named a new executive director. Her name is Elaine Anderson, and she succeeds Phil Connors, who accepted a similar position in another state. The board of directors would like your agency to write a news release announcing Anderson's hiring. The account executive who serves as a liaison to Volunteer Clearinghouse quickly agrees and turns to you.

It's 3 P.M., and the account executive would like the news release by 10 A.M. tomorrow.

It's the first assignment of your new job, and you want to do well. How and where do you start?

The Importance of Writing and Presentation Skills

"Writing is easy," said U.S. journalist and playwright Gene Fowler. "All you do is stare at a blank sheet of paper until drops of blood form on your forehead."[1]

We might update Fowler's description to include a computer screen, but his point remains: Good writing is hard work. In fact, more than one writer has compared the activity to spilling blood. Nobel Prize–winning novelist Ernest Hemingway declared, "Writing is easy. Just open a vein and bleed on paper."[2]

Whew! Tough business, this writing. Could anything be more challenging? Well, how about making a presentation? By yourself. In front of a lot of people. With your reputation and a potential client at stake. According to *The Book of Lists,* public speaking ranks number one on the list of people's greatest fears, ahead of heights, sickness, and even death.[3]

This chapter focuses on spilling blood and tackling terrors worse than death. In other words, this chapter focuses on writing and presentation skills. Why? Because they're at the heart of the practice of public relations. A Workinpr.com survey of almost 800 public relations managers found that "strong written/verbal communication skills" were the top job skills employers seek in entry-level employees. Also, between 80 and 90 percent of employers list experience, personality, and demeanor—key qualities for good presentations—as being among the most important factors in hiring decisions.[4] And employers say these qualities apply to all potential hires, not just entry-level applicants. Clearly, writing and presentation skills are prerequisites for success at every stage of a public relations career.

One objective of this chapter is to reduce the stress involved in writing and presenting by dividing those activities into small, achievable steps. Writing and presenting are processes. Rather than approaching them as jagged mountains to be scaled in one leap, we can learn to master writing and presenting by tackling them one step at a time—methodically climbing the mountain, so to speak, instead of trying to reach the top in one doomed jump.

However, this chapter doesn't pretend to tell you everything you need to know about writing and presenting. Those topics consume whole textbooks all by themselves. Instead, this chapter strives to cover the basics of writing and presenting, suggesting their fundamental importance to the profession of public relations. Let's begin with blood-spilling—that is, with writing.

A Context for Public Relations Writing

Journalists write to inform. Advertisers write to persuade. Informing and persuading are the respective contexts for the writing involved in those professions. What, then, is the context for public relations writing? In a sense, that question echoes one posed in Chapter 6: Are public relations practitioners objective communicators, like journalists, or are they persuasive advocates, like advertisers and lawyers? Our answer now—as it was then—is "none of the above." Public relations practitioners are neither journalists, nor lawyers, nor advertisers. They are relationship managers.

The context for public relations writing is relationship management. Sometimes the ethical management of relationships requires journalistic objectivity; other times, it may require persuasion. Often, it requires a little of both. As relationship-management tactics, public relations documents should address the values and interests of the writer's organization as well as the values and interests of the targeted public or publics. For example, a well-written news release certainly addresses the interests of the writer's organization: It communicates important information that the organization considers newsworthy. The same news release also addresses the interests of the news media, which rely on news releases to help them identify and communicate the news. Additionally, the news release addresses the interests of targeted publics within the news media's audiences—investors, perhaps, or local environmentalists. By addressing the individual interests of each of those parties, the news release maintains and even strengthens relationships that sustain the organization.

Think of our definition of public relations: *Public relations is the values-driven management of relationships between an organization and the publics that can affect its success.* Public relations writing supports that definition. Whatever the document may be—a speech, an annual report, or even an in-house memo—its aim is consistent: to be an effective tactic in the management of relationships vital to an organization's success.

The Writing Process

Writing a public relations document, whether it be a news release, a public service announcement, or something else altogether, can be intimidating. Writers respond to such anxiety in many ways. Sometimes they avoid the challenge by putting the

Good writing

> **"Good writing, like a good house, is an orderly arrangement of parts."**
>
> *Mortimer Adler*

is the core of effective corporate communication. Whether delivered in the form of a presentation, video, newsletter, annual report or other medium, most messages begin on a sheet of paper.

At Schaffner Communications we believe that good business communication belongs in the hands of skilled professional journalists, not of advertising copywriters who may sacrifice clarity for design, or aspiring novelists who could confuse the message with the medium.

Our clients agree. They recognize the need not only to master and tame the English language, but to conduct accompanying research, interviews and red pencil reviews that provide the framework for effective presentations. That's our style at Schaffner Communications.

Business communication, Schaffner-style, relies on pairing a client's message with the medium that's most appropriate for the audience and intent. Words are the heart of those messages, whether applied to printed, visual or audio materials.

Tools of the Trade

Good writing is at the core of effective communications programs, including all of the following:

Advertisements

Annual Reports

Books

Brochures

Columns

Correspondence

Documentation

Feature Stories

Flyers and Leaflets

Letters to the Editor

Magazine Articles

Manuals and Handbooks

Newsletters

Press Releases

Proposals

Public Service Announcements

Radio Copy

Scripts

Speeches and Presentations

Video News Releases

Brochure Chicago-based Schaffner Communications wins and keeps clients with its intense focus on good writing. (Courtesy of Schaffner Communications)

writing task off until the last moment. Or, conversely, perhaps they attack the challenge by flying to their computer keyboards and banging away. Both responses usually lead to frustration, however, not to good writing. Like public relations itself, writing is a process: It can't be started at the last moment, and it doesn't begin with your fingers flying over the keyboard. The **writing process** begins with values and ends with evaluation. Because writing is a process, its first step leads logically to a second step, which leads to a third, and so on.

The writing process, in fact, has something in common with Maslow's Hierarchy of Needs, presented in Chapter 5. As you'll recall, moving too high too fast in Maslow's hierarchy can be disastrous; the needs at each level of that pyramid must be fulfilled before you can move up to the next level. It's the same in the writing process: It's counterproductive to move to the fourth level, for example, when you haven't completed the first, second, and third levels. In fact, if you're stalled at a particular stage of a writing project, you should consider dropping down to the earlier levels. Perhaps a failure to complete one of them has led to your momentary dead end. At the very least, reviewing your progress may reveal a solution to your frustration.

Envisioning writing as a process can help you cope with the intimidation that sometimes accompanies important writing assignments. The writing process can help you avoid procrastination because it eases you into the actual writing; it helps you approach an assignment with confidence. And the writing process prevents you from wasting your time (and others' time) by jumping in too quickly and trying to write without adequate preparation. The writing process helps you tackle a writing assignment in a logical, productive fashion.

So what are the different stages of the writing process? As Figure 10.1 shows, the writing process for public relations consists of 10 stages. These stages, in order, are credibility, research, organization, writing, revision, macroediting, microediting, approval, distribution, and evaluation. Figure 10.1 also suggests that you should communicate with supervisors and/or clients—whoever is appropriate—as your writing assignment progresses. For a short newsletter story, communication with supervisors and/or clients might be brief: checking quotations, confirming deadlines, suggesting a new angle that your research has revealed, and submitting a draft before the deadline. But for a more extensive document, such as major sections of a corporation's annual report, communication might take the form of regularly scheduled meetings or a constant exchange of e-mail messages and rough drafts. Ask supervisors and clients how much communication they would like—and always inform them as new challenges and opportunities regarding an assignment arise.

Although our chapter focuses on the writing process within the context of public relations, the process applies to other situations, such as writing an advertisement, a short story, or even a love letter. However, some of the stages are more appropriate for public relations than for other writing situations; these stages include credibility, approval, and evaluation.

Let's now examine the individual stages of the writing process.

FIGURE 10.1   The Writing Process
Successful public relations writing begins with
credibility and ends with evaluating the success
of the written document. The 10 stages of the
writing process should be followed in order:
Research comes before organization, which
comes before writing, and so on. As the
document progresses, the writer should discuss
problems or new ideas with supervisors and/or
clients.

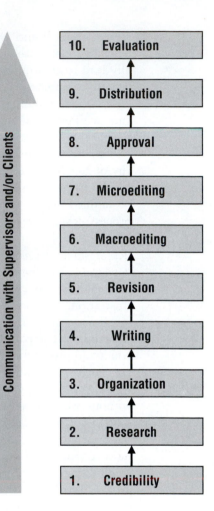

Credibility: Stage One of the Writing Process

This is *really* beginning at the beginning, but starting anywhere else would be misleading and counterproductive. As a communicator, you must have credibility, or there's no
point in trying to send a message. Clients and supervisors won't give an important writing assignment to an individual they don't trust. Receivers of a message may discount
it if they lack respect for the source. As we noted in Chapter 5, Aristotle praised the
strategies of appealing to an audience's intellect and to its emotions—but he said the
most powerful persuasive strategy of all often is the character of the communicator.

So how can you establish character? Actually, as you know, you've been doing
that since you learned to think for yourself and to make your own decisions. But
character isn't static. It grows—or diminishes. As a public relations practitioner, you
can "grow" and establish your character by testing your actions and those of your
employer against your own values, the values of your employer, the values of the pub-

lic relations profession (as stated in the ethics codes of organizations such as the Public Relations Society of America), and the values of the society in which you live.

In the scenario that opens this chapter, your character helped you move from being an intern to being a full-time employee. Your values-driven actions impressed the agency's partners so much that they paid you the ultimate compliment: They recruited and hired you.

Establishing character can't be an occasional thing. The values that surround and help give meaning to your life should be with you every day. One of the many

QuickBreak 10.1

WRITING FOR DIVERSE PUBLICS: TIPS FOR INCLUSIVE LANGUAGE

Public relations writing builds relationships. The careless use of language, however, can inadvertently exclude valuable members of important publics. To create inclusive documents, consider the following guidelines:[5]

- In documents that cite individuals as sources, draw upon diverse individuals. In many organizations and publics, it's easy to rely on a steady stream of white Anglo-Saxon males in their 40s and 50s. Not all qualified sources are of that race, ethnicity, gender, or age.

- Balance personal pronouns. For unnamed, generic individuals such as a supervisor or senator, balance the use of *he* and *she*. Don't, however, include illogical shifts. A hypothetical supervisor shouldn't change gender within a paragraph. Another solution is to use plural nouns—*supervisors* and *senators*—that can be replaced by *they*.

- Avoid words that describe particular relationships: *your wife, your husband, your boyfriend, your girlfriend, your parents, your children*. Female readers generally are excluded by *your wife*, just as male readers generally are by *your husband*. Let your targeted public be your guide as to what is appropriate.

- Know the dates of major religious holidays. When is Rosh Hashanah? When is Ramadan?

- Don't describe individuals by race, ethnicity, religion, age, sexual orientation, or physical or mental disability unless the information is relevant to your document's purpose. If an individual must be so described, consider applying the same exactness of description to every other individual mentioned in your document.

- If you are responsible for a document's design, apply your quest for inclusiveness to photographs and other visual representations of individuals. Even if you're *not* in charge of the design, don't hesitate to point out lapses of diversity.

A Bureau of Labor Statistics survey of almost 60,000 households revealed the following preferences in racial and ethnic terminology:[6]

- Blacks prefer *black* (44.15 percent) to *African American* (28.07 percent) and *Afro-American* (12.12 percent).

- Hispanics prefer *Hispanic* (57.88 percent) to *of Spanish origin* (12.34 percent) and *Latino* (11.74 percent).

- American Indians prefer *American Indian* (49.76 percent) to *Native American* (37.35 percent).

- Multiracial individuals prefer *multiracial* (28.42 percent) to *mixed-race* (16.02 percent).

Words have power. They can include—or exclude. Use them wisely.

payoffs of values-driven public relations is that it helps make you a credible, trust-worthy communicator.

Research: Stage Two of the Writing Process

Different public relations documents require different kinds of research: For example, a CEO's speech to a corporation's stockholders requires different research than an employee relations document on how to apply for a promotion. But regardless of what document they're preparing to write, public relations practitioners ask the following five questions.

1. WHAT IS MY PURPOSE IN WRITING?   In other words, what is the goal of this document? What does your organization hope this document will achieve? You should be able to answer this question with one clear, precise sentence. If that isn't possible, you don't understand the mission of the document, and you shouldn't proceed until you do.

For example, suppose that your supervisor asks you to write an employee newsletter story about your organization's new voluntary long-term disability insurance program. Great; but what's the goal? Should the story just inform employees about the new program? Or should it recruit them? Ideally, your supervisor can answer your questions—but if she can't, your story probably is on hold until you learn more about the story's precise purpose.

2. WHO IS MY TARGETED PUBLIC?   For most documents, this means *Who are my readers?* For the text of a speech or for a radio public service announcement, it means *Who are my listeners?* In all cases, it means *Who are the receivers of the message I intend to send?*

In Chapter 4 you encountered seven questions that public relations practitioners must answer to build successful relationships with important publics. These seven questions can help you answer *Who is my targeted public?*

- *How much can this targeted public influence my organization's ability to achieve its goals?* Because resources are limited, public relations practitioners must devote most of their attention and efforts to publics that can help their organization succeed.

- *Who are the opinion leaders and decision makers in my targeted public?* Can you appeal to those individuals without excluding other members of the targeted public?

- *What is the demographic profile of my targeted public?* What is the age range of its members? The education range? The male–female ratio? In other words, statistically speaking, who is your targeted public? What does **demographic information** say about your public's members?

- *What is the psychographic profile of my targeted public?* Are members of your targeted public politically conservative, liberal, or middle-of-the-road—or is the range too broad to generalize? Are they devoutly religious, assuredly secular, or scattered along the spectrum of religious intensity? **Psychographic information** includes data about what people believe, think, and feel.

- *What is my targeted public's opinion of my organization?* Are you approaching a friendly public, a neutral public, or a hostile public?

- *What is my targeted public's opinion of the subject I'm addressing?* How much do members of your targeted public already know about the subject you are preparing to address? Do levels of knowledge differ within your targeted public? You don't want to dwell on information they already know well; on the other hand, you don't want to make false assumptions about what you think they know. And beyond the targeted public's knowledge, what do its members *think* about your subject? Do its members agree, or do opinions vary?

These are six of the seven standard questions you can ask to help you answer, *Who is my targeted public?* The seventh question is so important that we reserve it for its own section, which follows: *What are the values and interests of my targeted public in this situation?*

3. WHAT ARE THE VALUES AND INTERESTS OF MY TARGETED PUBLIC IN THIS SITUATION?

One of the most important research functions in public relations writing is the identification of your targeted public's stake in your subject matter. Determining the targeted public's values and interests helps you do two things. First, you can quickly move to values and interests in your document, ensuring that your targeted public will pay attention (after all, its members have suddenly realized that you're addressing their concerns). Second, knowing your targeted public's values and interests can help you fulfill them, when possible. As you know, the best relationships in public relations are those in which both sides benefit: true win-win situations. You improve the odds of achieving a win-win relationship when you know your targeted public's stake in the relevant issue.

In Publicizing Volunteer Clearinghouse, our opening scenario, your consideration of your targeted public would provide extremely useful information for the news release you're about to write. You know that your targeted public is news media editors, and you know what they value: a newsworthy, objective, unbiased, local-interest story that they can deliver to their own audiences. You also know that they have a good opinion of Volunteer Clearinghouse and probably will use your news release—if you can meet their standards.

4. WHAT MESSAGE SHOULD I SEND?
You can answer this question by combining what you've learned from answering question 1 above (*What is my purpose in writing?*) and question 3 (*What are the values and interests of my targeted public in this situation?*). As you know from Chapter 8, a successful message combines the purpose of your document with the targeted public's values and interests.

Earlier, for example, we looked at a hypothetical situation in which you were asked to write an employee newsletter story on a new voluntary long-term disability insurance program. Your purpose, you learn, is to persuade employees to enroll in the program. But that's not your message; it doesn't yet have any appeal to the targeted public's values or interests. In researching your targeted public, you learn that your organization's employees have a powerful interest in the financial security of their families. *Now* you have a message: *Enroll in the new insurance program to provide additional financial security for your family.* You need not use those exact words, but that message needs to be the unmistakable theme of your newsletter story.

5. WHAT INFORMATION SUPPORTS MY MESSAGE?   What information does your organization want you to include in the document you're preparing to write? What information does your targeted public hope to learn from reading your document? Answers to those questions will guide you in your search for relevant information. In researching their stories, journalists seek specific information in six broad areas: *who, what, when, where, why,* and *how.* Those questions may not apply to every public relations writing situation, but asking them can help you anticipate the information requirements of your document.

With all this research gathered, you can turn with confidence to the next stage in the writing process: organization.

Quick ✔ Check

1. In what way is the writing process like Maslow's Hierarchy of Needs?
2. In the research stage of the writing process, what kinds of information should you gather about your targeted public?
3. In public relations, what qualities are essential in an effective message?

Organization: Stage Three of the Writing Process

The organization of a document should draw the targeted public's attention to the message and to the information that supports and develops it. Often, that means that the document moves gracefully but quickly to the message. Because the message directly targets the readers' or listeners' values and interests, the sooner we reach it, the sooner the targeted public knows why it should be reading, watching, or listening.

There are, however, exceptions to the general rule of moving quickly to the message. In bad-news situations, for example—in which you tell people something they don't want to hear—the message generally comes *after* a concise description of your reasons for the upcoming bad news. In other words, a quick explanation of *why* comes before you announce the bad news. If we simply announce the bad news first, our unhappy targeted public may tune out our explanation, and that could further damage our relationship. In rejecting employment applications, for example, many

Kids Cafe

ConAgra Foods' Feeding Children Better program is the national sponsor of Kids Cafes – kids-only afterschool meal programs that give kids free, nutritious meals in a safe and nurturing environment. In its first three years, the program will open at least 100 new Kids Cafes. 240 kids reported in with the following assessments:

For the **second year in a row**, the kids graded the Kids Cafe with high marks   *A*

59% of children said that their grades have improved since they began coming to the Kids Cafe   *A*

Pizza tops the list as the favorite Kids Cafe food   *A*

Eating food and **playing games** are the favorite Kids Cafe activities   *A*

Highlights Include

- **61 new** Kids Cafes funded by ConAgra Foods
- Each new Kids Cafe serves an average of **10-12,000 meals** to hungry kids each year
- Once all the 100 ConAgra Feeding Children Better Kids Cafes are opened, they are expected to serve a combined **1-1.2 million meals** per year

Quotes From Kids

What are you thankful for?

"I'm thankful for even getting to come here." **Brianna, age 8**

"I'm thankful that we get food so I can have it when I'm hungry." **Shirae, age 9**

"For my mom - she brought me to this great place that I'm thankful for this year." **Christopher, age 12**

"Clothes, food, shoes." **Jasmine, age 6**

Report Card   ConAgra Foods Feeding Children Better Foundation conducted research on the effectiveness of its Kids Café program for low-income schoolchildren. It transformed that research into a report card. (Courtesy of ConAgra Foods Feeding Children Better Foundation and Cone, Inc.)

organizations use business letters that place the *why* before the bad-news message: *Unfortunately, we have no positions open at this time. Therefore, we are unable to offer you a job.* The job applicant may not like the message, but at least he knows why his request cannot be satisfied.

Clearly, different documents are organized in different message-focused ways. But every document, no matter what its organization is, can benefit from an outline. Outlines needn't be the formal Roman-numeral lists that you learned to create in elementary school; a few scribbled notes for each paragraph may work just as well for you. And outlines aren't etched in stone: As you write a document, better ideas—and a better organization—may occur to you. But some form of outline, some written plan of how you're going to get from here to there, is essential. During spring break, for example, you wouldn't drive to some distant, sunny beach without a map. You *might* get there without one, but why waste time and risk failure? The same logic applies to writing. Use an outline.

In our Volunteer Clearinghouse scenario, the research you conducted in the previous stage of the writing process can now help you create an outline. You know that your targeted public consists of news editors, and you know that news editors want the news. Therefore, you decide to organize your news release in the **inverted pyramid** style of a traditional news story, with the most important information at the beginning and the least important at the end (see Figure 10.2). You review the most important details in the areas of who, what, when, where, why, and how, and you organize the details in terms of importance. You decide that your first paragraph needs to announce the most important news: The board of directors has hired Elaine Anderson to be the new executive director of Volunteer Clearinghouse. You decide that it's also important to describe briefly who Anderson is and when she'll begin her new job.

In your research you got a quotation about Anderson's abilities from the chairman of the board, but you decide to place that near the end of the news release. Although it's a good quotation, you decide that it's just not as important as the announcement of Anderson's hiring and the details about her qualifications for this new job.

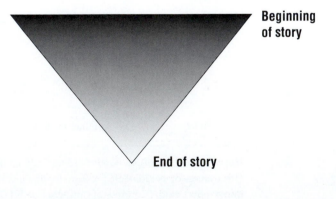

FIGURE 10.2   The Inverted Pyramid The inverted pyramid represents the traditional organization of a news story. Where the pyramid is widest, the information in the story is most important. The narrowing of the pyramid represents the decreasing importance of information as a news story progresses toward its ending. Thus, a traditional news story places the most important information at the beginning, which journalists call "the lead." In public relations, most news releases use the inverted pyramid organization.

CONTACT:
Patrick McMahon
(412) 762-2477
patrick.mcmahon@pnc.com

'PNC GROW UP GREAT' KICKS OFF WITH $500,000 IN GRANTS, MEDIA CAMPAIGN AND NEW VOLUNTEER POLICY
-- PNC rolls out nation's largest program of its kind to improve school readiness –

PITTSBURGH, March 24, 2004 -- "PNC Grow Up Great," the $100 million investment in early childhood education by The PNC Financial Services Group, Inc., was kicked off today with $500,000 in grants, an advisory council of experts and a print and broadcast media campaign to increase public awareness of the need to raise the nation's level of school readiness.

PNC created this program to better prepare children from birth to age five for school through grants to non-profit early education organizations, volunteerism, advocacy and awareness during the next 10 years. Joining PNC and its 24,000 employees are experts in the field, including Sesame Workshop, PBS member stations and Family Communications, Inc., the producers of "Mister Rogers' Neighborhood." Its first-year pilot program will focus on Head Start centers throughout Pennsylvania, New Jersey, Ohio, Kentucky and Delaware.

"As the largest school readiness program of its kind in the United States, PNC Grow Up Great will help our children, families and communities become smarter, stronger and healthier," said James E. Rohr, chairman and chief executive officer of PNC. "We see this program as an excellent investment in the future of the communities we serve. Improvements in school readiness will have a major impact on children's success in school and life."

Today, 80 percent of the nation's children spend up to 50 hours a week in "poor to mediocre" early childhood settings, according to the National Center for Education Statistics. Research also shows that a five-year-old from an underserved family starts school 18 months behind his or her peers in vocabulary development, which has a profound effect on reading ability and general comprehension.

- more -

www.pnc.com

The nonprofit educational organization behind
Sesame Street and so much more.
www.sesameworkshop.org

News Release   The headline and first words of a news release should quickly satisfy a journalist's desire for specific details about a newsworthy story. (Courtesy of PNC Financial Services Group, Inc.)

QuickBreak 10.2

TEN TIPS FOR WRITING BETTER SENTENCES[7]

1. *Challenge "to be" verbs.* Challenge *is, are, was, were, will be,* and every other form of the verb *to be.* Sometimes a *to be* verb best suits the needs of the sentence, but often you can find a stronger, more descriptive verb that might also shorten the sentence.

Original	Revision
He will be a good communicator.	He will communicate effectively.
We are inviting you. . .	We invite you. . .

2. *Use active voice.* In the **active voice,** the subject of the sentence does the action. In the **passive voice,** the subject receives the action.

Passive Voice	Active Voice
Our profits were affected by a sales slump.	A sales slump affected our profits.

Passive voice is grammatically correct, and it's the right choice when the action is more important than the action's doer. (Example: She was fired.) But passive voice can seem timid, and it requires a *to be* verb. Active voice is confident and concise.

3. *Challenge modifiers.* **Modifiers** (adjectives and adverbs) can strengthen a sentence by sharpening your meaning. But sometimes they prop up weak words, especially nouns and verbs. A precise, well-chosen word needs no modification.

Original	Revision
We are very happy.	We are ecstatic.
She ran fast.	She sprinted.

4. *Challenge long words.* If a long word or phrase works best, use it. Otherwise, use a shorter option.

Original	Revision
utilize	use
revenue-enhancement measure	tax

5. *Challenge prepositional phrases.* Avoid strings of prepositional phrases:

Your final outline might look something like this:

Paragraph 1:   Anderson hired for new exec director.
                Brief note on who she is.
                Brief note on what Volunteer Clearinghouse is.
                Note when she starts.

Paragraph 2:   Anderson's biography.

Paragraph 3:   She succeeds Phil Connors. Note where he's gone.

Paragraph 4:   Quote from board chairman.

Paragraph 5:   Note that anyone interested in volunteering with community service agencies can call the Volunteer Clearinghouse. List phone number and address.

Now you're organized. You know how to get from here to there. It's time to write.

Original	Revision
We will meet on Thursday in Centerville at the Lancaster Hotel on McDaniel Street near the harbor.	We will meet Thursday at the Lancaster Hotel, 1423 McDaniel St., Centerville.

Some prepositional phrases can be tightened into adjectives:

Original	Revision
I will present the report in the meeting on Thursday.	I will present the report in Thursday's meeting.

6. *Challenge long sentences.* How long should a sentence be? Long enough to make its point effectively—and no longer. Challenge any sentence that exceeds 25 words. Eliminate *to be* verbs and tighten prepositional phrases when possible.

7. *Avoid overused expressions.* Clichés such as "It has come to my attention" and "I regret to inform you" lack original thought. They sound insincere. Overused figures of speech, such as "He's a fish out of water," don't create the engaging image they once did.

8. *Avoid placing important words or phrases in the middle of a sentence.* The beginning of a sentence breaks a silence and calls attention to itself. The last words of a sentence echo into a brief silence and gain emphasis. The middle of a sentence generally draws the least attention.

9. *Keep the focus on the reader.* Tell readers what they want and need to know—not just what you want them to know. Keep the focus on how they benefit from reading your document.

10. *Read your sentences aloud.* Or at least whisper them quietly to yourself. That's the surest way to check for effective sentence rhythms. Reading aloud can also be an effective editing technique.

Writing: Stage Four of the Writing Process

Because you've completed the research and organization stages of the writing process, the question that now faces you isn't *What should I write?* Instead, it's *How should I write what's in my outline?* That difference doesn't make writing easy—but it certainly makes it easier. Having an outline allows you to begin anywhere. If you're intimidated by the importance of the first paragraph, start with the second: Your outline tells you what information to include.

Another strategy for getting started is simply to start: Write the first paragraph, no matter how bad it seems. Then stop and evaluate it. If it really is bad, why? What specifically is wrong with it? Are the sentences too long? Does the paragraph fail to move toward the targeted public's values and interests in this situation? Does it not follow your outline? Identifying specific problems helps you fix them. This process is similar to carving a statue out of stone: At first, all we have is an awkward chunk of rock. But by chipping away, little by little, we gradually create something that approaches our high standards.

For example, let's imagine that you roll up your sleeves and, with a quick glance at your outline for the Volunteer Clearinghouse news release, you just start writing:

> *The board of directors of Volunteer Clearinghouse has announced that Elaine Anderson will be that organization's new executive director. Anderson is the former supervisor of the Coxwold County Red Cross. Volunteer Clearinghouse coordinates the recruitment and training of volunteers for the agencies of the Coxwold County Social Service League.*

Not bad. But you quickly identify the small points that you don't like:

1. It takes 10 words before we get to the real news: Elaine Anderson is the new executive director. Can't we move faster to what will interest our targeted public of news editors?
2. The paragraph doesn't include Anderson's starting date.
3. The last sentence seems like an afterthought.

With the problems identified, you're ready to eliminate them. Your second draft might look like this:

> *Elaine Anderson, former supervisor of the Coxwold County Red Cross, will be the new executive director of Volunteer Clearinghouse, that organization's board of directors has announced. Anderson will begin her new job January 15. Volunteer Clearinghouse coordinates the recruitment and training of volunteers for the agencies of the Coxwold County Social Service League.*

That's better. There's room for improvement, but your first paragraph is now good enough to justify moving on to another section of your document. You'll get another chance to polish all sections of the document during the next stage of the writing process: revision.

Revision: Stage Five of the Writing Process

As writers consider revision, a seductive danger confronts them: the euphoria of creation. Good writers work hard to complete their first drafts, and when they're done, they're often relieved, excited, and justifiably pleased with themselves. *I've worked hard,* they think. *I've agonized over every sentence. I'm not going to change a thing, because this document is good!* That's the euphoria of creation: the feeling that your just-finished document is great and needs no revision. One of the few cures is to get away from the document for as long as possible. Put it aside, even if it's for only half an hour. Concentrate on something else. Let the euphoria of creation subside. Finally, reapproach your document with the faith that revision just might make it better.

That's the goal of revision: to make a good document even better. One way to improve a good document is to approach it with the reader's vision. In a book called *The Reader over Your Shoulder,* poet and novelist Robert Graves recommends imagining one of your intended readers leaning over your shoulder and saying, *But what does that mean? Can't this part be clearer? What's in this for me? What do I gain by reading this?*[8] Instead of banishing this annoying reader back to your imagination, do your best to satisfy his or her demands. Approach your document not as the writer but as a reader. Engage in a true *re*-vision.

A second method of revision is to test each sentence against the goal of the document. Your goal, probably, is to move your targeted public to an action or, at least, to an idea. As you reread your document, does *every* sentence work toward the goal? Could some sentences work toward the goal more effectively? Do some passages need to be longer and stronger? Are other passages needlessly repeating earlier points? One definition of poetry is "the best words in the best order." That's not a bad definition for a public relations document. Every word should contribute to the document's clear reason for existing.

Let's return again to our Volunteer Clearinghouse scenario. Having put your news release aside for about 45 minutes, you begin to reread it, imagining that the editor of a local newspaper is leaning over your shoulder. Because she's a journalist, she immediately tells you, *Give me specific details. No vagueness!* Your reader's vision leads you to reconsider your first sentence:

> *Elaine Anderson, former supervisor of the Coxwold County Red Cross, will be the new executive director of Volunteer Clearinghouse, that organization's board of directors has announced.*

You're specific about *who* and *what*—but exactly *when* was this announced? That's not clear. So to satisfy your reader's interest in getting the exact details, you revise the sentence:

> *Elaine Anderson, former supervisor of the Coxwold County Red Cross, will be the new executive director of Volunteer Clearinghouse, that organization's board of directors announced Monday.*

It's a small change, but it has a big impact: It helps to satisfy the needs of your readers. When you've worked through the entire document with a fresh perspective and tested each sentence against your goal, you're ready for the next stage of the writing process: macroediting.

Macroediting: Stage Six of the Writing Process

You've no doubt heard that a lawyer who represents himself or herself has a fool for a client. The same is partially true of editing: No writer should serve as the only editor of his or her writing. A qualified coworker should edit your document before you submit it to a supervisor or the client for approval. Does that mean that you as writer have no editing responsibilities? No: Your goal is to deliver a flawless document to the editor—and that means completing the first edit yourself. Your own edit should consist of two levels: the macroedit and the microedit.

Macroediting challenges the "big picture" of your document: the meaning, the organization, and the format. Among the important questions in a macroedit are

- Is the message of the document clear?
- Does the document answer a reporter's traditional questions: who? what? where? when? why? how?
- Is the document fair? (You don't have to present other points of view, but your document shouldn't distort reality, present half-truths, or ignore damaging information.)
- Does the document make any claims that seem unsubstantiated?
- Does the organization of the main points follow a logical order?
- Does one paragraph lead gracefully to the next?
- Is the format of the document correct? (For example, does the format of a news release identify a contact person?)
- Does the format assist the meaning? (For example, would internal headlines help?)

The macroediting stage is your last opportunity for significant rewriting before you deliver your document to others. If you are satisfied that the meaning, organization, and format are as good as they can be, it's time for the picky stage of the writing process: the microedit.

Microediting: Stage Seven of the Writing Process

Microediting means doing a sentence-by-sentence double-check of accuracy, spelling, grammar (including punctuation), and style. But by this point in the writing process, you've probably read your document at least a dozen times; you may even have parts of it memorized. This familiarity makes it hard for you to conduct an effective microedit: You may read what you *meant* to write instead of what you *accidentally* wrote. One way to increase your focus on the actual words in each sentence is to conduct the microedit backward, starting with the last full sentence. Moving through the document backward "defamiliarizes" it, helping you see what you've really written. When you're certain that the last sentence is flawless, move to the second-to-last sentence, and so on. As you might guess, proofreading backward isn't exciting, but it is effective.

To verify accuracy, double-check all names, titles, numbers—any fact that can be confirmed. Also double-check all spelling, punctuation, and common grammatical errors such as disagreements between verbs and their subjects. For style, verify that each sentence follows specific style guidelines preferred by its targeted public. In your Volunteer Clearinghouse news release, you probably would use Associated Press style, which many newspapers use. AP style, for example, asks you to abbreviate the words *street, avenue,* and *boulevard* when they're used with a specific street name and a specific address. Most news releases are written in newspaper style, which broadcast media rewrite to their specifications.

Imagine doing the microedit of your news release for Volunteer Clearinghouse. As you'll recall, you had revised your first sentence to this:

Elaine Anderson, former supervisor of the Coxwold County Red Cross, will be the new executive director of Volunteer Clearinghouse, that organization's board of directors announced Monday.

This would be the last sentence to undergo a microedit, because you wisely began at the end of the document and moved backward one sentence at a time. Stifling a yawn, you double-check the spelling of Elaine Anderson's name against her résumé—and your yawn turns into a gasp: Her first name is spelled *Elayne*. As you type in the correction, you're grateful that you edited the document yourself before submitting it to another editor. Good microediting helped save your credibility as a writer.

When the editing process is through, the document is ready for an important test: the approval stage of the writing process.

Approval: Stage Eight of the Writing Process

Chances are that you've been to a party in the past few months. Remember what you did before leaving your residence? You examined yourself in the mirror. You may even have asked a friend, "How do I look?" You wondered how others would react to you, and you did everything possible to ensure a good impression.

It's not that different with documents—except that, oftentimes, many people want to review a document before it is distributed to its targeted public: your supervisor, your client, anyone who is quoted, anyone who supplied important information, key department heads . . . the list can seem endless. It's as if a dozen friends and family members suddenly arrived and wanted to approve your appearance before you left for the party. And many of these reviewers have the power to insist on changes. In the workplace, your supervisor can assist you in determining which of the requested changes should be made.

Who is in charge of the approval stage? That depends on the company or organization, but in many cases the writer is in charge of securing approvals. The approval process involves knowing who needs to review the document, how soon each reviewer must respond, and who has the final say over requested revisions. Along with the document, each reviewer should receive a memorandum that politely specifies a deadline for response. An important strategy for the approval stage of the writing process is to keep a chart for every document, noting to whom it was sent, when it was sent, when it was returned, what revisions were requested, and what revisions were made.

The approvals list for the Volunteer Clearinghouse news release, for example, probably would include your supervisor, a representative of the clearinghouse's board of directors, and perhaps Elayne Anderson herself. Some documents, such as corporate annual reports, have much longer approvals lists; for example, lawyers and accountants read every annual report to ensure that it meets all its legal and financial reporting requirements.

For most public relations documents, a second round of approvals generally is not necessary unless substantial revisions were requested and made. However, be sure your supervisor grants final approval before you proceed to the next stage of the writing process: distribution.

VIAGRA FACT SHEET

Viagra™ (sildenafil citrate), now approved by the U.S. Food and Drug Administration, is a breakthrough treatment for erectile dysfunction, more commonly known as "impotence."

- Viagra is a tablet that works regardless of the underlying cause of ED. It was shown to be effective in men with ED associated with a [variety] of medical conditions, including diabetes, a variety of [...] neurogenic conditions, and depression.

- Viagra is not an aphrodisiac:
  It enables a man to respond naturally to sexual stimulation.

- Viagra is remarkably effective:
  The drug improved erections in approximately four of [...] it in clinical trials. Viagra is taken orally in 25-, 50-[...] about 1 hour before anticipated sexual activity.

- Viagra has been extensively tested:
  In trials worldwide more than 3000 men took [...] attempts resulted in successful sexual intercourse.

- Viagra works by increasing the blood flow [...] establishing and maintaining an erection; [...] The drug accomplishes this by sel[...] phosphodiesterase type 5, which h[...] monophosphate (cGMP), a necessary [...] flow into the penis. Viagra helps rest[...] in response to sexual stimulation.

- Viagra provides men with a marked [...] ED: Previous treatments involv[...] penis, the use of urethral supp[...] surgery, or the use of a vacuum [...] While other therapies prod[...] Viagra enables a man to res[...]

- The combination of Viag[...] blood pressure. Theref[...] nitrates in any form.

Pfizer Inc
235 East 42nd Street
New York, NY 10017

www.pfizer.com

Pfizer

News

For immediate release
March 27, 1998

Contacts:
Andy McCormick 212-573-1226
Mariann Caprino 212-733-5686

FDA APPROVES PFIZER MEDICINE VIAGRA FOR ERECTILE DYSFUNCTION

NEW YORK, New York -- The U.S. Food and Drug Administration has approved the breakthrough oral therapy Viagra (sildenafil citrate) for the treatment of erectile dysfunction, Pfizer Inc announced today.

Taken about an hour before anticipated sexual activity, Viagra is a tablet that works naturally with sexual stimulation. Viagra is effective in most men with erectile dysfunction (ED), the medical term for impotence, which is associated with a broad range of physical or psychological medical conditions.

Discovered and [...] Viagra is the first in a new class of medica[...] that improve bl[...] [...] inhibitors has been demons[...] patients.

"Viagra is a m[...] treats a medi[...] quality of li[...] Steere, Jr., [...] innovative th[...] underscores [...]

ERECTILE DYSFUNCTION PERSP[...]

The following selections are from letters that Pfizer has rec[...] past three years.

- "It may be difficult for someone who has not suffered with i[...] fully comprehend the effect of this condition on a person's life, [...] 'devastating' comes close to capturing the feeling..."

- "I suffer from impotence, erectile dysfunction or whatever oth[...] you may call it...I'm desperate...I want to walk with my head hig[...] like a whole man, not half of one..."

- "...I would very much like to know if [Viagra] would help a rectal c[...] patient now in remission eight years with a sigmoid colostomy. This [...] of surgery rendered me impotent..."

- "Before I took part in the [Viagra] study I was heavily depressed...T[...] feeling of being inadequate, even inferior, let alone impotent, w[...] unbearable..."

- "My boyfriend is a 45-year-old healthy male with an undiagnosable [...] impotence problem...We are desperately trying to find out if this new [...] product is going to be the answer to our prayers, or, if not, he must resign [...] himself to the fact that he will never be able to have his manhood back..."

- "...I am a healthy 50-year-old female involved for the past year with a [...] healthy 44-year-old male who suffers from impotence. We have been to [...] 11 doctors...We have had every kind of test imaginable done, and [...] suffered through many types of corrective action, none of which have [...] worked without great pain to one or both of us..."

- "...I've enjoyed a very active sex life until the past two years. I now feel [...] like less than half of a man, embarrassed so many times, actually getting [...] out of bed to hide in the bathroom and cry...."

References available upon request.   # # #

VIAGRA *(sildenafil citrate)*

NDC 0069-4210-30
30 Tablets
Viagra™ 50
(sildenafil citrate) tablets
50 mg*
Distributed by
Pfizer Pfizer Labs
Division of Pfizer Inc, NY, NY 10017

Media Kit Among the many written documents in the first media kit for the anti-impotence drug Viagra were a news release, a fact sheet, and a back-grounder that contained endorsements from satisfied consumers. (Courtesy of Pfizer, Inc.)

Distribution: Stage Nine of the Writing Process

Distribution differs from document to document. A news release can be hand-delivered, mailed, e-mailed, faxed, posted on a web site, or routed through online distribution services such as PR Newswire. A policy and procedure document telling employees how a certain process works can be placed in employee mailboxes or on desktops, e-mailed, posted on an intranet, placed in a binder in the organization's library, or even tacked onto an old-fashioned wall-mounted bulletin board. The writer may be in charge of all or some of the distribution, or distribution may be delegated to others.

As more and more distribution occurs through e-mail and web sites, however, writers are assuming increasing responsibility for distribution. With improvements in technology, distribution through cyberspace can be triggered by the push of a button. But therein lies a new problem for public relations practitioners. Should that message be posted on the organization's public web site—or, perhaps, should it be only on the intranet or extranet site? If the document is to be e-mailed within an organization, should everyone receive it—or just top management? More than one communicator has been embarrassed by accidentally posting a private document to every electronic mailbox within an organization. The ease of online communication is accompanied, unfortunately, by the possibility of instantaneous errors in distribution.

Even when distribution is delegated to others, the writer may want to double-check that it did occur. A sad truth is that the best writer and the most polished document in the world can be defeated by faulty distribution. Many writers, therefore, carefully monitor the distribution stage of the writing process. Double-checking distribution can be as simple as checking a web site or as complicated as driving to different office buildings to ensure that posters are properly displayed.

Despite the countless ways of distributing a document, a few facts hold true for every method: Whenever possible, a document should be delivered in the manner and at the time and in the place preferred by the targeted public. Don't hesitate to ask members of the targeted public about their preferences. When we're satisfied that our distribution method meets these public-focused criteria, we're ready for the final stage of the writing process: evaluation.

Evaluation: Stage Ten of the Writing Process

In earlier chapters, when we discussed the four-stage public relations process of research, planning, communication, and evaluation, we noted that although evaluation is mentioned last, it actually occurs throughout the public relations process. It's the same in writing: Evalutation is ongoing throughout the process. Above all, however, we evaluate at the end of the writing process to see whether our document succeeded. Did it address the targeted public's values and interests well enough to be read and acted upon? For example, did journalists use the news release we wrote for Volunteer Clearinghouse? If so, which media used it, and how many of our main points did the coverage include? In short, how well did we succeed? If some journalists chose not to use the news release, why not? Without excessively troubling the journalists, can we determine why our news release didn't become news in certain media? In the writing process, evaluation helps us to identify and reinforce what we did well—and to identify and not repeat any errors we may have made.

And now we're at the end of the writing process. At this point, it's only human to ask whether it's really worth working through all these stages. What's the reward for such a meticulous approach to writing? Fortunately, the rewards are many. Adhering to the writing process can help prevent the nausea that comes from staring at a computer screen as a deadline approaches and not knowing what to say. Within the framework of the writing process, should such a moment happen, we can drop back to previous levels, strengthen them, and then move forward again with confidence. Using the writing process can mean job security and promotability. As we note at the beginning of the chapter, public relations relies on skillful, precise use of language. Using the writing process, finally, can earn you respect as a thoughtful, professional writer who knows how to strengthen relationships with the magic of words.

Quick ✔ Check

1. How formal does a writer's outline need to be?
2. What is "the euphoria of creation"? How can its influence be diminished?
3. What questions should a writer ask in the macroediting stage of the writing process?
4. Why and how does a writer move backward in the microediting stage of the writing process?

Writing for the Ear

We've seen how the writing process works for documents designed to be read, such as news releases. But the writing process works equally well for documents designed to be *heard,* such as speeches and radio public service announcements. Documents designed to be heard, however, require special writing techniques to ensure that targeted publics easily comprehend the speaker's meaning. After all, unlike readers, listeners can't simply reread a paragraph or pause to decipher a challenging passage. Professional speechwriters, broadcast news writers, and other professionals who write for the ear have developed several guidelines for effectively conveying meaning to their listeners:

■ *Remember that the speaker has to breathe.* Use short sentences. Short sentences create frequent pauses, which allow the speaker to breathe. The pauses also give listeners a moment to consider the previous sentence. An average effective spoken sentence contains 9 to 10 words.

■ *Limit each sentence to one idea.* Avoid linking clauses together with coordinating conjunctions such as *and* and *but* or with subordinating conjunctions such as *be-*

GRAMMAR ON THE WEB

What's the difference between *who* and *whom*? How about *lay* and *lie*? Or *that* and *which*? Should an opening subordinate clause be set off by a comma—and what's an opening subordinate clause, anyway? Now imagine asking such questions in the middle of the night as you toil away at an important public relations document. Who can answer such questions when only you and the bakers in the local doughnut shop are awake?

Let the World Wide Web come to the rescue. The web abounds with sites sponsored by university writing centers, editing professors, and other cyberspace grammarians. Just go to your favorite search engine and type in the key word *grammar*.

Two of the best sites for college students have little in common except clarity and usefulness. The first is the first edition of the famous *Elements of Style* by William Strunk Jr., online at www.bartleby.com/141. Strunk clearly explains the blunt guidelines he offers, such as "Use the active voice" and "Omit needless words." The short, well-organized book closes with the sections "Words and Expressions Commonly Misused" and "Words Commonly Misspelled."

A second highly useful web site is *Guide to Grammar and Writing,* online at www.ccc.commnet.edu/grammar. This comprehensive, well-organized site can help answer your *who/whom, lay/lie,* and *that/which* questions. The site also includes quizzes, frequently asked questions, and links to other sites. Best of all, as a welcome relief, the entries are informal and reflect a sense of humor.

When questions of grammar arise, help may be only a few keystrokes away.

cause and *although*. By the time listeners receive the closing idea of a multiclause sentence, they may have forgotten the idea at the beginning.

■ *Use concrete words and images, not abstractions.* Clear, explicit language helps your listeners stay focused. They won't pause to try to decipher the meaning of vague, abstract language. Charles Osgood of CBS-TV and CBS radio so believes in the power of concrete, evocative language that he ends his television broadcasts with these words: "*See* you on the radio."

■ *Use precise nouns and verbs.* An imprecise verb needs an adverb to clarify its meaning. A vague noun needs an adjective to make it accurate. Choosing exactly the right word helps you create short, precise sentences. Avoid excessive use of *to be* verbs such as *am, is, was,* and *were.* Such verbs don't convey precise images to listeners.

■ *Challenge every word in every sentence.* Is each word necessary? Can a more precise noun eliminate the need for an adjective? Can you replace a long word with a shorter word without losing meaning? Spoken language is not the place to impress an audience with your knowledge of sesquipedalian (long) words.

■ *Spell out big numbers and give phonetic spellings for hard-to-pronounce words.* If the speaker stumbles, so do the listeners. Assist the speaker by providing pronunciation cues for big numbers and difficult names or words. For example, broadcast writers often write the number 5,200 as "52–hundred."

■ *Use traditional syntax (word order).* In the English language, the simplest sentences begin with a subject, which is followed by a verb, which in turn is sometimes followed by a direct object and perhaps an indirect object. Traditional word order offers the fewest roadblocks to understanding.

■ *Link sentences and paragraphs with clear transitions.* Often, you can create a clear **transition** by making the direct object of one sentence the subject of the following sentence. Note how objects become subjects in the following example: *In 1863 Abraham Lincoln wrote his greatest speech: the Gettysburg Address. The Gettysburg Address expresses principles that still guide us today. The most important of those principles is contained in the words "government of the people, by the people, and for the people."*

■ *Attribute direct quotations at the beginning of a sentence.* In written English, we often place the **attribution**—the *said Abraham Lincoln*—in the midst or at the end of a direct quotation. But listeners can't see quotation marks. Placing the attribution at the beginning of a quotation is the only way to signal clearly that the speaker is citing someone else's words.

■ *Introduce important points with general, descriptive sentences.* Let listeners know that an important point is coming. If a speaker simply says, *Sixty percent of our em-*

Public Service Announcement
Radio public service announcements demonstrate how writing meant to be read aloud differs from ordinary print writing. Note the repeated phone number and the brevity of sentences in the 30-second PSA. (Courtesy of the National Diabetes Education Program)

Medicare Benefits and Controlling Your Diabetes

Radio Public Service Announcements

"Good News"

In this spot, a mature adult woman calls her friend with some good news about new Medicare benefits. The listeners are engaged because they both have diabetes.

Good News :30 seconds

Woman 1:	*(ringing phone)* Hello?
Woman 2:	Hi, Laura. I've got good news. Medicare will now help us pay...
Woman 1:	*(interrupts her)* For our diabetes equipment and supplies... like glucose monitors, test strips and lancets.
Woman 2:	That's right. I learned about it by calling 1-800-438-5383. How did you know?
Woman 1:	The Internet – www.medicare.gov. What's that number again?
Woman 2:	1-800-438-5383. *(admiring)* The Internet? Laura, you're really something. *(They laugh)*
	FADE OUT.

ployees want better communication with top management, listeners may not retain the percentage as they absorb the rest of the sentence. We can assist our listeners by writing, *A high percentage of our employees want better communication with top management. Sixty percent of our employees say that top management should communicate more often with people in our organization.*

■ *Gracefully repeat main points.* Know the main points that you hope to convey, and seek opportunities to state them more than once.

■ *Avoid closing with "In conclusion."* Readers can see the end of a document coming. But how do listeners identify an upcoming conclusion? A return to the broad theme of the document—a restatement of the main point—can signal that the end is near.

■ *Break any of the above guidelines when doing so will assist the listener.* These are only guidelines, not rigid laws. Usually, these guidelines help convey meaning to the listener. In cases where they interfere with meaning, discard them.

Writing the spoken word well is an art, as is all good writing. Writing the spoken word, in fact, leads logically to our next section. Public relations professionals sometimes stand and deliver the words they have written. Sometimes they make presentations.

Quick ✔ Check

1. How many words are in the average effective spoken sentence?
2. In general, do adjectives and adverbs add to or detract from the effectiveness of spoken language?
3. What are transitions?
4. In spoken language, why should an important point be introduced by a general, descriptive sentence?

The Process of Successful Presentations

Comedian Jerry Seinfeld—someone who knows a thing or two about appearing before large groups—has no illusions about the difficulty of public speaking: At a funeral, he says, most of us would rather be the corpse than the person delivering the eulogy.[9] Cicero, the greatest of the Roman orators, wrote, "I turn pale at the outset of a speech and quake in every limb and in all my soul."[10] As we noted earlier, public speaking ranks number one among people's greatest fears.

Why the terror? Often, we fear making fools of ourselves—of being seen as impostors pretending to know something. Other times, we're afraid that the discomfort of being in front of a group will rattle us, making our voices tremble and our hands shake. People will see how nervous we are, and their awareness will intensify our nightmare. Make a presentation? No thanks. We'll schedule a root canal for that day (fear of dentists is not among people's top 14 fears).[11]

Values Statement 10.1

KELLOGG COMPANY

Based in Battle Creek, Michigan, the Kellogg Company produces breakfast cereals, toaster pastries, frozen waffles, bagels, cereal bars, and other food products. The Kellogg Company values statement includes this passage:

Integrity and Ethics

Integrity is the cornerstone of our business practice. We will conduct our affairs in a manner consistent with the highest ethical standards. To meet this commitment, we will:

Engage in fair and honest business practices.
Show respect for each other, our consumers, customers, suppliers, shareholders and the communities in which we operate.
Communicate in an honest, factual and accurate manner.

—Kellogg Company web site

Public relations practitioners, however, cannot avoid presentations. Clients want proposals. The news media want statements. Community groups want speeches. The question is not *Will we make presentations?* We will. Rather, the question is *How can we make successful presentations?* Our answer should sound familiar: A successful presentation requires research, planning, communication, and evaluation—the four stages of the public relations process. By the time you actually deliver your presentation, it should be an old friend. It should fit you and your targeted public like a pair of comfortable shoes. With presentations, familiarity doesn't breed contempt. Instead, your familiarity with your presentation, your audience, and even the room in which you'll be speaking breeds confidence and success. And it all starts with research.

Researching Your Presentation

Presentation research begins with knowing your targeted public. Who are its members? What values and interests unite them? Could cultural differences affect your presentation? What do they want from you? How long do they expect you to speak? If the situation permits such a request, don't hesitate to ask members of your future audience what they hope to learn from you. To create an effective message, you should combine audience research with another area of research: research into what you want to tell the audience. As you know, an effective message combines your purpose with the values and interests of the targeted public. During your presentation, if you consistently address the concerns of your audience, you can expect to be rewarded with eye contact, nodding heads, and attentive listeners.

Another aspect of audience research is identifying the decision makers and opinion leaders within your audience. Of course, you should maintain eye contact with and speak to everyone in the room. But at important moments in your presentation, you may want to focus extra attention on the people who can most help you achieve your goals.

Researching a presentation also involves learning about the room in which you'll be speaking. Is there enough space to allow freedom of movement as you speak? Are there windows that need to be shaded if you plan to project visuals onto a screen? Is there a screen? A projection system? A lectern? Answers to such questions not only improve the technical support of your presentation; they also increase your comfort level as you prepare for the presentation. You won't be walking into unknown territory.

Planning Your Presentation

Begin by planning to be yourself. Trying to be someone else during your presentation is stressful and distracting. You impress your targeted public more by addressing its values and interests than by maintaining icy composure at every moment. Have confidence in the message you create, and relax. Be yourself.

Planning includes message creation. Again, your message should combine your presentation's purpose with your audience's values and interests. Everything in your presentation should support the central, unifying theme of your message. But how long should "everything" be? Your research answers that question: Length is guided by what the audience wants. Ideally, a speech should take no more than 20 minutes and include no more than three main, message-related points. Presentation of a proposal to a client generally should take no more than one hour; anything longer might suggest a lack of respect for the client's time. During that hour, every point you make should be related to the central theme provided by your message. A brief statement to the news media may take only one minute. An educational presentation may take an entire day or two. Again, the ideal length for any presentation is established by the needs of the targeted public.

When you know the message and the length, you're ready to outline your presentation. Unless you're delivering a formal speech or a highly technical performance in which assistants trigger multimedia effects as you say specific words, experts suggest that you not have a word-for-word script. An outline allows you to maintain eye contact and helps you speak with—instead of read to—your audience. Many professionals recommend, however, that you memorize your introduction, your conclusion, and any important anecdotes. At those key moments, you want unflinching eye contact as you dazzle the audience with your sincere, articulate, and polished presentation.

Another aspect of planning for success is practice. And more practice. And even more practice. Practicing not only polishes your presentation; it also helps you become comfortable with it. And being comfortable with your presentation reduces the terror that freezes many of us at the mere thought of public speaking. Being comfortable with your presentation can actually make you eager to deliver it: You know it's good, you know you're ready, and (being human) you're eager for the praise you know you deserve. So practice. And then practice some more.

As you practice, try to duplicate the conditions and environment of the actual presentation. Practice in the room in which you'll make the real presentation. If that's not possible, practice in a similar room. Practice at the scheduled presentation time. If you intend to invite questions from your audience, have friends and coworkers observe your practice presentations and ask questions. Wear the comfortable clothing that you'll wear during the presentation—usually clothing at or just above the level of formality of your audience's attire. Use the technology and visual aids that you'll use in your actual presentation, and practice your solutions to sudden technological failures.

USING VISUAL AIDS.   Planned and used wisely, **visual aids** can enhance most presentations. Visual aids range from handouts to flip charts to overheads, slides, and com-

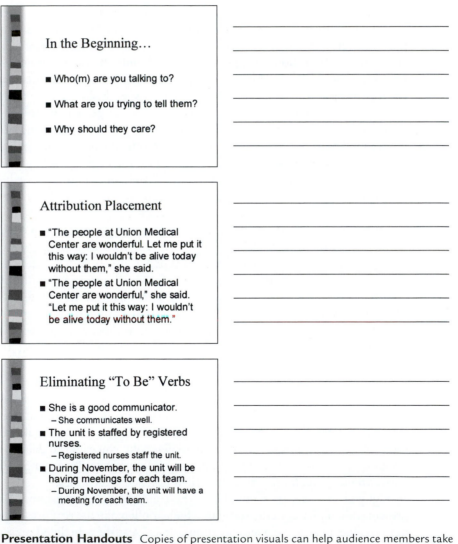

Presentation Handouts Copies of presentation visuals can help audience members take notes and focus on a speaker's message. Most slide-creation programs have special print functions for handouts.

puter projections. Recent studies show that well-designed visual aids can increase audience learning by 200 percent, increase audience retention of main points by 38 percent, and reduce explanation time by 40 percent.[12] Well-designed visuals are short and have headlines. Because you don't want your audience to read ahead of you, consider using a program such as PowerPoint, which allows you to use a computer projection system to build a visual one sentence or one image at a time. Although it's OK to look at your own visuals, don't turn your back and speak to them. Speak to your audience. If a gap occurs between one visual and the next, consider going to a blank screen—or covering your flip chart—so that an old visual doesn't become a distraction. And absolutely, positively avoid misspellings in your visuals.

Many audiences will be grateful for photocopies of visuals. Rather than interrupt your presentation to distribute them or make audience members wait until the presentation is over, have the attractively bound photocopies ready as the audience enters the room. Ideally, you have individualized both your visuals and the photocopies for this particular presentation. For example, if you're addressing your local chamber of commerce, the cover sheet of your bound photocopies should acknowledge that.

PLANNING FOR PROBLEMS.   You should also plan for trouble. If you're speaking from a script or an outline, you should have quick access to a second copy in case you misplace yours at the last moment. Ensure that extra lightbulbs are available for the projection system. If you're using a computer projection system, have overhead transparencies and access to an overhead projector in case your computer fails. If the journey to your presentation site involves airline travel, carry on—don't check—luggage that includes presentation materials. Otherwise, as you arrive in Barcelona to make your presentation, your visual aids may be 40,000 feet above Honolulu. Consider shipping bulky handouts or technology to the presentation site several days early to ensure that they arrive.

Your final moment of troubleshooting should occur approximately an hour before you start your presentation. Arrive early, and test the technology one last time. Double-check the location of your backup technology, such as an overhead projector and transparencies or a flip chart. Ensure that you have access to two copies of your outline or script.

Preparing for trouble also means being flexible. Know your presentation so well that you can cut it short if your hosts decrease your time allotment. Watch for any changes in your subject matter that might alter the direction of your presentation. For example, a potential client company suddenly facing a lawsuit over one of its products may be more interested in crisis communications counseling than in your scheduled presentation on a CD media kit for the now-notorious product.

Finally, if someone will be introducing you, consider writing a short introduction for that individual to use. He or she may appreciate the assistance, and you won't be surprised by an inadequate or a too-lavish introduction. Be sure to send that introduction to your introducer at least a week before your presentation.

Making Your Presentation

It's the moment of truth. You've been introduced, and you're the center of attention. After thanking the person who introduces you, pause a moment before you begin. Smile. Look at the people in the room. Show them that you're confident, that you're quietly excited about the information you're about to share. Maintain eye contact, and begin your memorized introduction.

Should you begin with a joke? Most experts say no. It's not worth the risk of failing and beginning the presentation with an awkward silence or strained laughter. A more effective opening strategy can be an anecdote with which your audience can identify. Another effective strategy is to begin by targeting your audience's concerns: Tell audience members exactly what you hope they gain from your presentation. After that, you may want to establish the basic guidelines of the presentation, such as when you'll take questions.

As you speak, continue eye contact, looking at one person at a time, gracefully forcing that person to realize that you are acknowledging and valuing his or her presence. Again, single out decision makers and opinion leaders for extra eye contact. Unless you are giving a formal speech, try not to anchor yourself to a lectern or a technology table. A handheld remote control can allow you to project visuals from any point in the room. If you move smoothly about the presentation area, the audience's eyes will follow you, helping everyone stay alert.

If your technology fails—and, eventually, in some presentation it will—don't try to hide the fact. You've prepared for this eventuality, and you're ready to handle it professionally. Acknowledge the failure; after all, everyone can see it. Toss off a quick joke, if appropriate, and move smoothly to your backup solution. Audience members probably are empathizing with you; it could just as easily be one of them suffering the failure. They'll be relieved and pleased to see you avoid panic. Your seamless move to an alternate plan will impress them, in part because it shows just how seriously you've taken this opportunity to speak with them. As we'll note in Chapter 12, sometimes a well-handled crisis creates a hero.

When possible, close your presentation by calling for questions. A question-and-answer session can emphasize one last time your respect for your audience's particular concerns. Don't finish with an answer, however. Instead, after you answer the final question, deliver a summary statement, a strong, planned "cap" for your remarks. In presentations that are *not* formal speeches, consider this closing tactic: After your final statement, clap your hands once, bow slightly, straighten, and, looking your audience in the eyes, say, with a smile, "Thank you very much." Your own clap and your slight bow just might trigger applause.

Formal speeches generally do not include a question-and-answer session. Instead, if you're presenting such a speech, deliver a strong conclusion and close with a simple "Thank you." Applause automatically follows most speeches.

However you conclude your presentation, keep an eye (subtly) on the clock. No one appreciates a presentation that runs past its allotted time. An overlong presentation can show a serious lack of respect for the audience, undermining the powerful

CONQUERING THE PRESENTATION JITTERS

"We have nothing to fear but fear itself," said President Franklin Roosevelt. Of course, Roosevelt referred to fear created by a faltering economy, but his shrewd comment also applies to presentations. Frequently, the presentation itself is not what we fear; instead, we fear appearing nervous and uncertain in front of others. We're unnerved by the fear that our hands will shake and our voices will tremble.

Expert presenters offer this advice about fighting stage fright:

- Practice in front of others. Present to test audiences before you present to the ultimate audience.

- Deliver the goods. If you're conveying useful information to your audience, its members will think you're great.

- As you present, maintain eye contact. Don't think about yourself; think about your audience. Talk to people, not to the walls, floor, or ceiling.

- Channel your nervous energy into movement. If appropriate, walk around as you speak. Address different sections of the room. Use hand gestures that complement your words.

- Realize that you are your own worst critic. Few people in the audience are evaluating your performance. Instead, they're evaluating the quality of the information they're receiving—so, again, deliver the goods.

- After a presentation, reward yourself with a special purchase or some other treat. Be grateful to the presentation for giving you the excuse for a minor extravagance.

One last bit of advice. Attack your fear. Seek opportunities to do presentations. Franklin Roosevelt *didn't* say, "Practice makes perfect"— but, once again, the phrase applies to presentations.

focus you've placed on addressing its values. Presentation coach Karen Susman recommends the following timing strategy: "Know your material and how long it takes to deliver. Follow the 75 percent rule. If you're scheduled to speak for one hour, plan 45 minutes of material. . . . Be so familiar with your presentation that you know where you can cut if you need to."[13]

After finishing your presentation, relax. That wasn't so bad, was it?

Evaluating Your Presentation

Don't bask in glory too long, though: Another presentation looms, and you can help make it great by applying what you've learned from your recent presentation and other past efforts. Wait 24 hours until the euphoria of finishing has passed, and then write yourself a memo, evaluating your recent presentation. What worked well? What didn't work as well as you had planned? How well did the technology perform? Did anything during the presentation surprise you? Was the audience responsive? If so, when? How do you know it was responsive? Did you finish on time? What questions and comments from the audience did you receive? When you've answered such questions, consider giving yourself a grade: *A* for excellent, *B* for good, and so on. Try to score a higher grade on your next similar presentation.

The ultimate evaluation, of course, comes from your targeted public. Did it receive and act on the message you delivered? If your presentation was a public relations tactic, did it help you achieve your objective? Ultimately, the success of your presentation must be judged by that standard.

Quick ✔ Check

1. Why is it important to be able to recognize the opinion leaders and decision makers in your audience?
2. Who determines the ideal length of a presentation?
3. Which parts of a presentation should be memorized?
4. What is the 75 percent rule for presentations?

Summary

The difficulty of writing and making presentations is matched by the importance of these two skills: They are core elements in the profession of public relations. Neither will ever be easy, but you can make them easier by following the process that each requires. Those processes are similar, moving through research, planning, implementation, and evaluation. Each stage must be completed before the practitioner can successfully grapple with the next stage. And after the last stage lies success.

As you gain more access to public relations professionals through guest lectures and internships, ask them when they last wrote a document or made a presentation. Their answers will underscore the importance of writing and presentation skills in the practice of public relations.

DISCUSSION QUESTIONS

1. Given what you know of writing for the ear, how would you rewrite the proposed first sentence of the Volunteer Clearinghouse news release to adapt it to a radio news story? Your final draft of the first sentence was *Elayne Anderson, former supervisor of the Coxwold County Red Cross, will be the new executive director of Volunteer Clearinghouse, that organization's board of directors announced Monday.*
2. Does the first sentence of the Volunteer Clearinghouse news release seem a little long? How might you shorten it? The text of the unrevised first paragraph of the news release appears on page 324.
3. Why do journalists prefer the inverted pyramid for news stories?
4. What is the difference between macroediting and microediting? Why aren't the two done simultaneously?
5. Have you ever approached a writing project without adequate preparation? How did you feel as you began writing? What were the results?

6. Can you quote memorable passages from famous speeches? How do those passages support or refute the guidelines for writing for the ear contained in this chapter?
7. Do you fear public speaking? If so, why? Be specific. Do you think the process for successful presentations outlined in this chapter could relieve some of your anxiety? Why or why not?

Memo *from the* Field

Regina Lynch-Hudson, President, The Write Publicist, Atlanta, Georgia

Regina Lynch-Hudson is founder and president of The Write Publicist in Atlanta. Self-described as "the quintessential American mutt," Lynch-Hudson has a 15-year track record of conceptualizing print media campaigns for people, places, products, and performances.

The Write Publicist's handling of the 1996 National Black Arts Festival (the largest biennial festival of its kind in the world) earned Best PR Campaign of the Year Award from the Atlanta Association of Media Women. Today, she pens *Regina Roams,* featured in *Arrivals,* the inflight magazine of AirTran Airways.

Admittedly, when I was asked to contribute to this public relations textbook, I wondered what I would communicate to wide-eyed, idealistic students, when my own career path has not been conventional. But then *public relations* is such an ambiguous term.

I regard public relations as an art form, combining some theory and a great deal of impressionism. From the subliminal theatrics required to deliver memorable presentations to the gut spontaneity of merging words that evoke reaction—a wordsmith's success isn't tied to academia alone. My own college years were short-circuited, due to a family tragedy. NEWS FLASH: Kidney dialysis patient brutally murdered leaving hospital. *Victim's daughter turns to writing for solace.*

Ongoing courses in consumer behavior, body language, and psychology melded with world travel, and an oftentimes nontraditional mélange of seminars, workshops, and lectures enhanced my perspective. I relied on creative ripeness and ravenous "literary consumption" to whet my writing skills.

You should also develop a penchant to read anything you can get your hands on—newspapers, magazines, menus, billboards, and direct mail. You never know when you'll be writing about an automotive manufacturer; a software company; a humanitarian organization; or a corporation with international reach. Subconsciously we all plunder our past for material—and in the profoundest, most unexpected way, up pops a tidbit of knowledge precisely when needed. Somewhere between writing's structure, public relations' principles, and imagination's abstractions, you'll discover a definite and confident style.

Be prepared to undergo years of clarifying and deepening your personal vision, of focusing your energies, of developing patience, just to objectively identify where *you* fit. Discovering one's strengths and weaknesses, maintaining one's commitment and capacity for learning, and perfecting one's craft are imperative in this business.

It's been said that life is a costume party and that we keep changing and changing and changing until we find the outfit that fits best. Some public relations practitioners blossom into world-class event coordinators. Many of us PR'ers are the "idea geniuses" who pen attention-grabbing news releases. Other PR-types possess a gift for gab and are better suited to "pitch" to editors or to deliver persuasive speeches. Tailor your career around a specialty that's a "fit," rather than with what the market seemingly needs. The market can be quite capricious. Embracing those skills that spur passion and inner solace, and daringly carving out a niche based on talents and interests, are not only necessary for productivity but are also necessary for longevity.

Poignancy sells. Regardless of the company or target audience, ability to elucidate a client, on paper, verbally, and even in your body language during oral presentations, requires varying degrees of ardor—delivered enthusiastically, succinctly, and with sincerity. Frankly, one must, to a certain extent, psychologically bond with the client's product or service to promote it. Genuineness is not easily feigned—unless you minor in drama and acting. And even then, audiences are not easily fooled over the long haul.

Originality rules. Oftentimes, originality implies being bold enough to go beyond accepted norms. It's how you pen (or peg) your clients as *distinct* that will brand them in the psyche of target audiences. Whether you are penning a proposal to reap sponsorship for an event, a speech to lure voters to a politician, or a script for a videotape to be used as a sales tool for a luxury resort, communicating what's "different" is fundamental. Knowing your clients enables you to gage how demonstrative you can be in your written, verbal, or pictorial personifcation of them. A bank or a life insurance company may require black-and-white doses of realism, whereas in promoting tourism, the arts, or food, you may add splashes of wit and whimsy.

Don't be afraid to stroke with a broad brush, to try new techniques, to make mistakes. Mistakes are the catalysts that germinate genius. There are no paint-by-number strategies for mastering public relations in the 21st century. The web and the 2000 Census reflect dramatic change in not only *how* we communicate but in the profile of who *we* are.

There's a big canvas out there, and, as Van Gogh illustrated, there is more than one way to paint a sunflower. Whether you work for a *Fortune* 500 giant or as a solo practitioner—it's how you distill millions of ideas and translate them into something cohesive that breathes life into the identity of your clients.

Case Study 10.1

Plastic Couple Splits

Fame can complicate romance. Just ask Jennifer Lopez and Ben Affleck, Nicole Kidman and Tom Cruise, or Barbie and Ken.

In case you missed the Valentine's Day 2004 news flash, Barbie dumped Ken, her steady guy for 43 years. Toy maker Mattel announced the dolls' breakup with a news release.

"With Ken, everything we did was on display," Barbie confided to reporter Jill Ingram of the *Asheville* (NC) *Citizen-Times.* "I mean, it's awful to have your breakup announced in a press release."

(At the end of her interview with Barbie, Ingram added this note: "Barbie can't converse. This interview is fake. I made the whole thing up. Please, oh please, let this disclaimer save me from the legal wrath of Mattel.")[14]

Executives at Mattel had better things to do than sue Ingram: They were busy counting the avalanche of news stories about Barbie's breakup. *PR Week* magazine estimated that the news release helped generate 500 broadcast stories and approximately the same number of print articles.[15] Internet company Terra Lycos, which monitors online searches, announced that within days of the breakup, *Barbie* had become one of the Internet's top 50 search terms. "Barbie was not even close to the list the previous week, but there she is at number 22 last week," the company reported. "We hope Ken has a good lawyer."[16]

Mattel, with the assistance of the Ketchum public relations agency, distributed the news release February 12, just before Valentine's Day and the American International Toy Fair in New York—an event that helps set trends in the toy industry.[17] Under the headline "The Storybook Romance Comes to an End for Barbie and Ken," the release began, "After more than 43 years together, Hollywood's quintessential 'doll' of a couple, Barbie and Ken, have decided to spend some time apart."[18]

Though journalists generally reject cute leads in news releases, the straight-faced treatment of the dolls as real people overcame journalism's preference for unadorned facts. Russell Arons, Mattel's vice president of marketing, became the celebrity couple's agent in the news release and offered this parody of the usual celebrity-split quote: "Barbie and Ken have always been an extraordinary couple. . . . And now they feel it's time to spend some quality time—apart."[19]

The news release not only made headlines around the world: It became part of the story. The release was discussed in the *New York Times,* the *Sunday Telegraph* of London, and the *Toronto Sun.* The *Post-Crescent* of Appleton, Wisconsin, mentioned the news release five times in one story, and the *Baltimore Sun,* in addition to mentioning the release, labeled the breakup a "pseudoevent" (see p. 273).

Mattel's news release even sparked other news releases that jumped aboard the breakup bandwagon. Reacting within 24 hours, 1-800-FLOWERS.COM issued a news release with this headline: "Ken Lost Barbie . . . Don't Lose Your Love This Valentine's Day." In the release, company CEO Jim McCann continued Mattel's "these are real people" charade: "If Ken had only visited us online or given us a call, we might have been able to help him."[20]

QualiLife Pharmaceuticals had a different romantic suggestion for the couple. Its news release, also distributed within 24 hours of the original, featured this headline: "Barbie & Ken Break Up After 43 Years: Did Her Sexual Dysfunction Play a Role?"

In the release's lead, the company offered an alternative to flowers: "As Mattel announces the breakup of Barbie and Ken, QualiLife Pharmaceuticals, developers of the female arousal fluid Zestra for Women . . . mourns what might have been." Noting that Barbie was 43, CEO Martin Crosby said, "Zestra increases and restores sexual pleasure for most women that experience a broad range of sexual difficulties related to perimenopause."[21]

But the Barbie–Ken breakup may have had more to do with sales than romance. Before the Valentine's Day split, business media were reporting that Barbie's sales had been disappointing for years, affecting Mattel's profits and prospects.[22] "We are not pleased," said Mattel CEO Robert Eckert.[23]

London's *Sunday Telegraph* concluded, "It will be . . . interesting to see if Barbie's breakup with Ken falls into the category of publicity stunt—designed to stir up a campaign prior to an imminent but tearful reconciliation and reunification—or whether this storied brand can truly be successfully repositioned for growth."[24]

Could Barbie lose her Malibu beach house and that cool pink car? Is Ken gone forever? And what about Blaine, the Australian surfer introduced in yet another Mattel news release?

At last report, Barbie had no comment.

DISCUSSION QUESTIONS

1. Can we judge the success of the Barbie breakup news release by the amount of media attention it generated?
2. Was Mattel wise to gamble with a "cute" news release?
3. Were the related news releases from 1-800-FLOWERS.COM and QualiLife Pharmaceuticals good for Mattel?
4. Was the Barbie–Ken breakup a pseudoevent? (You may wish to consult Quick-Break 9.1 on page 273.)
5. And, of course, the big question: Should Mattel have Barbie and Ken get together again?

Case Study 10.2

Online Outrage: Emulex and the Fake News Release

"In a moment of panic," said the lawyer, "this 23-year-old kid made a wrong decision that will affect him for the rest of his life. He is extremely remorseful for having been involved in these events. This was a response to a panic situation."[25]

That wrong decision cost investors millions of dollars and temporarily stole more than $2 billion in market value from an Internet communications company called Emulex.[26] The problem began with an abuse of the writing process and ended in a flurry of communication. In the end, good writing swept aside the bad—but only after what *Newsweek* called "one of the web's biggest-ever stock manipulation frauds."[27]

Mark Jakob, 23, triggered the hemorrhage of money in August 2000 with a fake news release. Concerned by losses related to Emulex stock that he owned, he wrote a news release falsely reporting that Emulex' CEO had resigned amid rumors of incorrect financial statements and an impending investigation by the Securities and Exchange Commission. Jakob then sent the news release to Internet Wire, a news release distribution company at which he had worked months earlier. At Internet Wire, he had been a news release processor, and his knowledge of the proper tone and format of news releases helped him give the bogus document an authentic appearance.[28] United Press International even reported that Jakob knew enough to include certain attachments that persuaded his former colleagues that Emulex really had sent the news release to Internet Wire for distribution. On August 25, Internet Wire distributed the news release to the world's financial news media.

Journalists scooped up the information and quickly relayed it to investors. Within hours, the false story of Emulex' woes had been reported by leading financial news media such as Bloomberg News, Dow Jones News Service, CBSMarketwatch.com, and CNBC. Emulex stock prices plummeted 60 percent in 15 minutes, from $110 a share to $43 a share. "The hoax . . . made news across the country by dissolving shareholder millions in minutes," *Investor's Daily* reported.[29] As Emulex investors learned of the plunging price, many sold immediately to prevent more substantial losses. Others had standing orders with their investment advisors to sell automatically if Emulex fell to a certain price.[30] When prices suddenly rose again as investors learned the truth, losses to Emulex investors exceeded $100 million.

"Some shareholders lost money saved for their children's college education, and for others it was a loss of a comfortable retirement that they had worked years to achieve," said James DeSarno of the FBI.[31]

Through a complex process called short selling, however, Jakob made money—albeit temporarily. His illegal manipulation of Emulex stock netted him almost $250,000.[32]

Writing had been used to attack Emulex, and the company used writing to regain the initiative. Less than an hour after learning of the bogus news release, Emulex had fired off its own news release setting the record straight and had posted a similar statement on its web site. In part, the release said, "The negative statements in this fictitious press release are categorically false."[33]

Internet Wire fought back with a news release of its own, which stated, in part, "It appears the hoax was perpetrated by an individual (or individuals) who falsely represented himself or herself as a public relations agency representing Emulex."[34]

Emulex CEO Paul Folino directed the crisis communications against stiff odds. Switchboards were jammed with panicked investors, his public relations manager was stalled en route to the office with a flat tire, and his chief financial officer was sailing off California's coast, out of range of his cell phone. One public relations practitioner called Folino's response "masterful." Folino's own assessment of his performance was more subdued. "That's what they pay me for," he said bluntly.[35]

Six days after the hoax began, the FBI arrested Mark Jakob. Working with the Securities and Exchange Commission, the FBI had traced the bogus news release to a computer at El Camino Community College in Torrance, California, where Jakob was a student. Six months later, he arranged a plea bargain with prosecutors, confessing his guilt in return for a prison sentence of 37 to 46 months.[36]

Other companies may need to learn from Folino's effective communication. "Disgruntled workers have found that the Internet makes it easy to take their frustration out by spreading false information in chat rooms or sending out fake news releases," reported the *New York Times* in 2001. In recent years, profits at Lucent Technologies slumped after a false news release, whereas another news release hoax boosted earnings at Pairgain, a manufacturer of Internet communications equipment. In both cases, federal authorities identified and filed charges against suspects.[37]

"The speed with which . . . the FBI and SEC exposed Jakob's criminal activities demonstrates our joint commitment to solving these fast-moving Internet crimes," said Alejandro Mayorkas, U.S. attorney for the Central District of California. "Those who seek to manipulate the market as Mark Jakob did should take heed of the years in federal prison that he faces in light of his conduct."[38]

DISCUSSION QUESTIONS

1. How does the concept of credibility, stage one of the writing process, apply to the key players in this case study: Mark Jakob, Paul Folino, Emulex, Internet Wire, and the financial news media?
2. How might the Emulex hoax have been prevented?
3. Emulex fought back mostly with written documents. What other tactics might it have used to counter the hoax?
4. The Emulex news release hoax may have damaged Internet Wire's relationships with important publics. If you were public relations director for Internet Wire, what relationships would you focus on, and what relationship-building tactics would you recommend?

Cyber Coach

Visit www.ablongman.com/guthmarsh3e for these study aids—and more:

- flashcards
- quizzes
- videos
- links to other sites
- real-world scenarios that let you be the public relations professional

KEY TERMS

active voice, p. 322

attribution, p. 332

demographic information, p. 316

inverted pyramid, p. 320

NOTES

1. Writerly Things, online, www.ecentral.com/members/writers/quotes/writers.html.

2. Nexxus: A Place for Poetry, online, www.sage.net/~sgreene/nexxus.

3. David Wallechinsky, Irving Wallace, and Amy Wallace, *The Book of Lists* (New York: William Morrow, 1977), 469–470.

4. "Workinpr.com State of the Industry Survey," Workinpr, 2003, online, workinpr. com; "Where the Jobs Are," PR News, 13 April 1998, online, LexisNexis.

5. Adapted from Charles Marsh, David W. Guth, and Bonnie Poovey Short, *Strategic Writing* (Boston: Allyn & Bacon, 2005).

6. Marsh, Guth, and Short, 20.

7. Adapted from Marsh, Guth, and Short.

8. Robert Graves and Alan Hodge, *The Reader over Your Shoulder,* 2nd ed. (New York: Vintage Books, 1979).

9. Rowena Crosbie, "Speak Your Way to Success," *Canadian Manager* 22, no. 4, 1997, online, LexisNexis.

10. Cicero, "Of Oratory," in *The Rhetorical Tradition,* eds. Patricia Bizzell and Bruce Herzberg (Boston: Bedford Books, 1990), 217.

11. Wallechinsky et al., 469–470.

12. Crosbie.

13. Karen Susman, "Six Key Indicators Guaranteed to Reduce Audience Stress and Increase Your Applause," *Records Management Quarterly* 31, no. 3, 1997, online, LexisNexis.

14. Jill Ingram, "What a Doll!" *Asheville* (N.C.) *Citizen-Times,* 5 March 2004, online, LexisNexis.

15. John N. Frank, "Mattel Makes Most of Barbie-Ken Breakup," *PR Week,* 23 February 2004, online, LexisNexis.

16. "The Passion of Christ Makes Top 10 Web Searches," news release issued by Terra Lycos, 24 February 2004, online, LexisNexis.

17. Holly Mullen, "Solo Barbie Makes Left, Right Happy," *Salt Lake City Tribune,* 17 February 2004, online, LexisNexis.

18. "The Storybook Romance Comes to an End for Barbie and Ken," news release issued by Mattel, 12 February 2004, online, LexisNexis.

19. "The Storybook Romance Comes to an End for Barbie and Ken."

20. "Ken Lost Barbie . . . Don't Lose Your Love This Valentine's Day," news release issued by 1-800-FLOWERS.COM, 13 February 2004, online, LexisNexis.

21. "Barbie & Ken Break Up After 43 Years: Did Her Sexual Dysfunction Play a Role?" news release issued by QualiLife Pharmaceuticals, 13 February 2004, online, LexisNexis.

22. Richard Siklos, "How the Marketing Men Destroyed a Profitable Romance," (London) *Sunday Telegraph,* 25 April 2004, online, LexisNexis.

23. Siklos.

24. Siklos.

25. Martin Stone, "Emulex Scammer to See Slammer," *Newsbytes,* 2 January 2001, online, LexisNexis.

26. Alex Berenson, "News Release Fakes Out Media, Upends Market," *New York Times,* 26 August 2000, online, LexisNexis.

27. Stone.

28. Alex Berenson, "Guilty Plea Is Set in Internet Hoax Case Involving Emulex," *New York Times,* 29 December 2000, online, LexisNexis.

29. Diane Lindquist, "Emulex Beat Hoax with Solid Product, Sales," *Investor's Daily,* 25 January 2001, online, LexisNexis.

30. Berenson, "News Release Fakes Out Media, Upends Market."

31. "Jakob Pleads Guilty to Fraud Charges in $110 Million Emulex News Hoax," *White-Collar Crime Reporter,* February 2001, online, LexisNexis.

32. "Jakob Pleads Guilty to Fraud Charges in $110 Million Emulex News Hoax."

33. Dick Kelsey, "Bogus News Release Sends Emulex Shares Plunging," *Newsbytes,* 25 August 2000, online, LexisNexis.

34. Kelsey.

35. Karen Alexander, "Quick Response Stems Damage to Emulex," *Los Angeles Times,* 1 September 2000, online, LexisNexis.

36. Berenson, "Guilty Plea Is Set in Internet Hoax Case Involving Emulex."

37. Berenson, "News Release Fakes Out Media, Upends Market."

38. Berenson, "Guilty Plea Is Set in Internet Hoax Case Involving Emulex."

chapter eleven

11

Public Relations in the Digital Age

objectives

After studying this chapter, you will be able to

- describe the changes—as well as the implications of those changes—that are occurring through the development of digital communications technology

- recognize the opportunities and challenges public relations practitioners face as a result of the Digital Age

- identify the many new strategies and tools practitioners now have for communicating with targeted publics

- appreciate that "new" doesn't always mean "better" and that in certain situations, traditional channels of communications are preferable to new high-tech channels

Differing Designs for the Future

scenario

Olds Young and Associates is one of the community's oldest architectural firms. One of the co-owners is Bud Olds, who founded the firm nearly three decades ago. The other owner is Betty Young, whose late father formed the original partnership with Olds.

In the five years since her father's death, Young has redirected the focus of the firm. Once known only as a local business, the firm has become nationally known for its designs of sports venues such as stadiums and arenas.

Because of increasing competition, your public relations agency has been asked to develop a public relations plan for Olds Young and Associates. As part of your initial research, you conducted separate interviews with the co-owners. It didn't take you long to discover a generation gap.

"We didn't use fancy public relations firms in the old days," said Olds. "If you wanted to generate new business, you went door-to-door and pressed the flesh. Who needs fancy PowerPoint presentations when a handshake and a smile will do the job? Don't let Betty talk you into proposing something as silly as DVD media kits. Most people in this town have never even heard of digital whatevers."

"Bud Olds has been like a second father to me," said Young. "But we need to bring this firm into the 21st century. The days of Magic Markers and flip charts are gone forever. I want to see us on DVDs. We have potential customers that we need to reach."

"I think this firm is getting too big for its britches," said Olds.

"I have some big plans for our firm's future," said Young.

You have a problem. You have asked for a joint meeting with Olds and Young. What are you going to tell them?

Welcome to the Revolution

Public relations was born in the Industrial Age and reached maturity in the Information Age. Now that we have entered a new era, the Digital Age, we can't help but marvel at how the profession—and society—is being transformed. As you prepare to enter the 21st-century workplace, you may be wondering how these changes will affect you and how you can better prepare for them.

It is easy for today's college students to take **digital** technology for granted. After all, you have known nothing else. However, the growth and influence of computer-readable communication has been nothing short of phenomenal. To put it into perspective, the college graduates of the mid-2000s entered elementary school in the early 1990s. In December 1990, about the time they entered grade school, there was only one web site in the world. It was located at CERN, the European Laboratory for Particle Physics. By January 2004, the number of web sites had grown to more than 46 million.[1] Experts estimate that Internet traffic doubles every 100 days.[2]

Consider the impact the digital revolution has on your life. You may use a debit card to buy meals and groceries. An electronic sensor on the windshield of your car may be the difference between zipping through highway traffic and waiting in line at a tollbooth. Instead of being burdened with your parents' large, bulky vinyl record collection, you may have a vast personal music collection with hundreds of selections on a pocket-size MP3 player. When your mom and dad were teenagers, they may have spent hours talking to each other and their friends on the family telephone—much to the chagrin of your grandparents. Today's teens are just as talkative. But they do so on their own wireless telephone, by e-mail, or through instant messages.

It is easy to be in awe of new technology. In many ways, technology can help us be more productive, healthy, happy, fulfilled, and self-confident. And technological advances have paralleled the tremendous growth of public relations. Practitioners have always been among the first to adapt technological advancements to their needs. Technology significantly contributes to every step of the public relations process: research, planning, communication, and evaluation. With a computer, a modem, and a telephone or cable line, today's practitioners have access to a world of information and opportunities.

The importance of new technology to the practice of public relations is reflected in the results of a joint PRSA-IABC survey. Respondents said technological advances have affected communication and public relations more than any other factor. Those surveyed cited the increased use of computer technology as the most significant development in recent years. One of every three practitioners questioned said he or she thinks technology offers the greatest opportunity for career advancement in the next five years.[3]

Messages and Media

New communications technology has made it possible for an instantaneous exchange of ideas and images with anyone in the world. At the dawn of the television age, Canadian philosopher Marshall McLuhan wrote that we are living in a **global village,** where everyone can share simultaneous experiences. On one occasion McLuhan said: "In our time, we have devised ways of making the most trivial event affect everybody. One of the consequences of electronic environments is the total involvement of people in people."[4]

McLuhan's theories were developed long before anyone had ever heard of the Internet. And when you take into account the increasing interactivity of media, the Canadian theorist's words seem to hold even deeper meanings. The world is now wired to a degree that perhaps even McLuhan could not have imagined. For many, the selection of the medium has become an even more important decision than the content of the message to be delivered.

But even the best communications media need content. Although selecting an appropriate channel is critical in successful communication, developing the message is also critical. And while it is true that the medium can alter the perception of a message,

Digital Media Kit The Walker Agency of Scottsdale, Arizona, earned headlines when it became the first agency to distribute a media kit on a "thumb drive." Walker also distributed the kit on a CD-ROM. (Courtesy of Yamaha and the Walker Agency)

News Release

Contact: Mike Walker — Walker Agency
(800) 248-9687 or mike@walkeragency.com

Yamaha's New Four-Stroke F250 Designed for Large Fishing Boats; Features Variable Camshaft Timing for Improved Torque

KENNESAW, Ga., 5/04 — In the 2002 model year, Yamaha Marine introduced the world's first four-stroke V6 outboards — the F225 and F200. For 2005, Yamaha is introducing a more powerful four-stroke V6 — the F250 — designed to power larger boats that need the additional fuel economy for longer runs compared to competitive two-stroke outboards. The F250 retains the same dedication to reliability, fuel economy and less noise as Yamaha's F225, but adds Yamaha's Variable Camshaft Timing to increase low and midrange torque for added performance.

The new F250 features a revolutionary system — Variable Camshaft Timing (VCT) — designed to increase low-end power for larger offshore fishing boats. The additional weight these boats possess requires the need for more low-end torque to get up on plane. The variable camshaft rotates in both directions to advance and retard intake camshafts to vary the intake timing. This variable timing increases volumetric efficiency in order to increase low and midrange torque.

How Variable Camshaft Timing Works

The Engine Control Module (ECM) directs the oil control valve to supply oil pressure inside the Variable Camshaft Actuator to advance and retard camshaft timing based on engine RPMs. When fully advanced, the camshaft advances 40 degrees, which opens and, in turn, closes the intake valves sooner. This advanced intake timing places the combustion chamber in valve overlap position, which increases intake and exhaust efficiency. Plus, the intake valve closing sooner helps build higher combustion-chamber pressure resulting in greater volumetric efficiency. The result is a 16 percent gain in torque in the 2000 to 3500 RPM range.

Yamaha's marine-inspired four-stroke V6 outboards were designed from the early design stages to be more compact and lightweight than other four-stroke outboards. Yamaha's engineers looked at the design of four-stroke automobile engines and came to the con[clusion] ... engine turned on its end was too large an engine block. The engine compartm[ent] ... [de]signed without affecting the car's performance. Boats do not h[ave] ... [ca]me in too many different sizes. In addition to being too ... [ou]tboard electronic components more susceptib[le] ...

"When it comes ... David Grigsby,
Yamaha's product man[ager] ... [four-]stroke 6-cylinder
engine even though o[ne] ... [po]wer without

Yamaha Marine Gr[oup] ...

[CD label:]
YAMAHA
When you want the best
2005 Press Kit
- more -
70 Chastain Road
For more information, contact:
Walker Agency
P.O. Box 14390 • Scottsdale, AZ 85267-4390
(800) 248-9687
(480) 948-3113 fax
www.walkeragency.com

[thumb drive:]
USB2.0
YAMAHA
256MB

the reverse also holds true. An appropriate message delivered via an inappropriate medium is just as ineffective as an inappropriate message delivered via an appropriate medium. Message and medium must be equal considerations in communication. If not, true communication does not occur.

The Role of Values in Message and Medium Selection

More to the point, the selection of both message and medium is closely tied to the values of the communicator, as well as to those of the targeted public. Those values are not linked to changes in technology. Instead, they are expressions of who we are and who we want to be. The first book ever produced in mass quantities was the Bible. Since the days of Gutenberg, millions of copies of the Bible have been produced using an increasing variety of media, including audiocassettes, videotapes, CD-ROMs, DVDs, and web sites. Despite the many advances in communications technology, the values expressed in the Bible have not changed.

For an example of how values dictate the message and the medium, let's revisit the architectural firm of Olds Young and Associates mentioned in this chapter's opening scenario. At the heart of the dispute between Olds and Young are conflicting values. Olds sees the firm as one with strictly local clientele. Young has a different vision—that of a firm competing on a global scale. Before any decisions can be made on *how* to communicate, the two partners must first reach a consensus on *what* to communicate and to *whom*. Only when those issues are decided is it appropriate to discuss messages and media.

Part of your job with Olds Young is to help the partners reach that consensus. Fortunately, you are not confronted with the necessity of choosing one option over the other. It is commonplace for different divisions within the same company to target different publics. If the architectural firm is willing to commit the necessary resources, *both* partners can have their way. Bud Olds can focus on local customers, using more personalized communication channels. At the same time, Betty Young can use more technologically advanced methods to reach out to clients more accustomed to communicating at that level. This is one generation gap that the sound application of public relations practices can close.

The point of this chapter is to put the Digital Age in perspective. Advanced technology is a useful tool in the practice of public relations. However, it is only a tool. Ultimately, the expression of our values determines how we use all the tools available to us.

The Digital Revolution

At the center of the explosion in communications technology is the *bit,* the basic element of transmission in digital communications. Nicholas Negroponte calls the bit "the smallest atomic element in the DNA of information."[5] Our increasing ability to transfer thoughts, images, and sounds into bits is changing the way we interact with our world.

The communications revolution of the late 20th century was a result of the ability to convert analog communication into digital formats. **Analog** communication relays all information present in the original message in the form of continuously varying signals. Those variations correspond to the changes in sound or light energy coming from the source.[6]

The conversion of analog communication into a digital format—into computer-readable bits—makes it possible to filter out unwanted information. Analog communication is like talking to a friend while seated in the stands of crowded Analog Stadium. You may have to strain to hear your friend above the cheering of the crowd, the noise of the game, and the whistling of the wind. At Digital Stadium, however, you would have no trouble hearing your friend. The crowd would grow silent, the game would cease, and the wind would stop blowing.

Digital communication also permits the simultaneous transfer of more information. Analog technology severely limited the number of calls a telephone company could transmit at any given moment. Essentially, telephone calls were handled one at a time along a vast copper wire network. With the introduction of digital communications and a fiber-optic network, the capacity of telephone communication systems dramatically multiplied.

Back at Analog Stadium, imagine what it would be like if thousands of people on one side of the field tried to communicate with a counterpart on the opposite side. It would be impossible to distinguish any one conversation in that din. However, it is a different story at Digital Stadium. Everyone on the east sideline would clearly hear their west sideline counterpart—and no one else!

We see this principle at work in television, through which it has become possible to transmit multiple programs on a cable TV or satellite channel that previously carried only one. Digital technology also makes it possible to store a remarkable amount of data in a relatively small space. For example, the typical music CD holds 783 million bytes of information.[7] A DVD of your favorite movie holds about seven times more data than a CD.[8]

To take it one step further, digital communication also makes it possible for many to simultaneously share information from a single source. This capability is evolving into an on-demand delivery system, which allows consumers to choose what they want, whenever they want. Instead of waiting around all day for your favorite movie to be broadcast at a specific time, eventually you will be able to download it from a programming source just as the pizza arrives!

Convergence and Hypermedia

Perhaps the most important consequence of the digital revolution is a **convergence of media.** As different media adopt digital technology in their production and distribution, barriers that have traditionally stood between them are tumbling down. Practically every medium we interact with now is digital, from the telephone on which we speak, to the music CD we listen to, to the Internet we surf. The television signal you receive in your home is very likely digital. And before long, all television signals will be digital. The newspaper, seemingly an artifact of 18th-century technology, is currently produced—and may soon be delivered to your "electronic doorstep"—digitally.

A more dramatic development is the convergence of traditionally distinct media into one form. Integrated multimedia incorporating digital audio, visual, and text information are called **hypermedia.** To see hypermedia in action, one need only log on to the web site maintained by the Cable News Network (www.cnn.com), one of the web's most popular sites. CNN Interactive combines text from magazines such as *Time* and *Sports Illustrated* with video and audio supplied by CNN. The site also provides links to other sites where more information on subjects of personal interest can be sought.

The potential application of hypermedia goes beyond the Internet. Think of what the week before the start of each school year is like. You have to run to the bookstore to purchase the textbooks you need for the coming semester. Depending on how many classes you are taking, this errand can bring new meaning to the idea of "carrying a full load." In the future, however, it may not be necessary to leave home. You will be able to download the contents of all your texts into a single device, a digital book. These textbooks will be unlike any you have ever seen. You will be able to highlight a word and have its definition appear. Instead of footnotes, links will take you to vast quantities of background information. Video and audio will be inserted to complement the text. When you finish your assigned reading, you will be able to use the same electronic book to download the daily newspaper or one of the best-selling novels of the day. Just how distant is this brave new world? It may be closer than you think. "By 2005, a quarter of textbook sales will be digital," said Dan O'Brien, senior analyst for Forrester Research. "It's not that digital textbooks will replace physical textbooks, but the opportunities there are much greater for this change to happen."[9]

Convergence Issues

Although the convergence of technology opens up a world of possibilities for the 21st century, progress does not come without its price. Only now are we beginning to understand the social ramifications of this new digital world. Convergence has raised numerous issues for public policy makers and individuals to address. Among those are questions about media mergers, personal privacy, job security, and intellectual property rights.

MERGERS OF MEDIA COMPANIES.   The convergence of communications technology has brought about a convergence of media companies; that is, media companies have merged for competitive reasons. These new giant media conglomerates now own the means of production and distribution of a wide spectrum of media. The largest of the media giants is Time Warner, which dropped AOL from its corporate name in 2003. Time Warner's vast corporate umbrella includes Time-Life Books, Home Box Office, Cable News Network, the WB Television Network, Castle Rock Entertainment, *Time, Fortune, Sports Illustrated,* New Line Cinema, Turner Network Television, the Atlanta Braves, Netscape Communications, and America Online.[10] According to

Time Warner's fiscal year 2003 annual report, the market value of the company was $72.30 billion.[11] In an earlier Securities and Exchange Commission filing, the company boasted that its global media empire reached consumers more than 2.5 billion times each month.[12]

Although a seemingly efficient arrangement, the concentration of numerous powerful channels of mass communication into the hands of a few corporations has caused some to worry. Some fear a loss of journalistic independence among the media outlets that have been consumed by these megamergers.

PRESERVATION OF PERSONAL PRIVACY.   The digital revolution has made it easier for people to gather, store, and transmit personal information. This is a matter of convenience for individuals as well as corporations. But there are risks. Even with sophisticated safeguards, digital information is not entirely secure. Privacy concerns extend to personal messages, whether sent via e-mail or wireless telephones. At a time when computer hackers are at least as knowledgeable as computer programmers, you never know who is accessing your private conversations. In the highly competitive economy of the 21st century, new technology opens the door to commercial espionage on an alarming scale.

JOB SECURITY.   The good news is that improved technology can make people more productive in the workplace. The bad news is that increased ability to do more with less lowers the demand for highly skilled workers. New communication technology is allowing many industries to outsource corporate functions. We have seen this in public relations, where many corporate public relations offices have been downsized. Much of the slack has been picked up on a per-job basis by independent consultants who do not receive any of the traditional corporate benefits (e.g., health coverage, retirement plans, or stock options). Then too, technological advances often disrupt successful companies, a phenomenon Clayton M. Christensen of the Harvard Business School has called "the innovator's dilemma" and about which he has written a book of the same name. The digital revolution has led to simpler, cheaper, and more user-friendly ways of doing things that can squeeze out the products of older companies. Although not a direct threat to public relations, these so-called disruptive technologies can threaten organizations in which it is practiced.[13]

PROTECTION OF INTELLECTUAL PROPERTY.   The fact that digital copies are both identical to original works and easy to alter poses a huge problem in the information age. A person's intellectual property has value. When others ignore copyright law (see Chapter 15) and use someone's intellectual property without permission or compensation, it is tantamount to theft. Today's digital technology makes it easier to copy and distribute the results of someone else's labors. This has always been a problem in the music industry, where the performances of top artists can be rapidly duplicated and shipped overseas for illegal sale in unregulated markets. And the problem is not limited to consumer goods. Specialized business software is also a prime target. In some instances, this piracy has national security implications.

Virtual Public Relations

Another byproduct of the digital revolution is the emergence of **virtual public relations,** the networking of small independent public relations consultants. Linked by telephones, fax machines, and the Internet, these informal practitioner networks successfully compete for business against traditional public relations agencies.

Here's how it works. A public relations consultant in Cincinnati has a client who needs to improve internal communications. This may require the services of a publications designer in Toronto, a freelance writer in London, a web developer in Sacramento, and an event planner in Charlotte. In many cases, these consulting arrangements are made on a project-by-project basis. However, in some virtual firms, such as INK, Inc. of Kansas City, Missouri, these widely scattered practitioners are full-time employees of an agency, one with its scattered operations linked by a secure intranet.

A reason virtual public relations is growing is its cost. "You can keep your overhead lower and pass that savings on to your clients," said Dick Grove of INK, Inc. Virtual agencies offer client discounts of up to 40 percent over traditional firms by sharing the money they save on office space. When Internet security company nCipher Corp., Ltd., switched to a virtual agency, public relations manager Claire Collins said, "It was not important to us to see what kind of desks they had or what their lobby looked like to gauge the level of their work as PR professionals."[14]

Another reason virtual agencies are becoming more attractive is the freedom they give to practitioners. "I've never been very good in the corporate structure," said Grove. "People are not geographically dependent."[15]

Quick Check

1. What is media convergence, and what are its implications?
2. What are hypermedia?
3. What is virtual public relations, and why is it growing in acceptance?

Computers and the Internet

Computers have been around for a lot longer than you may think. Charles Babbage, a mathematics professor at Cambridge University, created the first computer in 1822. It was a mechanical calculator he called a "difference engine."[16] By 1890, mechanical calculators were used to tabulate the U.S. Census.[17] Computers used by American and British code breakers gave the Allies a decisive edge over Axis powers in World War II. And though they were primitive by today's standards, computers played an indispensable role in helping humanity take its first voyages into space and its first steps on the moon in the 1960s.

However, it was in 1975, when the first personal computer was introduced, that the first seeds of the digital revolution were planted. Gone were the days when only the wealthiest corporations could afford their own computers, usually housed in big rooms. As these digital marvels became smaller and more affordable, they began showing up in homes and offices. Skeptics soon learned that these were more than just fancy typewriters. They could also analyze data, design publications, schedule meetings for several people at the same time, and communicate with others around the world.

The ability to link, or network, computers has created its own revolution. It is now possible to perform tasks at home or on the road that once could be done only in the office. One useful development has been the creation of the **personal digital assistant** or **PDA** (also known as a personal data assistant), a pocket-size information device that records handwritten scribbles and allows people on the move to stay in touch with various computer and telephone networks. Computer networks have also made it possible for many people, especially working or single parents, to earn a living without leaving their homes. Many companies allow some of their employees to telecommute, performing office tasks at home, but linked to the office by a computer and modem.

The impact of computer technology on the practice of public relations is undeniable. Public relations is about communicating, and computer technology has revolutionized communications. Computers have become critical in the preparation of messages delivered in the form of news releases, newsletters, and presentation slides. However, the role of computers in public relations extends far beyond message preparation. Computers also provide the delivery system for our messages, whether through e-mail, the Internet, or fax. Add to this the networking capabilities that make it easier for practitioners to operate outside the traditional office. Public relations practitioners have been quick to embrace each new technical achievement—because they, more than most, understand the value of exploring all methods of communication.

"Modern information technology is creating a new corporate communication landscape," according to Augustine Ihator of Western Kentucky University. "Computer technology has altered the power structure and relationship between corporations and their publics, stakeholders and the media."

"There is an emerging power sharing," Ihator wrote in *Public Relations Quarterly.* "Publics now have ready access to the mass media to tell their story from their own perspective and complain vehemently if necessary."[18]

And just where do these publics get this new access and power? It all comes through a cable or wireless link to the information superhighway, the Internet.

The New Town Commons

Before the digital revolution, the information revolution, the Industrial Revolution—and even before the American Revolution—people used to go the town commons to get the latest news. The commons, usually a town square or park in the center of the community, was a gathering spot for people to express themselves and hear the thoughts of their friends and neighbors.

In many ways, the **Internet** has become the town commons of the 21st century. This became evident in the hours following the September 11, 2001, terror attacks.

INK, INC.

INK, Inc., is a virtual public relations agency with its headquarters in Kansas City, Missouri—or wherever it chooses.

We Do the Job Others Can't

INK Inc. is a different kind of public relations firm. We don't bill by the hour, and we don't wax on for weeks about strategic positioning and research capabilities. We don't care about being the biggest firm with offices around the globe. We do care first and foremost about one thing above all else: achieving measurable results for clients.

Staffed exclusively by senior media professionals with actual newsroom experience, INK Inc. focuses on generating mainstream press coverage and placing stories in top-tier, national and international media. While we do offer a full range of services including broadcast production, writing, media training and special events, our specialty—and our bottom-line objective for every client—is publicity, or to put it bluntly, "getting ink."

—INK, Inc., web site

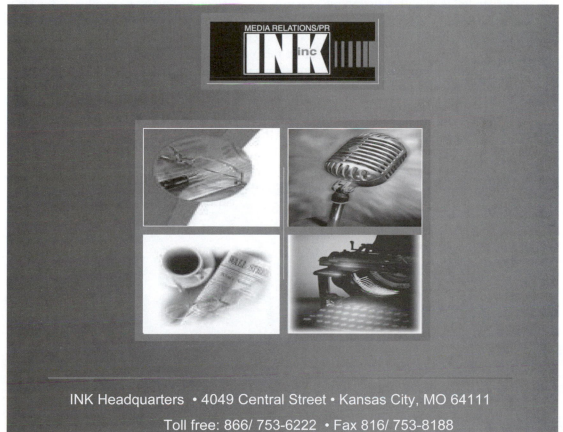

INK Headquarters • 4049 Central Street • Kansas City, MO 64111
Toll free: 866/ 753-6222 • Fax 816/ 753-8188

Downloadable Brochure Virtual public relations firms, such as the Kansas City–based INK, Inc., rely on digital technology to develop strategies and tactics for their clients. INK, Inc., also uses the Internet to distribute its own promotional materials, such as this online information kit. (Courtesy of INK, Inc.)

According to the Pew Internet & American Life Project (PIP), nearly three out of four Internet users used e-mail in some way related to the attacks.

"Perhaps the most significant development online after the attack has been the outpouring of grief, prayerful communication, information dissemination through e-mail, and political commentary," wrote PIP Director Lee Rainie one month after 9/11. "Others have gone to the virtual commons in chat rooms, bulletin boards, commemorative sites, and other online communities to describe their anguish, offer consoling words, broadcast their patriotism, and debate, even yell at times, about the meaning of September's events."[19]

The Internet traces its roots back to 1957 and the U.S.–Soviet space race. When the Russians launched the first artificial satellite into earth's orbit, the United States responded by creating the Advanced Research Projects Agency. ARPA's mission was to establish the United States' lead in the military use of science and technology.[20] Recognizing the need to link computers at research centers across the country with one another, the agency created ARPANET, the forerunner of today's Internet. At the urging of the federal government, colleges and universities began using APRANET for their own research purposes in the 1970s. When all of the interconnected research networks adopted a common computer communications language, TCP/IP (Transmission Control Protocol/ Internet Protocol), the Internet as we know it was born.[21]

At first the Internet remained primarily the domain of academics and researchers. Locating and accessing information from distance computers was both complicated and time consuming. The creation of the first network browsers at the University of

Sticker Thanks to the growth of the Internet, web-based companies such as Yahoo! have become household names. (Courtesy of Yahoo!)

Illinois simplified this. Researchers at CERN, the European Laboratory for Particle Physics, took things a huge step forward by creating an easy-to-use and graphics-friendly network, the **World Wide Web.** Suddenly, a world of information was at our fingertips. People embraced the Digital Age.[22]

The Birth of Cyber-Relations

In many ways, the Internet has helped to reduce the psychological distance that exists between an organization and the publics important to its success. Instead of being seen as a distant and obscure entity, the organization is now as close as the nearest computer screen. It is as if the Internet has become the organization's new front door and its **web site** the digital equivalent of the lobby, from which visitors are directed to various information sites within the organization. Interactive web sites allow visitors to communicate directly through e-mail links with key personnel within the organization. Through the integration of audio and video technology, visitors may be personally welcomed by the company CEO. For those looking for a particular nugget of information, many web sites are equipped with search engines that allow visitors to browse the entire site as well as company archives. It is even possible to take a virtual tour of an organization's facilities without leaving one's home. Add to this the role of corporate intranets and extranets (discussed in Chapter 9). Because of these innovations, once seemingly distant companies are now only a mouse click away.

This has led to what we have called **cyber-relations,** the use of public relations strategies and tactics to deal with publics via and issues related to the Internet.[23] While this term is not mutually exclusive of other forms of public relations, we use it to describe what has become a dynamic aspect of the practice of public relations with unquestionable social ramifications. With the rapid growth of the Internet over the past generation, practitioners have discovered that the web is often both the cause of and the solution to the challenges they face.

Because the Internet is practically everywhere—an estimated two-thirds of U.S. adults go online—it is an ideal medium for public relations practitioners.[24] But the web's omnipresence is also a challenge when it comes to targeting a specific audience. The Pew Internet & American Life Project says different people use the Internet in different ways: "High proportions of female Internet users have done activities such as seek health or religious information on the Internet, while a large percentage of males have sought news, financial information, sports news and political news." Other factors, such as race, household income, education, geography, and physical abilities, also influence the level of Internet activity.[25]

The Internet is also a growing beehive of financial activity known as **e-commerce.** According to that same Pew study, eight out of 10 Internet users have researched a product or service online. The number of people making online purchases rose 63 percent between 2000 and 2003. The most popular online transactions are ticket purchases or travel reservations, banking, and online auctions, such as eBay.[26]

It is important to place e-commerce in perspective. In terms of retail sales, it is a growing but still relatively small part of the economy. The U.S. Census Bureau estimated that e-commerce sales in the first quarter of 2004 totaled $15.5 billion, just 1.9 percent of total sales.[27] It also reported that business-to-business (B2B) activity totaled 92.7 percent of all e-commerce in 2002, representing $1.07 trillion of economic activity.[28]

Many small businesses believe that having a presence on the web is important. More than half of small business owners surveyed in 2003 agreed with the statement that their web site primarily provides company credibility. Two out of three small and medium-sized businesses with web sites regularly use e-mail to communicate with their customers.

"This research reinforces the growing importance of web sites to small business," said Joel Kocher of the online service company Interland. "As more and more consumers connect using the web, it's vital that small businesses gain an effective online presence."[29]

Individuals as Gatekeepers

In Chapter 5 we discussed the evolution of communication theory. As you may remember, theorists once believed that mass media could control the public opinion process. They thought that editors at newspapers, magazines, and radio stations dictated what information people received and when they received it. However, the growth in communications technology has changed all that. The magic bullet theory evolved into uses and gratifications theory—the belief that each person has become his or her own information gatekeeper and picks and chooses from a wide variety of information sources.

What does this mean for public relations? For starters, **push technology** allows information to be delivered or "pushed" directly to a user. By subscribing to various push services, individuals receive downloads of customized information. This can include news stories covering specific topics, sports scores, or the latest from the financial markets. If you represent a client that caters to people who travel extensively, a push service providing the latest in travel news and tips would be a cost-effective strategy for reaching this audience. What makes it most attractive is that it automatically delivers the information to an already receptive audience.

However, this also is an example of how communications innovations can mean both good news and bad news for public relations. Push technology may make it harder to get the attention of certain individuals. In the mass media, editors serve as information gatekeepers. But with push technology, individuals can become their own editors. That can make targeting publics more difficult. Opportunities for exposing your message may lessen. That, in turn, means making the best of the chances that remain.

Individuals as Publishers

Not only have individuals become information gatekeepers; they have also become self-publishers. Digital communications technology has made it possible for people to communicate more effectively and efficiently than ever. In the past, if your campus organization wanted to typeset and print a meeting notice for posting around campus, it was necessary to employ the services of a designer and the local photocopy shop.

BUILDING A BETTER WEB SITE

It seems as if everybody is on the Internet. However, it takes only a few minutes of Net surfing to learn that not all web sites are created equal.

If you are thinking about building a web site or are already on the Internet, knowing the best practices in cyberspace can be the difference between a site people want to visit and one that makes your organization look like a bunch of amateurs.

Before you do anything else, define your web site's purpose and audiences. The beauty of web sites is that they allow you to deliver multiple messages to multiple audiences. But who are these people, and what do you want to say?

As is true in other media, effective online communications should address the reader's self-interests. "It's important to let people know employees have pride in their organization, but do so subtly," said web content provider Carl Weinschenk. "People don't want to see a picture of your building or the employees white-water rafting in company T-shirts."[30]

Web sites can help build and maintain relationships. However, for that to happen, they have to be places people will want to visit more than once. To build a steady stream of repeat visitors, web sites must focus more on substance than flash. Sure, flashing text and spinning graphics may generate some hits. But if the content isn't updated regularly, visitors have no incentive to return. "Few things send as negative a message as a dated site," said Weinschenk.[31]

Your web site should also be user-friendly. Just ask anyone who has spent time twiddling his or her thumbs waiting for a graphics-heavy page to download. Visitors should be able to easily find the information they want. Organizing the homepage by audience-specific categories is one way to achieve this. Another is to design pages that do not require the user to scroll down for additional information.

Carefully plan your web site's hyperlinks. "Developing your links strategy is one of the most crucial elements involved in Internet marketing," said Susan Sweeney, author of *101 Ways to Promote Your Web Site.* "Appropriately placed, links can be a real traffic builder."[32] Exchanging links with professional, business, and trade associations can help drive new visitors to your site.

Good writers always consider the medium. According to a study by Sun Microsystems, individuals take 50 percent longer to read from a computer screen than from a printed page.[33] You need to keep sentences short, to-the-point, and in the active voice.

Web writing consultant Sara Means Geigel notes that web sites are nonlinear—you never know where readers may enter the site or where they may go. Because computer displays are typically horizontal, Geigel says web designers should not put an excessive amount of information on the screen. Web writers should also consider reader comfort. "You don't curl up with a web site on your favorite chair or sofa or in bed to read it like a good book," she said.[34]

Once you have created your web site, promote it. Place its address on all company communications, including company newsletters and advertising. It should be an integral part of each organization's branding.

Today, those tasks can be accomplished by just one person using a laptop computer and a printer. In the past, if your organization wanted to contact a large number of people off campus, the job might require the use of direct mail, advertising, or telephone solicitations—expensive and time-consuming procedures. Today, e-mail and faxes can do the job cheaper and quicker, though they would reach smaller, more targeted publics. In the past, only media moguls had the resources necessary to reach a worldwide audience. Today, all you need is your own web site.

Again, there is a downside. The fact that everyone can become his or her own publisher doesn't necessarily mean that he or she should. It will take you only a few minutes of surfing the World Wide Web to realize that there are a lot of people on the Internet with nothing to say. And sometimes what they have to say is downright vicious. Numerous organizations, the subjects of grievances imagined or real, have been victims of what one author has called **cybersmears**—the use of the Internet to attack the integrity of an organization and/or its products and services.[35]

Cybersmear tactics include the creation of what are called **gripe sites.** One example is "chasemanhattansucks.com," established by a disgruntled bank customer who said he had trouble removing an erroneous charge on his credit card account. What harm can one guy do? In its first two years of existence, that site recorded 300,000 hits.[36]

Another popular form of Internet self-publishing is the **blog,** a regularly updated online diary or news forum that focuses on a particular area of interest. At first, most blogs were created by web fanatics who had a story they wanted to tell. Blogs started catching on when reporters covering the Iraq war began posting their personal experiences. Employers are beginning to recognize their value as a communications tool.

"Employer interest currently is the highest that I've ever seen it," said Google's Jason Shellen. "The interest is mainly in developing blogs as external communication tools with customers and clients, though some employers are beginning to consider ways they can use blogs internally."[37]

One reason practitioners find blogs attractive is that they target specific audiences. Some practitioners have begun pitching stories to bloggers with similar interests. However, before taking the plunge, practitioners should do their research, read through the blog, and determine whether its environment is right for their message.

Perhaps an even bigger problem is that much of what is self-published, electronically or otherwise, does not go through the scrutiny that an editor applies to more traditional publications. Many self-published materials are inaccurate, incomplete, or biased—not to mention poorly written. Because of this, the need for constant monitoring of the Internet is growing. Organizations, especially publicly held companies, have a lot to lose from inaccurate information being flashed globally. The ease of self-publishing also brings into focus the need for rapid response plans to counter false or negative information on the Internet.

In his 1997 book *What Will Be,* Michael Dertouzos wrote that new communications technology will dramatically affect human behavior within organizations. With an increased ability to monitor all aspects of the organization, executives, Dertouzos said, will be able to hold their employees more accountable for their actions. He said this "will improve a firm's efficiency, even though its employees may be unhappy to have their individual work so open to inspection and critique."[38] Dertouzos also said the new technology will shift responsibility further down the corporate ladder, thus creating a greater need for employees to understand and embrace their organization's goals and values:

> For an organization to extract this increased decision power from its people, it will have to provide them with more knowledge about why some things are done and who does them, and why certain decisions are made and who makes them.[39]

With this growing reliance on employee communications, public relations will remain an important management responsibility in the 21st century.

Quick ✔ Check

1. What is cyber-relations?
2. What are some of the advantages and disadvantages public relations practitioners face as a result of digital communication technology?
3. What are blogs, and how are they used?

Other Internet Issues

For all the possibilities the Internet has created, it is still not the answer to all the problems that public relations practitioners face. Let's look briefly at a variety of Internet-related issues a practitioner should consider.

THE ONLINE GENERATION GAP.   The next time someone says "everyone's on the Net," you should politely beg to differ. Although the number of senior citizens using the Internet is rising rapidly, the fact remains that most still are off-line. According to a February 2004 survey, only 22 percent of Americans 65 or older had Internet access. "Most seniors live lives far removed from the Internet, know few people who use e-mail or surf the Web, and cannot imagine why they would spend money and time learning to use a computer," said Susannah Fox of the Pew Internet & American Life Project. However, she said as today's Internet users in their 50s get older, "they will be unlikely to give up their wired ways."[40]

THE GLOBAL DIGITAL DIVIDE.   Although the English-speaking people of the earth constitute only 8.7 percent of the world's population, they represent 35.8 percent of its Internet users. According to Global Reach, a global online marketing firm, Chinese language users are second at 14.1 percent, followed by Japanese at 9.6 percent, Spanish at 9.0 percent, and German at 7.3 percent.[41] This uneven Internet access is known as the **digital divide,** and it has great social and economic ramifications for the future. In addition to access, cultural considerations exist. "[A] low context society, such as the United States, wants the essence of a message clearly and quickly," wrote Western Kentucky's Ihator, "while [a] high context society, as in the Arab countries, appreciates the nuances and uses the physical context of the message to attribute meaning."

QuickBreak 11.2

THE MILLENNIUM BUG

To some people, Peter De Jager ranks right up there with Chicken Little, the boy who cried wolf, and the hyperbolic spin doctors of public relations.

De Jager was among the first to warn about the dangers of the Y2K computer problem. Writing in *Computerworld* in 1993, De Jager predicted that widespread disruptions would occur at midnight on New Year's Day 2000 because of outdated computers unequipped to deal with passage into the new millennium.[42] To give a simplistic explanation of the problem: The clocks on these antiquated computers would see the calendar click over to the year 2000, believe it was the year 1900, and shut everything down. Worse, others thought it would be—literally—the end of the world.

Lift your eyes from this page and look around. Still here? Of course you are. And that has led many to wonder whether De Jager, government officials, and the public relations in-

dustry didn't unnecessarily alarm the public. They also question whether the $500-billion price tag for inoculating the world—at an estimated $360 for every person in the United States—was too heavy a burden to pay for fixing the millennium bug.[43]

Needless to say, De Jager, the government, and the public relations industry disagree.

Although the world did not end, there were some glitches. In the United States, problems included a 30-minute power outage in Carson City, Nevada; a one-day delay in $50 million of Medicare payments; a brief breakdown of the 911 emergency telephone system in Charlotte, North Carolina; a three-hour cash-register-systems failure at the Godiva Chocolates store in New York; and the shutdown of 800 slot machines in Delaware. Problems elsewhere in the world included telephone outages in southern Australia, police department fax and telex system problems in Botswana, prison door sys-

INTERNET RESEARCH PROBLEMS.   As a research tool, the Internet is, in many ways, a mile wide and an inch deep. For all the information readily available online, the total represents only a small fraction of what can be gathered through more traditional forms of research. For example, many libraries do not have the necessary resources to digitize everything in their archives; a lot of vital information exists in print and on the shelves, but not online. Also, more can be learned through a personal examination of historical artifacts than by looking at digitized pictures of them. In addition, while an overwhelming majority of investors turn to company web sites to gather corporate information, a Burson-Marsteller study found that only one in five believes what he or she reads. Almost half of those polled said they considered newspapers and magazines to be the most credible source of information.[44]

UNWELCOME VISITORS.   Do you dread opening your e-mail in-box? Many do because of unsolicited **spam** e-mail, the cyberspace equivalent of junk mail. Spam has become so prevalent that it has created problems for legitimate web users. For example, spam-filtering software can't always differentiate a mailing from an unwelcome marketer and one's own student organization. And who hasn't heard from a grieving relative of a former African ruler wanting to use your bank account number to move gold out of the

tems failures in Canada, and the failure of eight traffic lights in Jamaica.[45]

"The premise is that there was no problem, that the only reason we spent this money is because people like myself convinced you to do it," De Jager said. "But the reality is they didn't spend money because we said there was a problem. They spent the money because they looked at their systems and went 'Oh my God, we have a problem.'"[46]

A congressional committee that monitored U.S. government efforts to prepare for Y2K agreed. "It is the Committee's judgment that the level of effort was justified," it said in its final report. "The risks and consequences of inaction were too dire to justify a lesser effort."[47]

Little did anyone know that the calamity they feared—and the need to use their Y2K plans—would come less than two years later. When terrorists attacked New York and Washington in September 2001, much of the world's normal operating systems were disrupted. But the *Wall Street Journal* reported two days after the attack, "For the most part, companies maneuvered safely through their respective shoals." Although the catastrophe forced companies to use what the newspaper called "a mixture of improvisation and managerial sleight of hand," most were able to maintain their operations. A spokesperson for SunTrust Banks Inc. of Atlanta noted that "Y2K gave us a great deal of experience and helped us polish our contingency procedures."[48]

As for the Chicken Little atmosphere that doomsayers thought would accompany the start of the new millennium, many credit public relations for keeping a lid on things. Although a few people hoarded food and locked themselves in bomb shelters, most people went about their lives on New Year's Day 2000 without a hint of concern.

country? Spamming doesn't build relationships—and can harm them. The Associated Press banned one public relations agency for sending too much "spam-like" e-mail.[49] Another new headache is **spim,** the unwelcome commercial use of instant messaging. However, we must guard against even more sinister visitors: **hackers,** who try to break into networked computer systems to either steal confidential information or just create mischief. And there are the ever-dangerous **computer viruses** that can attach to a person's e-mail address book and spread to computers around the world. They attack data and have already caused incalculable personal and global economic damage.

PASSIVE COMMUNICATION.   It is important to remember that the Internet is a passive way for an organization to communicate. People have to go to a web site; it does not automatically come to them. Although push technology allows organizations to send information via the Internet to subscribers, users must first sign up for the service. This is why the Internet is best used as a component of a larger integrated marketing communications plan (see Chapter 13).

CAREER IMPLICATIONS.   The rapid growth of the Internet has created a demand for college graduates capable of serving as webmasters. However, before you are tempted

The Library of Congress

THOMAS
Legislative Information on the Internet

In the Spirit of Thomas Jefferson, a service of The Library of Congress

Congress Now: House Floor This Week | House Floor Now | Senate Schedule: Majority   Minority

Search Bill Text 108th Congress (2003-2004):
Bill Number [   ]   Word/Phrase [   ]   Search   Clear

Quick Links: House | House Clerk | House Directory | Senate | Senate Directory | GPO

LINKS	LEGISLATION	*CONGRESSIONAL RECORD*	COMMITTEE INFORMATION
About THOMAS	**Bill Summary & Status** 93rd - 108th	**This Congress by Date**	**Committee Reports** 104th - 108th
THOMAS FAQ		**Text Search** 101st - 108th	**House Committees** Homepages
Congress & Legislative Agencies	**Bill Text** 101st - 108th	**Index** 104th - 108th	**Senate Committees** Homepages
How Congress Makes Laws: House | Senate	**Public Laws** 93rd - 108th	**Roll Call Votes** 101st - 108th	
Résumés of Congressional Activity			
Days in Session Calendar			
U.S. Code	Status of FY2005 Appropriations Bills		
Executive Branch	Appropriations Legislation FY1999-FY2004		
Judicial Branch	Presidential Nominations 100th - 108th		
State Resources	Treaties 90th - 108th		
Historical Documents			

The Library of Congress   Contact Us   Please Read Our Legal Notices

Thomas In an effort to bring government closer to the people of the United States, the Library of Congress has created Thomas, a source for legislative information on the Internet. Named in honor of Thomas Jefferson, the site transmitted almost 118 million files in 2003. Its web address is http://thomas.loc.gov. (Courtesy of Library of Congress)

to skip all your other studies to focus on developing web site programming skills, let us sound a cautionary note. One of the consequences of the advancement of technology is that, with the passage of time, it becomes more user-friendly. It may not be too long before anyone can create his or her own web site, thus pulling the rug out from under those who have only technical skills. Those who are more well-rounded will be able to cope with this change and thrive. They are the folks who will give web sites their substance. The bottom line, therefore, is that you should not give up on your studies quite yet.

Wireless Communications Technology

Another area in which technological advancements have had a tremendous impact on the practice of public relations is wireless technology. Our ability to communicate with others over great distances is no longer restricted by the length of a wire. The ability to communicate from anywhere using a variety of communication devices—telephones, computer modems, radios, video, facsimile (fax) machines, and satellites—has made us more mobile, responsive, and cost effective. Through the use of miniature transmitters and global positioning satellites, it is possible to locate the exact position of anyone and anything on the planet—particularly important in both commerce and travel. And what may have been the most important social, economic, and technological development of the 20th century, wireless communications technology, such as television, makes it possible for people in all corners of the world to share simultaneously in a common experience—in much the way the world watched in horror as terrorists attacked the World Trade Center and the Pentagon on September 11, 2001.

Look at what has happened in just the past few years. Because of the growth of the Internet, advancements in digital communications, and the availability of less expensive and more compact portable telephones, the demand for telephone service has exploded. It has been estimated that one in four of the world's 1.2 billion telephone subscribers has a mobile telephone.[50] Palm-sized computers, which serve as both portable telephones and fax machines, have become standard equipment for executives on the move.

The prevalence of cellular telephones became painfully obvious during the aforementioned terrorist attacks on New York and Washington, D.C. Passengers on the four hijacked jets and workers trapped in the World Trade Center used their telephones to deliver heart-wrenching farewells to loved ones. Evidence exists that passengers on one of the planes were prompted to confront their hijackers because of information received through wireless telephone communication. That plane crashed in western Pennsylvania, short of the terrorists' intended targets in Washington, D.C.

Just as important, the growth in cheaper, more accessible wireless communication is making the world a smaller place. Globally, there are currently telephone lines for only one person out of every eight. Most of these lines are located in the developed nations of the Western world. However, access to phones will change dramatically over the next quarter-century as developing nations embrace wireless communications technology. Frances Cairncross, senior editor of *The Economist,* has written that this

QuickBreak 11.3

SATELLITE MEDIA TOURS

In his movie role as Superman, the late actor Christopher Reeve could fly to any point on the globe in the wink of an eye. Despite a tragic horse-riding accident that left him quadriplegic, Reeve was still capable of traveling at "super-speed" to Barnes & Noble bookstores in different corners of the country to promote his book *Still Me.* And he did it without ever leaving a local TV studio.[51]

Satellite media tours, SMTs, have become a powerful tool of public relations. SMTs allow book authors, politicians, celebrities, and various experts to engage in one-to-one conversations with journalists. Instead of embarking on exhausting and time-consuming travel, a newsmaker can give "exclusive" interviews to reporters in dozens of cities in a single afternoon.

"SMTs save time and money by placing the interviews in a dozen or more markets in a matter of hours," said Nick Peters, vice president of the satellite distribution company Medialink. "Clients like it because it's cost-effective and exciting."[52]

As local television stations have expanded the amount of time devoted to local news program-

Satellite media tours make it possible for a newsmaker to meet individually with reporters all over the world at a fraction of the time and cost involved in a conventional media tour. (Courtesy of Medialink)

ming, SMTs have played an increasingly larger role. One survey discovered that of SMTs and

change will have significant geopolitical consequences. In her book *The Death of Distance,* Cairncross argues that the expansion of wireless technology will remove one of the Western world's key competitive edges, the vast superiority of its communications system. The worldwide economic impact of this shift in competitive equilibrium, she believes, will rival that of the collapse of communism.[53]

Quick ✔ Check

1. What are some ways public relations practitioners are using the Internet?
2. Despite its many advantages, why are some people reluctant to use the Internet?
3. What has been the impact of the growth of wireless communications?

video news releases that make the airwaves, 44 percent show up on locally produced morning news shows, compared with 37 percent shown during evening news shows, 29 percent during noontime newscasts, and 14 percent during late night.[54]

SMTs often serve a dual purpose, both giving practitioners access to a television audience and giving local stations access to big-name personalities they might not otherwise get. "Interviewing a hard-to-reach celebrity gives the station some clout," said one local television news producer in Decatur, Illinois. A satellite feed coordinator at a Miami, Florida, television station said, "If the SMT story is an 'evergreen' (a story with no time constraints on its use), it gives the station an option of using an interview on the weekends when we have a smaller staff on hand."[55]

When organizations face crises, every second counts. More and more, SMTs are becoming a preferred way for communicating when the heat is on. "Satellite media tours are about hard news," said Susan Silk, president of Media Strategy in Chicago. "There's no other way when things hit the fan but to have your guy's face on camera."[56]

No longer a novelty, SMTs are becoming more sophisticated. And they have to, considering the intense competition for valuable air time in this media-savvy world. Today, for example, the SMTs with extra impact are those that leave the studio and offer an exotic location as a backdrop. Former automobile executive Robert Eaton once did an SMT with U.S. television stations from the floor of the Tokyo Auto Show to highlight his company's entry into the Japanese car market. "When a story is making news from abroad, it certainly adds some panache to the SMT," said Sally Jewett, whose company produced the Eaton video. "It makes it irresistible."[57]

"The acceptance for SMTs is much higher than for VNRs in the larger markets," said Mark Denbo of West Glen Communications. "The real selling point is the ability to reach the top markets in a very short period of time with a concentrated message."[58]

Satellite Communications

On a summer afternoon in 1962, a wondrous event flickered across television screens in the United States and Europe. For the first time, viewers could see live television images from both sides of the Atlantic. The successful launch of Telstar, the first communications satellite, literally opened up a world of communications possibilities.

Today the earth is covered by a global geosynchronous satellite network that transmits our favorite television programs, telephone calls from overseas, computer data links, directions on how to get from one city to another, and even elevator music.

From the viewpoint of public relations practitioners, satellite technology provides the means for reaching a large audience when time is of the essence. It has played key

QuickBreak 11.4

VIRAL MARKETING

In word-of-mouth advertising, one person receives a tidbit of information and passes it along to a friend. Before you know it, the message has spread like wildfire.

That is essentially how **viral marketing** works. The thing that makes it different is that the information exchange takes place on the Internet. Much like a virus, it is spread via e-mail from person to person. Unlike a virus, the spread of information is intentional. Each person may pass the information along to many people. The information quickly multiplies and, so to speak, infects a large population.

Marketing Week has identified three basic types of viral e-mail. The first is the kind that no one wants to receive: from an antisocial prankster containing a computer-contaminating virus. The second is a genuinely noncommercial—sometimes anticommercial—message. For example, the magazine cited a June 2004 e-mail campaign to boycott several oil companies in protest of high gasoline prices. The third form of viral e-mail, one that appears to be growing in popularity, is the e-mail campaign that is ultimately commercial in intent.[59]

Pete Snyder, of the online marketing firm New Media Strategies, wrote that viral marketing brings great promise:

> Whether we call it buzz, peer marketing, chatter or online posting, [viral] marketing provides marketers with one-of-a kind, real time, dynamic access to users who are discussing a multitude of issues, products and services in their own unvarnished terms. More so, it allows what in the past was "the nameless, faceless corporation" to have real, honest and open exchanges with consumers and build valuable relationships for the future.[60]

Government and industry officials in Toronto, Ontario, launched a viral marketing campaign to counter a serious drop in tourism during 2003. Earlier that year, the region had a widely publicized outbreak of severe acute res-

roles in ending crises that threatened the financial stability of major U.S. corporations. It also played a pivotal role in U.S. military media relations during Operation Iraqi Freedom in 2003. Pentagon planners allowed embedded reporters to travel with troops and file live reports from the battlefield. Among the most memorable images of that conflict were live videos of U.S. armored divisions rolling through the desert toward Baghdad (see Case Study 12.2).

As noted in Chapter 9, one of the recent innovations in the use of satellite technology has been the satellite media tour (SMT). Let's say that your client is the publisher of a new book. Your goal is to generate publicity about the book that will, in turn, generate sales. It used to be that you and the book's author would have to pack your bags and go on the road for weeks, visiting bookstores and radio interviewers and journalists in city after city. Today, there is no need to travel any farther than a local television studio. From there, the author's words and image are beamed via satellite to waiting reporters in various locations across the nation. By prearrangement, each reporter is given a block of time to talk with the author. This gives the reporters what they want, an exclusive interview with the author. And it gives you what you

piratory syndrome, SARS, a pneumonia-like illness that claimed 40 lives in Canada and 916 worldwide. One official estimated that fears aroused by the epidemic cost the Toronto tourism industry $500 million in just a matter of months.[61]

In addition to regional advertising and special promotions that included a Rolling Stones concert, Toronto launched a viral marketing campaign—although, for obvious reasons, no one referred to it as such. It incorporated a promotion called the Kids Summer Road Trip. Canadian sports, media, and political celebrities sent e-mail postcards to potential visitors. The recipients were told that children 12 and under would receive free admission to several popular Toronto attractions. They were also encouraged to act as ambassadors and send the e-mail invitations along to friends and family.[62]

While viral marketing has great potential, it also has its critics. The European Commission adopted a Privacy and Electronic Communica-

tions Directive in 2003. Under these rules, commercial e-mails can be sent within the European Union only to consumers who requested them.[63] President George W. Bush signed similar legislation into law later that same year. The U.S. legislation prohibits senders of unsolicited commercial e-mail from disguising their identities by using false return addresses or misleading subject lines. The law also prohibits harvesting of e-mail addresses from web sites.[64]

However, these restrictions do not mean an end to the practice. Companies can still engage in viral marketing as long as they ask their customers' permission. As British online marketer Richard Bush noted, "We'd rather do a viral campaign that generated 1,000 qualified, opted-in e-mail addresses from 100,000 viral hits than have to deal with the 100,000 unqualified e-mail addresses."[65]

want, simultaneous publicity in numerous cities, without requiring you to spend a lot of time or money for travel.

SMTs have been used to publicize Super Bowl television commercials, attract viewers to the annual Jerry Lewis Labor Day muscular dystrophy telethon, promote new movies, and get voters to support candidates for the presidency of the United States. Although nothing is better than personal one-to-one contact, SMTs often provide an acceptable, cost-effective alternative.

Satellite technology has other valuable applications in the practice of public relations. Through satellite teleconferencing, organizations with widely dispersed operations can be linked for various purposes, including conducting sales meetings, training employees, and announcing important news. Satellites are used to transmit computer data between headquarters and regional offices. Companies in the information business, such as private weather services or financial market analysts, use satellites for getting their "product" to consumers. For more traditional manufacturers, global positioning satellites can track the product's progress from the factory to the warehouse to the store shelf. With the ability to react to changing global conditions becoming increasingly important, satellite technology has made it easier for organizations to keep an eye on world events. Satellite signals are used to activate pagers—even when you don't want to be found. And, yes, satellites are used for distributing that often annoying background music you hear when shopping at the mall.

Quick ✔ Check

1. In what ways can the Internet cause problems for an organization?
2. What are some ways public relations practitioners have used satellite technology?
3. What is viral marketing?

Why New Isn't Always Better

The introduction of new communications technology does not automatically spell doom for the old. Let's go back to Gutenberg's invention of the movable-type printing press in 1455. Many at the time predicted that it would mean the end of handwritten text. However, it had just the opposite effect. As vast quantities of inexpensive reading materials became more accessible, literacy rates grew; and, in turn, so did the calligraphic arts. Similarly, materials online and on CD-ROMs have not destroyed book sales. To the contrary, book sales to adults rose from 776 million in 1991 to more than 1 billion in 1995.[66]

The reason older technologies are able to survive the onslaught of newer technologies is that they are able to develop a niche in the new world order. Despite their use of 18th-century technology, newspapers continue to flourish in the 21st century. Why? Because they deliver something of value that consumers can't get elsewhere—in this case inexpensive and comprehensive coverage of local, regional, national, and global news. (We may, however, soon see the electronic delivery of newspapers.) Similarly, although many people thought radio would fade into oblivion after commercial television was introduced to the United States in 1947, it didn't; instead, radio evolved from a national source of entertainment programming into a local source of music and information. And the beat goes on.

In a public relations context, the introduction of new communications technology has created new ways of reaching and being reached by targeted publics. It is hard to imagine what life for the public relations practitioner was like without fax machines, cellular telephones, e-mail, and satellite media tours. But even in this age of technological wonders, it is equally difficult to envision the practice of public relations without some of the old standbys, such as brochures, media kits, news releases, and good old-fashioned face-to-face communication. Dertouzos wrote, "The Information Marketplace must be supported with all the traditional methods for building human bonds, including face-to-face, real-life experiences, if it is to serve organizations as more than a high-tech postal system."[67] The real challenge for the future is to stay up to date on what is new without forgetting what has worked well in the past.

As with all communication, the choice of communications technology ultimately comes down to recognizing one's audience and purpose. Public relations practitioners must understand their audience: What are its needs, what is its level of knowledge, and what are the best ways to reach it? Practitioners must also be clear about their purpose—especially because some media are better suited for some purposes than for others. The choice of which technology to adopt rests more on whether the technology works than on whether it is new.

Summary

The Digital Age has profoundly affected our personal and professional lives. The ability to reduce communication to a digital format has improved the speed and quality of communication. It has created a technological convergence of media, meaning that a communication used in one medium can be easily adapted for use in another. One place where this convergence occurs is the Internet, where words, sounds, and pictures can come together in one web site. Digital communication has led to the creation of virtual public relations agencies that provide the same services as those of traditional agencies but at a fraction of the cost. Other important advances have appeared in the areas of wireless communication, satellite communication, and computer technology.

While the Digital Age has brought many benefits, it also has raised a number of serious questions. Powerful channels of mass communication are being concentrated in the hands of relatively few corporations. Issues of privacy, job security, and protection of intellectual property also have been raised. And while it is important to keep up with technological advances, it is also important to remember that when it comes to deciding strategies and tactics, "new" doesn't always mean "better." Regardless of advances in technology, the decision about which message to deliver or which medium to use depends largely on the communicator's intended audience, purpose, and values.

DISCUSSION QUESTIONS

1. What is the Digital Age, and in what ways has it influenced your life?
2. In what ways has the introduction of digital communications technology influenced the practice of public relations?
3. What are some considerations public relations practitioners face when deciding whether to adopt new communications technology over more traditional channels of communication?
4. What are some of the ways public relations practitioners can use the Internet? Are there situations where the Internet may not be the best choice?

Memo
from the
Field

Craig Settles,
President,
Successful.com,
Oakland, California

As president and founder of Successful.com (formerly Successful Marketing Strategists), Craig Settles has developed and implemented innovative marketing campaigns for more than 18 years.

Potentially 60 million people will read articles and messages communicated about your organization in the first hours after a crisis—before you have any chance to impact the news coverage or shape those messages. Hard to believe?

Consider some of the findings of a recent survey of 600 journalists:

- 38 percent of news stories on print and broadcast media's web sites are run only on the web
- 42 percent of media outlets allow their web-site reporters to scoop their print or broadcast colleagues
- When news stories break about an organization, 37 percent of journalists will go first to the organization's web site if they can't reach someone at the company
- 27 percent of journalists would considering using an individual's chat room or newsgroup post as a main news source if confirmed by one other source, while 17 percent use the individual as a primary source
- 61 percent prefer to communicate with known and unknown sources by e-mail
- 65 percent of journalists use cell phones, and 25 percent use PDAs for work.

When they can't reach you on the phone, journalists are going to your web site first. If they can't find what they need, they're going somewhere else to someone whom you may have no influence over. And once they have a story, the news is immediate because the Net is immediate, and it's everywhere.

What's more, in this Internet age, individuals from anywhere and with no credibility can "manufacture" news during a crisis with a blog or rogue web site. Some credible news outlets, under the constant pressure of tight budgets, overworked staff, and endless news events, will give credence—and coverage—to these stories before verifying their validity.

To be an effective PR professional in this era when news is created and reported at "Net speed," you must become proficient at using Internet and wireless technologies to give your companies and clients a fighting chance. It's a brutal digital jungle out there.

Your Web Site—Ground Zero for Crisis Communication

The main Internet tool that will help better manage crisis communication is your press center, the area of your web site set aside exclusively for delivering information to, and building relationships with, journalists. Used effectively during normal times, this is where most journalists will come first during a crisis if they cannot reach you or another spokesperson by phone.

Other important Net tools include web broadcasts of live (also called streaming) or recorded audio and video messages posted in the press center. "Auditorium" software, such as Microsoft's Live Meeting, simulates a conference room on the web that journalists can log into at specified times. Their browsers take on the graphical appearance of an auditorium with seats as you use text, PowerPoint slides, audio, and interactive chat to communicate.

The section of your press center that contains your press releases should contain all crisis-related messages since this is likely the first place journalists will look when something breaks. All of the following suggested crisis-related material should be linked from a single web page.

> *Core information*—This should be all of the documents with main details about the crisis that enable journalists to write a complete story or at least present your point of view, if they can't reach a spokesperson.

> *Supporting information*—Copies of speeches by senior executives that pertain to the crisis should go here, as well as links to favorable articles as well as text from any TV or radio interviews (digitize these broadcasts if you can and post them). Company and product background material, if appropriate, should be here. Stock company video and audio files could be valuable.

> *Value-added information*—PowerPoint presentations, photos, contact info for industry experts, and other crisis-related materials that you will use in press conferences or individual meetings with journalists should be included in this section.

> *Interactive features*—If you have interactive features such as a chat room or auditorium software built into your press center, a crisis is an ideal time to roll these out. And try to get the highest-level senior executives that you can find into the picture.

Wireless Tools of the Trade

Help senior executives be more effective in a crisis by giving them PDAs with wireless service before a crisis happens. Some executives get only a few sheets of paper with a distilled list of procedures that they are expected to keep in wallets or purses. You should put everything associated with a crisis drill on short documents and store them on the PDA.

Most PDAs will do a good job of handling key crisis communication tasks. E-mail capabilities may drive the purchasing decision, so devices that allow users to receive e-mail without having to dial up and log into a network are best. Also consider where executives likely will be when a crisis erupts and whether a wireless carrier provides coverage to these areas.

The crisis com team is responsible for coordinating executive responses, preparing the resulting documents, communicating with the media, and possibly keeping employees updated, so you should pull out all of the stops when giving its members the right tools.

A smartphone (PDA and cell phone in one unit) is probably your best bet. Always-on e-mail delivery is important, so that makes devices such as the RIM BlackBerry or PalmOne Treo good choices.

Load these devices up with a streamlined version of the crisis com plan(s), contact data for executives, managers and web staff responsible for the press center, backup copies of data on executives' PDAs, press materials, and media contacts. Also include passwords and log-on procedures for your intranet if additional materials are stored here.

Two or three members of your crisis com team (I recommend everyone) should have wireless modems for their laptops. PDAs can be painfully slow for writing long documents. What's more, someone may need to FTP docs to the web team, and perhaps use a web editor to create press center documents.

Your web team should have laptops with wireless modems as well. If they're the ones who will physically post and remove data from the press center, they must be able to reach the site if they're at remote locations when a crisis strikes.

Within These Castle Walls—The Role of the Intranet

Your company's intranet should have an area for storing backup briefing documents and all other materials related to the crisis so executives and crisis com staff can reach them remotely if needed. Crisis communication documents sent to or from executives also should go here. Be sure to include a crisis com org chart and an executive org chart, since it's always nice to know who's responsible for what.

Set up intranet access to your media, analyst, and other important contact databases. If some of your team is stuck in various off-site locations when a crisis breaks, they can still keep in touch with the press. This is also good centralized backup for the team's PDAs.

When it's practical and tactful, you should include videos and pictures from the scene of the crisis in an executive briefing section, along with digitized plant maps, floor diagrams, or other visuals to help executives who are not on the scene better understand the situation. Add a discussion board in case executives want to have private threaded e-mail discussions with key managers (the crisis com team should have its own board).

Everything that you use or may use to supply or even rebuild your press center should go on the intranet. Your video, audio, and photo files all should be here, including those generated during the crisis. Many organizations create a "dark site," which is content prepared in advanced based on various crisis scenarios an organization expects to have.

These are just some of the technology options available, and they are continuously evolving. But it's not about what's hot and what's cool. It's all about what technology will keep you ahead of the curve when all hell breaks loose.

Case Study 11.1

Big Mama Is Watching

With more than 87 million of its citizens surfing the Net, China became the world's second-most wired nation in 2004, moving ahead of Japan and trailing only the United States. While that figure represents less than 7 percent of China's estimated 1.3 billion people, it is still an impressive 140 times higher than it was only six years earlier.[68]

The dramatic growth of the Internet is just one example of that ancient nation's push to become a world economic power in the 21st century. China stood for centuries as one of the world's leading civilizations. However, political and economic unrest in the 19th and 20th centuries slowed its progress and isolated it from much of the outside world. The communist takeover of China in 1949 placed the nation under the dictatorship of Mao Zedong, who imposed strict controls on everyday activities and cost the lives of tens of millions of people. His successor, Deng Xiaoping, gradually introduced market reforms that loosened the central government's control over the economy. Within two decades, China's economy quadrupled.[69]

According to the CIA's *World Factbook,* "Beijing says it will intensify efforts to stimulate growth through spending on infrastructure—such as water control and power grids—and poverty relief through rural tax reform aimed at eliminating arbitrary local levies on farmers."[70] The communist hierarchy also recognized the value of the World Wide Web in spurring economic growth. Chinese officials launched a Government on the Net program in 1999, in which 40 government agencies established an Internet presence. To promote Internet use, China's largest telecommunications provider launched a program that same year to provide higher-speed data lines and to reduce dial-up fees.[71]

"The government sees [Internet technology] as a driver of China's global competitiveness and a key to gaining international recognition," said Jay X. Hu, managing director of the U.S. Information Technology Office in Beijing.[72] In February 2002, Chinese Premier Zhu Rongji said, "The use of information technology is vital for the world economy and social development."[73]

Those efforts appear to have paid dividends. After 15 years of trying, China was finally admitted as a member of the World Trade Organization in 2001. Shanghai hosted the Asia-Pacific Economic Cooperation leaders summit that same year. China also won the highly coveted right to host to 2008 Olympic summer games.[74] However, these expressions of global recognition did not come without strings attached. To win approval from its critics, most notably the United States and the European Union, China promised to reform its economy, making it more open to the outside world. For the first time, the communist leadership had to pay heed to opinions of people outside their own regime.

This is where the Chinese leaders find themselves on the horns of a dilemma—a desire to introduce what is known as transparency into the nation's economy while maintaining tight controls over personal freedoms. The Internet has become a focal point of this conflict.

At the same time the communist regime has been encouraging its citizens to join the global Internet community, it has aggressively restricted what they can read or say about their government. Under regulations issued in 2000, Internet service and content providers are required to provide detailed records about their subscribers, including records of all web sites visited. The government prohibits the posting of "information that goes against the basic principles set in the Constitution" and "information that is detrimental to the honor and interests of the state." The measure also prohibits "information that undermines the state's policy for religions, or that propagates heretical organizations or feudalistic and superstitious beliefs"—specifically targeted against Falun Gong, a spiritual movement that the Chinese government has systematically suppressed.[75]

China employs an estimated 40,000 censors—derisively known as "Big Mamas"—to police the web.[76] They monitor web sites, chat rooms, and private e-mail. Much of the government's attention has focused on Internet cafes. Under the pretense of health and safety concerns, the government shut down 150,000 unlicensed cafes in 2003. Those remaining were required to install software that blocks 500,000 banned sites. That software also records attempted hits on banned sites and automatically forwards that information to "Big Mama."[77]

The crackdown continued into June 2004 when the Ministry of Information Industry unveiled a series of measures designed to control online chat rooms and bulletin boards. According to the government's official news agency, Xinhua, the measures aimed at "information threatening national security or social stability." The government also launched the Illegal and Harmful Content Reporting Center, a web site (http://net.china.cn) for people to complain to if they have seen something online that they believe is unlawful.[78]

"The public will be mobilized to supervise content on the Internet," Xinhua said. In a separate article, Chinese Internet service providers were encouraged to police themselves. "The basic principles of self-discipline for the Internet industry are patriotism, observance of the law, fairness and trustworthiness," the official news agency said.[79]

How serious is China about controlling Internet content? The Supreme People's Court has said, "In cases of a gross violation of law and where especially serious harm is caused to the state and people, law offenders may be sentenced to death and their properties will be confiscated by the state." The human rights organization Amnesty International reported that two members of Falun Gong imprisoned for Internet-related crimes have died in custody.[80]

The great unanswered question is whether China can manage the difficult balancing act of providing its citizens with economic freedom while depriving them of their basic human right to self-expression.

"Online freedom fighters—loose connections of Chinese dissidents and 'hacktivists' outside China—will continue to test the censors' ingenuity, while at home, Chinese 'netizens' will continue to push the envelope," wrote Beijing-based freelance writer Paul Mooney. "In the end, the Internet could prove too big to control."[81]

DISCUSSION QUESTIONS

1. Why should anyone outside of China be concerned about that government's attempts to control Internet content?
2. What are some of the tactics the Chinese government uses to try to control the Internet?
3. What are some of the contradictions in Chinese public policy that are pointed out in this case?
4. What do you believe is the answer to the "great unanswered question"—whether China can establish a free market economy while repressing political debate?

Case Study 11.2

Caught in the Eye of Hurricane Chad

Rather than listen to election-night returns from the 2000 presidential election, Craig Waters opted to watch *Gladiator* on pay-per-view television. In just a few short hours, he plunged into a public contest almost as ferocious as the one faced by the Russell Crowe character in the movie.

Waters, the director of public information for the Supreme Court of Florida, woke up the next morning with the rest of the nation to find that the presidential contest between George W. Bush and Al Gore was a virtual tie. Everything hinged on the Florida count. Bush led Gore by a razor-thin margin, and the numbers were in dispute. It was then that Waters—who had both journalism and legal training—knew that the attention of the world would soon fall upon a courtroom in Tallahassee and the seven justices he served.

"The court had been through election disputes before," Waters said. "But knowing full well that the presidency of the United States could hang on this one, I had some inkling at that point that this was going to be different."[82]

Was it ever. Journalists around the world called the Florida election dispute "Hurricane Chad"—named after the tiny, perforated pieces of paper that were supposed to form the holes in punch ballots. The degree to which a ballot was—or wasn't—punched became a national obsession. Terms such as *dimpled chad, pregnant chad,* and *hanging chad* were at the center of the debate over who would become the next president of the United States.

Fortunately for everyone involved, the Florida Supreme Court had aggressively pursued what became known as its Access Initiative in 1996. A survey at that time showed widespread public misunderstanding of the role of the court. Led by then–Chief Justice Gerald Kogan, the court realized that it had to do a better job of educating the media and the public. The court's response to this challenge led to the creation of two communication channels that served it well during the postelection drama of 2000.

The first channel was the World Wide Web. Waters said that his was the first court in the world to have its own web site. A media page on the web site was introduced

Florida Supreme Court spokesman Craig Waters *(center)* found himself to be the focus of world-wide attention during the disputed 2000 presidential election. His announcements of court rulings from the steps of the courthouse often marked major moments in the 36-day drama. (Courtesy of the Supreme Court of Florida)

two years later. This helped change the relationship between the court and reporters from one that had been reactive and negative to one that is generally proactive and positive.

During the 36-day dispute, the court placed the nearly 100 filings in the presidential election case on the web for immediate access by both the media and the public. This attracted millions of hits from Internet users around the globe. Careful planning anticipated the tidal wave of web surfers, and the site ran without interruption. The presidential election cases site remains intact today for historians and others curious about the events of that memorable period.

The second channel was television. Working with Florida State University, the court secured a $300,000 legislative grant in 1996 to permit live broadcasts of its proceedings. Four remote-control television cameras were installed in the courtroom. A transmission line was run from the courthouse to the nearby FSU Communications Center. From there, the pictures and sound were distributed worldwide on a state-owned satellite transponder.

During the days leading up to *George W. Bush, et al., Petitioners v. Albert Gore, Jr., et al.,* the court clarified and reinforced its channels of internal communications. Waters worked closely with the clerk of the court and the web master. He also worked out a system in which the seven justices reviewed and edited his public statements. Because the Code of Judicial Conduct governing behavior by judges forbade the justices from discussing pending cases, the task of speaking to the media fell on Waters' shoulders. Even then, his job was to announce judicial decisions—not to interpret them.

Despite the effectiveness of these communication channels, Waters and the court staff had to improvise. Up to 850 reporters and six dozen television satellite transmission trucks had descended upon a four-block area of central Tallahassee. In four downtown locations, officials established drop boxes that allowed reporters to plug into courtroom video and audio. They set up a temporary news conference area on the front steps of the courthouse. They positioned the television network camera pool in front of the building. An assembly line for distributing documents took over the courthouse lobby. Media were credentialed. Security measures were taken. Since the number of seats in the courtroom was limited, a media lottery for guaranteed seating was held. Waters also created an early warning system to give the television networks a 30-minute notice of upcoming court announcements.

And then came the day when the court's photocopier—in Waters' words—"crashed and burned." Because of the court's pioneering efforts in Internet use, Waters admits he underestimated the demand for paper copies. He hadn't counted on the hundreds of reporters coming into town without any Internet access. "They all wanted paper," Waters said.

When the photocopier broke down under the strain of the presidential dispute, drastic measures were taken. "We had to conscript secretaries and everyone we could to go to every copy machine available to use in the building," Waters said. He estimated that his team printed 800,000 photocopy pages during the five-week period.

Ironically, the so-called photocopier disaster had an upside. On the day of the meltdown, reporters using the web received court documents 90 minutes before those waiting on paper copies. As a result, the out-of-town reporters scrambled to get web connections, and the demand for paper copies eased.

Other challenges arose. During the election dispute, Waters received 15,000 e-mails—many of which were unfriendly. More than 700 incoming calls were charged to his cell phone account. Because of the flood of calls to his office from private citizens who had seen Waters on television, the court established a special telephone line for media use.

But even this outpouring of public comment had a positive aspect. "It provided me feedback that I wouldn't have had any other way," Waters said. "It gave me an insight into some of the misconceptions that were created in the public eye by whatever happened. . . . It allowed me to either go out and address the misconceptions the best I could or change the way I was presenting information so that the misconceptions were not created."

Because of the world's intense interest in the outcome of the presidential election, Waters became what one newspaper called "something of a cult figure." An Ohio tourist who was taking in the activity outside the courthouse said, "I want to see Craig Waters. I've seen him on television so much, I feel like he's my neighbor."[83]

Waters did not realize how closely the world was watching his every move until Thanksgiving week, when he commiserated with reporters concerned with the prospect of having to wait outside the courthouse through the holiday weekend. In an effort to reassure the media contingent, Waters said that he, too, would like to avoid missing Thanksgiving dinner with his Aunt Ethel in Alabama. By the time he returned to his office, Waters had received e-mails about his aunt. The BBC wanted to send a crew to Alabama to cover the family reunion. The *Miami Herald* published Aunt Ethel's Thanksgiving menu. She was also mentioned in the pages of the *New York Times* and by Diane Sawyer on *Good Morning America*.

In the end, the Florida Supreme Court received high marks for its handling of Hurricane Chad. "Florida has become the butt of many jokes because of a flawed election process," one newspaper columnist wrote. "But our open government laws, which make our officials operate in public and produce public records, have been widely praised by the national news media."[84]

"Every one of the 36 days I came to the office realizing that there were a thousand ways to fail," Waters said. "The fact that we were able to do what we did here speaks very loudly about the success of our overall policy of openness."

For the record, Craig Waters enjoyed *Christmas* dinner with Aunt Ethel.

DISCUSSION QUESTIONS

1. What values came into play that assisted the Florida Supreme Court in dealing with the intense pressure of world attention?
2. What role did technology play in this case? What were its limitations?
3. What publics did Craig Waters try to reach with his communications tactics? Why were those publics important to the Florida Supreme Court?
4. What lessons can others learn from the Florida Supreme Court's experience?

Cyber Coach

Visit www.ablongman.com/guthmarsh3e for these study aids—and more:

- flashcards
- quizzes
- videos
- links to other sites
- real-world scenarios that let you be the public relations professional

KEY TERMS

analog, p. 354

blog, p. 364

computer viruses, p. 367

convergence of media, p. 354

NOTES

1. Robert H. Zakon, "Hobbe's Internet Timeline," online, www.zakon.org/robert/internet/timeline.

2. Suzanne Sparks FitzGerald, "Predictions for the New Millennium—Have They Come True?" *Public Relations Quarterly* 48, no. 4 (winter 2003): 28–30.

3. "Profile 2000—A Survey of the Profession," *Communication World*, June–July 2000, A3, A18–A19.

4. Gerald E. Stearn, *McLuhan Hot & Cool* (New York: Dial, 1967), cited online, www.beaulieuhome.com/mcluhan/stearn.html.

5. Nicholas Negroponte, *Being Digital* (New York: Knopf, 1995), 14.

6. Joseph Straubhaar and Robert LaRose, *Communications Media in the Information Society* (Belmont, Calif.: Wadsworth, 1996), 16.

7. Marshal Brain, "How CDs Work," How Stuff Works, online, http://electronics.howstuffworks.com.

8. Karim Nice, "How DVDs Work," How Stuff Works, online, http://electronics.howstuffworks.com.

9. Kendra Mayfield, "E-Book Forecast: Cloudy," *Wired News*, 11 January 2001, online, www.wired.com.

10. "Who Owns What," Columbia Journalism Review, 23 June 2003, online, www.cjr.org/tools/owners.

11. *Time Warner FY 2003 Annual Report*, SEC Filing 10K, File No. 001-15062, online, www.sec.gov.

12. *AOL Time Warner 2000 Annual Report*, 1.

13. Paul T. Hill, review of *The Innovator's Dilemma, Education Week on the Web*, 14 June 2000, online, www.edweek.org/ew/ewstory.cfm?slug=40hill.h19.

14. Steve Jarvis, "Virtual Firms Win Respect for Performance, Savings Virtual Agencies Deliver Tangible Results," *Marketing News*, 8 July 2002, 4–5.

15. Dick Grove, telephone interview, 2 August 2004.

16. Straubhaar and LaRose, 288.

17. Straubhaar and LaRose, 292–293.

18. Augustine Ihator, "Corporate Communication: Challenges and Opportunities in a Digital World," *Public Relations Quarterly* 46, no. 4 (winter 2001): 15–18.

19. Lee Rainie and Bente Kalsnes, "The Commons of the Tragedy: How the Internet Was Used by Millions after the Terror Attacks to Grieve, Console, Share News, and Debate

the Country's Response," Pew Internet & American Life Project, 10 October 2001, online, www.pewinternet.org.

20. Zakon.

21. Mary Ann Pike, *Using the Internet with Windows 95* (Indianapolis: Que Corporation, 1998), 9–10.

22. Zakon.

23. David W. Guth and Charles Marsh, *Adventures in Public Relations: Case Studies and Critical Thinking* (Boston: Allyn & Bacon, 2005), 320.

24. Mary Madden and Lee Rainie, "America's Online Pursuits: The Changing Picture of Who's Online and What They Do," Pew Internet & American Life Project, 22 December 2003, online, www.pewinternet.org.

25. Madden and Rainie.

26. Madden and Rainie.

27. "Retail E-Commerce Sales in First Quarter 2004 Were $15.5 Billion," news release issued by the U.S. Department of Commerce, 21 May 2004, online, www.census.gov.

28. *E-Stats,* U.S. Department of Commerce, 15 April 2004, online, www.census.gov/estats.

29. "Survey Finds Web Sites Are Key in Driving Credibility, Marketing, for Small Business," *Public Relations Tactics,* November 2003, 18.

30. Carl Weinschenk, "10 Steps to Improving Web Content," *Public Relations Tactics,* November 2002, 22–23.

31. Weinschenk.

32. Joe Dysart, "Making the Most of Promotional Links," *Public Relations Tactics,* November 2002, 21.

33. Sara Means Geigel, "Web Writing That Wows," *Public Relations Tactics,* February 2003, 15.

34. Geigel.

35. Nicole B. Cásarez, "Dealing with Cybersmear: How to Protect Your Organization from Online Defamation," *Public Relations Quarterly* (summer 2002): 40–45.

36. Cásarez.

37. Bill Leonard, "Blogs Begin to Make Mark on Corporate Communications," *HRMagazine* 48, no. 4 (September 2003): 30.

38. Michael Dertouzos, *What Will Be: How the New World of Information Will Change Our Lives* (New York: HarperCollins, 1997), 210–211.

39. Dertouzos, 211–212.

40. Susannah Fox, "Older Americans and the Internet," Pew Internet & American Life Project, 25 March 2004, online, www.pewinternet.org.

41. "Global Internet Statistics (By Language)," Global Reach, online, http://global-reach.biz/globstats/index.php3.

42. Dominique Deckmyn, "De Jager Defends Y2K Hype," CNN Interactive, 4 January 2000, online, www.cnn.com/2000/TECH/computing/01/04/dejager.y2k.idg/index.html.

43. "Y2K Billions May Pay Dividends in the Long Run," CNN Interactive, 3 January 2000, online, www.cnn.com/2000/TECH/computing/01/03/y2k.long.term/:7Findex.html.

44. Howard Stock, "Web Site Users Don't Trust Corporate Content," *Investors Relations Business,* 27 October 2003, 1.

45. *Y2K Aftermath—Crisis Averted, Final Committee Report,* United States Senate Special Committee on the Year 2000 Technology Problem, 29 February 2000, 37–49.
46. Deckmyn.
47. *Y2K Aftermath—Crisis Averted, Final Committee Report.*
48. Daniel Machalaba and Carrick Mollenkamp, "Companies Struggle to Cope with Chaos, Breakdowns and Trauma," *Wall Street Journal,* 13 September 2001, B1.
49. Susanne Fitzgerald, "Predictions for the New Millennium—Have They Come True?" *Public Relations Quarterly* 48, no. 4 (winter 2003): 28–30.
50. Gregory C. Staple, ed., *TeleGeography 1996–97: Global Telecommunications Traffic Statistics and Commentary: TeleGeography* (Washington, D.C., 1997), xiii.
51. Sally Jewett, "What's 'In Store' for SMTs," *Public Relations Tactics,* July 1998, 20.
52. "Survey Finds Increasing Interest in Satellite Media Tours," Medialink news release transmitted on PR Newswire, 14 January 1992.
53. Frances Cairncross, *The Death of Distance: How the Communications Revolution Will Change Our Lives* (Boston: Harvard Business School Press, 1997), 28.
54. Nick Galifianakis, "Did You Know . . . Air Supply" (graphic), *Public Relations Tactics,* July 1998, 1.
55. "Survey Finds Increasing Interest in Satellite Media Tours."
56. Jodi B. Katzman, "Interactive Video Gets Bigger Play," *Public Relations Journal,* May 1995, 6.
57. Adam Shell, "Satellite Shorts," *Public Relations Tactics,* August 1996, 25.
58. Shell.
59. Robert Dwek, "Viral E-Mails Fast Becoming Marketing Tool of the Future," *Marketing Week,* 24 June 2004, 19.
60. Pete Snyder, "Wanted: Standards for Viral Marketing," *Brandweek,* 28 June 2004, 21.
61. Guth and Marsh, 312–316.
62. Guth and Marsh, 312–316.
63. "Special Report—Viral Marketing: Viral Strains," *Precision Marketing,* 9 July 2004, 17–18.
64. "Bush Signs Anti-Spam Legislation," Associated Press, 16 December 2003, online via *The Baltimore Sun,* www.sunspot.net.
65. "Special Report—Viral Marketing: Viral Strains."
66. Rebecca Piirto Heath, "In So Many Words: How Technology Reshapes the Reading Habit," *American Demographics,* March 1997, 39.
67. Dertouzos, 205.
68. "China Now Second-Most Wired Nation on the Globe," *China Daily,* 21 July 2004, online, LexisNexis.
69. *The World Factbook,* Central Intelligence Agency, online, www.odci.gov/cia/publications/geos/ch.html.
70. *The World Factbook.*
71. David James, "China's Love-Hate Affair with the Net," *Upside* 11, no. 8 (August 1999), 52–55.
72. James.
73. "State Control of the Internet in China," Amnesty International, November 2002, online, http://web.amnesty.org/web/content.nsf/pages/gbr_china_internet.

74. "Long Wait Over as China Joins the WTO," CNN, 10 December 2001, online, www. cnn.com.

75. "State Control of the Internet in China."

76. Paul Mooney, "Beijing's Internet Dilemma," *South China Morning Post,* 14 April 2004, 13, online, LexisNexis.

77. Alfred Hermida, "Behind China's Internet Red Firewall," BBC News, 3 September 2002, online, http://news.bbc.co.uk/1/hi/technology/2234154.stm.

78. "China Issues More Internet Regulations," Agence France Presse—English, 19 June 2004, online, LexisNexis.

79. "China Issues More Internet Regulations."

80. "State Control of the Internet in China."

81. Mooney.

82. Craig Waters, telephone interview by author, 20 August 2001.

83. Amy Driscoll, "Capitol an Offbeat Attraction," *Miami Herald,* 12 December 2000, online, www.simulsite.com/miami_herald.html.

84. Lucy Morgan, "As Glare Hits Court, Aide Shares the Light," *St. Petersburg Times Online,* 25 November 2000, online, www.sptimes.com/News/112500/Election2000.

12

Crisis Communications

After studying this chapter, you will be able to

- understand what crises are and how they develop

- recognize that crisis situations often create opportunities

- appreciate the importance of anticipating crises and planning for them before they happen

- explain the elements of an effective crisis communications plan

The Rumor

You are the head of corporate communications for a company that produces one of the nation's most popular snack foods. The company prides itself on making products that are both delicious and nutritionally sound. In your advertising you brag of using only natural ingredients with no artificial flavorings or other additives.

Recently a rumor cropped up on the Internet asserting that a leak from a nearby nuclear power plant has made most of your company's snack foods radioactive. Officials at the nuclear power plant say there has been no such leak. Despite this reassurance, the company has noticed a small decline in sales. To make matters worse, a producer from a nationally syndicated tabloid television show has called and wants to know whether it is true that the company's snack food products glow in the dark.

What are you going to do?

A New "Day of Infamy"

During the 20th century, U.S. citizens remembered December 7, 1941, the day Pearl Harbor was attacked, as a day of infamy. At the start of the 21st century, September 11, 2001, became a new day of infamy.

Approximately 3,000 people died and 8,700 were injured in the terrorist attacks on the World Trade Center, at the Pentagon, and on four hijacked aircraft. A bright

Firefighters placed a U.S. flag on the remains of the broadcast tower that once stood atop the North Tower of the World Trade Center. (Courtesy of the Federal Emergency Management Agency)

late-summer Tuesday morning was transformed into a time of unspeakable horror, remarkable bravery, tragic sorrow, and determined resolve. Although these attacks occurred in the United States, they were really an attack on the civilized world as people of more than 80 nationalities perished.

The shock wave from the events of those two chaotic hours were felt globally within minutes. Major financial markets closed. The Federal Aviation Administration ordered all planes in U.S. airspace to land immediately. The United States sealed its borders. Government agencies in Washington, D.C., abruptly shut down. The White House and the U.S. Capitol were evacuated. News sites on the Internet received a record number of visitors. Regular television programming gave way to nonstop news. Business meetings were cancelled. Major League Baseball postponed its entire schedule—followed soon thereafter by other professional and amateur sports. Stores sold out of their inventories of U.S. flags. Churches overflowed with mourners. People waited in long lines to donate blood to the American Red Cross.

But that's just the big picture. Dramas played out on a smaller scale in boardrooms and at watercoolers everywhere. Once the initial shock and sadness over the tragic deaths in New York, Washington, and western Pennsylvania subsided, the flood of questions began: Are any of our people in New York? Where are our employees who were traveling at the time of the attacks? How will this affect business or fund-raising? What would we do if our operations were disrupted or our facilities were destroyed? What would we have done if key officials of our organization were killed or incapacitated? What do we tell our employees? The questions just kept coming.

As we look back on the events of September 11, 2001, perhaps most memorable are *the things that did not go wrong.* More than 25,000 people in the WTC complex were saved by emergency personnel, many of whom lost their own lives. Most companies and organizations—even those located in the WTC and the Pentagon—resumed operations. The financial markets returned, as did baseball, football, and Broadway. The nation and much of the world united in a new determination to end terrorism and its causes.

We also remember the heroes—those who died and those who were left to rebuild. The personification of these heroes was New York City Mayor Rudolph Giuliani. Prior to the attack, he was seen by some as abrupt, abrasive, and callous—everything New York. However, his inspired leadership in the days and weeks following the catastrophe caused many critics to reevaluate the man they now called "Rudy." He was viewed as tough, resilient, and courageous—everything New York.

Other heroes emerged from everyday life, many of whom were public relations practitioners (see Case Study 16.2). In a time of chaos and fear, they kept their cool. They assessed the dangers and responded appropriately—just as they had planned. Although few could anticipate the toll of human suffering and physical devastation thrust upon them, many were prepared to act. They had emergency plans in place. As noted in Chapter 11, many dusted off their Y2K business recovery plans. Their employees had been trained. They knew what to do. And because these farsighted organizations had crisis communications plans, their stakeholders remained informed and—most important—remained calm.

Putting Crisis Plans in Action

The first job for those at ground zero in New York was to assess the human toll. More than 50,000 people regularly worked in the Twin Towers and other buildings in the WTC complex. In the confusion that followed the attacks, companies worked frantically to get a head count of employees. Because the first plane struck 1 World Trade Center at 8:45 A.M., just as people were arriving for work, there was no way to know how many people were at their desks.

It was the same story for many companies, as managers stayed up all night trying to reach employees by phone. Susan Zimmerman, human resources vice president at MassMutual Financial Group, said, "We would not rest until we knew everyone was safe."[1]

Even as managers sought to locate missing employees, the focus turned to letting important stakeholders know what was happening and how their companies were responding. During this crisis, public relations was not a luxury. The World Trade Center had been at the heart of the nation's—and arguably the world's—financial system. The list of tenants at the WTC complex read like a Who's Who of international commerce. The rapid dissemination of information was essential to avoiding a global economic panic.

The Internet and e-mail proved to be valuable tools in addressing investor concerns. Morgan Stanley, a brokerage and investment-banking firm, had 3,500 employees occupying 19 floors of 2 World Trade Center. Within hours of the attack, Chairman and Chief Executive Officer Philip Purcell, in a message posted on the Morgan Stanley web site, expressed his sympathy for the victims of the tragedy. He then said, "We want our clients to know today that in spite of this tragedy, all of our businesses are functioning and will continue to function."[2]

Communication played a critical role in both the grieving and recovery process. Cantor Fitzgerald, a bond trading company that lost 700 of its 1,000 employees in the disaster, established a family services center at the Pierre Hotel in Manhattan. It was there that Chairman Howard Lutnick, who had lost his own brother in the collapse of the towers, met with grieving relatives and surviving employees. "At the same time, his surviving lieutenants worked around the clock at backup offices in New Jersey and London to save Cantor's computer systems," the *Wall Street Journal* reported. "By Thursday morning, despite gaping holes in the staff, they had re-opened Cantor's electronic bond-trading network."[3]

If getting back to business just two days after this horrendous tragedy sounds cold to you, please remember this: Cantor Fitzgerald was a leading player in world bond markets, brokering trades on 75 percent of long-term U.S. treasury notes. Although the surviving Cantor employees wanted to get back to work as a tribute to their fallen comrades, much of the world's economy *needed* them back at work. It is a hard reality we all must face at some time or another: crises occur—and difficult as it may be, life goes on.

Crises Can Happen to Anyone

The world changed on that day of infamy. However, the unforgiving truth is that bad things do happen to good people. When we hear of misfortune happening to others, we may easily rationalize that "it couldn't happen here." However, recent history suggests otherwise:

- When a guest checked into a four-star hotel in Hong Kong, he had no idea that he would trigger an epidemic that would kill nearly 1,000 people on four continents.
- The chance to become the leader of the U.S. Senate escaped a Southern lawmaker when some ill-chosen words at a birthday party appeared to praise racial segregation.
- The joy of hosting the 2002 Winter Olympics soured when Salt Lake City organizing committee officials were swept up in a bribery scandal.
- The U.S. Forest Service found itself trying to put out two fires—the worst forest fire in Colorado history and the news that one of its own workers had started it.
- A transmission line problem in northern Ohio quickly escalated into the largest blackout in history—plunging 50 million people in the United States and Canada into darkness.

If anything, these and other incidents testify to this reality: Anything can happen. However unexpected, the sad truth is that most crises are not wholly unpredictable. Perhaps even sadder is the fact that many, if not most, are avoidable. By identifying and analyzing potential risks, we can eliminate many crises before they ever happen.

Quick ✔ Check

1. What steps did companies take in the hours following the September 2001 attack on the World Trade Center? What were the highest priorities of managers?
2. Why was it important for corporate executives to focus on business recovery so quickly after an incident that killed or injured thousands?
3. Are most crises unpredictable and therefore unavoidable?

The Anatomy of a Crisis

"If economics is the dismal science," disaster recovery consultant Kenneth Myers writes, "then contingency planning is the abysmal science. No one likes to look into the abyss."[4] But like it or not, crisis planning has become an imperative in the 21st century for big and small organizations alike. "Any small business owner who doesn't

QuickBreak 12.1

TEXTBOOK EXAMPLES: EXXON AND TYLENOL

Whenever people discuss the right way and the wrong way to conduct crisis communications, two names inevitably enter the conversation: Exxon and Tylenol.

Although both incidents date back to the 1980s, their lessons still meet the test of time. In fact, much of the growth in the science and practice of crisis communications can be traced to the spectacular successes and failures of these two companies. They constitute what we call—somewhat apologetically—textbook examples of crisis communications.

No one wants to be remembered for being the poster child for how *not* to act during an emergency, but that is the woeful legacy of Lawrence G. Rawl. He was chairman and chief executive officer of the Exxon Corporation when one of its tankers, the *Exxon Valdez,* spilled 11 million gallons of crude oil into the pristine waters of Alaska's Prince William Sound. Oil contaminated shorelines nearly 600 miles from where the tanker ran aground just after midnight on March 24, 1989.

Rawl declined to go to the accident site. Critics said he should have gone to Alaska and personally taken charge of the cleanup. "From a public relations standpoint, it probably would have been better if I had gone up there," Rawl later told *Fortune.* "But I would have used up a lot of people's time."[5]

Rawl waited one week before making his first public comment, in which he blamed U.S. Coast Guard and Alaskan government officials for holding up the cleanup. He came across in television interviews as combative, ill at ease, and unprepared. Exxon newspaper advertisements apologized for the oil spill but did not take responsibility for it. When the company announced that it would pass along spill-related expenses to customers as a "cost of doing business," angry consumers returned more than 45,000 credit cards.[6]

In an interview two months after the accident, Rawl said the spill and subsequent lawsuits would cost Exxon less than $1 billion.[7] In fact, a federal judge in Anchorage imposed $4.5 billion in punitive damages against Exxon in January 2004 on behalf of 32,000 fishermen and residents who had sued the company 15 years earlier. Exxon said it would appeal the decision.[8]

have a crisis management plan is derelict in his duties," says Martin Cooper of Cooper Communications in Encino, California.[9] As researchers Donald Chisholm and Martin Landau have pointedly noted, "When people believe that because nothing has gone wrong, nothing will go wrong, they court disaster. There is noise in every system and in every design. If this fact is ignored, nature soon reminds us of our folly."[10]

A series of surveys over the past two decades has unearthed a surprising pattern: Despite warning after warning, many organizations remain unprepared for crises and their consequences. In research conducted in the 1980s and 1990s, just over half of the organizations surveyed said they had written crisis plans. Only one-third of them said they had practiced them.[11]

One could logically assume that the 2001 terror attacks would have been a wake-up call. However, that does not appear to be the case. A Harris poll of senior executives in Fortune 1000 companies admitted that their companies were no better prepared for crises one year after 9/11 than they had been before.[12] The chairman of

The actions of James E. Burke stand in sharp contrast to those of Rawl. Burke was CEO of Johnson & Johnson when one of its most successful products, Tylenol, was involved in deadly product tampering crises in 1982 and 1986. On both occasions, Tylenol capsules were laced with cyanide by unknown perpetrators and placed on store shelves. Seven people died in the two incidents.

Within two weeks of the first Tylenol tampering incident, the value of Johnson & Johnson stock dropped $657 million. It was also estimated that the company had received as much as $300 million worth of negative publicity.[13]

The Food and Drug Administration advised against a massive product recall out of fear that doing so might spawn "copycat" crimes. However, Johnson & Johnson officials said they had no choice but to demonstrate their concern for consumer safety by recalling their product: Their values statement placed customer safety above all else. To further calm an uneasy public, Tylenol capsules were placed in triple-sealed safety packaging after the first incident. After the second, Johnson & Johnson replaced the capsule with tamper-proof caplets.

Burke took another important step to maintain his company's credibility. Early Johnson & Johnson statements indicated that there was no cyanide present in its manufacturing plants. However, that statement was wrong. Rather than risk discovery of this potentially damaging fact, the company immediately issued a news release correcting the error.

The textbook lessons of Exxon and Tylenol are clear. Companies that communicate quickly and compassionately with their stakeholders during crises have a far greater chance of saving their reputation—and their bottom line—than those that don't. People are more forgiving of those who admit their mistakes and move quickly to correct them than those who refuse to be held accountable and try to blame others. When the heat is on, success goes to those who keep cool and adhere to their values.

Lloyd's of London, an insurance company known for its high-risk policyholders, told the World Affairs Council in 2004 that four in 10 U.S. companies will face a serious crisis within five years, yet more than half have no crisis management plan.[14] Another report earlier that same year estimated a survival rate of less than 10 percent for businesses without a crisis management plan.[15]

What Is a Crisis?

The word *crisis*, just like the term *public relations*, is often misused by those who do not know it has a specific meaning. Everyone instinctively understands that flash floods, hurricanes, and earthquakes can usually be classified as crises. But what about a flat tire, missed homework, or being stood up on a date? Are these crises, too?

The difference between a **problem** and a **crisis** is a matter of scope. Problems are commonplace occurrences and fairly predictable. They usually can be addressed in a limited time frame, often without arousing public attention or without draining an organization's resources. On the other hand, crises tend to be less predictable. They require a considerable investment of time and resources to resolve and often bring unwanted public attention. And more than problems, crises can challenge an organization's core values.

Researchers Thierry C. Pauchant and Ian I. Mitroff have written that a crisis is "a disruption that physically affects a system as a whole and threatens its basic assumptions, its subjective sense of self, its existential core."[16] According to Pauchant and Mitroff, crises can threaten the legitimacy of an industry, reverse the strategic mission of an organization, and disturb the way people see the world and themselves.[17]

Steven Fink, a noted crisis consultant, has characterized crises as being prodromal situations (situations often marked by forewarning) that run the risk of

- escalating in intensity;
- falling under close media or government scrutiny;
- interfering with the normal operations of business;
- jeopardizing the positive public image enjoyed by a company and its officers; and
- damaging a company's bottom line.[18]

Laurence Barton refines the terminology even further, describing a crisis as a major event that "has potentially negative results. The event and its aftermath may significantly damage an organization and its employees, products, services, financial condition, and reputation."[19]

Crisis Dynamics

As you might imagine, crises come in many shapes and sizes. They can also influence public perceptions of organizations in vastly different ways. Some crises cast organizations in the role of *victim*. In other crises, organizations may be seen as the *villain*. And in a few cases, well-prepared organizations have emerged from crises in the role of *hero*.

Most people would rather be seen as a hero than as either a victim or a villain. At the same time, many people operate under a false assumption that crises and their consequences are unavoidable. However, public relations practitioners can do much to influence events before they happen and, in some instances, to avert crises altogether. That role of public relations is a focus of this chapter.

But before trying to change the course of events, we should understand the dynamics of a crisis. It is a mistake to believe that crises operate as randomly as next week's lottery. In fact, they follow predictable patterns. Although various researchers have adopted different terminology to describe these patterns, there is general agreement that crises tend to develop in four stages (Figure 12.1):

1. **Warning stage:** In reality, most crises don't "just happen." Usually, there are advance signs of trouble. At this stage, it may still be possible to avoid trouble, but the clock is ticking. This is a period in which we have an ability to be proactive and con-

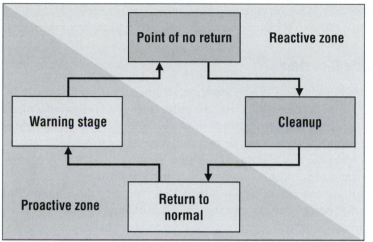

FIGURE 12.1 Crisis Dynamics

trol events *before* they happen. However, one of the greatest challenges in crisis communications is to recognize the potential for danger and then to act accordingly.

2. Point of no return: At this moment, the crisis is unavoidable, and we are forced to be reactive. Some damage will be done. How much remains to be seen and depends, to a large degree, on the organization's response. This is often the time when most of the stakeholders critical to the success of the organization first become aware of the crisis. And from this point on, they are watching very closely.

3. Cleanup phase: Even when the point of no return has been reached and the public spotlight shines upon the organization in crisis, an opportunity to minimize the damage remains. How long this period will last depends on how prepared the organization is to deal with the crisis. The cleanup phase is also a period of recovery and investigation, both internal and external. Fink says this is often the point at which the "carcass gets picked clean."

4. Things return to normal. If *normal* is defined as returning to the way things were before the crisis, then things probably will never be normal again. Following a crisis, operations may differ radically from before. New management may be in place. In addition to these changes, it is very likely that the organization learned valuable lessons. A vigorous evaluation of the organization's performance in dealing with the crisis can result in plans for coping with—or avoiding—the next crisis.

This brings us to an important point: The crisis dynamics model implies that this is a cyclical process, one in which we automatically move from one crisis to another. However, that doesn't have to be the case. Management has at least two opportunities to take steps to minimize or eliminate crises. One is identifying the warning signs of a looming crisis and taking forceful action before reaching the point of no return. The other comes after the crisis, when things return to normal. Management should then take the time to evaluate its performance and apply the lessons it learned. But if no such evaluation occurs, management runs the danger making the same mistakes and creating a new crisis. After all, history has a tendency to repeat. Just ask NASA.

A Tale of Two Shuttle Disasters

Two dates are forever burned into NASA's collective consciousness: January 28, 1986, and February 1, 2003. On the first date, the space agency experienced its first fatal in-flight accident when seven astronauts died in the explosion of the space shuttle *Challenger* shortly after liftoff. Seventeen years and four days later, another seven astronauts were lost when the space shuttle *Columbia* disintegrated during reentry following what had been a successful 17-day mission in earth orbit.[20]

While both tragedies came as a complete surprise to most people, a handful of NASA insiders knew that both shuttles had experienced problems that could lead to a catastrophe. Investigations of both accidents would attribute the failures, in part, to a NASA corporate culture known as "go fever": a strong desire to accomplish mission objectives on schedule without regard to NASA's long-standing value of putting safety first. In its report, the Columbia Accident Investigation Board said the disaster was "likely rooted to some degree in NASA's history and the human space flight program's culture."

However, from a public relations perspective, major differences separated the *Challenger* and *Columbia* accidents. Let's compare the two events and NASA's response to them during each of the four stages of crises.

WARNING STAGE

- *Challenger:* The explosion was caused by a failure of O-rings that sealed sections of the shuttle's solid-rocket boosters. The escaping propellant had the same effect on the shuttle's external fuel tank as a blowtorch on a gas tank. Engineers had identified the problem six months earlier and debated it as late as 12 hours before launch.

- *Columbia:* The shuttle's fate was sealed during liftoff when a chunk of insulating foam broke off the external fuel tank and struck the orbiter's left wing at almost 600 mph. It damaged some of the external tiles designed to protect the shuttle from the searing heat of reentry. NASA officials knew of the incident. After an internal debate, they decided that it did not pose a threat to the shuttle and its crew.

POINT OF NO RETURN

- *Challenger:* The shuttle exploded 71 seconds into the flight. The explosion was witnessed by millions on live television—including thousands of schoolchildren following the exploits of Christa McAuliffe, the first participant in NASA's Teacher in Space program.

- *Columbia:* The first signs of trouble appeared when temperature gauges on the left wing failed during reentry. Within a few minutes, all voice contacts and data were lost. Simultaneously, people on the ground watched a blazing trail of debris following the shuttle's flight path. Television cameras captured the disintegration of the orbiter over Texas.

CLEANUP PHASE

- *Challenger:* Despite a crisis plan that required an announcement of an in-flight death or injury within 20 minutes, NASA was silent for five hours. When officials held their first postaccident news conference, they promised a thorough investigation. But even then, they gave no information on the fate of the crew. That was left to President Ronald Reagan, who addressed a grief-stricken nation more than five hours after the explosion.

- *Columbia:* Within 15 minutes of the loss of shuttle data, NASA declared a "Shuttle Contingency" and posted an announcement on the agency's web site. Within 30 minutes, NASA spokesman Kyle Herring told NBC, "Obviously it is the break-up of something, and based on the timing it is more than likely that, yes, that is the shuttle."[21] Within four hours, President George W. Bush spoke to the nation, followed by NASA Administrator Sean O'Keefe. NASA then began a series of technical briefings on the accident.

NASA Administrator Sean O'Keefe briefs reporters on the investigation into the loss of the space shuttle *Columbia* and its seven-person crew. The agency's handling of media relations during this crisis contrasted sharply with relations following the *Challenger* accident. (Courtesy of NASA)

QuickBreak 12.2

ARE YOU READY?

While recent world events remind us of our own vulnerability, dozens of organizations have turned to the Internet to help people deal with whatever Mother Nature or people of ill will may throw in their direction.

The growth of the World Wide Web has created a cost-effective way to help public and private organizations reach large audiences with detailed emergency preparedness information. But like any other form of communication, the content of each organization's web site is determined by its mission and intended audience.

For example, the Department of Homeland Security's major focus is on terrorism. As part of its "Ready" campaign, the DHS uses a special web site, www.ready.gov, to advise people on how to prepare for a variety of unusual scenarios. "We know from intelligence reports that terrorists are working hard to obtain biological, chemical, and radiological weapons, and the threat of an attack is real," the web site proclaims. "One of the primary mandates of the Department of Homeland Security is to

educate the public, on a continuing basis, about how to be prepared in case of a national emergency—including a possible terrorist attack."[22]

Visitors to the DHS web site are invited to download the brochure "Preparing Makes Sense. Get Ready Now." It discusses potential threats, emergency supplies, where families should gather, and how to develop a family communications plan. It ends with the admonition "In all cases, remain calm."[23]

The Federal Emergency Management Agency (FEMA), another government agency, also has terrorism-related information on its web site, www.fema.gov. However, because the agency's mission covers both natural and human-created disasters, its web site content is broader than that on the DHS site. "Are You Ready? A Guide to Citizen Preparedness" includes information on a wide range of calamities including floods, tornadoes, hurricanes, hazardous materials incidents, accidents at nuclear power plants, and terrorism.

THINGS RETURN TO NORMAL

- *Challenger:* NASA's poor response to the crisis and subsequent loss of public confidence led to a White House decision to take the investigation out of the space agency's hands. An independent panel sharply criticized NASA management, resulting in the premature end of many promising careers.

- *Columbia:* NASA's quick response won it public praise. More important, it was allowed to conduct its own investigation of the accident. While the investigating board criticized NASA for "cultural traits and organizational practices detrimental to safety," the agency avoided the traumatic restructuring it had faced 17 years earlier.

That NASA won public praise for its response to the *Columbia* tragedy brings us to what may be the most important lesson in crisis communications: Not all outcomes of crises have to be bad. In fact, when managed properly, crises can bring opportunity.

"We know that disaster preparedness works," said former FEMA Director Joe Allbaugh. "FEMA's vision of a nation prepared is best achieved by your participation in community and family preparedness so that we are all better protected for every disaster."[24]

The American Red Cross is a private volunteer organization. As such, its disaster services web site (www.redcross.org) tends to have a more personal focus. While covering many of the same topics found on the DHS and FEMA sites, the Red Cross site also includes information on how to help children cope with disaster, animal safety tips, and how to minimize property damage and financial risks. It also contains a key message that the Red Cross constantly stresses: You have to be prepared to help yourself.

"Local officials and relief workers will be on the scene after a disaster, but they cannot reach everyone right away," the web site states. "Therefore, the best way to make your family and your home safer is to be prepared before disaster strikes."[25]

The Boy Scouts is a private organization created nearly a century ago to instill character and citizenship for boys growing into manhood. Its web site (www.scouting.org) is geared to the interests of its members and volunteers. Visitors to "Emergency Preparedness BSA" are told that "the emergencies of today's world demand more than ever that our young people and adults be trained as individuals and units to meet emergency situations."

In a reaffirmation of the organization's values, readers are told, "the basic aims of Scouting include teaching youth to take care of themselves, to be helpful to others, and to develop courage, self-reliance, and the will to be ready to serve in an emergency."[26]

And as you might expect from the Boy Scouts, a clear message to be prepared.

Crises Can Bring Opportunity

Gerald C. Meyers, a former automobile industry executive who has written and lectured extensively on the subject of crisis communications, says a "window of opportunity" opens during the warning and point-of-no-return stages of crises.[27] During these stages key stakeholders tend to sit back and withhold their judgment while placing the organization in crisis under close scrutiny. How long the window of opportunity remains open depends on the organization's reputation.

Meyers says seven potential benefits can be reaped from a crisis:[28]

1. *Heroes are born.* Crises can make people the focus of public attention. Those who respond well to that scrutiny are often seen as heroes.

2. *Change is accelerated.* People and organizations resist change. When change is suggested, you often hear, "But we have always done it this way." Crises often finally compel organizations and individuals who have lagged behind various social and technological trends to change the way they do things.

3. *Latent problems are faced.* When things are going well, it is easy to ignore some problems. This fact is reflected by the "if it ain't broke, don't fix it" mentality. During crises, however, organizations often have no choice but to tackle these problems head-on.

4. *People can be changed.* This item has a double meaning. On the one hand, it means that the attitudes and behavior of people can be changed, as has been dramatically demonstrated by society's loss of patience with sexual harassment in the workplace. However, "changing people" can have a pragmatic meaning: Sometimes it is necessary to replace some people with others who have a fresh perspective and new ideas.

5. *New strategies evolve.* Important lessons can be learned from crises. We often discover a better way of doing things or perceive new paths to opportunity.

6. *Early warning systems develop.* Experience is a wonderful teacher. If we know what the warning signs are, we can recognize a crisis on its way. As a child, you may have been told never to touch a pan on the stove without first checking to see whether the stove was hot. The same principle applies here.

7. *New competitive edges appear.* It has been said that nothing is more exhilarating than having someone shoot a gun at you and miss. Organizations and individuals often feel like this after surviving a crisis. The sense of teamwork and accomplishment that comes with a job well done often carries over to the next challenge. Because of the various changes that occur during the crisis cleanup, organizations are often better equipped to compete in the new environment.

Quick ✔ Check

1. What is the difference between a problem and a crisis?
2. Do crises follow a predictable pattern?
3. When comparing NASA's responses to the *Challenger* and *Columbia* disasters, what differences do you find? What issues, if any, still remain?

Crisis Communications Planning

Public relations, which by definition is a management function, plays a critical role during times of crisis. In an ideal setting, practitioners should be in a position to advise management before, during, and after each incident. Mayer Nudel and Norman Antokol, veterans of the U.S. Foreign Service, have written that communications specialists should be involved in every aspect of crisis communications.[29] Robert F. Littlejohn, who has experience in both academic and emergency management communities, favors the inclusion of a good communicator on a crisis management team, saying that strong communication skills are an essential quality of the team leader.[30]

Nobody likes to think about the consequences of disasters. However, the stark reality is that no one is immune to their effects. As the events of recent years have shown, crises can strike at any time and place. Public relations practitioners owe it to themselves, to their employers, and to all of their stakeholder publics to confront these unpleasant issues head-on and map out a course of action for dealing with crises that is consistent with their organization's values. In the final analysis, planning for a hurricane while it is still out at sea is a lot easier than when you are in the eye of the storm.

Effective crisis communications, like the public relations process as a whole, involves four steps: *risk assessment, crisis communications planning, response*, and *recovery*. Let's look more closely at each of these phases in turn.

Step One: Risk Assessment

At the heart of proactive crisis communications is **risk assessment:** the identification of the various threats under which an organization operates. Some potential crises are common to most organizations. These include problems created by bad weather, fires, financial difficulties, and on-the-job accidents. Other crises are more closely related to the specific nature of the product or service a given organization provides. These can include dangers inherent in the product/service itself (e.g., accidents involving public transportation or contamination of a food product) and toxic by-products from manufacturing processes (e.g., radiation from a nuclear power plant). Compared with private companies, publicly owned companies operate in an environment in which their crises are often more visible. The same holds true for well-known as opposed to lesser-known organizations. Sometimes crises have to do less with *what* business you are in than with *where* you are doing business. For example, the location of an office within a floodplain or in a country with an unstable political environment entails risks not faced elsewhere.

But the goal of risk assessment is not just the identification of potential hazards. Once a threat is identified, steps should be taken to eliminate or lessen it. The wisdom of this can be seen in the experiences of Nokia Corporation of Finland and Telefon AB L.M. Ericsson of neighboring Sweden. Both were leaders in the sale of mobile telephone handsets. Both relied on the same New Mexico semiconductor plant to supply them with computer chips. A March 17, 2000, lightning strike caused a fire that dramatically reduced the plant's ability to produce the critical components. Without the chips, neither company would be able to make its products. Because of more aggressive monitoring and better internal communication, Nokia officials recognized the crisis first. They immediately began working with the supplier on developing alternative sources of the computer chips. Ericsson officials were slower to react to the news out of New Mexico. By the time they realized the problem, it was too late. Nokia had effectively cornered the supply of the critical component and became the market leader. Ericsson's sales plunged. Remember: The best crises are those that are averted.

Many organizations can avert crises by clearly articulating and actively implementing their core values. By doing so, they can make all aware of the legal and ethical limits under which they choose to operate. This is much easier to do during a period of relative calm than it is during the heat of a crisis. Decisions made during a crisis without consideration of organization values can have long-term ramifications that can eventually trigger new crises.

A federal judge cited such a failure of values in a court ruling against A.H. Robins. In 1971 Robins introduced an intrauterine birth control device called the Dalkon Shield. Within three years the shield was being used by approximately 4 million women in the United States. However, doctors and consumers raised concerns about the device. Almost immediately complaints arose concerning infections, septic abortions, and infertility associated with the Dalkon Shield. Despite documented evidence that the product was potentially unsafe, the company took a hard-line approach and challenged every medical finding. In some cases the company even attacked the character of its accusers. In 1984 Federal District Judge Miles Lord summoned three company executives to his Minneapolis courtroom and told them, "You have taken the bottom line as your guiding beacon and low road your route." When Robins was acquired by American Home Products in December 1989, it agreed with the bankruptcy court to set aside $2.35 billion in a trust fund to settle the more than 6,500 claims.[31]

When undertaking a program of risk assessment, organizations can choose either to hire outside consultants or to perform an in-house evaluation. Some organizations, in fact, choose to do both. Often, outside consultants assume a training role after the planning is complete. These consultants can be expensive, costing from $5,000 to $15,000.[32]

For those who decide to do in-house planning and training, the development of a broad-based **crisis planning team (CPT)** is a logical step. The makeup of these teams varies. According to a National Association of Manufacturers study, the chief legal counsel is the company official most often assigned to the CPT, followed by the director of public affairs, the director of security, and the chief operating officer.

It is not enough for the management to dictate a crisis response to the rank and file. The plan will be more successful if employees have some ownership of it. For this reason, employees at all levels of the organization should take part in the risk assessment process. This brings different and valuable perspectives to the process. If two heads are better than one, think how much better the risk assessment can be if many heads contribute to the final product.

Quick ✔ Check

1. What are the four steps of the crisis communications process? Do these remind you of any other process you have seen?
2. What is risk assessment?
3. What role do values play in crisis communications?

THE CRISIS PLOTTING GRID

Steven Fink is a public relations and management consultant who has firsthand knowledge of crises. During the Three Mile Island nuclear power plant crisis in 1979, Fink provided valuable advice to Governor Richard Thornburgh of Pennsylvania that, in the long run, helped prevent public panic. In his 1986 book *Crisis Management: Planning for the Inevitable,* Fink developed a useful tool for risk assessment: the **crisis plotting grid** (Figure 12.2). By placing every potential crisis on the grid, an organization can easily identify the areas where its crisis planning is most needed.

The vertical axis of the grid, which runs from 0 to 10, represents the **crisis impact value (CIV).** Fink says you should respond to the following five questions for each potential crisis on a scale of 0 to 10, with 0 being the lowest level of impact on your organization and 10 being the highest:

1. If the crisis runs the risk of escalating in intensity, how intense can it get and how quickly can it escalate?

2. To what extent will the crisis fall under the watchful eye of key stakeholders, including the media, regulators, shareholders, and so on?

3. To what extent will the crisis interfere with the organization's normal operations?

4. To what degree is the organization the culprit?

5. To what extent can the organization's bottom line be damaged?

Add up the total from the five questions (maximum 50 points) and divide by 5. The resulting figure is the CIV for that potential crisis.

The horizontal axis represents the **crisis probability factor (CPF).** Determine the CPF for the crisis in question by estimating the probability of the crisis on a scale of 0 percent (absolutely no likelihood that the crisis will occur) to 100 percent (the crisis is an absolute certainty).

The CIV and CPF axes intersect at their midpoints (5 and 50 percent). Fink says the grid now becomes a barometer for crises facing an organization. Potential crises whose scores place them in the red zone are ones that present an organization with the greatest danger and require immediate attention. The next priority is to address crises that fall in the amber and gray zones. Potential crises located in the green zone shouldn't be ignored altogether but require less of your attention.

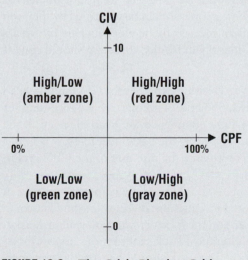

FIGURE 12.2   The Crisis Plotting Grid

Step Two: Developing the Plan

Crisis communications planning means developing communications strategies for identified risks—making as many decisions and taking as many steps as you possibly can *before* a crisis occurs. The best decisions are usually made when you have time to think through their ramifications.

Because crises vary in their scope and nature, it is best to have a flexible crisis plan that is not event specific. The contents of such a plan include crisis definitions, a list of crisis managers, stakeholder communication strategies, planned coordination and information sites, and an employee training program.

CRISIS DEFINITIONS.   Different people conjure up different images when they hear the phrase *public relations,* and the same is true when the word *crisis* is mentioned. A good crisis plan eliminates the guesswork as to whether something is "an incident" or "a crisis." One pharmaceutical manufacturer has a "decision tree" on the first page of its crisis communications plan in which a series of questions helps gauge the nature and intensity of each situation. Developing a common language is also critical for interactions with those outside an organization. Electric utilities with nuclear generators are required to ensure that public agencies, as well as people residing within 10 miles of these facilities, are familiar with terminology that relates to various emergencies and the possible responses to those emergencies.

A LIST OF INDIVIDUALS WHO WILL MANAGE THE CRISIS RESPONSE.   When possible, crises should not be allowed to keep an organization from conducting its daily operations. A special **crisis management team (CMT)** should be assigned the responsibility for monitoring and responding to any crisis. These people should be identified by their job titles, not by name—who knows whether Frank Jones will be working here two years from now? Backup persons should also be identified. Ideally, this team should consist of the following members:

- *The CEO or a designated crisis manager.* Deciding whether the CEO should head the CMT depends on the nature of the crisis. Sometimes no one else will do. In other instances, however, someone who has the CEO's confidence can head the team. If the presence of the CEO inhibits frank discussion among the CMT members, it is better to appoint a **crisis manager,** someone who represents the interests of the CEO and to whom is delegated decision-making authority.

What is not as clear is *when* the executive should publicly leap into the fray. A misjudgment can be very damaging. As noted in QuickBreak 12.1, Exxon Chairman Lawrence Rawl waited one week to comment on the *Exxon Valdez* oil spill in Alaska. He believed that public opinion issues should take a back seat to more important issues relating to the cleanup. "We thought the first task should be to assist our operating people to get the incident under control," Exxon President Lee Raymond told reporters. Based on public reaction, that was a mistake.

"When a major crisis occurs, the CEO must step out immediately into the glare of TV lights and tell the public what is being done to fix the problem," said Andy

Bowen of Atlanta-based Fletcher Martin Ewing Public Relations. "The CEO can't wait until all of the information is in."[33]

■ *Legal counsel.* Lawyers often present business communicators with their most difficult challenges during crises. Gerald Meyers, a veteran of many skirmishes with attorneys while he was head of American Motors, believes that the best advice is often to "cage your lawyers." He wrote, "Smart executives are not intimidated by lawyers who do not have to run the business once the legal skirmishing is over."[34]

This is not suggesting that legal counsel should be excluded from CMTs. Even their critics, including Meyers, say lawyers have an important role in crisis discussions and can provide valuable legal advice. But it is important to remember that the organization must answer to more than just a court of law. It also answers to the court of public opinion, where the judgment can be more devastating. That is why the legal and public relations counsels must have a good working relationship.

■ *Public relations counsel.* Public relations is a management function. In this capacity, the practitioner advises how best to communicate with important stakeholders and, when necessary, represents these stakeholders' views to the CMT. The public relations counsel also advises the CMT on public opinion and potential reactions to the proposed crisis responses. The public relations practitioner is also responsible for serving as the organization's conscience, making certain the organization's actions square with its stated values.

■ *Financial counsel.* Many crises have the potential for severely damaging the company's bottom line. Someone with hands-on knowledge of organization finances can be a valuable asset to the CMT.

■ *Appropriate technical experts.* These people may vary from crisis to crisis. After identifying the various threats to the organization, the crisis communications plan should then identify experts who can assist in the resolution of each type of crisis.

■ *Support personnel.* The CMT may require any of a variety of support services, including people with secretarial skills, people with computer skills, and artist–illustrators.

STAKEHOLDER COMMUNICATION STRATEGIES.   The plan should identify the various stakeholders who must be contacted and should provide appropriate telephone numbers, fax numbers, and e-mail addresses. Given adequate warning of a potential problem, some organizations prepare news releases and other stakeholder communications in advance.

The value of communicating with key stakeholders was demonstrated in October 2003, when destructive wildfires erupted throughout Southern California. San Diego Convention Center Corporation (SDCCC) officials realized that negative publicity could cause 15 groups to cancel multimillion-dollar trade shows and conventions. They moved quickly to reassure meeting planners through a series of telephone calls and e-mail updates. SDCCC also reassured the members of the American Society of Plastic Surgeons, which had already opened its meeting when the fires erupted. By keeping these stakeholders informed, SDCCC ensured that none of the conventions were canceled.[35]

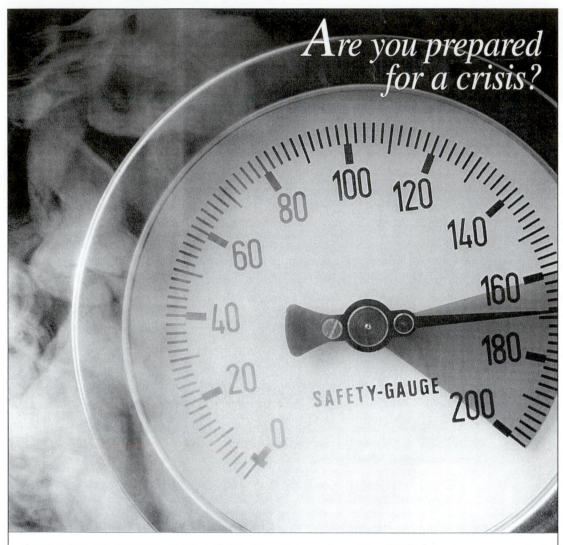

Advertisement Crisis communications consulting is one of the fastest-growing areas of public relations. (Courtesy of Barkley Evergreen & Partners)

Key stakeholders with whom organizations need to communicate during crises include the following:

■ *Employees.* This may be the most important group. Too often, employees are overlooked. Long after the reporters have left, these people remain. The plan needs to outline how employees will be notified of an emergency on short notice. It should also include plans for providing employees with updated information on a regular basis.

■ *The media.* It is critically important that an organization speak with one voice during a crisis. The plan should designate an official spokesperson. A procedure should be established for the timely release of information through news releases or regularly scheduled briefings. The plan should also include provisions for monitoring media reports. The establishment of a media information center (MIC) is discussed below.

■ *Other key stakeholders.* The plan should designate the individual or individuals responsible for serving as liaisons with people who require "special" attention. These key stakeholders include members of the board of directors, major stockholders, financial analysts, regulators/public officials, unions, and community leaders.

■ *The curious public.* Some crises attract a lot of public attention. In those cases, it is a good idea to have a rumor control center where people can telephone and have their questions promptly answered. This is a very useful mechanism for tracking down the source of erroneous information and squelching false rumors before they spread.

WHERE THE RESPONSE IS COORDINATED.   The CMT meets in what is called the **emergency operations center (EOC)**. The EOC is the command post for the organization's crisis response; therefore, it should be in a secure location. That doesn't mean that the meetings need to be held in Fort Knox. However, CMT members should be free to do their work without interruption and without the peering eyes of reporters, curious employees, and other rubberneckers. The meeting place should have adequate communications capabilities, including televisions and radios for monitoring the media (see Figure 12.3). It should also be close to the place where the media are briefed.

WHERE REPORTERS CAN GO TO GET INFORMATION.   The place set aside for meeting with reporters covering your crisis is the **media information center (MIC)**. The most important goal in its operation is to make the MIC the only place journalists can go for information during a crisis. When it comes to interagency and multiorganizational communication with the media, this is the place where all responding organizations ensure they are "singing off the same sheet of music." The MIC has to be close enough to the action to satisfy reporters, but far enough away to prevent journalists from getting in the way. A procedure for verifying the identity of working reporters, known as **credentialing,** should be established. Reporters and officials should have separate entrances into the building. Furnishings for the MIC should include a lectern

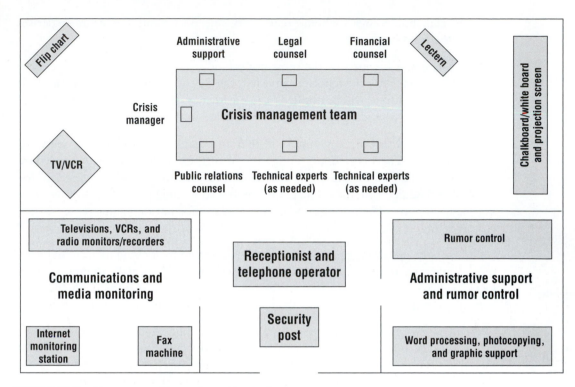

FIGURE 12.3   **Emergency Operations Center Layout**

or table capable of handling many microphones, adequate lighting and background for photography, tables and chairs for writing, access to telecommunications, and a place for distributing and posting news releases (Figure 12.4). The MIC should also be staffed at all times with a media center coordinator who can assist reporters in getting their questions answered.

THE ROLE OF THE INTERNET.   Organizations in crisis are increasingly turning to the Internet as a means of outreach. A web site can serve several audiences, including news media, employees, and others affected by a crisis. American Airlines made extensive use of the Internet in the months following the September 11, 2001, terrorist attacks. Facing possible bankruptcy, the world's largest airline used a special web site and e-mail to communicate with its employees—including 20,000 who had been laid off because of the attacks—and investors. When a would-be terrorist attempted to ignite a bomb hidden in his shoe on a Paris-to-Miami flight, the airline used the Internet in an unusual way. The FBI had imposed a news blackout. However, it allowed American to tell its employees that the security breach was the fault of French officials—not a result of the airline's actions. American posted the news on an employee web site, knowing that the news media were monitoring it and would report what it said.[36]

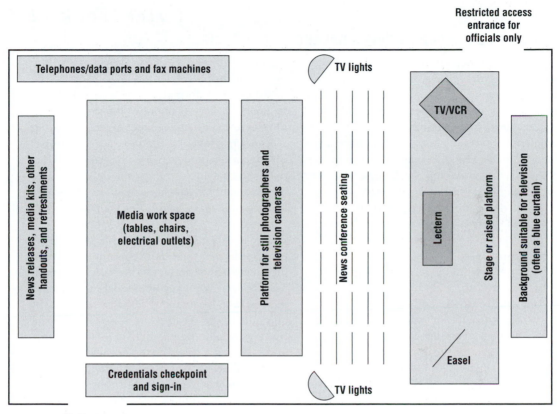

FIGURE 12.4   Media Information Center Layout

EMPLOYEE TRAINING.   Crisis communications training should occur as a normal part of employee orientation. Periodic reminders of each person's responsibilities also are in order—even if those responsibilities consist of nothing more than referring a matter to someone else. Mid- to upper-level managers should have more rigorous training, including tabletop exercises and role-playing scenarios. Part of this training should also focus on the language used and the information gathered when managers report a potential crisis. Inaccurate language and incomplete information can lead to misunderstandings that could cause an organization either to over- or underreact.

Every employee needs to know what to do when disaster strikes. Since Hurricane Andrew, one Miami law firm has issued a disaster-preparedness manual to all its employees. The manual includes emergency contacts, evacuation procedures, and instructions on what to do in the event of a variety of calamities. The firm has also set up an emergency telephone contact system so it can keep track of employees and their needs during crises.[37]

QuickBreak 12.4

THINGS TO DO *BEFORE* A CRISIS BREAKS

With an overwhelming consensus on the importance of a rapid response during a developing emergency, many actions can be taken before a crisis occurs. These include compiling organization data, training personnel, planning crisis center logistics, putting backups in place, developing internal communications channels, and providing psychological support for key publics affected by the crisis.

In advance of a crisis, key information about the organization needs to be at the public relations practitioner's fingertips. This ready-to-use data bank should include information on how many people an organization employs; a record of organization philanthropy and volunteer activity; a master list of all facilities (including names of plant managers, number of employees at each site, value of each plant for insurance purposes, and whether each facility is owned by a subsidiary or in a joint venture with another organization); profiles of products and services of the organization; and a historical overview of the organization.[38]

Additional information needs to include the home and office telephone numbers of key employees and a list of media contacts, including after-hours telephone numbers. Martin Cooper of Cooper Communications in Encino, California, recommends carrying in a wallet a list of names and home telephone numbers of lawyers, finance managers, and other members of the crisis team.[39]

Organizations that rely heavily on computers and data in their daily operations have an added burden of protecting their technological assets. Five steps recommended by *Nation's Business* are maintaining regular backups of computer data, disaster-proofing the office by putting computer equipment in less vulnerable areas, buying a generator to provide a backup source of electrical power, designing a mobile office plan that allows the business to pick up and move to an alternate location, and negoti-

---

Everyone needs to know whom they should call at the first sign of a crisis. The most important person in a crisis is often the first person to recognize it as such. That person's actions (or inactions) go a long way toward dictating the nature and quality of an organization's response. Employees should feel comfortable reporting trouble if even the slightest thing seems amiss. If the culture of the organization discourages such feedback, the organization may end up missing early warning signs that, if acted on, could have averted trouble.

Quick ✔ Check

1. What are the advantages of designating a crisis management team? Who should be in charge of it?
2. Why must a good working relationship exist between an organization's legal counsel and its public relations counsel?
3. What are some things one should do in anticipation of possible crises?

ating ahead of time to rent temporary office space should a disaster strike.[40]

More and more organizations are recognizing the value of providing support systems designed to help employees cope with the trauma that often accompanies crises. These are often easier to develop before problems occur. This support can take many forms. Simply providing food, clothing, or money to meet basic needs can go a long way toward restoring normalcy. In the wake of Hurricane Andrew, many Miami-area businesses came to the aid of their employees. One company estimated it spent more than $100,000 in labor and materials to help the families of 35 employees whose homes had been either severely damaged or destroyed by the storm.[41]

There are times, however, when food, clothing, and money are not enough to address the psychological trauma employees face. "Try to understand that there are bona fide stages of a disaster that people go through," said Pamela

L. Deroian, a clinical psychologist at the University of Miami. According to Deroian, reactions to disasters include a sense that life is out of balance, disbelief, sadness, anger, and survivor's guilt.[42]

Firms such as Crisis Management International, Inc., of Atlanta have a worldwide network of mental health professionals on contract and able to travel to the site of a disaster within hours. "Getting to people right away is the key," CMI President Bruce Blythe said. "You must make them feel safe and secure. You must let them know that someone cares." Among CMI's clients have been United Airlines, which hired the firm to counsel the survivors of a DC-10 crash in Sioux City, Iowa, and Standard Gravure Corporation, at which a disgruntled former employee walked into its Louisville, Kentucky, plant and shot and killed 7 employees, wounding 14 others.[43]

Step Three: Response

Crisis **response** is the execution of crisis communications strategies. If all the necessary steps have been taken, this is where the organization is rewarded for its hard work. Critical decisions on whom to call and how to respond have already been made. In some cases, actions may have already been taken to avert or minimize the crisis.

At the risk of being repetitive, the response phase is when employee training provides its greatest dividends. Employees who have been trained in how to respond—even if the preferred response is to defer to someone else—are less likely to make critical errors that compound a crisis. That is why it is important that every employee know what he or she should do.

However, just as with any public relations plan, a crisis communications plan must be flexible. Every crisis is unique. And although most crises are predictable, some are not. A crisis communications plan should guide, not dictate, the organization's response. It may be that because of some unanticipated factors, the organization's planned response may be inappropriate. The crisis in question could involve a group of stakeholders with whom the organization has little or no experience. And in some circumstances, such as the case of a catastrophic explosion, some of the response mechanisms anticipated in the plan may no longer be available.

Does this mean that a crisis communications plan is useless? Of course not. Think of a crisis communications plan in the same way a coach sees his or her game plan. Like a good game plan, a good crisis communications plan lays the foundation for success. All the training has been geared toward successful execution of the plan. However, both coaches and crisis managers can face circumstances that force them to change their plans. In sports, a key player may get hurt. In crisis management, some key decision makers may be unavailable. That may force some changes in the original plan, but the changes will be based on options and resources provided for in the plan. Even when one is forced to improvise, good planning can mean success.

Step Four: Recovery

When the immediate threat of a crisis ends, the natural instinct is to relax and to return to a normal routine. However, it is important to resist that temptation. There is an important final step: **recovery,** in which the organization should evaluate the quality of its response and take appropriate actions on the basis of lessons learned. The questions asked at the end of one crisis may make the difference in averting or minimizing the next crisis. Some questions that need to be asked are

- Were our actions during and after the crisis consistent with our organization's values?
- What aspects of the crisis did our plan anticipate? How can we build on these successes?
- What aspects of the crisis did our plan fail to anticipate? What changes do we need to make?
- How well did our employees perform? Were they adequately trained?
- What are the lingering effects of the crisis? Are there follow-up actions we should take?
- How have our stakeholders' views of the organization changed since the onset of the crisis?
- What actions can either take advantage of new opportunities created by the crisis or repair damage created by it?

Not every crisis response is successful. Some organizations are better prepared for crises than others. Some events are more unexpected than others. However, there is little sympathy or tolerance for those who fail to learn the lessons of the past. That is why a period of honest evaluation is absolutely essential. This point is reminiscent of the old saying "Fool me once, shame on you. Fool me twice, shame on me."

Crisis Planning Ethics

At a time when "big government" and "big business" are under increasing attack for being out of touch with the people, proactive crisis communications planning can be critical to an organization's continued success. Through this approach, many crises that confront organizations can be averted or, at least, minimized. However, many organizations' lack of planning for crises is a cause for great concern. Crises, as well as inappropriate responses to them, pose societal threats on a variety of levels. There are tangible losses associated with them, such as damage to property and financial setbacks. There are also intangible losses, as evidenced by the psychological damage to crisis victims and a loss of public confidence in organizations. Even more, who can determine a value and assess the cost when the outcome of a crisis is the loss of human lives?

Is crisis communications planning an ethical imperative? In the minds of researchers Pauchant and Mitroff, the answer is a resounding yes. Although they have a certain degree of "empathy" for those caught in the vortex of a crisis, they also express "moral outrage" when crises and their subsequent fallouts are preventable.[44]

Although PRSA's *Member Code of Ethics 2000* does not specifically mention crisis communications planning, one of the professional values it identifies is honesty. "We adhere to the highest standards of accuracy and truth in advancing the interests of those we represent and in communicating with the public," the code states.[45] That wording prompts the question "Can one claim to have acted in such a manner when one has failed to take reasonable precautions against predictable crises?"

It is not enough to develop technical contingencies to meet the logistical needs of an organization in crisis. Developing plans for communicating during times of stress is critical to the success, if not the very survival, of organizations. As one postmortem of Exxon's Alaskan oil spill noted,

> The *Exxon Valdez* spill clearly shows the penalty for perceived unreadiness in the face of an environmental disaster. But it also shows the importance of having insurance for when things go wrong. It would be unthinkable to go without liability insurance against claims for loss or negligence. Why then do some companies fail to take out strong public relations "insurance" for claims against image?[46]

Values Statement 12.1

DEPARTMENT OF HOMELAND SECURITY

Created in 2002, the Department of Homeland Security mobilizes and organizes efforts to secure the United States from terrorist attacks. A major reason for the establishment of the department was to unify a vast national network of organizations and institutions involved in efforts to protect the nation. Its headquarters are in Washington, D.C.

Vision: Preserving our freedoms, protecting America . . . we secure our homeland.

Mission: We will lead the unified national effort to secure America. We will prevent and deter terrorist attacks and protect against and respond to threats and hazards to the nation. We will ensure safe and secure borders, welcome lawful immigrants and visitors, and promote the free-flow of commerce.

—DHS Vision and Mission Statements
DHS web site

BIOLOGICAL THREAT

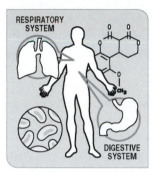

1. A biological attack is the release of germs or other biological substances. Many agents must be inhaled, enter through a cut in the skin or be eaten to make you sick. Some biological agents can cause contagious diseases, others do not.

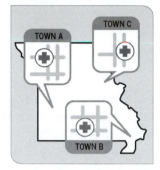

2. A biological attack may or may not be immediately obvious. While it is possible that you will see signs of a biological attack it is perhaps more likely that local health care workers will report a pattern of unusual illness.

3. You will probably learn of the danger through an emergency radio or TV broadcast.

4. If you become aware of an unusual or suspicious release of an unknown substance nearby, it doesn't hurt to protect yourself.

5. Get away from the substance as quickly as possible.

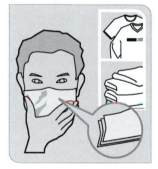

6. Cover your mouth and nose with layers of fabric that can filter the air but still allow breathing.

1

Poster The Department of Homeland Security provided this example of citizen preparedness information on its special web site, www.ready.gov. (Courtesy of the Department of Homeland Security)

Although ethical arguments might move some of the unconcerned and unprepared to action, tangible evidence of the consequences of such failures may prove more convincing.

Summary

Crises don't just happen. Usually warning signs indicate that trouble is on the way. Too often, however, people fail to recognize these signs. When this failure occurs, a considerable amount of an organization's time and resources must be spent dealing with a crisis.

Crises tend to develop in four stages: a warning stage, a point of no return, a cleanup, and a return to normalcy—although crises can alter what normalcy means for an affected organization.

Crises don't have to have exclusively negative outcomes. Good things can come out of a crisis—if an organization is prepared. But the sad truth is that most organizations are not. Many do not even have a written crisis communications plan. Among those that do, many have not properly trained their employees in its use.

Crisis communications planning is one of the most proactive things a public relations practitioner can do. However, it is not something he or she does alone. A good crisis plan is one that has been developed in collaboration with people throughout the organization *and* has the wholehearted support of top management. A good crisis plan also reflects an organization's values—and there is usually no more important time for communicating those values than during a crisis.

Good crisis communications planning begins with an honest assessment of the potential risks an organization may face. It follows with a plan that identifies the members of the crisis management team, key stakeholders, and the logistics necessary for a swift and appropriate response. The training of all employees is the key to a good response. Although the organization should be guided by its crisis communications plan, its response should not be dictated by it. As is the case with all plans, it should be flexible enough to address unanticipated circumstances. As the crisis ends and the organization moves into the recovery phase, it is important to evaluate what happened and why. This is the first step in preparing for—and possibly preventing—future crises.

DISCUSSION QUESTIONS

1. Can you name a crisis and identify how it proceeded through its four stages?
2. What are some lessons to be learned from the September 2001 terrorist attacks on New York and Washington, D.C.?
3. What do you think are some excuses organizations may proffer for not having adequate crisis communications plans? How would you counter those arguments?

4. Identify some crises that officials at your college or university might face. Where would you place each on Steven Fink's crisis plotting grid?
5. What role do organizational values play in crisis planning?

Memo *from the* Field

Wayne Shelor, Civilian Public Information Officer, Police Department, Clearwater, Florida

Wayne Shelor is the civilian public information officer for the Clearwater (Florida) Police Department and president of the 700-member National Information Officers Association (www.nioa.org), the nation's preeminent training organization for public safety spokespersons. Shelor's memo was written just days after his agency responded to its second hurricane in a month—and while he was closely monitoring the progress of a third storm. He proudly notes that he was a Boy Scout. And he certainly was prepared.

"Time and tide wait for no man."
    —William C. Somerville, English poet (1675–1742)

After a quarter-century in the field of information dissemination—10 years as a newspaper reporter and editor, and the past 15 as the spokesman for a metropolitan police department—I've found my strongest professional trait is that of crisis communications.

When the world is at its worst, I've discovered, I am at my best.

And, I learned early on, there's no time in the midst of a crisis to research or prepare. When a crisis unfolds, the media are *always* close behind, rolling in like an unstoppable hurricane-driven tide. And those who wisely took the time to *prepare* for worst case scenarios will avoid drowning in the sometimes suffocating publicity that is . . . public relations.

The media—particularly with the advent of cable news and satellite television trucks and the ubiquitous presence of the Internet—is a voracious beast that must be fed. Constantly.

When events break and a crisis looms, there's no time to stop and retreat, pause and prepare. If you don't feed the media beast, it will feed on you. Time is a media commodity that must be filled; if a public relations specialist doesn't supply pertinent, accurate, topical facts in a timely fashion, then the media will find someone, somewhere, to fill the time with speculation, opinion, and innuendo.

That's when reputations are ruined, careers are lost, and situations spiral out of control. Once that control is lost, it's rarely recovered.

As a Police Public Information Officer (PIO), I prepare constantly for the worst that can happen to my public safety agency. I read constantly (everything from newspapers and profession-related periodicals to myriad media Internet web sites and news portals), and I research what worked—and what failed—in high-profile cases around the nation.

Then I apply the lessons learned to the demographics and capabilities of my agency, its employees, and its policies and procedures. And my research and preparation have served me well:

- When a police officer shot dead an unarmed man at a wedding rehearsal dinner, the expedient, timely dissemination of factual information was handled so well that the region's "newspaper of record" wrote a positively glowing editorial about how the police dealt with an ugly situation.

- During a two-year, high-profile death investigation that garnered constant media scrutiny from around the globe, the sensitive case was protected—and the agency's sterling reputation left unsullied—because of the way information was (and was not) released.

- After Hurricane Andrew destroyed south Florida, we had a team dissect the public safety preparation and response policies of agencies across America and then develop what has been held out as the nation's most sophisticated and detailed disaster response and recovery plan.

There's no way anyone can ever anticipate every possible problem facing a business, organization, or public agency. Even plans such as our much-heralded Hurricane Response and Recovery policy are subject to changes in geography, manpower, funding, laws, infrastructure, government, and the strength and angle of attack of these unpredictable storms.

But we are *prepared* to address bad and sensitive situations.

Preparation involves everything from knowing the wants, needs, habits, styles, personalities, and practices of your various local media to anticipating and preparing for an eventuality that may not be likely, but is certainly possible. (I've never had one of my officers killed in the line of duty; it's really quite unthinkable within the law enforcement community. But it's a daily possibility, and as the PIO, I am prepared for everything from working with a mourning community to detailing for the family the scope and specifics of survivor benefits to the most-minute details of orchestrating a police funeral, including how to best accommodate the media. Were I to wait until it happens, I—and the entire department—would be overwhelmed.)

I learned long ago that the best public relations practitioners prepare themselves for the worst and invariably discover they're ready when the bad-but-not-the-worst unfolds. Every event and crisis situation "seasons" public relations specialists, and in time, they discover that panic and confusion are something they see only in the eyes of others, never in the mirror.

I've always found a healthy measure of comfort in that hard-earned self-confidence.

I've been practicing public relations for more than 15 years now and teaching the mechanics of media relations and crisis management for almost as long.

And my first admonition to those new to the profession is something I learned when I was but a lad: Always be prepared.

Case Study 12.1

Blame Canada

For Aunt Sheila, the answer to all problems, real and imagined, is to "Blame Canada." During the Blackout of 2003, a number of U.S. officials sang the same tune.

The difference is that the song from *South Park: Bigger, Longer and Uncut* earned its writers an Oscar nomination. The government and power company officials who wrongly suggested that the power outage was the fault of Canadian utilities received nothing in return but scorn.

A massive power failure struck eight Northeastern U.S. states and Eastern Canada on the afternoon of August 14, 2003. At the height of a summer heat wave and at the start of the evening rush hour, millions of people from Detroit to Toronto to New York were left in dark and wondering what happened. Unfortunately, government and power company officials did not shed very much light.

"The finger of blame for today's power outage is being pointed in two directions," reported MSNBC's Keith Olbermann. "In heat-wave-hit New York City, they say this all began in Ottawa with an overload of some kind. In Canada, the prime minister thinks it was a lightning strike at a plant in Niagara, New York."[47]

Actually, both versions were wrong. It took several months to unravel, but, in the end, a joint U.S.-Canadian task force determined that the power failure started outside Cleveland, Ohio. The North American Electric Reliability Council blamed the blackout on inadequate tree clearance along Akron-based FirstEnergy Corporation utility lines. The task force also cited other FirstEnergy technical and human errors for the blackout.[48]

While FirstEnergy acknowledges some problems with its electrical grid, it has always denied full responsibility for the Blackout of 2003. In the company's 2003 annual report, President and CEO Anthony J. Alexander told investors, "We remain convinced, as do other experts, that the August 14 outage cannot be explained by the events on our system alone or on any other single utility system."[49]

Whether FirstEnergy bears sole blame is a matter for technical experts to debate. However, when it comes to the public relations failure of August 14, 2003, there's plenty of blame to go around. One of the cardinal rules of crisis communications management is *don't speculate*. Unfortunately, speculation ran as hot as a summer evening without air conditioning.

The blame game appeared to start when New York City Mayor Michael Bloomberg told CNN in a live interview that the blackout had been caused by a lightning strike in Quebec. And just as the power failure cascaded like falling dominoes from Cleveland to New York, so did the "blame Canada" rumor. "We believe it was a cascading effect that may have originated in Canada," said Joy Faber of Consolidated Edison in New York. A spokesperson for New York Governor George Pataki blamed Canadian transmission lines. Even Senator Hillary Rodham Clinton, a New York Democrat, said, "Our best understanding is that whatever did happen to start these cascading outages began in Canada."[50]

While some Canadian officials did engage in finger pointing, many did not. When Ottawa Mayor Bob Chiarelli followed Bloomberg in an NBC interview in which the New York mayor repeated his earlier speculation, Chiarelli didn't blame anyone. "Governments must sit down and talk about how to fix this and fix long-term with backup generation."[51]

Crisis communications experts said many of the utility companies involved in the blackout did a terrible job of public relations. "I have very seldom seen organizations perform as poorly as they performed," said David A. Fuscus of the Washington-based Xenophon Strategies.[52]

"I was shocked and surprised that people were immediately making accusations and pointing fingers," said Catherine Bolton of the Council of Public Relations Firms. "They couldn't even tell us when we could have power back, so how could they already know whom to blame."[53]

Ironically, in the aftermath of this finger pointing, it was none other than Mayor Bloomberg who earned public praise. "Bloomberg's efforts to reassure the public and to restore order played well to a jittery public," reported MSNBC's web site.[54]

As you might imagine, some Canadians may have winced when they read that. And who could blame them?

DISCUSSION QUESTIONS

1. What do you consider to be the main lessons of the Blackout of 2003?
2. This case study says that a cardinal rule of crisis communications is *don't speculate*. But what should you do if someone casts blame on your company?
3. Suppose many people blamed your company for the blackout but a subsequent investigation cleared it of all allegations. Is it appropriate for you to say, in effect, "We told you so"?
4. Now that an independent organization has placed blame on FirstEnergy, should the Ohio-based utility apologize for the inconvenience it caused?

Case Study 12.2

Embedded Journalists

In no other time are values in greater conflict than during war. This is especially true in democratic societies, where the act of waging war is an expression of national policy. In open and free societies, people have a right to know how the conflict is going and about the manner in which it is being fought in their name.

The U.S. military has long struggled with the dual values of transparency and security. To put it another way, no one wants the enemy to see what troops are doing before they do it. Journalists, to their credit, understand this and are willing to work under some rules. However, the degree to which these restrictions are applied

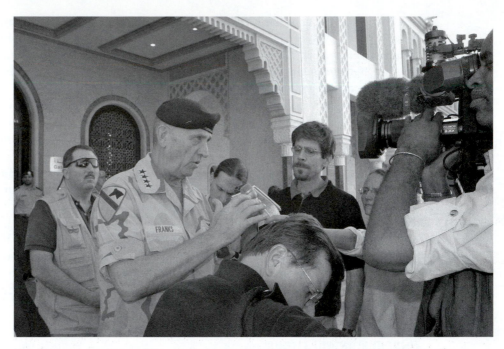

U.S. Commanding General Tommy Franks meets with reporters during Operation Iraqi Freedom. The Pentagon increased media access to the battlefield during the war to counter Iraq's propaganda and to garner public support. (Courtesy of the U.S. Department of Defense)

is often a flash point of conflict between the media and the military. During the Vietnam War, journalists had virtually unrestricted access to the battlefields. After U.S. troops withdrew from South Vietnam and it fell to the communists, many in the military blamed the news media for undermining American public support for the war.

"This opinion that the media lost the Vietnam War became deeply engrained in some of these officers and stayed with them as they rose through the ranks," wrote Robert S. Pritchard, former director of public affairs for the U.S. European Command.[55] As a result, tight restrictions limited journalists' access to future military operations, such as in Grenada in 1983 and during the first Gulf War in 1991.

During the buildup to the 2003 invasion of Iraq—the nation's most controversial war since Vietnam—Pentagon officials were concerned about public opinion both in the United States and abroad. Taking a page out of its own history—World War II, to be exact—the U.S. military agreed to give journalists largely unfettered access to the front lines by "embedding" them in individual units. This meant journalists would live and travel with the troops. It also meant that they would share the same dangers.

"The official rationale for the new policy is that the war in Afghanistan convinced the military brass that the best way to counter enemy propaganda about things like civilian casualties is to let credible reporters see for themselves," reported the *Columbia Journalism Review.*[56]

Victoria Clarke, the person most often credited with creating the embedded journalists policy, also wanted to show the human side of the armed forces. "It's a fundamental belief that the more news and information we provide, through a variety of media, the better off we are," said Clarke, who served as spokesperson for the Defense Department during the invasion. "Anytime you can give people an up-close and personal look at the U.S. military, you're having a good day."[57]

Though the notion of "bringing journalists along" was something untried during the Digital Age, it was hardly something new. It even predates World War II, when journalists reported from the front lines. "The strategy is simply classic public relations, the kind espoused by Ivy Lee," wrote *Public Relations Review* editor Ray E. Hiebert. "In the Rockefeller conflict with striking coal miners in Ludlow, Colorado, in 1913, with public opinion thoroughly against the Rockefellers and other mine owners, Lee invited reporters to come inside, talk to any officials, examine any documents, and observe the conflict firsthand.

"That proved to be the decisive strategy, gaining Rockefeller a rare sympathetic press, although pro-labor forces continued to castigate Lee for decades as a result."[58]

As the prospects for war in Iraq increased, the Pentagon announced its new policy to an appreciative, but skeptical, media. Journalists would be allowed to report events in "real time" without censorship. More than 600 journalists underwent a week of physical and procedural training—a sort of reporters boot camp. There were a handful of restrictions, such as not reporting specific locations and troop movements. Otherwise, reporters from around the world—even Al-Jazeera—were free to report as they pleased.

It was "old-fashioned war reporting, but with razzle-dazzle technology that brings it to our living room in real time," said *Washington Post* columnist Howard Kurtz.[59]

With the outbreak of war, the world witnessed events as never before. Viewers watched "live" as U.S.-led coalition forces raced across the Iraqi desert toward Baghdad. They saw troops battle for small towns, villages, bridges, and airfields. It was history as it was happening.

The first real test of the Pentagon's new openness came from an unanticipated event—a disgruntled U.S. soldier tossing hand grenades into the tents of officers in his own unit. "But the story behind the story was that as the first real test of the embedding process, it did work," said CBS embedded correspondent Mark Strassman. "The communication from them to us in terms of what was happening was great."[60]

While the embedding process appeared to work well, it wasn't without its critics. "You were put in a position where you would certainly not be antagonistic to the kids that you were involved with and admired," said embedded journalist George C. Wilson of the *National Journal.* "In effect, I was putting myself in a position to be a propagandist, which was great for the Pentagon, but not so great for the readers."[61]

There were other issues, as well. Because reporters covered the war from a limited perspective, that of the unit to which they were assigned, it was hard for them to see the big picture. Small victories or defeats were blown out of proportion. The speed of the invasion and earlier U.S. military operations may have also led to an unrealistic expectation that wars are won in a few days or weeks. President Bush fed this misconception when he declared the end of military operations on May 1, 2003. Continuing violence and mounting U.S. troop casualties more than a year later dogged the president as he sought reelection.

"Embedding in the Iraq war raised a host of arguments and controversies among journalists, but it succeeded beyond doubt as public relations," wrote Hiebert.[62]

"When a crippling public relations battle looms, the first issue is not who spins best, gets the best stories and wins the week," said Clark S. Judge, managing director of the White House Writers Group. "The issue is who becomes the standard of truth."[63]

DISCUSSION QUESTIONS

1. On what values do the U.S. military and media agree during a time of war? On what do they disagree?
2. From the Pentagon's perspective, what were the advantages and disadvantages of the policy of embedding journalists during the Iraq war?
3. Although many people disagreed with the decision to go to war with Iraq, does that make the policy of embedding journalists with the troops unethical?
4. What are some of the issues that arose out of the embedded journalist experience?
5. Can you describe the stages of crisis communications planning that went into the development of the embedded journalists policy?

Cyber Coach

Visit www.ablongman.com/guthmarsh3e for these study aids—and more:

- flashcards
- quizzes
- videos
- links to other sites
- real-world scenarios that let you be the public relations professional

KEY TERMS

cleanup phase, p. 397
credentialing, p. 409
crisis, p. 395
crisis communications planning, p. 406
crisis impact value (CIV), p. 405
crisis management team (CMT), p. 406
crisis manager, p. 406
crisis planning team (CPT), p. 404
crisis plotting grid, p. 405
crisis probability factor (CPF), p. 405

emergency operations center (EOC), p. 409
media information center (MIC), p. 409
point of no return, p. 397
problem, p. 395
recovery, p. 414
response, p. 413
risk assessment, p. 403
things return to normal, p. 397
warning stage, p. 396

NOTES

1. Matt Murray and Rick Schmitt, "For Bosses and Workers Alike, Getting Back to Work Takes Patience and Determination," *Wall Street Journal,* 12 September 2001, B1.
2. "Message from Morgan Stanley Chairman Philip Purcell," Morgan Stanley, 11 September 2001, online, www.morganstanley.com.
3. Carol Hymowitz, "In a Crisis, Leaders Put People First, But Also Get Back to Business," *Wall Street Journal,* 18 September 2001, B1.
4. Kenneth N. Myers, *Total Contingency Planning for Disasters* (New York: Wiley, 1993), 2.
5. "In Ten Years You'll See Nothing," *Fortune,* 8 May 1989.
6. Allanna Sullivan and Amanda Bennett, "Critics Fault Chief Executive of Exxon on Handling of Recent Alaskan Oil Spill," *Wall Street Journal,* 31 March 1989.
7. Sullivan and Bennett.
8. Adam Liptak, "$4.5 Billion Award Set for Spill of Exxon Valdez," *New York Times,* 29 January 2004, online, www.nytimes.com.
9. Jane Applegate, "Why Crisis Management Plans Are Essential," *Los Angeles Times,* 29 December 1989, D3.
10. Donald Chisholm and Martin Landau, "Set Aside That Optimism If We Want to Avoid Disaster," *Los Angeles Times,* 18 April 1989, sec. II, p. 7.
11. "Many Still Aren't Prepared," *Public Relations Journal,* September 1986, 16; David W. Guth, "Organizational Crisis Experience and Public Relations Roles," *Public Relations Review* 21, no. 2 (summer 1995): 123–136.
12. Leslie Brooks Suzukamo, "Gone in an Instant," *Kansas City Star,* 8 September 2003, B6.
13. "Tylenol Tries for a Comeback," *Newsweek,* 1 November 1982, 78.
14. "Businesses Neglecting Crisis Plans Levene," *Daily Mail,* 22 April 2004, 77, online, LexisNexis.
15. "Preparing for the Worst Times," *Financial Adviser,* 4 March 2004, online, LexisNexis.
16. Thierry C. Pauchant and Ian I. Mitroff, *Transforming the Crisis-Prone Organization* (San Francisco: Jossey-Bass, 1992), 12.
17. Pauchant and Mitroff, 15–16.
18. Steven Fink, *Crisis Management: Planning for the Inevitable* (New York: AMACOM, 1986), 15–16.
19. Laurence Barton, *Crisis in Organizations: Managing and Communicating in the Heat of Chaos* (Cincinnati: South-Western Publishing, 1993), 2.
20. Except where otherwise noted, facts and figures about the *Challenger* and *Columbia* disasters come from the report of the *Columbia* Accident Investigating Board, issued August 2003.
21. NBC coverage, approximately 9:30 A.M. EST, 1 February 2003.
22. U.S. Department of Homeland Security, online, www.ready.gov.
23. "Preparing Makes Sense. Get Ready Now," U.S. Department of Homeland Security brochure, online, www.ready.gov.
24. "Are You Ready? A Guide to Citizen Preparedness," Federal Emergency Management Agency, online, www.fema.gov.
25. "Disaster Services," American Red Cross, online, www.redcross.org/services/disaster.

26. "Emergency Preparedness BSA," Boy Scouts of America, online, www.scouting.org/pubs/emergency.

27. Heather Dewar, "Officials to Improve City Emergency Plan," *Baltimore Sun,* 27 July 2001, online, www.sunspot.net.

28. Gerald C. Meyers with John Holusha, *When It Hits the Fan: Managing the Nine Crises of Business* (Boston: Houghton Mifflin, 1986), 28.

29. Mayer Nudel and Norman Antokol, *The Handbook for Effective Emergency and Crisis Management* (Lexington, Mass.: D. C. Heath, 1988), 36.

30. Robert F. Littlejohn, *Crisis Management: A Team Approach* (New York: American Management Association, 1983), 18–32.

31. Barton, 48–50.

32. Applegate.

33. Andy Bowen, "Crisis Procedures That Stand the Test of Time," *Public Relations Tactics,* August 2001, 16.

34. Meyers, 232–236.

35. "San Diego Convention Center Corp: San Diego Wildfires 2003," Silver Anvil Award Profile No. 6BW-0411B02, Public Relations Society of America, online, www.prsa.org.

36. David W. Guth and Charles Marsh, *Adventures in Public Relations: Case Studies and Critical Thinking* (Boston: Allyn & Bacon, 2005), 307–311.

37. Sharon Nelton, "Prepare for the Worst," *Nation's Business,* September 1993, 22.

38. Barton, 175.

39. Applegate.

40. Rosalind Resnick, "Protecting Computers and Data," *Nation's Business,* September 1993, 25.

41. Nelton, 25.

42. Nelton, 23.

43. Keith Thomas, "Atlanta Firm Helps Workers Cope with Tragedy," *Atlanta Journal and Constitution,* 17 September 1989, A12.

44. Pauchant and Mitroff, 5–6.

45. *Public Relations Society of America Member Code of Ethics 2000,* online, www.prsa.org.

46. E. Bruce Harrison with Tom Prugh, "Assessing the Damage: Practitioner Perspectives on the Valdez," *Public Relations Journal,* October 1989, 42.

47. "Major Power Outage Hits the Northeast," MSNBC Special Report transcript, 14 August 2003, online, LexisNexis.

48. "Final Blackout Report Points to FirstEnergy, Lists 46 Steps to Improve Grid Reliability," *Electric Utility Week,* 12 April 2004, online, LexisNexis.

49. "Message to Shareholders," *FirstEnergy 2003 Annual Report,* FirstEnergy Corp., 3, online, www.firstenergycorp.com.

50. Ken Gray, "U.S. Officials Pin Blame for Blackout on Canada," *Vancouver Sun,* 16 August 2003, A3, online, LexisNexis.

51. Gray.

52. "2003 Postmortem: One PR Disaster After Another," *PR News,* 22 September 2003, online, LexisNexis.

53. "2003 Postmortem: One PR Disaster After Another."

54. "2003 Postmortem: One PR Disaster After Another."
55. Robert S. Pritchard, "The Pentagon Is Fighting—and Winning—the Public Relations War," *USA Today* (supplement), July 2003, 14, online, LexisNexis.
56. Andrew Bushell and Brent Cunningham, "Being There," *Columbia Journalism Review,* March/April 2003, 18–21.
57. Dale Eisman, "Clarke Discusses Revolution in War Reporting," *Virginian-Pilot,* 3 June 2003, A5, online, LexisNexis.
58. Ray Eldon Hiebert, "Public Relations and Propaganda in Framing the Iraq War: A Preliminary Review," *Public Relations Review* 29, no. 3 (summer 2003): 243–255.
59. Pritchard, 14.
60. *The NewsHour with Jim Lehrer* transcript, 21 April 2003, online, LexisNexis.
61. *The NewsHour with Jim Lehrer* transcript.
62. Hiebert, 249.
63. Hiebert, 249.

13

Public Relations and Marketing

objectives

After studying this chapter, you will be able to

■ describe recent changes in marketing

■ define integrated marketing communications

■ explain the differences between public relations, advertising, and marketing

■ describe marketing public relations

■ summarize the process of integrated marketing communications

Face the Music

What a dream job. You've just been appointed marketing director for a new chain of music stores that feature hard-to-find alternative rock CDs. Your company has opened stores in 12 major college cities around the United States.

Unfortunately, you've been hired only two months before the stores open. Now your associates are asking you for a marketing plan that will bring students flocking into the stores. Some associates want advertising; others prefer public relations. But, fortunately, you soon determine that everyone is flexible and eager to be innovative in the company's marketing efforts.

You have an adequate marketing budget but not enough money to advertise on national television or in magazines such as Spin.

What do you do?

Public Relations and Marketing

Let's begin by addressing a question you may be asking right now: *Why am I reading about marketing in a public relations textbook?*

Good question. Here are some answers:

- Marketing focuses on consumers, as does consumer relations, or customer relations, which is part of public relations. Traditional consumer relations tactics, such as product-oriented news releases, can work hand in hand with marketing tactics such as direct mail and in-store displays.

- Other areas of public relations, such as government relations and employee relations, can affect the success of marketing programs—and vice versa. Some of the biggest headaches in public relations, in fact, come from mishandled marketing programs that damage important relationships. For example, Major League Baseball struck out with a key public—baseball fans—during a joint-marketing agreement with makers of the movie *Spider-Man 2*. Fans tolerated ballpark signs and scoreboard movie clips—but they cried foul when promoters planned to put the Spider-Man logo on the bases. The webslinger who whipped the Green Goblin and Doc Ock couldn't conquer outraged fans of the national pastime. Major League Baseball retreated, and the games proceeded with web-free bases.[1]

- Marketing in the 21st century is undergoing dramatic changes. Far from just persuading consumers to buy products *now*, new marketing strategies seek to build long-term, productive relationships with consumers. That should sound a lot like public relations to you. These new relationship-oriented marketing theories signal a profound shift from the mass-marketing programs of the past.

The Decline of Mass Marketing

Life seemed easier when professionals in public relations and advertising believed they could rely on the awesome power of the mass media. When Company X wanted to sell its new and improved gizmo to millions of eager customers, it simply bought ads on the right TV and radio shows and did the same with a few newspapers and magazines that delivered huge audiences. Company X often tried to place news releases in the same media. With the boom of network television in the mid–20th century, such a marketing plan really seemed to work . . . for a while.

However, we're now witnessing the weakening of the mass media. In a world with hundreds of cable and satellite channels, the traditional television networks (ABC, CBS, NBC, Fox, and perhaps CNN and the WB) can no longer automatically deliver a mass audience. In addition, thousands of specialized e-mail or fax-delivered newsletters, web sites, and other new media have helped plow over the few broad paths that once reached millions of consumers. No longer can public relations and advertising profes-sionals reach a mass audience of consumers simply by placing news releases and ads in a few national print media and on the television networks your parents watched.

"It's time that public relations, advertising, sales promotion, and marketing pause for a reality check," says E. W. Brody, a respected public relations professor and practitioner.[2]

And what does our reality check reveal? These facts, says Brody:

- Mass media continue to proliferate (which leads to the next point).
- Audiences continue to fragment.
- New media, sometimes beyond practitioners' reach, are supplanting the old.
- Media that reach individuals one at a time with personalized messages are grow-ing in efficiency and effectiveness.

The Growth of Consumer-Focused Marketing

In this new reality, many organizations are decreasing their reliance on mass mar-keting. Instead, they are embracing what we will call consumer-focused marketing. Consumer-focused marketing uses a variety of media to build relationships with in-dividual consumers. In the past decade, one of the most popular forms of consumer-focused marketing has been **integrated marketing communications (IMC)**. In 2004, two-thirds of marketing executives in a national survey said they had increased their IMC efforts over the past year.[3]

IMC is distinctly different from mass marketing in five respects:

1. IMC practitioners focus on individual consumers. Products are developed to fill consumers' specific needs, and sales messages are created to target specific con-sumers' self-interests. (Because IMC targets consumers, not all of public rela-tions is part of IMC. Public relations, of course, targets other publics as well: employees, government officials, and stockholders, to name just a few.)
2. IMC practitioners use **databases** to target individual consumers rather than mass audiences. These databases contain a wealth of information on individual con-sumers' wants, needs, and preferences.
3. IMC practitioners send a well-focused message to each consumer through a va-riety of approaches: advertising, public relations, direct mail, and all other forms of marketing communications, including packaging and pricing.
4. IMC practitioners use consumer-preferred media to send their marketing messages.
5. IMC practitioners favor interactive media, constantly seeking information from consumers. Thus, media such as interactive web sites can be ideal for IMC.

Just as public relations has evolved over the decades, consumer-focused marketing is growing and changing. Although IMC is the best-known form of consumer-focused marketing, other forms exist, and they are helping to shape the future of marketing. IMC was preceded by database marketing, which helped turn marketing away from mass audiences and toward individuals. Other approaches that can be grouped under the broad umbrella of consumer-focused marketing include relationship marketing, customer relationship management (CRM), and integrated brand communication (IBC). QuickBreak 13.1 discusses similarities and differences among these new consumer-focused marketing approaches.

QuickBreak 13.1

IMC AND MORE

Databases and new methods of communication have revolutionized marketing. In the 1990s those two developments came together in integrated marketing communications (IMC), probably today's best-known consumer-focused marketing philosophy. But consumer-focused marketing includes other, closely related philosophies that you should know: database marketing, relationship marketing, customer relationship management (CRM), and integrated brand communication (IBC).

Database marketing. The new consumer-focused marketing philosophies began with database marketing. A computerized database can store vast amounts of information about individual consumers: what they buy, when they buy, how often they buy, how much they spend, how and how often your organization contacts them, and much more. "Database marketing," says management consultant Mindi McKenna, "involves the collection, storage, analysis, and use of information regarding customers and the past purchase behaviors to guide future marketing decisions."[4]

Relationship marketing. John Dalla Costa, president of the Center for Ethical Orientation, says that the true value of modern organizations "involves a return on relationship. . . . The worth of companies depends more and more on the worth of [their] varied relationships."[5] Relationship marketing looks beyond profits to individual relationships with specific consumers, all in the belief that if the relationships are good, profits automatically follow.

Customer relationship management. The Conference Board, a U.S.-based business-research association, defines CRM as "the business processes an organization performs to identify, select, acquire, develop, retain, and better serve customers. These processes encompass an organization's . . . engagement with its customers and prospects over the lifetime of its relationship with them."[6] CRM combines the technology of database marketing with the philosophy of relationship marketing to develop lifelong relationships with individual customers.

Integrated brand communication. According to marketing professors Don Schultz and Beth Barnes, integrated brand communication goes beyond IMC, which focuses on sales. It goes beyond CRM, which focuses on relationships between organizations and customers. Instead, IBC focuses on relationships between consumers and brands. Schultz and Barnes define brand as "the bond between the buyer and the seller."[7] In IBC, a brand is an individual consumer's perception of his or her relationship with a product or an organization. The goal of IBC is to discover each consumer's view of the brand and to align it with the organization's view. To do so, the organization must identify and integrate all forms of communication, sending one, clear message—just as in IMC.

These consumer-focused marketing strategies, including IMC, are closely related to one another. And with their increasing focus on building two-way, win-win relationships with important publics, they are closely related to public relations.

Public Relations, Advertising, and Marketing: Working Together

The three main pillars of IMC, as we said in Chapter 1, are public relations, advertising, and marketing. Although these three disciplines have much in common, much also differentiates them (Figure 13.1). Let's quickly review the definitions we established previously for each discipline:

> **Advertising** is the use of controlled media (media in which one pays for the privilege of dictating message content, placement, and frequency) in an attempt to influence the actions of targeted publics.

> **Marketing** is the process of researching, creating, refining, and promoting a product or service and distributing that product or service to targeted consumers. Marketing promotion disciplines include sales promotions (such as coupons), personal selling, direct marketing—and, often, aspects of advertising and public relations.

> **Public relations** is the values-driven management of relationships between an organization and the publics that can affect its success.

Advertising, marketing, and public relations follow the same process: research, planning, communication, evaluation. But unlike marketing, public relations focuses on many publics, not just on consumers. And unlike advertising, public relations doesn't control its messages by purchasing specific placements for them.

FIGURE 13.1   The Relationship among Advertising, Marketing, and Public Relations
Advertising, marketing, and public relations are three distinct professions with important areas of convergence. But not all advertising is marketing; nor is all public relations marketing.

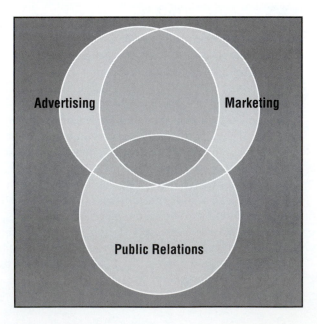

The Impact of Consumer-Focused Marketing on Public Relations

Consumer-focused marketing makes so much sense that some practitioners say, "We've been doing this for years. There's nothing new here." And, to some degree, they're right. Although certain aspects of IMC, for example, are relatively new, including the extensive use of databases and the use of new and innovative communications technologies, IMC is still based on a traditional commonsense approach familiar to most practitioners of good public relations: focusing on the values of a particular public and responding with a clear message.

But consumer-focused marketing *is* changing some aspects of public relations. The growing number of mergers of advertising and public relations agencies is evidence of this change. A generation ago, public relations constituted only a small portion of the activities of advertising agencies—almost an afterthought. But in recent years ad agencies have widened their range of services to better serve clients and to counter a decline in advertising's share of marketing budgets. Some agencies are expanding through mergers. Others are forming strategic partnerships with public relations agencies. Still others are building public relations departments from scratch. In some agencies, advertising and public relations divisions act as separate profit centers, partnering only when circumstances dictate the need for an IMC approach.

Consumer-focused marketing also is changing **marketing public relations,** the part of our profession that exists to promote organizations' products. More practitioners are learning—or at least learning about—disciplines such as direct mail, product packaging, and other forms of advertising and marketing. IMC, for example, is increasing the communications options of marketing public relations practitioners.

The Impact of Public Relations on Consumer-Focused Marketing

But the influence flows both ways: Public relations has also had a profound influence on consumer-focused marketing. Public relations professionals have always believed in breaking down publics into their smallest units, just as consumer-focused marketing does. And good public relations has always been two-way; the best practitioners have always listened—not just talked—to their publics. Two-way symmetrical public relations by definition seeks to identify and honor the values and interests of important publics. Critics of traditional marketing communications charge—perhaps not altogether fairly—that consumer values and interests were left out of the traditional marketing process. Those critics say that companies designed products and sent marketing messages with very little analysis of what individual consumers really wanted. Whether or not that's true, it is undeniable that consumer-focused marketing is increasing the power of the consumer in the marketing process.

Public relations practitioners seek communication with publics through media that those publics prefer; consumer-focused marketers do the same. Two-way symmetrical

Values Statement 13.1

J.M. SMUCKER COMPANY

The J.M. Smucker Company manufactures jams, jellies, preserves, ice cream toppings, and natural peanut butter. The company was founded in 1897 and is based in Orrville, Ohio.

Quality applies to our products, our manufacturing methods, our marketing efforts, our people, and our relationships with each other. We will only produce and sell products that enhance the quality of life and well-being. These will be the highest quality products offered in our respective markets because the Company's growth and business success have been built on quality. We will continuously look for ways to achieve daily improvements which will, over time, result in consistently superior products and performance.

At the J.M. Smucker Company, quality comes first. Sales growth and earnings will follow.

—Excerpt from "Our Basic Beliefs," J.M. Smucker web site

public relations involves the notion that sometimes an organization has to change to meet the needs of its publics, just as consumer-focused marketing involves realizing that a product may need to change. In fact, modern marketing's basic philosophy of respecting and listening to consumers may well be a contribution from the practice of successful public relations.

Differences between Public Relations and Consumer-Focused Marketing

A problem with some interpretations of consumer-focused marketing is the mistaken belief that all public relations is part of marketing communications. Knocking down that idea is easy. Marketing focuses on a very important public: consumers. But that's only one public. Public relations must focus on developing healthy long-term relationships with employees, stockholders, news media, and any other public essential to an organization's success. Certainly the two professions need to work together. But as Figure 13.1 indicates, public relations and marketing are distinct, complementary professions.

In *Excellence in Public Relations and Communication Management,* a landmark study on how award-winning public relations works, Professor James Grunig of the University of Maryland declares, "The public relations function of excellent organizations exists separately from the marketing function, and excellent public relations departments are not subsumed into the marketing function."[8] Nearly 20 years ago, a panel of public relations and marketing experts concluded that the two professions were "separate and equal, but related functions."[9] Jack Bergen, senior vice president of corporate affairs and marketing for Siemens, a multinational corporation, says, "PR people understand the richness of audiences that have an interest in a company; advertisers just focus on customers."[10]

Public relations isn't advertising or marketing. But public relations and consumer-focused marketing certainly share important values. Both focus on the needs and interests of a public or publics. Both try to listen as much as they speak. And both act to strengthen an organization.

Quick ✔ Check

1. How does consumer-focused marketing differ from mass marketing?
2. How and why does consumer-focused marketing use databases?
3. What are the differences among public relations, advertising, and marketing?

A Closer Look at Marketing

Before beginning this chapter, you probably had a basic understanding of marketing. After all, you encounter it every day. And earlier in this chapter, we defined marketing. But as you might suspect, we're about to tell you even more. Understanding how marketing works can make you a better public relations practitioner.

At its core, marketing means making the consumer want to buy your product. The so-called **marketing mix** consists of everything from product research and design to packaging, pricing, and product demonstrations. It even includes selecting the product's name. Years ago, marketing professors Jerome McCarthy and Philip Kotler defined the marketing mix with what they called the four P's of marketing:

1. *Product* (including name, design, and packaging)
2. *Price*
3. *Place* (where, exactly, can the customer buy it?)
4. *Promotion*

Public relations usually enters the marketing mix in the promotion category, and its importance is growing. In 2004, *PR Week* magazine and Manning Selvage & Lee, an international public relations agency, surveyed marketing executives and came to this encouraging conclusion: "Marketing executives said public relations is steadily gaining a larger and more strategic role in the marketing mix."[11]

One of IMC's greatest contributions to marketing is the belief that every bit of the marketing mix communicates to consumers. A product's name sends a message to the consumer, as do design, packaging, price, the place consumers purchase the product, and the promotions that publicize the product. Humor columnist Dave Barry accurately reported that North Dakota was considering a name change because the word *North* suggests cold, snow-swept plains to potential tourists. Barry then stretched the truth—but illustrated the communicative power of names—by adding, "In contrast, SOUTH Dakota is universally believed to be a tropical paradise with palm trees swaying on surf-kissed beaches."[12] Like names, price and place also can send consumers a message. A lavishly packaged product that sells for an eye-poppingly high price at the most exclusive store in town has a different image in consumers' minds than a product sold for 25¢ at the town's grungiest gas station.

One problem with traditional marketing, some critics say, is that these various forms of communication may be sending different messages about the same product. And if consumers don't have a clear vision of the product, they won't buy it.

For example, consumers may easily be confused by a product whose advertising suggests exclusivity and luxury—yet whose price suggests availability and cheapness.

"Most marketers send out a communications hodgepodge to the consumer, a mass message saying one thing, a price promo creating a different signal, a product label creating still another message, sales literature having an entirely different vocabulary, a sales force pitching nothing but 'price,' 'price,' 'price' to the retailer," say the authors of *Integrated Marketing Communications,* an excellent book on IMC. "Mixed-up, mass-directed, incompatible communication stems from the manufacturer's wishes rather than from customer needs."[13]

IMC tries to end that hodgepodge of messages by ensuring that every aspect of the marketing mix sends the same clear message to highly targeted consumers.

Marketing Public Relations

Before we take a closer look at how IMC in particular works, let's look at marketing public relations, which is the part of public relations that fits into marketing. Marketing public relations focuses on building relationships with consumers, with the intent, of course, of persuading them to buy a product.

Professional wrestler "Macho Man" Randy Savage helped Slim Jim meat snacks gain international exposure through an innovative marketing public relations appearance on ESPN's X-Games. (Courtesy of GoodMark Foods and Richard French & Associates)

ConAgra Foods, maker of Slim Jim products, uses marketing public relations, together with other IMC tactics, to gain market share in the multimillion-dollar meat snacks market. For example, knowing that sports broadcasters covering live events constantly need new and newsworthy information, ConAgra sent professional wrestler "Macho Man" Randy Savage, one of its celebrity endorsers, to ESPN's X-Games. Savage is news wherever he goes, and an ESPN broadcaster quickly grabbed the wrestler, who just happened to steer the on-air interview toward Slim Jim products.

How much did ConAgra pay ESPN for that international exposure? Zero. Zip. Nada.

The Macho Man's appearance was a form of media relations—of providing material that sports media want and need. And because Savage's appearance was product related, it became marketing public relations. A ConAgra representative credits the company's public relations agency with helping to create such innovative marketing public relations tactics.[14]

Other tactics in marketing public relations include:

- product- or service-oriented news releases and media kits;
- video news releases (VNRs) featuring newsworthy products or services;
- news conferences to announce significant new products or services;
- satellite media tours (SMTs), in which a spokesperson for a newsworthy product or service gives individual interviews to local television stations via satellite;
- displays at trade shows, where industry analysts and interested consumers gather to examine new products and services;
- special events designed to attract media attention to a particular product;
- spokesperson appearances in the media (including Internet chat rooms) and at special events; and
- communication efforts that target employees, investors, government regulators, and other publics besides consumers that can influence the success of marketing campaigns.

Marketing public relations can work alone or, better, as part of a marketing campaign. The public it targets is the consumer—sometimes through intervening publics such as the news media, where marketing public relations can win an independent, third-party endorsement for a product or service. Other parts of public relations certainly don't ignore the consumer; but, as we noted earlier, they generally work apart from marketing, targeting publics such as employees, the government, investors, and so on.

A Closer Look at IMC

Enough background. Let's jump into a deeper definition of integrated marketing communications. IMC, say the authors of *Integrated Marketing Communications*, is "planned, developed, executed, and evaluated with affecting one specific consumer behavior in mind, the process of making purchases now or in the future."[15]

Focusing on Individual Consumers

In IMC, individual consumers are the focus of thematically consistent messages sent through a variety of media. In fact, marketing professor Robert Lauterborn suggests that the traditional four P's of marketing have become the four C's:[16]

1. *Product* has become *consumer wants and needs:* These shape every aspect of the marketing process.
2. *Price* has become *consumer's cost:* For example, a price of $500 is a higher cost to a college student than it is to a movie star.
3. *Place* has become *convenience to buy.*
4. *Promotion* has become *communication:* This is two-way communication that actively seeks consumer input.

Sending thematically consistent messages through a variety of media may sound familiar. In Chapter 1, we discussed how an organization must identify its values and then ensure that all its actions, including its communications, are consistent with those values.

As we said earlier, IMC recognizes the ineffectiveness of trying to use only the old mass media to affect masses of people. Instead, IMC uses a variety of media to communicate with small groups and, ideally, individuals. For example, a combination of satellites, global positioning devices, and cell phones can allow marketers to send text messages to consumers as they near a favorite store. The messages can even offer discounts. "It drove me into the shop," said one recipient of such a message.[17]

Free-sample tactics often include rebate offers or other special-value promotions that gather information for databases. Databases are an indispensable element in IMC campaigns. As we've noted, computerized databases do more than record names, locations, phone numbers, and e-mail addresses; they can record when, where, and how a product was purchased. Databases also can record when and how consumers were contacted, when and how they responded, and what the organization and the consumer said. Every contact with a consumer becomes a chance to refine the database.

Sending One Clear Message

If the database lies at the heart of successful integrated marketing communications, so does the philosophy of sending one clear message—or, at least, thematically consistent messages—to consumers. Generally, marketing public relations helps send that one consistent message. However, with its expertise in supplying newsworthy stories to the news media, on some occasions marketing public relations may send a slightly different message than do the other tactics in an IMC campaign.

A classic example of how public relations can lead a campaign occurred when First Alert, Inc., maker of First Alert smoke detectors and carbon monoxide detectors, first prepared to market its carbon monoxide detectors. The marketing message of the First Alert carbon monoxide detector was simple: This product can save your life. But research revealed a problem: Wheatley Blair, Inc., the public relations agency

QuickBreak 13.2

THE FALL OF ADVERTISING?

Give a book a provocative title, and readers will come. For example, who wouldn't at least pick up a copy of author James Lee Burke's *In the Electric Mist with Confederate Dead*?

As noted in Chapter 1, the most provocative title in recent years for IMC practitioners may be Al and Laura Ries' *The Fall of Advertising and Rise of PR*. The father–daughter team of marketing consultants has made headlines with this claim: Public relations is more successful than advertising in introducing new brands.

"We're beginning to see research that supports the superiority of PR over advertising to launch a brand," the Rieses say. "A new study of 91 launches shows highly successful products are more like to use PR-related activities."[18] According to the Rieses, public relations tops other IMC disciplines for building credibility and generating word-of-mouth publicity; advertising is most successful in maintaining awareness of established brands.

Recent IMC research shows that 58 percent of marketing agencies increased the amount of time they spent seeking alternatives to advertising in 2004. In a study of 14 traditional marketing objectives, such as "building a brand's reputation" and "retaining customers," marketing executives believed public relations was the most effective discipline in eight categories; direct marketing was most effective in five; and advertising was most effective in one: "building awareness."[19] And public relations offers a financial advantage. "With one twentieth of your ad budget, you have a major PR program," says Jack Bergen, senior vice president of corporate affairs and marketing for Siemens, a multinational corporation.[20]

"Like Ries, I believe advertising has its place," says John Shattock of Shattock Communications and Research of New Zealand. "It should be a reminder of a perception that has already been established by more credible means. Public relations should come first, establishing perceptions and credibility."[21]

assisting in the launch of First Alert's new detector, discovered through research that the U.S. public didn't understand how dangerous carbon monoxide gas is.

"Most people didn't realize that every appliance in their home that runs on combustible fuel produces carbon monoxide every time it operates," said Bob Wheatley, a partner in Wheatley Blair. "They didn't understand that if appliances such as gas stoves, driers, fireplaces, furnaces, and water heaters aren't functioning properly, they can release into the home a gas that is odorless, colorless, and highly toxic."[22]

The bottom line of Wheatley Blair's research was this: Consumers might not respond to a marketing message stressing safety—because they didn't know that they were in danger.

Wheatley Blair and other members of the First Alert marketing team consequently crafted the following timetable and strategy. First, a public relations campaign targeting the news media would roll out. Mention of the First Alert carbon monoxide detector would be secondary; the campaign's primary goal would be to emphasize the threat of carbon monoxide poisoning. The detector itself then would

Carbon Monoxide Detector

Prevention for the number one cause of poisoning deaths in America.

First Alert
780 McClure Rd., Aurora, IL 60504-2495

FOR MORE INFORMATION CONTACT:
Laurel Blair, Bob Wheatley
Debbie Hanson, Sasha Spinner
312-337-7773

FOR IMMEDIATE RELEASE

CARBON MONOXIDE: AN INVISIBLE HEALTH HAZARD

Complaining that your meal last night made you woozy? Do you feel tired all the time? What abo...

getting rec... he onset of a viral infection may have

...soning at all. Carbon monoxide is the

...in America. At lower levels o...estion,

...cause the effects mimic flu...

...zziness and fatigue. Stud...

...medical professionals...

...orless, odorless toxi...

...ain damage and d...

...the body throug...

...armless, once...

...gen.

...water heate...

...able fuel s...

...ndidate for i...

...quate venting of appliances...

...angers, even air pressure changes inside you...

ascending flue gases back down your chimney, ca...

national health problem that is just beginning to...

-more-

Press representation for First Alert Carbo...
Wheatley Blair, Inc. • 325 West Huron, Suit...

Potential Carbon Monoxide Sources in the Home

Blocked chimney opening

...ged ...ney

Portable heater

Improperly installed kitchen range or cooktop vent

Gas clothes dryer

Operating barbeque grill in enclosed area such as the garage

Gas refrigerator

Gas or wood-burning fireplace

Leaking chimney pipe or flue

● Carbon monoxide detector locations

(For maximum protection, two carbon monoxide detectors are recommended per household; one located in the furnace room, the other near sleeping areas.)

Corroded or disconnected water heater vent pipe

Cracked heat exchanger

Information provided by First Alert.®

Questions & Answers about Carbon Monoxide Poisoning

How early warning can help save your life

Media Kit Materials Before safety-oriented advertisements for First Alert carbon monoxide detectors could work, consumers needed to learn of the dangers of the odorless, colorless, lethal gas. First Alert used media kits containing news releases, brochures, charts, and other material to inform news media about the dangers of carbon monoxide poisoning. (Courtesy of Wheatley Blair, Inc.)

be shipped to ensure availability. Finally, the advertising campaign would roll out in October, the beginning of the home heating season.

"For the ads to really work well, you needed to have a basic knowledge of what carbon monoxide is, where it comes from, and why it's bad for you," said Wheatley. "Otherwise, you're not going to get it. What we did was to generate newspaper and TV stories all over the country on carbon monoxide poisoning. A lot of the headlines were 'Silent, deadly killer is invading your home.'"

Radio and TV placements were also key to the public relations campaign. Wheatley Blair helped generate stories on CBS, NBC, and CNN network news.

Wheatley Blair's campaign included personal calls to science and home products editors, a comprehensive media kit, video news releases, sponsorship of interviews with scientists and medical personnel, and a toll-free information number.

Wheatley Blair's news-media strategy succeeded in raising public awareness of the dangers of carbon monoxide from 2 percent of consumers to 75 percent, and the entire First Alert IMC campaign was a success. Representatives of Wal-Mart told the makers of First Alert that the new carbon monoxide detector was the most successful new product introduction, up to that time, in the history of Wal-Mart's hardware/home products department. For its role in the First Alert campaign, Wheatley Blair won a Silver Anvil, the highest award bestowed by the Public Relations Society of America.

"What we did, in essence," said Wheatley, "was use public relations to approach media vehicles that were highly credible. And that created an environment in which the advertising could work harder and be more effective than it might have been."

In most IMC campaigns, public relations sends the same message that other elements of the marketing process send. But, as the First Alert example shows, marketing public relations is flexible. In fact, marketing professionals prefer public relations by a 2–1 ratio to advertising and direct marketing for so-called premarket conditioning.[23] By sending a slightly different preliminary message, public relations can help create receptivity for a subsequent IMC campaign.

Quick ✔ Check

1. What do public relations and IMC have in common? Is all of public relations part of IMC?
2. What are the four P's of marketing? What are the four C's of IMC?
3. What are some of the traditional tactics of marketing public relations?

How IMC Works

Professor Tom Duncan, author of *Principles of Advertising and IMC*, recommends starting an IMC campaign with an **IMC audit.** An IMC audit is similar in intent to the ethics audit (Chapter 6) and the communication audit (Chapter 7) we examined earlier in this book. As with all audits, the goal is to determine where an organization stands right now—and, perhaps, to make recommendations for future actions. Again and again, it's worth noting that the public relations process begins with good research. Duncan recommends an IMC audit that consists of five steps:[24]

1. Analysis of the communications network used to develop marketing communications programs
2. Identification and prioritization of key stakeholder groups
3. Evaluation of the organization's customer databases
4. Content analysis of all messages (ads, public relations releases, packaging, video news releases, signage, sales promotion pieces, direct response mailings, etc.) used within the past year
5. Assessment of knowledge of, and attitudes toward, IMC on the part of marketing managers, top management, and key agency managers

With the information a marketing team gathers from an IMC audit, it forms a good idea of the environment from which it intends to launch an IMC campaign. If that environment is favorable to an IMC campaign, great! Full speed ahead. But if the audit shows that an organization has no customer database and a hodgepodge of contradictory marketing messages, then it must make some technological and philosophical changes before it can launch a successful IMC campaign. Perhaps the organization must even reexamine its core values in light of the proposed IMC campaign.

Creating an IMC Campaign

With an IMC audit completed, we now know where we are. But how do we get to where we want to be? Using our knowledge of current resources and attitudes, how do we build a successful IMC campaign? The following seven strategies are among several recommended by Matthew P. Gonring, vice president of marketing and communication for Rockwell Automation:[25]

1. *"Create shared performance measures. Develop systems to evaluate communications activities,"* Gonring advises. Recall Chapter 8 on planning: We need to have a goal and measurable objectives to prove to others the effectiveness of our program. Setting precise sales goals may be too ambitious—but we can certainly specify the number and nature of relationships that we intend to create.

2. *"Use database development and issues management to understand your stakeholders."* Here's another expert telling us that a database is essential to a successful IMC campaign. A database details the individual consumer wants and needs that have been identified through interactive communication with consumers. Issues management, as we noted in Chapter 7, is a process of identifying and managing emerging issues that can affect your organization and the publics important to your organization.

3. *"Identify all contact points for the company and its products."* Some experts recommend an even broader look at contact points, or **contacts**. *"Contacts* will likely be a new term for many advertising and promotion people, particularly the way it is used in IMC,"* say the authors of *Integrated Marketing Communications.*

C Tactics To
miliarize consumers
h the new $50 bill,
U.S. Bureau of
graving and Printing
mmunicated through
ariety of media,
luding an interactive
b site and, pictured
re, news releases,
ool lesson plans,
d cashier posters.
urtesy of the
. Bureau of
graving and
nting)

The New Color of Money: Safer. Smarter. More Secure.

The United States government continues plans to issue currency with enhanced designs and security features. The government introduced a new $20 note design in 2003 and will continue with other denominations. A new $50 note will be introduced in late 2004, followed later by a new $100 note.

The new $50 design retains three of the most important security features that were first introduced in the 1990s and are easy to check: **a watermark, security thread and color-shifting ink.**

The New Color of Money
Safer. Smarter. More Secure.

Current Changes in Currency Design
Why a Newly Redesigned $50 Note?

LESSON PLAN

This lesson plan is designed to teach students about the features of the newly redesigned $50 note and offers educators the opportunity to teach U.S. history and economics at the National Standard level.

Reproduction is permitted and encouraged.
Available for download at www.moneyfactory.com/newmoney

The New Color of Money
Safer. Smarter. More Secure.

News Release

FOR IMMEDIATE RELEASE
TUESDAY, SEPTEMBER 28, 2004

www.moneyfactory.com/newn

CONTACTS:
Dawn Haley or Claudia Dickens, 202/874-3019
Bureau of Engraving and Printing

Rose Pianalto or Susan Stawick, 202/452-2955
Federal Reserve Board

Penny Kozakos, 202/530-4887
New Color of Money Media Support

Safer, Smarter, More Secure $50 Bill Issued
Banks to Begin Distributing the Redesigned Note Today

WASHINGTON – September 28, 2004 – Newly redesigned $50 notes arrive at banks ...ing today ready to make their way into circulation and consumer wallets. Today marks ...he Federal Reserve System distributes the new note to banks and thus into the public's

...ion, officials from the U.S. Department of the Treasury, Federal Reserve ...Secret Service were on hand for the first transaction using the newly ...ying homage to the symbol of freedom featured in the note's new ...officials used one of the first new $50 notes to buy an American flag ... Washington, D.C.'s Union Station.

...security features, subtle background colors of blue and red, ...d a small metallic silver-blue star. The new design is part ...s to stay ahead of counterfeiting and protect the

...cy is something the U.S. government takes ...tary for Domestic Finance at the Department ...rency regularly and enhancing security ... from would-be counterfeiters."

443

"We define a contact as any information-bearing experience that a customer or a prospect has with the brand, product category, or the market that relates to the marketer's product or service."[26]

4. *"Create business and communication plans for each local market."* As your IMC program improves, you may want to strive for the goal of developing a plan for every individual customer within your database. Ideally, all those messages to slightly different publics must be consistent with one another.

5. *"Create compatible themes, tones, and quality across all communications media."* Remember: All elements of the marketing process need to send consistent messages about your product.

6. *"Hire only team players."* Jealousy and insecurity can destroy an IMC campaign. Public relations practitioners can't always insist on using public relations tactics, nor can advertisers always insist on using advertising. Members of the IMC team must agree to use the messages and the media that consumers prefer.

7. *"Link IMC with management processes."* Robert Dilenschneider, the former head of Hill & Knowlton, one of the world's largest public relations agencies, offers solid advice: "Think in terms of what the manager wants to achieve, and tie everything you suggest to a financial or business result."[27]

If clearly identified consumer values, wants, and needs are shaping each step of your marketing process, from product design to follow-up after a purchase, the odds are good that you have a successful IMC campaign.

Applying IMC

Let's return to our music store scenario for a moment. What sorts of strategies and tactics might an IMC campaign include? After doing an IMC audit and learning that your organization will support an integrated marketing approach, you gain agreement on a consistent message to be sent to potential customers: "Hard-to-find music at hard-to-beat prices." A quick scientific survey of potential customers shows that this is an effective message. Your mission now is to deliver that message effectively and to bring buyers into your stores. Among the tactics you might consider are

- developing a web site and including its address in all your communications. A web site can be a highly interactive medium, and interactive media can generate information for the database you decide to build.

- placing ads in student newspapers. The ads include your web address and a coupon. Consumers who answer the few questions on the coupon get a 10 percent discount. The coupons provide more information for your database.

- sponsoring alternative rock concerts and passing out flyers with coupons.

- offering your store managers to local media as experts on little-known but high-quality bands. You particularly try to place the managers on call-in radio shows, where direct interaction with potential customers is possible.

DM: THE NEW KID IN TOWN

Direct marketing isn't really new, but recent technological advances have helped make DM the hottest thing in IMC.

In the words of the Direct Marketing Association, DM is "any direct communication to a consumer or business recipient that is designed to generate a response in the form of an order (direct order), a request for further information (lead generation), and/or a visit to a store or other place of business for purchase of a specific product(s) or service(s) (traffic generation)."[28] To that definition and its many parentheses, we would add that DM can use several different media for direct communication, including e-mail, postal mail, cell-phone text messaging, and telephone calls. In direct marketing, a company usually contacts a specific individual, bypassing all intermediaries such as retail stores or magazine advertisements.

As IMC practitioners seek cheaper, more effective alternatives to advertising (see Quick-Break 13.2), DM has come on strong. "Advertising's usage [has] slumped, largely at the expense of direct marketing's rise," *PR Week* magazine concluded in a study of IMC tactics.[29] Marketing executives report that DM has surpassed advertising for effectiveness in launching a new product, promoting a new product, and acquiring customers. And DM has increased its well-established leads in retaining customers and targeting niche audiences.[30]

In cyberspace, particularly e-mail, the laziest form of DM is called **spamming,** which involves sending the same promotional message to a long list of receivers, whether they're interested or not. In Europe, where cell phone use exceeds that of the United States, experts estimate that spam accounts for approximately 30 percent of text messages.[31] Although legislation to can spam is on the rise, some experts predict that the tactic eventually will self-destruct.

"The last time I checked," says marketing professor Stephen Hoch, "irritating people doesn't have a long-term benefit for anybody."[32]

- mailing a brief newsletter to all the names in your database. In the newsletter, you offer to e-mail the newsletter instead of mailing it. Consumers can request that service by visiting your web site. You could simply spam everyone in your database, but you wisely decide not to do so.

- launching a direct e-mail and text-messaging campaign that lets customers know when one of their favorite bands has released a new CD. You know each customer's favorite bands because that information is in your database. You use e-mail and text messaging because students move so often that street addresses are unreliable. And, of course, you send such messages only to students who agree, in advance, that they want them. In those messages you ask students to let you know whether they're interested in other bands as well.

For each of the above tactics, you also would establish some measures of evaluation. Evaluation of your tactics would help you determine which are most successful in helping your company achieve its marketing goals.

You can probably think of more and better ideas, but note what the tactics mentioned here have in common: They deliver approximately the same consumer-focused message, they tend to target individuals rather than mass audiences, they're not limited to traditional public relations and advertising tactics, they're interactive, and they seek information for an increasingly detailed database.

Hey, give yourself a raise.

Problems with 21st-Century Marketing

We hope you're excited about IMC, CRM, and the other approaches to consumer-focused marketing. However, we also hope that you're realistic. These relatively new approaches to marketing still face problems that can limit their effectiveness.

We've already hinted at one: jealousy, or so-called turf battles, with every member of the marketing team promoting only his or her own area of expertise. Only 21 percent of marketers say their IMC programs are "seamlessly integrated."[33] Bob Seltzer, head of IMC programs at public relations agency Ruder Finn, says, "Everyone understands that integration is smarter than isolation, but the desire to integrate hits the wall when one discipline has to fight the other for what they want."[34] Two tactics described earlier in this chapter—conducting an IMC audit and hiring only team players—can help eliminate this problem.

A second problem in consumer-focused marketing involves measuring results. The different professions of IMC tend to measure success differently. "One of the biggest obstacles to working with other disciplines is that we do not share a common ROI [return on investment] measurement vehicle," says Richard Mintz of public relations agency Burson-Marsteller.[35] However, marketing executives do give higher marks to public relations professionals than to advertisers for their efforts to document success or failure.[36]

A third problem in consumer-focused marketing is privacy. As noted in Quick-Break 13.4, the United States and the European Union have different standards regarding consumers' rights to privacy. And within the United States, concern for individual privacy increases as marketers seek more and more information on individuals. A survey of marketing professionals in the midwestern United States found that 74 percent favored government intervention to ensure additional privacy for consumers; only 7 percent strongly opposed government intervention. The authors of the study concluded, "The respondents . . . want legislation to protect privacy even though it might encroach upon their professional activities, partially to suppress their culpability and also because they desire such protections in their own lives."[37]

Finally, the very nature of consumer-focused marketing can be a problem. Excessive focus on consumers' desires could pull a company away from its core values. An organization that lives only to satisfy the whims of consumers may well lack the deeply felt, enduring values that characterize successful organizations. Consumer-focused marketing will succeed best when it operates on a solid foundation of organizational values. "The integrity of the corporation that stands behind the brand is even more important than the marketing or promoting of the brand itself," says

DATA DANGER: KIDS AND EUROPEANS

With its many divisions such as IMC, CRM, and IBC, consumer-focused marketing can certainly seem complicated. But we can console ourselves by remembering that one constant is the database, right?

Wrong, in some cases—particularly in marketing to U.S. preteens and marketing in Europe.

With the passage of the Children's Online Privacy Protection Act of 1998, the U.S. Congress and the Federal Trade Commission placed significant restrictions on database marketing to preteens. To gather and store data on children younger than 13, web site operators must, in most cases, get verifiable consent from the children's parents, allow parents to request that such information not be disclosed to third parties, allow parents to examine stored information on their children, and allow parents to delete any stored information and opt out of future collection of such data. In addition, web site operators must maintain the security of collected information and cannot make data collection a condition for entry into their web sites.[38]

Ditto for Europe—for consumers of all ages. The Directive on Data Protection of the European Union specifies that database marketers must have a consumer's permission to gather and store data on that individual; must allow consumers to review and correct database information; can use a database for one purpose only; and must get each consumer's permission to use a database for anything other than the original, single purpose.[39] Organizations that do not meet these requirements cannot use any form of database marketing in European Union nations.

A small loophole exists for U.S.-based companies doing business in the European Union. A so-called safe harbor agreement with European officials allows U.S.-based companies to import information from their European databases and use it according to U.S. laws—if they provide European consumers a chance to "opt out" of the new databases. High-tech giants with worldwide customers, such as Microsoft, Intel, and Hewlett-Packard, have sailed into the safe harbor.[40]

Meanwhile, New Zealand has adopted database laws similar to those of the European Union, and other countries are considering such restrictions.[41]

In case you're thinking you can't operate a database without enough lawyers to start a beach volleyball team, here's a contrarian opinion from marketing professor Peter Fader: You don't need all that information anyway. "I have heard industry professionals say that they have this huge data warehouse and 600 different measures," he says. "I say, 'Big deal, 595 of them are useless.' "[42]

Feel free to disagree—and think of a team name for those lawyers.

Frank Vogl, president of Vogl Communications in Washington, D.C. "So many people involved in the integrated marketing and communications of corporate brands have not paid adequate attention to the values that should be seen at the core of the brand itself."[43]

No one can deny that consumer-focused marketing faces serious challenges. However, at the beginning of the 21st century, the new, database-driven approaches to marketing offer significant opportunities for public relations practitioners.

Quick ✔ Check

1. What is an IMC audit? What steps does it involve?
2. In marketing, what is a contact or contact point?
3. Why are team players essential to a successful IMC campaign?

Summary

Consumer-focused marketing is not a passing fad. It's a growing reality for organizations that want their products to have clear, consistent, appealing images in the marketplace. It's also a growing expectation on the part of consumers, who seek more and more individual attention from organizations as new technologies make such communication possible. Unlike mass marketing, consumer-focused marketing begins not with a public but with an individual. Products are designed to accommodate, as much as possible, individual needs and desires. Sales messages focus on those same individual self-interests, which are discovered through two-way communication and are recorded in databases.

Integrated marketing communications unites a variety of communications tactics to address individual self-interests: advertising, public relations, marketing promotions, packaging, pricing, direct mail, and any other approach that can send an effective message to a potential customer. Despite the wide array of available tactics, the messages in an IMC campaign are integrated: Consumers should receive a consistent message about an organization's product or service. The message of an advertisement, for example, should be consistent with the message of the price and of a product-oriented news release.

Not all of public relations is part of consumer-focused marketing, of course. Marketing addresses one very important public: consumers. Public relations builds relationships with any public that can affect an organization's success, including employees, stockholders, and government regulators. But one of the most exciting areas in the future of public relations is its role in consumer-focused marketing. In the 21st century, marketing means building relationships with individual consumers, and that's good news for public relations.

DISCUSSION QUESTIONS

1. How are the philosophies of public relations and consumer-focused marketing similar? How are they different?
2. What is "integrated" about integrated marketing communications?
3. What are the benefits of using consumer-focused marketing instead of mass marketing?
4. Does IMC, as it is currently practiced, have any problems or potential problems?
5. How is an IMC audit similar to an ethics audit and a communication audit?

Memo *from the* Field

Vin Cipolla; Chairman
and CEO; HNW, Inc.;
New York and Boston

Vin Cipolla is chairman and CEO of HNW, Inc., a New York– and Boston-based marketing company that provides research, strategies, and tactics to help clients build lasting relationships with high-net-worth consumers. Its clients include UBS PaineWebber, Merrill Lynch, and Citigroup Private Bank. Cipolla is a Phi Beta Kappa graduate of Clark University.

There's a very good reason why integrated marketing has become so popular lately. Basically, without it, we marketers are doomed. In fact, when a company doesn't present a consistent marketing message to the public, it not only wastes a lot of money, it also risks its own reputation.

But that's not all. These days it's not enough for marketing functions like advertising, PR, and direct mail to work together. Now, marketing needs to be integrated throughout the entire company—with departments like customer service, sales, distribution, and manufacturing all working together on corporate objectives. The goal today is to make certain that everyone in the company is conveying the same message. Not just the marketing department.

Not convinced? Think about it. Imagine watching a heartwarming television advertisement promoting a particular airline's commitment to friendly service. Now, the next time you fly, you certainly expect that airline's in-flight personnel to be extra friendly, right? You certainly expect that airline to have spent as much effort maintaining high customer service standards as it did creating that expensive television advertisement.

The fact is, we expect more now as consumers than we did a few years ago. Interactive technology, web sites, and sophisticated database marketing have all raised the standard of customer service by facilitating dynamic two-way communication between business and consumers. Today it's not enough simply to sell products; companies must also build relationships with customers if they want to compete.

For example, consumers like to feel remembered and appreciated. That's one reason why some mail-order companies have started to track customer orders more effectively. Perhaps the next time you call, they may thank you for your repeat order and ask if you'd like the same size as before. It's that type of personal attention that is becoming the new norm.

That level of integration isn't easy to achieve. It requires a centralized database in which every customer contact position (e.g., billing, marketing, and service) is integrated so that valuable customer data is captured, analyzed, and maximized fully. That's a challenge. Maybe that centralized customer data isn't available yet. Or maybe it is, but the company doesn't know how to interpret it so the data provides valuable insight.

Another problem may be the company's own staff. Internal power struggles are responsible for the failure of many integrated marketing programs. Unfortunately, many employees aren't trained to work in cross-departmental partnerships. Finance managers speak a different language than marketing managers. Customer service has different priorities than sales. And rarely is there a company incentive for these disparate employees to work together in teams on company goals.

That's why the most successful companies have strong leadership at the top. Only the CEO or president has the authority to cross so many departmental borders. Without that senior-level support, a truly effective integrated marketing program will remain a distant dream.

So what does all this mean for you? It means your job just became a lot more difficult. Now you don't just need to work well with other marketing divisions. You also need to work well with customer service, billing, and distribution too.

The more you understand how the entire company functions, the better you'll perform your own job. The more you understand what these various managers consider important, the easier a time you'll have working with them on the corporate goals. And, finally, the more you understand how emerging technology is impacting marketing, the more successfully you'll play by today's new marketing rules.

As you take on the challenge, I wish you all the luck in the world.

Case Study 13.1

Revolvolution

In the movie *Crazy People,* comedian Dudley Moore played an advertising executive who disavows exaggeration and pledges that his advertisements will feature only the truth. His new slogan for Volvo automobiles? "Boxy—but good."

Audiences laughed, but Volvo executives groaned.

They groaned again when Robert Sevier, author of *Integrated Marketing for Colleges,* said, "If you want safety in cars, it's Volvo."[44]

Ask any baby boomer about Volvo's image, and you'll probably get an answer like this: "Well built, very safe—but they look like a shoebox on wheels."

Volvo executives have nothing against safety; their cars are renowned throughout the world for engineering that protects drivers and passengers. But they wanted a broader image. They wanted a new generation of consumers to think of Volvos as—stylish.

Enter a "revolvolution," Volvo's term for the expansion of its image. In 2001, Volvo launched a high-tech integrated marketing communications campaign "to redefine the way the Volvo brand is viewed by consumers."[45]

Volvo tied the campaign to one of the biggest media events of the year: college basketball's March Madness national tournament. One lucky basketball fan would win a Volvo S60 sports sedan, the car designed to prove that Volvos could be both safe and stylish. On March 15, Volvo launched an integrated series of tactics that featured a consistent message and that strove to lead consumers to a Revolvolution web site. Once at the web site, consumers could fill out a simple survey and enter other contests with prizes such as tickets to the tournament's championship game. Information from that survey would, of course, go into Volvo's consumer database.

Public relations kicked off the campaign. Through PR Newswire, a news release distribution service, Volvo sent online news releases describing the campaign and the contests to automotive and technology journalists throughout the United States.

Next came television commercials. Volvo ran the ads throughout the basketball tournament, promoting the S60 and directing viewers to the Revolvolution web site, where they could enter the contests. The company also announced the national winner of the S60 during a live webcast on its Revolvolution site.

Volvo placed web ads on CBS's Sportsline.com, a web site operated by the television network that broadcast the tournament. Like the television ads, the web ads directed consumers to the Revolvolution web site.

WebTV viewers were able to use their interactive televisions to click through Volvo ads and enter the S60 contest. Similar technology allowed users of wireless personal digital assistants and telephones to enter Volvo's contest. When sports fans used those devices to check game scores, they received brief invitations to enter the contest. Consumers who submitted entries without visiting the Revolvolution web site received e-mails informing them of the site and of the opportunities to complete a survey and enter additional contests.

Despite this diversity, the tactics had much in common. Most targeted individuals, not mass audiences; most were interactive and sought additional information from consumers; and, in the best spirit of integrated marketing, all delivered a consistent message: The S60 was safe and stylish.

"The language and the graphics and so forth were very branded to Volvo," said Arthur Ceria, interactive creative director of Fuel North America, one of the agencies that assisted Volvo with the campaign.[46]

Volvo also tried to ensure that neither the campaign nor the requests for information annoyed consumers. "This integrated campaign was all about not being intrusive," Ceria said. "We weren't pushing the users to go through a long experience. It was up to them to decide what information they wanted to give."[47]

Volvo's IMC campaign seems to be working. Beginning in April 2001, when the March Madness promotion ended, Volvo reeled off five straight months of improved sales, culminating in record sales for August 2001. And among the sales leaders was the S60. "Business was very impressive across most of our car lines," said Vic Doolan, CEO of Volvo Cars of North America. "However, the V70 Cross Country and the S60 are really distinguishing themselves."[48]

Volvo's image problems may have become famous in a movie called *Crazy People,* but thanks to an integrated marketing campaign that emphasized one clear message, that largely targeted individual consumers, that built and used a database, and that integrated a variety of interactive tactics, the only crazy people around may be the ones who still think Volvos are boxy and boring.

DISCUSSION QUESTIONS

1. Has Volvo's revolvolution succeeded? What is your image of Volvo cars?
2. What qualities made Volvo's revolvolution marketing campaign an IMC campaign?
3. Why do you think the revolvolution campaign began with public relations tactics?
4. In your opinion, was Volvo gambling by avoiding conventional media in favor of high-tech new media?
5. Can you name other products that have sought to change or expand their images? Did they succeed?

Case Study 13.2

Flunking History: Umbro and the Holocaust

Reebok, a manufacturer of athletic shoes and apparel, won a place in marketing's mythical Hall of Shame in 1997 when the company named a women's running shoe the Incubus.

Reebok representatives said they chose Incubus because it sounded like *incubate.* The name, they hoped, would evoke images of warmth and rebirth.[49]

They should have checked a dictionary. Here's how the *American Heritage Dictionary* defines *incubus:* "an evil spirit believed to descend upon and have sexual intercourse with women as they sleep."

The marketing misfire earned international headlines, gained a spot on several "year's dumbest ideas" lists, and even became a staple in college textbooks. Shoe marketers probably scared their new employees with the story, right?

Not at Umbro, apparently. In 2002, the British manufacturer of sports gear attracted international notoriety for naming a running shoe the Zyklon. In German, *zyklon* means *cyclone*—but during World War II, Zyklon B was the name of a gas used to murder millions of Jews and other prisoners in Nazi concentration camps. The deadly brutality of the camps and their gas chambers became known as the Holocaust.

When the Simon Wiesenthal Center, an international Jewish human rights organization, expressed outrage, Umbro quickly confessed ignorance. "The naming of the shoe is purely coincidental and was not intended to communicate any connotations," said an Umbro representative.[50]

"Umbro dropped the name but had no explanation," reported a columnist for United Press International. "It probably sounded cooler than their original choice, Black Plague #7."[51]

Other observers were equally stunned:

- "It's sick when you think about it," said a 78-year-old concentration camp survivor whose mother and two younger sisters died in Nazi gas chambers. "It is also very unprofessional."[52]

- "Considering the care with which companies normally choose titles for their products, I also find it hard to believe Umbro's assertion that the naming of the shoe was 'purely coincidental,'" said a Wiesenthal Center representative. "Any investigation of the word, on the Internet for example, quickly reveals its links to the Holocaust."[53]

- "How on earth did Umbro's marketing people, who are paid a fortune to think up new product names, fail to realize that this one could cause massive offense?" asked a London newspaper. "Do they know nothing about history?"[54]

Umbro lacked a good explanation. "I don't think the person who named them knew what it would mean to some people," said an Umbro representative. "We are currently looking at who chose it, but I can tell you it wasn't chosen deliberately for its unfortunate meaning. I think in the future, we will be checking the names we use more carefully."[55]

To that last comment, an Australian newspaper responded, "Too bloody right."[56]

If Umbro decides to learn from history, it might want to study Reebok's response to the Incubus debacle. Reebok may have helped restore its reputation by accepting responsibility and truly apologizing. "We apologize," said a Reebok representative in response to the crisis. "Certainly it is very inappropriate."[57]

In contrast, Umbro seemingly chose to apologize not for its action but, rather, for the offense its action "may" have caused. "I would like the opportunity to express our sincere regret that the Zyklon name may have upset someone," said an Umbro representative.[58]

College students generally take two or three history courses during their undergraduate years. Umbro and the ill-fated Zyklon provide an example of why those courses matter.

DISCUSSION QUESTIONS

1. How is a product's name part of an integrated marketing communications campaign?
2. What is your opinion of Umbro's response to the disaster?
3. If you had been an Umbro official at the time, what actions, if any, would you have suggested to end the problem and repair the damage?
4. What stories have you heard about other badly named products?

Cyber Coach

Visit www.ablongman.com/guthmarsh3e for these study aids—and more:

- flashcards
- quizzes
- videos
- links to other sites
- real-world scenarios that let you be the public relations professional

KEY TERMS

advertising, p. 432
contacts, p. 442
customer relationship management (CRM), p. 431
database marketing, p. 431
databases, p. 430
direct marketing, p. 445
IMC audit, p. 441
integrated brand communication, p. 431

integrated marketing communications (IMC), p. 430
marketing, p. 432
marketing mix, p. 435
marketing public relations, p. 433
public relations, p. 432
relationship marketing, p. 431
spamming, p. 445

NOTES

1. "Spider-Man Can't Steal Bases," *Promo,* June 2004, 11.
2. E. W. Brody, "PR Is to Experience What Marketing Is to Expectations," *Public Relations Quarterly* 39, no. 2, 1994, online, LexisNexis.
3. "Marketing Executives Report Rise in Use of Public Relations Marketing Mix," news release issued by Manning Selvage & Lee, 18 May 2004, online, LexisNexis.
4. "Will Database Marketing Work in Health Care?" *Marketing Health Services* (fall 2001), online, LexisNexis.
5. John Dalla Costa, *The Ethical Imperative* (Reading, Mass.: Addison-Wesley, 1998), 178.
6. "Customer Relationship Management Programs: New Hot Business Issue," news release issued by PR Newswire, 28 August 2001, online, LexisNexis.
7. Don E. Schultz and Beth E. Barnes, *Strategic Brand Communication Campaigns* (Lincolnwood, Ill.: NTC Business Books, 1999), 44.
8. William P. Ehling, Jon White, and James E. Grunig, "Public Relations and Marketing Practices," in *Excellence in Public Relations and Communication Management,* ed. James E. Grunig (Hillsdale, N.J.: Lawrence Erlbaum, 1992), 390.
9. Glen M. Broom, Martha M. Lauzen, and Kerry Tucker, "Public Relations and Marketing: Dividing the Conceptual Domain and Operational Turf," *Public Relations Review* (fall 1991): 224.
10. "The Route to the Consumer," *PR Week,* 17 May 2004, online, www.prweek.com.
11. "Marketing Executives Report Rise in Use of Public Relations Marketing Mix."
12. Dave Barry, "North Dakota Name Change Lacks Direction," *Lawrence Journal-World,* 12 August 2001, 9B.
13. Don E. Schultz, Stanley I. Tannenbaum, and Robert F. Lauterborn, *Integrated Marketing Communications* (Chicago: NTC Business Books, 1993), 22.

14. Betsy Spethmann, "Jerky Match," *Promo,* February 2000, online, LexisNexis.
15. Schultz, Tannenbaum, and Lauterborn, 107.
16. Schultz, Tannenbaum, and Lauterborn, 12–13.
17. Patricia Odell, "Text Messaging Gets a Cautious Reception in the U.S.," *Promo,* May 2003, 25.
18. Al Ries and Laura Ries, "Part 1: The Fall of Advertising," Ries & Ries Focusing Consultants, online, www.ries.com.
19. "The Route to the Consumer."
20. "The Route to the Consumer."
21. John Shattock, "The Fall of Advertising and the Rise of PR," Shattock Communications and Research, online, www.shattock.net.nz.
22. Bob Wheatley, telephone interview by author, 24 March 1994.
23. "The Route to the Consumer."
24. Tom Duncan, "Is Your Marketing Communications Integrated?" *Advertising Age,* 24 January 1994, online, LexisNexis.
25. Matthew P. Gonring, "Putting Integrated Marketing Communications to Work Today," *Public Relations Quarterly* 39, no. 3 (1994), online, LexisNexis.
26. Schultz, Tannenbaum, and Lauterborn, 51.
27. Cliff McGoon, "Secrets of Building Influence," *Communication World,* March 1995, 18.
28. "What Is 'Direct Marketing'?" Direct Marketing Association, online, www.the-dma.org.
29. "The Route to the Consumer."
30. "The Route to the Consumer."
31. Brian W. Kelly, "Becoming Inevitable," *Promo,* April 2004, AR19.
32. "State-of-the-Art in Direct Mail: Getting Ever Closer to the Customer," Knowledge@Wharton, 24 March 2004, online, www.knowledge.wharton.upenn.edu.
33. "Marketing Executives Report Rise in Use of Public Relations Marketing Mix."
34. "Working with Ad Agencies," *PR Week,* 19 July 2004, online, LexisNexis.
35. Sherri Deatherage Green, "PR Leads the Way," *PR Week,* 21 June 2004, online, LexisNexis.
36. "The Route to the Consumer."
37. Stuart L. Esrock and John P. Ferré, "A Dichotomy of Privacy: Personal and Professional Attitudes of Marketers," *Business and Society Review* (spring 1999): 113, 121, 123.
38. U.S. Federal Trade Commission, "You, Your Privacy Policy, and COPPA," U.S. Federal Trade Commission, online, www.ftc.gov.
39. Eve M. Caudill and Patrick E. Murphy, "Consumer Online Privacy: Legal and Ethical Issues," *Marketing and Public Policy* (spring 2000): online, LexisNexis; Ross D. Petty, "Marketing without Consent: Consumer Choice and Costs, Privacy, and Public Policy" (spring 2000): online, LexisNexis; Bodo Schlegelmilch, *Marketing Ethics: An International Perspective* (London: International Thomson Business Press, 1998), 100.
40. Thomas Weyr, "U.S., E.C. Bicker over Free Data Flow," *DM News,* 9 April 2001, online, LexisNexis.
41. Schlegelmilch, 101–102.
42. "State-of-the-Art in Direct Mail: Getting Ever Closer to the Customer."
43. "Enviro Activists Use Ethics to Drive Powerful PR Strategies," *PR News,* 12 March 2001, online, LexisNexis.

44. Jamie Smith, "Put Out the Word: University Sets Branding Example," *Marketing News TM,* 7 May 2001, online, LexisNexis.

45. "Volvo Cars of North America Pioneers World's First Fully Integrated Interactive Television Advertising Promotion," a news release issued by Volvo Cars of North America, 16 March 2001, online, LexisNexis.

46. Sandy Hunter, "Interactive: Some of Those Clever Folks Bent on Dragging Advertising into the 21st Century Speak Out," *Boards,* 1 May 2001, online, LexisNexis.

47. Hunter.

48. "Volvo Continues to Post Record Sales," news release issued by Volvo Cars of North America, 4 September 2001, online, LexisNexis.

49. "Foot in Mouth," *Financial Times,* 24 February 1997, online, LexisNexis.

50. Jonathan Petre, "Protests by Jews Halt the Zyklon Sports Shoe," (London) *Daily Telegraph,* 29 August 2002, online, LexisNexis.

51. Joe Bob Briggs, "Joe Bob's Week in Review," United Press International, 16 January 2003, online, LexisNexis.

52. Graham Hiscott, "Umbro Drops Name after 'Nazi Gas' Blunder," Press Association, 28 August 2002, online, LexisNexis.

53. Hiscott.

54. Victor Lewis-Smith, "Sporting Soles of Indiscretion," (London) *Mirror,* 14 September 2002, online, LexisNexis.

55. "Fury Over Nazi Gas Sports Shoe Name," BBC, 29 August 2002, online, www.news.bbc.co.uk.

56. David Moore, "Fascist Fashion Fad Flops," *Townsville* (Australia) *Sun,* 31 August 2002, online, LexisNexis.

57. Helen Kennedy, "Reebok Exorcises Its Shoes," (New York) *Daily News,* 20 February 1997, online, LexisNexis.

58. Tovah Lazaroff, "Zyklon Beige Sport Shoe Renamed," *Jerusalem Post,* 29 August 2002, online, LexisNexis.

Cross-Cultural Communication

objectives

After studying this chapter, you will be able to

- describe broad areas that historically have distinguished one culture from another

- explain the differences between a culture and a public

- discuss traditional obstacles to successful cross-cultural communication

- describe a nine-step process organizations and individuals can use to achieve effective cross-cultural communication

East Meets West

You are the new senior communications specialist for a multinational producer of breakfast cereals. Your company is based in the United States, and you are eager to begin traveling internationally. You've been to Mexico and Canada but have never been overseas. The director of corporate communications has just

scenario

asked you to launch a magazine for employees in the three countries in which your company operates: the United States, Spain, and Japan.

You quickly learn the names of the company's senior communications officials in Spain and Japan and, with the director's permission, invite them to the United States to help plan the magazine. You know that a lot rides on the success of these meetings. You're new with the company, and you want to impress your employers. Your guests from Spain and Japan report to you, and you don't want them to entertain doubts about their new boss. And you know that the director of corporate communications wants a great magazine that will impress the company's chief executive officer.

As the three-day meeting approaches, you're excited as you review the preparations. You've scheduled a comfortable meeting room, reserved tables in your city's best restaurants, and arranged entertainment for two evenings. You're startled, however, when a colleague asks about cultural differences.

Cultural differences? You will be dealing with individuals from highly developed economies who, in addition to their native languages, speak fluent English. Could there really be important cultural differences? And could those differences affect the success of your magazine project?

That's a risk you must avoid, but what can you do? How do you cope with the challenges of cross-cultural communication?

Cultures: Realities and Definitions

The job seemed easy for the U.S.-based poultry company: It wanted to translate its English-language slogan—"It takes a tough man to make a tender chicken"—into Spanish. But the Spanish rendition may have startled Hispanic consumers: "It takes a sexually aroused man to make a chick affectionate."[1]

Affection was in short supply when media giants America Online and Time Warner merged in 2001, creating what could have been a textbook example of synergy: Time Warner's magazines, music, movies, and TV shows delivered to homes through AOL's computer access. Instead, in the words of the *Los Angeles Times,* the merger produced "a paralyzing culture clash."[2] London's *Guardian* newspaper called it "a bloody culture clash" and concluded "the biggest merger in media history turned out to be a nightmare."[3] Analysts believed that AOL's arrogance clashed with Time Warner's sense of superiority—a conflict that turned ugly when, in a high-level staff meeting, an AOL executive coldly ordered a Time Warner executive "to fetch some more documents."[4] Stockholders lost more than $173 billion as the company's share price tumbled from approximately $50 to less than $20.[5]

Promoters of a Seattle-area rave—a huge, uninhibited dance party—unintentionally offended Muslims when they lifted Arabic passages from the Koran, the holy book of Islam, to decorate a brochure. Devout Muslims honor the Koran so much that they wash their hands and mouths three times before touching and reading from the book.

"This is a disgrace to Islam," said a spokesman for a Seattle mosque. "The activities in raves are totally immoral."

The brochure's designer apologized and confessed that he found the passages in a school textbook. "We had no idea what any of it meant," he said. "It looked good on [the brochure]. It is a beautiful language. And we had a desert and a camel in there. It was a theme."[6]

The theme of these three anecdotes is cross-cultural communication. Each of these damaging mishaps occurred when different cultures intentionally or unintentionally met. In each case, important values were at issue. Those values grew, in part, out of **demographics** (nonattitudinal characteristics), **psychographics** (attitudinal characteristics), and **geodemographics** (characteristics based on where a person or group lives). But the values grew from more than these three "-graphics." The values shaped and were shaped by unique cultures.

The term **culture,** in the sense of a group of people unified by shared characteristics, defies precise definition. "It seems obvious from the use of the word in our everyday language that it is impregnated with multiple meanings," says Anindita Niyogi Balslev of the Center for Cultural Research in the Netherlands.[7] In fact, as early as 1952 scholars had identified more than 150 definitions of *culture.*[8] The *Dictionary of Anthropology* defines a culture as "a social group that is smaller than a civilization but larger than an industry,"[9] with *industry* being an anthropological term for a small community. A culture, therefore, is usually larger than a public. In fact, a culture may consist of countless different publics, all of which are influenced by the traits of that culture.

Why study cross-cultural communication? "Now, more than ever before in human history, more people are coming into contact with people from cultures other than their own," says Robert Gibson, author of *Intercultural Business Communication.* Gibson cites several reasons for the growth of cross-cultural contacts, including improved travel methods, the Internet, and increasingly diverse workforces.[10] To that list, we might add the increasing number of mergers and acquisitions in the business world, the growth of democratic governments around the world, and the consequent increase in international trade. Many of these forces help fuel **globalization,** the growing economic interdependence of the world's people.

Communication errors such as those of the poultry company, AOL and Time Warner, and the Seattle rave occur because, in the words of Stephen Banks, author of *Multicultural Public Relations,* "scant attention is paid in research or practice to the predicaments of culturally diverse populations and the necessity for learning to communicate effectively across cultural differences."[11] In 2001, a representative of the National Association of Corporate Directors recommended that, to negotiate successfully with diverse cultures throughout the world, each U.S. business should create an Office of Foreign Affairs to study trends, politics, moods, and opinions in regions where the business wishes to operate.[12] The authors of this book respectfully suggest that such an office should already exist: the organization's public relations department.

International Public Relations

Not all cross-cultural communication involves relationships between two nations. For example, the union of AOL and Time Warner involved the awkward merger of two business cultures. And the wealth of ethnic groups within the United States, Canada, and other nations can make cross-cultural communication an everyday experience. In the current global economy, however, when public relations practitioners study unfamiliar cultures, they often are studying consumers and business partners in other nations. "Cultural diversity and identity," says the author of *Multicultural Public Relations,* "tend strongly to conform to national borders."[13] For example, a recent survey of European tourists found that 25 percent of visitors to Italy went there hoping for a love affair with an Italian male. Only Italy's natural beauty scored higher; the lovers outscored museums and other attractions. Right or wrong, a large percentage of European tourists believe that romance and passion are cultural characteristics of Italian males.[14]

Musician Randy Newman has a satirical song that envisions the world becoming "just another American town"—a humorously offbeat premise for a song but a disastrous notion for international public relations. If the world were a town, it would be stunningly diverse—not at all a representation of a culture familiar to most students. A popular children's book, *If the World Were a Village,* shows that if Earth were a village of 100 people, current demographic ratios would make the village look like this:[15]

- 24 residents would have no electricity; most of the others would use it only at night to light their homes.
- 22 would speak Chinese; 9 would speak English; 7 would speak Spanish.
- 20 would earn less than a dollar a day.
- 17 would not be able to read or write.
- 10 would be younger than 5 years old; 39 would be younger than age 19; 1 would be older than age 79.
- 7 would own a computer.

Successful international public relations recognizes such diversity and attempts to create harmonious, productive relationships through well-researched cross-cultural communication.

Cultural Attributes

Without a research strategy, studying a different culture can seem impossible. Where do we start? What information should we gather? Fortunately, social scientists and business experts have created systems for categorizing important cultural attributes. One of the best-known systems was created by marketing professional Marlene Rossman.[16] Rossman's system distinguishes among cultures by analyzing attitudes regarding eight characteristics. Let's examine each to see how it can differ from culture to culture.

Attitudes about Time

Different cultures have different attitudes about time. In some Latin American nations, a dinner party scheduled for 8 P.M. may not really begin until near midnight. In other cultures, arriving later than 8 P.M. would insult your hosts. In some cultures, a designated time is a flexible guideline; in others, it is a specific target. On a working vacation in Zurich, Switzerland, one of your authors was warned by Swiss colleagues to avoid the center of the city on a particular Thursday afternoon; college students would be holding a spontaneous demonstration at that time, he was told. A scheduled spontaneous demonstration: something to be expected from a nation famed for making clocks and other timepieces.

In a study of national attitudes toward time, *American Demographics* magazine reported that, of 31 nations studied, Switzerland ranked first in terms of a rapid, time-oriented pace of life. The United States ranked in the middle at number 16, and Mexico ranked last. In general, Japan and Western European countries had the fastest pace of life. Developing nations in Africa, Asia, the Middle East, and Latin America had the slowest, most flexible pace.[17]

In our East Meets West scenario, differing attitudes toward time could affect the success of your meetings. Like North Americans, Japanese tend to be punctual about business meetings. If a meeting is scheduled for 9 A.M., businesspeople in Japan and the United States generally are ready to sit at the table and begin at that hour. In Spain, however, businesspeople are more casual about specified starting times. Roger Axtell, author of *Do's and Taboos around the World,* says that in Spain "the only time punctuality is taken seriously is when attending a bullfight."[18] Is that wrong? No: It's just different.

And how about early-afternoon meetings? No problem for your Japanese guest, but will your Spanish guest expect a traditional siesta at that time? In Spain and several other nations in Europe and Latin America, businesses often close from lunch until late afternoon.

Attitudes about Formality

Should you address a new business associate from another nation by his or her first name? Should you hug? Bow? Shake hands? The answers depend, of course, on cultural preferences. As a rule, however, formality is safer than informality in new business relationships.

Syrians often embrace new acquaintances. Pakistanis shake hands, though never a man with a woman. Zambians shake hands with the left hand supporting the right. Norwegians rarely use first names until relationships are well established. Japanese almost never use first names in business settings.

What do cross-cultural experts say about the visitors you're expecting for your magazine-planning meeting? A warm handshake and even an accompanying pat on the back would be acceptable as you greet your Spanish visitor. The Spanish make no distinction about shaking hands with men or women. With your Japanese guest,

A Quieter Quack When AFLAC, a leading international insurance company, recently cast its famous duck in Japanese TV commercials, the company introduced a kinder, gentler quack. Japanese culture frowns on yelling, an AFLAC representative explained. (Courtesy of American Family Life Assurance Company—AFLAC)

however, be prepared to bow, even though he or she may offer to shake hands. You can flatter your Japanese guest by bowing first. In Japan, the person who initiates a bow is acknowledging the high social status of the other person. If you exchange business cards with your Japanese visitor, bow slightly and extend yours with both hands. You should accept your visitor's card in the same manner and should look at it respectfully after receiving it.[19]

Attitudes about Individualism

People in the United States pride themselves on the rugged individualism that turned a diverse group of immigrants into a powerful nation of highly mobile individuals. It's comparatively rare in our society to live one's life in the town of one's birth surrounded by family. Other cultures, however, especially those of Asian and Hispanic origin, often place more emphasis on preserving extended families. Chinese names, for example, place the family name before the individual name.

Japanese businesspeople in particular see themselves as part of a team; in fact, only 8 percent of Japanese adults say they respect entrepreneurs.[20] An individual may speak on behalf of an organization, but not until he or she has painstakingly built consensus on the issue under discussion. The Japanese call the consensus-building process *nemawashi*; it precedes virtually all important organizational decisions. "As a result," says Sanae Kobayashi, an executive with LBS Company in Tokyo, "decision making in Japanese organizations usually takes more time than it does in the West. However, as compensation, in Japan the execution is made with more speed and completeness."[21]

Because of the importance of *nemawashi* throughout their culture, the Japanese are reluctant to say no. In your magazine-planning meeting, for example, it would be

unusual for your Japanese guest to veto a particular proposal. Instead, he or she might meet the idea with thoughtful silence and a polite "If only . . ."

Attitudes about Rank and Hierarchy

In cultural terms, rank and hierarchy extend beyond organizations: They exist within society itself. India, for example, still struggles to overthrow a traditional caste system of Brahmans—often Hindu priests—at the top and so-called untouchables at the bottom. Knowing the social status of a business associate and understanding the consequent signs of respect he or she expects can be essential to successful cross-cultural communications. For example, your Spanish guest would be honored to be seated at your right during meals—a sign of respect in Spain. And when you initiate a bowing sequence with your Japanese guest, you courteously suggest that he or she outranks you.[22]

Attitudes about Religion

Knowing the religious conventions and traditions of a culture can help prevent unintended errors that can hamper cross-cultural communication. For example, Muslims fast from dawn to sunset during the holy month of Ramadan. Inviting an Islamic business associate to a working lunch during that time could inadvertently suggest a lack of respect for his or her religious beliefs. The Jewish Sabbath extends from Friday evening to Saturday evening and, in Judaism, is a day of rest. Scheduling a Friday evening business dinner in Israel, where Judaism is the dominant religion, could be a serious cultural faux pas.

In the tense days after the terrorist attacks of September 11, 2001, President George W. Bush referred the upcoming U.S. response as "this crusade, this war on terror."[23] Americans might have viewed the comment as reassuring—but in the Middle East, many Muslims viewed it differently. "You can't say *crusade* if you want the Muslim world on your side," explained ABC News reporter John Donovan.[24] Muslims in the Middle East consider the Crusades of the Middle Ages a time of religious oppression when Christians and Muslims battled over territory sacred to both religions. Bush showed a greater awareness of Islam when he invited leaders of that religion to the White House for a dinner marking the end of Ramadan.[25]

Attitudes about Taste and Diet

For many public relations practitioners, cuisine is the reward for mastering the subtleties of cross-cultural communication. Perhaps it's arroz con pollo (chicken with

QuickBreak 14.1

THE MELTING-POT MYTH

Much of this chapter focuses on cultures beyond the borders of the United States. Can we assume, then, that the United States is a uniform hot-dogs-and-apple-pie culture? Hardly.

In *America's Diversity,* a study of 200 years of U.S. Census data, the Population Research Bureau reported, "Residential separation of the races continues to be so pronounced that sociologists Douglas Massey and Nancy Denton have called it 'American Apartheid.'"[26] (Apartheid is the former South African policy of enforced separation of races.) A national survey of U.S. citizens indicates that *apartheid* may be too strong a word for some: 38 percent want a more uniform culture; 31 percent want cultural differences to remain; and 29 percent lack strong opinions on the matter.[27]

But can culture and race really be linked? Studies show that race can indeed be an indicator of a unique culture. A recent survey of racial and ethnic groups within the United States, for example, concluded that blacks, Asians, Hispanics, and non-Hispanic whites (a U.S. Census Bureau designation) spend their time in different ways. Asians spend more time each week on education than do blacks, Hispanics, or whites. Blacks devote more time to religion each week than do the other racial and ethnic groups. Hispanics spend more time caring for their children than do the other groups. Whites spend more time at work than Asians, blacks, or Hispanics.[28]

"The trend in every aspect of American life is toward greater cultural, ethnic, and linguistic diversity," says marketing expert Marlene Rossman. "Not only are minority groups increasing in size, they are also not assimilating the way many minority and ethnic (especially immigrant) groups did in the past. . . . Our cultural model is becoming the mosaic, not the melting pot."[29]

rice) in Costa Rica or couscous in Algeria or bratwurst in Germany or grits in the southern United States. The culinary diversity of the world's cultures is dazzling and gratifying—but also rife with opportunities for serious blunders. Religion and other cultural influences often prohibit the consumption of certain foods. Hindus don't eat beef; cattle are exalted in that religion, which encompasses the belief that souls return to earth again and again as different life forms. Strict Judaism forbids the consumption of pork products and shellfish, which are considered unclean.

Attitudes about Colors, Numbers, and Symbols

What's the unlucky number in mainstream U.S. culture? Thirteen, of course. How about in Japanese culture? It's four. One of your authors learned that the hard way when he titled an article for a multinational corporate magazine "Four from Japan." Every culture develops an unofficial language of colors, numbers, and symbols that often speaks louder than words. For example, the logo of the HSBC Group, one of the world's largest financial institutions, is a red hexagon. HSBC began in Hong Kong and Shanghai, where red is considered a lucky color. But when HSBC expanded to the Middle East, it learned that red was a symbol of conflict. In that region of the world, HSBC chose to use its secondary colors, black and gray.[30]

Symbols can be just as fraught with meaning as colors and numbers. For example, most of us interpret the thumbs-up symbol used for case studies in this book as a sign of approval. In Australia and Nigeria, however, the symbol and the gesture mean anything but approval. In those societies, the upward thumb is an obscene sign of disrespect.[31]

Attitudes about Assimilation and Acculturation

How quickly can members of one culture adjust to the traditions of another? How accepting are people of new ideas and nontraditional thinking? Such flexibility can help characterize a culture. The more a culture resists outside influences, the more powerful its own traditions can become. The French Academy, for example, which is the legal watchdog of the French language as it's spoken in France, has officially banned English terms such as *hot dog* and *drugstore*. Russian President Vladimir Putin has begun a similar anti-English campaign, instituting fines and even imprisonment for Russians who used English derivatives such as *biznismeni* for *businessmen*.[32] More tolerant is the attitude of former South African President Nelson Mandela, who drew cheers from young adults attending an R.E.M. concert in London by declaring, "I am now almost 100 years old, but I am so proud because my roots are in South Africa but my gaze reaches beyond the horizon to places like Britain where we are tied together by unbreakable bonds."[33]

Sometimes assimilation and acculturation occur so gradually that the process escapes our notice. More than one observer, for example, has noted that U.S. dominance of the technology and content of the Internet is subtly piping U.S. influences into offices and homes around the world. Says Andre Kaspi, a professor at the Sorbonne in Paris, "You have to know English if you want to use the Internet. . . . The main difference now in favor of American culture is the importance of technology—telephone, Internet, films. . . . American influence is growing. It's so easy to get access to U.S. culture; there are no barriers."[34]

No doubt true. But any public relations practitioner who assumes that the world has become one big U.S.-based culture runs the risk of studying a different phenomenon: the culture of the unemployment line.

To Rossman's list of eight characteristics, we might add one more: attitudes about business communication. For example, although executives in the United States and Canada frequently use voice mail and e-mail, executives in European nations generally prefer "real-time," simultaneous communications; thus the use of cell phones in Europe exceeds usage in United States and Canada. Executives in France and Germany, however, prefer paper-based communications to other forms; their use of postal services and fax machines exceeds usage rates in other nations.[35] Part of successful cross-cultural communication involves learning how members of other cultures prefer to receive their business messages.

1. What is the purpose of the analytical system created by Marlene Rossman?
2. Would it be fair to say that the United States is all one culture? Why or why not?
3. What is the difference between a culture and a public?

Cross-Cultural Communication: Definitions and Dangers

Clearly, this chapter uses the term *cross-cultural communication* to refer to exchanges of messages among the members of different cultures. But it's worth stopping to ask what, exactly, is meant by **cross-cultural.** Many sociologists and communication specialists use the term *intercultural* to denote exchanges of various kinds between cultures. Your authors, like many public relations practitioners, prefer the term *cross-cultural* because it prompts an image of crossing a border, of going into partially unknown territory. *Cross-cultural* urges caution and encourages you to stay constantly aware of the obstacles to successful communication between members of different cultures.

And what do we mean by **communication?** We mean more than words can say. In Chapter 13, for example, we noted that every aspect of a product sends a message to consumers. Besides the verbal messages of news releases and advertisements, a product's price, packaging, and distribution all send nonverbal messages to potential purchasers. Consumers in West African communities were horrified when one U.S. company tried to sell its popular brand of baby food in their stores. The labels featured a smiling baby—very popular in the United States, but intensely disturbing in a culture that relies on pictures to identify the contents of jars and cans.[36] Briefly, by *communication,* we mean any exchange of information—verbal and/or nonverbal—between the sender and the receiver of a message.

Encoding and Decoding

In Chapter 5 we examined a basic **communication model,** which, as you'll recall, looks like this:

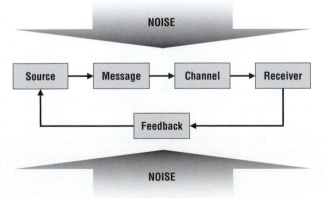

More complex versions of this basic model include two elements that become particularly important in communication between cultures: encoding and decoding. **Encoding** involves the sender's selection of words, images, and other forms of communication that create the message. **Decoding** involves the receiver's attempt to produce meaning from the sender's message. With those additional elements, the communication model looks like this:

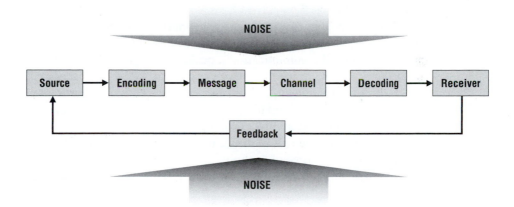

In successful cross-cultural communication, senders must understand how a message will be decoded before they can effectively encode it. The perils of encoding errors are illustrated by yet another U.S. company's adventures abroad. When the Coca-Cola Company translated its name into Chinese, the phonetic version—KeKou Kela—instructed Chinese consumers to "Bite the wax tadpole."[37] It's hard to guess who was most surprised by that particular cross-cultural encoding–decoding glitch.

Even though an organization's message may need different encodings for different cultures, the message should ideally remain shaped by the values that unite the organization. A successful organization cannot embrace one set of values with the elderly in South Africa, a different set of values with women in China, a third set of values with Russian immigrants in Australia, and so on. Such duplicity would be more than dishonest; maintaining so many different personalities would be exhausting. In successful organizations, all messages emanate from a set of clearly understood core values, as well as from the business goals that grow out of those values. Says Jean-Louis Tronc, director of human resources and corporate communications for DuPont de Nemours of France, "There are a certain number of global values within a company which must remain the same everywhere."[38] As we note many times throughout this book, successful public relations is a values-driven process.

Gestures and Clothing

Our broad definition of communication also applies to interpersonal communication. Our gestures, clothing, and expressions can be every bit as communicative as our words. In Taiwan, blinking at someone is considered an insult. In the Islamic faith, shoes are absolutely forbidden on the grounds of mosques. In many Asian cultures, shoes are removed and left at the front doors of residences. The A-OK expression made by forming a circle of the thumb and forefinger and raising the other three fingers is, like thumbs-up, a sign of approval in the United States. But in Japan it's a symbol for money. In Australia and some Latin American nations, it's an obscene gesture. During a 1950s visit to a Latin American country, Vice President Richard Nixon grandly made the A-OK gesture—and was stunned by an immediate chorus of boos.[39]

Because people from almost every culture use their hands when they speak, gestures—more so than clothing or expressions—can send unintended messages during cross-cultural communication. Speaking to a group of journalists in the Central Asian nation of Kyrgyzstan, one of your authors illustrated a point by bringing one fist down on top of the other two or three times. Halting in midsentence, his shocked interpreter leaned over and hissed in his ear that he was signaling, in the crudest possible way, that he wanted to make love to his audience. Fortunately, your author's stricken expression led his audience to forgive him with friendly laughter. That story has two morals: Cross-cultural mistakes can be very embarrassing—and people can be very forgiving if they sense your good will.

Stereotyping

Another sure ticket to failure in cross-cultural communication is **stereotyping:** the assumption that all members of a particular culture act, think, feel, and believe in the same way. Are all Hispanics family-oriented? Are all Swiss punctual? Are all Japanese polite? Are all U.S. citizens blunt? Do all teenagers like loud music? Do all baby boomers like the Beatles? Cultures *do* exist, but they consist of individuals, none of whom are exactly alike. "After all," says Harvard Professor H. L. Gates Jr., "culture is always a conversation among different voices."[40]

Finally, public relations practitioners should be prepared for the distinct possibility that their colleagues from different cultures *also* are studying cross-cultural communication. Your Japanese guest, for example, may insist on shaking hands rather than bowing. Your Spanish guest may ask for an early-afternoon meeting to show his or her willingness to adapt to your culture. So who prevails in such complicated situations? Often, it's easiest to follow the culture of the host, but the host still should seek opportunities to honor the cultures of his or her guests. An abundance of courtesy is a good beginning for cross-cultural communication.

Cross-cultural communication has become an unavoidable challenge for the public relations profession. One recent study shows that two-thirds of international business mergers fail because "cultures and people are often incompatible, national differences emerging."[41] Says Elizabeth Howard, principal partner of an international consulting firm, "Today it is difficult, probably impossible, to find a business that has not been affected in one way or another by the new global economy." Indeed, it's not unusual for farmers from the midwestern United States to find themselves part of trade delegations in Asia or Latin America, seeking new markets for

U.S. agricultural products. And those farmers, like others engaged in cross-cultural business discussions, constantly confront the question posed by sociologist and anthropologist David Howes: "What happens when the culture of production and the culture of consumption are not the same?"[42]

These cultural gulfs must be bridged if the producers and the consumers are to achieve their goals. In the next section we offer a nine-step process that can help organizations and individuals achieve successful cross-cultural communication.

Quick ✔ Check

1. What do *encoding* and *decoding* mean?
2. Should an organization's core values change as it communicates with different cultures?
3. What does *stereotyping* mean? How can it threaten successful cross-cultural communication?

Achieving Successful Cross-Cultural Public Relations: A Process

At this point in our chapter, two facts are clear: Cross-cultural communication can be difficult—and it is inevitable. Painstaking encoding and decoding of cross-cultural messages have become everyday challenges. Given that reality, how can public relations practitioners in the 21st century become effective cross-cultural communicators? We recommend a process consisting of nine stages: awareness, commitment, research, local partnership, diversity, testing, evaluation, advocacy, and continuing education. We begin with awareness. If public relations practitioners aren't sensitive to the presence or potential difficulties of a cross-cultural encounter, they have little hope of communicating effectively.

Stage One: Awareness

You can start enhancing your awareness of cross-cultural situations right now—by studying a foreign language and enrolling in liberal arts courses that allow you to explore the traits and traditions of other cultures. If your college or university has an international students association, consider joining it. If it has a study abroad program, plan to spend a semester in another country. Higher education offers you rare opportunities to discover that the rest of the world doesn't think, act, dress, eat, and communicate as you do.

Achieving fluency in a foreign language can keep you from being the butt of an old joke that remains all too current. As the joke goes, someone who speaks

QuickBreak 14.2

DIVERSITY IN PUBLIC RELATIONS

"To be more effective in our increasingly socially complex society," says Reed Byrum, former president of the Public Relations Society of America, "achieving diversity is more than just a matter of inclusiveness. The public relations profession needs to vigorously recruit minorities into the profession and into leadership positions."[43]

So is public relations an ethnically, culturally diverse profession? In a word, no.

Sensitivity regarding this shortcoming led to a tense exchange of viewpoints at a recent forum sponsored by *PR Week* magazine.

"What's your percentage?" asked a public relations practitioner of another, who had praised his agency's commitment to diversity. "One in two? One in five? One in 10? I don't think so."

"My point is a simple one," the other practitioner responded. "I do think we're trying."

"Trying versus committed to me are two different things," said the frustrated first speaker.[44]

Diversity figures for the public relations profession are notoriously difficult to establish. Rough estimates offer this assessment: African Americans constitute fewer than 5 percent of public relations professionals, Hispanic Americans fewer than 3 percent, and Asian Americans fewer than 2 percent.[45] The U.S. Bureau of Labor Statistics offers a slightly more optimistic view of a wider field, "advertising and related professions": The bureau reports that 9 percent of practitioners are Hispanic and 6 percent are African American.[46] None of these totals reflect the diversity of the U.S. population: 13 percent Hispanic, 12 percent African American, and 4 percent Asian American.[47]

A 2003 survey by the Public Relations Society of America indicates that government agencies, corporations, and associations fare better in attracting minority practitioners than do agencies.[48] The PRSA survey also found that only 16 percent of practitioners believed that most organizations offer special programs to develop and retain the minority-group employees they currently have.[49]

The diversity outlook in public relations does contain some bright spots, however. PRSA's National Diversity Committee annually identifies and rewards that organization's most diverse local chapters.[50] And in 2004, the Hill & Knowlton public relations agency launched Growth through Recruitment and Diversity (GRAD), a program of college visits, internships, and mentoring.

Ellen Shedlarz of Hill & Knowlton notes that promoting diversity within public relations is more than just the right thing to do: It's good for business. "Our client base is very diverse," she explains. "If we don't have the same diversity in our employee base, we won't connect as strongly."[51]

three languages is trilingual; someone who speaks two languages is bilingual; someone who speaks one language is a U.S. citizen. English indeed has become the language of international commerce, but learning to speak the language of a foreign business acquaintance—even if you master only a few key phrases—may heighten your sensitivity to cross-cultural issues. More important, perhaps, learning a second language can improve the success of your cross-cultural communication by creating good will. On business in Paris, one of your authors was able to persuade a new acquaintance to work late by using his shaky knowledge of French, gained in college. When the Parisian apologized, in English, for missing a deadline, your author was able to respond *C'est la même chose pour tout le monde, n'est-ce pas?*—roughly, "It happens everywhere, doesn't it?" The Parisian was surprised that an American could speak even bad French. The conversation sputtered along in French until the amused Parisian switched back to English and agreed to stay late to finish the project.

Organizations throughout the United States are imitating the college experience by sponsoring courses in multiculturalism and cross-cultural communication. Burson-Marsteller and Hill & Knowlton, two of the largest public relations agencies in the world, routinely organize multiday courses to sensitize executives to cross-cultural realities and possibilities. Such sessions include problem-solving exercises, case studies, role playing, and other techniques that immerse participants in cross-cultural communication situations.[52]

Another powerful way to increase sensitivity is to diversify the workplace, bringing multiculturalism and cross-cultural communication into the everyday business of the office. This strategy will be discussed in greater detail below.

Stage Two: Commitment

Reporters have a technique called "parachute journalism"—dropping into a locality the reporter doesn't know well to write a quick story about that same little-known locality. Journalists aren't proud of parachute journalism. Nor should public relations practitioners be proud of using a similar strategy in their profession: parachuting, so to speak, into a little-known culture to do some hit-and-run relationship building. Successful cross-cultural communication requires personal commitment, as well as commitment from an organization's highest levels, to doing the arduous background work that allows the effective encoding and decoding of messages to and from another culture.

Stage Three: Research

Commitment implies a willingness to do the research demanded by successful cross-cultural communication. Standard reference sources for this research include magazines such as *Communication World* and *American Demographics* online; books such as Roger Axtell's *Do's and Taboos around the World* and *Gestures: The Do's and Taboos of Body Language around the World*; and online resources such as the web site sponsored by the International Trade Administration, a division of the U.S. Department of Commerce. The ITA web site includes information on business etiquette in almost every nation around the world. Hosting a meeting for colleagues from Botswana? Confirm your meeting 24 hours ahead of time, and don't be offended if your guests arrive late. Don't call them by their first names until they initiate that practice, and don't schedule the meeting for September 30: That's Botswana Day. Need more information? See the ITA web site at www.ita.doc.gov.

QuickBreak 14.3

WHAT'S YOUR CL RATING?

We could be talking about crude language here—or Courtney Love. But we're not.

Research by a consortium of international business communicators has identified six stages of cultural learning—CL, for short:[53]

1. The *Local Expert* stage, characterized by *ignorance* and a "people are really all alike" attitude toward cross-cultural communication.

2. The *Tourist* stage, characterized by *realization* and a "they are different from us" attitude toward cross-cultural communication.

3. The *Curious Sojourner* stage, characterized by *understanding* and an "I'm studying the differences" attitude toward cross-cultural communication.

4. The *Bicultural Expert* stage, characterized by *synthesis* and an "I'm finding some good combinations" attitude toward cross-cultural communication.

5. The *Integrator* stage, characterized by *selection* and a research-based "I know what will work" attitude toward cross-cultural communication.

6. The *Leader* stage, characterized by *deftness* and a "making it happen" attitude toward cross-cultural communication.

You don't need complex logic (yet another CL) to know that successful public relations practitioners score closer to CL6 than to CL1.

As you encounter examples of cross-cultural communication throughout this chapter, can you assign CL ratings for the primary communicators?

And—can't lie—what is your CL rating?

Believe it or not, the Central Intelligence Agency also makes available some of its highly detailed data on different nations around the world. Check out the CIA's *World Factbook* at www.cia.gov/cia/publications/factbook.

A good reference librarian can steer you to other current sources. Such research might help you remember to take off your shoes when you enter the hotel room of your Japanese guest in our East Meets West scenario.

Stage Four: Local Partnership

No matter how much research you conduct, you'll never know as much about a foreign culture as does someone reared in it. When an organization begins a long-term cross-cultural relationship, it should consider bringing a member of that culture onto its communications team. "You must have representation on the ground in different parts of the world, but you should be extremely cautious about hiring a major global PR agency," says Robert Wakefield, former chairman of the International Section of the Public Relations Society of America. "Instead, tap into the worldwide network of small local agencies or talented native PR consultants who can guide you through the maze of PR issues in their own country."[54]

Stage Five: Diversity

Not all different cultures are beyond the borders of the United States. As Quick-Break 14.1 notes, the United States is hardly a melting pot; instead, it's a mosaic of different cultures. Diversity within an organization's public relations team can help ensure successful cross-cultural communication at home. Furthermore, it can increase an organization's awareness of cultural differences, which benefits communication both at home and abroad. Pitney Bowes, a multinational company examined in Case Study 14.1, believes that a diverse workforce boosts company profits.

Stage Six: Testing

As every actor knows, it's better to bomb in rehearsal than on opening night. When possible, test your relationship-building tactics on trusted members of the culture you plan to address. For example, in this chapter's East Meets West scenario, you could show a detailed itinerary of your business and entertainment plans to natives of Japan and Spain. You just might learn, for example, that Spanish business dinners don't begin until late evening—often past 9 P.M.—and that Japanese business dinners can go on for hours and often end in nightclubs.[55]

Stage Seven: Evaluation

A constant goal in public relations is to learn from our successes as well as from our mistakes. As soon as possible, public relations professionals should evaluate the effectiveness of completed cross-cultural communication efforts, seeking ways to reinforce the good and revise the bad. In the East Meets West scenario, for example, did your Japanese guest wince when you offered her a gift as you met her at the airport? Your consequent research might show that although the Japanese enjoy receiving gifts, they often are embarrassed if they cannot reciprocate immediately.[56] The gift may have been a blunder, but it was a valuable misstep: It taught you to be sensitive to the intricacies of offering a gift to a member of another culture.

Stage Eight: Advocacy

Cross-cultural communication works best when an entire organization commits to it. Commitment requires a persistent focus, and a persistent focus requires an advocate. Perhaps that advocate can be you. Says international communication consultant Mary Jo Jacobi:

> No matter where a multinational company operates, it must remain conscious of the fact that it has audiences in many other parts of the world and that whatever its executives do and say locally could have far-reaching ramifications and business implications. As a result, we must seek to ensure that we communicate a consistent message worldwide, particularly on sensitive matters. Getting this clearly in the minds

PARA PUBLICACIÓN INMEDIATA

<u>**PARA MÁS INFORMACIÓN:**</u>
Mirna Aceituno, McDonald's
(630) 623-6432

Michael Delgado, VPE Public Relations
(626) 403-3200, Ext 217

LOS NUEVOS Y CALIENTITOS SÁNDWICHES DE DESAYUNO McGRIDDLES® DE McDONALD'S® SON VERDADERAMENTE INGENIOSOS

Los Clientes Ahora Tienen Una Manera Conveniente de Disfrutar Sus Sabores de Desayuno Favoritos

OAK BROOK, Ill.—(9 de junio de 2003) — Pregunta: ¿Qué es ingenioso, innovador y delicioso? Respuesta: ¡Los nuevos sándwiches de desayuno McGriddles de McDonald's! Una nueva comida agregada en forma permanente al menú, los sándwiches de desayuno McGriddles proporcionan una manera ingeniosa para que los clientes disfruten de hotcakes dorados (horneados con el dulce sabor de miel) y diversas combinaciones de salchicha, tocino crujiente, huevos y queso derretido en un conveniente sándwich. A partir del 10 de junio de 2003, los clientes de McDonald's de todo el país podrán disfrutar de estas creaciones únicas en los restaurantes McDonald's participantes.

Las tres variedades de estos sándwiches de desayuno nuevos y calientitos consisten en dos hotcakes tiernos y dorados, horneados con el delicioso sabor de miel, y la opción de salchicha; salchicha, huevo y queso o tocino, huevo y queso. Los sándwiches de desayuno McGriddles de salchicha están disponibles a un precio sugerido al público de $1.59 y las otras dos sabrosas variedades están disponibles a un precio sugerido de $2.19 (los precios y la participación pueden variar).

"Estos nuevos sándwiches de desayuno son de verdad únicos en la categoría de desayuno", dijo Max Gallegos, director de marketing, McDonald's EE.UU. "Ningún otro restaurante los ofrece y en los restaurantes de todo el país donde se realizaron pruebas piloto, los McGriddles han deleitado a nuestros clientes con su combinación única de deliciosos sabores. Esta es otra manera en que McDonald's responde a los gustos del consumidor, proporcionando una novedosa opción de desayuno".

News Release The growing power of Hispanic markets in the United States has led progressive companies such as McDonald's Corporation to issue news releases in Spanish. For an English-language version of this news release, see page 294. (Courtesy of Valencia, Pérez & Echeveste Public Relations)

QuickBreak 14.4

DOUBLE-WHAMMY CULTURE CLASH

Merging two company cultures into one new business can be tough. But when those two companies come from different nations, the merger faces a cultural double-whammy. A classic corporate culture clash occurred when German car manufacturer Daimler-Benz bought U.S.-based Chrysler Corporation in 1998.

"These two cultures . . . were bound to collide," said a former U.S. auto executive.[57]

"Problems are caused when an acquirer's corporate culture fails to mesh with that of its new subsidiary," wrote a British business analyst. "That's the biggest single risk in all cross-border acquisitions."[58]

Still, optimism abounded when the two companies joined forces. "The merger of Daimler and Chrysler was hailed as a marriage made in heaven," reported a British financial analyst. "But the honeymoon was shortlived."[59] Within three years, the new DaimlerChrysler was worth only half its initial value, key Chrysler executives had resigned, and the new company was preparing to close six Chrysler factories.[60] Observers inside and outside the company knew what to blame: clashing cultures.

"[Germans] can't understand this cultural mentality that is forever focusing on the bottom line and quarterly results," said an industry consultant.[61]

"German workforces expect to be consulted at all stages of any strategic deal, while at Chrysler the unions aim to beat down the management and vice versa," said another.[62]

"In the case of DaimlerChrysler, there was a total clash of cultures," said a British business professor.[63]

All sides should have listened to an investment banker who had worked with both companies before the merger. "It could take them at least a year to learn each other's true character and identity," the banker warned. "That's why these transatlantic mergers are always trickier than they look on paper."[64]

of colleagues is one of the most important roles that we, as professional communicators, must undertake.[65]

Stage Nine: Continuing Education

The cross-cultural seminars at Burson-Marsteller and Hill & Knowlton are examples of continuing education, as are exchanges of executives between local branches of multinational companies. Other forms of continuing education can be as simple as reading international publications, watching international television programming, attending lectures, or—gasp!—returning to a university for an occasional night course on a foreign language or an unfamiliar culture. Fortunately, learning doesn't stop at graduation. It's a big, exciting world out there, burgeoning with opportunities for anyone who can cross its boundaries with knowledge, diplomacy, and confidence.

ТОРГОВЛЯ С АМЕРИКОЙ

СПРАВОЧНИК ПО ПРОГРАММАМ ПРАВИТЕЛЬСТВА США

Публикация BISNIS -
Службы деловой информации о странах Содружества независимых государств
Министерства торговли США

Business Guide An indication of the increasing importance of cross-cultural communication is this U.S. Department of Commerce Russian-language publication, *Doing Business in America*.

Quick ✓ Check

1. In the nine-step process for successful cross-cultural public relations, what does local partnership mean? Why is it necessary?
2. What sources could you consult for information on the cultures of other countries?
3. Specifically, how does cross-cultural communication mean more than international communication?

Summary

As we noted in Chapter 11, a generation ago Canadian philosopher Marshall McLuhan argued that the world was becoming a "global village." In many ways, he was right. Modern technology can make communication between Kenya and China faster and easier than the task faced by a 19th-century Toronto resident who simply wanted to deliver a message across town. Yet the global village is hardly a community in the traditional sense. Every street has its own customs, biases, traditions, fears, religion, diet, and language. Every street, in other words, has its own culture.

If the global village is to thrive, those streets need to learn to communicate with one another. The conversations won't be easy. We need only to read a daily newspaper to see that the conversations often fail. We can increase the chances of success, however, by learning a process for effective cross-cultural communication—a nine-step process that begins with awareness and includes commitment, research, local partnership, diversity, testing, evaluation, advocacy, and continuing education. That process needs well-educated, talented, versatile communicators. In fact, the process of cross-cultural public relations needs you.

Cross-cultural communication is so essential to the present and future of public relations that we're not yet ready to put the subject aside. We will return to it in Chapter 16, in which we'll examine predictions for the increasing diversity of publics around the world.

DISCUSSION QUESTIONS

1. Besides the gaffes mentioned in this chapter, what cross-cultural communication errors have you heard of? Have any happened to you?
2. What is a culture? What other definitions besides those offered in this chapter can you find? How do *you* define a culture?
3. How might you respond to a colleague who makes the following statement: "You're wasting your time with that cross-cultural stuff. We're all humans, and we're a lot more alike than we are different."
4. In the East Meets West scenario, would it be smarter to meet separately with your international visitors from Japan and Spain? Why or why not?
5. What cross-cultural educational opportunities exist at your college or university? Are you taking advantage of them?

Memo
from the
Field

Bill Imada, President,
IW Group, Los Angeles,
California

Bill Imada is the president and founder of IW Group, a Los Angeles–based advertising and public relations agency specializing in the Asian American market. The agency represents a variety of major corporations and governmental agencies, including AT&T, Northwest Airlines, Merrill Lynch, Washington Mutual, Chevron Corporation, and the American Legacy Foundation.

Values play a critical role in the way people think, react, relate, communicate, and make decisions. As a student of public relations, take a moment to think about the values that shape your own personality and the way you make decisions in life. As the authors of this book clearly note, there are a host of common values that people around the world share. When you walk into a room filled with nationals from Japan, Spain, or any other country in the world, consider all of the values you might share first. You will be pleasantly surprised by the number of values you have in common with your colleagues from another country or even another neighborhood or community. Your efforts to communicate will be made easier and more enjoyable when you find the values that bring you together. Afterwards, take time to discover the things that make you different and unique. Celebrate what you have learned from one another, and share what you have learned with others.

As you move forward with your studies in public relations and communications, take a moment to think about some of the values you may take for granted. In this chapter, the authors talk about the concept of time. Many people from Western countries often talk about the lack of time we have to accomplish things. Americans, for instance, often say "time flies." On the contrary, many Latin American and Asian cultures may say "time walks." From a cultural point of view, which phrase is right? Both are right. How might this concept of time influence the way you interact and negotiate with your counterparts from Japan and Spain?

Now think of some other values that shape your views on life and ask yourself and your classmates to evaluate how these values might influence the way you think, react, relate, communicate, and make decisions. What thoughts come to mind when you think of these values: independence, family, sales, and equality.

Now ask people from other cultures to talk with you about their views on these values. I think you will find their answers enlightening and thought-provoking.

The authors also talk about the significance of gestures in other cultures. It is important to note that gestures are an important method of communicating in many cultures around the world. In Japan, public relations professionals often say that the Japanese can say "no" 40 different ways without even uttering the word. Facial expressions, hand movements, and body positions can signal a variety of different messages. As public relations practitioners, it is essential for you to learn how gestures can and will play a role in cross-cultural communication.

Lastly, think about what you have learned in the past about getting from one point in life to another. What did your teachers, professors, and parents tell you about getting from point A to point B? You and your classmates may say that the best way to get from point A to point B is a straight line. Why? Because it is considered the most efficient, cost-effective, and timely way to reach your desired destination. As you move forward in your public relations career, remember that there can be many different and unique ways to get from one point to another—and not necessarily by taking the direct approach. The most effective public relations practitioners will recognize early on that there are a myriad of different ways to reach where you'd like to go. Take time to explore each route. You'll be pleased that you did.

Case Study 14.1

Pitney Bowes Sends a Message

Sixty years ago, the sales team of a U.S.-based multinational company attended an awards ceremony at a prestigious hotel. Nothing unusual about that. One member of the team was black, and the hotel refused to admit him. Unfortunately, nothing unusual about that either. "Whites Only" policies characterized some U.S. businesses until the 1960s. What happened next, however, *was* unusual. Led by the company chairman, the entire sales team walked out of the hotel and refused to attend the ceremony.[66]

What kind of company would risk offending clients, industry partners, and social leaders to stand up for equal rights and the value of diversity? A company named Pitney Bowes.

In terms of equal rights and the value of diversity, much has changed in 60 years. Pitney Bowes' values haven't. The company remains a worldwide leader in creating a diverse workforce.

"For over 50 years, a key component of our successful business model has been an employee population that reflects the global marketplace," says Pitney Bowes Chairman and CEO Michael Critelli. "We believe that the diversity of thought and life experience in our employee population helps us produce superior products and services."[67]

Pitney Bowes is a $5-billion-a-year developer and supplier of message- and document-management systems. Its customers include more than 2 million businesses in more than 130 countries around the world. To cope with such a diverse customer base, Pitney Bowes aggressively seeks a diverse workforce. Minority employees constitute more than 40 percent of the company's personnel. More than 20 percent of the management staff consists of minority employees.[68] "Our executive leadership team is over 50 percent people of color and/or non–U.S. born," Critelli says.[69]

To maintain and strengthen productive relationships among its diverse work-force, Pitney Bowes follows a process familiar to students of public relations: research, planning, communication, and evaluation.

The company's diversity-related research began in 1987 with the goal of identifying barriers that prohibited the advancement of women and minority-group employees. In that year, Pitney Bowes created the Women's Resource Group and the Minority Resource Group to spearhead research efforts. To study the business value of diversity, Pitney Bowes launched a research project with the University of Pennsylvania in 1996.

As its research began to highlight areas for improvement, Pitney Bowes initiated the planning phase. It created a Diversity Task Force to develop specific objectives for promoting diversity at all levels of the company. One element of the plan recommended that Pitney Bowes' top managers present annual diversity-promotion plans with measurable objectives.

As one of the world's top message-management companies, Pitney Bowes didn't lack ideas for communicating its diversity objectives to employees. Internal newsletters routinely cover diversity issues; every training session for new managers includes a Managing Diversity segment; and the company crafted a short, memorable diversity policy featured in a variety of media, including its web site: "Diversity is essential to innovation and growth. Pitney Bowes encourages and maintains diversity in every aspect of its operations, from our own workforce to the customers, business partners, and communities with whom we work." Pitney Bowes' main "Statement of Value," which it features on its web site, in its annual reports, and in other media, also bluntly states, "We value diversity."[70]

Finally, Pitney Bowes evaluates the success of its research, planning, and communication. Every year, each business unit within the company submits a report showing the degree to which it achieved its specific diversity objectives. Top managers also review the impact of the company's overall diversity policies on profits, employee advancement, diversity of business partners, and other areas.[71]

As a result of its dedication to diversity, the company routinely wins praise from its own employees, magazines such as *Business Week,* books such as *The 100 Best Companies to Work For in America,* and organizations such as the National Urban League. That praise soared in 1998 and 1999 when five different magazines, including *Hispanic* and *Working Woman,* named Pitney Bowes a top company for minority-group employees.

Michael Critelli emphasizes that his company's successful quest for diversity is fueled by more than morality. Pitney Bowes also firmly believes that diversity strengthens important relationships with customers and business partners. "We clearly recognize the growth opportunities that diversity creates," he says, "not only in expanding our market access but in widening our base of mutually beneficial relationships, especially with minority- and women-owned companies."[72]

Critelli also believes that a diverse management team increases Pitney Bowes' international competitiveness. When he announced the promotion of Keith Williamson, a high-ranking black manager, to the position of president of the company's

Capital Services division, he praised Williamson's "extensive legal and tax knowledge and sound business judgment." But he added, "His appointment underscores Pitney Bowes' belief that leveraging the diversity of our employees helps us sustain our competitive leadership."[73]

DISCUSSION QUESTIONS

1. The Pitney Bowes sales team risked social condemnation when it walked out of that 1940s awards ceremony. What did it gain?
2. Pitney Bowes believes that diversity makes good business sense. What is its logic?
3. Women are not a minority group. Why does Pitney Bowes include them in its diversity programs?
4. In your opinion, do Pitney Bowes' actions live up to the company's diversity policy "Statement of Value"?
5. How does the specificity of Pitney Bowes' diversity plans help the evaluation process?

Case Study 14.2

Zakazukha!

Two cheers for *Expert,* the magazine named Russia's best business periodical by the Russian Managers Association. *Expert* has more than 70,000 readers in Moscow alone, and it won top honors for "brand awareness, authority, inspired confidence, and depth of analysis."[74]

But why not three cheers? In a word, *zakazukha.*

Zakazukha is the Russian word for payments to journalists—often from public relations practitioners—to win favorable or prevent negative news media coverage. "In a study on business and the media published this year [2003]," wrote the *Moscow Times,* "the [Russian Managers Association] estimated that *zakazukha* articles account for about 30 percent of all stories published."[75]

Recent news reports suggest that *zakazukha* is a standard tactic in Russian media relations:

■ In Moscow, an investigative journalist has been charged with blackmailing a local business leader. Pay $100,000, she allegedly told the man, or she'd feature him in a devastating exposé.[76]

■ A Russian journalist has admitted accepting money for a favorable article on a fitness club owner—and accepting a 30 percent discount for illegal, unlicensed cosmetic surgery at the club to repair his broken nose (broken by the angry target of a non-*zakazukha* story). The journalist alleges that when he later wrote about the illegal surgery, thugs hired by the club owner beat him (no report on whether they rebroke his nose).[77]

■ To test journalists' willingness to be partners in *zakazukha,* a Russian public relations agency sent a bogus news release, detailing the opening of new business,
to Moscow news media. "More than half of the publications that received the
release initiated negotiations to run the story in exchange for cash," reports *PR
Week* magazine.[78]

The prestige of Russian news media has sunk so low that when a Russian pulp
mill hired public relations agency Fleishman-Hillard to help thwart a violent hostile
takeover, the agency decided to target the most credible news media in Russia: foreign media. "We determined [the Moscow bureaus of foreign media] to be a potentially potent counter-weapon because those Western institutions had a much greater
degree of credibility and authority not only here in the West but also in Russia," said
Andrew Kattel, senior vice president of international business communications at
Fleishman-Hillard.[79]

In 2002, the International Public Relations Association conducted a survey of
public relations professionals in 52 nations—and learned that *zakazukha* had spread
throughout Eastern Europe. "*Zakazukha* is a common practice," said a Ukrainian
practitioner. "We have the law on advertising which directly forbids [publishing] materials paid for by an advertiser without making it clear that it was paid. This law is
widely ignored."[80]

Said a Croatian practitioner, "Some journalists openly demand goods or services
in exchange for not publishing negative stories (even made-up negative stories) about
the company/organization."[81]

The IPRA survey revealed these discouraging facts about *zakazukha* and media
relations in Eastern Europe:[82]

■ Only 13 percent of Eastern European practitioners believe that journalists are not
influenced by *zakazukha.*

■ 41 percent of Eastern European practitioners believe that journalists often accept
money in return for publishing news releases. In contrast, no North American
practitioners in the survey—literally 0 percent—believed that North American
journalists often accept money to do so.

■ Eastern European practitioners believe that their regional news media are less reliable than news media from other regions.

By participating in *zakazukha,* practitioners undermine the credibility of the
news media, damaging an important part of democracy and eliminating news media's
ability to supply reputable third-party endorsements. "The credibility of any publication can only be based on its independent objectivity," says Frank Ovaitt, of the
U.S.-based Crossover International agency. "As long as the practice of illicit paid-for
editorial continues in any marketplace, the local public can never have confidence in
what they read."[83]

Russian journalist Alexei Pankin sees the damage of *zakazukha* firsthand. "This
total lack of trust on all sides," he says, "has become a heavy cross to bear today,
at a time when business is taking its first steps toward social responsibility and the

demand for reliable information, whether it be positive or negative, is very much on the rise."[84]

DISCUSSION QUESTIONS

1. What do you know of the history of journalism in Russia? Could that history help explain *zakazukha*?
2. If you had a Russian client and a journalist in that nation demanded *zakazukha* to prevent a negative story, what council would you offer your client?
3. What do you know about the values of the U.S.-based Society of Professional Journalists? What is its stance on *zakazukha*?
4. What international public relations practices besides *zakazukha* concern the International Public Relations Association? (A visit to the organization's web site, www.ipra.com, can help you answer this question.)

Cyber Coach

Visit www.ablongman.com/guthmarsh3e for these study aids—and more:

- flashcards
- quizzes
- videos
- links to other sites
- real-world scenarios that let you be the public relations professional

KEY TERMS

communication, p. 466
communication model, p. 466
cross-cultural, p. 466
culture, p. 459
decoding, p. 467
demographics, p. 459

encoding, p. 467
geodemographics, p. 459
globalization, p. 459
psychographics, p. 459
stereotyping, p. 468

NOTES

1. Marlene Rossman, *Multicultural Marketing* (New York: Amacom, 1994), 6.
2. Chris Gaither and Sallie Hofmeister, "What Should Happen to AOL?" *Los Angeles Times,* 21 April 2004, online, LexisNexis.
3. Owen Gibson, "The Arrogance Has Gone," (London) *Guardian,* 14 July 2003, online, LexisNexis.
4. Sherryl Connelly, "The Bigger They Fall," (New York) *Daily News,* 28 July 2003, online, LexisNexis.
5. Gaither and Hofmeister.

6. Mike Lindblom, "Muslims Protest Koran Use in Rave Ad," *Seattle Times,* 10 February 2001, online, LexisNexis.

7. Anindita Niyogi Balslev, ed., *Cross-Cultural Conversation* (Atlanta: Scholars Press, 1996), 10.

8. Stephen P. Banks, *Multicultural Public Relations*, 2nd ed. (Ames: Iowa State University Press, 2000), 9.

9. Charles Winick, *Dictionary of Anthropology* (Totowa, N.J.: Littlefield, Adams, 1972), 144.

10. Robert Gibson, *International Business Communication* (Oxford: Oxford University Press, 2000), 3.

11. Banks, ix.

12. John Budd Jr., "Opinion . . . Foreign Policy Acumen Needed by Global CEOs," *Public Relations Review* (summer 2001): 132.

13. Banks, 105.

14. "Italian Stallions," *Times* (of London), 1 May 2001, 17.

15. David J. Smith and Shelagh Armstrong, *If the World Were a Village* (Toronto: Kids Can Press, 2002).

16. Rossman.

17. Robert Levine, "The Pace of Life in 31 Countries," *American Demographics,* November 1997, 20.

18. Roger Axtell, *Do's and Taboos around the World,* 3rd ed. (New York: Wiley, 1993), 68.

19. Much of the information in this section comes from two excellent books by Roger Axtell: *Do's and Taboos around the World* (note 18) and *Gestures: The Do's and Taboos of Body Language around the World* (New York: Wiley, 1991).

20. Budd, 131.

21. Sanae Kobayashi, "Characteristics of Japanese Communication," *Communication World,* December/January 1996–97, 15.

22. Axtell, *Gestures,* 150.

23. *ABC World News Now,* 9 January 2002, online, LexisNexis.

24. *ABC World News Now.*

25. Johanna Neuman, "Bush's Inaction over General's Islam Remarks Riles Two Religions," *Los Angeles Times,* 23 November 2003, online, LexisNexis.

26. Daphne Spain, "America's Diversity: On the Edge of Two Centuries," *Reports on America* 1, no. 2 (Washington, D.C.: Population Reference Bureau), 7.

27. Spain, 7.

28. John Robinson, Bart Landry, and Ronica Rooks, "Time and the Melting Pot," *American Demographics,* June 1998, 20.

29. Rossman, 6, 12.

30. Mary Jo Jacobi, "Communications without Borders: Thinking Globally While Acting Locally" (speech delivered to the 1998 annual meeting of the International Public Relations Association, London, 17 July 1998).

31. Axtell, *Gestures,* 50.

32. Alice Lagnado, "Putin to Purge Russian Tongue of Foreign Elements," *Times,* 1 May 2001, 16.

33. Adam Sherwin, "Mandela Steals Show in Trafalgar Square," *Times,* 30 April 2001, 8.

34. Mark Rice-Oxley, "The American World," *Seattle Times,* 18 January 2004, online, LexisNexis.
35. "Pitney Bowes Messaging Study Reveals Hidden Cultural Pitfalls for Communicating with Colleagues and Customers outside the United States," news release issued by Pitney Bowes, 31 July 2000, online, www.PitneyBowes.com.
36. David Howes, ed., *Cross-Cultural Consumption* (London: Routledge, 1996), 1.
37. Naseem Javed, "Naming for Global Power," *Communication World,* October/November 1997, 33.
38. Maud Tixier, "How Cultural Factors Affect Internal and External Communication," *Communication World,* February/March 1997, 25.
39. Information in this paragraph comes from Axtell's *Do's and Taboos* and *Gestures* (notes 18 and 19 above).
40. Henry Louis Gates Jr., "Whose Culture Is It, Anyway?" *Cast a Cold Eye* (New York: Four Walls Eight Windows, 1991), 263.
41. Budd, 126.
42. Howes, 2.
43. "Public Relations Society of America Finds Progress of Industry in Diversity Efforts 'Mixed' in Landmark Survey," news release issued by the Public Relations Society of America, 22 August 2003, online, www.prsa.org.
44. "*PR Week* Regional Forum," *PR Week,* 12 July 2004, online, LexisNexis.
45. John Graham, "Opportunities for Firms and Clients Abound If We Stick to Our Principles," *PR Week,* 8 December 2003, online, LexisNexis.
46. Mindy Charski, "In Search of Diversity," *Adweek,* 2 August 2004, online, LexisNexis.
47. Charski.
48. "Public Relations Society of America Finds Progress of Industry in Diversity Efforts 'Mixed' in Landmark Survey."
49. "Public Relations Society of America Finds Progress of Industry in Diversity Efforts 'Mixed' in Landmark Survey."
50. "PRSA National Diversity Committee," Public Relations Society of America, online, www.prsa.org.
51. Charski.
52. Susan Fry Bovet, "Firms Send Promising Internationalists to 'College,'" *Public Relations Journal,* August/September 1994, 28.
53. Gibson, 19.
54. Cynthia Kemper, "Challenges Facing Public Relations Efforts Are Intensified Abroad," *Denver Post,* 1 March 1998, online, LexisNexis.
55. Axtell, *Do's and Taboos,* 68, 89.
56. Ibid., 90.
57. Peter Jennings, Bob Jamieson, and Bob Woodruff, *ABC World News Tonight,* 25 January 2001, online, LexisNexis.
58. Peter Martin, "Shoals across the Pond," *Financial Times,* 2 June 2001, online, LexisNexis.
59. Widget Finn, "Mind the Culture Gap," *Daily Telegraph,* 14 June 2001, online, LexisNexis.
60. Jennings, Jamieson, and Woodruff; William Drozdiak, "Alacatel Aims to Purchase Lucent," *Washington Post,* 29 May 2001, online, LexisNexis; "When Business Pops the Question," *Engineer,* 18 May 2001, online, LexisNexis.

61. Jennings, Jamieson, and Woodruff.

62. Finn.

63. Andrew Leach, "DaimlerChrysler Just the Latest Example of a Merger Most Foul," *Daily Mail,* 21 January 2001, online, LexisNexis.

64. Drozdiak.

65. Jacobi.

66. "Diversity Initiatives," Pitney Bowes, online, www.pitneybowes.com.

67. "Pitney Bowes Celebrates Diversity around the World," news release issued by Pitney Bowes, 29 February 2000, online, www.pitneybowes.com.

68. "Pitney Bowes Names Keith Williamson President of Capital Services Division," news release issued by *Business Wire,* 31 March 1999, online, LexisNexis.

69. "Pitney Bowes Celebrates Diversity around the World."

70. Pitney Bowes, www.pitneybowes.com.

71. Pitney Bowes, www.pitneybowes.com.

72. Pitney Bowes, www.pitneybowes.com.

73. "Pitney Bowes Names Keith Williamson President of Capital Services."

74. Igor Semenenko, "Expert Gets Top Spot in Business Media Survey," *Moscow Times,* 23 July 2003, online, LexisNexis.

75. Semenenko.

76. Frank Brown, "A Free Press for Sale," *Newsweek,* 28 June 2004, online, LexisNexis.

77. Brown.

78. Ian Hall, "Ceyda Aydede, IPRA—IPRA Chief Aydede's on a Global Mission, *PR Week,* 13 December 2002, online, LexisNexis.

79. "Navigating the Rough-and-Tumble World of International PR," *PR News,* 22 September 2003, online, LexisNexis.

80. "Examples of Unethical Media Practice," International Public Relations Association, online, www.ipra.org.campaigns/icmt/examples.htm.

81. "Examples of Unethical Media Practice."

82. "IPRA Campaign for Media Transparency," International Public Relations Association, online, www.ipra.org.

83. "Unethical Media Practices Revealed by IPRA Report," news release issued by the International Public Relations Association, online, www.ipra.org/campaigns/icmt/docs/press2.htm.

84. Alexei Pankin, "No Foothold for Trust in Vicious Media Circle," *Moscow Times,* 27 May 2003, online, LexisNexis.

Public Relations and the Law

objectives

After studying this chapter, you will be able to

- understand the differences between and the regulation of political and commercial speech

- appreciate how privacy and copyright laws affect the practice of public relations

- identify the higher burden of proof public officials and public figures have in libel cases

- recognize the increasing role public relations has in the judicial system

Working in a Minefield

scenario

It has been a bad day at the Ferndale Corporation's investor relations office, and it almost got worse.

Your headache began when the corporate attorneys called and said that you would have to prepare a news release announcing the chief executive officer's sudden, unexpected resignation. Ferndale's revenues have fallen dramatically in recent months, and the board of directors wants to move in a new direction before the next annual meeting.

When you go to brief the staff on what is happening, you find a colleague downloading music from the Internet. She tells you "downloading music doesn't hurt anybody." But you know differently.

As you sit down to write the news release about the CEO's departure, a number of questions come to mind. What should I say? What can I say? What must I say? Three questions similar in structure, but entirely different in their legal ramifications.

On top of everything, the timing for this could not be worse. The annual report is due at the printer this afternoon. Can you delay it?

It's times like these that everyone needs to talk to a friend. Your best friend from college is an investment analyst at a local stock brokerage firm. But before you start dialing, you suddenly hang up the telephone. You realize that you almost made the biggest mistake of your life, one that could have landed you in prison.

You think to yourself, "It's like working in a minefield."

A Parade of Corporate Horrors

The next time someone tells you that the "whole world changed in 2001," remember that the terrorist attacks of September 11 were not the *only* events that shook public confidence. In the wake of a series of corporate financial scandals, lawmakers, regulators, and investors began scrutinizing businesses more closely than ever. And if the folks in the boardrooms want to know why they are now under intense public scrutiny, they have no one to blame but themselves.

The first shock came with the sudden collapse of the Enron Corporation. Within a six-week period, the value of stocks in the Houston-based energy trading company plummeted from more than $80 a share to less than $1 each. At the heart of the controversy was the company's failure to accurately disclose its financial situation. Enron officials acknowledged that they used a complex web of partnerships to overstate profits by more than $580 million over a four-year period. The partnerships allowed Enron to keep a half-billion dollars in debt off its books. That, in turn, allowed the company to continue to acquire credit it needed to run its business. Investment analysts first began questioning Enron's financial statements in early 2001. The scheme fell apart when Enron's main rival backed out of a merger deal and the company was forced to announce a stunning $638 million third-quarter loss in October of that year.

The most difficult aspect of this scandal has been the plight of Enron's 20,000 employees. Many lost their jobs. But that wasn't the worst of it. While the value of Enron stocks dropped, the company barred employees from selling shares from their retirement accounts under the guise of switching to a new plan administrator. In practical terms, the employees lost all their retirement funds. In contrast, Enron executives cashed out more than $1 billion in company stocks. Another 600 employees received $100 million in bonuses in November 2001—less than one month before the company filed for bankruptcy.[1]

Unfortunately, that was just the beginning of a parade of corporate horrors. Here's a sampling:

■ Adelphia Communications Corporation, once the nation's sixth-largest cable-television company, filed for bankruptcy in 2002 after government investigators discovered that the company's CEO used more than $2 billion to finance family loans. In 2004, a federal jury convicted Adelphia's founder and his son of trying to loot the company of millions of dollars.[2]

■ Telecommunications giant WorldCom, Inc., fired its chief financial officer in 2002 after uncovering improper accounting of $3.8 billion in expenses. Less than a month later, the company filed for bankruptcy protection—surpassing Enron as the largest corporate bankruptcy in U.S. history. Several WorldCom executives were arrested. Some pleaded guilty to securities fraud and making false statements. Meanwhile, thousands of workers were laid off their jobs.[3]

■ The former CEO and CFO of Tyco were indicted in 2002 for stealing $600 million in company funds. The government alleged that the money was used for, among other things, $11 million in art and other furnishings, a $6,000 shower curtain, a $2.1 million Italian vacation, and a $19 million interest-free loan to purchase a Florida home. The defendants didn't deny using the money for lavish parties and personal pleasures. They said they had a legal right to do so.[4]

■ Frank Quattrone, one of Wall Street's biggest names in technology stocks, was convicted of obstructing a grand jury, obstructing federal regulators, and witness tampering in May 2004. The charges stemmed from a government investigation into the Credit Suisse First Boston Bank and whether it took kickbacks from investors seeking tips on hot public stock offerings.[5]

In Chapter 6 of this book, we discussed the ethics of public relations. We also said that one shouldn't confuse ethics with the law. However, in this chapter, we discuss the legal environment in which public relations is practiced. Because of widely publicized examples of corporate greed, public relations practitioners face an increasingly hostile environment. That's not just because much of what was done was morally questionable. It was also illegal.

Public Relations, the Law, and You

At this point, you may be wondering: "What does all of this have to do with public relations?" The answer: plenty. Public relations practitioners are supposed to manage relationships between organizations and their many stakeholders. In publicly held corporations such as those we mentioned, relationship management is more than a moral issue—it is a legal imperative. And while none of the aforementioned executives were public relations professionals, one wonders where each organization's practitioners were. Did they have access to the corridors of corporate power? Did they have the ear of executives? And if they did, what did those practitioners say and do? Could history have been different?

According to the Administrative Office of the U.S. Courts, the federal courts experienced an across-the-board increase in the number of appellate, civil, criminal, and bankruptcy filings during fiscal year 2002. Most categories registered all-time highs. A large portion of that activity was in the civil courts, which recorded a record 274,841 filings—up nearly 20 percent over the previous decade.[6] And these figures do not even take into account lawsuits filed in state and municipal courts. Like it or not, this is the reality of today's society.

This fact should not be lost on public relations practitioners. They are often thrust into the limelight when their employer's actions face legal challenges. Practitioners also require an intimate knowledge of the laws governing what they may or must say or do in a variety of situations. For example, a certain degree of exaggeration is perfectly acceptable at times. However, at other times it is not. Depending on whom the practitioner is representing, some information can be considered public (for all to see) or very private.

The challenge for public relations practitioners is to understand the many laws and regulations that govern or, at least, influence their practice. Unfortunately, at least one study suggests that many practitioners do not have a good understanding of the laws and regulations governing the public relations profession. More than half the practitioners questioned in one survey indicated they had no familiarity with SEC regulations. In the same survey, more than 48 percent said they were not familiar with laws relating to professional malpractice, 45 percent were not familiar with laws governing financial public relations, and 40 percent were not familiar with laws pertaining to commercial speech. These responses led the author of the study to this conclusion:

> The finding that most practitioners are only somewhat or not at all familiar with important legal issues, combined with the finding that most of their work is either not reviewed or subject to limited review by legal counsel, suggests that many public relations practitioners may be placing both themselves and their clients at risk of legal liability.[7]

Attorney Morton J. Simon said that public relations practitioners "can and have cost companies millions of dollars. While the incidence of legal implications [to the practice of public relations] may vary, their importance when they exist cannot be minimized."[8]

Public Relations and the First Amendment

As noted in Chapter 3, the most important event in the development of public relations in the United States was the adoption of the **First Amendment** to the Constitution. The freedoms guaranteed by the First Amendment provide the framework for the nation's social, political, and commercial discourse:

> Congress shall make no law respecting an establishment of religion, or prohibiting the free exercise thereof; or abridging the freedom of speech, or of the press, or the right of the people peaceably to assemble, and to petition the Government for a redress of grievances.[9]

In the more than two centuries since its adoption, a great deal of thought and debate has surrounded what the First Amendment does and does not guarantee. There have been many instances in which free expression has come in conflict with other social interests. Does a person's First Amendment right to freedom of speech supersede someone else's Sixth Amendment right to a trial by "an impartial jury"? Does freedom of expression allow one to yell "fire" in a crowded theater? Clearly, the freedoms embodied in the First Amendment are not absolute. It has been left up to the courts, and, ultimately, the Supreme Court, to decide on the amendment's limits.

Political versus Commercial Speech

Although public relations enjoys certain protections under the First Amendment, these rights are not without some limitations. The practice of public relations often falls into a gray area between what the law characterizes as political speech and commercial speech. **Political speech** is defined as expression associated with the normal conduct of a democracy—such as news articles, public debates, and individuals' expressions of their opinions about the events of the day. In general, the U.S. Supreme Court has been reluctant to limit political speech. Justice William Brennan wrote in 1964 that there is a "profound national commitment to the principle that debate on public issues should be uninhibited, robust, and wide-open, and that it may well include vehement, caustic, and sometimes unpleasantly sharp attacks on government and public officials."[10]

Commercial speech, which is defined as expression "intended to generate marketplace transactions," is more restricted.[11] In fact, for much of the nation's history, commercial speech has been treated by courts as if it were unprotected by the First Amendment. In 1976, however, the Supreme Court ruled that a Virginia law prohibiting pharmacists from advertising prescription drug prices was unconstitutional. In doing so, the court recognized limited First Amendment protection for "pure commercial speech":

> Generalizing, society also may have a strong interest in the free flow of commercial information. Even an individual advertisement, though entirely "commercial," may be of general public interest. . . . And if it is indispensable to the proper allocation of resources in a free enterprise system, it is also indispensable to the formation of intelligent opinions as to how that system ought to be regulated or altered. Therefore, even if the First Amendment were thought to be primarily an instrument to enlighten public decision making in a democracy, we could not say that the free flow of information does not serve that goal.[12]

Supreme Court Justice Harry Blackmun also wrote in *Virginia State Board of Pharmacy v. Virginia Citizens Consumer Council Inc.,* "In concluding that commercial speech, like other varieties, is protected, we of course do not hold that it can never be regulated in any way. Some forms of commercial speech regulation are surely permissible."[13] Two years later, in *First National Bank of Boston v. Bellotti,* the Court also affirmed that corporations do enjoy some rights of political speech.

The Supreme Court further defined the limits of commercial speech in the 1980 case *Central Hudson Gas & Electric Corp. v. Public Service Commission of New York.* In that case, Central Hudson Gas & Electric successfully challenged a state ban on promotional advertising by electric utilities. The Court said that there are times when restrictions on commercial speech are justified because they serve certain social interests. In *Central Hudson,* however, the justices felt that the regulation in question was "more extensive than necessary to serve that interest." The Court sided with the utility, saying that the government interest could have been accomplished with less restrictive regulation.[14] The Court clarified what it meant by "not more extensive than necessary" in 1989, when it ruled that the government can "reasonably" restrict commercial speech, even when other means can achieve the "substantial governmental interest" involved.[15]

In recent years, commercial speech has been under attack in several quarters. One case in particular, *Kasky v. Nike,* had the potential for reshaping commercial speech law for decades (see QuickBreak 15.1). However, it became a moot issue when the two parties settled out of court. Other decisions have been more favorable to the business community. The Supreme Court ruled in June 2000 that state governments may not place greater restrictions on tobacco advertising than those required by federal law. The U.S. Court of Appeals in New York in 1998 overturned a state liquor authority ban of certain Bad Frog Beer labels—ones that featured a frog making what many people consider an obscene gesture.[16]

Is public relations considered political speech, or is it considered commercial speech? The answer largely depends on the public being targeted, the purpose of the message, and the court's interpretation. Despite this somewhat murky answer, two things are very clear. First, there are limits to both political and commercial speech. And second, public relations practitioners need to know what those limits are.

Quick ✔ Check

1. Why do the authors of this book describe the environment in which public relations practitioners operate as "increasingly hostile"?
2. What is the difference between the ways the U.S. Supreme Court has treated cases involving political speech and those involving commercial speech?
3. Is public relations considered political speech, or is it considered commercial speech?

The Key: Know Your Own Business

It is not suggested here that every public relations practitioner should be ready to take the state bar exam. However, you don't have to be a lawyer to have a good working knowledge of the law. And that understanding should begin in the workplace. All public relations professionals need to know the laws and regulations that govern their organization.

Many of these laws and regulations relate to the handling of private information. For example, hospital public information officers need to know the rules pertaining to the confidentiality of patient records. Most of the information found in a patient's

KASKY V. NIKE

When California antiglobalization activist Marc Kasky sued Nike and five of its corporate officers under the state's Business and Professional Code in 2000, he launched a battle that threatened to shake the foundations of corporate speech law and the practice of public relations.

Kasky claimed that Nike had made false and misleading statements in a public relations campaign that answered critics of its overseas labor practices. In response to charges that Nike products were being produced by underage, unpaid workers in harsh conditions, the company retained GoodWorks International, cochaired by former U.S. United Nations Ambassador Andrew Young. The consulting firm found no evidence of widespread abuse of workers. When Nike publicized these findings, Kasky sued. The activist not only wanted the corporation to "disgorge all monies" received through the allegedly illegal practices, but he wanted Nike to undertake "a court-approved public information campaign" to correct the record on its overseas practices.[17]

Nike argued that the First Amendment protected its public relations campaign. It said companies must be free to explain their actions to customers, investors, and anyone else. The case drew little attention—it earned only one sentence in the second edition of this book—when two lower courts sided with Nike. However, when the California Supreme Court said that the messages in question were "made in the context of a modern, sophisticated public relations campaign intended to increase sales and profits by enhancing the image of a product or of its manufacturer or seller," the court,

in essence, ruled that Nike's public relations campaign did not have First Amendment protection and was subject to state law.[18]

What had been a fairly obscure legal matter was suddenly on everyone's radar screen. Public relations, advertising, media, and business organizations filed legal briefs urging the U.S. Supreme Court to overturn the decision. Among the public relations organizations that entered the fray were the Public Relations Society of America, the Council of Public Relations Firms, the Arthur Page Society, the Public Affairs Council, and the Institute for Public Relations.

"Those of us who assist companies in gathering and disseminating information related to their businesses have always relied upon the same First Amendment protections as those who openly criticize Nike and other corporations," said PRSA President and CEO Reed Bolton Byrum. "Without that protection, there will be a serious impact on all aspects of corporate communications."[19]

At first, the U.S. Supreme Court agreed to hear the case. Then the justices sent it back to California. Before a final decision was rendered, the two sides settled out of court. The company agreed to pay $1.5 million in workplace program investments and to continue existing after-hours worker education programs.[20] While the legal precedent still stands in California, for the rest of the country, nothing— at least from a legal standpoint—has changed. However, most observers agree that *Kasky v. Nike* muddied the waters of corporate speech law for years to come.

file is considered private. An improper release of that information could open the practitioner and the hospital to civil or criminal litigation.

The actions of practitioners can also be controlled by the legal status of the organizations they represent. Government practitioners must learn that all their records are open to public inspection, except records specifically exempted by law. The best-known federal law guaranteeing access to government information is the **Freedom of Information Act (FOIA)**. The FOIA applies to all federal agencies and departments except the president and his advisers, Congress and its subsidiary committees and agencies, and the federal judicial system.[21] Although there are specific exemptions to the FOIA, a vast majority of federal government records are available for anyone to inspect. Similar laws covering records held by state and local governments have been enacted nationwide. State and federal "sunshine" laws also require that meetings of government agencies at which official decisions are made must be open to the public. However, as is the case with open records laws, specific exemptions permit some government business to be conducted in private.

Practitioners employed by nongovernmental organizations enjoy a much greater degree of privacy than do their government counterparts. However, even they may be governed by state and federal requirements relating to disclosure (a concept that we discuss later in greater depth), taxation, and ethical conduct. For example, people hired for the purpose of influencing the actions of state and federal officials must register as lobbyists. Practitioners representing the interests of governments or organizations based outside the United States must also register as foreign agents. Both lobbyists and foreign agents must file periodic reports on their activities with designated agencies.

Federal Agencies That Regulate Speech

The federal government does not license public relations practitioners. Several federal agencies, however, do have a major impact on the practice of public relations. These agencies create and enforce regulations designed to protect the public's best interests. These rules often cover company or organization communications, especially in areas considered to involve commercial speech. Four of the most prominent of these agencies are the Federal Trade Commission, the Securities and Exchange Commission, the Federal Communications Commission, and the Food and Drug Administration.

The Federal Trade Commission

When public relations practitioners promote a particular product or service, their actions may fall under the watchful gaze of the **Federal Trade Commission (FTC)**. The FTC was established in 1914 "to ensure that the nation's markets function competitively . . . are vigorous . . . and free of undue restrictions."[22] The commission is the source of most federal regulation of advertising. However, it also has jurisdiction over product-related publicity generated by public relations practitioners.

The Federal Trade Commission Act empowers the FTC to "prevent unfair methods of competition, and unfair or deceptive acts or practices in or affecting commerce."[23] This includes advertisements and publicity that may be considered false or misleading, including claims that are unsubstantiated, ambiguous, or exaggerated. The FTC is especially sensitive when the product or service being promoted may adversely affect personal health or when it requires a considerable investment of money before the consumer can determine its effectiveness.

If the FTC believes a violation of the law has occurred, it may obtain voluntary compliance through what is known as a **consent order.** However, if such an agreement cannot be reached, the commission can take a complaint before an **administrative law judge.** This person hears testimony and reviews evidence, much like the judge and jury in a civil or criminal case. An administrative law judge can issue a **cease and desist order.** This decision can be appealed to the full commission, then to the U.S. Court of Appeals, and ultimately to the U.S. Supreme Court. If the FTC's ruling is upheld, it can then seek **injunctions, consumer redress,** and **civil penalties** through the federal court system. In the case of ongoing consumer fraud, the FTC can go directly to federal court in an effort to protect consumers.[24]

The Securities and Exchange Commission

As a result of the 1929 stock market crash that triggered the Great Depression, the federal government closely monitors the financial affairs of publicly traded companies. Congress created the **Securities and Exchange Commission (SEC)** in 1994 to "administer

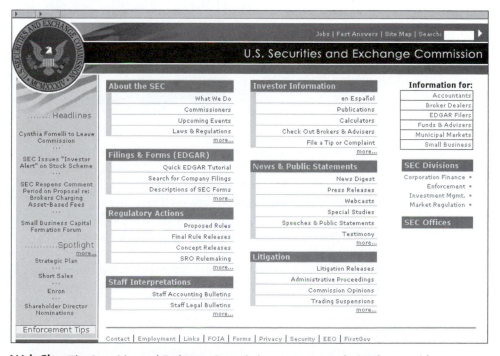

Web Site The Securities and Exchange Commission operates a web site that provides access to a variety of public records and updated information on federal regulations. (Courtesy of the U.S. Securities and Exchange Commission)

Annual Report Publicly held businesses such as the Sonic restaurant chain are required by law to inform shareholders about the company's financial health and other issues that could affect the value of the shareholders' investments. (Courtesy of Sonic, America's Drive-In)

federal securities laws and issue rules and regulations to provide protection for investors and ensure that the securities markets are fair and honest."[25] In other words, the SEC's job is to see to it that everyone is operating on a level playing field. It does so by ensuring that investors can base their decisions on timely and accurate information.

The concept of **disclosure** is the foundation of SEC regulation. Under the Securities Act of 1933, publicly held companies—companies that issue financial securities, such as stocks and bonds, for public sale—have an obligation to disclose frankly, comprehensively, and immediately any information that is considered important to an investor's decision to buy, sell, or even hold the organization's securities.

As mentioned at the beginning of this chapter, cases such as Enron, WorldCom, and Aldelphia have focused intense public scrutiny on corporate disclosure. However, the SEC addressed the issue of fair disclosure a year before the news about Enron's problems surfaced. Before it issued **Regulation FD** (Fair Disclosure), companies often provided selective tidbits of information to favored analysts and money managers to curry favor among major investors. These companies may have been operating within the *letter* of existing disclosure law, but they were clearly outside of its *spirit*. However, Regulation FD, along with amendments to the SEC's disclosure rules, tightened disclosure loopholes. When the new rules were adopted, the SEC announcement said, "We believe that the practice of selective disclosure leads to a loss of investor confidence in the integrity of our capital markets."[26]

Congress further tightened disclosure rules in 2002 by passing the **Sarbanes-Oxley Act.** Under its provisions, CEOs and CFOs are held personally accountable for the truthfulness of corporate financial statements. Violators face up to 20 years in prison and a $5 million fine. The law limits the ability of company officers and their families to sell stock when employees are blocked from doing so. It created new laws against destroying, altering, or falsifying records in an attempt to impede investigations. It also required companies to annually publish a code of ethics.[27]

Although companies are required to file a large variety of reports with the SEC and other federal agencies, the most recognizable channels of disclosure are Form 10-K to the SEC and the annual report to shareholders. Publicly held corporations

Form 10-K Publicly held corporations such as Microsoft are required to file a Form 10-K every year. The form also has to be included in the company's annual report, which must reach shareholders within 15 days of the annual meeting. (Courtesy of the U.S. Securities and Exchange Commission)

QuickBreak 15.2

SEC RULE 10b-5

Any practitioner engaged in financial public relations must study SEC Rule 10b-5, which prohibits fraudulent or misleading corporate communications in matters that could affect investment decisions. Rule 10b-5 states that it is illegal "to make any untrue statements of a material fact or to omit to state a material fact necessary in order to make the statements made, in light of the circumstances under which they were made, not misleading." The rule also prohibits "any act, practice, or course of business which operates or would operate as a fraud or deceit upon any person, in connection with the purchase or sale of any security."[28]

One area in which this rule has a major impact on the practice of public relations is insider trading. That was the issue in 1985, when the SEC filed charges against Anthony M. Franco, the owner of a Detroit public relations firm and national president-elect of the Public Relations Society of America. The SEC complaint stemmed from a news release Franco had prepared in which his client, Crowley, Milner and Company, announced its intentions to buy another firm, Oakland Holding Company.

The SEC suit claimed that Franco purchased 3,000 shares of Oakland Holding Company stock in anticipation of making a sizable profit upon the public announcement of the proposed buyout. When the unusual transaction caught the attention of American Stock Exchange officials, Franco rescinded the trade. He claimed that his stockbroker had acted without his authorization. The SEC suit was resolved when Franco signed a consent decree, in which he did not acknowledge any wrongdoing but promised to obey the law in the future. When the affair became public knowledge in 1986, *after* he had assumed the PRSA presi-

dency, Franco was forced to resign that post. Threatened with action by the PRSA Board of Ethics, he also resigned his membership in October 1986.[29]

Rule 10b-5 is also important in the area of timely and accurate disclosure. This was a central issue in a 1968 landmark case involving the Texas Gulf Sulfur Company. TGS geologists discovered a major deposit of valuable minerals in eastern Canada in November 1963. During the five months between the discovery and its public announcement, a handful of TGS executives—the few people who knew the secret—bought more than 20,000 shares of company stock. To squelch rumors of a major ore strike, TGS issued a news release on April 12, 1964, that said, in part, "The drilling done to date has not been conclusive."[30] Four days later, a second news release announced a major ore strike. An appeals court eventually ruled that the April 12 news release was misleading and a violation of Rule 10b-5. Many of the TGS executives involved in the incident were fined and ordered to repay profits made as a result of the inside information.

PRSA's *Member Code of Ethics 2000* addresses these issues under the section dealing with the disclosure of information. It lists among its guidelines that members shall "be honest and accurate in all communications" and "investigate the truthfulness and accuracy of information released on behalf of those represented." The code cites as an example of improper conduct "Lying by omission: A practitioner for a corporation knowingly fails to release financial information, giving a misleading impression of the corporation's performance."[31]

annually file a **Form 10-K** with the SEC. In it, a company is required to disclose specific information about its financial health and direction. This includes annual and multiyear reports on net sales, gross profit, income, total assets, and long-term financial obligations. The 10-K report also includes a management discussion and analysis of the company's financial condition.

Form 10-K usually provides the basis for the more familiar corporate **annual report,** which has to be in the hands of shareholders no less than 15 days before the corporate annual meeting. Typically, these annual reports are written and designed to make the investor feel good about his or her decision to own stock in the company. But serious investors and analysts look beyond the color pictures printed on glossy paper. They focus on Form 10-K, which is often inserted at the back of the annual report and printed on plain paper. All the small print may seem like gobbledygook, but it *is* necessary; and the information required in Form 10-K also has to be included in the annual report. Among the SEC requirements for an annual report are

- audited financial statements;
- supplementary financial information, such as net sales, gross profits, and per-share data based on income or loss;
- management discussion and analysis of the company's financial condition and any unusual events, transactions, or economic changes;
- a brief description of the company's business (products and/or services);
- the identities of company directors and executive officers; and
- a description of any significant litigation in which the company or its directors or officers are involved.

This is only a thumbnail sketch of SEC annual report reporting requirements.[32] It is a good idea to check with the SEC each year to keep up with changes in disclosure requirements.

Another SEC regulation that every practitioner needs to know is SEC Rule 10b-5, which prohibits, among other things, **insider trading** (see QuickBreak 15.2). Indirectly, that is what got Martha Stewart into trouble in 2004. A person violates insider trading rules if he or she buys or sells securities on the basis of insider information not available to other investors. Stewart was convicted of misleading federal investigators about selling shares of ImClone, a pharmaceutical company—just before the government announced an unfavorable ruling on one of the company's experimental drugs. An investigation alleged that inside information may have come from ImClone founder Samuel D. Waksal, a close friend.[33]

If the public is to have confidence in the nation's financial institutions, everyone has to play by the same rules. As the SEC states on its web site, "Because insider trading undermines investor confidence in the fairness and integrity of the securities markets, the [SEC] has treated the detection and prosecution of insider trading violations as one of its enforcement priorities."[34]

The Federal Communications Commission

Public relations practitioners who work for political candidates or whose clients may be subject to public criticism should be familiar with the federal agency that has regulated the nation's broadcast media since 1934, the **Federal Communications Commission (FCC)**. Originally created as the Federal Radio Commission in 1927, the FCC has the primary responsibility for ensuring the orderly use of the nation's airwaves in the public interest. Because a finite number of radio wave frequencies are available for public use, radio and television stations operate under licenses granted by the federal government. In contrast, print media face relatively little government oversight because of historic precedents and First Amendment protections. Since the Telecommunications Act of 1996, broadcast licenses are granted for a period of eight years and may be renewed after a review of the licensee's performance.

Public relations practitioners representing political candidates should also be aware of section 315 of the 1934 Communications Act, better known as the **equal opportunity provision.** Whenever a legally qualified candidate for public office appears

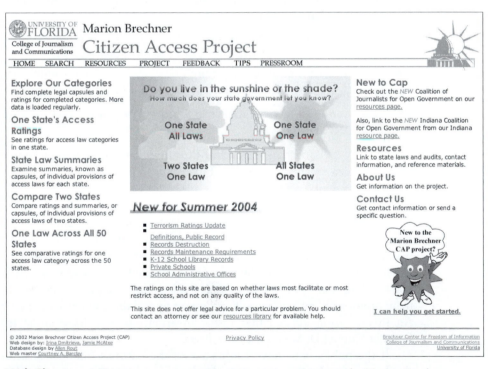

Web Site In an effort to encourage more transparent government, the Marion Brechner Citizens Access Project has created a web site where visitors can research and compare local, state, and federal open records and meetings laws. (Courtesy of the Marion Brechner Citizens Access Project)

Values Statement 15.1

FEDERAL COMMUNICATIONS COMMISSION

The FCC was established by the Communications Act of 1934 and is charged with regulating interstate and international communications by radio, television, wire, satellite, and cable. Its five commissioners are appointed by the president and confirmed by the Senate for five-year terms. Only three commissioners may be representatives of the same political party, and none may have any financial interest in commission-related business.

It is the mission of the Federal Communications Commission to ensure that the American people have available—at reasonable costs and without discrimination—rapid, efficient, nation- and world-wide communication services; whether by radio, television, wire, satellite, or cable. *47 U.S.C. §151—Title 1, Section 1 of the Communications Act of 1934, as amended.*

—Strategic Plan FY 2003–FY 2008
Federal Communications Commission

in a radio or television broadcast, all other candidates for that office must be afforded equal opportunities for access. It means that if a candidate appears in a broadcast at no cost, all other qualified candidates for that office must be offered the same opportunity. Under another provision of the law, legally qualified candidates must be allowed to purchase commercials at the station's lowest advertising rate.

Section 315 is usually applied to political advertising but can also be triggered by the appearance of a qualified candidate in a product commercial, a public service announcement, or entertainment programming. However, there are exemptions to the rule. The equal time provision does not apply when a candidate appears in a bona fide newscast, news interview, news documentary, or on-the-spot coverage of a bona fide news event.

Under what is known as the **personal attack rule,** stations are required to provide free air time to persons who have been the subject of a broadcast character attack. Unlike section 315, the personal attack rule does not necessarily require equal air time. In other words, if the character attack occurred during a prime-time television show, the station does not have to offer the exact same time slot. The station is obliged only to offer a "reasonable" opportunity for response. If the rule sounds vague on what is "reasonable," that is because it is. It is also an area of the law under constant review.

An ongoing controversy facing the FCC is the proposed easing of broadcast ownership rules. Under the old rules, media companies were not allowed to own broadcast stations that reached more than 35 percent of the U. S audience. They also faced limits on how many stations they could own in the same market. The broadcast networks said that they needed wider audience access to compete in today's media-rich environment. However, a large coalition of opponents that cut across the political spectrum opposed the change. Those groups, including PRSA, said this growing media concentration threatened to reduce the diversity of voices in the media.[35] After high-level bargaining, Congress eventually agreed in 2003 to raise the cap to 39 percent. However, in June 2004, a federal appeals court struck down a proposed rule change that would have allowed companies to own more stations in the same market.[36]

Another hot-button issue involving the FCC is a regulation making it unlawful to send an unsolicited advertisement to a facsimile (fax) machine without prior written permission from the recipient. Fines could range up to $500 for each violation.[37] The rule, scheduled to go into effect in early 2005, has been opposed by a variety of business interests, especially professional associations such as PRSA that use fax messages to communicate with their members.[38] This regulation has also been the target of lawsuits. But unlike the broadcast ownership rules, opponents have not been successful in striking down the "junk fax" rule.[39]

The Food and Drug Administration

As public relations ventures deeper into the integrated marketing of products and services, practitioners are having to familiarize themselves with the regulations of yet another federal agency, the **Food and Drug Administration (FDA)**. The FDA was created to "protect, promote, and enhance the health of the American people." The agency has responsibility for ensuring that "foods are safe, wholesome, and sanitary; human and veterinary drugs, biological products, and medical devices are safe and effective; cosmetics are safe; and electronic products that emit radiation are safe."[40]

The area in which public relations practitioners are most likely to encounter this agency is in the promotion of products or services that are regulated by the FDA. The FDA enforces laws and regulations designed to ensure that regulated products are "honestly, accurately, and informatively represented."[41] FDA rules include restrictions on the labeling and promotion of prescription drugs. Both advertising and public relations professionals working in the health-care field must be aware of these limitations.

The FDA's Division of Drug Marketing, Advertising, and Communications (DDMAC) oversees prescription drug promotional labeling and advertising. Advertising includes commercial messages broadcast on television or radio, communicated over the telephone, or printed in magazines and newspapers. According to regulations, drug ads or promotions cannot be false or misleading and cannot omit material facts. Companies are required to submit their direct-to-consumer (DTC) ads to the FDA at the time they begin running. However, some companies seek prior approval.

"We look at a lot of DTC ads before they run," says Kathryn J. Aikin, of DDMAC. "Manufacturers typically want to be sure they're getting started on the right foot."[42]

Quick ✔ Check

1. Why is it important for public relations practitioners to understand the laws and regulations that govern their organizations?
2. Which federal agency serves as a watchdog against false and misleading advertising claims?
3. What does *disclosure* mean, and why are disclosure rules so vigorously enforced?

Libel

Another area in which public relations practitioners may be restricted in their use of free expression involves **libel,** which is loosely defined as "a false communication that wrongfully injures the reputation of others."[43] To put it another way, when you bad-mouth someone, you had better have your facts!

There are two major reasons why public relations practitioners need to have a good understanding of libel law. First, they need to know that there are limits to free speech, especially when it involves another person's or company's reputation. They also need to understand that the courts have—under certain circumstances—given people great latitude in expressing their opinions on matters of public concern.

The Burden of Proof in Libel

Before 1964, people seeking damages under a claim that they had been libeled needed to prove five things: defamation, publication, identification, damage, and fault. These five things are known as the **burden of proof.**

DEFAMATION.   Defamation is any communication that unfairly injures a person's reputation and/or ability to maintain social contacts. Untruthful allegations that someone is a Nazi or has AIDS are examples of defamatory statements. It is also possible to defame a company, product, or service. In determining whether defamation has occurred, the court takes into account the context in which the statement was made, asking questions such as whether a reasonable person would understand the comment to be a parody or a joke. A truthful statement cannot be considered defamatory. Also, under the law you cannot defame a dead person.

PUBLICATION.   Publication is the communication of a defamatory statement to a third party. Don't let the term *publication* fool you. This burden of proof is not restricted to print media; it is met regardless of the communication channel used. Another important concept closely related to this is the *republication rule*. If you repeat a defamatory statement made by someone else, *you* can be subject to a separate libel claim, even if you accurately quoted the original source. However, there are exceptions to the republication rule. For example, you may accurately repeat a defamatory statement contained in an official court document or during a meeting of an official governmental body such as Congress.

IDENTIFICATION.   Identification is the requirement that the person or organization alleging libel has to be identified in such a way that a reasonable person could infer that the defamatory statements applied to the plaintiff. This is easy to prove when names are used. However, this requirement can also be satisfied when no names are mentioned, if the defamatory statement provides information that can lead a reasonable person to believe it describes a particular individual or organization. It is even possible to defame members of a group. An allegation that someone at your college is a crook probably does not satisfy this burden. However, an allegation that someone in your family is a crook probably does.

DAMAGE.   There has to be evidence that the person or organization suffered injury or **damage** as a result of the defamation. This is not limited to financial injury, such as the loss of a job. Damage can also consist of loss of social esteem, such as losing all of your friends. Although this kind of damage may be intangible, juries have been known to give out some very high monetary awards as compensation for loss of social esteem.

FAULT.   A plaintiff can demonstrate **fault** by proving that the defamatory statement is untrue. (Remember, a truthful statement is not defamatory.) Before 1964, the burden was on the defendant to show that the statement was true. Even if the statement was made as a result of unintentional error, the fact that an error was made was all that really mattered. However, it is on this burden of proof—fault, or falseness—that in 1964 the Supreme Court made what many have argued was one of its most significant rulings involving freedom of expression. In that ruling the Court articulated the doctrine of *actual malice,* to which we now turn.

Actual Malice

In the case of **The New York Times v. Sullivan,** the Court set a higher burden of proof in libel cases involving public officials. It also shifted the burden of proving the falsity of a statement to the plaintiffs. In essence, the justices said public officials had to show not only that the statements made about them were not true but that the source of those statements knew—or should have known—they were not true. This higher burden of proof is known as **actual malice,** which the Court defined as knowing falsehood or reckless disregard for the truth.

Why did the Supreme Court make it harder for public officials to sue for libel? The case came out of the civil rights struggle of the 1960s. A civil rights group had run a full-page advertisement titled "Heed Their Rising Voices" in the *New York Times*. In the ad the group accused Montgomery, Alabama, officials of illegally suppressing lawful dissent. The basic thrust of the advertisement was accurate. However, some of the statements made in it were not—such as the number of times Martin Luther King Jr. had been arrested (four, not seven as stated in the advertisement). Because of the republication rule, Montgomery Police Commissioner L. B. Sullivan decided to sue the newspaper for libel. The purpose of this tactic was clearly understood by all: to make the nation's news media think twice before accepting the word of civil rights advocates. A jury awarded Sullivan $500,000 in damages, and the Alabama Supreme Court upheld the ruling. The U.S. Supreme Court, however, overturned the decision in a 5–4 vote.

In writing for the Court, Justice William Brennan said this higher burden of proof was necessary to guarantee healthy public debate:

> A rule compelling the critic of official conduct to guarantee the truth of all his factual assertions—and to do so on pain of libel judgments virtually unlimited in amount—leads

to . . . "self-censorship." Allowance of the defense of truth, with the burden of proving it on the defendant, does not mean that only false speech will be deterred. . . . Under such a rule, would-be critics of official conduct may be deterred from voicing their criticism, even though it is believed to be true and even though it is in fact true, because of doubt whether it can be proved in court or fear of expense of having to do so. . . . The rule thus dampens the vigor and limits the variety of public debate. It is inconsistent with the First and Fourteenth Amendments.[44]

Subsequent court decisions have defined a **public official** as a person elected to public office (and potentially criticized in that role) or anyone who has significant public responsibility and is engaged in policy making. In another decision, *Gertz v. Robert Welch, Inc.,* the Supreme Court extended the actual malice burden to libel cases involving **public figures**—people who have widespread notoriety or have injected themselves into a public controversy in an attempt to influence its outcome. The Reverend Jesse Jackson may not be a public official, but when it comes to civil rights, he is considered a public figure.

This takes us back to something we stated earlier: People are often given great latitude in expressing their opinions on matters of public concern. As hard a pill as it may be to swallow, there is often little that public relations practitioners can do when they or their bosses are harshly criticized in the media. If a boss qualifies as either a public official or a public figure, then he or she is part of the public discourse and must meet a higher burden of proof, actual malice, to sue successfully for libel. Although a few public officials and public figures have won libel cases, most have not.

Other Forms of Libel

In the mid-1980s the courts handled two libel cases under common law rules. Common law consists of legal rules and principles that originate from judicial decisions, as opposed to those that are enacted by legislators or regulatory agencies.[45] The nature of these **common law libel** cases raises a red flag for business communicators because both cases involve everyday business practices in which human nature can lead to "mistakes." Several elements of these cases are of particular note. First is the lack of constitutional protection. Communication of "a private matter" is not protected by the First Amendment; in these cases, therefore, the plaintiff needed to show only negligence to win punitive damages. Second, in one of the cases the plaintiff won damages on defamatory but true information that exceeded the company's privilege to share such information.

The first case involved the credit reporting firm Dun & Bradstreet, which had issued an erroneous credit report on Greenmoss Builders, a building contractor. The Supreme Court ruled that this was a "private matter" not involving "matters of public concern" and permitted Greenmoss to recover $50,000 in presumed damages and $300,000 in punitive damages.[46] Although a complicated decision, the ruling appears to exclude nonmedia defendants from constitutional protection.

The second case involved a DuPont company memo following the firing of an employee for sexual harassment. The memo referred to the recent firing and then restated company policies and procedures regarding the issue. Eventually word of the firing, including the identity of the former employee, spread through the community. The former employee sued DuPont for common law libel and won. The court ruled that the company had gone too far in identifying the ex-employee to those who did not need to know his name. The ruling came despite the fact that the information about the employee was true, and despite the company's recognized privilege to pass that information around on a need-to-know basis. Thus, in this common law libel case, truth was *not* a defense. True information that exceeds privilege, in this case someone's legitimate need to know, can cost your company in libel damages.

A recent addition to libel law is **food disparagement laws**—known informally as "veggie libel laws." Although these laws may sound somewhat frivolous, the reason for their creation is not. They are the outgrowth of aggressive news reporting that has had a negative effect—sometimes fair, sometimes unfair—on the marketplace. The first of these laws resulted from a 1989 controversy in which the CBS news magazine program *60 Minutes* ran a story linking the use of the pesticide Alar on apples to cancer in children. The report resulted in a sharp drop in apple sales. Growers sued CBS and lost. However, the incident spawned the adoption of food disparagement laws in more than a dozen states.[47] In the most famous of the veggie libel cases, talk show host Oprah Winfrey successfully defended herself against a suit brought by the cattle industry in 1996. Winfrey had suggested on her show that U.S. beef was not safe to eat. When beef prices fell as a result of what has been called "the Oprah effect," the Texas beef producers sued. However, they met the same fate as the apple growers and lost.[48]

Privacy

Libel is not the only area of the law to distinguish between truly private individuals and persons in the limelight. This distinction is also evident in privacy law. The legal debate over an individual's right to privacy is very complicated and, in many instances, unresolved. It often surprises people to discover that the U.S. Constitution does not specifically mention an individual's right to privacy. However, such a right has developed over the years through the passage of laws and through judicial decisions. As a general rule, private individuals have an easier time suing for invasion of privacy than do public figures.

The Four Torts of Privacy

Although the word *privacy* has one meaning in common everyday usage, it carries a different meaning when used in a legal context. *Black's Law Dictionary* has defined **privacy** as "the right to be left alone; the right of a person to be free from unwarranted publicity."[49] The law recognizes four torts, or wrongful acts, that constitute an invasion of privacy: intrusion, false light, publication of private facts, and appropriation.

QuickBreak 15.3

THE PURSUIT OF PRIVACY

The *right* to privacy and the *reality* of privacy are two very different concepts in the Digital Age. In a world with a 24-hour news cycle and thousands of reporters needing to fill news holes, woe to anyone who unwittingly becomes a subject of media attention. It can be a suffocating experience.

Just ask Richard Jewell. He worked as a security guard in Centennial Park during the 1996 Summer Olympics in Atlanta. On a Friday night during the games, Jewell spotted a green backpack, suspected that it was a bomb, and helped hurry enough people from the scene that only one person was killed when it exploded. At first he was hailed as a hero. But when the media identified him as a suspect, he and his family suffered 88 days of unrelenting scrutiny.

"He would appear to be the victim of the beast that the media can turn into when there is blood in the water," *USA Today* reported years later. "The images of Jewell wading through the world press to get to an FBI interview never die."[50]

Jewell was eventually cleared of wrongdoing in the Centennial Park blast. Someone else was arrested. Several media organizations chose to settle libel suits brought by Jewell. One is still wending its way through the courts.[51]

The lines between legitimate news interest and prurient curiosity are often blurred. Consider the matter of Dale Earnhardt's autopsy photos.[52] When the racing legend tragically died from injuries received in the last lap of the 2001 Daytona 500, questions arose about NASCAR's official explanation for the driver's death, a seat belt failure. The *Orlando Sentinel*

had reported that four drivers had recently died as a result of violent head whip, a preventable injury. In an effort to confirm its suspicions, the newspaper submitted a public records request for Earnhardt's autopsy photos. Although the *Sentinel* said it would not publish the photos, the family fought the request out of a fear that the photos would wind up on the Internet.

What followed was a flurry of legal and legislative activity. In court, the newspaper won a partial victory when it agreed to the selection of an independent medical doctor to examine the photographs under court supervision. The expert confirmed the newspaper's suspicion that violent head whip, not seat belt failure, was to blame. As a result, NASCAR reversed an earlier decision and required head and neck restraints for drivers.

However, in the court of public opinion, the Earnhardt family was a clear winner. Because of an outpouring of public outrage, state lawmakers passed the Florida Family Protection Act within 39 days of the crash. The bill severely restricts media access to autopsy photos. A Florida student newspaper challenged the constitutionality of the law all the way to the U.S. Supreme Court and lost.

And we haven't even begun to discuss hackers and eavesdropping technology that invade our privacy in ways we can't even imagine. The right and reality of privacy continues to evolve in the Digital Age. As with most other social conflicts, the issues will eventually boil down to a question of values.

INTRUSION.   Intrusion is defined as an improper and intentional invasion of a person's physical seclusion or private affairs. This area of privacy law hinges on whether a person has a reasonable expectation of privacy. Examples of intrusion involve trespassing on private property and illegally bugging telephone conversations. But if a television crew positioned on a public sidewalk photographed you inside your home through an open window, that would not, in a legal sense, be considered intrusion.

FALSE LIGHT.   You can be sued if you present someone in a **false light,** even if the communication in question isn't defamatory. For example, a picture of a man holding a mug of water in his hand is not, in and of itself, defamatory. But if the man is a member of a religion that prohibits its followers from drinking alcohol, and if the picture's caption implies that he is enjoying a beer, that could result in a claim of false light invasion of privacy. Categories of false light are distortion (the unintentional distortion of reality), fabrication (knowing falsehood perpetrated through alteration or embellishment of the facts), and fictionalization (publication of something, usually a book or movie, that is presented as fiction but closely mirrors real life).

PUBLICATION OF PRIVATE FACTS.   **Publication of private facts** involves the public disclosure of true personal information that is embarrassing and potentially offensive. The courts have ruled, in essence, that we are entitled to keep some secrets about ourselves. However, to make a successful claim under this tort, a plaintiff must show that the information is neither newsworthy nor from a public record. If an ordinary person drinks too much in the privacy of his or her home and doesn't break any laws, it is likely that the courts will consider this private information. However, if this same person is an elected official and gets picked up for drunken driving, his or her drinking problem becomes a public matter.

APPROPRIATION.   **Appropriation** is defined as the commercial use of someone's name, voice, likeness, or other defining characteristics without consent. For example, entertainer Bette Midler was once forced to tone down her stage act because she too closely mimicked the voice and mannerisms of legendary actress Mae West. "The Divine Miss M" herself later successfully used this aspect of privacy law to prevent a Midler sound-alike from appearing in an advertisement. The commercial use of a person's likeness without consent is often referred to either as *misappropriation* or as infringement of an individual's *right of publicity*. This right does not necessarily end with a person's death. In several states, California among them, the deceased's heirs retain the "right of publicity." However, the courts have said that in some circumstances a claim of misappropriation is not valid. For example, news content is not considered a commercial use. Nor is it considered a commercial use when a media outlet uses a likeness in promoting itself. Written consent is the best protection from a claim of misappropriation.

Privacy Issues in Public Relations

Privacy issues can arise in countless aspects of the practice of public relations. Practitioners routinely prepare news releases, publicity photos, videos, newsletters, annual reports, brochures, posters, and web sites for public dissemination. An invasion of privacy suit can originate from any of these communications.

One area in which the practitioner has to be especially sensitive to privacy rights is employee relations. "It should not be assumed that a person's status as an employee waives his/her right to privacy," writes Frank Walsh, an expert in public relations law. "However, there are circumstances in which the employment relationship may provide an implied consent or waiver sufficient to invalidate an invasion of privacy suit."[53]

Privacy concerns also come into play when reporters make inquiries about employees. There are restrictions on the kinds of employee information that can be made public. The laws vary by location and profession. Typically, practitioners are limited to confirming a person's employment, job title, job description, date hired, and, in some cases, date terminated. A good guideline to follow: Check first with the personnel or human resources department about what is considered public or private employee information.

The growth of the Internet has raised many workplace questions. For example, the degree to which an employer may monitor an employee's e-mail may depend on whether a reasonable expectation of privacy exists. In some corporations employees are told that their e-mail will be monitored. Other companies, in search of time-wasting and inappropriate behavior, regularly review printouts of the web sites their employees visit while on the job.

Copyright

Although privacy protections are not specifically mentioned in the U.S. Constitution, **copyright** protections are. Copyrights protect original works from unauthorized use. Central to any discussion of copyright protections is the concept of **intellectual property,** which federal law defines as "original works of authorship that are fixed in a tangible form of expression." Copyrights cover seven forms of expression: literary works; musical works; dramatic works; pantomimes and choreographic works; pictorial, graphic, and sculptural works; motion pictures and other audiovisual works; and sound recordings.[54] Because the development of digital technology has made it nearly impossible to tell a copy from an original, the protection of intellectual property is a legal area of vital importance.

Copyright concerns about protecting one's own property and respecting the rights of others are a common issue for public relations practitioners. Copyright law confronts us all in many different ways every day. Is it all right to take a funny editorial cartoon published in the morning newspaper and reprint it in the company newsletter? Can someone use one company's products to promote another's without permission? Is it legal to take an image off a web site and use it in another medium? Are you allowed to photocopy this book?

Copyright Guidelines

As is true with other aspects of public relations law, the best place to get answers to these and other questions about copyrights are people who have expertise in this area—in this case, copyright lawyers and the U.S. Copyright Office. That said, some general rules of copyright are worth remembering:

■ Copyright protection exists from the moment a work is created in a fixed, tangible form. In other words, the law presumes that a work becomes the intellectual property of the author at the moment of its creation.

■ Copyrights do not protect works that have not been fixed in a tangible form of expression. Although it is possible to copyright an author's written description of a particular location, that does not prohibit someone else from offering a different description of the same setting.

■ If a work is prepared by someone within the scope of his or her employment, it is considered **work for hire** and becomes the intellectual property of the employer. The work belongs to the employer if it was produced while the employee was "on the clock." Even after hours, the employer retains the rights if company resources (such as computers or copiers) were used.

■ It is possible for the copyright owner, such as a photographer or writer or artist, to grant limited use of the work while retaining copyright ownership.

■ Copyrights do not protect ideas, methods, systems, processes, concepts, principles, and discoveries. They do, however, protect the manner in which these are expressed.

■ Government documents and other publicly owned works may not be copyrighted.

The Digital Millennium Copyright Act

The ability to make exact copies of digital files without any measurable decline in quality is one of the great blessings of the Digital Age. However, in the view of copyright holders, it is also one of the great curses.

As noted in Chapter 11, digital technology has made it easier to copy and distribute the fruits of someone else's labors. This is of particular concern to the entertainment and computer software industries, which have seen their intellectual property rights eroded by the manufacturing and distribution of illegal copies.

These industries use special technology designed to foil piracy. For example, when a Hollywood movie studio distributes its latest movie on DVD, it encrypts the data on the disk to prevent unauthorized copying. That should be enough. However, in a world in which the frontiers of computer knowledge are breached every day, it is not. To use an analogy, locksmiths would face the same problem if every time they built a better lock, someone came along behind them and built an even better key.

In an effort to address this problem, the U.S. Congress passed the **Digital Millennium Copyright Act** (DMCA) in 1998. The DMCA established new rules for downloading, sharing, and viewing copyrighted material on the Internet. It made it a crime to circumvent antipiracy measures built into most commercial software, videos, and

ONLINE MUSIC PIRACY

Of all of the issues discussed in this chapter, the one that strikes closest to home for many readers is the battle over intellectual property. Of course, it is not often thought of in those terms. Many young people see it as the clash between the music industry and consumers over downloading music on the Internet. To some, this issue is nothing more than an attempt by the rich to get richer. But the music industry sees it as theft and estimates annual losses from piracy at $4.2 billion worldwide.[55]

In many instances, the law on intellectual property is clear. According to the U.S. Copyright Office, "Copyright is a form of protection provided by the laws of the United States (title 17, U.S. Code) to the authors of 'original works of authorship,' including literary, dramatic, musical, artistic, and certain other intellectual works. This protection is available to both published and unpublished works."[56]

Protection of intellectual property was included in the original draft of the U.S. Constitution. But that was before the Digital Age, the Internet, and the creation of technology that makes it easy to create and globally distribute perfect reproductions.

This is where the legal waters are muddy. At first, the music industry targeted file-sharing services such as Napster. The courts ruled that these services were guilty of abetting copyright infringement because they operated from a central server. However, when companies such as Grokster, KaZaA, and Morpheus moved to more decentralized peer-to-peer (P2P) technology, the music industry hit a snag. Citing the so-called 1983 Betamax case, the courts ruled that these P2P companies have no more control over the actions of consumers than manufacturers of home video recorders.[57]

That legal setback forced the music industry to take the controversial step of suing its own customers. The Recording Industry Association of America filed 261 copyright infringement lawsuits in September 2003.[58] RIAA claimed its lawsuits targeted people who illegally distributed, on average, more than 1,000 music files for millions of other P2P network users.

This tactic brought the music industry both scorn and embarrassment—especially when the media learned that one defendant was a 12-year-old New York honors student.[59] However, the lawsuits also had the desired effect: One study reported that the percentage of online Americans downloading music files had been cut in half in the three months after RIAA filed its lawsuits.[60]

DVDs. It also outlawed code-cracking devices used to copy software illegally. Violators can be fined up to $2,500 for each violation.

The law has its critics. Academics, computer researchers, and librarians argue that DMCA limits their right to copy and share a limited amount of material for educational and noncommercial purposes. "The DMCA is not really a copyright statute," said intellectual property attorney Richard Horning. "It's an access control statute."[61] However the law provides some exemptions to some of these same groups, including limited institutional liability for violations committed by college faculty and students. While several attempts have been made to amend DMCA, those efforts have been successfully opposed by the music and movie industries.[62]

Fair Use

The courts have said it is all right to use copyrighted works without their owners' permission in some circumstances. These instances fall under the concept known as **fair use,** which the law has said is the use of copyrighted material "for purposes such as criticism, comments, news reporting, and teaching."[63] Again, fair use is a very complex area of the law. However, it is usually considered fair use if the copyrighted work is used for an educational as opposed to a commercial purpose.

The degree to which the copyrighted material is copied and the effect on its potential market value also affect whether a claim of fair use is valid. It is probably safe for professors to photocopy a paragraph from a book and distribute the copies to their classes. Copy shops have stopped reproducing book chapters for professors using course packets, however, because the courts have ruled that this practice harms the book's potential market value.

In a ruling that further defined fair use rights, the U.S. Supreme Court strengthened the rights of freelance writers in 2001. The court ruled by a 7–2 margin that major publishing companies may not reproduce the work of freelancers in electronic form without their consent. The effect of the ruling was to give the writers a voice in whether their work, originally published in one form, could be electronically published in an online database. As a practical matter, the Court's ruling largely affects only that material produced in the pre–Internet era—before freelance contracts specified whether the material could be used online.

Public relations practitioners often claim fair use when taking a quotation from a copyrighted publication for use in a news release, brochure, report, or speech. (For example, we have engaged in this practice in writing this book.) However, a claim of fair use cannot be made without appropriate attribution of the copyrighted material to its owner. As your writing and editing teachers will remind you, this is just one more reason why it is necessary to use quotation marks and to properly cite sources of information.

Protecting Your Intellectual Property Rights

To assert a right of copyright protection, the work in question should bear a copyright notice that cites the year of the copyright and the name of its owner. An example: Copyright © 2005 Joan Q. Public. An even more complete way of securing copyright protection is to register a work within three months of its creation with the U.S. Copyright Office, Library of Congress, 101 Independence Ave. S.E., Washington, D.C. 20559-6000. There is a $30 nonrefundable fee for basic registrations. Although registration is not required to claim ownership, it is required to bring an infringement of copyright lawsuit.

As a result of legislation proposed by the late Congressman Sonny Bono, a California Republican—the guy from Sonny and Cher for those who know pop music history—the owners of copyrighted works retain their rights longer than in the past. According to the U.S. Copyright Office web site: "As a general rule, for works created after January 1, 1978, copyright protection lasts for the life of the author plus an additional 70 years. For an anonymous work, a pseudonymous work, or a work made for hire, the copyright endures for a term of 95 years from the year of its first publication or a term of 120 years from the year of its creation, whichever expires first."[64] The U.S. Supreme Court upheld the change in 2003. That decision relieved executives at the Walt Disney Corp., who were in danger of losing control over their most identifiable icon, Mickey Mouse.[65]

Similar to copyrights are trademarks and service marks. Both protect intellectual property rights. **Trademarks** (™) protect names, designs, slogans, and symbols that are associated with specific products. When you see the symbol ®, that indicates that the trademark is registered with the U.S. Office of Patents and Trademarks. For example, pick up a 12-ounce can of Coca-Cola®. Both the name Coca-Cola® and its derivative, Coke®, are registered trademarks. So is the design of the can and style of the lettering. When organizations want to protect names, designs, slogans, and designs associated with a particular service, they apply for a **service mark,** indicated by the symbol ˢᴹ.

Quick ✔ Check

1. What is the higher burden of proof that public officials and public figures must meet to make a claim of libel?
2. In terms of privacy law, what is appropriation?
3. What steps have been taken to protect intellectual property rights on the Internet?

Litigation Public Relations

Every time you turn on your television, somebody's on trial. And we are not just talking about reruns of network television dramas such as *The Practice, Matlock, Law & Order,* or *Perry Mason.* We are seeing real people, real issues, and real-life drama. Whether O. J. Simpson, Martha Stewart, Kobe Bryant, or Michael Jackson, it seems as if *everyone* is in court. There's even Court TV—all trials all the time. With the convergence of the Digital Age and increased camera access to courtrooms during the last decade, we have entered what the *New York Times* has called "the era of the lawyer as press agent."[66] We have also seen the birth of a new branch of public relations: **litigation public relations (LPR).**

Litigation public relations is the use of mass communication techniques to influence events surrounding legal cases. Although it often focuses on lawyers' dealings with reporters, including preparation of news releases, coaching for interviews, and monitoring media, LPR can also involve the use of other public relations practices. These include focus groups and surveys as well as courtroom exhibit preparation.

Public Relations as a Legal Strategy

A rash of high-profile cases—most notably the double-murder trial of O. J. Simpson—has brought the ethics of LPR practitioners into question. It is an ethical controversy rooted in the Constitution. The First Amendment guarantees freedom of speech and of the press. The Sixth Amendment guarantees fair and open trials. In this age of pervasive media, these two social interests often come into conflict.

While serving as chairman of the Criminal Justice Standards Committee of the American Bar Association (ABA), William Jeffress Jr. said, "A lot of us think defense attorneys and prosecutors shouldn't be playing to the press and becoming public relations agents for their clients."[67] One New York judge complained, "Lawyers now feel it is the essence of their function to try the case in the public media."[68]

Not surprisingly, some lawyers vigorously defend the use of public relations in connection with their practices. The late William M. Kunstler, who served as defense counsel in some of the most controversial trials of the past generation, believed that the use of pretrial publicity was necessary to balance scales of justice he thought were tipped unfairly toward the prosecution. "Whenever and wherever practicable, fire must be met with fire," Kunstler wrote.[69]

Because few states have laws that limit what prosecutors and defense attorneys can say before trial, it is generally left to state bar associations to regulate pretrial comment.[70] Most of these regulations mirror Rule 3.6 of the ABA's Model Rules of Professional Conduct. The rule states that "a lawyer shall not make an extrajudicial statement that a reasonable person would expect to be disseminated by means of public communication if the lawyer knows or reasonably should know that it will have a substantial likelihood of materially prejudicing an adjudicative proceeding."[71] However, this rule is rarely enforced. "It's hard to prove that some out-of-court statement has an impact on a trial," said New York University law professor Stephen Gillers. "So, essentially, there's a rule but there really isn't any rule."[72]

The waters were muddied even further by the U.S. Supreme Court in June 1991, when the Court reversed sanctions against a Nevada attorney who had conducted a news conference to counter negative publicity about his client. In *Dominic P. Gentile v. State Bar of Nevada*, the Court said the rule, as interpreted by the Nevada state bar, was too vague. In his opinion for the majority, Justice Anthony M. Kennedy wrote, "In some circumstances press comment is necessary to protect the rights of the client and prevent abuse of the courts."[73]

The Use of LPR Tactics

One survey of trial lawyers suggests that although most do not, as a rule, use mass communication techniques in their practices, a majority approve of their use. Nine out of 10 litigators surveyed said that in certain circumstances it is appropriate to speak to the media on behalf of a client. And by a more than 2–1 ratio, those who were surveyed and expressed an opinion said they thought the media had been fair

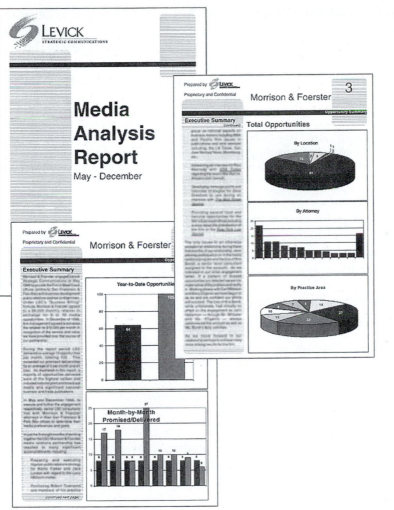

Media Analysis Report A media analysis report can help litigation public relations practitioners show clients the effectiveness of media relations strategies and tactics. (Courtesy of Levick Strategic Communications)

in reporting cases in which they had personally been involved. Still, most lawyers appear to be uneasy about being under the glare of the media.[74]

When public relations practitioners are engaged in LPR, they usually work for the lawyer, not the client. LPR practitioners often aid in pretrial research by using public opinion polls and focus groups to determine the mood of the jury pool. Lawyers sometimes use this information to test specific approaches that may be employed in court. Practitioners often coach both lawyers and clients on how to deal with the media, how to be interviewed, and how to be proactive in defending their reputation. A practitioner's roles also may include preparation of courtroom exhibits; service as a contact point for the media; and, in the most controversial aspect of LPR, assistance in efforts to influence the jury pool before a trial ever takes place.

Even when the practitioner works independently of a lawyer, it is often the lawyer who has the closest access to the client. The reason for this is simple: The lawyer, not the practitioner, has legal immunity. One very public example of this surfaced in 1998, when then–presidential spokesman Mike McCurry told reporters that he had not asked President Clinton about his relationship with a White House intern. McCurry said he did not want to be subpoenaed by the special prosecutor investigating the allegations surrounding Clinton:

> On matters like this that are going to be under investigation, I think it could conceivably jeopardize the legal representation the president is entitled to, so I choose not to ask him directly about these things and rely on what counsel tells me. And then we work with the president to figure how we're going to respond to questions.[75]

For any practitioner, the reality of this lawyer–client **privilege** issue can be difficult to swallow—especially when it runs counter to the professional need to have direct access to management. It was especially frustrating for McCurry, who told reporters at one White House briefing, "I think you all know the constraints that I'm laboring under here, and I don't want to belabor the pain and anguish I feel."[76]

Is LPR in Society's Best Interests?

Is LPR a good thing for our society? No pun intended, but the jury is still out. On the one hand, people and companies should have every right to defend their reputations in the court of public opinion. However, many are bothered by attempts to use extrajudicial statements (statements made outside a court) to influence proceedings inside the court.

One place where that happens with increasing regularity is the Internet. According to a study released in 2004, a growing number of defendants are taking their side of the story to the web.[77] For example, when Michael Jackson was arrested on child molestation charges in November 2003, his publicist posted his defense on MJJ-Source.com, "The Official Source for Michael Jackson News and Information." The site contained an open letter to his fans, news releases, background materials, and downloadable court documents. According to the authors of that study, "The analysis revealed that standard litigation public relations standards transfer well to the Internet and suggests that such web sites are a promising means for disseminating and controlling a client's message."[78]

It all comes down to the difficult balancing act left us by the framers of the Constitution. A built-in conflict exists between the First and Sixth Amendments. Judges, lawyers, and public relations practitioners must carefully navigate these uncharted waters. We must also remember that, as public relations practitioners, we have our own codes of ethics to uphold. The PRSA *Member Code of Ethics 2000* says that practitioners must "serve the public interest by acting as responsible advocates for those we represent." The code also says that "a member shall preserve the integrity of the process of communication." Though not explicit statements on LPR, they do, nevertheless, provide meaningful guidance.

In these muddy and uncharted waters, professional and personal values are the best guide as to what is best for our clients and for society.

Quick ✔ Check

1. What is litigation public relations?
2. Why must litigation public relations practitioners sometimes deal only with lawyers instead of the lawyers' clients?
3. What are the arguments for and against the use of litigation public relations?

Summary

As a result of the "corporate horrors" of recent years, public relations practitioners face pressure to operate within both the letter and the spirit of the laws governing their profession. Practitioners must follow a wide array of rules and regulations that cover practically every aspect of their professional responsibilities. Unfortunately, many appear woefully ignorant of these laws.

First Amendment protection for the practice of public relations lies in the gray area between political and commercial speech. The underlying purpose of each communication determines the degree of constitutional protection it enjoys. In addition to constitutional issues, laws govern various aspects of specific businesses. Among the most notable of these are disclosure laws pertaining to publicly held companies. Practitioners also are often confronted by a need to understand libel, privacy, and copyright laws. In the case of libel and privacy laws, they also need to understand the different burdens of proof for public and private individuals. The growth of the Internet and digital technologies have triggered legal issues undreamt of a generation ago.

Public relations is having a growing—and not necessarily positive—effect on our civil and criminal justice systems. The practice of litigation public relations is expanding dramatically—thanks in part to the built-in conflict that exists between our constitutional freedom of expression and our constitutional right to a fair and open trial. Here, as in other areas of public relations, we should be guided by our values.

DISCUSSION QUESTIONS

1. Devise a response to this statement from a fellow public relations practitioner: "This is the United States. I have freedom of speech. I can say whatever I want on behalf of my clients."
2. How do federal agencies regulate commercial speech?
3. What is the burden of proof for libel? Are all persons treated the same under libel law?
4. How do privacy rights affect the practice of public relations?
5. What are some tasks undertaken by a practitioner of litigation public relations? Under what constraints do LPR practitioners operate?

Memo
from the
Field

James F. Haggerty, Esq.;
President; The PR
Consulting Group, Inc.;
New York, New York

James F. Haggerty, president and CEO of The PR Consulting Group, is an attorney with more than 18 years of experience in marketing, public relations, and public affairs. Among the nation's best-known experts in litigation communications, Haggerty has also earned a national reputation in professional services marketing, public affairs, and crisis management.

The intersection of public relations and law continues to widen, as interest in legal matters and legal media coverage grows. Unfortunately, the intersection is often littered with blind spots, potholes, and other hazards. For the PR practitioner with the right skills, however, it can be an avenue to a unique public relations career, combining media, law, regulation, government affairs, and public opinion in a way that is fast-paced, challenging and, in the end, extremely satisfying.

Law now permeates most aspects of our lives, and media and news coverage are no exception. Watch CNN, MSNBC, or Fox News long enough and you begin to appreciate just how much legal news coverage is a part of our lives. A Court TV producer recently told me that the network became so successful that *all* news is now Court TV. She wasn't very far from the truth.

The ramifications for the public relations field are enormous. You don't have to be a lawyer to excel in this field, but nearly all PR practitioners at some time in their careers will now find themselves immersed in legal issues—or butting heads with the lawyers representing their client. Lawyers who still feel "no comment" is always the best response.

My company spends 70–80 percent of its time advising clients in the relatively new public relations specialty called litigation public relations. It combines the best elements of crisis communications, public affairs, and litigation strategy. In litigation public relations, it is not enough to deliver media coverage or other PR "results"—you've got to deliver coverage that helps to meet the client's litigations goals: whether it is discouraging legal action before it is filed, creating the proper atmosphere for a beneficial settlement, or controlling the effect on the client's reputation as a case moves to trial and beyond.

You need the ability to sift through 100-page legal filings for the sentence or two that catches the real "story" behind the case. You need the confidence to deal with lawyers and argue for a communications strategy that will enhance the litigation strategy. And you need to pick your media targets carefully: Giant media lists and mass-produced press kits are usually the exception rather than the rule.

But here's a fact most lawyers won't tell you: Sometimes what happens in the court of public opinion can be more important than what happens in the court of law.

An example: We recently worked with a client who spent eight years tangled in oppressive litigation with a large multinational corporation. Although the company's lawyers were doing an excellent job, the legal wrangling seemed endless. The other side's strategy was to bury the company in legal filings and discovery requests until virtually all of the defendant's resources were focused on fending off what was, at best, a very weak case. The litigation was sapping the lifeblood of a company that didn't have the resources to match the much larger multinational.

Then we got involved. Six months later, the case was withdrawn, with a simple joint statement that the parties would "agree to disagree."

How did this happen? In looking at the situation, we reasoned that the one thing that would stop the multinational plaintiff from continuing its frivolous litigation was a severe blow to the company's reputation. They needed to look not just wrong on the law but foolish for continuing what was obviously a mean-spirited, vindictive lawsuit designed to crush a smaller competitor. So we worked with thousands of pages of legal documents to assemble the kind of information that would convince an influential columnist to write an opinion piece exposing the true story of the case. Then we showed the column to an Associated Press reporter, who wrote a story on the column itself. The AP story was picked up in about a half-dozen cities nationwide. An editorial writer in one of the key trade publications covering the industry saw the AP story and wrote a very damaging editorial exposing the company's tactics. And so on.

It wasn't long before the multinational began to see that continuing the lawsuit was getting in the way of its own business goals. At that point, the plaintiff realized it was far easier to quit than to fight!

This is the value of litigation public relations. And while we usually can't have that kind of impact on every case, we can ensure that we create the kind of positive conditions that facilitate the best possible result for our clients: allowing them to get the litigation behind them and get back to the *real* work of their company or organization.

Case Study 15.1

Higher Standards?

The theme of the Bank of America's 2002 annual report was "Higher Standards." Chairman, CEO, and President Kenneth D. Lewis said it reflected the "company's commitment to the idea that in every endeavor, there is always an opportunity to raise the bar, to do something better than has ever been done before."[79]

In his letter to shareholders, Lewis took note of what he called "a crisis of public confidence in the ability of American corporations to govern themselves effectively and ethically." He said that Bank of America (BA) would aggressively promote its core values and its recently updated code of ethics.

"But we also know that actions speak louder than words," Lewis wrote. "And so, we foster a culture of openness, in which healthy debate is encouraged and associates are expected to blow the whistle on improper activity."[80]

Unfortunately for BA, someone had already blown the whistle. The Securities and Exchange Commission (SEC) received an anonymous letter during the summer of 2001 accusing BA of improper late-day trading and improper market timing.[81] In simpler terms, the complaint boiled down to giving a handful of investors an unfair advantage.

The timing of the transaction is critical. When someone purchases mutual fund shares after 4 P.M. Eastern U.S. Time—when the New York markets close—the law requires that they be priced at the *next day's* closing value. What the anonymous letter alleged—and the SEC later confirmed—was that BA allowed certain preferred customers to buy mutual fund shares at *that day's* closing price. That means that if the price went up overnight, the buyer got a bargain not available to all investors.[82]

With the anonymous letter were copies of e-mails that documented BA's actions. In November 2001, SEC staff asked BA to turn over the e-mails of seven senior managers from the previous three years. One e-mail in particular, which the bank's director of marketing had sent via blind copies to other senior executives, was of special interest.[83] To put it simply, it was the smoking gun.

What the SEC staff did not know was that BA had also received a copy of the anonymous letter. The company knew exactly what the SEC investigators sought.[84] What followed was a series of stalling and delaying tactics that, in the end, backfired.

BA responded to the government's document request by saying that it could produce e-mails for the previous five months, but that the restoration of earlier e-mails from backup tapes would incur an "unreasonable amount of time, labor, and expense."[85] The company did not disclose that it had already restored the critical e-mail exchange, the so-called smoking gun. The e-mail was retrieved from the backup tape and then deleted.[86]

After receiving only a fraction of what it had requested by May 2002, the SEC again directed BA to turn over all documents in a timely matter. By October, the bank's attorney announced that the firm had fully complied with the government's request. However, it had not—the smoking gun e-mail was still missing. The SEC staff questioned a former company official under oath on October 28 and learned that BA did, in fact, have copies of the missing e-mail, as well as a copy of the anonymous letter that triggered the investigation. Bank officials later blamed "a technical glitch" for the failure to produce the documents.[87]

This pattern of delay continued. In December, the SEC again ordered BA to turn over the documents—only to learn a month later that some of them had been destroyed.[88] Another handover of additional documents in early February 2003 was still incomplete. As if to add insult to injury, SEC auditors flew from Washington to San Francisco later that month to examine what they had been led to believe were the remaining documents. Only after the auditors arrived from their cross-country trip did they learn that the company had known for months that hundreds of documents the auditors had expected to examine were "missing."[89]

To make a long story short, it wasn't until December 23, 2003—more than two years after the initial SEC staff request—that BA handed over all of the pertinent e-mails, including the smoking gun. BA fired several employees who had been embroiled in the scandal.[90] Armed with the evidence, the SEC began to piece together the whole story—not only the improper late-day trading that sparked the investigation, but also the subsequent cover-up.[91]

On May 10, 2004, the SEC announced that Bank of America had agreed to an official censure and a $10 million civil penalty as part of an out-of-court settlement. The commission found that BA "repeatedly failed to promptly furnish documents requested by the staff, provided misinformation concerning the ability of production status of such documents, and engaged in dilatory acts that delayed the investigation."[92]

The other shoe fell a few days later, when BA announced that it agreed to pay $375 million in shareholder repayments and civil penalties to settle impending securities fraud charges. Eight members of the bank's board of directors were also required to leave their positions within a year.[93]

"I believe that we will be judged not by the actions of a few of our associates, but rather by the way we responded as a team to a violation of our shared values," Bank of America CEO Lewis told shareholders in the company's 2003 annual report. "We will have no tolerance for decisions or actions that fail to put the interests of our customers, associates, and shareholders first."[94]

DISCUSSION QUESTIONS

1. From both legal and ethical perspectives, what did Bank of America do wrong?
2. What is the harm in a publicly held company like Bank of America giving its best customers an advantage in stock market transactions? Doesn't a special relationship deserve special treatment?
3. What is your reaction to statements made in Bank of America's 2002 and 2003 annual reports?
4. This case study does not mention the actions of any public relations practitioners. Why do you think the authors chose to include it?

Case Study 15.2

In Search of Sunshine

One of comedian George Carlin's characters from his classic standup routines is "Al Sleet, your hippy-dippy weatherman." Al, it seems, is just a few fries short of a Happy Meal. So it comes as no surprise when the hippy-dippy weatherman says, "Tonight's forecast: Dark. Continuing mostly dark through the night. Turning to scattered light at dawn."[95]

However, when University of Florida Professor Bill Chamberlin tells you that the forecast for accessing public records in a particular state is "dark," he is not joking. Instead, he and other like-minded individuals are making a statement about the value of citizen access to public records in a democracy.

Chamberlin is the director of the Marion Brechner Citizen Access Project (MBCAP), a research unit of the Brechner Center for Freedom of Information at the university's College of Journalism and Communications. According to the MBCAP's web site, its goal is "to allow citizens and public officials to better understand public access to local government information in all 50 states."[96] The project is named for Marion B. Brechner, a central Florida broadcasting executive and philanthropist who contributed $600,000 for its creation in 1999. She and her late husband, Joseph L. Brechner, long active in press freedom causes, had given more than $1 million for the creation of the Freedom of Information Center in 1985.[97]

"Any element of government control over information flow means that the coyote is in charge of the chicken barn," Chamberlin said. "Any government control over what information governments disclose and do not disclose to the public means a serious risk to our representative democracy."[98]

Brechner Center personnel often answer queries from the public, journalists, officials, and policy advocates. Chamberlin said that many of these questions in the early 1990s centered on which states had the best and worst laws granting public access to government records. With the help of Brechner's contribution and early support from the Knight Foundation, MBCAP was born and a massive research effort was launched.

Under Chamberlin's direction, UF graduate students examined public records and open meetings laws nationwide. "For the research, we used only graduate students with legal research training, given the sensitivity of putting legal material on the web," Chamberlin said. This involved research of each state's constitutional provisions and laws. It will eventually include reviews of relevant appellate court decisions.

The MBCAP's Sunshine Advisory Board evaluated this information in a variety of categories. For each, the 11-member board rated various state laws on a seven-point scale developed by Chamberlin and several research consultants. The highest ratings went to the states with the fewest barriers to public access to government records. Each of the scale's seven rating points is represented with a weather icon.

For example, the MBCAP staff researched the number of hours public records are available for citizen inspection. None of the states earned either a "sunny" (7), or completely open, rating. Nor did any receive a "mostly sunny" (6), or mostly open, rating. Fourteen states were rated as "sunny with clouds" (5), meaning that public records in those states are somewhat open. Nearly half of the states were rated as "party cloudy" (4), meaning the public records are "neither more open nor more closed." MBCAP rated record access in three states and the District of Columbia as being "cloudy" (3), or somewhat closed. Nine states were rated as "nearly dark" (2), or mostly closed. No states received a "dark" (1), or completely closed, rating.[99]

Each state's ratings are entered into an interactive database on MBCAP's web site. Visitors can study the transparency of individual states or compare ratings among states. The site also serves as a clearinghouse of freedom of information research from other organizations with similar interests, such as the Reporter's Committee for Freedom of the Press and the Society of Professional Journalists.

"We are regularly called by freedom of information activists, journalists, and state legislators interested in changing the law in their state," Chamberlin said. "They are anxious to learn what other states are doing and which states have the laws that most encourage access."

Chamberlin said that the MBCAP has focused its attention in recent years on the impact the War on Terrorism has had on state public records law. Democracies have had to strike a delicate balance between two of their core values, public safety and open government, he explained.

"Scholars and FOI activists have found that in the face of terrorism threats, state lawmakers from many states are shutting down access to a wide range of information, including security response plans and criminal investigations," Chamberlin said. "It may seem intuitively responsible to protect information that would assist terrorists."

However, Chamberlin added that shielding the public from the actions of government officials "may do more harm than good" because the public can't pressure officials to correct security flaws if it doesn't know about them.

Despite having relatively modest resources for the pursuit of its vital mission, the MBCAP continues to operate from its Florida office with one goal in mind: to make every state a sunshine state.

DISCUSSION QUESTIONS

1. Why is access to government information important to public relations practitioners?
2. Identify the four steps in the public relations process as they relate to the Marion Brechner Citizen Access Project.
3. What role do values play in this case study?
4. Given what has been described as "relatively modest resources," how would you promote the mission of the MBCAP?

Cyber Coach

Visit www.ablongman.com/guthmarsh3e for these study aids—and more:

- flashcards
- quizzes
- videos
- links to other sites
- real-world scenarios that let you be the public relations professional

KEY TERMS

actual malice, p. 504

administrative law judge, p. 495

annual report, p. 499

appropriation, p. 508

burden of proof, p. 503

cease and desist order, p. 495

civil penalties, p. 495

commercial speech, p. 491

common law libel, p. 505

consent order, p. 495

consumer redress, p. 495

copyright, p. 509

damage, p. 504

defamation, p. 503

Digital Millennium Copyright Act, p. 510

disclosure, p. 496

equal opportunity provision, p. 500

fair use, p. 512

false light, p. 508

fault, p. 504

Federal Communications Commission (FCC), p. 500

Federal Trade Commission (FTC), p. 494

First Amendment, p. 490

Food and Drug Administration (FDA), p. 502

food disparagement laws, p. 506

Form 10-K, p. 499

Freedom of Information Act (FOIA), p. 494

identification, p. 503

injunctions, p. 495

insider trading, p. 499

intellectual property, p. 509

intrusion, p. 507

libel, p. 503

litigation public relations (LPR), p. 513

The New York Times v. Sullivan, p. 504

personal attack rule, p. 501

political speech, p. 491

privacy, p. 506

privilege, p. 516

publication, p. 503

publication of private facts, p. 508

public figures, p. 505

public official, p. 505

Regulation FD, p. 496

Sarbanes-Oxley Act, p. 497

Securities and Exchange Commission (SEC), p. 495

service mark, p. 513

trademarks, p. 513

work for hire, p. 510

NOTES

1. "Explaining the Enron Bankruptcy," CNN, 12 January 2002, online, www.cnn.com.
2. "Adelphia Communication Milestones," *Washington Post,* 8 July 2004, online, www.washingtonpost.com.
3. "WorldCom Company Timeline," *Washington Post,* 11 May 2004, online, www.washingtonpost.com.
4. "The Tyco Mistrial: An Unfortunate Ending," *New York Times,* 3 April 2004, C4, online, LexisNexis.
5. "Former Tech Banker Quattrone on Trial," *Washington Post,* 2 May 2004, online, washingtonpost.com.
6. "Caseload in Federal Courts Still Rising," news release issued by the Administrative Office of the U.S. Courts, 18 March 2003, online, www.uscourts.gov.

7. Kathy R. Fitzpatrick, "Public Relations and the Law: A Survey of Practitioners," *Public Relations Review* (spring 1996): 1–8.

8. Morton J. Simon, *Public Relations Law* (New York: Meredith, 1969), 4.

9. *The Constitution of the United States and The Declaration of Independence* (Commission on the Bicentennial of the United States Constitution, 1992).

10. *The New York Times Co. v. Sullivan,* 376 US 255, 270 (1964).

11. *Virginia State Board of Pharmacy v. Virginia Citizens Consumer Council, Inc.,* 425 US 764, 765 (1976).

12. *Virginia State Board of Pharmacy v. Virginia Citizens Consumer Council, Inc.*

13. *Virginia State Board of Pharmacy v. Virginia Citizens Consumer Council, Inc.*

14. *Central Hudson Gas and Electric Corp. v. Public Service Commission of New York,* 447 US 557, 100 S. Ct. 2343 (1980).

15. John D. Zelezny, *Communications Law: Liberties, Restraints, and the Modern Media* (Belmont, Calif.: Wadsworth, 1997), 361; based on *Board of Trustees v. Fox,* 492 US 469, 480 (1989).

16. Robert S. Greenberger, "More Courts Are Granting Advertisements First Amendment Protection," *Wall Street Journal,* 3 July 2001, B1.

17. Karla K. Gower, "*Kasky v. Nike, Inc.*: The End of Constitutionally Protected Corporate Speech?" paper presented at the Association of Educators in Journalism and Mass Communications Annual Conference, Kansas City, Mo., August 2003.

18. Gower.

19. "PRSA Presses Supreme Court to Protect Free Speech Right for American Business," news release issued by the Public Relations Society of America e-mailed to its membership, 3 March 2003.

20. "Nike, Inc. and Kasky Announce Settlement of *Kasky v. Nike* First Amendment Case," Nike news release, 12 September 2003, online, www.nikebiz.com.

21. David W. Guth and Paul Wenske, *Media Guide for Attorneys* (Topeka, Kan.: Kansas Bar Association, 1995), 28.

22. Federal Trade Commission, www.ftc.gov.

23. FTC web site.

24. FTC web site.

25. Securities and Exchange Commission, online, www.sec.gov.

26. Final Rule: Selective Disclosure and Insider Trading, 17 CFR Parts 240, 243, and 249; release Nos. 33-7881, 34-43154, IC-245999, File No. S7-31-99. RIN 3235 AH82, www.sec.gov.

27. "The Laws That Govern the Securities Industry," Securities and Exchange Commission, online, www.sec.gov/about/laws.shtml.

28. Zelezny, 331; 17 C.F.R. § 240.10b-5 (1992).

29. Dennis L. Wilcox, Phillip H. Ault, and Warren K. Agee, *Public Relations Strategies and Tactics,* 3rd ed. (New York: HarperCollins, 1992), 142–143.

30. *Securities and Exchange Commission v. Texas Gulf Sulfur,* 446 F. 2nd 1301 (2nd Cir 1966).

31. Public Relations Society of America, *Member Code of Ethics 2000,* online, www.prsa.org/codeofethics.html.

32. Robert W. Taft, "Discretionary Disclosure," *Public Relations Journal,* April 1983, 34–35.

33. "A Chronology of ImClone and Martha Stewart," *Washington Post,* 8 July 2004, on-line, www.washingtonpost.com.

34. SEC web site.

35. "Public Relations Society of America Strongly Supports the Overturning of FCC Ownership Rules by the U.S. Third Circuit Court of Appeals," news release issued by the PRSA, 25 June 2003, online, www.prsa.org.

36. Seth Sutel, "Court Throws Out FCC's Media Ownership Rules," Associated Press, 24 June 2004, online, LexisNexis.

37. "Unwanted Faxes: What You Can Do," Federal Communications Commission, online, www.fcc.gov.

38. "FCC Delays Amended Fax Advertisement Regulations," news release issued by the PRSA, 19 August 2003, online, www.prsa.org.

39. Penny Brown Roberts, "Judge Rules Junk Faxes Not Protected Speech," *The Advocate* (Baton Rouge, La.), 6 August 2004, 1A, online, LexisNexis.

40. Food and Drug Administration, online, www.fda.gov.

41. FDA web site.

42. Carol Rados, "Truth in Advertising: Rx Drug Ads Come of Age," *FDA Consumer,* July–August 2004, online, www.fda.gov.

43. Zelezny, 519.

44. *The New York Times Co. v. Sullivan,* 376 US 254, 279 (1964).

45. This information on common law libel has been graciously supplied by Associate Professor Thomas W. Volek of the University of Kansas.

46. *Dun & Bradstreet v. Greenmoss Builders,* 472 US 749 (1985).

47. Adam Cohen, "Trial of the Savory," *Time,* 2 February 1998, 77.

48. "Texas Jury Has No Beef with Oprah," Associated Press story reported in the *Lawrence* (Kansas) *Journal World,* 27 February 1998, 3A.

49. *Black's Law Dictionary,* 5th ed. (St. Paul: West, 1979), 1075.

50. Mike Lopresti, "Eight Years After Atlanta, Closure Difficult for Jewell," *USA Today,* 17 August 2004, 11D.

51. "Wrongly Suspected Richard Jewell," Court TV, online, www.crimelibrary.com.

52. David W. Guth and Charles Marsh, *Adventures in Public Relations: Case Studies and Critical Thinking* (Boston: Allyn & Bacon, 2005), 283–286.

53. Frank Walsh, *Public Relations & the Law* (New York: Foundation for Public Relations Education and Research, 1988), 15.

54. I. Fred Koenigsberg, *How to Handle Basic Copyright and Trademark Problems, 1991* (New York: Practising Law Institute, 1991), 31.

55. Anti-Piracy Update, Recording Industry Association of America, n.d., online, www.riaa.com.

56. "Copyright Basics," U.S. Copyright Office, online, www.copyright.gov/circs/circ1.html.

57. Mark Thyer, "Understanding and Dealing with Common Peer-to-Peer (P2P) Application Security," *Information Systems Security,* Nov./Dec. 2003, 42–51.

58. "64 Individuals Agree to Settlements in Copyright Infringement Cases," news release issued by the Recording Industry Association of America, 29 September 2003, online, www.riaa.com.

59. "Downloading Girl Escapes Lawsuit," Associated Press, as reported on CBSNews.com, 9 September 2003, online, www.cbsnews.com.

60. "Pew Internet Project and Comscore Media Metrix Data Memo," Pew Internet & American Life Project, January 2004, online, www.pewinternet.org.

61. Cade Metz, "Congress Revisits the Copyright Act," *e-Week*, 17 May 2004, online, LexisNexis.

62. Andrea Foster, "Library Groups Join Effort to Ease Copyright Law's Restrictions on Digital Sharing," *Chronicle of Higher Education*, 9 July 2004, 31.

63. Walsh, 61.

64. "Copyright Basics."

65. Gina Holand, "High Court Backs Longer Copyrights," *Kansas City Star*, 16 January 2003, C1.

66. Jan Hoffman, "May It Please the Public: Lawyers Exploit Media Attention as a Defense Tactic," *New York Times*, 22 April 1994, B1.

67. B. Drummond Ayres, "Simpson Case Has California Debating Muzzles for Lawyers," *New York Times*, 21 August 1994, sec. 1, p. 40.

68. Hoffman.

69. William M. Kunstler, "The Lawyer: 'A Chill Wind Blows,'" *Media Studies Journal* (winter 1992): 79.

70. Ayres.

71. Rule 3.6 (subsection a), *American Bar Association Rules of Professional Conduct*, 1983.

72. Ayres.

73. *Dominic P. Gentile, Petitioner v. State Bar of Nevada, U.S. Supreme Court Reports*, 115 L Ed 2nd, 888–912.

74. David W. Guth, "The Acceptance and Use of Public Relations Practices among Kansas Litigators," *Public Relations Review* (winter 1996): 341–354.

75. White House press briefing, 23 January 1998, 1:35 P.M.

76. Karen Tumulty, "Caught in the Town's Most Thankless Job," *Time*, 9 March 1998, 68.

77. Bryan H. Reber, Karla K. Gower, and Jennifer A. Robinson, "The Internet and Litigation Public Relations," paper presented to the Public Relations Division, Association for Education in Journalism and Mass Communications, Toronto, Canada, August 2004.

78. Reber, Gower, and Robinson.

79. *Bank of America 2002 Annual Report*, 1.

80. *Bank of America 2002 Annual Report*, 2.

81. "In the Matter of Banc of America Securities LLC," Admin. Proc. File No. 3-11425, Securities and Exchange Commission, 10 March 2004, 2, online, www.sec.gov.

82. Adam Shell, "Anatomy of a Trick Trading Scheme," *USA Today*, 5 September 2003, 1B.

83. "In the Matter of Banc of America Securities LLC," 3.

84. "In the Matter of Banc of America Securities LLC," 3.

85. "In the Matter of Banc of America Securities LLC," 4.

86. "In the Matter of Banc of America Securities LLC," 4.

87. "In the Matter of Banc of America Securities LLC," 4.

88. "In the Matter of Banc of America Securities LLC," 5.

89. "In the Matter of Banc of America Securities LLC," 6.

90. *Bank of America 2003 Annual Report,* 3.

91. "In the Matter of Banc of America Securities LLC," 8.

92. "SEC Brings Enforcement Actions Against Banc of America Securities for Repeated Document Production Failures During a Pending Investigation," news release issued by the U.S. Securities and Exchange Commission, 10 March 2004, online, www.sec.gov.

93. "SEC Reaches Agreement in Principle to Settle Charges against Bank of America for Market Timing and Late Trading," news release issued by the U.S. Securities and Exchange Commission, 15 March 2004, online, www.sec.gov.

94. *Bank of America 2003 Annual Report,* 3.

95. George Carlin, *George Carlin/FM & AM,* from the comedy routine "The 11 O'clock News," Little David Records, 1972.

96. Marion Brechner Citizen Access Project, online, www.citizenaccess.org.

97. Marion Brechner Citizen Access Project web site.

98. All direct quotes from Bill Chamberlin come from an e-mail exchange on 27 August 2004 unless otherwise noted.

99. Marion Brechner Citizen Access Project web site.

chapter sixteen

Your Future in Public Relations

After studying this chapter, you will be able to

- understand better the forces that are shaping the future of society

- recognize the trends that are changing the practice of public relations

- recognize the leadership role women and minority practitioners are playing and will play in public relations

- pinpoint steps you can take today to secure a successful future in public relations

The Government Contract

scenario

The excitement of your agency's winning a big contract from a new client has begun to wear off. The reality of this opportunity is settling in—and you re-alize you need to hire four more people to handle the increased workload.

Besides you, the agency that you head has 10 people: three white females, two Hispanic females, three white males, one black female, and one black male. Your new client, a government agency, requires that its contractors have diverse workplaces that mirror the gender and racial makeup of society at large.

After advertising the positions in local and professional publications, you have determined that only four of the applicants meet your highly technical minimum education and experience requirements. However, all four finalists are white males.

You are committed to cultural diversity in the workplace; you were particularly hoping to hire an Asian American practitioner. Both your client and various community groups are closely watching your hiring practices and insist on diversity. However, you have conducted what you considered an open and fair recruitment process. You also have four qualified applicants ready to go to work and a bunch of work piling up. What are you going to do?

What's Next?

Public Relations Tactics, a monthly publication of the Public Relations Society of America, celebrated its 10th anniversary in July 2004 by boldly predicting what the profession would look like in the year 2014. However, in a strategically wise move, the editors also reminded their readers of some past predictions that didn't pan out:

- "This 'telephone' has too many shortcomings to be seriously considered as a means of communication. The device is inherently of no value to us."—*Western Union internal memo, 1876*
- "This wireless music box has no imaginable commercial value. Who would pay for a message sent to nobody in particular?"—*NBC founder David Sarnoff's associates in response to his pushing for investment in radio in the 1920s*
- "Who the hell wants to hear actors talk?"—*H. M. Warner, cofounder and president of Warner Brothers, 1927*
- "We don't like their sound, and guitar music is on the way out."—*Decca Recording Company rejecting the Beatles, 1962*
- "There is no reason anyone would want a computer in their home."—*Ken Olson, founder and chairman of Digital Equipment, 1977*[1]

Oops!

Obviously, there is peril in predicting the future. But everybody does it because we all have a stake in it. No one has a greater personal interest in your future than you. After all, isn't going to college about getting yourself ready for the challenges of the future? (OK, at least *one* of the reasons?)

How does one go about predicting the future, especially the future of a dynamic profession such as public relations? We'd hope that by this point of the semester—assuming that you haven't been reading this book backward—that you would understand that the answer to any question about how anyone gets started doing anything has a one-word answer: *research.* Understanding the past and the present is the key to predicting the future. Social forces shaped public relations during its first century and will continue to do so in its second.

GUNGGONGGUANXI

No discussion of the globalization of public relations is complete without focusing on the People's Republic of China. The profession is beginning to blossom in what most Western practitioners view as a contradictory and complicated environment.

First, some background on China may be helpful. Slightly smaller in landmass than the United States, China has more than four times the population. Communists under Mao Zedong seized control of China after World War II. This brought the political repression resulting in the loss of tens of millions of lives (see Case Study 11.1). Mao's successor, Deng Xiaoping, introduced market-based reforms and decentralized economic decision-making. As a result, the Chinese economy quadrupled in size during that last two decades of the 20th century.[2]

China is engaged in a very difficult balancing act. On the one hand, its communist leaders want to maintain strict political control over the people. However, they also see the growth of a free-market economy as the answer to the many problems that plague the world's most-populous nation. In this environment, the recently introduced profession of public relations—what the Chinese call *gunggongguanxi*—is developing.[3]

According to the China International Public Relations Association (CIPRA), annual public relations revenues in China grew by 32 percent in 2003 to an estimated 3.3 billion yuan ($397 million in U.S. currency). CIPRA estimated that there were more than 1,500 public relations companies operating in China during 2003, with the total number of practitioners exceeding 15,000. The association also predicted that the profession would grow by another 30 percent in 2004.[4]

One sign of the emergence of Chinese public relations was the creation in 2003 of Xinhua PR Newswire. A joint venture of the Xinhua Financial Network (XFN)—a Hong Kong–based financial services and media company—and the London-based PR Newswire Association, Xinhua PR Newswire assists companies in writing and distributing financial news releases within China and around the world. This first-of-its-kind network serves 500 newspapers and 1,500 specialized industry publications throughout China.[5]

Because of the communist regime's desire to maintain tight social controls, the government closely regulates public relations activities. An example was the release of industry guidelines by the China International Public Relations Congress in 2004. Under the "Service Guidance of the PR Industry," Chinese agencies are required to have standard service procedures and provide clients with standard proposals within certain fee limitations.[6] And as noted in Case Study 11.1, the government's control of the information flow extends to the Internet, where misuse could result in the death penalty.

Beyond political considerations, Chinese public relations practitioners also face cultural hurdles. The very concept of *gunggongguanxi*, which loosely translates into penetrating one's personal networks, clashes with another Chinese value, *guanxi*, defined as obligations associated with close personal relationships. The difference in the two concepts amounts to doing business based on *what* you know versus doing it based on *whom* you know.[7] There is also a Chinese cultural need for modesty that stems from Confucius's belief that people lose stature by promoting their own accomplishments.[8] If you are someone who believes that, then publicity, a favorite tactic in public relations, is one of the last things you want to do.

Social Forces and Public Relations

Public relations—now and in the future—cannot operate in a vacuum. Just as its practitioners seek to exert influence on various aspects of society, social forces are at work that influence the profession. Understanding those forces is a key to unlocking the mysteries about the future of public relations.

The Global Spread of Democracy

One powerful social force is the global spread of democracy. Much of the history of the 20th century centered on the worldwide struggle against forces of tyranny and oppression. Most of that century's wars and great social movements grew out of a desire either to gain or to protect individual freedoms. With the end of the Cold War between democracy and communism, many nations embraced democratic institutions and ideas for the first time.

The changeover from an authoritarian to a democratic society is not easy. Democracy is more than just a set of rules. It is a way of life. Imagine what it would be like to live in a society where the government watched over every aspect of your life. For as long as you can remember, someone was always telling you what you could do, think, or say. Now imagine what it would be like to have all those restrictions suddenly lifted. After the euphoria of liberation had dissipated, you would confront the cold reality of your new way of life. Before, someone else made your decisions for you. Now, you have to make your own choices and live with the consequences of those choices.

To ease this transition, many public and private agencies have engaged in aggressive programs of education and technical support in the newly emerging democracies. At the forefront of these efforts have been journalists, marketers, and public relations practitioners teaching the virtues of free expression. By the thousands, these professionals have crisscrossed the globe in an effort to instill democratic values and traditions in places where historically there have been none. The challenge is to do so in a culturally sensitive manner. The fact that something works well in the United States does not necessarily mean it will work somewhere else. The most successful efforts at spreading democracy have been those mindful of local traditions and values.

Quick ✔ *Check*

1. What is *gunggongguanxi?*
2. What are some challenges facing the development of public relations in the People's Republic of China?
3. How has the end of the Cold War influenced the global growth of public relations?

Globalization

Another major social force influencing the future of public relations is **globalization.** The United Nations Development Program defines globalization as "the growing interdependence of the world's people through shrinking space, shrinking time, and disappearing borders."[9] With each passing day, the peoples of the earth are being drawn closer together by a vast array of forces. We live in a world where the economies of different nations are inexorably linked. Advances in communications technology have made it possible for us to know what is happening on the opposite side of the world instantaneously. Improvements in transportation have made it possible for you to travel in mere hours distances that took your grandparents weeks and months to cover.

Working in combination, these forces have given us a sense of **interconnectedness** and created a world of opportunities for public relations practitioners. Marshall McLuhan's global village (which we discussed in Chapters 11 and 14) has, in many ways, become a reality. Targeting certain audiences and effectively reaching them are, in many ways, easier than ever. But as we already have discussed in Chapter 11, these advances have also forced practitioners to face serious challenges and make some difficult choices. Thanks to the global reach of digital telecommunications, crises can now spread at the speed of light. And in a world in which the Internet makes it possible for anyone with a "cause" to become a self-publisher, it is becoming more difficult for organizations to identify potential threats.

Although some see globalization as an opportunity, others see it as a threat. Still others see it as both. Antiglobalization forces are concerned that the world's richest nations exploit the poorest in the name of economic development. They are concerned about the relocation of manufacturing jobs to poorer countries where laborers receive only a fraction of pay and have fewer human rights protections than their counterparts in industrialized nations. The exploitation of natural resources and the resulting damage to the environment are also a concern. In addition, technology and knowledge gaps are widening between rich and poor nations. Although it is difficult to gauge the strength of antiglobalization forces, they have made their voices heard. Massive protests in cities hosting international trade meetings have become commonplace in recent years.

The Changing Face of the United States

Interconnectedness means more than international relations, however. One need only look at the changing face of the United States. During the Industrial Revolution in the late 1800s, most of the immigration into this country came from Europe. The predominance of new arrivals from Europe remained fairly consistent for decades. But by the 1980s there had been a shift. Of the nearly 20 million foreign-born residents counted by the U.S. Census in 1990, 44 percent were added in the 1980s. Of the new arrivals, almost half came from Latin America and nearly one-third from Asia. According to the 1990 census, three out of every four persons living in the United States were of white European ancestry. By the middle of the 21st century, that group is expected to shrink to just over half the U.S. population.[10]

Booklet and Brochures With the assistance of Valencia, Pérez & Echeveste Public Relations, the California Department of Health Services prepared these recipes and good nutrition tips for Hispanic consumers. (Courtesy of Valencia, Pérez & Echeveste Public Relations)

The 2000 census provides a snapshot of the changes in U.S. society. The nation's population on April 1, 2000, was 281,421,906, a 13.2 percent increase over the 1990 census. Although the "white" population continued to constitute the largest racial group, its percentage of the total population had slipped from 80.2 percent in 1990 to 75.1 percent in 2000. For the first time in the nation's history, people of "Hispanic or Latino" origin were counted as the nation's largest minority group, totaling 35,305,818 or 12.5 percent of the U.S. population. They edged past the "black or African American" population, which totaled 34,658,190 or 12.3 percent of the population.[11]

In an ideal world, public relations should mirror the societies it serves. However, several studies have all come to the same conclusion: People of color are underrepresented in the profession. This issue confronts you as the head of the fictional agency in the opening scenario of this chapter: You are being torn by competing values. On the one hand, you believe in the value of a multicultural workplace and know that the client and community expect it. On the other hand, you question the fairness to the four individuals who followed the rules you established and emerged as finalists. And not to be forgotten is the competing value of getting the job done.

This is a very real-life scenario; it has no easy answers. The choices are difficult:

1. You could turn down the contract and avoid the hassles. But this could have a devastating effect on employee morale and could damage your agency's ability to compete for major contracts in the future.
2. You could hire the four white males and defend the decision on the basis of sticking by the rules you established at the outset. However, you would do so at the risk of alienating the community and, possibly, losing the contract.
3. You could reopen the search from scratch and expand the geographical area in which you advertise the positions. This might bring in more qualified candidates who are women or persons of color. But it might not, and you would run the risk of losing the candidates you have already identified.
4. You could hire one or two of the finalists and expand the search for the remaining positions. This might ease the immediate situation; but, for reasons already mentioned, there is no guarantee that this course will lead to a long-term solution.

There is no one correct answer. It all comes down to which value you hold highest. The first option seems the least viable: You wouldn't have sought the contract if you didn't value entrepreneurship and the business it would bring to your agency. The second option indicates that the integrity of the process you established is your highest value. The third option places multiculturalism at the top of your list of values. Many would choose the fourth option because it has the appeal of addressing all three values: entrepreneurship, fairness, and multiculturalism. Of course, it is a compromise without any permanent guarantees. But it still has the advantage of leaving your options open.

The Growth in World Population

Another factor with significant implications, both for the practice of public relations and for society as a whole, is the rapid growth of the world's population. That there will be a lot more of us in the 21st century is a sobering fact in and of itself. But it is the nature and the consequences of the growth that bring the greatest challenges.

World population growth will be dramatic in the coming decades. The U.S. Census Bureau estimates that the current population of the United States is approximately 295 million. By the year 2050, that number is expected to climb to 420 million, a 42 percent increase. In comparison, the current world population is estimated at 6.5 billion and projected to be 9.1 billion in 2050, a 40 percent increase.[12]

There is another way to look at this. See Table 16.1 for a list of the 10 most populated nations on Earth in the year 2000. Now compare those rankings with the projections for the year 2050 in Table 16.2 (p. 538). You may be thinking to yourself, "That's interesting. But what does it have to do with me?" In a word: Plenty.

With the world's population growing rapidly—especially in nations outside the industrialized West—the competition for Earth's limited resources is becoming more vigorous. In the best of all possible scenarios, this means increased economic trade and international cooperation—activities that the practice of public relations can help foster. However, in the worse of all possible scenarios, the intense competition for Earth's dwindling resources could lead to wars, terrorism, and other forms of social unrest. The constructive application of public relations in its role as a catalyst for consensus is critical in helping human populations avoid these dire outcomes.

The growth in world population also foreshadows future environmental problems. The air we breathe, the water we drink, and the land on which we depend for our food are all threatened by an encroaching human population. One of the most immediate concerns is the loss of tropical rain forests, which are being clear-cut and burned to make way for people, animals, and crops. By destroying these rain forests, humanity is losing an irreplaceable source of numerous species of health-giving

| TABLE 16.1 | The Ten Most Populated Nations on Earth in the Year 2005 |

RANK	COUNTRY	POPULATION
1	China	1,306,313,812
2	India	1,080,264,388
3	United States	295,734,134
4	Indonesia	241,973,879
5	Brazil	186,112,794
6	Pakistan	162,419,946
7	Bangladesh	144,319,628
8	Russia	143,155,362
9	Nigeria	140,601,615
10	Japan	127,417,244

THE HISPANIC AND LATINO FACTOR

There's a quiet revolution under way in the United States, one that moves to a decidedly Latin beat.

The 2000 Census showed that for the first time, persons of Hispanic or Latino origin had become the nation's largest minority group, representing 12.5 percent of the total population. By 2050, the government estimates that Hispanics and Latinos will constitute 24.4 percent of the U.S. population.[13]

This growing prominence can also be seen in the marketplace, where the Selig Center for Economic Growth predicts that "the immense buying power of the nation's Hispanic consumers will energize the U.S. consumer market as never before."[14] The center estimates that Hispanic-Latino economic clout will be more than $1 trillion in 2008. That is a 357 percent increase since 1990, compared to 136 percent for remaining consumers.[15]

The growing influence of the Hispanic and Latino community has caught the attention of the public relations industry. Practitioners are adjusting their approach to a rapidly diversifying marketplace. "It's not do-goodism," said Ofield Dukes, chairman of the Public Relations Society of America's National Diversity Initiative. "It's a matter of economics."[16]

Diversity is often easier said than done. Something as simple as assigning an adjective to describe this community is fraught with peril. While many use *Hispanic* and *Latino* as if they are interchangeable, they are not. *Latino* refers to the Spanish- and Portuguese-speaking people of the western hemisphere. *Hispanic* is associated with Spain and the Iberian Peninsula.[17] The distinction is important to many.

"People from Latin America have immigrated to the U.S. because of hardships, dictatorships, drugs, poverty and the search for the American dream," said Venus Gines, founder of a Latino health awareness group. "Immigrants from Spain, a European, industrialized nation, usually don't come to this country hungry."[18]

Targeting this public is very complicated. It includes people from many countries and cultures. Mexican Americans constitute nearly three-quarters of the Hispanic and Latino population in the United States. Another 11 percent are of Puerto Rican heritage. Seven percent come from Central and South America. Five percent have ties to Cuba.[19]

There is also the language barrier. Not every word easily translates from English into Spanish. For example, Bayer Corporation executives trying to promote an antacid product were surprised to learn that Spanish has no word for heartburn. "We had to define what heartburn was," said one Bayer official.[20]

Then there is the challenge of adapting to cultural nuances. "When you're scheduled to be at a 2:30 meeting, it's OK to show up at 2:55," said account planner Sharon Brunot-Speziale, an Anglo American working at a Chicago Hispanic-Latino advertising agency. "I don't have that sense of urgency and Type A behavior that I've had in other positions."[21]

Many experts agree that success in communicating with a diverse audience starts with a diverse workforce. "Having a team of people with diverse backgrounds and perspectives is a business mandatory," said Kathy Bremer of Porter Novelli Public Relations. "Effective communication begins with understanding the client's business and target audiences."[22]

TABLE 16.2	The Ten Most Populated Nations on Earth in the Year 2050	
RANK	**COUNTRY**	**POPULATION**
1	India	1,601,004,572
2	China	1,424,161,948
3	United States	420,080,587
4	Indonesia	336,247,428
5	Nigeria	307,420,055
6	Pakistan	294,995,104
7	Bangladesh	279,955,405
8	Brazil	228,426,737
9	Congo (Kinshasa)	181,260,098
10	Mexico	147,907,650

herbs and flowers, not to mention oxygen. Many of the people who clear-cut and burn the rain forests are not evil. They are just poor and looking for a way to improve their lives. Many companies, such as McDonald's, have developed partnerships that promote alternatives to the destruction of the environment. These and other public relations activities can serve as models for future environmental cooperation.

In addition to these global trends, major changes are taking place within the United States that will have a dramatic impact on future public relations practitioners in this country: the aging of the U.S. population. The **baby boom generation,** born between 1945 and 1964, will place a tremendous strain on the generations that have followed. Baby boomers will start reaching retirement age in 2010. Between 2010 and 2030, the percentage of people age 65 and older will grow from 13 percent to almost 20 percent. During that same time frame, the number of people age 85 and older living in the United States will grow from just under 4.2 million to more than 6.2 million.[23] From a political and social standpoint, this means that issues important to older citizens—issues such as Social Security, health care, and the stability of personal investments—will take on increasing importance.

However, the graying of America will have an even deeper impact on today's college students. The percentage of **breadwinners,** people between the ages of 18 and 65 who typically make up the nation's labor pool, is declining. The U.S. Census Bureau estimates that breadwinners will constitute 60 percent of the U.S. population in 2010. By 2030, that estimate dips to 54 percent.[24] In other words, a smaller percentage of breadwinners will carry most of the tax burden for the rest of the nation. That trend, in turn, has a variety of implications for the future—including the likelihood that cost-effective public relations will become increasingly important.

WHAT WOULD JESUS DRIVE?

When is green *really* green? And when it comes to the environment, is public relations part of the problem, part of the solution, or both?

Modern public relations and the environmental movement both evolved during the early 20th century. Theodore Roosevelt, if he were alive today, would probably be considered an environmental activist. But he also had considerable public relations savvy (see Chapter 3). Roosevelt effectively marshaled public opinion in May 1908 when, for the first time, he brought all the states' governors together at the same place to discuss the preservation of the nation's natural resources. According to public relations historian Scott Cutlip, it may well have been the White House Conference of Governors on Conservation that "embedded the word *conservation* into the nation's vocabulary."[25]

And since the 1960s, the environmental movement has played a significant role in the nation's social and economic development. Businesses and industries are no longer judged on their profitability alone. They are now held accountable for how environmentally friendly they are. This change has contributed to what many have called **green public relations.**

The 3M Company was among the first of the major corporations to reap the benefits of going green. Its 3P program, which stands for "Pollution Prevention Pays," was launched in 1975. Developed by two environmental engineers and an environmental communications specialist, 3P projects saved 3M more than half a billion dollars during the program's first 15 years—and have earned the company praise from environmental groups and the media. In 1990, 3M launched a new environmental effort, 3P Plus, by investing $150 million to reduce hazardous air emissions at its manufacturing facilities.[26]

Many in the environmental movement do not share the same enthusiasm for green public relations. In fact, they have another term for it— **greenwash.** San Francisco–based CorpWatch, which opposes what it calls "corporate-led globalization," gives out bimonthly Greenwash Awards to companies its says "put more money, time, and energy into slick PR campaigns aimed at promoting their eco-friendly images than they do to actually protecting the environment." Some of its "winners" include the Nuclear Energy Institute, the American Chemistry Council, and British Petroleum.

The degree to which the environment has become a public relations battleground came into focus during the controversial "What Would Jesus Drive?" public awareness campaign in 2002. On the surface, it may seem odd—even irreverent—to ask such a question. It was raised by the Pennsylvania-based Evangelical Environmental Network (ENN), which contended that vehicle choices are moral decisions. ENN specifically targeted sport utility vehicles (SUVs), which it said hurt the environment by increasing pollution and oil dependence.

"We are spreading the word that to love our neighbors and care for creation, automakers and politicians need to build cars that reflect our moral values," said the Reverend Jim Ball of ENN.[27]

A pro-SUV organization, the Sport Utility Vehicle Owners of America, countered with its own full-page ad in *USA Today* that asked "What Would Jesus (Rivera) Drive?" A smiling, waving man named Jesus Rivera was shown standing in front of his seven-year-old SUV. The ad said he had logged 150,000 miles in his SUV, through snow and in transporting his seven grandchildren.

"For millions of people like Jesus Rivera, it's all about safety, utility and versatility," the ad said. It went on to urge SUV owners to protect their rights.[28]

Quick ✔ Check

1. Why is an increasing marketing focus being placed on the Hispanic community in the United States?
2. What are the implications of the higher population growth rate in non-Western nations?
3. What effect will the aging of the baby boom generation have on society?

Feminization of the Workplace

"Over the past three decades, a significantly greater proportion of women have participated in the American workforce," reports the U.S. Bureau of Labor Statistics in its 2004 publication *Women in the Labor Force: A Databook*. "In addition, women have made substantial inroads into higher-paying occupations during this time." The report notes that 60 percent of women over the age of 16 participate in the workforce, compared with just 43 percent in 1970. The proportion of women employed as managers, administrators, or executives has doubled during the past two decades. From 1979 to 2002, women's real earnings (adjusted for inflation) increased by 27 percent, while men's real earnings increased by just 1 percent.[29]

It is easy for today's students to take for granted something that was relatively new just a generation earlier: the presence of women in the workplace. This movement—what some have called the **feminization** of the workplace—has dramatically changed our social and political landscapes. Women constitute more than 51 percent of the nation's population. They are an increasingly powerful political force. Despite these positive trends, there is still need for improvement in significant areas such as workplace sexual harassment and **salary equity,** equal pay for equal work.

According to *Women in the Labor Force,* women's earnings in 2002 were 78 percent of men's. Female college graduates had median earnings of $809 a week, compared with $1,089 for men.[30] In a separate report, the Bureau of Labor Statistics said that the median weekly earnings for women managers in marketing, advertising, and public relations in 2002 was $874, just 69.2 percent of the $1,262 weekly earning for male managers.[31]

Findings in a 1986 study commissioned by the International Association of Business Communicators suggested that the field was becoming a **velvet ghetto**—an employment area in which women hold the numerous lower-paying technical positions and men predominate in the few high-paying managerial positions.[32] As one researcher noted:

> This "feminization" of the field has been heralded by some. Women, they argue, are uniquely suited for public relations because of their natural orientation toward "relationships" and their facility with verbal tasks. More often, though, women's entrance into public relations has been viewed with concern. People worry that so many women in the field will lower salaries and frustrate public relations' efforts to be taken seriously as a management function. These fears are bolstered by extensive research that shows women

SEXUAL HARASSMENT

According to the U.S. Equal Employment Opportunity Commission (EEOC), sexual harassment is a form of sex discrimination that violates Title VII of the Civil Rights Act of 1964. The EEOC defines workplace **sexual harassment** as "unwelcome sexual advances, requests for sexual favors, and other verbal or physical conduct of a sexual nature . . . when submission to or rejection of this conduct explicitly or implicitly affects an individual's employment, unreasonably interferes with an individual's work performance or creates an intimidating, hostile or offensive work environment."[33]

According to the EEOC, 13,566 sexual harassment cases were filed with federal and state agencies during fiscal year (FY) 2003. That's almost a 14 percent rise over the previous decade. However, there is a silver lining: It was the third straight year that figure had declined. The agencies found "no reasonable cause" in 46.1 percent of the cases. Some 21.2 percent involved settlements or withdrawals with benefits. Nevertheless, sexual harassment is expensive. More than $50 million was awarded to victims of sexual harassment in FY 2003—and that figure does not count any monetary awards obtained through litigation.[34]

Although there are legal remedies for dealing with blatant sexual harassment, many victims are reluctant to report it because of a fear of damaging their careers. Then there is a more covert form of harassment, dubbed by some as **lookism,** which is defined as a tendency to focus more on a woman's appearance than on her job performance. In one focus group a female practitioner complained that she had to fight the perception of some of her older male colleagues that a woman traveling by herself or out alone after dark is "available."[35]

Sexual harassment in the workplace threatens more than just employees. Companies that do not take steps to enforce sexual harassment policies face increasing risk of stiff financial penalties. In an effort to force companies to take this problem more seriously, Congress amended the Civil Rights Act in 1991. The amendment made it possible for successful plaintiffs to collect not only lost wages but also up to $300,000 in punitive damages against offending companies.[36] The U.S. Supreme Court has also weighed in on this issue. The court said an employer is responsible for sexual harassment committed by a supervisor even if the employer was unaware of the supervisor's behavior. The Court also ruled that workers can still file sexual harassment charges against supervisors even in the absence of adverse job consequences.[37]

It should be noted that sexual harassment is not just about men acting inappropriately toward women. According to the EEOC, men filed 14.7 percent of sexual harassment claims in FY 2003. The U.S. Supreme Court has also recognized that illegal harassment can occur between people of the same sex.[38]

Public relations practitioners will play a critical role in eliminating this offensive behavior from the work environment—both inside and outside their profession. As the EEOC has noted, employers "should clearly communicate that sexual harassment will not be tolerated."[39] That's one of the jobs of public relations.

The only way to rid the workplace of sexual harassment is to create a company culture that makes it taboo, said Naomi Earp, vice chair of EEOC. She believes that antiharassment-policy education should be a part of every employee's regular training.[40]

"Management should talk about [the antiharassment policy] the way they talk about productivity and attendance," says Michael Fetzer of the EEOC's Cleveland office. "Otherwise, people won't think it's really that important to the company leadership."[41]

lag behind their male peers in salary and advancement. And this gender gap cannot be explained by age, level of education, or years of experience.[42]

Nearly two decades later, the IABC Research Foundation revisited its velvet ghetto study. While some of the fears raised in the earlier report did not come to pass, researchers said there were still economic and social barriers for women in public relations to overcome:

- While women continued to dominate the public relations industry, evidence suggested that the feminization of the field may have peaked in the 1990s and that the percentage of male practitioners was beginning to slowly build by approximately one-half a percent per year.

- The velvet ghetto predicted that the feminization of public relations could lead to salary declines. That did not happen. But, as we have already shown, women continue to make less than their male counterparts.

- Access to senior management by women practitioners appears to have declined over the past two decades. In the velvet ghetto report, half of the respondents said they reported directly to the CEO. However, *IABC Profile 2002* placed that figure at only 35 percent.[43]

PRSA conducted a similar inquiry. In its *Year 2000 Gender Study*, researchers concluded that men averaged about $17,000 more in annual salary than women, "even after years of experience, age, job interruptions and education were accounted for." However, in terms of promotion, the researchers said "participants are more unsure now than they were five years ago about the existence of a glass ceiling for women."[44]

The gender debate took on new life during 2000, when Harold Burson, founder and chair of Burson-Marsteller, suggested that a public relations industry dominated by women may not be a good thing. "Unless more men are attracted to public relations, it runs the risk of being regarded as a 'woman's job,'" Burson said. Although some women agreed with Burson, others strongly disagreed. "That's not even a point for discussion," said Sabrina Horn, head of a San Franciso–based agency.[45]

Even those who agree that gender discrimination exists often disagree on how to rectify the situation. Some argue that women should seek out more professional expertise—that improving their strategic and professional skills will allow them to compete at the same level as men. Others argue that women should push for **empowerment**—not only ensuring that they have the tools for success, but also demanding to be included in decision making.[46] Although sincere people may argue about which is the best path to take, none disagree on the common goal: equity.

A hopeful sign can be found in a gender study on job satisfaction among public relations practitioners. Although men and women viewed job satisfaction from decidedly different perspectives, evidence supported a growing respect for each other. "Both groups appear to be willing to respect the other, and, perhaps more importantly, to engage in dialogue on the issues in ways that will result in collaboration and benefits for both," the study said. "The willingness on both sides to work toward just

Values Statement 16.1

LEAGUE OF WOMEN VOTERS OF THE UNITED STATES

The League of Women Voters encourages informed and active participation of citizens in government and influences public policy through education and advocacy.

The goal of the League of Women Voters of the United States is to empower citizens to shape better communities worldwide. We are a nonpartisan political organization.

We:

- act after study and member agreement to achieve solutions in the public interest on key community issues at all government levels.

- build citizen participation in the democratic process.

- engage communities in promoting positive solutions to public policy issues through education and advocacy.

We believe in:

- respect for individuals.

- the value of diversity.

- the empowerment of the grassroots, both within the League and its communities.

- the power of collective decision making for the common good.

We will:

- act with trust, integrity and professionalism.

- operate in an open and effective manner to meet the needs of those we serve, both members and the public.

- take the initiative in seeking diversity in membership.

- acknowledge our heritage as we seek our path to the future.

—"Vision, Beliefs and Intentions,"
LWV web site

solutions is especially critical at this point in the evolution of a workplace where people can be satisfied."[47]

Quick  Check

1. What is the meaning of the phrase *velvet ghetto?*
2. What are the differing views on how to level the playing field for men and women in public relations?
3. What is workplace sexual harassment?

Where Public Relations Is Headed

As modern public relations moves into its second century, the signs are generally positive. As it did during its first century, the profession of public relations has to adapt to a changing social environment. However, not everything will change. There will be a continuing need for the profession to address some of the same old questions, including those relating to its ethical standards and its social value. Let's survey briefly some of the key trends for the future of public relations.

GROWTH.   According to the Bureau of Labor Statistics, "Keen competition will likely continue for entry-level public relations jobs, as the number of qualified applicants is expected to exceed the number of job openings." However, before you start re-thinking your career choice, you should know that the bureau reports in its *Occupational Outlook Handbook, 2004–05* that "opportunities should be best for college graduates who combine a degree in journalism, public relations, advertising, or another communications-related field with a public relations internship or other related work experience. Employment of public relations specialists is expected to increase faster than the average for all occupations through 2012."[48] Increasingly, this growth is being reflected in boardrooms, as more and more organizations recognize the profession's role in enhancing and maintaining relationships with key stakeholders.

THE STRUGGLE FOR CREDIBILITY.   After 100 years, the modern profession still isn't sure what it wants to call itself. Because people who do not understand the profession have used *public relations* as a pejorative term since the time of Edward Bernays, many organizations have shied away from that phrase. Others have said the term is too broad or too narrow, depending on the context. By one accounting, "corporate communications" and "communications departments" outnumbered "public relations departments" at *Fortune* 500 companies by a 2–1 margin.[49] Concerns about the profession's credibility may be at the heart of this issue. The Public Relations Society of America Foundation created the National Credibility Index to track the way U.S. citizens perceive information sources. The good news: Many public relations tactics received a high index rating. The bad news: Public relations practitioners were rated near the bottom—below student activists, candidates for public office, and famous athletes.[50] Despite this apparent ambivalence, signs indicate that the profession is earning respect in surprising places. When Al and Laura Ries wrote *The Fall of Advertising and the Rise of PR* in 2002, they challenged the conventional wisdom that public relations plays second fiddle to advertising when it comes to launching or repositioning brands. They cite the Internet as proof of the power of public relations. "Amazon, eBay, Yahoo!, Priceline and even AOL benefited from enormous amounts of publicity," Al Ries said. "Sure, they may have done some advertising, but it was PR that built those brands."[51]

GREATER INTEGRATION.   Public relations activities are being more closely aligned with those of marketing and advertising. As we discussed in Chapter 13, the concept of integrated marketing communications (IMC) is the current rage. But as we also discussed, differences of opinion exist regarding just where public relations fits in the mix. Some see public relations as an element under a broad marketing umbrella. Others (your authors among them) see public relations practitioners as using a separate management discipline whose values often coincide with those of marketers. Regardless of one's point of view, one fact is undeniable: Today's clients are demanding more than just the persuasive messages of advertising and marketing. They also want the credibility that comes through third-party endorsement. For that, they need public relations. This is especially true when it comes to cause-related marketing, something for which public relations is well suited. According to New Jersey public relations executive John Rosica, "Cause-related marketing can increase brand equity, create a more positive image for corporations and establish a preferred brand name with customers and potential customers."[52]

GREATER ACCOUNTABILITY.   The profession of public relations is under greater scrutiny than ever before. "There's an increased emphasis on accountability, measuring success in every way we can," said Pat Stocker, director of executive programs at the College of Business and Management at the University of Maryland.[53] Katie Paine of Delahaye Medialink, a public relations measurement and analysis firm, said, "I don't think that there's a program proposed any more that doesn't have a measurement element."[54] However, accountability now extends beyond an organization's bottom line. Ever since Ralph Nader's assault on General Motors in the mid-1960s, the public has expected organizations to reflect social values. Corporations are expected to value public interest as well as profitability. The role of public relations practitioners is well suited for monitoring the conduct of organizations. At the same time, however, practitioners must hold themselves to those same high standards. Failure to do so has often given the profession a bad name. Accountability in public relations also requires that practitioners enthusiastically embrace equal opportunity without regard to gender, race, religion, national origin, or sexual orientation. That aspect of accountability will require aggressive recruitment of a more inclusive workforce, one that mirrors the diversity of society.

TARGETING.   As a result of social and technological changes, we are living in a world of increasingly fragmented values and desires. Public opinion and public policies are being ruled by ever-shifting and constantly self-defining coalitions of interests. At the same time, the explosion in the number of communication channels has dispersed audiences. The challenge for public relations practitioners is clear: Reaching key publics in the future will require more targeted approaches. Designing those approaches, in turn, requires a greater precision in research methodologies and planning strategies.

RAPID RESPONSE.   In the race to influence public opinion, time is an enemy. President Abraham Lincoln concerned himself with stories that appeared in the daily newspaper. President Franklin Roosevelt had to respond to stories on hourly radio newscasts. Today the president is confronted with minute-by-minute developments in stories on 24-hour news channels and the Internet. The window of opportunity for getting across one's point of view is narrowing. By implication, this means that public relations practitioners must plan even further ahead. They must do a better job of anticipating events that could shape the public view of their organization. For that reason, issues management skills will in all likelihood become increasingly important.

A NONTRADITIONAL WORKPLACE.   While it is doubtful that a government agency has done a survey to support this hypothesis, it is very likely that there has been a sharp increase in the number of people wearing fuzzy slippers to work. That's because more than 20 million people spend some time every week working in the comfort of their own homes. According to the latest government figures, 15 percent of U.S. workers do some work at home as part of their primary job. While half of those surveyed were wage and salary workers who took work home on an unpaid basis, 17 percent said they had a formal arrangement to be paid for work they did at home.[55] *PR Week* reports that telecommuting has become a popular solution for public relations agencies looking to keep employees who have undergone a change in lifestyle, such as having a baby or moving to a rural area. "You have to accommodate talent," explained New York public relations executive Kimberley White. "That often means putting up with where that talent decides it wants to live."[56] However, telecommuting is not the only change in the workplace. As already noted, the labor pool is becoming more diverse in its gender and racial composition. By the time your children graduate from college, the workplace will have a very different look and feel.

VISION.   The demands of a rapid-paced society tend to focus on the problems of the moment and to ignore the potential challenges of the future. The charge of short-term thinking is often leveled against business and industry in the United States. Public relations practitioners share responsibility for this state of affairs. With public relations practitioners being held more accountable for a company's bottom line, many move from one planning cycle to another without having a real sense of direction. What organizations—and practitioners—need is a sense of vision. They need to have a sense of where they want to be 5, 10, and 20 years down the road. Here is where values, research, and strategic planning pay dividends. A longer-term outlook also requires practitioners to demonstrate that they have what is commonly referred to as "backbone"—the courage to stand by their vision. Backbones do have flexibility, however; visions can change.

Quick ✔ Check

1. What trends are influencing the future of public relations?
2. In what ways will public relations practitioners be held more accountable in the future?
3. What is meant by the need for "vision"?

Your Future in Public Relations

By now it should be obvious that modern public relations is a profession that continues to evolve as it moves into its second century. That is what makes it both challenging and exciting. Every day in public relations brings with it a new adventure.

YOU ARE THE FUTURE

You are the future of public relations.

As you make the transition from college life into a career in this dynamic profession, it is OK to pause for a moment and take a deep breath. After all, you are about to embark on a wonderful journey—but to where? No one knows for sure. But some pretty smart people have put some thought into what your future will hold. And they see a world of both opportunities and challenges.

"The PR industry has the chance to become the communications tool of choice in the next decade," said Richard Edelman, president and CEO of Edelman Public Relations Worldwide. "The opportunity for PR stems from the absence of trust in institutions and the splintering of audiences among various forms of media."[57]

Edelman based his prediction on the fragmentation of media, which he said has led to "information overload" and the creation of "individual webs of trust and triangulation among multiple sources of information." His reasoning: If organizations can establish credibility, they could become a part of these "webs of trust." That, he said, is the opportunity and challenge facing public relations.[58]

And how can future practitioners help establish this credibility? Mark Weiner, CEO of Delahaye Medialink Worldwide Communications Research, said, "Match ethics with the delivery of meaningful business outcomes, and you'll earn credibility."[59]

According to a study of future trends conducted on behalf of the IABC Research Foundation, "An opportunity exists for communication professionals to change their roles. Communication officers are in the best position to provide information for leaders that flags new trends and anticipates potential changes on the horizon." This prediction was based on interviews with more than 30 senior practitioners and survey responses from more than 1,000 IABC members.[60]

However, with this shot of optimism comes a dose of reality. "Communication professionals need to increase their ability to measure results more concretely," the study said. "Proving the economic value of the communication function is becoming increasingly important." But that's the rub: Only 17 percent of the survey participants said they use before and after assessments to gauge communication performance.[61]

Gary Grates, head of the General Motors Corporation executive and financial communications group, wrote in *Public Relations Quarterly* that practitioners must learn to sense and respond to changes in the environment: "In a way, we must become social scientists in our jobs, able to discern what people are looking at, listening to, and believing in."[62] Practitioners need to focus on problem solving, he said. "The wise firm will, in the long run, achieve greater profitability and stronger relationships by focusing on finding the solution instead of packaging the sell."[63]

The values and lifestyles of today's college graduates will also shape the future. According to Mike Marino, former head of human resources for Burson-Marsteller/New York, new practitioners are already beginning to question the traditional workweek and workplace. "In order to be able to effectively attract and retain this segment of the population," he said, "employers—including agencies—will need to adopt more flexible work arrangements."[64]

See, you are already molding the future of public relations.

Are you ready for it? The short answer is no—at this stage of your academic and professional life, you probably are not quite ready. But the good news is that if you continue doing the right things, you will be.

Your decision to earn a college degree was the first big step in the right direction. Although exceptions to the rule exist, a college diploma is usually necessary if you are going to make the first cut in the employment process. As to what kind of degree you obtain, that is probably less important than what you studied in earning the degree. Not everyone in the profession has received a degree in public relations. And although the study of public relations is traditionally centered in either journalism or communications studies programs, degrees from other departments can also lead to successful public relations careers.

So what constitutes a good educational foundation for the practice of public relations? Educators and practitioners at a 1998 conference on public relations education said a student seeking a public relations career should earn a degree that "reflects an integration of a broad education with a liberal arts orientation." According to the conferees, that "broad education" should include a theoretical understanding of the processes of communication, the liberal arts, the social sciences, sociopolitical trends, general business practices, and "the principles and skills specific to the profession of public relations."[65]

Perhaps the best news from that conference, "Dialogue on Public Relations Education," was the release of survey results showing practitioners and educators in general agreement about the preparation students need for a career in public relations. The survey identified the three most highly desired qualifications for entry-level employees: having news release writing skills, being a "self-starter," and having critical thinking and problem-solving skills. Unfortunately, that same survey suggested that educators and practitioners were not wholly satisfied with the skills graduating students possessed in those three areas.[66] Significantly, each of these skills involves knowledge above and beyond that taught in public relations classes. A well-rounded college education is the basis for success. The implication for today's college students is clear: Treat all your course work as if it were relevant to your major. It is!

Internships—supervised workplace experiences—also figure prominently in public relations career preparation, especially in light of corporate downsizing and the growth of virtual public relations. More than ever, internships give students the opportunity to get hands-on experience in a wide range of public relations activities. Think of internships as an extension of a college education—with one major difference: The "classroom" is the real world. If you are not certain what kind of public relations you want to practice—agency, government, nonprofit, or corporate—having several different internships during college can give you a taste of the different aspects of the field.

Internship experience can be crucial in getting that first job. "Internships are becoming vital to obtaining employment," reports the Bureau of Labor Statistics. "Employers seek applicants with demonstrated communication skills and training or experience in a field related to the firm's business—information technology, health, science, engineering, sales, or finance, for example."[67]

Membership in student public relations organizations also provides a good foundation for a public relations career. Some schools have **Public Relations Student Society of America (PRSSA)** chapters, which are affiliated with PRSA. IABC also sponsors student organizations. Other student groups operate independently. Whatever route one chooses, these student organizations can provide valuable job/internship information, networking opportunities, and professional experience that can be listed on a résumé. Some professional organizations give students who were active in their school's public relations organization a membership discount upon graduation. These student groups also offer opportunities for getting together with people who share common career interests. However, as with other student organizations, what you get out of any such group largely depends on what you put into it.

The Future of Values-Driven Public Relations

Some view the future with hope. Others fear the future. Either way, like it or not, the future is coming.

What kind of future lies ahead? At best, we can only make educated guesses. In QuickBreak 16.5, we choose to leave the prognostications to others. Perhaps our time is better spent on the present and on the things we can do today to prepare ourselves for tomorrow.

Each of us perceives the future in different ways. That's because we are unique individuals who view the world through different prisms. For that reason, the best preparation for the future is getting to know the one individual who will exert the most influence over the future as you will know it. In other words, the person you most need to get in touch with is yourself.

At the risk of being too philosophical, what is life but a series of choices? Some choices, such as what to have for lunch or what color socks to wear, are not particularly challenging. Other times we are confronted with choices that can quite literally mean the difference between life and death. The funny thing about choices, however, is you can't always know the ultimate outcome of what may seem at the time to be the most trivial of decisions. Those are the decisions that steer us to unexpected paths in our lives. The best we can hope for is developing the habit of making good decisions.

That is why values are important. Values are the road map by which we, both as professionals and as individuals, chart a course into the future. Having values alone is not a guarantee of taking a smooth road. In fact, sticking to values can lead to a more treacherous road than traveling down the path of least resistance. But at least when we stick to our values we *know* we may be headed down a bumpy road. Often the path of least resistance does not turn out to be as smooth as it looks.

After a century of modern public relations, it is somewhat disheartening to know that practitioners are still compelled to demonstrate their worth to employers, clients, coworkers—and even to themselves. In the words of a Public Relations Society of America report on the stature of the profession,

> Public relations has evolved from a fringe function to a basic element of society in a comparatively short period of time, despite a number of handicaps. One of the greatest of these is the field's failure to act according to its own precepts. It has allowed prejudices against it to persist, misconceptions to entrench themselves and weaknesses within the field to be perceived as endemic. Public relations, like most elements of society, is now confronted with critical questioning. Its practitioners are questioning its stature and role as pointedly as outsiders. Like other elements of society, it must respond to its challengers or lose even its present stature and role. That role must be clarified; its goals must be set; its practitioners must earn optimal stature; means to achieve the goals must be established.[68]

In its own way, this report, prepared by PRSA's College of Fellows, is a plea for the very same concept advocated throughout this book: *values-driven public relations*. It is a recognition—and a warning—that until practitioners fully embrace the relationship-building values on which this profession was supposedly built, our period of self-doubt will continue.

Granted, that's a heavy load to place on the shoulders of someone still in college. However, real change can occur if we remember that 21st-century public relations will be built one person at a time.

As you ponder the many choices that await you, here are some guidelines to help you steer down the uncertain paths of the future:

■ *Be true to your values.* If you can't be true to yourself, then to whom can you be true? If something doesn't pass the "Can you look at yourself in the mirror?" test, don't do it.

■ *Pay your dues.* No one is going to hand you the keys to the executive washroom—at least not yet. Hard work and personal commitment are your investments in the future. Your time will come.

■ *Make your own luck.* A wise person once said that luck is where opportunity meets preparation. Circumstances may place you in the right place at the right time. But it will be your talent and professionalism that will keep you there.

■ *Learn from your mistakes.* Mistakes are often more instructive than successes. If you are willing to look objectively at a situation and, when necessary, shoulder the blame, it is unlikely that you will make the same mistake again.

■ *Celebrate victories.* Just as it is important to learn from mistakes, it is important to accept credit when credit is due. You want to encourage success, not ignore it. Life is too short not to enjoy the good times. Don't take them for granted.

■ *Keep learning.* Your education is just beginning. The world is rapidly changing, and you need to keep up with it. Don't pass up opportunities to learn something new; you never know when this knowledge will come in handy. Knowledge is power.

■ *Command new technology—and don't let it command you.* Technological advances offer new and exciting ways to reach out to targeted publics. However, having the ability to use a new technology doesn't mean we should. Values, audience, and purpose should govern our decisions on which channels we choose.

■ *Pass it on!* It is very likely that you will owe some aspect of your career advancement to mentoring from a more experienced practitioner who took you under his or her wing. The best way you can honor that special person is to become a mentor yourself and show someone else the ropes.

■ *Maintain perspective.* Former University of North Carolina basketball coach Dean Smith retired with the most victories in the history of major college basketball. But he lost quite a few games as well. That's why he once told a reporter that he didn't treat every game as if it were a life-or-death situation. "If you do," Smith said, "you will be dead a lot."

■ *Exercise your rights as a citizen—especially your First Amendment rights.* Freedom can't be taken for granted. It must always be defended and used responsibly. That's why it is important that you vote and speak out on important issues. That is also why you should resist anyone who tries to curb someone else's freedoms. How do you know that your freedoms won't be next on someone's hit list?

One practitioner at a time. That is how values-driven public relations will be established during the modern profession's second century.

Summary

As modern public relations moves into its second century, it has the potential to do both good and harm in society. Its good rests in the profession's ability to bring people together to reach consensus. However, some applications of public relations have been used to block consensus.

Major social forces are shaping the future. Among them are the global spread of democracy, the economic and cultural effects of globalization, the growth in world population, and the increasing feminization of the workplace. The growing presence of women has had and will continue to have a dramatic effect on the field of public relations. Although women in public relations continue to face the same challenges as women everywhere, there appears to be a consensus for addressing salary equity and sexual harassment issues in the industry.

The growth of public relations is expected to continue in the foreseeable future. Public relations will continue to work closely with other marketing disciplines—all of which will be held more accountable. Many of the old problems of the past, such as the search for respect, credibility, and ethics, will continue. Although the workplace in which public relations is practiced may change, the profession's need to adhere to enduring values remains constant.

DISCUSSION QUESTIONS

1. What social, political, or demographic trend will have the most significant impact on the practice of public relations in the 21st century? Please explain your reasoning.
2. How will world and national population trends affect public relations?
3. What steps do you think are necessary to make the profession of public relations more inclusive and representative of the population as a whole?
4. What steps are you taking to prepare for a career in public relations?
5. In a constantly changing world, what role will values play in the future of public relations?

Memo
from the
Field

Sarah Yeaney,
National President
PRSSA 2004–2005

Sarah Yeaney, national president, comes to PRSSA from Penn State University (PSU). Yeaney is majoring in public relations and business. An advocate of the society and its educational benefits, she was elected in March 2004 to serve as president of the 2004–2005 National Committee. Yeaney has been involved in public relations activities since her freshman year at PSU. She had previously served as national vice president of member services in 2003–2004. She had hands-on involvement with member recruitment, retention, and scholarship promotion. Yeaney also had internships with public relations agencies Hill & Knowlton in New York and Fleishman-Hillard in Washington, D.C., during her senior year.

It was the trademark press conference that launched Johnson & Johnson's sales instead of plummeting them after bottles of Tylenol poisoned consumers. The pill-shaped paperweight that a J&J executive waived in the air did more for the company's ratings than any scientific research could. The speech also turned the heads of business owners everywhere toward the evolution of public relations.

Now more than ever companies see communications as a need for survival. As a student, it is a challenge—and an opportunity—to harness this time of change and turn it into success. Here are a few pointers to help:

1. *Think outside of the box—or the classroom.* The role of public relations has forced education outside of textbooks; the mutually advantageous definition is only a starting point. Although professors set the stage for outlining the industry's experience, no curriculum can match the ever-changing demands of communications. It would be impossible for teachers to take in the daily modifications of public relations and incorporate them into lesson plans. However, joining an organization can provide you with that outlet. The Public Relations Student Society of America offers members

the opportunity to learn and grasp the industry. Workshops, lectures, and national events address the current forces that are shaping public relations and what you can do to stay abreast of the wave.

2. *Just do it.* Because public relations is hard to define, you will receive no better education other than experience. Employers crave résumés loaded with internships that have already prepared a student for the fast-paced communications world. As internships become more coveted, finding them has become a résumés race just like entry-level positions. However, joining student clubs and writing their communications can help. Nonprofit organizations or student newspapers and magazines are other areas to consider.

3. *Read—and not just textbooks.* Knowing what a press conference is may be important, but knowing the one that launched an IPO announcement is crucial. Becoming a consumer of the media will help you understand how business operates. In turn, the way business runs dictates the role public relations will play in achieving business objectives. Get your news from more than one source; diversity in thought creates winning strategies in more than one audience.

4. *Talk it out.* Many people in this field often say "it isn't just what you know, but who you know." Mentors not only help with internship searches but also provide advice on how to pave your professional path. Mentors often listen to ideas and help you find experiences that cater to your interests. PRSSA's professional society, PRSA, is one such example of a mentor pool. The parent society hosts more than 20,000 professionals from a variety of public relations interests that range from technology to academic careers. Most important, all of them are eager to help students who have taken the initiative to jump-start their own career paths.

The issues in this chapter will help you further understand public relations' role at the decision-making table. Read it more than once and walk away with a motivation to want to read more. Remember, the best part about public relations is the opportunity to cut and paste your interests into a career that is exciting and different each day. Good luck, and I'll see you in the field.

Case Study 16.1

Shared Sacrifice?

It takes only one misstep to undo months of hard work. Just one miscalculation, regardless of intentions, can turn a hero into a heel overnight. And as frustrating as it can be, it remains a hard fact of life that the management of relationships also requires the management of perceptions.

Just ask American Airlines.

Few companies have faced the trauma the world's largest airline confronted in autumn 2001. The trouble started on September 11, when two of the airline's flights were hijacked and turned into weapons of mass destruction. American Flight 11 out of Boston was deliberately crashed into the North Tower of the World Trade Center in New York. American Flight 77 was flown into the Pentagon near Washington. All civilian air traffic was grounded for four days. Many airlines already faced economic strife. With flights being curtailed and travelers frightened of what might happen next, the airline industry teetered on the brink of financial ruin.

But then came more. In October, flight attendants on a Los Angeles to Chicago flight subdued a disturbed man who tried to break into the cockpit. On November 12, American Flight 587 crashed shortly after takeoff from New York's John F. Kennedy International Airport. Though not terrorism-related, the crash rattled an already nervous nation.

And then came even more. Passengers and crew aboard an American flight from Paris to Miami subdued a man trying to ignite a bomb hidden in this shoe. Just a few days later, a U.S. Secret Service agent of Arab-American descent was removed from a flight at Baltimore-Washington International Airport after the crew accused him of being hostile.[69]

Despite this unprecedented series of crises, American successfully navigated through the storm. Less than two weeks after the terrorist attacks, the company and other airlines successfully lobbied Congress for $5 billion in direct federal aid and another $10 billion in loan guarantees. While some in Congress expressed concerns about bailing out an industry that had faced financial problems before the attacks, the overwhelming consensus was that the nation's economy was at risk. "If planes don't fly, the whole economy shuts down," said Senator Jay Rockefeller, a West Virginia Democrat.[70]

Even with the bailout, American faced some hard choices. The company was forced to lay off 20,000 of its 128,000 employees and to reduce the size of its fleet.[71] To ease the burden, American Chairman and CEO Don Carty announced on October 4 that he and the airline's board of directors had offered to serve without compensation through the end of the year. "Perhaps no group is more keenly aware of our problems than our Board members," Carty said. "It is particularly meaningful for them to forgo compensation for the remainder of the year."[72]

The airline also created a special "American Heroes" web site through which employees could make payroll deductions or contribute lump-sum donations to the families of those killed in the attacks and to assist employees who had been laid off. Carty said the web site was established after he had received thousands of e-mails from employees volunteering to take pay cuts.[73]

The company struggled through 2002 and 2003. AMR, the airline's parent company, reported total losses of $5.8 billion during that period. Some 7,000 more employees were laid off.[74] In its 2002 annual report, American said it had to reduce its annual operating costs by $4 billion "in order to become competitive and sustain its operations." Half of those cuts came through a series of cost-reduction measures.[75] Once again, American turned to its employees for help. It asked its unions and employees for approximately $1.8 billion in permanent annual savings through "a combination of changes in wages, benefits, and work rules."[76] At first the airline's three major unions agreed. Then the wheels almost fell off the deal.

Shortly after the unions had agreed to the concessions, published reports indicated that the airline had given seven of its executives bonuses of up to twice their annual salaries during 2002. The airline had also started putting money into a trust fund to protect the pension benefits of 45 executives.[77] The company said the actions were necessary "to retain key executives" and ensure American's stability. The leaders of two unions threatened to reopen the contract vote. American Airlines officials had no choice but to cancel the executive bonuses.[78]

Carty admitted that he had given misleading information to his management team, including communications employees. "I fell short in conveying to my management team and our spokespeople that I had not fully briefed our union leaders on my discussions," he said.[79]

"Mr. Carty's strength is that he is an honest man," American corporate spokesman Gus Whitcomb said. "Now we hope that we have enough time to allow individuals who are understandably angry to set emotion aside and realize that bankruptcy is as ugly an alternative today as it was a week ago."[80]

"No reasonable person can blame the union members for being outraged," editorialized the *Buffalo News*. "Carty has apologized, but an apology is not the same as accountability. His indefensible action has endangered the airline's survival. Is this really the man who should be running the business?"[81]

Apparently not. The leaders of the unions decided to stick with the original labor agreement on April 25, 2003—one day after Carty resigned as chairman and CEO.

DISCUSSION QUESTIONS

1. Were American Airlines executives wrong to take steps to ensure the stability of the company's leadership? What, if anything, should they have done differently?
2. Carty apologized for his actions. In light of his leadership of the company through perilous times, shouldn't that have been enough to save his job?
3. At the start of this case study, the authors write that "the management of relationships also requires the management of perceptions." Do you agree with this statement? Why or why not?
4. If you were in charge of the airline's corporate communications office, what actions would you have recommended to repair the damage to relationships created by the dispute over executive bonuses? Which relationships, in particular, needed attention?

Case Study 16.2

PR in the Face of Terror

The first challenge was to survive. Many did not.

For the survivors of September 11, 2001, the second challenge was to move beyond the terror and pick up the pieces of a world suddenly gone mad. Many did just that. Public relations played an important role in the recovery.

Much has been (and will be) written about the heroes of that infamous day. Terrorists hijacked four passenger jets and turned them into weapons of mass destruction. Within a span of two horrific and chaotic hours, New York's World Trade Center was destroyed, the Pentagon in Washington was severely damaged, an airliner crashed in western Pennsylvania, and thousands of innocent people—people who were guilty of nothing more than being in the wrong place at the wrong time—were dead.

And the world was a much different place.

Cantor Fitzgerald, one of the nation's largest bond dealers, employed 1,000 people on the top four floors of the WTC's North Tower. Rescue officials believe that none of the more than 700 Cantor employees in the office on September 11 escaped the building before its collapse. Edelman Public Relations Worldwide helped the shattered company coordinate its initial response to the tragedy. Approximately 50 Edelman employees volunteered at bereavement centers established at nearby hotels for the families of the dead and missing. Edelman also coordinated television interviews for Chief Executive Officer Howard Lutnick, who arrived at the WTC just as the first plane struck.[82]

"We've got to make our company be able to take care of my 700 families," Lutnick said. One of those families belonged to his younger brother Gary, a Cantor employee trapped in the North Tower.

Two days after the attack, the bond market reopened. So did Cantor Fitzgerald.

Morgan Stanley, a major financial brokerage, was the largest tenant of the WTC, with 3,500 employees. Most of its employees survived, thanks to fortunate timing and geography. Its offices were located in the South Tower, the second building hit. Unlike those of Cantor Fitzgerald, Morgan Stanley's offices were below the impact point. Those two factors gave Morgan Stanley employees enough time to scramble to safety.

The job for Morgan Stanley's corporate communicators was twofold: They needed to address the human tragedy that had befallen their company and they had to reassure frightened customers that their investments were safe.

"We have all been saddened and outraged by the attack on America, and extend our deepest sympathies and prayers to all of the people affected," Morgan Stanley Chairman Philip Purcell said in a statement posted that afternoon on the company's web site. "All our clients should rest assured that their assets are safe and our Financial Advisors will soon be in contact with our individual investors to answer questions and address their concerns."[83]

Shortly after the attack on the World Trade Center, a hijacked jet slammed into the Pentagon. The White House, the Capitol, and dozens of other government buildings were evacuated. However, the United States government continued to function. Spokespersons for the Federal Aviation Administration announced an unprecedented grounding of all commercial air traffic in the United States. U.S. Securities and Exchange Commission Chairman Harvey L. Pitt issued a statement assuring a nervous nation that the disruption of the financial markets was "a temporary phenomenon."[84]

Even while fire and rescue crews searched a collapsed and burning section of the Pentagon for their fallen comrades, Defense Department and military officials conducted media briefings in another part of the building. "It's an indication that the

Just hours after a terrorist attack on the Pentagon left almost 200 people dead, U.S. Secretary of Defense Donald Rumsfeld briefs news media in another part of the building. (Courtesy of the U.S. Department of Defense)

United States government is functioning in the face of this terrible act against our country," Defense Secretary Donald H. Rumsfeld said. "The Pentagon is functioning. It will be in business tomorrow."[85]

The need to communicate with stakeholders was especially acute for officials at Chicago-based United Airlines and Fort Worth–based American Airlines. Their crews and passengers had been victims, and their aircraft had been the instruments of the terrorists' deadly plot. The two companies had to communicate immediately to a wide range of stakeholders, including relatives of the victims, employees, news media, and federal investigators. They also had a number of key messages to deliver, including sympathy and support for the victims' families and cooperation with federal authorities. Both airlines mobilized their employees in response to the tragedies. Some went to the departure and destination airports of the four flights. Others staffed emergency hotline telephones. The airlines also dispatched technical teams to crash sites to assist federal investigators.

"I know that I speak for every employee at American Airlines when I extend our deepest sympathy to those who lost a loved one, family member, or friend on American Airlines Flight 11, American Airlines Flight 77, United Airlines Flight 93, United Airlines Flight 175, or at the sites of these tragic accidents," said CEO Donald J. Carty in a statement posted on the company's web site.[86]

On his company's web site, United CEO James E. Goodwin expressed similar sentiments. And like his counterpart at American, Goodwin pledged full support for victims' families. He added, "We are also making every resource available at our company to assist all of the relevant authorities—including the FBI—with the ultimate goal of bringing to justice the individuals or organizations responsible for these horrific criminal acts."[87]

The ripple effects of the terrorist attacks were felt in many places. An example is the National Association of Insurance Commissioners, an information clearinghouse for state insurance regulatory agencies, headquartered in Kansas City, Missouri. NAIC's Securities Valuation Office was in 7 World Trade Center, a building that caught fire and eventually collapsed following the attack. All the company's New York employees survived. By following a crisis plan initially developed as a defense against the millennium bug (see Chapter 11), NAIC was able to recover critical computer records before the building lost electrical power.

"We developed our Business Recovery Plan with the idea that it would ready us for any emergency situation that would cause loss of a critical service, loss of access to a facility, or loss of a facility itself," said NAIC's Executive Vice President and CEO Catherine J. Weatherford. "The concept we developed went beyond the scope of just responding to Y2K. . . . However, none of us could have anticipated the type of tragedy that would afflict our nation on September 11."[88]

Following the attacks, public relations practitioners played a role in the nation's recovery. In the New York area, the Public Relations Society of America organized volunteers to help companies needing communications. The International Association of Business Communicators offered crisis resources to its members at no charge. Several New York public relations agencies helped find office space for practitioners displaced from lower Manhattan. On The Scene Productions and Medialink made their satellite uplink facilities available to those affected by the WTC disaster "at substantial discounts."[89] When it really mattered, the public relations community had no competitors, just colleagues.

The role of public relations in a time of national distress was captured by PRSA Chair and CEO Kathleen L. Lewton in a message to members just two weeks after the attacks:

> As always in time of tragedy, PR professionals have been in the midst of the maelstrom, in many capacities. Serving as spokespersons for hospitals, airlines, and governments; handling media inquiries and releasing statements for companies directly impacted; managing efforts to reach employees at remote locations; providing agency support for clients in crisis—as the tragedy unfolded, even those of us who were watching from afar were well aware that behind the scenes, there were thousands of public relations people hard at work, trying to cope.
>
> Our profession is such that in times of crisis, we are essential. We can never step back or step aside, we can never demur, we rarely even have the chance to ask for a moment to reflect and grieve. Our companies and organizations and communities rely on our skills most in times of disruption and peril, and I know that I speak for the entire public relations profession when I offer our admiration and our commendations to the colleagues who labored so tirelessly and so heroically in the first days of the crisis, and to all those who today are working to help our nation recover.[90]

Among those killed on United Flight 93 was public relations practitioner Mark Bingham. Although his actions did not involve the practice of public relations, his role in the events of September 11 may have been more significant than any other practitioner.

We may never know exactly what happened on Flight 93. Based on information gleaned from cellular telephone conversations between passengers and family, Bingham was among a group of passengers who said they would try to overpower the hijackers. The plane crashed approximately 80 miles southeast of Pittsburgh, Pennsylvania, killing all on board. Authorities believe that the hijackers were foiled in their attempt to attack the White House or the U.S. Capitol.

September 11, 2001, was the nation's bloodiest day since the Civil War. Ironically, Flight 93 crashed in the state that was home to that conflict's most celebrated battle. In giving what Abraham Lincoln described in the Gettysburg Address as "the last full measure of devotion," Mark Bingham embodied the practitioner's commitment to serving the public interest.

DISCUSSION QUESTIONS

1. What lessons can public relations practitioners learn from the events of September 11, 2001? How do you think practitioners performed?
2. Why do you think American Airlines and United Airlines used their web sites to deliver messages to stakeholders? What other tactics/media could have been used?
3. At a time of great calamity, such as the terrorist attacks on New York City and Washington, D.C., what role does public relations play?
4. Is a practitioner's advocacy on behalf of a client's interests inconsistent with broader public interests during national emergencies? Where does the commitment to the client end and the commitment to the broader public interest begin? How do one's personal interests figure into the equation?

Cyber Coach

Visit www.ablongman.com/guthmarsh3e for these study aids—and more:

- flashcards
- quizzes
- videos
- links to other sites
- real-world scenarios that let you be the public relations professional

KEY TERMS

baby boom generation, p. 538
breadwinners, p. 538
empowerment, p. 542

feminization, p. 540
globalization, p. 533
green public relations, p. 539

greenwash, p. 539

interconnectedness, p. 533

internships, p. 548

lookism, p. 541

Public Relations Student Society of
America (PRSSA), p. 549

salary equity, p. 540

sexual harassment, p. 541

velvet ghetto, p. 540

NOTES

1. Reid Goldsborough, "Unpredictions," *Public Relations Tactics,* July 2004, 25.

2. *The World Factbook,* Central Intelligence Agency, 18 December 2003, online,
www.odci.gov/cia/publications/factbook.

3. David Weiner, "Can Canadian PR Help China Break into the World Market?" *Strategy,*
20 October 2003, online, LexisNexis.

4. "PR Sector Building Reputation," *China Daily,* 27 August 2004, online, LexisNexis.

5. "Xinhua PR Newswire Launches Corporate Information Distribution Network to Reach
over 2,000 Chinese Media Outlets," PR Newswire, 22 July 2003, online, LexisNexis.

6. "New Guidance to Standardize China's Public Relations Industry," *China Daily,*
26 June 2004, online, LexisNexis.

7. Weiner.

8. Weiner.

9. *Human Development Report 1999,* United Nations Development Program, online,
www.undp.org/hdro.

10. Alejandro Portes, ed., *The New Second Generation* (New York: Russell Sage Foundation, 1996), 54–81.

11. Data from the 1990 census and 2000 census, U.S. Census Bureau, online, www.census.gov.

12. U.S Census Bureau, International Database, updated 30 April 2004, online, www.
census.gov.

13. U.S. Census Bureau, online, www.census.gov.

14. Jeffrey M. Humphreys, *Georgia Business and Economic Conditions,* Selig Center for
Economic Growth, Second Quarter 2003, vol. 63, no. 2, 6.

15. Humphreys, 6.

16. Leon Stafford, "Missing Out on the Trend; Diversity Focus Can Open Doors," *Atlanta
Journal-Constitution,* 27 October 2002, 1F, online, LexisNexis.

17. Yolanda Rodriguez, "Hispanic or Latino? It All Depends," *Atlanta Journal-Constitution,*
10 December 2003, 6F, online, LexisNexis.

18. Rodriguez.

19. Linda P. Morton, "Targeting Hispanic Americans," *Public Relations Quarterly* 47,
no. 3 (fall 2003): 46–48.

20. Stafford.

21. Mindy Charski, "Crossing Cultures," *AdWeek,* 3 May 2004, online, LexisNexis.

22. Stafford.

23. U.S. Census Bureau.

24. U.S. Census Bureau.

25. Scott M. Cutlip, *The Unseen Power: Public Relations, a History* (Hillsdale, N.J.: Lawrence Erlbaum, 1994), 31.

26. Lowell F. Ludford, "3P Program Pays Off in Cost Savings of $500 Million for 3M," *Public Relations Journal,* April 1991, 20–21.

27. Dee-Ann Durbin, "SUV Supporters Counter Jesus Ads," Associated Press, 13 July 2003, online, LexisNexis.

28. Durbin.

29. *Women in the Labor Force: A Databook,* U.S Department of Labor, Bureau of Labor Statistics, February 2004, online, http://stats.bls.gov/cps/wlf-databook.htm.

30. *Women in the Labor Force: A Databook.*

31. "Highlights of Women's Earnings in 2002—Report 972," U.S. Department of Labor Bureau of Labor Statistics, September 2002, online, http://stats.bls.gov.

32. L. L. Cline et al., *The Velvet Ghetto: The Impact of the Increasing Percentage of Women in Public Relations and Organizational Communications* (San Francisco: IABC Research Foundation, 1986).

33. "Facts about Sexual Harassment," U.S. Equal Employment Opportunity Commission, online, www.eeoc.gov/facts/fs-sex.html.

34. "Sexual Harassment Charges EEOC & FEPAs Combined: FY 1992–FY 2003," U.S Equal Employment Opportunity Commission, 8 March 2004, online, www.eeoc.gov/stats/harass.html.

35. Linda Hon, "Toward a Feminist Theory of Public Relations," *Journal of Public Relations Research* 7, no. 1 (1995): 33–34.

36. Barry S. Roberts and Robert A. Mann, "Sexual Harassment in the Workplace: A Primer," *University of Akron Law Review,* online, www.uakron.edu/lawrev/robert1.html.

37. The applicable cases are *Faragher v. City of Boca Raton,* 118 S. Ct. 2275 (1998) and *Burlington Industries Inc. v. Ellerth,* 118 S. Ct. 2257 (1998).

38. The applicable case is *Oncale v. Sundowner Offshore Services, Inc.,* 118 S. Ct. 998 (1998).

39. "Facts about Sexual Harassment."

40. Candace Goforth, "Changing the Workplace Culture Can Help Stop Sexual Harassment," 5 November 2003, *Akron Beacon Journal,* online, LexisNexis.

41. Goforth.

42. Linda Hon, "Feminism and Public Relations," *The Public Relations Strategist* 1, no. 2 (summer 1995): 20.

43. Heidi P. Taff, "Times Have Changed? IABC Research Foundation's 'The Velvet Ghetto' Study Revisited," *Communication World,* February/March 2003, 10–11.

44. Elizabeth L. Toth and Linda Aldoory, *Year 2000 Gender Study,* Public Relations Society of America, 2001, online, http://PR-education.org/prsa2000genderstudy.htm.

45. Hampson.

46. Hon.

47. Shirley A. Serini et al., "Watch for Falling Glass . . . Women, Men and Job Satisfaction in Public Relations: A Preliminary Analysis," *Journal of Public Relations Research* 9, no. 2 (1997): 116–117.

48. *Occupational Outlook Handbook, 2004–05 Edition,* U.S. Department of Labor, Bureau of Labor Statistics, online, http://stats.bls.gov/oco/ocoso086.htm.

49. Cynthia Fritsch, researcher, "'Communications' Tops 'PR' by 2–1 Margin at Fortune 500," *O'Dwyer's PR Services Report,* February 1996, 1.

50. National Credibility Index, Public Relations Society of America, online, www.prsa.org/nci/nci.html.

51. Sean Callahan, "B to B Q&A: Proclaiming the 'Fall of Advertising'; Controversial New Book Argues That Public Relations Is the Best Way to Launch a Brand," *BtoB,* 14 October 2002, 3.

52. "Targeting, Relationship-Building Define Marketing Today," *PR News* 52, no. 13, 25 March 1996, online, LexisNexis.

53. "Targeting, Relationship-Building Define Marketing Today."

54. "Measurement Driving More PR Programs," *PR News* 52, no. 12, 18 March 1996, online, LexisNexis.

55. "Work at Home in 2001," news release by U.S. Department of Labor Bureau of Labor Statistics, 1 March 2002, online, http://stats.bls.gov.

56. Paul Cordasco, "Telecommuting Helps PR Firms Keep Their Top Talent at Home," *PR Week—U.S. Edition,* 20 October 2003, 10.

57. Paul Holmes, "Embracing the Paradox of Change," *The Holmes Report,* 12 March 2001, online, www.holmesreport.com.

58. Holmes.

59. Mark Weiner, "The External Factors Shaping Public Relations in 2014," *Public Relations Tactics,* July 2004, 29.

60. Katherine Woodall, "What Will the Future Hold? Study Reveals Opportunities for Communicators," *Communication World,* February/March 2003, 18–21.

61. Woodall.

62. Gary F. Grates, "Through the Look Glass. Seeing the Future of Public Relations Relevance," *Public Relations Quarterly* (fall 2003): 15–19.

63. Grates.

64. Mike Marino, "Questions Abound for the PR Office of 2014," *Public Relations Tactics,* July 2004, 24.

65. "Outcomes Task Team Report," report of National Communication Association 1998 Summer Conference: Dialogue on Public Relations Education, Arlington, Virginia.

66. Don W. Stacks et al., "Perceptions of Public Relations Education: A Survey of Public Relations Curriculum, Outcomes, Assessment, and Pedagogy," released at the National Communication Association 1998 Summer Conference: Dialogue on Public Relations Education, Arlington, Virginia, 10 July 1998.

67. *Occupational Outlook Handbook, 2004–05 Edition.*

68. "Excerpt from Report on Stature of PR: Factors Inhibiting Stature and Role of PR," *O'Dwyer's PR Services Report,* March 1992, 31.

69. David W. Guth and Charles Marsh, *Adventures in Public Relations: Case Studies and Critical Thinking* (Boston: Allyn & Bacon, 2005), 307–311.

70. "Bush Signs Airline Bailout Package," CNN, 23 September 2001, online, www.cnn.com.

71. Guth and Marsh.

72. "Employees of American Airlines, American Eagle, TWA and AMR Board of Directors Chip In to Help American Through Financial Crisis," news release distributed via PR Newswire, 4 October 2001, online, www.prnewswire.com.

73. "Employees of American Airlines, American Eagle, TWA and AMR Board of Directors Chip In to Help American Through Financial Crisis."

74. Guth and Marsh.

75. AMR Corporation Form 10-K for the Fiscal Year Ended December 31, 2002, U.S. Securities and Exchanges Commission, file number 1-8400, online, www.sec.gov.

76. AMR Corporation Form 10-Q for the Quarterly Period Ended March 31, 2003, U.S. Securities and Exchanges Commission, file number 1-8400, online, www.sec.gov.

77. "American Airlines Blunder," editorial, *Buffalo News,* 24 April 2003, B10, online, LexisNexis.

78. AMR Corporation Form 10-Q for the Quarterly Period Ended March 31, 2003.

79. "Comms Team Trying to Help American Avoid Chapter 11," *PR Week—U.S. Edition,* 28 April 2003, 2.

80. "Comms Team Trying to Help American Avoid Chapter 11."

81. "American Airlines Blunder."

82. "Cantor Fitzgerald Turns to Edelman," *O'Dwyer's PR Daily,* 21 September 2001, online, www.odwyerpr.com/0921cantor.htm.

83. "Message from Morgan Stanley Chairman Phillip Purcell," Morgan Stanley, 11 September 2001, online, www.morganstanley.com.

84. Statement by SEC Chairman Harvey L. Pitt (2001-90), U.S. Securities and Exchange Commission, 11 September 2001 online, www.sec.gov.

85. Transcript of Department of Defense News Briefing on Pentagon Attack, U.S. Department of Defense, 11 September 2001 (6:42 P.M. EDT), online, www.defenselink.mil.

86. "A Message from American Airlines Chief Executive Officer Don Carty," American Airlines, 11 September 2001, online, www/aa.com.

87. "A Message from United Airlines CEO James E. Goodwin," United Airlines, 11 September 2001, online, www.ual.com.

88. Catherine J. Weatherford, interview by authors, 28 September 2001.

89. "PR Community Pitches In," *O'Dwyer's PR Services,* 13 September 2001, online, www.odwyerpr.com/0913pr_community.htm.

90. E-mail message of Kathleen Larey Lewton, APR, Fellow PRSA Chair and CEO, Public Relations Society of America, 26 September 2001.

Appendix

Member Code of Ethics 2000

Approved by the PRSA Assembly, October 2000

Preamble

Public Relations Society of America Member Code of Ethics 2000

>   Professional Values
>   Principles of Conduct
>   Commitment and Compliance

This Code applies to PRSA members. The Code is designed to be a useful guide for PRSA members as they carry out their ethical responsibilities. This document is designed to anticipate and accommodate, by precedent, ethical challenges that may arise. The scenarios outlined in the Code provision are actual examples of misconduct. More will be added as experience with the Code occurs.

The Public Relations Society of America (PRSA) is committed to ethical practices. The level of public trust PRSA members seek, as we serve the public good, means we have taken on a special obligation to operate ethically.

The value of member reputation depends upon the ethical conduct of everyone affiliated with the Public Relations Society of America. Each of us sets an example for each other—as well as other professionals—by our pursuit of excellence with powerful standards of performance, professionalism, and ethical conduct.

Emphasis on enforcement of the Code has been eliminated. But, the PRSA Board of Directors retains the right to bar from membership or expel from the Society any individual who has been or is sanctioned by a government agency or convicted in a court of law of an action that is in violation of this Code.

Ethical practice is the most important obligation of a PRSA member. We view the Member Code of Ethics as a model for other professions, organizations, and professionals.

PRSA Member Statement of Professional Values

This statement presents the core values of PRSA members and, more broadly, of the public relations profession. These values provide the foundation for the Member

Code of Ethics and set the industry standard for the professional practice of public relations. These values are the fundamental beliefs that guide our behaviors and decision-making process. We believe our professional values are vital to the integrity of the profession as a whole.

ADVOCACY

We serve the public interest by acting as responsible advocates for those we represent.

We provide a voice in the marketplace of ideas, facts, and viewpoints to aid informed public debate.

HONESTY

We adhere to the highest standards of accuracy and truth in advancing the interests of those we represent and in communicating with the public.

EXPERTISE

We acquire and responsibly use specialized knowledge and experience.

We advance the profession through continued professional development, research, and education.

We build mutual understanding, credibility, and relationships among a wide array of institutions and audiences.

INDEPENDENCE

We provide objective counsel to those we represent.

We are accountable for our actions.

LOYALTY

We are faithful to those we represent, while honoring our obligation to serve the public interest.

FAIRNESS

We deal fairly with clients, employers, competitors, peers, vendors, the media, and the general public.

We respect all opinions and support the right of free expression.

PRSA Code Provisions

Free Flow of Information

CORE PRINCIPLE

Protecting and advancing the free flow of accurate and truthful information is essential to serving the public interest and contributing to informed decision making in a democratic society.

INTENT

To maintain the integrity of relationships with the media, government officials, and the public.

To aid informed decision-making.

GUIDELINES

A member shall:

> Preserve the integrity of the process of communication.
>
> Be honest and accurate in all communications.
>
> Act promptly to correct erroneous communications for which the practitioner is responsible.
>
> Preserve the free flow of unprejudiced information when giving or receiving gifts by ensuring that gifts are nominal, legal, and infrequent.

EXAMPLES OF IMPROPER CONDUCT UNDER THIS PROVISION:

A member representing a ski manufacturer gives a pair of expensive racing skis to a sports magazine columnist, to influence the columnist to write favorable articles about the product.

A member entertains a government official beyond legal limits and/or in violation of government reporting requirements.

Competition

CORE PRINCIPLE

Promoting healthy and fair competition among professionals preserves an ethical climate while fostering a robust business environment.

INTENT

To promote respect and fair competition among public relations professionals.

To serve the public interest by providing the widest choice of practitioner options.

GUIDELINES

A member shall:

> Follow ethical hiring practices designed to respect free and open competition without deliberately undermining a competitor.
>
> Preserve intellectual property rights in the marketplace.

EXAMPLES OF IMPROPER CONDUCT UNDER THIS PROVISION:

A member employed by a "client organization" shares helpful information with a counseling firm that is competing with others for the organization's business.

A member spreads malicious and unfounded rumors about a competitor in order to alienate the competitor's clients and employees in a ploy to recruit people and business.

Disclosure of Information

CORE PRINCIPLE

Open communication fosters informed decision making in a democratic society.

INTENT

To build trust with the public by revealing all information needed for responsible decision making.

GUIDELINES

A member shall:

> Be honest and accurate in all communications.
>
> Act promptly to correct erroneous communications for which the member is responsible.
>
> Investigate the truthfulness and accuracy of information released on behalf of those represented.
>
> Reveal the sponsors for causes and interests represented.
>
> Disclose financial interest (such as stock ownership) in a client's organization.
>
> Avoid deceptive practices.

EXAMPLES OF IMPROPER CONDUCT UNDER THIS PROVISION:

Front groups: A member implements "grass roots" campaigns or letter-writing campaigns to legislators on behalf of undisclosed interest groups.

Lying by omission: A practitioner for a corporation knowingly fails to release financial information, giving a misleading impression of the corporation's performance.

A member discovers inaccurate information disseminated via a web site or media kit and does not correct the information.

A member deceives the public by employing people to pose as volunteers to speak at public hearings and participate in "grass roots" campaigns.

Safeguarding Confidences

CORE PRINCIPLE

Client trust requires appropriate protection of confidential and private information.

INTENT

To protect the privacy rights of clients, organizations, and individuals by safeguarding confidential information.

GUIDELINES

A member shall:

> Safeguard the confidences and privacy rights of present, former, and prospective clients and employees.
>
> Protect privileged, confidential, or insider information gained from a client or organization.
>
> Immediately advise an appropriate authority if a member discovers that confidential information is being divulged by an employee of a client company or organization.

EXAMPLES OF IMPROPER CONDUCT UNDER THIS PROVISION:

A member changes jobs, takes confidential information, and uses that information in the new position to the detriment of the former employer.

A member intentionally leaks proprietary information to the detriment of some other party.

Conflicts of Interest

CORE PRINCIPLE

Avoiding real, potential, or perceived conflicts of interest builds the trust of clients, employers, and the publics.

INTENT

To earn trust and mutual respect with clients or employers.

To build trust with the public by avoiding or ending situations that put one's personal or professional interests in conflict with society's interests.

GUIDELINES

A member shall:

> Act in the best interests of the client or employer, even subordinating the member's personal interests.
>
> Avoid actions and circumstances that may appear to compromise good business judgment or create a conflict between personal and professional interests.
>
> Disclose promptly any existing or potential conflict of interest to affected clients or organizations.
>
> Encourage clients and customers to determine if a conflict exists after notifying all affected parties.

EXAMPLES OF IMPROPER CONDUCT UNDER THIS PROVISION:

The member fails to disclose that he or she has a strong financial interest in a client's chief competitor.

The member represents a "competitor company" or a "conflicting interest" without informing a prospective client.

Enhancing the Profession

CORE PRINCIPLE

Public relations professionals work constantly to strengthen the public's trust in the profession.

INTENT

To build respect and credibility with the public for the profession of public relations.

To improve, adapt, and expand professional practices.

GUIDELINES

A member shall:

Acknowledge that there is an obligation to protect and enhance the profession.

Keep informed and educated about practices in the profession to ensure ethical conduct.

Actively pursue personal professional development.

Decline representation of clients or organizations that urge or require actions contrary to this Code.

Accurately define what public relations activities can accomplish.

Counsel subordinates in proper ethical decision making.

Require that subordinates adhere to the ethical requirements of the Code.

Report ethical violations, whether committed by PRSA members or not, to the appropriate authority.

EXAMPLES OF IMPROPER CONDUCT UNDER THIS PROVISION:

A PRSA member declares publicly that a product the client sells is safe, without disclosing evidence to the contrary.

A member initially assigns some questionable client work to a non-member practitioner to avoid the ethical obligation of PRSA membership.

Resources

RULES AND GUIDELINES

The following PRSA documents, available online at www.prsa.org, provide detailed rules and guidelines to help guide your professional behavior. If, after reviewing them, you still have a question or issue, contact PRSA headquarters as noted below.

PRSA Bylaws

PRSA Administrative Rules

Member Code of Ethics

Questions

The PRSA is here to help. If you have a serious concern or simply need clarification, please contact Kim Baldwin at (212) 460-1404.

PRSA Member Code of Ethics Pledge

I pledge:

To conduct myself professionally, with truth, accuracy, fairness, and responsibility to the public; To improve my individual competence and advance the knowledge and proficiency of the profession through continuing research and education; And to adhere to the articles of the Member Code of Ethics 2000 for the practice of public relations as adopted by the governing Assembly of the Public Relations Society of America.

I understand and accept that there is a consequence for misconduct, up to and including membership revocation.

And, I understand that those who have been or are sanctioned by a government agency or convicted in a court of law of an action that is in violation of this Code may be barred from membership or expelled from the Society.

_____

Signature

_____

Date

Glossary

Terms in the Glossary match those of the Key Terms section in each chapter and reflect the usage in the text. Thus, some entries in the Glossary are singular and others are plural.

account executive   The individual at a public relations agency with the responsibility for managing a client's account and the people working on that account.

Accredited Business Communicator (ABC)   Designation given to accredited members of the International Association of Business Communicators.

Accredited in Public Relations (APR)   Designation given to accredited members of the Public Relations Society of America.

active public   A group whose members understand that they are united by a common interest, value, or values in a particular situation and are actively working to promote their interest or values.

active public opinion   Expressed behavioral inclination exhibited when people act—formally and informally—to influence the opinions and actions of others.

active voice   A grammatical term designating that, within a sentence, the subject does the action denoted by the verb (see *passive voice*). In most grammatical situations, writers prefer active voice to passive voice.

actualities   Recorded quotable quotes or sound bites supplied to radio stations on cassette tape or via a dial-in phone system or a web site.

actual malice   The higher burden of proof that public officials and public figures must satisfy in libel cases: In addition to showing that a defamatory statement is false, a public figure must also show knowing falsehood or reckless disregard for the truth.

ad hoc plan   A plan created for a single, short-term purpose; from the Latin phrase meaning "for this purpose only."

administrative law judge   The presiding officer in hearings about alleged violations of government regulations. This person hears testimony and reviews evidence, much like the judge and jury in a civil or criminal case. If federal regulations are at issue, this judge's decision can ultimately be appealed in the federal court system.

advertising   The process of creating and sending a persuasive message through controlled media, which allows the sender, for a price, to dictate message, placement, and frequency.

advertising value equivalency (AVE)   A calculation of the value of publicity based on the advertising rates and the amount of media coverage received.

agenda-setting hypothesis   The idea that the mass media tell us not what to think, but what to think about. This hypothesis is the most widely accepted view of how mass media interact with society.

analog   Transmitted in the form of continuously varying signals. Those variations correspond to changes in sound and light energy coming from the source.

annual meeting   A once-a-year informational conference that a publicly held company must, by law, hold for its stockholders.

annual report   A once-a-year informational statement that a publicly held company must, by law, send to its stockholders.

appropriation   A tort in libel law. In this context, it is the commercial use of someone's name, voice, likeness, or other defining characteristic without the person's consent.

association magazines   Magazines for members of associations, such as the American Library Association.

attitude   A behavioral inclination.

attributes   Characteristics or qualities that describe an object or individual, such as gender, age, weight, height, political affiliation, and religious affiliation.

attribution   The part of a sentence that identifies the speaker of a direct quotation. In the sentence *"Public relations is a values-driven profession," she said,* the words *she said* are the attribution.

aware public   A group whose members understand that they are united by a common interest, value, or values in a particular situation but who have not yet formed plans or acted on their interest or values.

aware public opinion   Expressed behavioral inclination that occurs when people grow aware of an emerging interest.

baby boom generation   People born between 1945 and 1964. The name comes from the record post–World War II surge in population. As the baby boomers reach retirement age early in the 21st century, they are expected to place a tremendous strain on services geared toward the elderly.

backgrounder   A document that supplies information to supplement a news release. Written as publishable stories, backgrounders are often included in media kits.

belief   A commitment to a particular idea or concept based on either personal experience or some credible external authority.

Bernays, Edward L.   The man often acknowledged as the "father of public relations"—a notion he openly promoted. In his landmark 1923 book *Crystallizing Public Opinion,* Bernays coined the phrase "public relations counsel" and first articulated the concept of two-way public relations. Bernays was a nephew of noted psychoanalyst Sigmund Freud.

bill inserts   Leaflets or other marketing documents that can be included with the bills that a company sends to its customers.

bivariate analysis   Analysis of research data that examines two variables.

blogs   Regularly updated Internet diaries or news forums that focus on a particular area of interest.

boundary spanning   The function of representing a public's values to an organization and, conversely, representing the values of the organization to that public.

brainstorming   A collaborative and speculative process in which options for possible courses of action are explored.

branding   The process of building corporate and product identities and differentiating them from those of the competition.

breadwinners   People between the ages of 18 and 65 who typically constitute the labor force. As the so-called baby boom generation reaches retirement age, the percentage of breadwinners relative to the total U.S. population will decline.

b-roll   Unedited video footage that follows a video news release. Rather than use the VNR as provided, some television stations prefer using b-roll footage to create their own news stories.

B2B   Abbreviation for "business-to-business."

burden of proof   The legal standard a plaintiff must meet to establish a defendant's guilt. For example, to prove a case of libel, the plaintiff must show defamation, identification, publication, damage, and fault or actual malice.

business-to-business communication   The exchange of messages between two businesses, such as a manufacturer and a distributor.

business-to-business relations   The maintenance of mutually beneficial relations between two businesses, such as a manufacturer and a distributor.

categorical imperative   A concept created by Immanuel Kant; the idea that individuals ought to make ethical decisions by imagining what would happen if a given course of action were to become a universal maxim, a clear principle designed to apply to everyone.

cause marketing A concerted effort on the part of an organization to address a social need through special events and, perhaps, other marketing tactics.

CD-ROM The acronym for "compact disc–read-only memory," a medium for storage of digital data. It is a popular format for storage of music, computer software, and databases. CD-ROMs are increasingly popular among public relations practitioners for the distribution of multimedia and interactive communications.

cease and desist order An order issued by an FTC administrative law judge upon a ruling that a company or individual has violated federal laws governing marketplace transactions, including advertising.

census Survey of every member of a sampling frame.

channel The medium used to transmit a message.

civil disobedience Peaceful, unlawful action designed to affect social discourse and/or change public policy.

civil penalties Penalties imposed under civil law for the violation of government regulations. These penalties usually involve the levy of a fine or placement of certain restrictions against the individual or organization found to be in violation.

cleanup phase The third stage of a crisis. During this stage, an organization deals with a crisis and its aftermath. How long this period lasts is influenced by the degree to which the organization is prepared to handle crises.

client research The gathering of information about the client, company, or organization on whose behalf a practitioner is working. Typically, this information includes the organization's size, products or services, history, staffing requirements, markets and customers, budget, legal environment, reputation, and mission.

closed-ended questions Questions for which the response set is specifically defined; answers must be selected from a predetermined menu of options.

cluster sampling A sampling technique used to compensate for an unrepresentative sampling frame. It involves breaking the population into homogeneous clusters and then selecting a sample from each cluster.

coalition building Efforts to promote consensus among influential publics on important issues through tactics such as face-to-face meetings.

cognitive dissonance The mental discomfort people can experience when they encounter information or opinions that oppose their opinions.

commercial speech Expression intended to generate marketplace transactions. The U.S. Supreme Court has recognized a government interest in its regulation.

commitment The extent to which each party in a relationship thinks that the relationship is worth the time, cost, and effort.

Committee for Public Information (CPI) Committee created by President Woodrow Wilson to rally public opinion in support of U.S. efforts during World War I. Often referred to as the Creel Committee, it was headed by former journalist George Creel and served as a training ground for many early public relations practitioners.

common law libel Libel defined by judicial rulings rather than by legislators or regulators; can occur in private communications, such as internal business memoranda.

communal relationship A relationship characterized by the provision of benefits to both members of the relationship out of concern and without expectation of anything in return.

communication The exchange of information, verbal and nonverbal, between individuals. Also the third step in the four-step public relations process. Because the process is dynamic, however, communication can occur at any time.

communication audits Research procedures used to determine whether an organization's public statements and publications are consistent with its values-driven mission and goals.

communication model A diagram that depicts the elements of the process of communication.

communications grid A tool used during communication audits to illustrate the distribution patterns of an organization's communications. The various media used are listed on one axis, stakeholders important to the organization on the other.

communications specialist   Job title given to some public relations practitioners, whose jobs usually entail the preparation of communications.

community relations   The maintenance of mutually beneficial contacts between an organization and key publics within communities important to its success.

compliance-gaining tactic   An action designed to influence the behavior of a person or public. Ideally, the action is consistent both with an organization's goals and values and with the person's or public's self-interests and values.

components of relationships   As defined by researchers Linda Childers Hon and James E. Grunig, the six key components that should be used in measuring the strength of a relationship: control mutuality, trust, satisfaction, commitment, exchange relationship, and communal relationship.

computer viruses   Software programming that attaches to a computer user's e-mail address book and is spread to computers around the world. Often the product of mischief, they have been known to erase or damage data on the computers they infect.

confidence levels   The statistical degree to which one can reasonably assume that a survey outcome is an accurate reflection of the entire population.

consent order   Ruling issued by the FTC when a company or individual voluntarily agrees to end a potentially unlawful practice without making an admission of guilt.

consumer redress   Compensation for consumers harmed by misleading or illegal marketplace practices. Under federal law, consumer redress can be sought by the Securities and Exchange Commission.

consumer relations   The maintenance of mutually beneficial communication between an organization and the people who use or are potential users of its products and/or services.

contacts   In marketing, all informative encounters, direct or indirect, that a customer or potential customer has with an organization's product or with the organization itself.

contingency plan   A plan created for use when a certain set of circumstances arises. Crisis communications plans are examples of contingency plans.

contingency questions   Questions that are asked on the basis of questionnaire respondents' answers to earlier questions.

controlled media   Communication channels, such as newsletters, in which the sender of the message controls the message as well as its timing and frequency.

control mutuality   The degree to which parties in a relationship agree on and willingly accept which party has the power to influence the actions of the other.

convenience sampling   The administration of a survey based on the availability of subjects without regard to representativeness.

convergence of media   A blending of media made possible by digitization. As different media adopt digital technology in their production and distribution processes, the differences among them become less apparent, and various media begin to incorporate one another's characteristics.

coorientation   A process in which practitioners seek similarities and differences between their organization's opinions regarding a public and that public's opinion of the practitioners' organizations.

copyright   A legal designation that protects original works from unauthorized use. The notation ©, meaning copyright, indicates ownership of intellectual property.

corporate social responsibility   An organizational philosophy that emphasizes an organization's obligation to be a good corporate citizen through programs that improve society.

credentialing   A process for establishing the identity of people working in an otherwise restricted area. Usually used in connection with reporters, credentialing involves issuing passes or badges that give access to an area such as a media information center.

crisis   An event that if allowed to escalate can disrupt an organization's normal operations, jeopardize its reputation, and damage its bottom line.

crisis communications planning   The second step in effective crisis communications. In this step practitioners use the information gathered during risk assessment to develop strategies for communicating with key publics during crises; they also train employees in what they are supposed to do in a crisis.

crisis impact value (CIV) The vertical axis on Steven Fink's crisis plotting grid. Specific questions are used to measure the impact a given crisis would have on an organization's operations.

crisis management team (CMT) An internal task force established to manage an organization's response to a crisis while allowing other operations to continue.

crisis manager The person designated as the leader of a crisis management team. When this person is not the chief executive of an organization, he or she is usually someone appointed by the chief executive.

crisis planning team (CPT) A broad-based internal task force that develops an organization's crisis communications plan.

crisis plotting grid A risk assessment tool developed by crisis planning expert Steven Fink for prioritizing crisis communications planning needs.

crisis probability factor (CPF) The horizontal axis on Steven Fink's crisis plotting grid. It is an estimate of the probability that a given crisis will occur.

cross-cultural Occurring between members of different cultures.

Crystallizing Public Opinion Book authored by Edward L. Bernays in 1923, in which the term *public relations counsel* first appeared. In the book Bernays also became the first to articulate the concept of two-way public relations.

cultural relativism The belief that no culture or set of cultural ethics is superior to another.

culture A collection of distinct publics bound together by shared characteristics such as language, nationality, attitudes, tastes, and religious beliefs.

customer relationship management (CRM) The use of individual consumer information, stored in a database, to identify, select, and retain customers.

cyber-relations The use of public relations strategies and tactics to deal with publics via and issues related to the Internet.

cybersmears Instances of using the Internet to unfairly attack the integrity of an organization and/or its products and services.

damage A burden of proof in libel. In that context, to prove damage is to demonstrate that the person or organization claiming libel suffered injury as a result of defamation.

database marketing The use of individual consumer information, stored in a database, to help plan marketing decisions.

databases Structured data storage and retrieval systems. In certain situations, such as with commercial online databases, these systems can be accessed by multiple computer users simultaneously.

decision makers Any persons or group of people who make decisions for publics.

"Declaration of Principles" Ivy Ledbetter Lee's 1906 articulation of an ethical foundation for the yet-to-be-named profession of public relations. In his declaration Lee committed his publicity agency to a standard of openness, truth, and accuracy—one that was not, unfortunately, always met.

decoding The process of deriving meaning from a message.

defamation A burden of proof in libel. In that context, defamation is any communication that unfairly injures a person's reputation and ability to maintain social contacts.

demographic information Data on nonattitudinal characteristics of a person or group, such as race, gender, age, and income.

dichotomous questions In a questionnaire, either/ or questions such as yes/no and true/false items.

diffusion theory A belief that the power of the mass media rests in their ability to provide information; individuals who act upon that information then influence the actions of others in their peer group or society.

digital Transmitted in a computer-readable format. Digital information is easy to use in a variety of media.

digital divide The term used to describe the uneven distribution of Internet access along geographical and socioeconomic lines.

Digital Millennium Copyright Act   A federal law enacted in 1998 that established rules for downloading, sharing, or viewing copyrighted material on the Internet. It also makes it a crime to circumvent antipiracy and code-cracking measures.

direct marketing   The delivery of individualized advertising to consumers one at a time, as opposed to mass advertising.

disclosure   The full and timely communication of any information relevant to investors' decisions to buy or sell stocks and bonds; a legal obligation of publicly held companies.

domestic publics   Groups that are united by a common interest, value, or values in a particular situation and that exist primarily within an organization's home country.

downsizing   Reduction in an organization's workforce. Because of economic globalization and technological advances during the last quarter of the 20th century, organizations were forced to do more with fewer employees to remain competitive.

DVD (digital video—or versatile—disc)   A computer disk that stores multimedia messages in a digital format.

e-commerce   Financial activity conducted on the Internet.

e-mail   A process by which a written message is sent electronically via computer to a receiver or receivers.

emergency operations center (EOC)   The place where a crisis management team meets to develop its response to a crisis. It is in a secure location, one where the CMT can work free from interruptions.

employee relations   The maintenance of mutually beneficial relations between an organization and its employees.

empowerment   The process through which an individual or a public gains power and influence over personal and/or organizational actions.

encoding   Selecting words, images, and other forms of communication to create a message.

equal opportunity provision   The requirement that legally qualified candidates for public office be afforded equal access to broadcast media. This provision does not apply if a candidate's appearance is in the context of news coverage.

ethical imperialism   The belief that a particular set of ethics has no flexibility and no room for improvement.

ethics   Beliefs about right and wrong that guide the way we think and act.

ethics audit   A process through which an organization evaluates its own ethical conduct and makes recommendations to improve it.

ethos   An Aristotelian term denoting persuasive appeal based on a speaker's character and reputation.

evaluation   The fourth step of the public relations process. However, because public relations involves a dynamic process, evaluation can occur at any time.

evaluation research   Fact-gathering designed to help a practitioner determine whether a public relations plan met its goal(s) and objectives.

exchange relationship   A relationship characterized by the giving of benefits to one party in the relationship in return for past benefits received or for the expectation of future benefits.

executive summary   A description, usually one page in length, covering the essentials of a public relations proposal.

external publics   Groups that are united by a common interest, value, or values in a particular situation and that are not part of a public relations practitioner's organization.

extranets   Controlled-access extensions of organizations' intranets to selected external publics such as suppliers.

fact sheet   A who-what-when-where-why-how breakdown of a news release. Unlike a news release, a fact sheet is not meant for publication; instead, it gives just the facts of the story contained in the news release. Fact sheets are often included in media kits.

fair use   A legal principle stating that portions of copyrighted works can be used without the owner's permission under certain conditions. Commonly, fair use includes noncommercial news reporting and certain educational purposes.

false light A tort in privacy law. A person can be sued for invasion of privacy if he or she presents someone in a false and offensive light, even if the communication in question isn't defamatory.

fault A burden of proof in libel cases involving private individuals. In that context, to prove fault (falseness) is to show that a defamatory statement is untrue.

Federal Communications Commission (FCC) A federal agency established to ensure the orderly use of the nation's broadcast airwaves in the public interest.

Federalist Papers Essays written to New York newspapers by John Hamilton, James Madison, and John Jay under the nom de plume "Publius" in support of ratification of the U.S. Constitution. The essays have been called "the finest public relations effort in history."

Federal Trade Commission (FTC) A federal agency established to ensure a competitive marketplace. The FTC is the source of most federal regulation governing advertising.

feedback The receiver's reaction to a message.

feedback research The examination of evidence—often unsolicited—of various publics' responses to an organization's actions. This evidence can take many forms, such as letters and telephone calls.

feminization The process through which the increasing influence of women is felt upon social, political, and economic issues.

First Amendment The constitutional guarantee of freedom of expression, freedom of the press, and freedom of religion. Its ratification in 1789 is considered the most significant event in the development of public relations in the United States.

focus groups An informal research method in which interviewers meet with groups of selected individuals to determine their opinions, predispositions, concerns, and attitudes.

Food and Drug Administration (FDA) A federal agency established to protect, promote, and enhance the health of the people of the United States. The FDA regulates the promotion of food, drug, and cosmetic products and services.

food disparagement laws Laws adopted in several states to protect products and services from defamatory statements that damage their market value; also known as veggie libel laws.

formal research Research that uses scientific methods to create an accurate representation of reality.

Form 10-K A comprehensive financial disclosure form that publicly held companies are required to file annually with the SEC.

Four-Minute Men A speakers' bureau utilized by the Committee for Public Information (Creel Committee) during World War I. Its members would make short presentations in support of the U.S. war effort during the four-minute intermissions between reels at movie theaters.

framing Communicating an idea in such a manner that an audience, either intentionally or unintentionally, is influenced by the way it is imparted.

Freedom of Information Act (FOIA) A federal law requiring all government documents, except those covered by specific exemptions, to be open for public inspection.

gatekeepers Members of the news media, such as editors, who determine which stories a given medium will include.

geodemographics A marketing term for the examination of behavioral patterns based on where people live.

globalization The growing economic interdependence of the world's people as a result of technological advances and increasing world trade.

global village Concept first articulated by Canadian communications theorist Marshall McLuhan, suggesting that because of advances in telecommunications technology, we live in a world in which everyone can share simultaneous experiences.

goal The outcome a public relations plan is designed to achieve.

golden mean A concept created by Aristotle and Confucius. In Aristotelian ethics, the golden mean is the point of ideal ethical balance between deficiency and excess of a quality—for example, between deficient honesty and excessive honesty.

government relations The maintenance of mutually beneficial relations between an organization and the local, state, and federal government agencies important to its success.

grassroots lobbying Organized efforts by ordinary citizens to influence legislative and regulatory governmental processes.

green public relations Public relations activities geared toward demonstrating an organization's commitment to the environment. Increased environmental commitment is sometimes referred to as "going green."

greenwash A term environmentalists use to describe disinformation disseminated by an organization in an effort to present an environmentally responsible image.

gripe sites Web sites dedicated to airing complaints, either real or imagined, against individuals or organizations.

hackers Individuals who seek unauthorized access to web sites and computer networks. Sometimes the motivation is personal amusement. However, a hacker's purpose may be to steal, alter, or damage data.

hypermedia Integrated multimedia incorporating audio, visual, and text information in a single delivery system.

identification A burden of proof in libel. To prove identification is to show that a reasonable person would infer that a defamatory statement applies to the plaintiff.

IMC audit An organization's examination and analysis of its own marketing communications: procedures, databases, personnel, messages, and so on.

independent endorsement Verification by a disinterested outside party, which can lend credibility to a message, as when the media decide to air or publish a news story based on an organization's news release.

independent public relations consultant An individual practitioner who is, in essence, a one-person public relations agency providing services for others on a per-job basis, contract, or retainer.

Industrial Revolution The period in the 19th and early 20th centuries during which the United States and other Western nations moved from an agricultural to a manufacturing economy.

informal research Research that describes some aspect of reality but does not necessarily create an accurate representation of the larger reality.

injunctions Court orders that prohibit the enjoined person from taking a specified action.

insider trading The purchase or sale of stocks or bonds on the basis of inside information that is not available to other investors. It is a violation of federal law and professional codes of ethics.

instant messaging An electronic process that allows two or more people to conduct a real-time, written conversation via computer.

institutional investors Large companies or organizations that purchase stocks and other securities on behalf of their members, usually in enormous quantities.

integrated brand communication The coordination of an organization's marketing communications to clarify and strengthen individual consumers' beliefs about a particular brand.

integrated marketing communications (IMC) The coordinated use of public relations, advertising, and marketing strategies and tactics to send well-defined, interactive messages to individual consumers.

intellectual property Original works of authorship that are fixed in a tangible form of expression.

interconnectedness The effect of a variety of forces that tend to draw the people of the world closer together. These forces include technological advances, world population growth, and multiculturalism.

internal publics Groups that are united by a common interest, value, or values in a particular situation and that are part of a public relations practitioner's organization.

International Association of Business Communicators (IABC) The world's second-largest public relations professional association, with approximately 12,500 members. It was founded in 1970 and is headquartered in San Francisco.

international publics   Groups that are united by a common interest, value, or values in a particular situation and that exist primarily beyond the boundaries of an organization's home country.

Internet   A global network, originally created for military and scientific research, that links computer networks to allow the sharing of information in a digital format.

internships   Temporary, supervised workplace experiences that employers offer students. Some interns work for academic credit. Others receive a nominal wage for their services. Internships are considered a valuable precursor to a public relations career.

intervening public   Any group that helps send a public relations message to another group. The news media are often considered to be an intervening public.

intranet   A controlled-access internal computer network available only to the employees of an organization.

intrusion   A tort in privacy law. In that context intrusion is defined as an improper and intentional invasion of a person's physical seclusion or private affairs.

inverted pyramid   A symbol that represents the traditional organization of a news story. In a traditional news story, the most important information occurs within the first few sentences; as the story progresses, the information becomes less important.

investor relations   The maintenance of mutually beneficial relations between publicly owned companies and shareholders, potential shareholders, and those who influence investment decisions.

issues management   A form of problem–opportunity research in which an organization identifies and analyzes emerging trends and issues for the purpose of preparing a timely and appropriate response.

latent public   A group whose members do not yet realize that they share a common interest, value, or values in a particular situation.

latent public opinion   A behavioral inclination that exists when people have interest in a topic or issue but are unaware of the similar interests of others.

Lee, Ivy Ledbetter   Author of the "Declaration of Principles" in 1906. Lee became the first practitioner

to articulate a vision of open, honest, and ethical communication for the profession—but became known by his critics as "Poison Ivy" for not living up to those standards.

libel   A false communication that wrongfully injures the reputation of another. To make a successful claim of libel, a plaintiff must meet the requirements of a five-point burden of proof.

litigation public relations (LPR)   The use of public relations research, strategies, and tactics to influence events surrounding legal cases.

lobby   In a public relations context, an organization that exists solely to influence governmental legislative and regulatory processes on behalf of a client. The word *lobby* may also be used as a verb to denote the act of lobbying.

logos   An Aristotelian term denoting persuasive appeal to the intellect.

lookism   A covert form of sexual harassment: attention that focuses more on a woman's appearance than on her job performance.

macroediting   A stage in the writing process in which the writer examines the "big picture" of a document, including format, organization, and completeness of information.

magic bullet theory   The belief that the mass media wield such great power that by delivering just the right message, the so-called magic bullet, the media can persuade people to do anything.

manipulation   In a public relations context, an attempt to influence a person's actions without regard to his or her self-interests.

marketing   The process of researching, creating, refining, and promoting a product or service and distributing that product or service to targeted consumers.

marketing mix   The four traditional aspects of marketing: product, price, place (distribution), and promotion.

marketing public relations   The use of the public relations process to promote an organization's goods or services.

Maslow's Hierarchy of Needs Developed by psychologist Abraham Maslow, a multitiered list of ranked factors that determine a person's self-interests and motivations. Under Maslow's theory, people must meet their most basic needs before acting on less pressing needs.

media advisory A fact sheet that is faxed or e-mailed to news media to alert them of a breaking news story or an event they may wish to cover.

media information center (MIC) A place where a large number of reporters can gather to collect information on a crisis. It should be close to, but separate from, the emergency operations center established for the crisis.

media kit A package of documents and other items offering extensive coverage of a news story to the news media. A media kit contains at least one news release as well as other materials, such as backgrounders, fact sheets, photo opportunity sheets, and product samples.

media relations The maintenance of mutually beneficial relations between an organization and the journalists and other media people who report on its activities.

message The content of a communication that a sender attempts to deliver to a targeted receiver.

microediting A stage in the writing process in which the writer examines each sentence of a document for factual accuracy as well as correct grammar, spelling, punctuation, and style.

mission statement A concise written account of why an organization exists; an explanation of the purpose of an organization's many actions.

modifiers Words or phrases that develop the meaning of another word, such as an adjective that modifies a noun or an adverb that modifies a verb.

monitoring In the context of issues management, the sustained scrutiny and evaluation of an issue that could affect an organization.

Monroe's Motivated Sequence Created in the mid-1920s by Purdue University Professor Alan H. Monroe, a five-step process (attention, need, satisfaction, visualization, and action) that organizes persuasive messages.

multivariate analysis Analysis of research data that examines three or more variables.

mutual fund managers Individuals responsible for purchasing stocks and other securities on behalf of a mutual fund's investors; the investors participate by purchasing shares in the fund.

news conference A structured meeting between an organization's representative(s) and the news media for the purpose of providing information for news stories.

news release A client-related news story that a public relations practitioner writes and distributes to the news media.

The New York Times v. Sullivan Landmark 1964 U.S. Supreme Court ruling that established a higher burden of proof in libel cases brought by public officials.

noise In the context of the communication model, distractions that envelop communication and often inhibit it. Noise can be both physical and intangible. It is sometimes referred to as static.

nonprobability sampling The process of selecting a research sample without regard to whether everyone in the public has an equal chance of being selected.

nontraditional publics Groups that are united by a common interest, value, or values in a particular situation but that are unfamiliar to an organization, but with which the organization now has a relationship.

n-step theory A theory of mass communications suggesting that the mass media influence opinion leaders, who change from issue to issue, and that these opinion leaders, in turn, wield influence over the public.

objectives Specific milestones that measure progress toward achievement of a goal. Written objectives begin with an infinitive, are measurable, and state a specific deadline.

Office of War Information (OWI) An agency created by President Franklin Roosevelt to disseminate government information during World War II. Headed by former journalist Elmer Davis, it was a training ground for future public relations practitioners. It evolved after the war into the United States Information Agency.

open-ended questions Questionnaire items for which the number of possible answers is undefined and unrestricted.

opinion An expressed behavior inclination.

opinion leaders Individuals to whom members of a public turn for advice.

outcomes The actions of a targeted public generated as a result of a tactic or program.

outputs Measures of activity associated with implementation of a particular tactic or program.

passive voice A grammatical term designating that, within a sentence, the subject does not do the action denoted by the verb (see *active voice*). Instead, the subject is affected by the action denoted by the verb, as in *She was hired*. In most grammatical situations, writers prefer active voice to passive voice.

pathos An Aristotelian term denoting persuasive appeal to the emotions.

personal attack rule An FCC requirement that broadcast stations provide free air time to persons subjected to a character attack during a presentation on a public issue.

personal digital assistant (PDA) A handheld wireless communication device that incorporates the functions of a conventional notebook into a small computer.

persuasion In a public relations context, an attempt to influence a person's actions through an appeal to his or her self-interest.

photo opportunity sheet A document that promotes the visual interest of an upcoming event. Photo opportunity sheets are sent to photojournalists and television stations. When appropriate, photo opportunity sheets are included in media kits.

pitch letter A letter sent by a public relations practitioner to a journalist, often on an exclusive basis, describing a newsworthy human-interest story whose publication would generate helpful publicity for an organization.

planning The second step in the four-step public relations process. Because the process is dynamic, however, planning can actually occur at any time.

point of no return The second stage of a crisis. Once this moment is reached, a crisis becomes unavoidable.

political action committees (PACs) Organizations representing particular special interests that collect money and contribute it to political candidates.

political speech Expression associated with the normal conduct of a democratic society. The U.S. Supreme Court historically has been reluctant to regulate it.

Potter Box A tool designed by Harvard Professor Ralph Potter for ethical decision making. Using the Potter Box involves defining an ethical issue and then identifying competing values, principles, and loyalties.

press agentry/publicity model A form of public relations that focuses on getting favorable coverage from the media. In this model, accuracy and truth are not seen as essential.

press secretary The individual given the responsibility to speak for and handle media inquiries on behalf of a political or government official.

primary public Any group that is united by a common interest, value, or values in a particular situation and that can directly affect an organization's pursuit of its goals.

primary research Original research not derived from the results of any earlier researcher's efforts.

privacy A person's right to be left alone and be free from unwarranted publicity.

privilege Exemption of certain communications from court-ordered disclosure. For example, communication between a client and his or her attorney is considered privileged. However, communication between that same client and a public relations practitioner may not be privileged, and the practitioner could be required to testify.

probability sampling The process of selecting a research sample that is representative of the population or public from which it is selected.

problem A commonplace occurrence of limited scope. People often confuse problems with crises.

problem–opportunity research The gathering of information to answer two critical questions at the outset of any public relations effort: What is at issue, and what stake, if any, does our organization have in this issue?

Progressive Era   Running from the early 1890s until the start of World War I, a period in which a series of political and social reforms, primarily in the United States, occurred in reaction to the growth of business and industry during the Industrial Revolution.

propaganda   A systematic effort to disseminate information, some of which may be inaccurate or incomplete, in an attempt to influence public opinion. A propagandist advocates a particular idea or perspective to the exclusion of all others.

proposal   A formal document that details specific, goal-oriented public relations tactics recommended for a client.

pseudoevent   A special event, often of questionable news value, created for the purpose of attracting the attention of the news media.

psychographic information   Data on attitudinal characteristics of a person or group, such as political philosophy and religious beliefs.

public   In a public relations context, any group of people who share a common interest, value, or values in a particular situation.

public affairs officer   The person responsible for maintaining mutually beneficial relations between a government agency or official and important publics. The term *public affairs* is also used by some nongovernment organizations as a synonym for government relations or community relations.

publication   A burden of proof in libel. In that context, publication is the communication of a defamatory statement to a third party.

publication of private facts   A tort in libel law. In that context, publication of private facts involves the public disclosure of personal information that is embarrassing and potentially offensive.

public figures   For the purposes of libel law, individuals who have widespread notoriety or who inject themselves into a public controversy for the purpose of influencing its outcome.

public information model   A form of public relations that focuses on the dissemination of objective and accurate information.

public information officer   The individual given the responsibility to speak for and handle media inquiries on behalf of a government agency.

Publicity Bureau   The first public relations agency, founded by George V. S. Michaelis and two partners in Boston in 1900.

public official   For the purposes of libel law, any individual elected to public office and/or with substantial public decision-making or policy-making authority.

public opinion   The average expressed behavioral inclination.

public relations   The management of relationships between an organization and the publics that can affect its success. The term to describe the emerging profession was first used in 1923 by Edward L. Bernays in *Crystallizing Public Opinion*.

public relations agency   A company that provides public relations services for other organizations on a per-job basis, by contract, or on retainer.

public relations managers   Practitioners whose job responsibilities are more strategic than tactical in nature. These practioners solve problems, advise others, make policy decisions, and take responsibility for the outcome of a public relations program.

Public Relations Society of America (PRSA)   The world's largest public relations professional association, with approximately 20,000 members. Founded in 1947, it is headquartered in New York.

Public Relations Student Society of America (PRSSA)   An organization for public relations students. It is affiliated with the Public Relations Society of America.

public relations technicians   Practitioners whose job responsibilities are more tactical than strategic in nature. Their primary role is to prepare communications that help execute the public relations policies of others.

public service announcements (PSAs)   Broadcast announcements made on behalf of nonprofit organizations or social causes. Because of legal requirements to serve the public interest, the broadcast media do not charge for PSAs, as they do for commercial announcements. This term is also used to describe free advertising space granted by print media; however, the print media are under no legal requirement to provide the space.

push technology   Computer software that permits users to customize information received automatically from the Internet.

rating scale questions   Questionnaire items designed to measure the range, degree, or intensity of respondents' attitudes on the topic being studied.

receiver   The person or persons for whom a message is intended.

recovery   The fourth and final step in effective crisis communications. In this step practitioners evaluate the quality of the organization's response to a crisis and take appropriate actions as a result of the lessons learned.

Regulation FD   A regulation issued by the U.S. Securities and Exchange Commission in 2000 designed to tighten corporate disclosure requirements.

relationship management   The use of public relations strategies and tactics to foster and enhance the shared interests and values of an organization and the publics important to its success.

relationship marketing   Placing relationships with individual consumers above profits, in the belief that good relationships lead to increased profits.

representative sample   Population sample selected by procedures that ensure that all members of the population or public being studied have an equal chance of being chosen for the sample. A representative sample must also be sufficiently large to allow researchers to draw conclusions about the population as a whole.

research   The first step of the public relations process. However, because the public relations process is dynamic, research can occur at any time.

research strategy   A plan that defines what the researcher wants to know and how he or she will gather that information.

resource dependency theory   The premise that organizations form relationships with publics to acquire the resources they need to fulfill their values.

response   The third step in effective crisis communications. In this step practitioners utilize their crisis communications plan.

return on investment (ROI)   A business concept for getting more out of something than the original cost.

rhetoric   The use of communication for the purpose of persuasion. In some of its applications, the practice of public relations is a rhetorical activity.

risk assessment   The first step in effective crisis communications. In this step practitioners identify potential hazards their organization may face.

salary equity   Equal pay for equal work.

sample   In a research context, the segment of a population or public being studied to enable researchers to draw conclusions about the public as a whole.

sampling frame   The actual list from which a research sample, or some stage of the sample, is drawn.

Sarbanes-Oxley Act   Legislation passed by Congress in 2002 that holds corporate officials personally accountable for the truthfulness of corporate financial statements.

satellite media tour (SMT)   A series of interviews with reporters in different cities, conducted by means of satellite technology; the newsmaker stays in one location, eliminating expensive and time-consuming travel.

satisfaction   When used in the context of Monroe's Motivated Sequence, the process of presenting an audience with a solution to a problem that has already been identified. When used in the context of measuring the strength of relationships, a reference to the degree to which the benefits of the relationship outweigh its costs. When used in the context of Mick Jagger, something of which he "can't get no."

scanning   In the context of issues management, the process of identifying future issues that could affect an organization.

secondary publics   Groups that are united by a common interest, value, or values in a particular situation and that have a relationship with a public relations practitioner's organization, but which have little power to affect that organization's pursuit of its goals.

secondary research   Research utilizing information generated by someone else, sometimes for purposes entirely different from your own; also known as *library research*.

Securities and Exchange Commission (SEC)   A federal agency that administers federal securities laws to ensure that the nation's securities markets are fair and honest.

Seedbed Years   A term coined by public relations historian Scott Cutlip that refers to the period during the late 19th and early 20th centuries in which the modern practice of public relations emerged.

service marks   A legal designation indicated by the symbol ^{SM} to protect names, designs, slogans, and symbols associated with a particular service.

sexual harassment   Unwelcome sexual advances. Workplace sexual harassment is harassment that may affect an individual's employment, unreasonably interfere with an individual's work performance, or create an intimidating, hostile, or offensive work environment.

simple random sampling   A basic and often impractical form of probability sampling that involves assigning a number to every person within the sampling frame, followed by random selection of numbers.

situation analysis   In a written public relations proposal, a statement that accurately and objectively describes an opportunity or threat for which public relations actions are recommended.

soft money   Money donated to national political parties for general expenses. Legislation passed in 2002 restricted such donations but allowed contributions to local political parties and national political conventions.

source   The originator of a message.

spamming   The mass distribution of an advertising-oriented e-mail message.

spim   The unwelcome commercial use of instant messaging.

spin   A popular term used to describe the framing of a message in what the source considers the most desirable context.

spin doctor   A popular term coined by *New York Times* editorial writer Jack Rosenthal in 1984 to describe the activities of political public relations practitioners.

special event   A planned happening that serves as a public relations tactic.

stakeholder   A public that has an interest in an organization or in an issue potentially involving that organization.

stakeholder research   Research that focuses on identifying and describing specific publics important to the success of an organization.

standing plan   A plan that remains in effect over an extended period of time. Its tactics are routinely reenacted to sustain fulfillment of the plan's goal(s) and objectives.

statement of purpose   In a written public relations proposal, a declaration that the proposal presents a plan to address a given situation.

stereotyping   The assumption that all members of a particular group or culture are the same and act in the same manner.

strategies   General descriptions of how practitioners propose to achieve a plan's objectives.

survey research   Formal research conducted through the use of carefully selected population samples and specifically worded questionnaires.

SWOT analysis   An assessment of the strengths, weaknesses, opportunities, and threats that an organization has or could confront.

systematic sampling   A probability sampling technique that uses a standardized selection process to create a sample that is both representative and easy to develop. At its most basic level, systematic sampling involves the selection of every Kth member of a sampling frame.

tactics   Specific recommended actions designed to help an organization achieve the objectives stated in a public relations plan.

text messaging   The process of sending a written message from one cell phone to another.

things return to normal   The fourth and final stage of a crisis. During this stage the immediate threat created by the crisis is over, but its lingering effects are still felt. Although things may have returned to "normal," normality now may be much different from what it was before the crisis.

third-party endorsement Verification of a story's newsworthiness that the news media provide when they publish or broadcast the story. Appearance in an uncontrolled news medium lends credibility to a story, because the media are neither the sender nor the receiver but an independent third party.

trade magazines Magazines for members of particular trades or professions, such as carpenters or lawyers.

trademarks A legal designation indicated by the symbol ® that protects names, designs, slogans, and symbols associated with specific products.

traditional publics Groups that are united by a common interest, value, or values in a particular situation and with which an organization has an ongoing, long-term relationship.

transition A device that clarifies the introduction of a new topic within a document. One traditional transition device is a sentence that shows the relationship of the previous topic to the new topic. Such a sentence follows the previous topic and precedes the new topic.

transparency A quality achieved when organizations and individuals conduct business openly and honestly without hidden agendas.

trust The willingness of one party in a relationship to open itself to the other.

two-step theory A theory of mass communication suggesting that the mass media influence society's opinion leaders, who, in turn, influence society.

two-way asymmetrical model A form of public relations in which research is used in an effort to persuade important publics to adopt a particular point of view.

two-way symmetrical model A form of public relations that focuses on two-way communication as a means of conflict resolution and for the promotion of mutual understanding between an organization and its important publics.

uncontrolled media Communication channels, such as newspaper stories, in which a public relations practitioner cannot control the message, its timing, or its frequency.

units of analysis What or whom a researcher is studying in order to create a summary description of all such units.

univariate analysis Analysis of research data that examines just one variable.

Universal Accreditation Program The availability of PRSA accreditation to members of eight additional public relations organizations; established in 1998.

uses and gratifications theory The belief that people have the power to pick and choose the mass media channels that, in turn, influence their actions.

utilitarianism A philosophy developed by Jeremy Bentham and John Stuart Mill that holds that all actions should be directed at producing the greatest good for the greatest number of people.

values The fundamental beliefs and standards that drive behavior and decision making. They are also the filters through which we see the world and the world sees us.

values-driven public relations The values-driven management of relationships between an organization and the publics that can affect its success.

values statement A written declaration of the principles that an organization will strive to follow in all its actions.

variables The logical grouping of qualities that describe a particular attribute. Variables must be exhaustive (incorporating all possible qualities) and mutually exclusive.

veil of ignorance A term and concept created by philosopher John Rawls. The veil of ignorance strategy asks decision makers to examine a situation objectively from all points of view, especially from those of the affected publics.

velvet ghetto Situation that exists when women predominate in lower-paying technical or middle-management jobs, with men dominating upper-level managerial positions.

video news releases (VNRs)   Videotaped news stories that an organization produces and distributes to the news media. VNRs often include b-roll footage.

viral marketing   Public relations or marketing information that is spread from person to person via e-mail.

virtual organizations   Temporary organizations formed by smaller units or individuals to complete a specific job.

virtual public relations   A term used to describe the work of many small public relations consultancies; as a result of advances in communications technology, these consultancies can have the look, feel, and service capabilities of much larger public relations agencies.

visual aids   Displays presented to an audience to enhance the meaning of a speaker's words. Visual aids can include computer projections, slides, flip charts, handouts, and overhead-projector transparencies.

vox populi   Latin for "voice of the people." The phrase refers to the importance of public opinion.

warning stage   The first stage of a crisis. If warning signs are recognized and appropriate action is taken quickly, the negative effects of a crisis can be averted or minimized.

webcast   Audiovisual telecasts, usually live, delivered through a web site.

web site   A series of computer files maintained by an organization or individual that can be accessed via the Internet. Web sites are created to project an organization's image and to share information with various publics. They are also useful for marketing goods, services, or ideas and for generating feedback.

work for hire   Anything prepared by someone within the scope of employment and, therefore, considered the property of the employer.

World Wide Web   A graphics-oriented computer network developed in 1991 that made the Internet more accessible and attractive and helped spur its rapid development.

writing process   An organized system for producing effective public relations documents. The writing process begins with the credibility of the writer and moves through 10 separate steps: credibility, research, organization, writing, revision, macroediting, microediting, approval, distribution, and evaluation.

Index

Text Credits

p. 13, courtesy of J.C. Penney Company; pp. 22–24, courtesy of Judith T. Phair; p. 38, reprinted with permission from the Public Relations Society of America (www. prsa.org); pp. 49–51, courtesy of John Echeveste; pp. 81–83, courtesy of Edward M. Block; p. 111, courtesy of PepsiCo, Inc., Worldwide Code of Conduct; pp. 125–127, courtesy of David A. Narsavage; p. 157, courtesy of the Provincial Emergency Program; pp. 159–161, courtesy of René Pelletier; p. 185, courtesy of Goodwill Industries; pp. 190–193, courtesy of Cone, Inc.; p. 208, courtesy of the Institute for Public Relations; pp. 228–230, courtesy of Leslie Gaines-Ross; pp. 259–261, courtesy of Timothy S. Brown; p. 275, courtesy of Johnson & Johnson; pp. 300–301, courtesy of Shirley Barr; p. 334, courtesy of Kellogg Company; pp. 341–342, courtesy of Regina Lynch-Hudson; p. 359, courtesy of INK, Inc.; pp. 376–378, courtesy of Craig Settles; pp. 418–419, courtesy of Wayne Shelor; p. 434, Copyright © The J.M. Smucker Company; pp. 449–450, courtesy of Vin Cipolla; p. 456, courtesy of Special Olympics, Inc. "Special Olympics" is a trademark and tradename owned by Special Olympics, Inc.; pp. 478–479, courtesy of Bill Imada; pp. 518–519, courtesy of James F. Haggerty, photo by Matt Flynn; p. 543, courtesy of the League of Women Voters of the United States; pp. 552–553, courtesy of Sarah Yeaney; pp. 564–570, reprinted with permission from the Public Relations Society of America (www. prsa.org).

CASE STUDIES PORTFOLIO

Julius Caesar wrote, "Experience is the teacher of all things" in *De Bello Civili* more than 2,000 years ago. And it is true that people often learn best by doing. However, that's not always practical, especially for young public relations practitioners at the beginning of their careers. This is why case studies, detailed examinations of the experiences of others, are useful. Studying others' experiences brings to mind George Santayana's famous quotation, "Those who do not learn from history are doomed to repeat it." The history of public relations is filled with valuable lessons of spectacular successes and stunning failures.

You will find 24 such stories in this special appendix to *Public Relations: A Values-Driven Approach*. In keeping with the philosophy guiding the 32 case studies within the chapters, each case in this portfolio examines the application of public relations strategies, tactics, and values. These are examples in which the application—or misapplication—of public relations affected the outcome of real-world challenges. They encompass many aspects of public relations, including media relations, event planning, litigation public relations, cross-cultural communication, government public relations, and crisis communications. Each case provides valuable insight into the challenges today's practitioners face.

Some of these cases cover recent events, such as Hurricane Katrina and the political activism of Bono, the Irish rock star. Others are updated versions of cases that appeared in earlier editions of this book, including "Citizens for a Free Kuwait" and "Using Public Relations to Ban Landmines." All of them tell a story in which public relations—or a lack of public relations—made a difference.

As you read these case studies, please apply the theories and concepts you have learned in this book. Did the practitioner or organization follow the four steps of the public relations process? Were research and planning adequate? Were communications properly targeted? What values, if any, were followed? What would *you* have done differently to gain a more favorable outcome?

All of this brings us back to one more famous quotation, from author Pearl S. Buck: "One faces the future with one's past." That's the real beauty of case studies: from one you can shape the other.

Case Studies Portfolio

The Lessons of Katrina

As a child, you may have heard the fable of the Dutch boy who averted a flood and saved his community by sticking his finger in a leaky dike. But as we learned in the wake of Hurricane Katrina, finger-pointing alone is not enough.

According to the National Hurricane Center (NHC), "Katrina was one of the most devastating natural disasters in United States history."[1] The storm packed 125-mile-per-hour winds when it made landfall south of New Orleans on August 29, 2005. Four months after the catastrophe, the death toll stood at more than 1,300 with hundreds still missing. The NHC also estimated property damage at $75 billion, making Katrina the most costly natural disaster in U.S. history.[2]

Although the disaster area was equal in size to the United Kingdom, much of the world's attention focused on New Orleans. At first, it looked as if Crescent City had weathered the storm. However, the levee system protecting New Orleans—a Gulf Coast city that lies mainly below sea level—failed. Nearly 80 percent of the city flooded under as much as 20 feet of water. An estimated 1.5 million people were displaced.[3]

Compounding this misery was an inadequate response and poor crisis communications on the local, state, and federal government levels. Risk assessment and preparing for the worst are the essence of crisis planning. Communicating those plans to key stakeholders—most notably the victims—is critical. However, a week would pass before many received relief. There were dead bodies abandoned on city streets. This human drama played out on live television to a worldwide audience. And the same question was asked time and time again: How could this happen in America?

Katrina was much more than a public relations failure. It was a system failure. "This country's emergency operations, awesome in their potential, are also frighteningly interdependent," *Time* reported in a post-storm analysis. "At every level of government, there was uncertainty about who was in charge at crucial moments."[4]

One of Katrina's lessons was to learn from the past. For example, there was a need for reliable interagency radio communications. Following the terrorist attack on the World Trade Center four years earlier, lives were lost and rescue efforts hampered because police, fire, and ambulance workers were unable to talk with one another. *The 9/11 Commission Report* called for "improved connectivity in public safety communications."[5] This was not done. The resulting confusion delayed getting help to Katrina's victims.

It was also painfully obvious that there had been inadequate emergency planning. New

Orleans officials had used the Louisiana Superdome as a shelter during Hurricane Georges in 1998. At that time, they were criticized for not making adequate preparations. Seven years later, conditions at the stadium were no better. The city had failed to stockpile food, fuel, and other supplies necessary to do the job.[6]

Perhaps most damning was a lack of leadership. As *Time* noted in its analysis, "Leaders were afraid to actually lead, reluctant to cost businesses money, break jurisdictional rules or spawn lawsuits. They were afraid, in other words, of ending up in an article just like this one."[7]

Regarding failed leadership, there's plenty of blame to spread around. New Orleans Mayor Ray Nagin was slow to order an evacuation but quick to blame others. E-mails from the office of Louisiana Governor Kathleen Blanco painted the picture of an administration that appeared to be more concerned with boosting its image than providing disaster relief. President George W. Bush appeared to be out of touch when he praised FEMA Director Michael Brown for doing "a heck of a job" in responding to Katrina despite mounting evidence to the contrary.

"There was no one who was able to balance compassion for the victims with a sense of hope, direction and confidence," said Ed Nicholson, director of media and community relations for Tyson Foods.[8]

Katrina became a perceptual crisis fed, in part, by competitive, around-the-clock news coverage that sometimes distorted reality. The situation at the New Orleans Convention Center is a prime example. Public safety officials were unaware of thousands of refugees stranded there without adequate food and water—until they finally saw it live on television. However, it since has been documented that TV reports of widespread shootings and assaults at the convention center were exaggerated.

Even with the best planning and response, Hurricane Katrina would have been a tragic event. However, the pain was unnecessarily compounded by the government's inability to adequately communicate with the people it is supposed to serve. Joe Trahan, a noted New Orleans media trainer and educator, put it best when he observed, "If you can't or don't communicate, the frustration and anger will get out of control."[9]

DISCUSSION QUESTIONS

1. What were some of the specific failures of government officials in their response to Hurricane Katrina?
2. The case study criticizes some officials for "pointing fingers" at one another. However, isn't assigning blame part of the evaluation process?

3. Using the crisis communications model in Chapter 12, can you identify the four stages of the New Orleans crisis?
4. Do you agree that there was a failure of leadership when it came to the government's response to Hurricane Katrina? Why or why not?

NOTES

1. Richard D. Knabb, Jamie R. Rhome, and Daniel P. Brown, *Tropical Cyclone Report— Hurricane Katrina, 23–30 August 2005,* National Hurricane Center, 20 December 2005, 1.
2. Knabb, Rhome, and Brown, 11–12.

3. Knabb, Rhome, and Brown, 9.

4. James Carney, "Four Places Where the System Broke Down," *Time,* 19 September 2005, 34–41.

5. *The 9/11 Commission Report—Final Report of the National Commission on Terrorist Attacks on the United States,* Executive Summary, 2004, 20.

6. Knabb, Rhome, and Brown, 37.

7. Carney, 36.

8. Ed Cafasso, "Going Back to Basics: Hurricane Katrina Illustrates the Importance of Aligning Action and Communications," *Public Relations Tactics,* October 2005, online reprint, www.prsa.org.

9. Cafasso.

Parrott Talks; Rand McNally Listens

Geography students must have heaved a sigh of relief when the 20th century gave way to the new millennium. The 1990s had been a dizzying decade for mapmakers: the disintegration of the Soviet Union; the reunification of Germany; land transfers in the Middle East; the status of Parrott, Virginia; China's reacquisition of Hong Kong; border disputes in South America . . .

Wait a minute. Parrott, Virginia?

That's right. Thanks to a 10-year-old boy and a values-driven company that realized how one small public can connect with others, Parrott—population 800—is now on the map.

Chris Muncy, a fourth-grader from Mishawaka, Indiana, was a mapmaker's dream. By kindergarten, he knew all his state capitals, and every summer, before visiting his grandparents in Parrott, he'd get out his family's *Rand McNally Road Atlas* to trace each bend in the road of the upcoming journey.

But Chris had a problem: Parrott wasn't on the map.

"For years people groused about not being in the atlas," confessed one resident of Parrott. "You kind of assume they didn't want you to be on their map. And what could we do?"[1]

Chris knew what to do: He sent a letter to Rand McNally, publisher of the best-selling *Rand McNally Road Atlas.* "I'm going to get a road atlas every year for the rest of my life," he wrote. "I want you to put in the town

where my grandpa, great-grandma, grandma and uncle live. It's called Parrott, Virginia."[2]

Founded in 1856 and based in Skokie, Illinois, Rand McNally isn't exactly a small company. It has offices throughout the United States and Canada, and it produces thousands of print and electronic maps for those countries. In other words, a letter from a 10-year-old boy about his grandparents' hometown could easily be ignored. But Rand McNally's response was consistent with its clearly stated values:

> Our products bring the world to its people. They lend insight and understanding to global geopolitical events, unlock the power of a child's imagination, help travelers manage journeys more efficiently, deliver new vistas that lead to incisive learning, and drive the commerce of nations.[3]

Instead of replying with a regretful form letter, Rand McNally studied Parrott, Virginia. Though the town was small, it did qualify for inclusion in the *Road Atlas.* In fact, there was just enough room between the towns of McCoy and Belspring to include a small black dot labeled "Parrott." And so Rand McNally helped "unlock the power of a child's imagination" and put Parrott on the map.

But the story doesn't stop there. In honoring its values and satisfying the desires of one tiny public, Rand McNally attracted the attention of a few larger publics: the readers and viewers of *ABC World News Tonight, People* magazine, United Press International, and newspapers from Boston to San Diego. (Yes, Rand McNally did issue a news release announcing the story of how Parrott came to be on the map.)

The residents of Parrott held the first parade in the town's two-century history, and the grand marshal, waving proudly from a fire engine, was Chris Muncy. An official of Rand McNally attended and presented Chris with a new *Road Atlas*. And in that atlas, of course, was a new dot labeled Parrott. There to record it all were journalists from major news media throughout the United States.

The story of Chris Muncy, Parrott, and Rand McNally received two full minutes of coverage on *ABC World News Tonight*. It received a spread, with photos, in *People* magazine. United Press International put the story on its newswire, and news media throughout the nation informed their audiences about a boy, a town, and a company that listens and responds. That's a lot of publicity for satisfying the needs of one seemingly uninfluential public.

At the end of the parade in Parrott, Chris surveyed his success and pronounced it "Pretty neat!"[4]

The public relations staff at Rand McNally probably agreed.

DISCUSSION QUESTIONS

1. Was Chris Muncy a public? Can a public have only one member?
2. Should Rand McNally have issued a news release? Doesn't that seem like bragging?
3. Why was Chris Muncy's story so appealing to national news media?
4. How do you suppose Rand McNally's public relations team learned about Chris' letter?
5. Rand McNally is a privately held company; it doesn't have stockholders. Why, then, does it value positive national publicity?

NOTES

1. "Thanks to Chris Muncy, the Tiny Town of Parrott, Va., Now Rates a Spot on the Map," *People*, 15 October 1990, online, LexisNexis.
2. "Thanks to Chris Muncy."
3. Rand McNally, online, www.randmcnally.com.
4. Janet Sutter, "Kid Gets Credit for Geographic Breakthrough," *San Diego Union-Tribune*, 3 October 1990, online, LexisNexis.

The Dog That Didn't Bark: Abercrombie & Fitch and MADD

In one of Sherlock Holmes' most famous cases, "Silver Blaze," Holmes solves a mystery by noting what *didn't* happen: A dog that should have barked did not. The story doesn't mention public relations, but it contains a valuable lesson for today's practitioners: They should be ready to bark, figuratively speaking, at bad guys and bad ideas.

Like the dog in "Silver Blaze," the public relations team that serves Abercrombie &

Fitch—a popular retailer of clothing for the college-age market—didn't bark when it should have. In summer 1998, A&F published almost 1 million copies of its 200-plus-page back-to-school catalog. Amid the apparel and well-toned models was a section titled "Drinking 101." Containing recipes for alcoholic beverages with names such as Woo-Woo and Brain Hemorrhage, the two-page spread urged, "Rather than the standard beer binge, indulge in some creative drinking this semester."

A&F's hangover began July 16 when the national office of Mothers Against Drunk Driving retaliated with a furious news release. "This catalog is among the most blatantly irresponsible pieces of marketing we have ever seen," declared Karolyn Nunnallee, MADD's president at the time. Noting that most college undergraduates are below the legal drinking age, Nunnallee added, "This catalog shows not only a total disrespect for the law, but a complete disregard for the well-being of [A&F's] customers." The MADD news release capped that quotation with statistics regarding the number of drinking-and-driving deaths for youths under age 21.[1]

Let's pause here to ask an important question. The notorious catalog was a *marketing* action, not a public relations tactic. Why, then, might some consider it a failure of public relations?

As noted in Chapter 8 and elsewhere in this book, the well-informed voice of the public relations team should be heard as an organization considers future courses of action. Ideally, no other area of the organization better understands the publics that influence and are influenced by the organization's actions—including its marketing actions. As A&F's 1998 back-to-school catalog demonstrates, a marketing blunder can have severe consequences for public relations. It can damage relationships with activist groups, the news media, customers, and other publics whose actions help spell success or failure for the organization.

The day after MADD's news release, NBC's *Today* show featured a live interview with Nunnallee, MADD's angry and articulate president. Host Matt Lauer read a lengthy statement from A&F that said, in part, "We condemn irresponsible and illegal drinking." However, Lauer closed the segment by saying, "We want to mention one more time that the folks at Abercrombie and Fitch denied our request for an interview on the subject."[2]

NBC Nightly News also covered the story, as did the Associated Press and Reuters, an international news service.[3] In an AP story, Nunnallee continued MADD'S attack: "This catalog is an abomination."[4] She asked A&F to cease distribution of the catalog, send letters of apology to catalog recipients, and devote at least one page in the next four catalogs to the problems of underage drinking.

A&F stumbled a bit as it began to implement public relations tactics to minimize the damage. In its first response to MADD's fury, an A&F representative said, "The catalog is out the door."[5]

However, A&F quickly issued its statement to NBC's *Today* show, and within six days of the MADD news release, A&F had added a page to its online version of the catalog. Under the heading "Be Smart," a statement read, "We don't want to lose anybody to thoughtlessness and stupidity. For some, part of college life includes partying and drinking—be smart, and be responsible."[6]

Within nine days of MADD's news release, the Associated Press reported, A&F had agreed to attach stickers with the Be Smart message to catalogs in its stores and to send postcards bearing the same message to catalog subscribers.

"In retrospect, the company feels that it should have initially provided a balance in that story," said a company representative.[7]

In other words, the dog should have barked before it was too late.

DISCUSSION QUESTIONS

1. Should Abercrombie & Fitch have sent a representative to appear on NBC's *Today* show with the MADD president? Why or why not?
2. Suppose that, in a similar situation, a marketing department says, "We know our customers, and this won't offend them. Let's distribute the catalog." What should be the response of the public relations department?
3. What other groups besides MADD might have been offended by the "Drinking 101"
spread? Can you name any publics that would approve of the spread?
4. Do you think A&F's public relations tactics did enough to defuse the situation? If not, what else would you have recommended?
5. Could the controversial A&F catalog actually have been a *good* public relations tactic? After all, it brought a great deal of media attention to the retailer and its catalog.

NOTES

1. "MADD Calls on Retailer to Pull Catalog Encouraging Underage Drinking," Mothers Against Drunk Driving news release, 16 July 1998, online, www.madd.org.
2. NBC *Today* show, 17 July 1998, online, LexisNexis.
3. *NBC Nightly News,* 16 July 1998, online, LexisNexis. Mark Williams, "Catalog Controversy," *Marketing News,* 14 September 1998, online, LexisNexis. Reuters, 17 July 1998, online, LexisNexis.

4. "Riding This Trend, Retailer Draws Fury," *Chicago Tribune,* 25 July 1998, online, LexisNexis.
5. "Short Cuts," *Newsday,* 18 July 1998, online, LexisNexis.
6. Abercrombie & Fitch web site, www.abercrombie.com. Date confirmed by A&F Web Team e-mail to authors, 22 July 1998.
7. "Riding This Trend, Retailer Draws Fury."

Canada's Family Channel Battles Bullies

A recent worldwide survey asked 26,000 adults to name the friendliest nation on Earth. The top answer? Think hockey, maple leaves, and maybe even actors Jim Carrey and Mike Myers. Think Canada.[1]

Even the world's friendliest nation, however, can contain an oddly discordant note: Think bullies. Research shows that 20 percent of Canadian youths ages 4 to 19 have been bullied continually for two or more years.[2]

"Bullying is about behavior," says middle-school teacher Bill Belsey, president of Bullying.org Canada. "And we can change behavior."[3]

Although changing a public's behavior may not be as easy as Belsey thinks (see Chapter 8), he has good reason for optimism. His partner in the crusade to end bullying is a media giant: Canada's Family Channel, a subsidiary of Astral Media that reaches more than 5 million homes in that nation.

Why would a for-profit media outlet join a grassroots organization to combat a problem that could hardly affect its bottom line?

In a word, values.

"If it's important to kids, it's important to us," says Joe Tedesco, vice president and general manager of the Family Channel. "The majority of our viewers are Canadian kids, and bullying is an issue that faces every kid at one time or another."[4]

In "The Way We Do Business: Our Guide to Ethical Business Conduct," Astral Media specifies its commitment to corporate social responsibility:

> We are committed to being a responsible corporate citizen of the communities in which we reside. We will strive to improve the well-being of our communities through the encouragement of employee participation in civic affairs and through corporate philanthropy.[5]

In 2005, additional research by the Family Channel and the Canadian Initiative for the Prevention of Bullying identified a strategy that might reduce bullying:

- When an observer objects, bullying stops within 10 seconds in 57 percent of incidents.
- In 85 percent of bullying situations, observers are present.
- When observers are present in a bullying situation, they object only 25 percent of the time.[6]

"Family Channel and Bullying.org are trying to change 'bystander' behavior by showing kids examples of how they can act differently and diffuse bullying situations," says Belsey. "We are not asking kids to get involved in a physical way but rather to reach out to victims and show bullies that their actions will not be tolerated."[7]

At the center of the intervention strategy is a pledge that the Family Channel and Bullying.org encourage young Canadians to take:

> This is for me, my friends today, and my friends tomorrow. I think being mean stinks. I won't watch someone get picked on, because I am a do-something person—not a do-nothing person. I care. I can help change things. I can be a leader. In my world, there are no bullies allowed. Bullying is bad. Bullying bites. Bullying bothers me. I know sticking up for someone is

the right thing to do. My name is _____. And I won't stand by. I will stand up.[8]

To promote the pledge and encourage intervention in bullying situations, the Family Channel has helped implement the following public relations tactics:

- a National Bullying Awareness Week, launched in 2003
- a Bullying.org web site where youths can take the pledge and share advice
- television public service announcements showing youths intervening in bullying situations and taking the pledge
- a video news release showing the launch of Bullying Awareness Week at an elementary school in Ontario
- media interviews with young stars of Family Channel shows such as *Radio Free Roscoe*
- news releases announcing National Bullying Awareness Week

In the first National Bullying Awareness Week, 55,000 Canadian youths took the pledge. "The message of the pledge," says Belsey, "is to encourage kids to be leaders and not followers and set an example that bullying is not cool."[9]

In 2005, the Canadian Public Relations Society honored the Family Channel and its anti-bullying campaign with the Award of Excellence for Community Relations.

"As long as they're bringing it to the forefront for people to hear and learn about . . . ," says Ali Mukaddam, a star of *Radio Free Roscoe*, "then it's just a good thing."

DISCUSSION QUESTIONS

1. Family Channel and Bullying.org want to change a public's behavior. What does public relations research say about their chances of success?

2. In addition to the tactics used by the Family Channel to promote the pledge and encourage intervention in bullying situations, what other tactics would you recommend?

3. If you were public relations director of the Family Channel, how would you answer possible stockholder concerns about using corporate resources for charitable activities that don't directly boost the bottom line?

4. Do you believe that ethical companies benefit financially? Do you prefer to do business with ethical companies?

NOTES

1. "It's Official—Australia Is All about the Food, Footy, and Fame," Global Marketing Insight news release, 22 February 2006, online, LexisNexis.

2. "Survey Finds That Children Are Often Bullied for an Extended Period of Time," Family Channel news release, 14 November 2005, online, LexisNexis.

3. Todd Saelhof, "Bully Effort Scares Up Help," Calgary Sun, 16 November 2004, online, LexisNexis.

4. "Family Channel Takes a Stand against Bullying," Family Channel news release, 8 November 2004, online, LexisNexis.

5. "The Way We Do Business: Our Guide to Ethical Business Conduct," Astral Media web site, www.astralmedia.com.

6. "Survey Finds That Children Are Often Bullied for an Extended Period of Time."

7. "Family Channel Takes a Stand against Bullying."

8. Stephanie McGrath, "Fighting Words," Toronto Sun, 21 November 2004, online, LexisNexis.

9. "Family Channel Takes a Stand against Bullying."

Sowing Seeds of Discontent

It is known as the "Terminator" and has nothing to do with Arnold Schwarzenegger's classic sci-fi movie. But to many farmers and environmentalists around the world, it is just as scary.

We are not talking about killer robots. This Terminator is a genetically engineered seed designed to render the seeds of its offspring sterile. Doing so would block farmers from saving the seeds and ensure that agribusiness companies have a steady source of income.

To companies such as Monsanto, one of the world's largest seed companies, Terminator technology seemed to make good business sense. By developing seeds resistant to its own herbicides ("Roundup Ready" seeds), Monsanto had created markets for both products. But developing the Roundup Ready technology cost millions of dollars. The Terminator—officially known as Technology Protection System—was designed to protect that investment.

However, some have not shared Monsanto's enthusiasm. "The small farmers in the developing world who still rely extensively on their ability to hold back their seeds . . . who can get wiped out by one bad season, would suddenly find themselves with no seeds for the next year and no money to buy new seeds," said Ismael Serageldin of the World Bank.[1]

To others, the environmental risks of this technology are even greater. Some environmentalists fear that cross-pollination of genetically altered crops with those in neighboring fields could result in widespread crop damage. An even broader concern is that the spread of Monsanto's new technologies could result in a lack of biodiversity, which, in turn, could result in crop failures and famine.

For many, the controversy over Terminator technology became symbolic of a larger debate over the use of genetically modified (GM) food. "In Europe and developing countries, genetic engineering is viewed not just as scientific advancement but as a social force that controls people and what they grow," the *St. Louis Post-Dispatch* reported. "For those who think that way, the Terminator has become a powerful symbol."[2]

Another issue that dogged Monsanto was consumer safety. Research on the long-term effects of GM food was inconclusive. Undaunted, the company proclaimed the safety of its products in public statements and advertising. But those tactics came under attack. The United Kingdom Advertising Standards Authority (ASA) accused Monsanto of misleading the public about the safety of GM products. The ASA upheld 81 complaints about misleading newspaper advertisements. It was particularly critical of the company's claims that its GM tomatoes were proven to be safe, even though the tomato had not been approved in 20 countries and was not available in the United Kingdom.[3]

Monsanto was publicly embarrassed when an environmental group disclosed that the caterers at the company's British headquarters had banned some GM foods from the employee canteen.[4] *Time* also awarded Monsanto the dubious distinction of having the year's worst public relations, saying "the firm acted more like a chemical company than a food giant and failed to convince consumers of the benefits of GM products."[5]

In October 1998, scientists and farm economists at the World Bank in Washington voted to ban the use of the Terminator in their projects. The USDA received more than 2,000 letters and e-mails from 55 nations opposing its use.[6]

On October 6, 1999, Monsanto Chairman Robert Shapiro announced that the company would not pursue commercial development of Terminator technology and accepted personal blame for his company's poor public relations performance. As if to give special emphasis to his mea culpa, Shapiro made his remarks at a Greenpeace business conference in London.

"We have irritated and antagonized more people than we persuaded," Shapiro said. "Too often we forgot to listen."[7]

The company subsequently introduced "The New Monsanto Pledge," which included a commitment to "dialogue, transparency, respect, sharing, and delivering benefits."[8] The company also created a series of advisory panels so it could open a dialogue with a variety of stakeholders.

"Monsanto's decision is at least a recognition that it has heard the public outcry and that the public has a role in how the technology develops," said Dr. Jane Rissler of the Union of Concerned Scientists.[9]

Monsanto has kept its pledge, saying that it is "engaged in dialogue with experts and interested parties to learn technology applications that might be available and how they might be used to address biotech stewardship, maintenance of intellectual property rights, and protection of the rights and needs of farmers." However, as recently as 2006, Monsanto would not sell its genetically engineered seeds to farmers unless they contractually agreed to these terms: "To use Seed containing Monsanto Technologies solely for planting a single commercial crop. Not to save any crop produced from Seed for planting and not to supply Seed produced from Seed to anyone for planting other than to a Monsanto licensed seed company."[10] According to the Center for Food Safety, a nonprofit environmental-advocacy group, "Monsanto has an annual budget of $10 million and a staff of 75 devoted *solely* to investigating and prosecuting farmers" who may have violated their contracts.[11] To date, according to the center, Monsanto has filed lawsuits against more than 145 farmers.[12]

DISCUSSION QUESTIONS

1. Could Monsanto have avoided public controversy over the Terminator without undermining its own business interests and values?
2. Is it wrong for companies such as Monsanto to aggressively protect their business interests in the face of a consumer backlash?
3. What methods of research would you have conducted if you were in charge of the company's public relations?
4. Did Monsanto cave in to public pressure at the expense of its belief in production of genetically modified food products?

NOTES

1. Erin Hayes, "Seeds of Controversy," ABC News.com, 2 August 1999.
2. Bill Lambrecht, "Critics Vilify New Seed Technology That Monsanto May Soon Control," *St. Louis Post-Dispatch*, 1 November 1998, online, www.stltoday.com.
3. "U.K. Slams Monsanto Publicity," *Chemical Week*, 12 April 2000 (as quoted on Findarticles.com, www.findarticles.com).
4. Lyndsay Griffiths, "Double Standard? Monsanto's British HQ Caterer Bans Genetically Modified Food," Reuters, 22 December 1999 (as posted on ABCNews.com).
5. "The Best (and Worst) of 1999," *Time*, 20 December 1999, online, www.time.com.
6. Lambrecht.
7. John Vidal, "We Forgot to Listen, Says Monsanto," *The Guardian*, 7 October 1999, online, www.guardian.co.uk.
8. "The New Monsanto Pledge," Monsanto web site, www.monsanto.com.
9. " 'Terminator' Victory a Small Step in a Long War," Environmental News Network, 7 October 1999, online, www.cnn.com.
10. "2006 Monsanto Technology/Stewardship Agreement," online, www.farmsource.com/images/pdf/2006%20EMTA%20Rev3.pdf.
11. "Monsanto vs. U.S. Farmers," Center for Food Safety, online, www.centerforfoodsafety.org/pubs/MonsantoExSum1.14.2005.pdf.
12. "Monsanto vs. U.S. Farmers."

No News Is Bad News: Media Relations at the Atlanta Olympics

As the world begins to look toward Beijing for the 2008 Summer Olympic Games, veteran sports reporters who rely on world-class media relations during the Olympics may still be looking back, with a shudder, to Atlanta.

Reporter Mike Downey of the *Los Angeles Times* summed up media relations at the 1996 Summer Olympic Games in one word: "confused."[1]

Was Downey too harsh—or too polite? You decide:

■ At his first meeting with a reporter from the *Atlanta Journal-Constitution*, the head of the Atlanta Committee for the Olympic Games (ACOG) pronounced, "We don't have to tell you a damned thing."[2]

- Reporters were assigned hotel rooms far from the athletic action. Highlights of the bus system provided for the media included:[3]
  - A bus driver who had never driven on a major highway. She panicked and turned back. Reporters on board missed a world record at the rowing venue.
  - A completed journey to a lake where a major competition was occurring. Right lake, wrong side.
  - Bus drivers who refused to stop in midroute. One journalist pried open a bus door with photographic equipment. Another pretended to be sick in order to get off the bus.
- Atlanta's mayor "lightheartedly" recommended that journalists be taken to the shooting venues and used as targets.[4]

How could media relations at the Atlanta Olympics have gone so wrong? The journalists themselves may have had the best answer. "It is generally agreed," wrote a reporter for *Scotland on Sunday,* "that bad planning lies at the heart of the city's problems."[5]

Perhaps the worst element of ACOG's media relations was also the most important: getting the facts to the reporters. For that, ACOG was relying on a sophisticated computer system supplied and staffed by IBM. IBM designed the system to gather information at the athletic venues and immediately translate it into a new format for newspapers.[6] From the beginning, there were three problems:

- Information in the system jammed. There was input but sometimes no output.[7]

- Information was sometimes wrong. One boxer was listed as two feet tall. Another athlete's age was recorded as 97.[8]

- Information that did emerge wasn't in the format that newspapers preferred. "Many of the . . . problems were a case of pro-

gramming a computer to format a certain sport's information one way, while newspapers were expecting it another way," reported *USA Today*[9] on this clear case of neglecting a public's values.

"We went expecting high tech, and we got Third World," said the United Press International's top sports editor. "Basically, nothing was working."[10] International media agencies from Japan to England began to demand refunds for the exclusive access they had purchased.[11]

What caused the system failure? Journalists from around the world began reporting that IBM had not adequately tested the system.[12] To its credit, IBM immediately dispatched extra workers, including a public relations team. By the end of the Olympics, most of the system was performing efficiently—but journalists by then had begun inventing new acronyms and interpretations for ACOG. Among the favorites were A-CLOG and Atlanta Can't Organize the Games.[13]

If officials with ACOG were unhappy, officials with the International Olympic Committee (IOC) were aghast. After the closing ceremonies in Atlanta, the IOC summoned representatives of the international news media and IBM to London to discuss how a repeat performance of the technological glitches could be avoided. At the same time, the IOC Press Commission met in Lausanne, Switzerland, to specify what lessons could be learned from ACOG's performance.[14]

The Atlanta Olympics did provide the world with unforgettable moments of athletic drama. But a poorly planned relationship with the news media began with ACOG's top official saying, "We don't have to tell you a damned thing" and ended with this epitaph from the *New York Times:* "Many in Atlanta are starting to realize that the worldwide media criticism, whether deserved or not, may have long-term consequences."[15]

DISCUSSION QUESTIONS

1. If you had been an ACOG public relations official, how might you have persuaded that organization's leaders that the media are an important public?
2. If you had been an ACOG public relations official, how might you have responded to the mayor's joke about using journalists for target practice?
3. In terms of public relations, what did IBM do wrong and what did it do right in regard to its Olympics computer system?

4. Was it fair of the news media to publish and broadcast so many negative accounts of ACOG's media relations? Weren't the media there to report on the athletic events?
5. Besides the journalists themselves, what other publics should have been important in ACOG's media relations plan?

NOTES

1. Mike Downey, "Bum Steers in 'Bumfoozled' Atlanta," *Los Angeles Times*, 23 July 1996, online, LexisNexis.
2. Melissa Turner, "Media and the Olympics: Post-Games Fallout of Worldwide Bad Press," *Atlanta Journal-Constitution*, 20 October 1996, online, LexisNexis.
3. Kirk Bohls, "Atlanta Is Gigantic Mess That Isn't Moving," *Austin American-Statesman*, 24 July 1996, online, LexisNexis.
4. Kevin Sack, "Atlanta Bristles at All the Criticism," *New York Times*, 25 July 1996, online, LexisNexis.
5. Tom Knight, "Payne and Suffering Inflicted on All in Problem Games," *Scotland on Sunday*, 28 July 1996, online, LexisNexis.

6. Kevin Maney, "IBM: The Mad Scramble Olympic Crucible Tests Corporate Giant's Mettle," *USA Today*, 2 August 1996, online, LexisNexis.
7. Maney.
8. Maney.
9. Maney.
10. Turner.
11. Knight.
12. Turner; Maney; Knight.
13. Eric Adler, "A Big Stink Rises over Transportation; Buses Break Down, Streets Jam Packed, People Stranded," *Kansas City Star*, 23 July 1996, online, LexisNexis.
14. Turner.
15. Sack.

Corporate Podcasting

If you were web surfing on February 10, 2005, and happened across the Oregon-based *Northwest Noise*, you might have thought that the end of the world was near. The editor of the popular blog proclaimed, "Just now, as I look out my window and, yes, yes, there are pigs flying and a fat lady is singing."[1]

What, you may ask, provoked such a reaction? That was the day General Motors entered the world of podcasting and, in turn, transformed what many saw as a vehicle for counterculture into a mainstream medium.

Podcasting, both as a term and practice, emerged in 2004. It is a marriage of the words *iPod*, Apple's revolutionary digital audio player, and *broadcasting*. Podcasts are audio files that sound like radio programs downloaded to computers or portable digital devices for on-demand listening. At the outset, podcasting was the domain of the eclectic, including what the *New York Times* described as "programs of weird monologists and couples capering, complaining and exposing their personal lives in ostentatiously appalling ways."[2] However, by April 2005, it was estimated that more than 6 million U.S. adults had downloaded podcasts—and that number was expected to rapidly grow.[3] The practice had become so prevalent that the editors of the *New Oxford American Dictionary* named *podcast* their Word of the Year for 2005.[4]

General Motors, for many a symbol of staid conservative corporate values, entered the world of podcasting in connection with the 2005 Chicago Auto Show. In a five-minute presentation, GM North America President Gary Cowger introduced the 2006 Cadillac DTS and Buick Lucerne sedans. It was a no-frills production absent of music and sound effects.[5] Many in the podcast community were not impressed.

"Kinda looks like the time when ol' Dad put on the gangsta wear and hoodie, and tried to bust a rhyme," wrote software developer Dave Ritter. "You had to give him points for trying, but no matter how hard he tried to be hip, it wasn't going to fly."[6]

Despite the initial criticism of GM's first efforts in the new medium, the company logged approximately 10,000 downloads of the podcast within the first month of its release.[7] As the company increased both the quality and quantity of its podcast offerings, the number of downloads soared, an estimated 75,000 during August 2005.[8]

While these figures look impressive, what do they *really* mean? As is often a challenge with many public relations tactics, the tangible impact of podcasting is difficult to measure. How can one equate downloads with sales figures, especially with high-end purchases such as automobiles? And as is true with any individual tactic that is part of an integrated marketing communications campaign, how does one measure its effectiveness in motivating the consumer when working in combination with other tactics?

"No one knows the impact of podcasts, or even how many hits constitute a success," said Travis Austin, director of creative services for the Washington-based Strat@comm agency. "Finding the right length and frequency to hold an audience in this format has not been established."[9]

Even with a lack of measurement, podcasts offer companies something they lack in traditional broadcast media. "Companies are completely losing control of their messages, and one way to get into the game is by blogging and podcasting," said GM Director of New Media Michael Wiley. "The companies that are early adopters stand tremendous opportunity to be winners in the long run."[10]

Other advantages to podcasts are that they are relatively inexpensive and that their audience is self-selecting, meaning that people are already interested in the topic when they choose to download. "It is an interesting way to connect with niche audiences," Wiley said.[11]

Within a year of GM's first podcast, some of the biggest names in business and industry had jumped on the bandwagon. Disneyland celebrated its 50th anniversary with a series of podcasts recorded in the amusement park. The major broadcast networks began offering downloads of audio and video versions of their news and entertainment programming. IBM uses podcasts as an internal communications tool, one that reaches 7,000 employees weekly at an annual savings of $700,000 in conference-call costs.[12]

Some bloggers—including some on GM's *FastLane Blog*—said they feared the introduction of corporate marketing messages into what they saw as an alternative to commercial broadcasting. In other words, they were concerned that corporations will dominate the new medium. GM's Wiley dismisses that argument, noting that the audience has ultimate control.

"If you don't want to listen to it, don't," he said.[13]

DISCUSSION QUESTIONS

1. What are the advantages and disadvantages of podcasting?
2. Does a traditional company such as General Motors take a risk in adopting cutting-edge communication tactics such as podcasting?
3. What differentiates a good podcast from a poor one?
4. Is podcasting a suitable tactic for both internal and external publics?

NOTES

1. "GM Starts a Podcast," *Northwest Noise,* 10 February 2005, online, www.northwestnoise.com.
2. Virginia Heffernan, "The Podcast as a New Podium," *New York Times,* 22 July 2005, E1.
3. "Data Memo: Podcasting," Pew Internet & American Life Project, April 2005, online, www.pewinternet.org.
4. Nathan Bierma, "At Random—'Podcast' Is Word of the Year," Knight Ridder/Tribune Business News wire, 28 December 2005, via LexisNexis.
5. John Couretas, "Podcast Is New GM Marketing Tool," *Automotive News,* 14 March 2005, 25.
6. Jamie Smith Hopkins, "Corporations Podcast Their Marketing Nets," Knight Ridder/Tribune Business News wire, 11 December 2005, via LexisNexis.
7. Couretas, 25.
8. Hopkins.
9. John Guiniven, "Podcast as a PR Tool: What Do You Need To Know?" *Public Relations Tactics,* September 2005, online reprint, www.prsa.org.
10. Hopkins.
11. Couretas, 25.
12. Hopkins.
13. Couretas, 25.

Citizens for a Free Kuwait

Most of today's college students remember that the United States and its allies invaded Iraq in 2003 and ousted dictator Saddam Hussein in hopes of seizing weapons of mass destruction that, as it turned out, were not there. However, many may not recall that more than a decade earlier the difference between peace and war may have also rested on what was—or wasn't—inside Iraq.

This much is not in dispute: Within hours of Iraq's August 2, 1990, occupation of Kuwait, a campaign was under way to convince the American people of the need to use military force against the invaders. An organization calling itself Citizens for a Free Kuwait hired public relations giant Hill & Knowlton to marshal public support for war. Over the next five months, an effective—and ultimately successful—campaign was waged. A coalition of Western and Arab nations led by the United States launched a war to liberate Kuwait on January 17, 1991. It lasted only six weeks and ended with Iraq's withdrawal from Kuwait.

In many ways, the Hill & Knowlton campaign was fairly traditional. It included special observances on 20 college campuses, a day of prayer observed in churches nationwide, the delivery of media kits to reporters, and the distribution of thousands of "Free Kuwait" T-shirts and bumper stickers. Hill & Knowlton also hired a public opinion research firm, the Wirthlin Group, to take the public's pulse and to learn what might sway people to support military intervention. Although public opinion was decidedly against going to war to protect the supply of oil, research uncovered sentiment that suggested war may be more acceptable if it were aimed at ending atrocities.

This brings us to the most controversial aspect of the Hill & Knowlton campaign. On October 10, 1990, a 15-year-old Kuwaiti girl, identified only as Nayirah, tearfully testified before the Congressional Human Rights Caucus about Iraqi atrocities she said she had seen at a Kuwait City hospital. Her family name was concealed, ostensibly to protect relatives still living in occupied Kuwait. In her statement, Nayirah said, "I saw the Iraqi soldiers come into the hospital with guns, and go into the room where fifteen babies were in incubators. They took the babies out of the incubators, took the incubators, and left the babies on the cold floor to die."[1]

What was called the "incubator incident" became a rallying cry for war. President George H. W. Bush mentioned the incident several times during public debate. It was cited in United Nations debate. Seven U.S. senators mentioned the incident before voting in favor of a resolution that gave the president legal authority to use force against Iraq. That resolution had passed the Senate by only five votes.

Although there is substantial evidence of Iraqi atrocities against civilians during its occupation of Kuwait, there is no tangible evidence that the incubator incident ever happened. Independent human rights organizations were unable to verify Nayirah's account. An ABC News crew that entered Kuwait as the country was being liberated found the incubators right where they were supposed to be.[2] The story's credibility was further undermined when it was learned that the only person claiming direct knowledge of the incident, Nayirah, was actu-

ally the daughter of Saud al-Sabah, Kuwait's ambassador to the United States.

There are other disturbing aspects. Hill & Knowlton was accurate in noting that Citizens for a Free Kuwait had a broad-based membership representing both people in and outside of Kuwait's government. However, it is also true that of the nearly $12 million raised by the committee for the pro-war campaign, $11.8 million came from Kuwait's ruling family.[3]

Although there was nothing illegal in the arrangement, it was not widely known that the Congressional Human Rights Caucus—the group that sponsored Nayirah's testimony—maintained free office space in Hill & Knowlton's Washington offices. Because the Congressional Human Rights Caucus is a private foundation and not an official committee of Congress, witnesses could say anything they wanted under oath without any threat of prosecution.

A Kuwaiti dentist, who claimed to be a surgeon, repeated the incubator story in testimony before the United Nations Security Council on November 27, 1990. He claimed to have supervised the burial of 120 newborn babies who had died as a result of the alleged atrocity. However, confronted with his testimony after the war, the dentist admitted that he had no direct knowledge of the incubator incident.[4]

"The first casualty when war comes is truth," said Senator Hiram Johnson when the United States entered World War I in 1917. But truth can be elusive. It is not likely that the incubator story, in and of itself, made the difference between peace and war. There were other political, social, economic, and military issues involved in the decision. However, one thing is certain: The ethical standards of public relations practitioners became the focus of international debate.

DISCUSSION QUESTIONS

1. Was the decision to hide Nayirah's identity appropriate? Do you feel the concealment made any difference in the debate on whether the United States should go to war against Iraq?

2. Citizens for a Free Kuwait listed dozens of members from all walks of life. However, a large majority of its funding came from the Kuwaiti royal family. Is it appropriate to characterize this group as a "grassroots" organization?

3. Suppose, for a moment, that the incubator story was false. Would public relations practitioners be justified in using it to achieve what they may see as a moral purpose, the liberation of Kuwait?

4. If you had been hired to represent Kuwait, what tactics would you have used to sway public opinion in favor of U.S. intervention?

5. Do any of the issues raised in the case study have any relevance to the ongoing controversy surrounding the 2003 invasion of Iraq?

NOTES

1. John Martin, "The Plan to Sell the War," *20/20*, 17 January 1992.
2. Martin.
3. Martin.
4. Martin.

Wrestling for Success

In 1986, Syracuse University All-American wrestler Wayne Catan took the mat against world champion Yury Voroboiev. Catan came in second.

A month earlier, he had wrestled in his weight-class finals at the National Collegiate Athletic Association championships. He came in second.

Catan graduated and entered public relations. In 2000, he was nominated for *PR Week* magazine's Solo Practitioner of the Year award. He came in second.

Then one of Catan's biggest clients, Pets.com (famous for its mascot, a sock-puppet dog) went out of business—a loss of almost $250,000 a year in revenues. In 2001, Catan was again nominated for Solo Practitioner of the Year. He won.

Wayne Catan is a winner.

As the president, writer, researcher, secretary, coffee maker (and only employee) of Catan Communications in New Jersey, Catan doesn't believe in accepting defeat. "Every day when I wake up, whether I'm sick, tired, or cranky, I've got to hit the pavement," he says.

In naming Catan Solo Practitioner of the Year, *PR Week* noted that Catan "grapples with the mundane tasks that large agencies usually pay other people to do—filing, answering phones, compiling media lists, writing his own press releases, and making all of his own pitch calls."[1]

Does Catan's never-ending search for new business mean that he must occasionally compromise his values? Not even close. In 1998, Catan resigned as the public relations consultant for a well-known boxing promoter whose fighter had just lost to heavyweight champion Evander Holyfield. Catan quit after refusing to issue a statement accusing Holyfield of illegal punches. When the promoter disregarded Catan's advice and publicly condemned Holyfield, Catan became his own client, issuing the following statement: "[The fighter] lost, and I want every sports writer and client to know that [I] did not release the protest statement."[2] Catan's accountant might have winced at the financial loss, but public relations practitioners applauded his integrity. "Sports Publicist KO's Boxing Promoter" read the headline in a prominent public relations newsletter.[3]

Catan doesn't fire all his clients. He's enjoyed national successes with

■ Pet Sitters International, an organization of professional "babysitters" for pets. Catan helps with the annual "Take Your Dog to Work Day." He became a media favorite when he was asked to explain the exclusion of cats: "There are still cat box issues to deal with."[4]

■ Sabol Sports, creator of the Puffer, a golf putter whose shaft holds up to four cigars. Catan helped win mentions in news media including *Sports Illustrated, Parade, USA Today,* AP, CNN, and CNBC.[5]

Journalists and public relations practitioners still wonder whether one of Catan's most notable consulting efforts was a real lawsuit or a publicity tactic. The media attention began when Pets.com, a Catan client, sued comedian Robert Smigel for reportedly saying that the company stole the idea for its sock-puppet dog from Smigel's Triumph, the Insult Comic Dog. Triumph was a popular puppet on NBC's *Late Night with Conan O'Brien.*

"We didn't make this up," said Catan, defending the lawsuit. "They started it."[6]

Whether the legal battle was a true grudge match or an inspired promotional idea, the news media noticed. "Sock Puppet Suit Gets Pets.com Good Press" declared one headline.[7] Predictable pun-filled headlines followed, including "TV Dog Puppets Engage in Hand-to-Hand Combat" and "Pets.com Poop$ on Conan's 'Pup' Pet."[8] Catan and his client steadfastly upheld the legitimacy of the lawsuit, which they eventually settled out-of-court.

The high-profile dogfight lost energy when Catan's client went out of business—just months before he won the *PR Week* Solo Practitioner of the Year award.

As a former collegiate athlete, Catan probably dreads sports clichés, but he might agree that success isn't a destination; it's a journey. Decades ago, after his heartbreakingly close loss to world champion Yury Voroboiev, Catan said, "I hate when I lose—but I thought I did pretty well. I've been improving every match. It's only a matter of time before the tables are turned. Things are getting closer."[9]

That attitude, more than any gold medal, makes Wayne Catan a winner.

DISCUSSION QUESTIONS

1. What qualities does Wayne Catan have that make him a successful public relations practitioner?
2. What are the advantages and the disadvantages of being an independent public relations consultant?
3. If you had been asked to issue the statement condemning Evander Holyfield, would you have resigned? Why or why not? Does Values Statement 2.1 (p. 38) affect your decision?
4. Would you have advised Pets.com to sue Robert Smigel? Why or why not?

NOTES

1. "Solo Practitioner of the Year 2001," *PR Week,* online, www.prweekus.com/us/events/awards2001/solo.htm.

2. Jack O'Dwyer, "Sports Publicist KO's Boxing Promoter," *Jack O'Dwyer's Newsletter,* 14 October 1998, online, LexisNexis.

3. O'Dwyer.

4. Jeffry Scott, "Take Your Dog to Work Day," *Atlanta Journal and Constitution,* 10 April 2001, online, LexisNexis.

5. "Profiles of Sports PR Firms," *O'Dwyer's PR Services Report,* December 1998, online, LexisNexis.

6. Chris Clancy, "Sock Puppet Suit Gets Pets.com Good Press," *O'Dwyer's PR Services Report,* June 2000, online, LexisNexis.

7. Clancy.

8. Michael Precker, "TV Dog Puppets Engage in Hand-to Combat," *Dallas Morning News,* 29 April 2000, online, LexisNexis; Bill Hoffman, "Pets.com Poop$ on Conan's 'Pup' Pet," *New York Post,* 26 April 2000, online, LexisNexis.

9. Rich Cimini, "A Moral Victory for the U.S.," *The Record,* 1 April 1986, online, LexisNexis.

Ghost Story: A Questionable Tactic Haunts Medical Journals

Professor Adriane Fugh-Berman has encountered a ghost—twice. A professor of physiology and biophysics at Georgetown University School of Medicine, Fugh-Berman received an e-mail from a major international pharmaceutical company in 2004. The message offered her an article, already researched and written, that she could revise, if she wished, and submit to a medical journal under her own name. Journal articles can help professors gain promotion to higher ranks and higher salaries.

The professor looked at the article, which touted one of the company's drugs, but refused to submit it under her name. A short while later, however, she encountered the article again. This time, it carried another medical researcher's name: It had been submitted to a prestigious medical journal, and the journal's editors were consulting Fugh-Berman to see if the article merited publication. Rather than examine the article, she told the editors about the ghost.[1]

The ghost, of course, was a ghostwriter. Ghostwriting is a time-honored activity within public relations: Practitioners write speeches for executives, news releases without personal bylines, and a host of other documents for which others often receive the credit. Such ghostwriting is standard procedure. But some ghosts are scarier than others: Editors of medical journals maintain that ghostwriting in the medical profession, especially when the ghostwriter is paid by a pharmaceutical company attempting to secretly promote its own products, is unethical and dangerous.

"Scientific research is not public relations," explains Robert Califf, vice chancellor of clinical research at Duke University. "If you're a firm hired by a company trying to sell a product, it's an entirely different thing than having an open mind for scientific inquiry. . . . What would happen to a PR firm that wrote a paper that said this product stinks?"[2]

Unfortunately, the ghost that appeared twice before Fugh-Berman may have lots of company. "I believe 50 percent of articles on drugs in the major medical journals are not written in a way that the average person would expect them to be," says David Healy, professor of psychological medicine at the University of Wales. "The evidence I have seen would suggest there are grounds to think a significant proportion of the articles in journals . . . may be written with help from medical writing agencies. They are no more than infomercials paid for by drug firms."[3]

Paraphrasing the charges of yet another angry medical professor who had seen a ghost, a *New York Times* reporter wrote, "Public relations firms hired by drug companies—furtive spin doctors—are ghostwriting articles in the journals to suit clients' interests."[4]

A 1998 survey published in the *Journal of the American Medical Association* found that ghosts had written at least 11 percent of articles in the top U.S. medical journals.[5] "It introduces another bias into the whole clinical drug trial picture," says Professor Thomas Bodenheimer of the University of California at San Francisco. "So . . . the American public and the physicians in the United States are not going to know, really, the true facts about the drugs."[6]

To combat ghostwriting, medical journals and medical researchers have enlisted their own writing skills: They are asking pharmaceutical companies and their ghostwriters to follow to a written ethics code known as *Good Publications Practice: Guidelines for Pharmaceutical Companies*. In part, that document states:

- The Acknowledgments section of a paper should list those people who made a significant contribution to the study but do not qualify as authors. It should also be used to acknowledge the study's funding and the [pharmaceutical] company's involvement in the analysis of the data or preparation of the publication. . . .

- The named author(s)/contributors should approve the final version of the manuscript before it is submitted.

- The contribution of the medical writer should be acknowledged.[7]

By listening to their target audience—medical editors—and following the provisions of such ethics codes, public relations practitioners can help lay this ghost to rest.

DISCUSSION QUESTIONS

1. Is it ethical, in your opinion, for public relations practitioners to ghostwrite articles that tout a pharmaceutical company's product?
2. Is all ghostwriting in public relations unethical? Is it unethical for a public relations practitioner to write a speech for which another individual receives credit?
3. The vice chancellor of clinical research at Duke University suggests that a public relations agency that ghostwrote an honest article about a defective drug would lose its pharmaceutical client. What should public relations practitioners do when their research reveals that a pharmaceutical client's drug may have defects?
4. Would it be ethical for a public relations practitioner, in the employ of a pharmaceutical company, to openly assist a professor in writing a medical-journal article about one of the company's products?

NOTES

1. Anna Wilde Mathews, "At Medical Journals, Writers Paid by Industry Play Big Role," *Wall Street Journal*, 13 December 2005, A1.
2. Mathews, A1.

3. Antony Barnett, "Revealed: How Drug Firms 'Hoodwink' Medical Journals," *The Observer*, 9 December 2003, online, http://observer.guardian.co.uk.

4. Lawrence K. Altman, "The Doctor's World: Some Authors in Medical Journals May Be Paid by 'Spin Doctors,'" *New York Times*, 4 October 1994, online, LexisNexis.

5. Melody Petersen, "Madison Ave. Has Growing Role in Business of Drug Research," *New York Times*, 22 November 2002, online, LexisNexis.

6. Mathews, A1.

7. Elizabeth Wagner, Elizabeth A. Ford, and Leni Grossman, "Good Publication Practice for Pharmaceutical Companies," *Current Medical Research and Opinions* 19, no. 3 (2003): 153.

Ashland's Apology

It is easy to image that life might have been a lot easier for Lawrence G. Rawl if he had behaved more like John R. Hall.

Rawl was the chairman and chief executive officer of the Exxon Corporation in March 1989, when one of his company's oil tankers ran aground and spilled 11 million gallons of crude oil into the pristine waters of Alaska's Prince William Sound. In the immediate wake of the accident, Rawl and his company were combative, uncommunicative, and unapologetic.

Rawl stayed away from the disaster site. He waited a week to speak to the media. When Rawl finally spoke, he blamed federal and state officials for delaying the cleanup. Reacting to Rawl's delay, one Wall Street analyst said, "This is a real black eye for the company."[1]

At the time, Rawl estimated that the oil spill and subsequent lawsuits would cost Exxon less than $1 billion.[2] Fifteen years later, a federal judge in Anchorage imposed $4.5 billion in punitive damages on behalf of 32,000 Alaskan fishermen and residents.[3] That judgment is still under appeal. The company has also reported that it already has paid approximately $3.5 billion for the cleanup and in other lawsuits.[4]

Contrast Rawl's actions with those of Hall, who in January 1988 was chief executive officer of Ashland, Inc. It was at that time—14

months before the Alaskan oil spill—that a storage tank owned by Ashland collapsed and spilled 750,000 gallons of diesel fuel in the Monongahela and Ohio Rivers near Pittsburgh. Although the amount spilled was only a fraction of the size of the Alaskan spill, the potential impact was much greater because the spill threatened the source of drinking water for millions of people.

Like Rawl, Hall was initially inclined to stay away from the disaster site. Within 24 hours, he changed his mind and flew to Pittsburgh to survey the damage and meet with reporters. "Our company had inconvenienced the lives of a lot of people," Hall said. "I felt it was only right to apologize."[5]

"This honesty and openness is the wave of the future in crisis news media relations," wrote Bill Patterson in *Disaster Recovery Journal*. "And the surprising result of candor is that an executive's credibility is enhanced among those who matter most—employees, customers, stockholders and the media."[6]

Just as in the Exxon case, Ashland was not without blame. The collapsed storage tank had been rebuilt from a 40-year-old tank without a written permit. The evidence also suggested that inadequate testing had been conducted on the rebuilt tank prior to its being put into operation.

"The negligent conduct by Ashland which allowed the tank to collapse not only caused extensive environmental damage and widespread community dislocations, but also risked serious or fatal bodily injury," said an official state report on the incident. "The collapse could have been and should have been averted."[7]

Instead of dodging the issue, Hall accepted responsibility. "If we made mistakes, we have to stand up and admit them," he said.[8]

Ashland paid $1.25 million in fines for violating state laws and $2.75 million to settle damage claims that had been filed by state officials. Nearly half of this payout was used for a detailed study of fish and wildlife living in the oil spill region.[9] In the end, the cleanup and subsequent lawsuits cost Ashland more than $30 million.[10]

Patterson, who trains business executives on the best ways to deal with crises, had high praise for Hall. "His company took its lumps, but negative news coverage and editorials were greatly reduced because of his openness and candor," Patterson said. "You can't escape the crisis, but you can mitigate the final damages and restore credibility by showing compassion and concern."[11]

One can only wonder how much more it would have cost if John Hall had taken Exxon's approach. By acting quickly and accepting responsibility, Ashland avoided many of the mistakes Exxon would make a year later and became an often-cited example of corporate responsibility.

Ashland merged its refining, marketing, and transportation assets with Marathon Oil in 1997 to become Marathon Ashland Petroleum, LLC. Marathon bought out Ashland's shares in this partnership and changed the company's name to Marathon Petroleum Company, LLC, effective September 1, 2005.[12] No longer in the oil business, Ashland now focuses on the chemical and transportation-construction industries.

DISCUSSION QUESTIONS

1. Why are some companies cast as villains in the court of public opinion while other companies, facing similar circumstances, are seen as heroes?
2. It is often said that "perception is reality." Do you agree or disagree? Why?
3. If you were the CEO of Exxon at the time of the Alaskan oil spill, what might you have done differently?
4. Why are values important to the practice of public relations, and to what degree did Ashland and Exxon communicate their values?

NOTES

1. Ellen Benoit, "The Valdez Legacy," *Financial World,* 27 June 1989, 82–83.
2. "In Ten Years You'll See Nothing," *Fortune,* 8 May 1989, 50–54.
3. Adam Liptak, "$4.5 Billion Award Set for Spill of Exxon Valdez," *New York Times,* 29 January 2004, online, www.nytimes.com.
4. "ExxonMobile Sets Valdez Record Straight," ExxonMobile news release, 6 October 2004, online, www.exxonmobil.com/Corporate/Newsroom.
5. Clare Ansberry, "Oil Spill in Midwest Provides Case Study in Crisis Management," *Wall Street Journal,* 8 January 1988, A21.
6. Bill Patterson, "Crisis Communication, The Community, and SARA Title III," *Disaster Recovery Journal* 3, no. 4, online, www.drj.com/drworld/content/w1_053.htm.

7. Tank Collapse Task Force, Pennsylvania Department of Environmental Resources, *Report of the Investigation into the Collapse of Tank 1338*, June 1988, online, www.dep.state.pa.us/dep/PA_Env-Her/ashland.htm.

8. Ansberry, A21.

9. Marylynne Pitz, "Fish Return after '88 Oil Spill, Study Says," *Pittsburgh Post-Gazette*, 9 October 1998, online, www.post-gazette.com.

10. "Settlement Reached in Suits Related to Pittsburgh Spill," *Wall Street Journal*, 8 November 1989, A1.

11. Patterson.

12. "Marathon Completes Acquisition of Ashland's Interest in Marathon Ashland Petroleum," Marathon Petroleum Company news release, 30 June 2005, online, www.mapllc.com.

A Technology-Driven Tragedy

NBC's web site "Everest Assault '96" promised visitors "all of the excitement, but none of the risks" that go with attempts to scale the world's largest mountain.[1] Tragically, that promise was fully met.

On May 10, 1996, nine people from four expeditions died when they were caught in a violent blizzard near the summit of Mount Everest. And while NBC's web site made Internet history by providing the first accounts of the horrible events unfolding in the Himalayas, the chilling reality is that the presence of the web site and NBC correspondent Sandy Hill Pittman were contributing factors in the disaster.

Depending on the commentator's point of view, Pittman has been described as either a millionaire, a socialite, or as a social climber. However, there was one indisputable fact: Pittman was not a newcomer when it came to mountain climbing. By the time of her ill-fated assault on Everest, she had successfully scaled six of the highest mountains in the world. She wanted Mount Everest to be her seventh.

Reaching the place where heaven meets earth requires a team effort. For every person who achieves the summit, there are dozens more left behind in base camps down the mountain who hand-carry the tons of food and supplies required for an Everest assault.

Added to this tonnage was Pittman's 40-pound satellite telephone—her link to the NBC web site, which served as a resource for educators, journalists, and novices following her progress up the mountain.

Forty pounds may not sound like much. However, in an environment where every ounce results in the consumption of precious energy and oxygen, it represented a substantial burden. Sherpa Lopsang, who carried the equipment up the mountain for Pittman, was exhausted when he reached Base Camp Three, 24,000 feet above sea level. Although he initially refused to carry the burdensome device any farther, he later changed his mind after discussing the situation with expedition leader Scott Fischer. Ironically, the satellite telephone failed to work when it arrived at Base Camp Four, the final staging area for the assault on the summit.

Pittman herself had difficulty during her climb to Base Camp Three, still nearly a mile below the summit. Several accounts confirm that Pittman had to be "short-roped," a technique in which a weak climber is tied to a stronger climber. In fairness, Pittman has said she didn't ask to be short-roped.

That Pittman was singled out for special treatment is not disputed. The reason was the publicity that she would bring to Fischer and his commercial climbing enterprise, Mountain Madness Guided Expeditions. Fischer, who would die on the mountain, reportedly said, "If I can get Sandy to the summit, I'll bet she will be on TV talk shows. Do you think she will include me in her fame and fanfare?"[2]

The disaster of May 10 cannot be traced to a single incident. It was, quite literally, a tragedy of errors. Key preparations for the final push to reach the summit were left undone. The climbers left Base Camp Four behind schedule. Because of the number of expeditions to Everest, the progress of climbers was hindered by what some have called a traffic jam at the top of the world. The leaders of various expeditions, concerned about publicity and client satisfaction, violated their own safety rules. Climbers lingered at the summit three hours past an agreed upon 2:00 P.M. deadline for turning around and returning them to camp. And as day was turning into night, a killing blizzard engulfed Everest. Nine-teen people were stranded on the mountain without shelter or bottled oxygen. Only 10 returned.

Since the accident, much of the blame has been focused on Pittman and the drive for publicity her technology-enhanced presence fueled. As one publication noted, "Otherwise-sophisticated Manhattanites blame Pittman for killing 'all those people on Everest.'"[3] This is not entirely fair. Although even she might admit to making some mistakes on the mountain, others made far more catastrophic decisions. However, her silence upon returning to the United States did not help her cause.

No one person is responsible for the tragedy on Mount Everest. At the core of this disaster was a clash of values. No one suspected that this clash would become a life-or-death struggle. At several critical junctures, a reckless desire to succeed overshadowed what was supposed to be the real purpose of journey: to safely climb to the top of Mount Everest and live to tell about it.

DISCUSSION QUESTIONS

1. Discuss the pros and cons of Sandy Hill Pittman's presence on the ill-fated Mount Everest expedition. What, if anything, might you have done differently?
2. What lessons do you think public relations practitioners can learn from this disaster?
3. Do you agree with the authors that this tragedy was caused by "a clash of values"? To what values are they referring? Explain your reasoning.
4. Can you think of any other circumstances in which the desire for publicity comes into conflict with other values?
5. If you had been in Sandy Hill Pittman's shoes, how would you have handled the criticism she received upon returning to the United States?

NOTES

1. Pam Snook, "Web Site Breaks News of Mount Everest Tragedy," *Public Relations Tactics* (August 1996): 6.
2. Jon Krakauer, *Into Thin Air* (New York: Villard, 1997), 170.
3. Deborah Mitchell, "Pitons Are Served," *Salon,* June 1997, online, www.salonmagazine.com/june97/media/media970611.html.

Pro Bono: Bridging the Cultures of Rock and Politics

The world's news media call him "a political coalition builder" and a "hyper-agent."[1] The *New York Times* credits him with spearheading "a worldwide public relations campaign." Reporter Ed Bradley of the CBS program *60 Minutes* said, "He gets a lot of credit for lobbying President Bush. They've met several times."[2]

Oh, and he also performs with a band. He's Bono, lead singer and songwriter of U2, the Irish rockers who rival Madonna for creative longevity.

Bono as a public relations practitioner? Maybe not quite. But to fight AIDS and poverty in developing nations, Bono has crafted a variety of relationship-building tactics to win resources from wealthy nations. He has hosted special events, delivered speeches to world leaders, and created photo opportunities by telephoning a U.S. president live from stage and lending a pope his ever-present sunglasses. And he uses the language of his target publics: "When I'm speaking to corporate America," he says, "I always talk about countries being brands."[3]

For helping to raise billions of dollars for the world's poor, Bono and Microsoft's Bill and Melinda Gates were named *Time* magazine's 2005 Persons of the Year. So you'd think Bono's life, to quote a U2 song, might be "the sweetest thing." But you'd be ignoring the perils of cross-cultural communication.

In a scathing article titled "Saint Bono the Martyr," London's *Daily Mail* underscored the challenge of living on stage and in the corporate boardroom: "His obsession with changing the world has alienated both band-mates and fans. Could it now spell the end of the U2 singer's career?"[4]

Even less tolerant of Bono's cross-cultural odyssey was the *Ottawa (Canada) Sun:* "We resent spoiled brat rock stars . . . trying to dictate government policy decisions and telling us how to spend federal dollars."[5]

Less inflammatory critics still note the improbable clash of Bono's two worlds. CNN labels Bono and President George W. Bush the "odd couple."[6] The *New York Sun* calls Bono and a leading economist "an unlikely pair."[7] Melinda Gates herself said, "We'd certainly never had a rock star to the house before . . . but the whole reason we got together is because we have this joint cause."[8]

Bono himself tackles the cultural divide by confronting it head-on. In a meeting with President Bush and congressional leaders, he said, "I'm the first to admit that there's something unnatural, unseemly, about rock stars mounting the pulpit and preaching at presidents. . . . Talk about a fish out of water. . . . Yes, it's odd having a rock star here—but maybe it's odder for me than for you."[9]

Bono might also be the first to admit that he sometimes stumbles in the alien cultures of world politics and corporate boardrooms. In one of his first meetings with President Bush, he says he pushed so relentlessly for more AIDS-relief money that Bush finally pounded the table to silence him. "He banged the table to ask me to let him reply," Bono recalls. "I was very impressed that he could get so passionate. And let's face it: Tolerating an Irish rock star is not a necessity of his office."[10]

An entire nation may have wanted to pound a collective fist when Bono—still seeking funds for the world's poor—declared, "Ireland is now the richest country in the European Union, second only to Luxembourg—and Luxembourg isn't really a country."[11]

To critics in Luxembourg and elsewhere, he concedes, "I'm sick of Bono—and I'm Bono."[12]

He says he worries that his band-mates are "sick of the sight of me shaking hands with politicians."[13] Ironically, just as some scorn a rocker turned lobbyist, others decry the president's pal who still rocks: "He has courted ever greater risks to his street reputation," notes the *International Herald Tribune*.[14]

Why invite such culture clashes? One answer might be his success: "Bono charmed and bullied and morally blackmailed the leaders of the world's richest countries into forgiving $40 billion in debt owed by the poorest," *Time* declared in its story naming him one of its 2005 Persons of the Year.[15]

Bono himself believes that, if world poverty declines, he'll be remembered for his communications in just one culture: rock and roll. "Oddly enough," he says, "I think my work, the activism, will be forgotten. . . . I hope it will because I hope those problems will have gone away. But our music will be here in 50 years' and 100 years' time."[16]

DISCUSSION QUESTIONS

1. Do you agree with the *New York Times* that Bono's fund-raising efforts can be called public relations? Why or why not?

2. Are the worlds of rock and roll and of politics and corporations really different cultures? Why or why not?

3. As Chapter 14 notes, stereotyping can interfere with successful cross-cultural communication. In what ways, if any, has stereotyping hurt Bono's fund-raising efforts?

4. Before reading this case study, what were your impressions (if any) of Bono? Do his relationships with Bill Gates and George W. Bush hurt his credibility as a rock star?

NOTES

1. Eric R. Danton, "The Many Faces of Bono," *Hartford (Connecticut) Courant,* 1 December 2005, online, LexisNexis. Alexandra Marks, "Celebrity Hyper-Agents Transform Philanthropy," *Christian Science Monitor,* 19 September 2005, online, LexisNexis.

2. Transcript, *60 Minutes,* CBS, 5 February 2006, online, LexisNexis.

3. Joel Selvin, "U2's Bono Makes Fiery Case," *San Francisco Chronicle,* 11 November 2005, online, LexisNexis.

4. Paul Scott, "Saint Bono the Martyr," *Daily Mail,* 24 December 2005, online, LexisNexis.

5. "Act Like Pro, Bono," *Ottawa Sun,* 7 July 2005, online, LexisNexis.

6. Transcript, "The Situation Room with Wolf Blitzer," CNN, 2 February 2006, online, LexisNexis.

7. John P. Avlon, "The Rock Star and the Economist," *New York Sun,* 7 October 2005, online, LexisNexis.

8. Jamie Wilson Washington, "Melinda, Bill and Bono are Time's People of the Year," *The Guardian,* 19 December 2005, online, LexisNexis.

9. Bono, "Bono's Prayer for Africa," *The Record* (Kitchener-Waterloo, Ontario), 18 February 2006, online, LexisNexis.

10. George Rush and Joanna Molloy, "When Dubya Silenced Bono's Vox," *New York Daily News,* 26 January 2005, online, LexisNexis.

11. Richard Kay, "Bono's Little Bit of Bother," *Daily Mail,* 23 February 2006, online, LexisNexis.

12. "They Said What?" *The Journal* (Newcastle, England), 31 December 2005, online, LexisNexis.

13. "The Lobbyist Rock Star," CNN.com, 16 April 2004, online, LexisNexis.

14. Brian Lavery, "The Irish Love U2, Except When They Don't," *International Herald Tribune*, 28 June 2005, online, LexisNexis.

15. Desmond Butler, "Bill and Melinda Gates, Bono named *Time*'s Persons of the Year for Work on Poverty," Associated Press, 18 December 2005, online, LexisNexis.

16. *60 Minutes*.

Poison Postcards in Kansas

A public relations document reflects the values of the organization that created it. Sometimes, however, that reflection can become so distorted that it forces an organization to reappraise the values that unite it. A case in point: political mudslinging—the practice of smearing an opponent with charges often unrelated to current political issues. Can mudslinging really create a distorted reflection of personal or organizational values? Ask a group of Kansans who gained an unexpected education in hardball politics.

Anonymous postcards began arriving in Kansas voters' mailboxes during the long hot summer of 1998. In one case, they accused a candidate for the state legislature of failing to pay child support. In a second case, they accused another state-legislature candidate of ties to extremist neo-Nazi groups. In yet another case, they informed voters about the bankruptcy of a state Board of Education candidate. Court records proved the truth of the child-support and bankruptcy charges. Two of the three candidates were defeated in their primary elections.

"Pure garbage," scoffed the only targeted candidate to win his election.[1]

Who launched the anonymous mailings? Who, in the words of the surviving candidate, threw the garbage? The answer startled many Kansans: the Kansas chapter of the National Education Association, the state's largest teachers organization. That revelation even surprised many of the organization's members. One member expressed the wish that KNEA had handled the campaign differently: "We should have been up front that it was us from the start."[2]

Concurrent discussions within the Public Relations Society of America reflected that commitment to openness. In 1998, PRSA members were discussing a new ethics code that would become that organization's "Member Code of Ethics 2000." One provision of the full code, printed in its entirety in the appendix (pp. 564–570), holds that members should "reveal the sponsors for causes and interests represented."

The anonymity of the attacks was only the beginning of the problem for many KNEA members. Some charged that such campaign tactics shouldn't have been used at all. After conversations with teachers throughout the state, KNEA's president admitted, "The message was pretty clear that the tactic was not one that was viewed as appropriate by members of this organization."[3]

As news of KNEA's sponsorship of the postcards spread throughout the state, it became obvious that KNEA's leadership had little oversight of the organization's communications. The *Topeka Capital-Journal* reported that when the KNEA president was asked about the postcards, he replied that "he didn't know enough about the mailings to say who was involved in their development."[4] The president later added that "neither he nor members of the board [of directors] had advance knowledge of what was in the mailings." The president attributed the mailings to KNEA's political director, who had worked in conjunction with an independent political consultant.[5]

That lack of oversight allowed KNEA's communications to contradict its values. "The issue with our members was that we didn't focus on the issues that were important to them," said KNEA's president. "What they wanted to know about candidates wasn't whether or not they had filed for bankruptcy but whether they took positions that were supportive of quality schools and strengthening the profession."[6]

The power of the written word created KNEA's problem. It was only fitting, therefore, that KNEA used the written word to reassert its core values and rededicate itself to values-driven actions. In a letter to the organization's 24,000 members, KNEA's president wrote:

> It is clear that many members were embarrassed, offended or angered by an approach which contradicted the standards and values the association should be reflecting. In the future, we will guarantee that the members of KNEA will have oversight of and provide direction for the activities conducted by our association. We have learned a very important lesson, and, as is sometimes the case, learned it the hard way.[7]

DISCUSSION QUESTIONS

1. If KNEA had followed the 10 stages of the public relations writing process (see Chapter 10), would the original postcards have been mailed? Why or why not?
2. It is not illegal for independent organizations such as KNEA to sponsor anonymous political messages. Is it unethical? Why or why not?
3. In your opinion, are personal attacks effective in political campaigns?
4. KNEA's president quickly admitted that the organization had made an error. Was that a wise decision? In your opinion, did his quick confession hurt KNEA's reputation? Or did it strengthen it?
5. The "poison postcards" clearly embarrassed KNEA. Did anything good come out of this episode?

NOTES

1. "KNEA Drops Negative Tactics," *Topeka Capital-Journal,* 15 August 1998, online, LexisNexis.
2. "KNEA Drops Negative Tactics."
3. "KNEA Drops Negative Tactics."
4. "Cook Lashes Out at Foes," *Topeka Capital-Journal,* 13 August 1998, online, LexisNexis.
5. "KNEA Drops Negative Tactics."
6. "KNEA Drops Negative Tactics."
7. "KNEA Drops Negative Tactics."

The High Price of Sexual Harassment

On its web site, Mitsubishi Motors North America proclaims that "respect is the guiding principle" of its "commitment for making diversity work." The company also notes that since 1998, the Mitsubishi Motors USA Foundation has recognized 26 outstanding women in 15 states as "Unsung Heroines" for their many contributions to improving the lives of others.[1]

While Mitsubishi takes pride in its diversity efforts, it has good reason to continue them—34 million reasons to be exact: The company was once forced to pay a $34 million settlement in a federal sexual harassment class action lawsuit.[2]

In 1996, the U.S. Equal Employment Opportunity Commission charged that Mitsubishi (then known as Mitsubishi Motors Manufacturing of America) had discriminated against as many as 700 women employed at its Normal, Illinois, assembly plant over a six-year period.[3] As early as 1992, female employees began to complain of crude and obscene behavior on the assembly line by some of their male counterparts. However, appeals to management and the union local appeared to fall on deaf ears. When a class-action lawsuit was filed on behalf of 29 women at the plant in 1994, some of the women were allegedly targeted for reprisals.

The company's response has become a textbook example of what *not* to do. When EEOC officials arrived at the plant to investigate the complaints, they were astonished to see that the company hadn't even bothered to clean up sexually explicit graffiti from the workplace.

This feeling was reinforced when Gary Shultz, Mitsubishi general counsel and manager of public relations, chose to attack the accusers. Shultz organized a march and demonstration in front of the EEOC offices in Chicago, giving employees who marched a day off with pay. Telephone lines were set up at the plant so workers could call politicians to complain about how the government was threatening both car sales and American jobs. And, as Michael Major noted in an analysis of this case for *Public Relations Tactics*, "In case these messages were too subtle for some people, the company underlined its point by letting it be known that they were seeking gynecological and other personal records from the women who filed the complaints."[4]

The response to the company's slash-and-burn strategy was predictable: Key stakeholders were outraged. Robert Irvine, president of the Louisville-based Institute for Crisis Management, said, "By drawing attention to where so many allegations are being made, the company was, in effect, signaling that where there's so much smoke, there must be fire." Crisis expert Robin Cohn of New York added, "By going out with both barrels after the EEOC, [Shultz] was alienating the very people he has to work with, and giving them publicity they may not have gotten otherwise."[5]

Within 24 hours of the ill-conceived march on the EEOC office, the head of MMMA's parent company, the Mitsubishi Corporation in Japan, tried to defuse the controversy by condemning sexual harassment and expressing hope that the matter could be "solved quietly."[6] That didn't happen. A nationwide boycott of Mitsubishi products, led by the Reverend Jesse Jackson and the National Organization for Women, was launched. NOW named Mitsubishi a "Merchant of Shame."[7]

After the company agreed to a series of sweeping reforms authored by former U.S. Labor Secretary Lynn Martin, the boycott was suspended in January 1997. However, the controversy continued. Less than a year later, one company executive claimed that he resigned rather than give in to pressure to deceive reporters about MMMA's lack of progress in addressing sexual harassment. Arthur Zintek, vice president and general manager of human resources, wrote in his resignation letter, "Deception does not align with either my values or the stated values of the company." When the letter was released to the public as part of a federal court filing, MMMA officials denied that they had tried to mislead reporters and said the letter distorted a complicated issue.[8]

The company finally settled the case on June 10, 1998. Court-appointed monitors reported two years later that "Mitsubishi is in compliance with the decree, has sexual harassment in the plant firmly under control, and has made commendable progress in improving its systems for preventing such behavior and dealing with it appropriately when it occurs."[9]

EEOC Chairwoman Ida L. Castro said, "While this report shows that Mitsubishi has made substantial progress in ridding pervasive sexual harassment from its workplace, the Commission will remain vigilant in monitoring its employment practices in accordance with the landmark settlement of two years ago."[10]

DISCUSSION QUESTIONS

1. How would you have advised Mitsubishi to respond to the allegations of sexual harassment?
2. If a company or organization feels it is being wrongly accused of some wrongdoing, how aggressively should it defend itself to key stakeholders?
3. Was the sexual harassment crisis Mitsubishi faced avoidable? What steps could have been taken to defuse the controversy?
4. Is it appropriate for a company such as Mitsubishi, with a history of sexual harassment, to now promote its diversity efforts?

NOTES

1. "Diversity," Mitsubishi Motors North America web site, online, www.mitsubishicars.com/company/diversity.html.
2. Joint Motion for Entry of Consent Decree. *Equal Employment Opportunity Commission, plaintiff, v. Mitsubishi Motor Manufacturing of America, f/k/a "Diamond-Star Motors Corporation," defendant, and International Union, UAW and its Local Union 2488.* Case No. 96-1192. United States District Court for the Central District of Illinois, Peoria Division.
3. Kathleen Behof, "Mitsubishi Faces Record Sexual-Harassment Suit," CNN Interactive, 9 April 1996, online, www.cnn.com.
4. Michael J. Major, "Mitsubishi's PR Strategy Stalls," *Public Relations Tactics* (June 1996): 1.
5. Major, 1.
6. Major, 1.
7. "Viewpoint: Mitsubishi Joins Smith Barney as Merchant of Shame," National Organization for Women web site, May 1997, www.now.org.
8. Rochelle Sharpe, "Mitsubishi Unit Deceived Press, Ex-Official Says," *Wall Street Journal*, 12 January 1998, A22.
9. "Monitors Say Mitsubishi in Compliance with EEOC Consent Decree; Sexual Harassment 'Firmly Under Control' at U.S. Plant," U.S. Equal Employment Opportunity Commission news release, 6 September 2000.
10. "Monitors Say Mitsubishi . . ."

March of Dimes

One of the greatest ironies of the 20th century was that a man who successfully hid his physical disabilities from most Americans was also the most visible spokesperson in the fight against the disease that had crippled him.

Franklin Delano Roosevelt was the only person elected president of the United States four times. From his inauguration in March 1933 until his death in April 1945, FDR held a commanding presence in the minds of U.S.

citizens. Historians consider him among the greatest of presidents for having led the United States through the Great Depression and to the brink of victory in the Second World War.

He is also remembered for his courage in overcoming polio (poliomyelitis), a viral disease that attacks the central nervous system and can lead to paralysis and death. Children were most often the victims of the disease, which is transmitted through contaminated food and water. When FDR contracted polio at the age of 39 in 1921, he lost the use of his legs. But with careful event planning, the assistance of the Secret Service, and the acquiescence of the news media, the extent of Roosevelt's physical disability was unknown to most people.[1]

While FDR may have hidden his own physical limitations, he was not shy in showing his support for others who had suffered the same fate. Initially, his efforts centered on Warm Springs, Georgia, where he had first gone in 1924 to bathe in the area's therapeutic warm spring waters. Roosevelt purchased the property in 1926. A year later, with the help of former law partner Basil O'Connor, FDR established the nonprofit Warm Springs Foundation as a center for polio therapy and research.[2]

With the onset of the Great Depression, the Warm Springs Foundation faced severe financial difficulties. A nationwide series of "Birthday Balls" was organized on January 30, 1934, coinciding with President Roosevelt's 52nd birthday. The "Birthday Balls" ranged from a lavish gala at New York's Waldorf-Astoria to a wheelchair dance for patients at Warm Springs.[3] The event was promoted with the slogan "Dance so that others may walk." It was so successful that it was repeated for several years.[4]

"Birthday Balls exploited the prestige of the presidency to collect monies for the Warm Springs Foundation," wrote media historian Douglas Gomery. "It was often difficult to tell the difference between these polio balls and similar fund raisers staged by the Democratic Party."[5]

While the close connection between charity and politics may have been coincidental, it is undeniable. While Roosevelt had genuine sympathy for polio victims, being seen as their champion also helped his public image. Gomery wrote that several interest groups, especially the entertainment industry, embraced the "Birthday Balls" as a means to gain favor from the Roosevelt administration.[6]

The relationship between FDR and the entertainment industry spawned the signature fund-raising campaign for which Roosevelt is best remembered, the March of Dimes. Roosevelt established the National Foundation for Infantile Paralysis on January 3, 1938. It marked the first time that a permanent self-sustaining source of medical research funding had been based on small individual contributions rather than on money given by a few wealthy patrons. Eddie Cantor, a 1930s film and radio star, called this grassroots fund-raising effort the "March of Dimes," a play on words mimicking the name of a popular newsreel series of the day, *The March of Time*. Cantor asked the public to send dimes to the White House to support polio research.

Two days after Cantor's initial radio appeal, the White House received 30,000 pieces of mail, virtually all of which had coins taped to the letters. The next day, the White House received 150,000 letters.[7] This is especially impressive when you consider that a dime in the 1930s was the equivalent of $1.27 in today's money. "The March of Dimes had become the most beloved (and richest) charity in the USA with coffers brimming over with totals measured in the millions of dollars," Gomery wrote.[8]

The story did not end with FDR's death on April 12, 1945. On the tenth anniversary of Roosevelt's passing, March of Dimes officials announced that a polio vaccine developed by Dr. Jonas Salk with their support was both safe and effective. As a result, the threat of polio has been virtually eradicated in most of the world.

This grassroots fund-raising effort that tapped into the generosity of a nation at the height of its worst economic crisis has had one other lasting imprint. To commemorate Roosevelt's crusade against polio, the U.S. Mint began issuing dimes with FDR's image on January 30, 1946, the 64th anniversary of his birth.

DISCUSSION QUESTIONS

1. In your opinion, why was the March of Dimes so successful—especially in the midst of the Great Depression?
2. In hindsight, does Roosevelt's decision to hide his personal disability undermine his credibility as a champion of polio victims?
3. The case mentions the relationship between the charity and partisan politics. What were the benefits and risks of this relationship?
4. At the time of its creation, what made the March of Dimes unique among medical research charities?

NOTES

1. "Franklin Roosevelt Founds March of Dimes—January 3: This Date in History," History Channel, online, www.historychannel.com/tdih.
2. "The March of Dimes Story," March of Dime web site, www.marchofdimes.com.
3. Douglas Gomery, "Health Politics and Movie Power," *Historical Journal of Film, Radio and Television* 15, no. 1 (1995): 127–128.
4. William H. Helfand, Jan Lazarus, and Paul Theerman, "'. . . So That Others May Walk': The March of Dimes," *American Journal of Public Health*, 1 February 2002, 158.
5. Gomery, 128.
6. Gomery, 131.
7. Gomery, 131.
8. Gomery, 132.

The Nestlé Boycott

The Nestlé company's marketing of powdered infant formula in developing nations has been at the center of a global controversy for nearly three decades—and there is no end in sight.

Health-care professionals and religious organizations have expressed concern that the powdered formula must be mixed with water, and water in developing countries is often un-clean. This can make infants seriously ill. Another concern is the cost of the powdered formula, which can represent a substantial percentage of a consumer's income in poor nations. In an attempt to make the powder last longer, mothers might consider watering down the ingredients, unwittingly starving their children to death.

However, one practice particularly angered industry critics. It had become common practice for Nestlé and other manufacturers to have "milk nurses" or "mother craft workers" in white uniforms travel to villages to sell the product. Although these salespeople were usually trained nurses, critics complained that the uniforms lent a false air of authority to the sales pitch. With these salespeople being paid on commission, critics raised concerns about a built-in conflict of interest.[1]

Because of such marketing practices, Nestlé has been the target of a worldwide boycott since 1977, with the exception of a four-year hiatus in the mid-1980s. As public awareness of the controversy grew, several major multinational organizations took up the fight. One of them was the Interfaith Center on Corporate Responsibility (ICCR). One of the tactics ICCR used was to purchase shares of stocks in the publicly held companies that manufacture the powdered formula. This gave critics legal access to shareholder meetings and allowed them to vote on company practices at annual shareholder meetings.

"A massive sales campaign presently encourages poor mothers to abandon breast feeding for this more expensive, mechanically complex and less healthful method," wrote the ICCR's Leah Margulies. "There could be no more dramatic illustration of manufacturing a need that wasn't there."[2]

Other organizations, including the United Nations and the World Health Organization, took up the cause. The WHO/UNICEF International Code of Marketing of Breastmilk Substitutes, adopted by the World Health Assembly (WHA) in 1981, supported a ban of all promotion of bottle feeding and set out requirements for labeling and information on infant feeding.

Nestlé opted for a far more confrontational approach. It vigorously combated a series of shareholder fights designed to spotlight its questionable marketing practices. Nestlé was unwilling to compromise and challenged critics on every point. This led to an international boycott of Nestlé products, which ran from 1977 until 1984. It ended when the company said it would follow the terms of the WHA code. Company critics claim the boycott cost Nestlé "several billion dollars in lost sales and additional expenses."[3]

The story does not end here. The Nestlé boycott was reinstated in 1988 when critics claimed the company violated its promises by supplying free samples of baby formula to hospitals in developing nations. Although Nestlé acknowledged providing some supplies to hospitals, a company spokesman called the boycott "stupid" and said it wouldn't change the company's marketing practices.[4]

The company has tried to address the boycott with no success. It reportedly rejected one public relations firm's proposals because they were too militant.[5] In 1991, the company launched an advertising and health-clinic poster campaign promoting breast feeding. Although the campaign received some praise, cynics noted that it was targeted at women who got free infant formula from the government. Nestlé's competitors supplied that formula. In part because of the ongoing controversy, Nestlé does not have any government contracts.[6]

In recent years, Nestlé commissioned an independent audit of its infant formula marketing practices in three African nations. In a report entitled *The Nestlé Commitment to Africa*, the company implies that auditors found Nestlé practices in compliance with WHO guidelines.[7] However, the International Baby Food Action Network reported in 2004 that Nestlé was the source of more violations than any other company.[8]

"On the face of it, the boycott has done Nestlé little harm," the *Financial Times* reported in 2004. The newspaper noted that the value of company stock has risen nearly 1,600 percent since the beginning of the boycott and that Nestlé consistently ranks in the top 20 of the newspaper's annual list of most-respected companies. "But it cannot be much fun being the object of so much dislike for so long, particularly as Nestlé says infant formula accounts for no more than 1 per cent of its revenues," the newspaper said.[9]

"Nestlé could go to 20 PR agencies and 19 of them would give the same advice: stop marketing this stuff," one crisis management expert said. "The trouble is, that is not what management wants to hear."[10]

DISCUSSION QUESTIONS

1. Despite a generation of protests against its marketing of infant formula, Nestlé remains a very profitable company. In what way, if any, do you think the company has been hurt by this issue?

2. The case mentions that Nestlé rejected one public relations agency's proposals because they were too militant. One of those proposals was for Nestlé to try to infiltrate opposition groups. What do you think of this tactic?

3. Do infant formula manufacturers bear any moral responsibility if consumers misuse and are hurt by misuse of a safe product? Can you think of any other products that may fall into this category?

4. Has the boycott against Nestlé been a success or a failure? What do you think of the practice of using an economic boycott as a tactic to influence a company's actions?

NOTES

1. Allen H. Center and Frank E. Walsh, *Public Relations Practices: Managerial Case Studies and Problems,* 3rd ed. (Englewood Cliffs, N.J.: Prentice-Hall, 1985), 366.

2. Leah Margulies, "Baby Formula Abroad: Exporting Infant Malnutrition," *Christianity and Crisis,* 10 November 1975, 264–267.

3. Laurie Duncan, "Group Calls for Resumption of Nestlé Boycott; Says It Broke Promise Not to Promote Baby Formula in Third World," *Los Angeles Times,* 5 October 1988, sec. 4, p. 1.

4. Duncan.

5. "Plan Is Nestlé's Best PR," *Journal of Commerce,* 7 August 1989, 5A.

6. Bradley Johnson, "Nestlé Ads Pitch Breast-Feeding," *Advertising Age,* 2 December 1991, 40.

7. *The Nestlé Commitment to Africa,* Report Summary, October 2005, Nestlé S. A., online, www.nestle.com/Our_Responsibility/Africa+Report/Overview/Africa+Report.htm.

8. "Breaking the Rules, Stretching the Rules 2004," International Baby Food Action Network, web site, www.ibfan.org/english/codewatch/btr04/btr04contents.html.

9. Michael Skapinker, "How Baby Milk Marketing Fed a Long-Life Campaign," *The Financial Times* (London), 26 May 2004, 16.

10. "Plan Is Nestlé's Best PR."

Reebok and the Incubus

George Santayana may not be your favorite philosopher, but we bet you've heard one of his most famous sayings: "Those who do not learn from history are doomed to repeat it." If you've read "Flunking History: Umbro and the Holocaust" (Case Study 13.2), you may have asked yourself how a company could select such a catastrophically bad name for a new product—especially when Umbro could have learned from Reebok's earlier debacle.

The weird tale of Reebok and the Incubus broke on February 18, 1997, when *ABC World News Tonight* closed with this story:

> Finally, this evening, the great shoe mess and how the giant maker of sports shoes, Reebok, stepped right into it. When we heard today from our affiliate in Phoenix, Arizona, about what Reebok had called one of its running shoes for women—well, even Reebok agreed it was a mess. ABC's Judy Muller on the strange case of the Incubus.[1]

Why a strange case? And what's an incubus? The answers to those questions describe a marketing campaign gone awry.

Reebok makes athletic shoes and athletic apparel. Like all organizations, it also sometimes makes mistakes. And sometimes it makes a doozy.

In the mid-1990s Reebok launched a new running shoe for women: the Incubus. In 1996, it shipped more than 50,000 pair at a retail price of $57.99.

So what does *incubus* mean? (We'll offer a hint here: The name was not a reference to the California-based alternative-metal band.) London's *Financial Times* reported that Reebok chose the word because it sounded like *incubate*, a name that the company's marketers hoped would conjure up images of comfort and rebirth.[2]

Sounds reasonable. But what does *incubus* mean? Before using it, Reebok did ensure that the name wasn't trademarked.

That was prudent. But, really, what does *incubus* mean? Fortunately, while the name was on the shoebox and in marketing materials, it wasn't on the shoe itself.

Enough stalling. What does *incubus* mean? Turns out no one at headquarters had consulted a dictionary. Had Reebok marketers

done so, they might have encountered this definition from *The American Heritage Dictionary:* "Incubus: An evil spirit believed to descend upon and have sexual intercourse with women as they sleep."[3]

On *World News Tonight,* Judy Muller shared a similar definition with America.

"I'm horrified, and the company is horrified," a Reebok representative immediately told reporters. "How the name got on the shoe and went forward, I do not know. We are a company that has built its business on women's footwear, so to do anything that's denigrating to women is not what we're about."[4]

The day after the fateful ABC broadcast, another Reebok representative added, "We apologize. Certainly it is very inappropriate. . . . Obviously, it became very apparent to us yesterday why nobody else [had trademarked] the name."[5]

"What are the lessons here?" asked *The Naming Newsletter,* a marketing publication, in a retrospective of product-name disasters. "First, if you're tempted to use an obscure or unusual word (like *Incubus*), be absolutely, positively certain you know what the word means. Look it up. In a good dictionary. On Google.com."[6]

In selecting *Incubus* for a name, Reebok's marketers sought to convey a consistent image of warmth and nurturing for the company's new shoe. Instead, the name undercut that brand message with suggestions of evil and terror.

As all young romantics know, Shakespeare's Juliet innocently said, "What's in a name? That which we call a rose / By any other name would smell as sweet." Marketers, however, are supposed to know better. When Juliet ignored the power of names and what they stand for, she helped bring about her own death. Reebok's tragedy wasn't exactly of Shakespearean proportions, but it's a safe bet that every marketer in the company now has a dictionary within easy reach.

DISCUSSION QUESTIONS

1. How is a product's name part of an integrated marketing communications campaign?
2. What do you think of Reebok's response to the disaster?
3. If you had been a Reebok official at the time, what actions, if any, would you have suggested that the company take to end the problem and repair the damage?

4. Compare this case with Case Study 13.2 ("Flunking History: Umbro and the Holocaust"). What similarities and differences do you find in how the two companies created and responded to the crises?
5. What stories have you heard about other badly named products?

NOTES

1. Judy Muller and Peter Jennings, *ABC World News Tonight,* 18 February 1997, online, LexisNexis.
2. "Foot in Mouth," *Financial Times,* 24 February 1997, online, LexisNexis.
3. *The American Heritage Dictionary,* 3rd ed. (Boston: Houghton Mifflin, 1992), 916.
4. Ann Gerhart and Annie Groer, "The Reliable Source," *Washington Post,* 20 February 1997, online, LexisNexis.

5. Chris Reidy, "Reebox Kicks Itself over Name with Bad Fit," *Boston Globe,* 20 February 1997, online, LexisNexis.
6. "More Painful Lessons from the 'Oops' File: Watch What You Say," *The Naming Newsletter,* second quarter 2003, online, www.namingnewsletter.com.

Eight First Dates and Two Awards: Fleishman-Hillard Prompts Young Singles to Shout Yahoo!

In retrospect, doing the downward dog in front of national news media and millions of viewers may not have been the best idea, but scheduling nine romantic dates in three days can scramble the best of brains.

The dog (a yoga position) and dates were part of a special event designed to attract media attention to Project: Real People, a 2004 advertising campaign for Yahoo! Personals, an online dating service hosted by the popular web portal. The ad campaign would feature 50 real subscribers to Yahoo! Personals. To launch the campaign, public relations agency Fleishman-Hillard helped Yahoo! create a special event: Julie Koehnen, a 39-year-old Hollywood screenwriter and one of the 50 subscribers featured in the ads, would live—and date—for three days under a billboard on Los Angeles' Sunset Boulevard.

While living on an elevated platform beneath the billboard, which featured her photograph and the confession that she was "looking for a few good dates," Koehnen would go online and select eight Yahoo!

Personals subscribers for dates, inviting her favorite back for a ninth date. And the world could watch it all via a live webcast on Yahoo!

The Yahoo! team did show some mercy: Koehnen could depart for her real home at night. But from 7 A.M. to 7 P.M. for three days, she would eat, go online, date, work, date, exercise, be interviewed, date, doze, and date for all the world to see.

"The immediate interaction with people was amazing," Koehnen said of her three-day marathon. "They'd e-mail me while I was up there and respond as fast as I read their messages on the web cam. The Internet is so fast and visceral."[1]

If the Internet was fast and visceral, the traditional media weren't far behind. On day one of the special event, TV trucks from local stations and national networks arrived in the predawn darkness. "I got a phone call at 4:30 in the morning that the trucks were there and I had to get ready for interviews right away," Koehnen said. "I thought I'd just be hanging out with the Yahoo people, but this was really huge."[2]

To promote the special event, Fleishman-Hillard used other public relations tactics. Before the event, it prepared video b-roll footage, distributing it to local and national media via satellite and disk. It also prepared and distributed a media advisory/photo opportunity sheet headlined "Los Angeles Single Searches for Love on Yahoo! Personals atop Sunset Strip Billboard." Finally, the agency helped sponsor a contest on a Los Angeles radio station, with the winner gaining one of the eight dates.

Though it called the special event "a live ad," *Adweek* magazine noted the importance of public relations in attracting news media: "Because PR determines the success of a live ad, novelty and originality are crucial."[3]

Not only did novelty, originality, and romance flourish—among Koehnen's billboard dates were a police officer, a surfer, and a race-car mechanic—so did media coverage and activity on the Yahoo! Personals site. The special event generated almost 350 stories in 100 U.S. media markets, gaining exposure to a potential audience of 126 million. Traffic on the dating web site jumped almost 20 percent from the previous two-week period; subscriptions jumped 27 percent during the same period. The webcast recorded more than 500,000 hits.[4] *Promo* magazine named the billboard extravaganza its 2004 Campaign of the Year,[5] and the Public Relations Society of America honored Fleishman-Hillard with a 2005 Silver Anvil, the society's top award, in its special events category.[6]

And the downward dog? It was a yoga position that Koehnen assumed during an early-morning workout—a position that involved inadvertently aiming her posterior at the news media. "I don't think I'll do that again," she told a reporter from Reuters, an international news service.[7]

On a brighter note, the story might have a Hollywood ending for screenwriter Koehnen: As this book goes to press, she and the winner of the ninth date are still together.[8]

DISCUSSION QUESTIONS

1. Recall the discussion of special events and so-called "pseudoevents" from Chapter 9. Was the Yahoo! billboard tactic a pseudoevent?

2. *Adweek* magazine called the special event "a live ad." Was the event an advertisement? Would that mean it wasn't public relations?

3. If you had been able to help Fleishman-Hillard promote the special event, what tactics besides the b-roll, media advisory, and radio contest might you have used?

4. Using the communication model described in Chapters 5 and 9, can you describe source, message, channel, receiver, feedback, and noise for this special event?

NOTES

1. Betsy Spethman, "Getting Personal," *Promo,* 1 December 2004, online, LexisNexis.
2. Spethman.
3. Joan Voight, "Living It Up," *Adweek,* 26 September 2005, online, LexisNexis.
4. Fleishman-Hillard, "Yahoo! Personals Takes Online Dating to New Heights," PRSA Silver Anvil 2005 competition entry, online, www.prsa.org.
5. Spethman.
6. Fleishman-Hillard.
7. "Love Writ Large," *Sydney Morning Herald,* 9 January 2004, online, LexisNexis.
8. Spethman.

The Lion Roars

When the North Carolina–based Food Lion grocery store chain was accused by a network news show of selling spoiled meat to its customers, the company fought back using a unique—and controversial—legal strategy.

Food Lion unknowingly hired a reporter, armed with a hidden television camera, in the meat departments of two of the chain's stores. During her brief 11 days on the job, reporter Lynne Neufer Litt collected more than 50 hours of videotape. That footage was the foundation of a 1992 *Prime Time Live* investigative report that purportedly showed Food Lion workers engaged in unsanitary meat-handling practices.

Immediately after the program was broadcast, Food Lion President and Chief Executive Officer Tom Smith said, "This stuff belongs in the tabloids, along with Elvis and UFO sightings."[1] Despite Smith's reassurances, Food Lion stock dropped 10 percent of its value the very next day.

"The program, shades of Upton Sinclair's 1906 *The Jungle,* shocked an enormous audience and jolted an industry," reported the *Columbia Journalism Review.*[2]

Food Lion officials felt the report was false and inspired by the program's quest for higher ratings. The subsequent release of hidden camera footage not broadcast also suggested that selective editing may have presented a distorted picture of reality. The company also noted that the source of most of the allegations had been the United Food and Commercial Workers Union, which had for a decade unsuccessfully sought to unionize Food Lion stores. The union had coached Litt on how to pose as an experienced meat cutter and had arranged a phony letter of reference to help her gain employment with Food Lion.

However, instead of suing the network for libel, the supermarket chain filed a $30 million lawsuit alleging that ABC had violated federal racketeering laws by using fraudulent means to gain employment for a reporter. A libel action would have required Food Lion to prove that ABC was guilty of actual malice, which is defined as knowing falsehood or reckless disregard for the truth. Fraud—in this case the manner in which the reporter obtained employment with Food Lion—would be much easier to prove.

Food Lion's unusual legal strategy provoked its own public debate. "I think primarily . . . Food Lion knew that as a public figure it would have an almost insurmountable burden of proof in the court to show that ABC knew or had reason to know that what it was publishing was untrue," said Jane Kirtley of the Reporter's Committee for Freedom of the Press. "The fascinating thing about this is as a legal matter in court Food Lion has not challenged the accuracy of the story."[3]

"In many ways this case is highly unusual if not absolutely unique," said Hugh Stevens, counsel for the North Carolina Press Association and a local counsel for ABC. "It certainly punishes the news media for what is a truthful report about a matter of public interest because of the way it was gathered."[4]

William S. Weiss, a New Jersey-based public relations consultant, had a different perspective on the case. Writing in *Public Relations Tactics,* Weiss said, "Obviously jurors were more disgusted by the fraudulent and illegal ways *Prime Time Live* obtained its evidence, and by the network's refusal to use video showing employees behaving responsibly."[5]

Initially, the unusual legal strategy appeared to have paid off for Food Lion. A North Carolina jury sided with the supermarket chain and awarded Food Lion $5.5 million in damages. First Amendment experts and the media criticized the decision, claiming that it would have a chilling effect upon investigative journalism. Washington-based attorney Bruce Sanford said, "It's punishing the messenger plain and simple."[6] However, the jurors did not see it that way. "The media has the right to bring the news, but they have guidelines too," said jury foreman Gregory Mack. "When you look at a football game, you see boundaries all around. You go out of bounds, you go out of bounds."[7]

In the end, both sides claimed victory. In October 1999, the U.S. Court of Appeals for the Fourth Circuit reduced the damage award to $2: $1 for the employee's breach of loyalty and $1 for trespass. Ironically, the court threw out the fraud claim, and the remainder of the compensatory and punitive damages, because Food Lion had failed to assert a claim of libel. However, the court also rejected the network's claim that its hidden-camera news-gathering technique had First Amendment protection. In essence, the court said that ABC could have done its job without using questionable tactics.[8]

DISCUSSION QUESTIONS

1. Should Food Lion have challenged *Prime Time Live* on the truthfulness of its reporting, or was the company right to adopt this unusual legal strategy?
2. How would you have handled a similar situation, in which a television reporter used a hidden camera to present an unflattering—and possibly inaccurate—picture of your company?
3. Suppose you work for a company and find out that a hidden television camera has caught your employees doing something illegal. The program is scheduled to air in a few days. How would you handle this situation?

NOTES

1. Statement by Tom E. Smith, President and CEO of Food Lion, in Response to ABC's *Prime Time Live* Food Lion Segment, PR Newswire, 5 November 1992.

2. Russ W. Baker, "Truth, Lies and Videotape," *Columbia Journalism Review.* July/August 1993, online, www.cjr.org.

3. Transcript, *NewsHour,* Public Broadcasting System, 15 January 1997, online, www.pbs.org.

4. April Jones, "No Special Privileges," *The UNC Journalist* (spring 1997): 9–12.

5. William S. Weiss, "Food Lion Jury Roars at 'Primetime Live'," *Public Relations Tactics* (August 1994): 1.

6. Paul Nowell, "Food Lion Wants More Time," Associated Press report, online, www.abcnews.com

7. "Experts: Public Is Loser in Food Lion Verdict," CNN, 23 January 1997, online, www.cnn.com.

8. Barbara Wartelle Wall, "Food Lion vs. ABC: A Good News/Bad News Decision," Gannett News Watch, online, www.gannett.com/go/newswatch/99/October/new1029.htm.

Using Public Relations to Ban Landmines

When representatives of 121 nations gathered in Ottawa, Canada, in 1997 to sign a treaty banning the use of landmines, the ceremony signaled the success of grassroots public relations in marshaling worldwide public opinion.

Antipersonnel landmines, buried just below the ground's surface and triggered when someone steps on them, continue the horrors of war long after the last battles are fought. Some of the landmines are abandoned, while others are forgotten or lost. Regardless of the reason they are left behind, the mines have taken a terrible toll. At the time of the treaty signing, it was estimated that up to 100 million landmines in 69 countries killed or maimed more than 25,000 people a year—an average of one person every 22 minutes.[1]

The International Campaign to Ban Landmines (ICBL) started in 1991 as a three-person effort in a Vermont farmhouse and ultimately grew into a worldwide network of more than 1,000 organizations. Thanks to the efforts of ICBL, the nations of the world not only banned landmines but pledged $500 million to aid in their removal. And ICBL and its coordinator, Jody Williams, won the 1997 Nobel Peace Prize.

At first, the organizers relied heavily on fax machines and telephones to get their message to like-minded organizations, elected officials, the news media, and other opinion leaders. However, Mary Wareham, coordinator of the U.S. Campaign to Ban Landmines, an ICBL member organization, said e-mail soon played an increasingly important role. "It's fast, convenient, easy to use, and it's cheap," Wareham said.[2]

Robert Muller, president of the Vietnam Veterans of America Foundation, whose organization was an early supporter of the landmine ban, told the *New York Times* that the Internet was another key to the ICBL campaign's success. "The fact that we can move information around at immediate speed and low cost is the key to moving any massive group of organizations and people."[3]

By May 1996, ICBL had grown to a coalition of 500 nongovernment organizations in 30 countries. Within eight months, those numbers would double. "We created the momentum for this political process," Wareham said.[4]

A major boost to the ICBL's campaign came in February 1997, when Britain's Princess Diana traveled to Angola and later to Bosnia to observe the clearing of landmines and to meet with their victims. Reporters and photographers who had chronicled every aspect of her failed marriage to Prince Charles followed her to the minefields and, in turn, brought the issue of landmines to the world's attention.

Shortly after Diana's death in a Paris car crash, the leader of a British ICBL affiliate said, "Probably her greatest legacy has been the massive increase in interest she has generated in this subject."[5] Ironically, the princess died just as an 89-nation conference convened in Oslo, Norway, to draft the treaty. After three weeks of intense negotiations and lobbying, the conferees agreed to a document that called for a complete ban of the use of landmines within a decade.

Even with this success, some work remained unfinished. Several major military powers, including the United States and China, refused to sign the treaty for a variety of reasons. For example, the United States claimed the limited use of landmines to protect American outposts in Cuba and along the Demilitarized Zone between North and South Korea was justified. ICBL continued to lobby the United States and Canada after the December 1997 treaty signing ceremony in Ottawa.

The Norwegian Nobel Committee recognized the campaign to rid the world of landmines by awarding it the Nobel Peace Prize in 1997. The committee decided that the ICBL and Williams should equally divide the $1 million award that goes with the prize. Moments after the award was announced, Williams told reporters she was "a little stunned."[6]

"The mobilization and focusing of broad popular involvement which we have witnessed bears promise that goes beyond the present issue," said Norwegian Nobel Committee Chairman Francis Sejersted during the Nobel ceremony in Oslo in December 1997. "You have not only dared to tackle your task, but also proved that, the impossible is possible."[7]

Since winning the Nobel Peace Prize, Williams has served as a campaign ambassador for the ICBL, speaking on its behalf all over the world. She is also a distinguished visiting professor of social work and global justice in the graduate school of social work at the University of Houston.[8] As of September 2005, 147 countries had ratified the landmine treaty. However, that list did not include the United States, the Russian Federation, or the People's Republic of China.[9]

DISCUSSION QUESTIONS

1. The Internet, including e-mail, is credited with much of the success of the ICBL's campaign against landmines. Do you feel the group could have been as successful without these communications tools? How could it have been done without the Internet?

2. Is it appropriate to call this campaign "successful" in light of the refusal of the United States and other major military powers to sign the antilandmine treaty? Why or why not?

3. How pivotal was Princess Diana's role in development of the treaty? Do you think the

timing of her death had any effect on the outcome?

4. What is your opinion of the use of celebrities and special events to call attention to worthy causes that might otherwise go unnoticed?

5. Can the United States offer a values-based defense of its refusal to sign the treaty? What might that defense be?

NOTES

1. "121 Nations Sign Historic Landmine Treaty," CNN Interactive, 10 September 1997, online, www.cnn.com.
2. K. C. Wildmoon, "Peace through E-Mail," CNN Interactive, undated, online, www.cnn.com.
3. Wildmoon.
4. Wildmoon.
5. "Princess Diana's Anti-Mine Legacy," CNN Interactive, 10 September 1997, online, www.cnn.com.
6. "Anti-Mine Activists Win Nobel Peace Prize," CNN Interactive, 10 October 1997, online, www.cnn.com.
7. Presentation Speech by Professor Francis Sejersted, Chairman of the Norwegian Nobel Committee, on the occasion of the award of the Nobel Peace Prize for 1997, Oslo, 10 December 1997, online, http://nobelprize.org/peace/laureates/1997/presentation-speech.html.
8. Jody Williams biography, International Committee to Ban Landmines web site, www.icbl.org.
9. "Landmine Monitor Report 2004," International Committee to Ban Landmines web site, www.icbl.org.

False Hope

An explosion rocked a Sago, West Virginia, coal mine on the morning of January 2, 2006. Thirteen miners were trapped 260 feet below ground. Company, local, state, and federal authorities immediately began a frantic effort to rescue the men.[1] The mine's owner, International Coal Group (ICG), also activated its crisis communications plan. Company officials conducted regular news briefings, counseled the miners' families, and cooperated with state and federal regulators. The company received high marks for its initial crisis response.[2]

That changed just before midnight on Wednesday, January 3. Within a three-hour period, the families experienced the joy of being told that 12 of the 13 miners had sur-

vived—only later to suffer the shock and grief of learning that 12 of the 13 had died. Like the mining families who had just realized their worst fears, people around the world began asking the same question: How could this miscommunication have happened?[3]

A visibly shaken ICG President Ben Hatfield met with reporters on the day after the disaster and explained how poor communications conspired with good intentions. By the early evening hours of Wednesday, rescuers had already found the body of one of the miners near the site of the initial blast. The fate of the remaining 12 miners was unknown. Shortly before 11 P.M., rescue workers wearing full-face oxygen masks radioed the rescue command center that they had found the missing miners.[4]

In a muffled, barely audible voice over a crackling radio, a member of the rescue team announced that they had found the missing men. Six minutes later, an emergency medical technician radioed the rescue team and asked "And what I am telling them?" The rescuer replied, "Twelve, and they're bringing them out." When the EMT said, "And they're all alive," the rescue worker replied, "Uh, as far as I know."[5]

According to Hatfield, this exchange was heard on an open speakerphone in the command center. And as might be expected after 36 hours of nearly unbearable tension, the place erupted into a spontaneous celebration of joy and relief. Several people in the command center—exactly who is not known—could not wait to share the good news with the anxious families. In violation of the ICG's crisis response plan, they pulled out their cell phones and announced that the miners had been rescued.

The news spread like wildfire to the nearby Sago Baptist Church, where most of the trapped miners' family and friends had waited for news. According to media reports, a man burst through the front door of the church and screamed "They've found them! All 12 are alive!" The church bell tolled as the crowd cheered, wept, prayed, and sang the hymn "How Great Thou Art." A friend of three of the trapped men proclaimed, "There still are miracles!"[6]

Back at the command center, a different picture was emerging. The rescuers had initially thought that the miners were unconscious but

alive. However, 45 minutes later, the rescue team radioed that only one of the miners appeared to be alive. The company immediately dispatched more medical teams to the mine.

Hatfield was aware of the premature celebration back at the church and did not want to confuse matters by releasing unverified information. He decided to wait until he was certain of his facts. Three hours after the first erroneous report, Hatfield went to the church to tell the crestfallen families that only one of the 12 miners had survived.

Hatfield later said that he asked a state trooper to call the church and warn the families that the company was trying to sort out conflicting information. However, that was not done. If he had to do it all over again, Hatfield said that he, personally, would have gone to the church sooner and warned the people.

"In the process of being cautious, we allowed the jubilation to go on longer than it should have," Hatfield said.[7]

While ICG rightfully accepted blame for what turned out to be a cruel mistake, it shares it with others. The news media quickly accepted as fact unverified reports from unofficial sources. West Virginia Governor Joe Manchin, who initially questioned the validity of the reports, admitted that he "got caught up in the euphoria" and helped to spread the false rumor.[8]

The fact is that people heard what they desperately wanted to hear. No one wanted to compound the families' grief with a glimpse of false hope. But that's what happened when some well-intentioned people failed to follow the company's crisis communications plan.

DISCUSSION QUESTIONS

1. The case suggests that some of the families' heartache could have been avoided if "well-intentioned people" had followed the company's crisis communications plan. Where, specifically, did they fail to follow the plan?

2. How could ICG have improved its communications with the families?

3. Should ICG seek to share the blame with the news media for spreading the false rumor?

4. Knowing what you now know about the events at the Sago Mine, what would you have done differently had you been in charge of crisis communications?

NOTES

1. Vicki Smith, "12 Miners Found Dead After Rescue Effort," *Lawrence Journal-World,* 5 January 2006, 1.

2. Jim Jordan, "Mining Company Lost Control, Experts Say," Knight Ridder, 4 January 2006, online, www.charlotte.com.

3. Bob Dart, "Company Knew Report Was Wrong," *Kansas City Star,* 5 January 2006, 1.

4. Allen G. Breed, "Answers to Foul Up in Mine Disaster Sought," Associated Press, 6 January 2006, online, http://abcnews.go.com.

5. "Sago Mine Emergency Call Transcripts," ABC News, 5 January 2006, online, http://abcnews.go.com.

6. Breed.

7. Breed.

8. Breed.

Cloudy Days for Sunbeam

Earlier in this textbook, Chapter 15, "Public Relations and the Law," opens with "a parade of corporate horrors"—a hall of shame that includes the financial misdeeds of Enron, WorldCom, Tyco, and other scandal-ridden companies of recent years. But that ignominious march began long before Enron. A decade ago, the Sunbeam Corporation became a less-than-shining participant in the parade.

In the mid-1990s Sunbeam, a maker of home appliances, was a favorite of financial analysts, who advise investors on which stocks to buy, sell, or avoid altogether. The company had hired Albert Dunlap, a tough CEO with a reputation for turning around faltering companies. And the analysts applauded in February 1998 when Sunbeam released information on its plans to acquire three other consumer-products companies. Sunbeam's future looked bright.

But then the storm clouds rolled in.

Scarcely a month after announcing the acquisitions, Sunbeam shocked investors and investment analysts with word that it expected to lose money in the first quarter of the new fiscal year and had fired its executive vice president for consumer products.

"To analysts who have praised Sunbeam . . . the most alarming aspect of [the] announcements was how little warning the company had given to investors," declared the *Wall Street Journal.*[1]

And those analysts weren't happy.

"There really is a credibility issue," said one.

"The investment community has been blindsided," said another.[2]

Matters soon worsened. After a meeting that Sunbeam organized to reassure investment analysts, Dunlap confronted an analyst who had recommended that his clients sell their Sunbeam stock. According to the analyst,

Dunlap "grabbed me by my left shoulder, put his hand over his mouth and near my left ear and said: 'You son of a bitch. If you come after me, I'll come after you twice as hard.' "[3]

But it was *Barron's*, a weekly investment newspaper, that did the heavy hitting. Less than a month after Dunlap's reassurances to analysts, Barron's charged that Sunbeam had misled investors and analysts by using "artificial profit boosters" to sweeten the previous year's impressive profits. The devastating story concluded, "[Dunlap's] enemies, including disenchanted shareholders, angry security analysts, and bitter former employees, are growing in number. . . ."[4]

Finally, distrust of the financial picture painted by Dunlap's team spread to Sunbeam's board of directors. *Business Week* magazine reported that board members felt "betrayed" and "misled about the company's financial condition."[5] The board fired Dunlap, disavowed his financial projections, and issued the remarkable statement that Sunbeam's official financial report from the previous year "should not be relied upon."[6]

Dunlap's problems didn't end with being fired. On May 15, 2001, the U.S. Securities and Exchange Commission issued a news release that began with this ominous paragraph:

> The Securities and Exchange Commission today filed a civil injunctive action in U.S. District Court in Miami, Florida, against five former officers of Sunbeam Corporation and the former engagement partner on the Arthur Andersen LLP audits of Sunbeam's financial statements. The Commission alleges that the Defendants engaged in a scheme to fraudulently misrepresent the Company's results of operations in connection with a purported "turnaround" of the Company. When Sunbeam's "turnaround" was exposed as a sham, the stock price plummeted, causing investors billions of dollars in losses.[7]

Dunlap was charged with five separate violations of U.S. securities laws. In 2002, he reached a settlement with the SEC in which, without stipulating either guilt or innocence, he agreed to never again serve as an officer of a publicly held company and to pay a penalty of $500,000.[8]

The moral of Sunbeam's story? Like most other publics, investment analysts, investors, the SEC, and members of boards of directors don't like to be left in the dark.

DISCUSSION QUESTIONS

1. Shouldn't public relations practitioners keep quiet when there's bad news that could affect the performance of their company's stock? Why not let investment analysts discover the news on their own?

2. Why, in your opinion, did Sunbeam's board of directors issue the remarkable statement that the company's financial report from the previous year might be unreliable?

3. If you were an investment analyst, what would be your response to a company executive who swore at you and threatened you?

4. Are the financial analysts who monitored Sunbeam partly to blame for being deceived? How about board of directors members? After all, in its scathing report about Sunbeam's finances, Barron's used information that anyone can acquire through the web site of the Securities and Exchange Commission (www.sec.gov).

5. This case occurred in 1998. As described in Chapter 15, what federal legislation now exists that might have prevented the Sunbeam scandal?

NOTES

1. Douglas A. Blackmon, "Sunbeam Shares Dive as Investors Doubt Dunlap," *Wall Street Journal,* 6 April 1998, A16.
2. Blackmon, A16.
3. John A. Byrne, "How Al Dunlap Self-Destructed," *Business Week,* 6 July 1998, 60.
4. Jonathan R. Laing, "Dangerous Games: Did 'Chainsaw Al' Dunlap Manufacture Sunbeam's Earnings Last Year?" *Barron's,* 8 June 1998, 19.
5. Byrne, 64.
6. "Sunbeam Audit Committee to Conduct Review of Company's 1997 Financial Statement," Sunbeam, news release, 30 June 1998.
7. "SEC Sues Former Top Officers of Sunbeam Corporation and Arthur Andersen Auditor in Connection with Massive Financial Fraud," Securities and Exchange Commission news release, 15 May 2001, online, www.sec.gov.
8. "Former Top Officers of Sunbeam Corp. Settle SEC Charges," Securities and Exchange Commission news release, 4 September 2002, online, www.sec.gov.

Inside the Body Shop

In 1976, Anita Roddick opened a small shop in Brighton on the southern coast of England. She called it The Body Shop and stocked it with a different kind of skin and hair-care products: Packaging was minimal and environmentally sensitive. The products hadn't been tested on animals. Advertising shunned artificially beautiful, impossibly thin models. Whenever possible, product ingredients came from developing countries that desperately needed markets for those materials.

That was the beginning of a small empire that today includes more than 2,000 shops in more than 52 countries.

The values of The Body Shop aren't vague: They're written for all to see in the company's Values Statement, Mission Statement, and Trading Charter. In pursuit of those values, The Body Shop has supported the missions of organizations such as Greenpeace and Amnesty International. In the 1990s, the company began a campaign to save the planet's rain forests.

But high standards invite scrutiny. The Body Shop got smacked in the face by such scrutiny in "Shattered Image: Is the Body Shop Too Good to Be True?"—a devastating article in *Business Ethics* magazine. In short, the story charged that The Body Shop wasn't living up to its high ideals.

Roddick and her husband, Gordon, initially lashed out at the criticism. Then, to prove to themselves and others that The Body Shop wasn't founded upon hypocrisy, they launched one of the first and most painstaking ethics audits (see Chapter 6) in corporate history.

The Body Shop had previously conducted environmental audits to ensure that it was meeting the goals of its Earth-friendly policies. Now it undertook to produce a comprehensive values report consisting of three audits: a social audit, an environmental audit, and an animal protection audit.

The Roddicks also commissioned a separate, independent audit to be done wholly by an outside team. Titled *The Body Shop International Social Evaluation,* the report was written by Kirk Hanson, a senior lecturer at the Stanford Graduate School of Business. Significantly, Hanson was a member of the editorial advisory board of *Business Ethics* magazine, which published the highly critical evaluation of The Body Shop's fulfillment of its written ethics code.

Hanson interviewed more than 300 people and spent almost a year in researching and writing his report, which judged The Body Shop's performance in 39 distinct categories.[1] Performance in each category was rated from five stars (performance much better than comparable companies) to one star (performance much worse than comparable companies). His conclusion?

> Overall, I believe The Body Shop demonstrates greater social responsibility and better social performance than most companies of its size. Certain dimensions of its social behavior, however, raise concerns and should be addressed promptly by the company. Other aspects of its social record are about the same as other companies and must be improved if the company seeks to distinguish itself as a leader in social responsibility. The Body Shop has made mistakes in the past, but its management today has committed itself to correcting those errors.[2]

Seeming to address the criticisms in the *Business Ethics* article, Hanson added:

> The company has been subject to many charges of irresponsible behavior over the past two years. Many of these charges have no merit whatsoever. Others I have been unable to verify and have found still others to be accurate but greatly overblown in their significance. A few of the charges do have substance and are addressed in this report. . . . I am convinced the company and its employees are genuinely committed to making The Body Shop a force for social change.[3]

In Hanson's report, The Body Shop scored particularly well for its clear, ambitious written values. Hanson saved his harshest criticism for the company's reaction to customer complaints and negative publicity.

Having been through such extensive audits, is The Body Shop now a perfectly ethical company? Of course not. No organization is. As noted in Chapter 6, living by an ethics code is a never-ending process, not a finished piece of work. But by doing its own rigorous internal ethics audit and by commissioning an in-depth external ethics audit, The Body Shop set an admirably high standard for other companies to follow.

DISCUSSION QUESTIONS

1. In your opinion, should The Body Shop have ignored the charges of unethical behavior and waited for the storm to pass?
2. Why do you think The Body Shop conducted its own audit in addition to Hanson's independent audit?
3. The Body Shop put Hanson's report on its web site. Was this a good idea, given that the report did criticize some aspects of the company?
4. Did The Body Shop risk charges of buying off a critic by hiring Hanson, who had ties to *Business Ethics* magazine?
5. The Body Shop's commitment to its values costs money. Is it worth it? Why or why not? What benefits might The Body Shop receive for its values-driven behavior?

NOTE

1. Kirk Hanson, *The Body Shop International Social Evaluation*, 1995, The Body Shop web site, www.thebodyshop.com. Posted 1995.
2. Hanson.
3. Hanson.